AF663451

RAIMON PANIKKAR

Opera Omnia (Vol. 10)

Philosophy and Theology

Part 1

The Rhythm of Being

I left Europe (for India) as a Christian, I discovered I was a Hindu and returned as a Budhhist, without ever having ceased to be Christian.

RAIMON PANIKKAR

RAIMON PANIKKAR

Opera Omnia

(18 Books in 12 Volumes)

Edited by

MILENA CARRARA PAVAN

ISBN : 978-81-208-4225-0

1. Mysticism and Spirituality

1.1 : Mysticism, Fullness of Life

1.2 : Spiritualiy, the Way of Life

2. Religion and Religions

3. Christianity

3.1 : The Religion

3.2 : A Christophany

4. Hinduism

4.1 : The Vedic Experience : Mantramanjari

4.2 : The Dharma of India

5. Buddhism

6. Cultures and Religions in Dialogue

6.1 : Pluralism and Interculurality

6.2 : Interculural and Interreligious Dialogue

7. Hinduism and Christianity

8. Trinitarian and Cosmotheandric Vision

9. Mystery and Hermeneutics

9.1 : Myth, Symbol, and Ritual

9.2 : Faith, Hemencutics, and Word

10. Philosophy and Theology

10.1 : The Rhythm of Being

10.2 : Philosophical and Theological Throught

11. Sacred Secularity

12. Space, Time, and Science

RAIMON PANIKKAR

Opera Omnia (Vol. 10)

Philosophy and Theology

Part 1

The Rhythm of Being

Edited by
MILENA CARRARA PAVAN

Forewords by
KAPILA VATSYAYAN
DR. KARAN SINGH

Motilal Banarsidass Publications

MOTILAL BANARSIDASS
PUBLICATIONS
4741/23, Ansari Road, Daryaganj, New Delhi - 110002 (India)
Email: *mlbd@mlbd.com* | *sales@mlbd.com* | *exports@mlbd.com*
Website: *www.mlbd.com*

Philosophy and Theology
by
Raimon Panikkar

First Indian Edition Published in 2024

Published in India by Motilal Banarsidass Publications

ISBN : 978-81-96165-38-3 (HB)
ISBN : 978-81-208-4225-0 (Set)

FOR SALE IN INDIA ONLY

Printed and bound in India

To
Scott Eastham

Pūrṇam adaḥ pūrṇam idam.
pūrṇāt pūrṇam udacyate.
Pūrṇasya pūrnam ādāya,
pūrṇam evāvaśiṣyate.

That is Wholeness, this is Wholeness,
From Wholeness comes Wholeness.
If Wholeness is taken from
Wholeness, Wholeness still remains.

Upanishadic Invocation

Acknowledgments

Many friends have helped me in the long period I took in drafting and rewriting this book between giving the initial Gifford Lectures on which it is based in 1989, too many to list them all. Nevertheless, I must acknowledge the special assistance of the following friends and colleagues: Joseph Cunneen, Joseph Prabhu, Bill Burrows, Roger Rapp, Ignasi Boada, Milena Carrara, and Scott Eastham, to whom I have dedicated *The Rhythm of Being*.

Series Foreword

All the writings it is my privilege and responsibility to present in this series are not the fruit of mere speculation but, rather, autobiographical—that is, they were first inspired by a life and praxis that have been only subsequently molded into writing.

This Opera Omnia ranges over a span of some seventy years, during which I dedicated myself to exploring further the meaning of a more justified and fulfilled human lifetime. I did not live for the sake of writing , but I wrote to live in a more conscious way so as to help my fellows with thoughts not only from my own mind but also springing from a superior Source, which may perhaps be called Spirit— although I do not claim that my writings are in any way inspired. However, I do not believe that we are isolated monads, but that each of us is a microcosm that mirrors and impacts the macrocosm of reality as a whole—as most cultures believed when they spoke of the Body of Âiva, the communion of the saints, the Mystical Body, karman, and so forth.

The decision to publish this collection of my writings has been somewhat trying, and more than once I have had to overcome the temptation to abandon the attempt, the reason being that, though I fully subscribe to the Latin saying scripta manent, I also firmly believe that what actually matters in the final analysis is to live out Life, as witnessed by the great masters who, as Thomas Aquinas remarks in the Summa about Pythagoras and Socrates (but not about Buddha, of whom he could not have known), did not write a single word.

In the twilight of life I found myself in a dark forest, for the straight path had been lost and I had shed all my certainties. It is undoubtedly to the merit of Sante Bagnoli, and of his publishing house Jaca Book, that I owe the initiative of bringing out this Opera Omnia, and all my gratitude goes to him. This work includes practically all that has appeared in book form, although some chapters have been inserted into different volumes as befitted their topics. Numerous articles have been added to present a more complete picture of my way of thinking , but occasional pieces and almost all my interviews have been left out.

I would like to make some practical comments which apply to all the volumes:

1. In quoting references, I have preferred to cite my previously published works following the general scheme of my publications.
2. Subject matter rather than chronolog y has been considered in the selection, and thus the style may sometimes appear uneven.
3. Even if each of these works aspires to be a self-sufficient whole, some ideas recur because they are functional to understanding the text, although the avoidance of unnecessary duplication has led to a number of omissions.
4. The publisher's preference for the Opera Omnia to be put into an organic whole by the author while still alive has many obvious positive features. Should the author outlive the printer's run, however, he will be hard put to help himself from introducing alterations, revisions, or merely adding to his original written works.

I thank my various translators, who have rendered the various languages I have happened to write in into the spirit of multiculturalism—which I believe is ever relevant in a world where cultures encounter each other in mutual enrichment, provided they do not mislay their specificity. I am particularly grateful to Milena Carrara Pavan, to whom I have entrusted the publication of all my written works, which she knows deeply, having been at my side in dedication and sensitivity during the last twenty years of my life.

R.P.

DR. KARAN SINGH

3, NYAYA MARG
CHANAKYAPURI
NEW DELHI-110 021

Raimon Panikkar was one of the outstanding scholars of the 20th century. His work on Hindu texts, particularly his remarkable rendering of the Rig Veda in Mantramanjari stand as a monument to his scholarship. Equally at ease in Hinduism and Christianity, Panikkar was one of those rare scholars who was a bridge between the Indic and Abrahamic religion. He was a vibrant personality with whom I had many creative conversations on Hinduism and comparative religion.

Karan Singh
Dec. 20, 2018

TEL. : (011) 2611-5291, 2611-1744, FAX (91-11) 2687-3171, 2462-7102
Email : karansingh@karansingh.com

Foreword

I am happy to respond to the request of Dr Milena Carrara Pavan, President, Fundacio Vivarium Raimon Panikkar, Tavertet Spain, to write a Foreword to the Opera Omnia, the Collected Works, of the great scholar and an extraordinary human being. Raimon Panikkar. It was a privilege to know Panikkar for many decades. The publication marks the centenary year of his birth.

The Opera Omnia ranges over a span of some seventy years of Raimon Panikkar's exploration and includes practically all that has appeared in book form. His reach is incomparable. The titles of the twelve volumes, being published in India by Motilal Banarsidas Publishers and mentioned below, make more explicit his depth and the razor-sharp intellect.

Mysticism and Spirituality
Religion and Religions
Christianity
Hinduism
Buddhism
Cultures and Religions in Dialogue
Hinduism and Christianity
Trinitarian and Cosmotheandric Vision
Mystery and Hermeneutics
Philosophy and Theology
Sacred Secularity
Space, Time and Science

It is no accident that Panikkar wanted to begin the publication of his Opera Omnia with the volume on Mysticism and Spirituality, Fullness of Life. He wrote:

"Actually, whenever I had an intuition I almost always started to write a new hook, or at least an article, with the aim of cheeking, clarifying, deepening and eventually formulating my experiences — although I then gave them a philosophical slant, which I believe is an indispensable form of expression".

He added:

"I cannot recall when frst had the experience of advaita – which, together with the trinitarian experience, is perhaps my fundamental experience. They certainly go back to when I was very young, however, perhaps long before I had heard the name of advaita". (Raimon Panikkar and Milena Carrara, A Pilgrimage to Kailash, MLBD 2018, pp. 116 - 117.)

Each of Panikkar's writings can be considered a step of his long pilgrimage on earth, a physical step in time and space in human history, and a philosophical-spiritual step, by considering philosophy not as the 'love of knowledge' but as the 'knowledge of love,' and being aware – to use the last words of his philosophical testament. The Rhythm of Being – that more important than the tree of knowledge is the tree of Life.

To achieve fullness of life Panikkar always considered indispensable for him to be in dialogue with religions and cultures, expressions of man in his inexhaustible search for that harmony, which unites the earthly and the heavenly.

Simone Weil, in Letter to a Priest, sets as one of the conditions for embracing the Church the possibility of adopting without reserve the conviction that "Every time a man has, with a pure heart, called upon Osiris, Dionysius, Krishna, Buddha, the Tao, etc., the Son of God has answered him by sending the Holy Spirit".

This list of overlapping names and cultures seems to have been truly incarnated in the life and writings of Raimon Panikkar. With his heart set on a conversation between Hinduism. Buddhism and Christianity, the child of which would inherit the spiritual genetics of all the three while adding something new, he projected on the outer world, representing frst and foremost a complex interior knot, a personal challenge, as we can see more clearly in his diaries.

Once Panikkar said:

"A book is a drop in the ocean of public opinion, a true prayer [is] a glass, but a book that is the fruit of contemplation can be a wholesome rain". What about the 12 volumes of his Opera Omnia? I will say, not the wholesome rain of one day but of a rich season and we are so grateful to him for them.

Panikkar consistently and all alone pursued a path of rigorous thinking, articulating a vision for the future of humanity. He covered all major issues of philosophy and theology, all areas of human life and has something to say that is prophetic and makes us think in a creative way. He was blessed with an inter-cultural and inter-religious background coupled with an intense commitment to academic pursuits, which brought together his whole life experience and bore fruit in his writings.

* * * *

On personal note, as I glanced through the contents of some of the volumes, my memory understandably made me travel through several decades of my friendship and communication with Raimon Panikkar. I had seen him as a researcher and scholar in the Banaras Hindu University where his sharp intellect was interacting with others. I had met him in conferences in India, Europe and the USA. Also. I visited him in his home in Travertet, Spam where he had fnally settled.

I shall never forget my walk with him in Travertet over the cliff with tin deep gorge below. This was to be my last meeting with him, As we walked in silence, there was communication beyond words. In Travertet he had set up his Vivarium Foundation, and devised an ecumenical gathering like a satsang with incense sticks burning, where people came and he read out to them ranging from Bible, Upanishads, and from the texts of all religions. I recall his having once said: "I left Europe (for India) as a Christian. I discovered I was a Hindu and returned as a Buddhist, without ever having ceased to be a Christian".

I also recall the three or four occasions where I was a listener – participant to his presentations and his mode of communication. I refer to his participation in two conferences on the 'Concepts of Space' and 'Concepts of Time' (organized by the Indira Gandhi National Centre for the Arts in Delhi in 1987/1990). In the frst conference on Space, his assertion that "there is no Outer without Inner Space" brought back the primacy of human consciousness. In the seminar on 'Concepts of Time', which had the privilege of having the presence of His Holiness the Dalai Lama, he said to the audience: "the experience of time is intrinsically connected with the awareness of life and of reality. It is pervious to any epistemological split between subject and object... and there is no possible phenomenology of time because its awareness cannot be encompassed in one single act of consciousness. Consciousness itself is temporal.... But Reality is not exhausted in time alone. And we moderns can only with diffculty accept a non-dualistic relation with an inseparable and yet distinct dimension of reality: Time and Timelessness".

I would like to recount two other occasions, one in Europe and one in

India. 1 had gone to Switzerland to attend an international conference on the Dialogue of Religions under the auspices of Global Dialogue, where the Participants included Raimon Panikkar and Grevel Lindop, a renowned English poet. There was the opportunity of taking a trip with them on a ropeway. As we ascended, our conversation transcended the earthly to reach the spiritual. We shared the experience, yet we were making our own individual journeys. Panikkar refected on life. The going up and coming down was for him the levels of life in its ascension and descent. For Lindop it was poetry and painting. For me I was re-living the experience of the mountains, of the Himalayas.

I remember my visit with Raimon Panikkar, a Roman catholic priest, and Father Andrei Scrima, of the Greek Orthodox Church, to Paramacharya Sankaracharya, a most revered Hindu seer of the Kanchi Mutt, in the outskirts of Chennai in South India. It was like a reversal of roles, with the Paramacharya, sitting on a hay stack, giving a discourse on matters of philosophy and religions, to these two, seemed like his disciples, looking up and listening to the master. All the borders of religion and faith melted in a moment and just dissolvedv.

I might add here that the India International Centre organized an international conference in 2013 on Raimon Panikkar, participated by his contemporaries and some of his disciples and pupils, beside Madame Milena Carrara Pavan. The resultant publication, which I co-edited with Professor Côme Carpentier de Gourdon, was appropriately titled 'Raimundo Panikkar – A Pilgrim Across Worlds'.

The present generation and the future generations will be grateful to Dr. Milena Carrara Pavan and the Fundacio Vivarium Raimon Panikkar and the Motilal Banarsidas Publishers, for making available the writings of a most extraordinary human being of the twentieth century. Raimon Panikkar does not claim to be a reformer nor is he an iconoclast. He does not see any one side, regarding others as adversaries. He builds on the foundations of the past and nuances the traditional concepts and reinterprets them in the light of the contemporary situation he faces. He is a bridge-builder between cultures and religions.

KAPILA VATSYAYAN

Life Trustee and Past President, India International Centre,
and Chairperson, IIC-International Research Division.
Formerly: Secretary, Department of Culture, Government of India,
Academic Director, Indira Gandhi National Centre for the Arts,
Member of Parliament,
and Member, UNESCO Executive Board.

June 21, 2018

Foreword

He submitted to the music, yielded
To the dictation of a song, listening with rapt attention
Became, like his lyre, its instrument."
Czeslaw Milosz, "Orpheus and Eurydice"

It was the late Ewert Cousins, one of the pioneers of interfaith dialogue in the twentieth century, who as early as 1992 in his book *Christ of the 21st Century* formulated the thesis that we are at the dawn of the Second Axial Age, and that Raimon Panikkar is one of its paradigmatic and pioneering thinkers. The notion of the First Axial Age was put forward by Karl Jaspers in *The Origin and Goal of History*, the idea of an axial period pointing to one of the fault lines of history. Referring to and describing the period from roughly 800 to 200 bce, Jaspers pointed to the distinctive and formative religions and the associated forms of consciousness that came into being at this time—from Zoroaster in Persia, Vedic Hinduism, Buddhism, and Jainism in India, the Hebrew prophets, particularly Isaiah, Amos, and Jeremiah in Israel, the rise of the Socratic-Platonic-Aristotelian phase of Greek philosophy in Athens, and finally the emergence of the great teachers of the Chinese tradition, Laotze, Confucius, and Mencius, the canonical figures of Chinese philosophy. Jaspers's thesis was that this period not only marked a dividing line in terms of the growth and development of human consciousness but also shaped it for the next two and a half millennia.

The distinctive mark of First Axial Age consciousness was that it was personal, self-reflective, and inner-directed in contrast to the mythic, ritualistic, tribal, and collective forms of consciousness in the pre-Axial period.[1] Whether one refers to the Delphic injunction to "Know thyself,"

1 See Shmuel Eisenstadt, "The Axial Age: The Emergence of Transcendental Visions and the Rise of Clerics," *European Journal of Sociology* 23, no. 2 (1982): 294-314; and idem, *The Origins and Diversity of Axial Age Civilization*, ed. S. N. Eisenstadt (New York: State University of New York Press, 1986). Also Robert Bellah's early and pioneering article "Religious Evolution," *American Sociological Review* 29 (1964): 358-74, and his forthcoming book on religious evolution.

the Upanishadic notion of the *atman*, the Buddhist idea of *anatta*, or the early Chinese ideas of "selfcultivation" and the "heart-mind," the emphasis is on individual identity and individual moral responsibility. While this shift of consciousness away from the tribal and ritualistic to the individual and moral brought about the growth of "interiority," and psychological and moral ideas of authenticity, autonomy, and integrity, and opened up many possibilities, it also closed off others and had some negative consequences. It produced, for example, many of the dualisms that we live with today between body and spirit, earth and heaven, individual and society, transcendence and immanence, and between the so-called secular and the so-called sacred.

The Second Axial Age, which Cousins, like others, sees dawning, is marked by the possibility of a depth encounter of world religions. Religions, of course, have always traveled and affected one another, but what distinguishes this new encounter is a dialogical attitude that conforms to what the Jesuit paleontologist Pierre Teilhard de Chardin called "center-to-center unions." This is how Cousins glosses Teilhard:

> By touching each other at the creative core of their being, they release new energy which leads to more complex units. Greater complexity leads to greater interiority which, in turn, leads to more creative unions. Throughout the process, the individual elements do not lose their identity but rather deepen and fulfill it through union. . . .The more "other" they become in conjunction, the more they find themselves as "self." At this point of history because of the shift from divergence to convergence, the forces of planetization are bringing about an unprecedented complexification of consciousness through the convergence of cultures and religions.[2]

Panikkar for at least sixty years of his life has engaged in such "center-tocenter unions" between no fewer than four traditions: Christianity, Hinduism, Buddhism, and modern science [he has a doctorate in chemistry together with doctorates in philosophy and theology]. While in this book he writes in a largely philosophical register, he also makes clear that the ground and springboard of his thought is spiritual experience filtered through metaphysical reflection. One reason why reading Panikkar is as challenging as it is rewarding is because of his mastery of different disciplines and multiple cultural idioms expressed at a high level of philosophical abstraction. It is nonetheless worth the effort because he deploys his vast learning and religious

2 Ewert Cousins, *Christ of the 21st Century* (Rockport, Mass.: Element Books, 1992), 8-9. Cousins had, however, referred to Panikkar as a "mutational man" as early as 1979. See idem, "Raimundo Panikkar and the Christian Systematic Theology of the Future," *Cross Currents* 29 (1979): 143.

experience to meet some of the urgent challenges of our age in a daring and almost prophetic manner. At a time of a much-heralded postmodern "return to religion," much of it still vague and tentative, Panikkar actually offers bold alternatives that attempt to diagnose our religious condition and meet our spiritual needs. It is a mark of the sad insularity and provincialism of the modern Western academy that many of its practitioners are largely unaware of the vast body of religious thinking in other parts of the world. They could do worse than study Panikkar, a thinker with whom Martin Heidegger had conversations for over twenty years, but about whom he was characteristically silent in his published work.

This book had its origin in Panikkar's Gifford Lectures, delivered in Edinburgh in 1989 under the title "Trinity and Atheism: The Dwelling of the Divine in the Contemporary World." The long gestation, remarked on in the preface, allowed him to incorporate issues of Christology and theological anthropology that he pursued in his *Christophany: The Fullness of Man* (Maryknoll, N.Y.: Orbis Books, 2004), as well as questions about God published as *The Experience of God: Icons of the Mystery* (Minneapolis: Fortress Press, 2006), to mention only two of his recent publications in English. The real reasons for the delay in publication, however, have more to do both with the depth at which Panikkar deals with ultimate questions and with his firm policy of publishing only what he has vividly experienced in some fashion.

What for long has driven and unified Panikkar's thinking has been his cosmotheandric vision of reality, what he calls the "trinity" of cosmic matter, human consciousness, and divine presence in co-constitutive relationality. These three basic and irreducible dimensions of reality interpenetrate one another and exist only in relation to one another:

> There is a kind of *perichōrēsis*, "dwelling within one another," of these three dimensions of Reality: the Divine, the Human, and the Cosmic.[3]

And then again:

> There is no matter without spirit and no spirit without matter, no World without Man, no God without the universe, etc. God, Man, and World are three artificially substantivized forms of the three primordial adjectives which describe Reality.[4]

3 Panikkar, "The Myth of Pluralism: The Tower of Babel—A Meditation on Non-Violence," *Cross Currents* 29, no. 2 (1979): 214-16.

4 Panikkar, "Philosophy as Lifestyle," in *Philosophers on Their Own Work* (Berne: Peter Lang, 1978), 206.

Panikkar's use of the theological term *perichōrēsis*, taken from the discussions about the Trinity by the Greek Fathers and paralleling in a loose manner the three moments of the eternal dance of Śiva Nataraja—creation, destruction, and preservation, is deliberate and is designed to articulate four closely related aspects of reality: (1) its "trinitarian" structure, (2) its differentiated unity, (3) the open-ended character of reality, and (4) its essentially rhythmic quality.

1. The "Trinitarian" Structure

The main thesis that Panikkar wants to proffer here is the triadic structure of Reality comprising the Divine, the Human, and the Cosmic in thoroughgoing relationality. In saying that "God, Man, and World are three artificially substantivized forms of the adjectives which describe Reality," Panikkar is pointing to his own version of the Buddhist *pratityasamutpada*, the espousal of what he calls "radical relativity." There are no such things or beings as God or Man or World considered as completely independent entities. Not only are they dependent on one another, but this dependence is structural, that is, constitutive of their being. Panikkar coins the term "interindependence" to express this relationship.

To concerns about the appropriateness of taking a Christian theological symbol to describe what is essentially a philosophical and poetic vision, Panikkar makes at least three responses. First, the symbol of the Trinity is not a Christian monopoly, but in fact is common in many other traditions. Second, the relationships and movements within the Trinity provide a precise and vivid model for the dynamism of the different dimensions of Reality that Panikkar wants to articulate. Rowan Williams, the current archbishop of Canterbury and a significant theologian in his own right, has captured this dynamism well in a perceptive essay on Panikkar entitled "Trinity and Pluralism," in which he writes:

> For Panikkar, the Trinitarian structure is that of a source, inexhaustibly generative and *always* generative, from which arises form and determination, "being" in the sense of what can be concretely perceived and engaged with; that form itself is never exhausted, never limited by this or that specific realization, but is constantly being realized in the flux of active life that equally springs out from the source of all. Between form, "logos," and life, "spirit," there is an unceasing interaction. The Source of all does not and cannot exhaust itself simply in producing shape and structure; it also produces that which dissolves and re-forms all structures in

> endless and undetermined movement, in such a way that form itself is not absolutized but always turned back toward the primal reality of the source.[5]

Third, even for Christians, Panikkar feels that the doctrine of the Trinity should not be treated, as it often is, as a recondite teaching about the inner life of God cut off from the rest of life and experience. Rather, so potent and rich a symbol it is that it invites further deepening and development, preferably by intercultural and interreligious communication. Panikkar is by no means alone in wanting to articulate the logic of the Trinity philosophically, and with reference to the whole of reality. Thus, Hegel likewise saw the Christian Trinity as the *Grundstruktur* for his entire dialectic and conceived of his philosophy as a translation of the doctrinal core of Christianity.[6] Of course, Panikkar's is a quite different philosophical style than Hegel's, but the aim in both cases is the same—to "expand" and articulate Christian doctrine as a model of Reality. In offering the Christian symbol of the Trinity as a resource for interpreting reality, and in showing its homeomorphic equivalence to the Hindu notion of *advaita*, Panikkar is engaging in what in contemporary parlance would be called comparative theology. In this theology symbols of particular traditions are shared with the idea of testing their applicability and fruitfulness to contexts beyond their original ones. This is a process that Panikkar describes as "mutual fecundation."

2. Its Differentiated Unity

Pluralism, as Panikkar construes it, mediates between sheer plurality and multiplicity on the one hand and the monism of the One on the other. Reality is neither one nor many, but rather non-dual [*advaita*]. What from one perspective looks plural is from another perspective a unity expressing the interdependence and the interrelatedness of all things and the co-arising of all processes. This marks a significant shift from the way pluralism is metaphysically thematized in the western philosophical tradition, as the problem of the "One and the Many" (*hen kai polla*), and the attendant difficulties of construing the "and." Is the One above the Many (Plato)? In the Many (Hegel)? The source of the Many (Plotinus)? The real ground for the Many (Spinoza)? Beyond the Many (Kant)? Panikkar, who inclines to the Buddhist ontology of relations and processes rather than of substance, sees

5 Rowan Williams, "Trinity and Pluralism," in *Christian Uniqueness Reconsidered: The Myth of a Pluralistic Theology of Religions,* ed. Gavin D'Costa (Maryknoll, N.Y.: Orbis Books, 1990), 3.

6 Jorg Splett, *Die Trinitaetslehre GWF Hegels* (Freiburg: Herder Verlag, 1965).

the One as both grounding differences as well as emerging in and through them.

Again, Rowan Williams captures the particular cast of Panikkar's thinking well:

> the heart of this ontology could be summarized by saying that *differences matter*. The variety of the world's forms as experienced by human minds does not conceal an absolute oneness to which perceptible difference is completely irrelevant. If there is a unifying structure, it does not exist and cannot be seen independently of the actual movement and development of differentiation, the story of life-forms growing and changing.[7]

3. The Open-Ended Character of Reality

Like Whitehead, Panikkar stresses the unfinished, continually developing, and ever new character of reality:

> I am not only saying that everything is directly or indirectly related to everything else: the radical relativity or *pratityasamutpada* of the Buddhist tradition. I am also stressing that this relationship is not only constitutive of the whole, but that it flashes forth ever new and vital in every spark of the real.[8]

Panikkar's thoughts here evoke the famous hymn to the freshness of life of the nineteenth-century literary critic, Walter Pater:

> The service of philosophy, of speculative culture towards the human spirit, is to rouse, to startle it to a life of constant and eager observation. Every moment some form grows perfect in land or face; some tone on the hills or the sea is choicer than the rest; some mood or passion or insight or intellectual excitement is irresistibly real and attractive to us—for that moment only. Not the fruit of experience, but experience itself is the end. . . . How should we pass most swiftly from point to point and be present always at the focus where the greatest number of vital forces unite in their purest energy? To burn always with his hard, gemlike flame, to maintain this ecstasy, is success in life.[9]

---

7 Williams, "Trinity and Pluralism," 5.

8 Panikkar, *The Cosmotheandric Experience*, ed. Scott Eastham (New York: Orbis Books, 1993), 60.

9 Walter Pater, "Conclusion," in *Studies in the History of the Renaissance* (New York: Oxford University Press, 1919), 194.

This is the recognizable anthem of an aesthete. While endorsing this aesthetic attitude, Panikkar provides a philosophical ground to it by his idea of *creatio continua*, the radical newness of each moment and phase of reality as it unfolds in unpredictable ways.

4. The Rhythmic Character of Reality

Rhythm is what Panikkar calls a human invariant, a universal condition that all human beings embody. We sleep and wake up and structure our days in a certain rhythm. Human rhythm in turn mirrors and adjusts itself to cosmic rhythms: the rhythm of day and night, the rhythm of the seasons, the rhythm of music and dance, the harmony of the universe. But more than that, Panikkar posits rhythm in Being itself, a rhythm in which we humans participate and which we co-create.

> Life is a dance. . . . This choral dance is a combination of harmony and rhythm, Plato says. It reminds us of the Trinitarian *perichōrēsis*, the cosmic and divine dance. Śiva is Nataraja, the dancing god. The dance is his creation. Dance is practically for all popular religions the most genuine human sharing in the miracle of creation. . . . We all participate in rhythm because rhythm is another name of Being and Being is Trinity.[10]

The trinitarian structure of reality not only allows for but invites differentiation and diversity. Nonetheless, the Trinity is unbroken because the three dimensions of reality in their relationality do not fragment or break up reality into parts. The life of the Whole courses through each and every one of its manifestations. This is the basis of the distinction Panikkar makes between the *pars pro toto* (the part standing for the whole, which it obviously cannot because it is a part) and the *totum in parte*, the Whole expressed and manifested in the part, which Panikkar's notion of full-fledged relationality tries to capture. He takes pains to distinguish his holism from what he calls the "totalitarian temptation." To speak of reality as a whole is not to speak of the whole of reality. It is rather the attempt to discern the unity that underlies the differentiation. Likewise, the cosmotheandric intuition is the awareness of the undivided reality of the whole.

> In sum, we can speak about the Whole only if in a certain way we can discover the unfolding of the Whole in its particular manifestations and this is possible only because each of us is a sort of image of the Whole—*quemadmodum omnia*. This forces us to recognize that

10 Panikkar, *The Rhythm of Being*, 37.

> any discourse about the Whole is necessarily provisional because the Whole itself has no extrinsic limits.[11]

This cosmotheandric vision which has in its present form emerged out of long years of prayer and reflection is not, however, offered as just a private image or an arbitrary fiat. On the contrary, it has developed in awareness of and in dialogue with the long history of reflection about the Ultimate in both the East and the West. In calling Panikkar one of the pre-eminent thinkers of the dawn of the Second Axial Age, Ewert Cousins was claiming both that we are living in a mutational moment in human history, a moment of inter-religious convergence, and that Panikkar is a spiritual mutant, "one in whom the global mutation has already occurred and in whom the new forms of consciousness have been concretized."[12]

Among these new forms of consciousness are the equal importance given to all three intertwined centers of reality—God, World, and Man—and the associated notion of "sacred secularity." This explicitly contradicts the dualism of the so-called sacred and the so-called secular, because there is nothing in this nondual interrelatedness that is not sacred.

The cosmotheandric model also contradicts, or at least puts into question, the long history of theism. In this book, Panikkar offers us a Nietzschean "genealogy" of theism, tracing its origin to the Parmenedean equation of Thinking and Being, developed further in the laws of non-contradiction and the "excluded middle," and receiving one of its clearest expressions in Leibniz's Principle of Sufficient Reason.

> It is important to note the profound and paradoxical affinity between Theism and rationalism—to the point that Reason has dethroned God and taken its place in many offshoots of modern culture. What is "according to reason" amounts to the "will of God." Reason demands the *reductio ad unum*, the concurrence of thoughts to a certain unity— otherwise there would be no possible understanding of anything. Reason as God reigns supreme and is the source of truth, morality, and law. Reason, like God, is the principle of order. . . . Scientific atheism could be cursorily described as the replacement of the God Principle by the Principle (of) Reason.[13]

Both rationalism and theism are shown to be problematic and inadequate for our present and future spiritual needs. Rationalism shuts out

11 Ibid., 29.

12 Cousins, *Christ of the 21st Century*, 73.

13 *Rhythm*, 117.

the affections of the heart and the *esprit de* finesse, as Pascal long ago argued. Even more dangerously, it closes itself off from the wisdom of the "third eye," or of mystical intuition. One of Panikkar's signal contributions in this area is to insist on the prevalence of such intuition not only in well-known mystics, but also in common experience. Mystical insight is a potential everyone has, but under the sway of a rationalistic culture the ability is sadly underdeveloped. As for theism, tied as it is in the West to forms of rationalism, it is put into question not only by modern science but also by visions of reality coming from the apophatic religious traditions of both West (as in Pseudo-Dionysius and Meister Eckhart) and East.

> I have been suggesting that theisms as such do not exhaust the human ways to encounter the divine Mystery. The world of theisms has been a domain of great power. Theism has persisted for millennia, and will no doubt continue to survive in some form. "Right" or "wrong" are inapplicable epithets here. The world of theism is a universe in itself which selects its own criteria for judging what is right and wrong. Yet theisms no longer seem able to satisfy the most profound urges of the contemporary sensibilities both in the civilizations that first nurtured these theisms, and in others as well. The world of theism is not alone in facing religious problems, as well as vital metaphysical issues. In short, the divine Mystery remains a mystery.[14]

Let me conclude this foreword with a comment about the rather abrupt epilogue that Panikkar provides in place of what originally would have been chapter 9, entitled "The Survival of Being." That chapter in a sense was to be Panikkar's attempt at a full-fledged eschatology dealing with both the end of time and the time of the end. Panikkar has always been critical of linear models of time and of eschatologies that push fulfillment, human and cosmic, into the future. By contrast, his notion of "tempiternity" insists with Plato that time is the moving image of eternity and that Being lives not in time but with time. Our human life on earth is thus not to be seen as a linear progression toward God or nothingness but rather embodies a rhythm in which every moment is inhabited by its other eternal dimension. His is, if you want, a "realized eschatology," which urges us to discover and live in the present the fullness of life. Hence, the primacy of hope in his thinking. Hope for him, however, is not oriented toward expectations of the future, but rather to the invisible in the present, to the inner dimension of the real revealed to or intuited by the third eye.

14 Ibid., 171.

In response to his critics, perhaps, in the original chapter 9 he did speculate about the future, but came to realize that these were empty speculations. As he says in the epilogue, "I must admit that all ultimate problems cannot have ultimate answers, but we can at least be aware of the problem we have presented. We have touched the limits of our intelligence and we must stop here." As another philosopher reminds us: "Whereof we cannot speak, thereof we must be silent."

Joseph Prabhu
Philosophy Department
California State University Los Angeles

Preface

A. Locus Philosophicus

It is an honor for me to deliver these most prestigious lectures. All the more since these are to be the centennial lectures. I am standing on a podium from which, for an entire century, many great scholars have spoken. I am aware of my responsibility. I happen to be the first catalan, the first spaniard, the first indian, and, with one recent exception from the Middle East, the first asian. I feel I should try to convey something of the wisdom of all those countries and continents.[1]

It is hardly necessary to begin these lectures by analyzing the approximately 150 courses given on the fate of Lord Gifford's notion of "Natural Theology" over the intervening hundred years. It is enough to recall the fundamental changes in western society from the end of the last century to the infancy of the new millennium. Today's concerns may still echo many of the old disputes about "reason and faith," "natural and christian theology," "the rational foundations of morality," "modern science and religion," and the like, but the fundamental problematic has changed.

The world itself has changed. Much has happened in this century, much that is new: two World Wars and over a hundred major armed conflicts since

1 Two decades have elapsed since these lectures were delivered. They were given orally and the speeches recorded. After my revision of the lecture notes, a student of mine and friend, Professor Scott Eastham, who attended the lectures, polished and edited them. He prepared a text for publication, and I thank him heartily for his work. Still later others helped me in my revisions, the last of whom is another dear friend, Roger Rapp. If I allowed the text to lie dormant for such a long period, the reason was twofold. On the one hand, the fact that I do not sever action from contemplation led me to other activities. On the other hand, as has happened with most of my writings, I prefer to let initial enthusiasm subside and allow the filter of time to discern what is abiding and what is mere passing fashion. This second reading has consisted in trimming here and there, in clarifying some thoughts, and eventually adding a good number of pages, which then called for the polishing style of Joseph Cunneen, to whom I am profoundly indebted. I am also grateful for the long patience and continuing confidence of Orbis Books, which have respected this long delay. I hope that neither Bill Burrows nor the reader will regret it.

1945 have ravaged the earth, colonial empires have disappeared, technocracy has spread over the entire planet, religious traditions have mingled, whole peoples have been uprooted, mentalities have changed. All this has brought us to the brink of a mutation much deeper than a merely cultural reorientation and much more than a mere change in our feelings about the world. Could it be that reality itself is shifting profoundly, and that we are changing with it? A "paradigm shift" will not be adequate to understand this. We require a transformation, a *meta-noia* in the literal sense of overcoming the *nous*.

Such a change comes about not because new things appear in the panorama, but because the panorama itself has been transformed. Detecting such a shift may well correspond to the deepest concern of Lord Gifford, who encouraged us to tackle reality itself with assumptions different from those customarily employed by the representatives of the church and academy of his time.

No less a genius than William James began his Gifford Lectures in 1901 by admitting: "It is with no small amount of trepidation that I take my place behind this desk, and face this learned audience." I spare you a description of my own feelings, but I am reminded of Chuang Tzu's saying: "The restful mind of the sage becomes the mirror of the universe."

In order to speak properly one ought to be inspired; that is, the Spirit should come upon the speaker. So said Isaiah,[2] and Christ concurred.[3] *Minutis minuendis*, the Spirit has also to come upon us, she has to anoint us, empower us to say and to hear those very words that will release the fearful from their fear, give self-confidence to the meek, and liberate the oppressed from every form of oppression, even that of thought itself. This appeal is always pertinent in the academic community; today it takes on a burning urgency.

As far as possible, I would like to draw on the human experience of roughly the last six thousand years, allowing the wisdom of historical Man to crystallize in holohedral form so as to offer the possibility of overcoming (not negating) history, and thus entering a new phase in the very life of reality. My *locus philosophicus*, therefore, will not be solely in the domain of the concepts that form the common currency of our times, but in the realm of symbols that may more appropriately describe the situation of humanity over its entire historical period. I would like to fathom the underlying myth, as it were, and be able to provide elements of what may be the emerging myth for human life in its posthistorical venture.

---

2 Is LXI, 1.

3 Lk IV, 18 ff.

On the one hand, I am not trying to say something new. I do not wish to contribute to the alienation produced by the obsessive search for novelties. My originality, if any, will be that of going to the origins—not to do archeology or to make anachronistic interpretations, as if the beginnings were always exemplary, but to perform the task of a latter-day hunter-gatherer, re-collecting life from the stupendous field of human experience on Earth since the days when our ancestors felt the need to consign their adventures to that mature fruit of language which we call script. This is our historical period.

On the other hand, all that I intend to convey is brand-new in the sense of the *creatio continua*, as will be explained later on. The ideas here expressed are not the fruit of a dialectical mind making use of induction or deduction from ancient and contemporary sources. Rather, having paid respect to forebears and peers, I offer the harvest of a personal experience which has been later checked and criticized by the wisdom of all those whom I have had the privilege to hear or to read.

It is a misleading commonplace to say that we should say what the ancients would say, were they in our situation. This procedure begins with a mistaken assumption that betrays one of the many myths of modernity. We need to overcome the idea of time, as if real time were independent of the things and events connected with it. If those ancient sages were to live in our times, they would not be the same sages intact with just some slight adjustments or an added degree of temporal maturity. Socrates without all of his temporal and spatial environment would not be Socrates at all. A Jesus *redivivus* would not be the living Christ. Time is not an accident to life, or to Being. We cannot be satisfied with either continuing or reforming the old. Each existence is *tempiternal*, as we shall explain later, and with this observation we have already reached our topic of the "Rhythm of Being," which is ever old and ever new.

Our task and our responsibility are to assimilate the wisdom of bygone traditions and, having made it our own, to allow it to grow. Life is neither repetition nor continuation. It is growth, which implies at once rupture and continuity. Life is creation.

If creation is an act of contemplation, as Plotinus says, real growth would be to reenact in a contemplative way our partnership in the very creative activity of reality:

> And Nature, asked why it brings forth its works, might answer, if it cared to listen [to our queries] and to speak: It would have been better not to ask but to understand and to be silent just as I myself am silent and have no habit of talking.

The philosopher goes on, questioning Nature and answering in her name:

> And what have we to understand? This; that whatsoever comes into being is my vision, seen in my silence. . . . The geometricians from their vision draw their figures: but I draw nothing: I just contemplate [θεωρούσης] and the figures of the material world take being as if they fell from my contemplation.[4]

I could have cited Śankarāchārya and others, but this may be enough to establish the climate Lord Gifford desired "for 'Promoting, Advancing, Teaching, and Diffusing the study of Natural Theology' in the widest sense of that term."

Yet this is only half of the picture since we should not assume a linear and external conception of time as if each temporal moment were just the logical and "inertial" continuation of the one before, as opposed to time being an aspect of ourselves, and of everything, living in the Rhythm of Being, as we shall explain later.

We are not cybernetic machines, merely following the laws of action and reaction in a sophisticated manner. It is not only the artist who creates. Everyone of us is a co-creator, as Bonaventure asserted when expanding on an idea of Saint Paul.[5]

B. A Note on Language

1. This book is written in *koinē* english, not in american, british, or indian english—although sometimes I feel that my english is as brown as my skin. Not being a national language, english welcomes as insiders quotations from other sources and makes room for references to places other than "Central Park" or "Piccadilly Circus" and to poets other than Yeats and Shakespeare.

2. Almost every line of this work is pregnant with echoes and presences of a number of writers East and West, modern and ancient, scientific and humanistic. Furthermore, hardly any word has been used without at least a conscious resonance of its etymology. Except for direct quotations I have decided to suppress most footnotes. No bibliography at the end would be sufficient to give an idea of the background of the text. I am not alone in

---

4 Plotinus, *Enneads*, III, 8, 4: Τί οὖν συνιέναι; Ὅτι τὸ γενόμενόν ἐστι θέαμα ἐμὸν σιωπώσης, καὶ φύσει γενόμενον θεώρημα, καί μοι γενομένηι ἐκ θεωρίας τῆς ὡδὶ τὴν φύσιν ἔχειν φιλοθεάμονα ὑπάρχειν. Καὶ τὸ θεωροῦν μου θεώρημα ποιεῖ, ὥσπερ οἱ γεωμέτραι θεωροῦντες γράφουσιν ἀλλ' ἐμοῦ μὴ γραφούσης, θεωρούσης δέ, ὑφίστανται αἱ τῶν σωμάτων γραμμαὶ ὥσπερ ἐκπίπτουσαι.

5 1 Cor III, 9; 1 Thes III, 2 (συνεργοί).

this habit. Without going back to the Renaissance, modern philosophers like Descartes, Leibniz, Kant, Spinoza, Schopenhauer, and so many others are full of implicit and explicit references to many other sources. The foreign words intercalated here and there are intended to be like windows inviting the reader to look into the riches of other traditions. Let us not forget that any authentic word is the crystallization of a collective experience, sometimes of millennia of condensed human wisdom. At the price of increasing its density, this text would like to help overcome the still reigning monoculturalism that makes western culture the only point of reference. Furthermore, the quotations of the classics also have a definite political intention. Technocracy is so demanding and absorbing that modern education throughout the world, which has adopted the western model, has hardly time for, and little interest in, truly philosophical studies. We should not idealize the past, but neither should we fall prey to the powers that be which consciously or unconsciously encourage "free and critical" thinking only provided that the present-day status quo is not intelligently challenged.

3. The following is a more delicate problem. English is a very flexible and rich language, but it cannot overstep its own boundaries. The ways of speaking are not irrelevant; they correspond to ways of understanding. Against the modern positivistic and colonialistic belief, it is a plain fact that not all is translatable in any given language. Language is not just a formal system of signs, and even if it were, many languages would mean many such systems. The ways of thinking and reaching intelligibility are not the same in all peoples. I shall pose a single example.

The common way of modern western writing (speaking is more versatile) follows a straight line of exposition: one thought after the other in an ordered procession with as few meanders as possible and without coming back to a developed idea to illumine it from behind after the main thought has been expressed. In this way of writing, our memory should not be strained, and "we" want one orderly thought to march behind the other.

The normal way of many languages (perhaps closer to the oral tradition) is more circular and involute—not, tellingly enough, in the pejorative modern meaning of the word. Words are not necessarily concepts, and they connote as much as they denote. The meaning of a word is not necessarily exactly the same as the concept that the word may name. The meaning is what is meant by a mind, which does not need to be an "objective mind." Moreover, there are meanings that can be conveyed only by a cluster of words. Human speech does not always need to be a melody. It can also be a symphony.

There is more, however, and this is intrinsically related to the topic of this book. The very process of understanding is a rhythmic process between the three dimensions of reality intimated by the author, on the one hand, and the interpretative action of the reader assimilating what can be only suggested, on the other. The traditional prohibition of writing down the words of wisdom, notwithstanding later exceptions and exaggerations, was not just to keep the common folk ignorant, but because scriptures, being necessarily frozen words, cannot convey the multidimensionality of the trialogue between the speaker, the hearer, and the things themselves as reflected in the different awarenesses of the partners—as Plato himself insinuated.[6]

4. Present-day north american english makes a radical distinction between humans and other creatures (a stone, a flower, and an elephant are "its"), and does not distinguish gender from sex. The moon, symbol of femininity for the latin vernaculars (*la luna*, *la lune*), is the masculine *der Mond* in many a germanic language, which names instead the sun using the feminine gender (*die Sonne*), which in turn is the symbol of masculinity for the latin languages (*el sol*, *le soleil*). No italian will imagine that *la sentinella* or *la guardia* is necessarily a woman. In english, beauty, love, and justice are neither masculine nor feminine, unlike in many languages; instead, he and she apply almost exclusively to sexual differences, when reifying the person and speaking of it as an object. "I" and "Thou," on the other hand, refer to the integral person without differentiation between "he" and "she." I am pleading for an *utrum* (both, as well as) besides the neuter (*ne utrum*, neither nor). But this will take time, like the reintroduction of the grammatical dual, which would facilitate the *advaitic* language. The dual is neither singular nor plural (the parents are neither the father nor the mother alone). In spanish *mis padres* means both my father and my mother. We should avoid divisive language without falling into dualistic expressions. We should not give the males the exclusive claim on the meaning of Man.

For reasons that may become obvious later on I also use the expressions "humans" and "human being(s)" only sparingly as if any one of us were solely the numerical member of a class, degrading thus the unique dignity of everyone of us to be "beings" of a formal series.

5. There is still another, almost imperceptible, difficulty. The english language, both the more ancient british and the more recent north american, has practically all modisms and grammatical expressions shaped from and for a worldview that is not cross-cultural and certainly does not fit with the new insights I want to convey. Long sentences are unbearable today, while short ones were of crude taste in years past, but my difficulty is more than

6 Plato, *Phaedrus* 275 a; VII *Epistola* 334 a.

one of style and fashion. We may not like "progress," but still we say "to move ahead"; we do not have to assume that "bigger" is better, but still we have to say "grand" and "magnificent." I may say that history is not about the past, but about the present appearing in the present as time past, but I will have to give "historical" explanations if I want to be understood. I may try to avoid the word "God" on certain occasions, but we cannot do without theistic (or anti-theistic) language. I may try to explain that we are not isolated individuals and that even Man without the Cosmos below and the Divine above (two biased metaphors again) is only an abstraction, but I will have to use the words Cosmos, Man, and God as substantives and not as relations. We are conditioned by language, but even if I were to write in a non–indo-european language unknown to me (and to most of my readers), I would face similar difficulties since each language shapes and is shaped by a particular worldview. My defense of the "radical relativity" goes in that direction, but even then we need some referents and the referents vary and are also relative.

Have I then to fall into utter silence? Or into the pit of relativism, which amounts to chaos and total lack of communication? My way out is rather a way in—another metaphor that favors, perhaps unnecessarily, immanence and interiority. In simple words (again unintentionally assuming that simplicity is "better" than complexity), I follow a way of patience, contingency, and humility.

Patience, learning how to endure the imperfection and the provisionality of every word, statement, and thought while knowing that for the time being those expressions may be the bearers of what they attempt to convey.

Contingency, because no expression is self-sufficient, being always dependent on the whole and touching "truth," "reality," "Being," . . . at any single point.

Humility, aware of the *humus* (earth) that *homo* (man) is, that all our words are concrete, that is, that they "grow together" (*con-crescare*) with all our particular worldviews.

Keeping this in mind I abandon the pretension to any absolutism and feel encouraged to speak out my own insights, convinced that the role of the listener is as important as that of the speaker.

C. Perspective of the Book

A personal "confession" may not be out of place after almost twenty years of planning and writing this work. During these long, all too long, years my great temptation has been to jump into the contemporary discussion swirling about the burning questions of justice, political problems, sociological questions, linguistic analyses, ethical issues, and the like, and take stances that descend into the *palestra* of our present times. No need to cite scores of names of those who have been engaged in this noble task. I join the chorus of voices that call for a radical transformation of our dominant culture. Nonetheless, here I timidly venture a solo, which fortunately is not alone. I do not ignore the importance of contemporary thought—being a person who loves the world and sponsors a sacred secularity. Yet my perspective, while taking contemporary thought into account as much as possible, is somewhat different. It is neither about "oriental thought," whatever that may be; nor is it pure *Seinsmetaphysik*, in spite of the ambiguity of the word.

The perspective of this book is twofold. First, it tries to overcome the monoculturalism of our present times, even though I have to use the consecrated words of western tradition if I am to make sense to most readers. My horizon is mainly that of the indo-european world from which I draw most examples and the majority of the words. Vast fields of human experience remain outside this angle of vision in spite of my efforts also to make some sense of the sensibilities of peoples belonging to other cultures. I should make clear from the very beginning that words like "World," "Being," and "God" claim to have a universal meaning. This is not the case; such words convey only one vision. This awareness that there are no cultural universals may shed some light for some of our contemporaries at this historical juncture. Here I understand history more as a manifestation of the "timeless," or even as the "timeful" in time, rather than as a narrative of events and their connection.

It is for this reason that most of the words here are used as symbols and not as concepts. Symbols are neither purely objective nor merely subjective. They require the participation of the subject discovering in the symbol an (also) objective reality. This is why human thinking is essentially dialogical.

Furthermore, interculturality does not mean that we deal mainly with the problems of other cultures as we see them, but that we try to integrate the ways of thinking of other peoples into a contemporary intelligible language, as much as this is possible for us.

This leads us now into the other perspective of this book: it purports to be a contemplative work. The long delay in publication has helped me delete any sentence that is not the fruit of an experience. No word should be uttered if not out of contemplation, but no contemplation is possible if it is not the fruit of action. Action means life, and life is not life if not lived to the full— and thus also consciously, as much as possible. Yet experience needs to be expressed and interpreted. Expressions are contingent and interpretations are not infallible.

"*The Dwelling of the Divine* in the Contemporary World" was the original title of the Gifford Lectures. In spite of having changed the title, for reasons that may become obvious, the leading thread of the entire work continues to be the same. I do not develop a cosmology or an anthropology, but rather present a theology—if I were to abide by the usual division of knowledge, which I do not accept if such a division is interpreted as a compartmentalization of reality, and this is already one of the reasons for changing the title.

This book would also like to be an answer to the thousands of unanswered letters that have been present in my spirit as I have rethought these lectures.

In reworking these lectures I have also renewed my communion with the innumerable brethren from past and present with whom I have been able to enter into a living and loving dialogue. I feel this book is a communitarian enterprise.

Tavertet
Pentecost 2009

Gods, angels, and spirits,
present here & now—
Human beings, and every living thing,
attending here & now—
Benches, walls, stones, and sacred spaces,
abiding here & now—

May my words be in Harmony
with the entire Universe,
contribute to its Justice,
enhance its Beauty,
and be spoken in Freedom,
so that Peace may draw
closer to our World.

Amen

Contents

Abbreviations of Titles of Texts Used in References

Books of the Bible

Acts	Acts of the Apostles
Am	Amos
Col	Colossians
1 Cor	1 Corinthians
2 Cor	2 Corinthians
Dt	Deuteronomy
Ex	Exodus
Ez	Ezekiel
Gn	Genesis
Heb	Hebrews
Is	Isaiah
Jas	James
Jb	Job
Jer	Jeremiah
Jn	John
1 Jn	1 John
2 Jn	2 John
3 Jn	3 John
Lk	Luke
Mk	Mark
Mt	Matthew
Phil	Philippians
Phlm	Philemon

Prv	Proverbs
Ps(s)	Psalms
1 Pt	1 Peter
Rom	Romans
Rv	Revelation
Sir	Sirach
1 Thes	1 Thessalonians
1 Tm	1 Timothy
2 Tm	2 Timothy
Wis	Wisdom
Zec	Zechariah

Other Classic Texts

AV	Atharva Veda
BG	Bhagavad Gītā
Bodh	Bodhicaryāvatāra
BS	Brahma Sūtra
BU	Bṛhadāranyaka Upaniṣad
Conf.	Augustine, *Confessions*
CU	Chāndogya Upaniṣad
Denz	Denzinger, *Enchiridion Symbolorum*
Dham.	Dhammapada
DS	Denzinger-Schönmetzer, *Enchiridion Symbolorum*
Enn	Enneads of Plotinus
IsU	Īṣa Upaniṣad
JaimUB	Jaiminīya Upaniṣadbrāhmaṇa
KathU	Kaṭha Upaniṣad
KausU	Kauśītāki Upaniṣad
KenU	Kena Upaniṣad
KrV	Kritik der reinen Vernunft
MaitU	Maitrāyaṇi Upaniṣad
MandU	Māṇḍūkya Upaniṣad
MB	Mahābhārata

Met.	Aristotle, *Metaphysics*
MK	Mūlamadhyamaka Kārikā
MunU	Muṇḍaka Upaniṣad
PG	*Patrologia cursus completus, Series Graeca* (ed. Migne)
Phys.	Aristotle, *Physics*
PL	*Patrologia cursus completus, Series Latina* (ed. Migne)
Poet.	Aristotle, *Poetics*
Pol.	Aristotle, *Politics*
PrasU	Praśna Upaniṣad
Ram	Rāmāyana
RV	Rig Veda
SB	Śatapatha Brāhmaṇa
SN	Samyutta Nikāya
SU	Śvetāśvatara
Summ.	Thomas Aquinas,
Theol.	*Summa Theologiae*
TB	Taittirīya Brāhmaṇa
TMB	Tāṇḍiya Mahābrāhmaṇa
TU	Taittirīya Upaniṣad
Tuscul.	Cicero, *Tusculanae Disputationes*
VS	Vedānta Sūtra
YS	Yoga Sūtra

I
Introduction

μελέτατο πᾶν
"Cultivate the whole"[1]

A. All or Nothing

Cal fer pura a tot o re
la jugada, com si ho fos:
qui no mori d'amorós,
l'amor no el prendrà a mercè.

You've got to play the game
for keeps, all or nothing:
If you won't die for love,
love won't lend you its wings.[2]

—Carles Riba

These lectures represent both daring and danger. Either they will convey a wisdom that has been gestating for millennia and assimilate the insights of our ancestors by extracting their *rasa* (sap, quintessence), which still retains its fragrance for our world, or else they will fail to achieve this aim and will be nothing more than interesting *doxai* (opinions).

It is also true, however, that every tradition has warned us not to pretend to unravel the mystery of the universe, not to search for things above ourselves or beyond our powers.[3] Teachers of all sorts have repeated the refrain that one must curb—or, as they may prefer to say, educate and train—the enthusiasms of the best students. In short, the untrodden path is a contradiction in terms. If it is a path, it is not untrodden; if it is untrodden, it is not a path. Yet, as the *Dhammapada* says, "there are no tracks in the

1 Periandros of Corinth (although other interpretations are possible).

2 Carles Riba, *Salvatge cor* (Barcelona: Edicions 62, 1974), XXVI.

3 V. gr. *Sirach* III, 22.

sky,"[4] or as St. John of the Cross writes, "on the summit there is no way,"[5] because at that level the very idea of way is inapplicable. There is no way, not because it is untrodden, but because there is nowhere to go once the goal has been reached, or rather, once way and goal merge. The ultimate *upāya* is *anupāya*, the last way or means [to realization] is no-way; there are no means, as Abhinavagupta says.[6] The same insight also reverberates in chinese wisdom and among christian, muslim, and many other mystics. Life as rhythm needs no way.

On the other hand, practically all masters say that to pretend we have reached *nirvāṇa*, that we are realized souls, that *satori* is already behind us, is yet another contradiction. The very fact of affirming it proves that we have not yet attained the realm of the ineffable. No realized person would ever say so.

This is the challenge of the "all or nothing" voiced above by the catalan poet, who invokes a multisecular wisdom: The enterprise may fail. It will certainly fail if we do not dissolve the dilemma, overcome dialectics, and convert logical contradiction into an experiential polarity wherein the "all" is the other "side" (*alter*, not *aliud*) of "nothing." *Śūnyatā*, emptiness, is not Non-Being interpreted as the contradiction of Being. Here, the english word "nothingness," unlike the spanish *nada*, may be misleading. We should be able to overcome (not deny) the "mental," to speak and think in symbols instead of only using concepts, and to some degree unfold qualified tautologies in order to reach wholeness together and enjoy its radiance. The *metanoia* of the Gospels means more than a "change of mind"; it means to "overcome the mental."

This risk of all or nothing is real and concrete to me. After a lifetime of study, after an effort to assimilate the honey of wisdom (the *madhu* of the Upanishads) from as many human phyla as I could, dare I now present a vision that is not a system? Am I able to offer a real symbol and not merely a sterile sign? Will this meditation bear a fruit that stems not from me but from the very Life of Being?

An immediate response, not totally convincing, is that this enterprise is not so new or daring after all, but simply an effort to bring about a certain harmony in the human experience. This would be fair justification. I claim no more than to continue tradition, to reinterpret the traditional wisdoms

4 *Dham* XVIII, 20.

5 St. John of the Cross, *Ascent of Mt. Carmel*, Frontispiece.

6 Abhinavagupta, *Tantrāloka* I, 45.

of our ancestors from the extraordinary vantage point of our times. It is easy to criticize Plato and to find fault with Śankara, but this is possible not only because we are heir to centuries of decantation, but also because they are thinkers on whom we still lean in order to overcome their own philosophical schemes.

Yet this response, if not wrong, is not totally convincing for those, at least, who are aware of the myth of history. We are historical beings, but we are more (not less) than history. I mentioned the idea of a *creatio continua*, as the radical newness of each "moment"—not only of time but also of space, and ultimately of reality. Reality has no inertia, like a body moving in an empty space and along a neutral time, because space and time already belong to reality. Passing from time *b* to time *c* is as mysterious and "new" as coming to time *b* from time *a*.

Speaking in the language of our times, we may say that we are at a crossroads not only in human destiny but in the very history of reality. These are the "signs of the times" that I will attempt to under-stand by standing under the spell, the beauty, the truth, and also the burden of that selfsame Destiny which I am trying to detect under the metaphor of rhythm. Or is it more than a metaphor? Rhythm may perhaps lead us further up (*meta-phorein*), but further than Being? Or is Being itself a metaphor? For Nothingness? *All, or Nothing? This is the issue: to overcome the dilemma!*

1. The Choice of the Topic

The most excruciating decision for me has been choosing the topic, the *topos*, the place from where to say "it." Closely tied to this is the method of approach and exposition. I am aware that the etymology of choice discards whim, even my own will, but suggests taste and enjoyment (*gustare, jușate*). I have to choose what I "perceive" as the most important topic objectively (I need a clear insight) and subjectively (I must have a pure heart). No minor challenge indeed.

Our topic is about the very meaning of reality, but to ask about the "meaning" of a thing is different when asking about reality because we cannot make reality an object that would leave the (asking) subject outside it. The solution to the question about reality is bound to dissolve, to disappear as a question, and to reach a "new innocence." So our question has to emerge from reality itself through us, who are also real. If reality is not to become a mere abstraction, we need to incorporate our vision of the concrete reality we perceive, especially when that reality is human. How do we see it?

In a world of crisis, upheaval, and injustice, can we disdainfully distance ourselves from the plight of the immense majority of the peoples of the world and dedicate ourselves to "speculative" and/or "theoretical" issues? Do we not thereby fall prey to the powers of the status quo, which, in some countries at least, are willing to leave intellectuals in peace provided they do not upset the System? Can we really do "business as usual" in a world in which half of our fellow beings suffer from Man-made causes? Is our theory not already flawed by the praxis from which it proceeds? Are we not puppets in the hands of an oppressive System, lackeys to the powers that be, hypocrites who succumb to the allure and flattery of money, prestige, and honors? Is it not escapism to talk about the Trinity while the world falls to pieces and its people suffer all around us? Is this not merely regression to a pre-scientific and pre-critical attitude? Is indulging in speculation about such seemingly impractical ideas not a betrayal of those who still expect some saving power from humanistic studies? Is, for instance, the Trinity any help in the planetary ecological crisis?

I expect to demonstrate that the *importance* of this topic relates directly to the *urgency* of our present human and earthly predicament.

The question of science and technocracy, which has been occupying my thinking for many years, may seem more urgent, but in the final analysis the problem of the Divine is synonymous with the ultimate meaning of Life. The topic is not a theological quibble or a merely conceptual lucubration. It stands for the final question of Man when confronted with a challenge to the very meaning of being human, real, and alive—in other words, when confronted with the problem of Being and its survival.

All of us would do well to recall the protests of the powerless against the powerful for their silences, complicities, and outright crimes. We are all co-responsible for the state of the world. Today's powers, though more anonymous and more diffused, are quite as cruel and terrible as the worst monsters of history. What good is a merely intellectual denunciation in countries where we can say anything we like because it is bound to remain ineffectual? Our nominalistic world drowns words in the sea of its own techno-babble. There is little risk in denouncing provided we do not lift a finger. Is it not sheer hypocrisy just to "denounce" in order to tranquilize our conscience?

Do we really take the peoples of the world into consideration? Have we seen the constant terror under which the "natives" and the "poor" are forced to live? What do we really know about the hundreds of thousands killed, starved, tortured, and *desaparecidos*, or about the millions of displaced and homeless people who have become the statistical commonplaces of the mass media? In this just elapsed century of "civilized Man" and "planetary civilization" there have been over a hundred million people slaughtered in wars. We have *not* progressed—not even economically. We live in a world in which during the 1980s there were over three million deaths in warfare (over two thousand every day), two and a half million of whom were civilians. In the same period, the GNP of Africa and Latin America *decreased* by 15 percent—which, if we discount the wealthy elites, probably means a 30 percent decrease for most of the people. At present, after more than twenty years of "technological progress," the situation is even worse.

The problem is urgent. Our good intentions are not enough, and these very intentions are not without presuppositions. Rather, we must assume that the role of the philosopher is to search for a truth (something that has saving power) and not to chase after irrelevant verities. We must assume, moreover, that the ivory tower mentality is an escapism, and that intellectuals ought to be incarnated in their own times and have an exemplary function. This further implies that the task may not be merely rational, and that the elaboration of an overall vision of reality is relevant for human life because we are more than rational animals and we are certainly more than mere machines. As Nietzsche says, "Because you lie about that which is, you do not catch the thirst for that which should be."[7] If we are too comfortably seated on our social privileges, our intellectual inertia will prevail and we just will not see the real situation. We do not want to see it because we are living a lie, as Christ said[8] long before Nietzsche.

Without this thirst for "living waters" there is no human life, no dynamism, no change. Thirst comes from lack of water. We have all kinds of soda pop, which may satisfy our immediate taste for superficial explorations, but they cannot quench our existential thirst for the reign of justice. Without this thirst we simply do not see the real predicament of the world nor do we realize the drastic changes (the radical *metanoia*) we must undertake both inside and outside ourselves. We are dealing with something that is more than an academic challenge. It is a spiritual endeavor to live the life that has been given us.

Now the foremost way to communicate life is to live it, but this life is neither exclusively public domain nor merely private property. Neither withdrawing from the world nor enmeshing ourselves in it is the responsible human attitude, although obviously we must respect individual options. How

---

7 Nietzsche, *Grossoktavausgabe*, XII, 279: "Weil ihr über das, was ist, lügt, darum ensteht/ euch nicht der Durst nach dem was werden soll."

8 Jn VIII, 44.

then do we answer to the cries of the peoples that our present "cybernetic" civilization tries to keep away from the public eye by isolating them into "third worlds" of all sorts? I ask this in spite of well-intentioned friends who advised me to spare such reflections in a respectable academic work.

Neither an accurate analysis of the ills of the world nor a violent attack against the unjust status quo will be truly effective. Need we say that all the saints and prophets have failed? If they preached an earthly paradise, it has not come to be even after at least six thousand years. No Messiahs sacred or profane have delivered the goods. This past century has been, in the evaluation of many thinkers of the right and of the left, one of the worst periods in human history. Evil offers neither religious consolations nor unconscious excuses. If those prophets preached otherworldly compensations or offered *karmic* explanations, such teachings have lost credibility for the majority.

History shows that when good management is too successful, a positive reform too drastic or a just victory too glamorous, then almost automatically abuses, exaggerations, and injustices set in. Christians know what happened when the Cross of Christ became the hilt of a victorious sword. Could it perhaps be that the message of the sages was directed not toward bringing back a historical paradise, but toward helping us to open a "third eye" by which we could see and live another dimension of reality? The experience of this third dimension, without alienating us from the world, allows us to live a full and realistic life in this world of ours. It liberates us from the despair of impotency and the anxiety of a barren existence. It does not prevent us from shedding tears, but as the spirituality of the *bodhisattva* and the Sermon on the Mount assure us, tears are not an obstacle to experiencing joy and peace. Furthermore, this experiential vision, liberating us from all fear, empowers us to work for the enhancement or perhaps transformation of the human condition. As the jewish legend says, only a handful of saints sustain the world. This book does not want to be an exercise in futility or a display of information. We shall still return to its aim.

* * *

Thinking through the topic, I have often wondered whether I was trying to cover so much ground that I would be obliged to treat everything superficially. How can one dispatch monotheism in a single chapter, for instance? I was tempted to abandon such an ambitious project and to concentrate instead on a single subtopic, thus seemingly gaining in depth what I would lose in breadth.

Three motives have sustained me against yielding to the demon of discouragement. One is very personal. If in the sunset of my intellectual and spiritual life I still have to renounce the Whole and be satisfied with partial achievements, there must be something wrong—either with myself or with the very method for discovering the meaning of life as a whole. When are we to come of age? Or, christianly speaking, for when and whom have we reserved the Resurrection?

The second motive is intellectual; it contests the validity of the facile simile regarding depth and breadth. Philosophical activity is not like scientific inquiry; everything is interconnected. You cannot investigate a portion of reality without being involved with all of it. In a word, the vision of the whole is not the sum of its parts. It is another type of vision. Yet, in spite of all the delays and complications in preparing the ground, and irrespective of the difficulty of putting my message into languages that are so unaccustomed to *śabdabrahman* (ultimate words), what I have to say is relatively simple. There is farsighted wisdom in Lord Gifford's will in which he called for delivering popular lectures. He was encouraging us to say things that will truly be significant for people's lives.

The third motive is political. Consciously and/or unconsciously, the status quo can be maintained more easily if the citizens of the world are kept busy with their own specializations and are deprived of the intellectual instruments and political means to challenge the present state of affairs. We are allowed to complain in our specialized fields and even to suggest changes, but the power of the dominating culture discourages and makes it almost impossible to have a view of the Whole. Reforms are welcome, but transformation is mistrusted.

Our present-day civilization cynically asks: How can anybody have the ambition of knowing everything? I reply: How can anybody resign themselves to going through this life without knowing what is to be known in order to be a whole person?

I would like to help awaken the dignity and responsibility of the individual by providing a holistic vision. We are not ants. To use an old initiation formula, each of us is a "king, a prophet, and a priest"—which could be interpreted as saying that freedom is our personal calling.

In short, *the choice of the topic* is determined by the need to overcome the inertia of the mind, the laziness of our hearts, and the fear in our lives, thus contributing to the freedom of our being. The choice of the *topic* is not prompted by a desire simply to defend the individual freedom on which our responsibility rests, but rather to inquire about that selfsame *freedom of Being* on which our human and cosmic dignity is grounded.

2. *The Context*

The "nuclear threat" should not be minimized and the human predicament cannot be ignored; a "business-as-usual" mentality is irresponsible. In choosing an apparently theoretical topic, however, I am not in the least departing from the concrete human condition of our times. Yet, we should have no fear of either individual or collective death.

The Trinity, as we shall see, is immediately relevant to the political, economic, and ecological predicament of the earth. Which world is being menaced? What is this world that we inhabit? Who is being threatened? It is no excuse to say, "All these are theoretical questions, but the bomb and the poor are real whether we care about them or not, whether we believe in them or not." One may equally well retort that God is as real as the bomb, or that the *brahmaloka* (world of Brahma, heaven) is as much of a fact, for believer and unbeliever alike. We should not present world problems from the perspective of only one worldview.

I am too conscious of the "concordant discord" of our times to assume that I speak only for myself in an individualized way. I am an inheritor of and a speaker for multitudes of fellow beings living through the same modern predicament. I am not claiming that the *nous poiētikos* of Aristotle, the *illuminatio* of Augustine, the *intellectus agens* of Thomas Aquinas and Ibn Rushd, the transcendental imagination of Kant, the *esse intentionale* of the neo-thomists, the *Dasein* of Heidegger, and so on, are all the same notions or respond to a similar problematic. However, I am saying, first, that these apparently abstruse theories have a practical relevance for our lives; second, that there is a "discordant concord" in all these *homeomorphic equivalents*; and third, that this continuous discontinuity of traditions might constitute a symphony if we could "hear" the ideas of these thinkers in a creative way.

Already in the fifth century BC Heraclitus wrote: "invisible harmony [is] more powerful than the visible."[9] This greek idea was also widely accepted by the latins and continued during the Renaissance preceding the humanistic theme of the *concordia discors*.[10] This is a pertinent idea now that the enthusiasms of the self-appointed "Enlightenment" have subsided, and we may be better able to entertain the idea that what we call *the* "world" is not all that there is to it.

---

9 Heraclitus, *Fragm*. 54: ἁρμονία ἀφανὲς φανερῆς κρείτον.

10 Seneca in the first century wrote: "Tota haec mundi concordia ex discordibus constat" ("The entire harmony of the world consists of discordant elements"). Seneca, *Naturalium quaestiones* VII, 27, 4.

I join here the *philosophia perennis*, not in any sectarian sense, nor as an immutable interpretation or monopolistic appropriation, but by joining the voices of tradition in a critical attitude of listening to what has gone before and of participating in "handing over" (*tradere*) the accumulated wisdom of bygone ages. Man, like a plant, also has roots. An uprooted philosophy is all too easily carried away by the weakest winds of fashion. *Perennis* does not mean everlasting or immutable. The very word (*per annus*) suggests, like the "seasonal course of the stars" of Cicero,[11] an accommodation to all the seasons, the rhythms of the year. Nor should we forget the image of a revolving and passing thing contained in the very word *annus* (year).

* * *

We have to overcome the assumption that anything important should be complicated. On hearing an updated version of the ptolemaic system, the thirteenthcentury king of Castille, Alfonso X el Sabio, said that if he had been the dear God, he would have made things a good deal less complicated. Modern science, however, consciously or unconsciously, cultivates a sort of *disciplina arcani*, only for the initiated. You cannot pretend to understand anything of molecular biochemistry, for instance, if you are not well trained in at least three disciplines.

Human wisdom is not like that. It is like the Gospel, understandable to all because it concerns all. Of course, this does not mean that strenuous work is not needed before formulating or transmitting it, or that it can easily be received by hearts and minds stuffed with egotism and vanity. Nor does it mean that words are not necessary or that many of the present-day languages have not undergone a considerable impoverishment which makes them unfit for dealing with metaphysical and spiritual matters.

Many of those people who busy most of their time with the rich technocratic complex of modern culture have lost a sense of the cosmic and mystical dimensions of life. Modern Man is mainly *homo habilis* (skillful Man), and the intellectual *homo sociologicus*, or at most *politicus*. Most discussions among "educated" elites revolve around political events as presented by the mass media. People will attack or defend the present-day system, but the horizon within which the very problematic is viewed will be the sociopolitical (economic) context, perhaps with a fringe of ethical nuance. But there it stops. At a more intimate level, the modern mentality recognizes personal problems with metaphysical overtones every day, but these retain only individualistic interest. It is a telling paradox that the universal God (if he exists) has been tolerated as a private concern.

11 Cicero, *Natura Deorum* II, 56: *perennis stellarum cursus.*

Perhaps people interested in metaphysical questions have always been a minority. The difference, however, is that not so long ago these speculative problems were seen to be intimately connected with practical and political questions. Today they seem only a luxury for unoccupied minds. When the women in the marketplace were discussing the filioque in the fourth century in Asia Minor, they might not have understood the intricacies of trinitarian theology, but they sensed very clearly that those theoretical issues had a direct bearing on their own lives. The "heresies" of centuries past were also political problems. We should be aware that we always speak from within a given context, and that we must stand somewhere in order to "under-stand."

Our context is the overall situation of contemporary Man in our world.

3. *The Aim*

In a more academic mood I would have written "The Pretext." A transparent hermeneutic of a *text* needs to know not only its *context* but also its *pretext*. What is our aim?

Archaic Man had an orientation in life. Life was not easy or at the service of the individual. The world was perhaps even more a "vale of tears" than for some of our contemporaries, but it all had a meaning, a coherent narrative, an intentionality. This meaning was cosmic, indeed theocosmic. Everything was part of a cosmic cycle, the result of *karma*, past actions, the will of the Gods, the *daivā*su*ram* struggles (of good and evil spirits), the destiny of Heaven, the decree of Providence, or the like.

Historical Man has tried to put human destiny into human hands. For a long while now, people have lived under the myth or "spell" of history, which is seen as the unfolding of the highest intelligence, the field of *dharma*, the anteroom of the city of God, the manifestation of the Spirit, or even the triumph of the fittest. Human life is seen as a struggle for the future, as a search for a place in history (even if in a low key). Today history is becoming democratized; it no longer depends theoretically on the whims of *brahmins* and *kṣatriyas*, priests and nobility, or even of the Deity. Anyone can become not only president of the republic but a voter in the universal human poll, or a bit player in the great mass media spectacle. History is this screen where the "divine" and/or "human" comedy is being played out.

Both myths have collapsed. Eternal returns, *kalpas*, cosmic liturgies, *axes mundi*, and the like become less and less plausible, even for those who still live in such cultural universes. The manifestation of God in History, the universal democracy, the value of the individual, and the meaningfulness of history are no longer readily credible. Marxism may have been the last intellectual effort to rescue human optimism in history. Spartacus, in the slave war against Rome in the first century BC, was defeated; for one victorious David there were hundreds, if not thousands, of victorious Goliaths; 85 percent of the indigenous population of America was wiped out—if not by guns, then by the biological and cultural viruses that the conquerors carried with them. There have been many slave rebellions before and after Spartacus, and plenty of atrocities before and since the conquistadors, but the consciousness of this recurring pattern is relatively new. These crimes were not the exceptions but the rule. Even today. No need to go back to witch-hunts and the slave trade: Auschwitzes, Gulags, repressions, and "sanctions" of all kinds, from both the right and the left, the massive presence of two billion of our fellow beings eking out their lives today in subhuman conditions (at a time when we boast of being able technically to solve all their problems), have so thoroughly undermined the belief in the saving power of history—whether as the will of God, the manifestation of Absolute Spirit, or the dawn of a utopian Future—that the very idea of Christendoms, Sacred Empires, World Democracies and global Orders as the collective construction of a better future has lost appeal and credibility. Its last bulwark seems to be the promised paradise of globalization, which finds increasing resistance and may soon be abandoned.

In any case, technocracy is still the prevailing myth. It promises immediate gratification of immediate needs, even if these are artificially created. Technocracy, however, is not a Messiah for the future, but a Santa Claus for the present—and for the majority of people it does not deliver the goods. Ecological consciousness, genetic engineering, science fiction, and escapist drugs, heterogenous as they may seem, all have in common this disenchantment with history and the dream of taking our destiny into our own hands, but the ground is shifting beneath our very feet. In brief, an orientation does not seem to come from above nor are we able to orient ourselves from below.

What, then, is a plausible narrative for humanity today?

My first aim would be to contribute to such an orientation, but my fear is that today we need something more; the very Orient has faded away for many. The dawn does not chase away the clouds, and when a certain light appears we know neither where it has come from nor where it leads. Things are visible, we analyze and even enjoy them, but we do not see the sun, even if we have powerful telescopes.

The original title of these lectures was "The Dwelling of the Divine in the Contemporary World," but the problem is that God has become a superfluous hypothesis for the prevalent modern civilization. The trains run, the planes fly, the skyscrapers stand, telecommunications work, independently of whether or not God exists.

Obviously, I cannot disperse the clouds or change the course of the sun. Nor is my aim to preach resignation or rebellion. We need first to describe the *topos*, the locus where this Orient may shine. This Orient is neither merely outside nor exclusively inside us. The dwelling place of the Divine is no-where, perhaps because it is now-here.

I could try to express the same aim in a single word: *hope* !

What our contemporaries most lack is hope. Everybody has faith—in one thing or another. Love, of all sorts, is also present everywhere. We believe in so many ideas and love so many things, but our culture has little hope. Most people drag their feet along without much enthusiasm and need a variety of stimuli to go on living with a certain joy. Existence, for many has become boring, when not a burden. Here we need to dispel a misunderstanding: hope is not of the future. Hope should not be confused with a certain optimism about the future which only betrays a pessimism about the present. Hope is not the expectation of a bright tomorrow. *Hope is of the invisible.*

Love is more directly related to the first eye, the sensitivity of the senses, although it can soar up to the *amor Dei intellectualis* (intellectual love of God) of a Spinoza. Faith is closer to the reality opened to the second eye, the intellectual aspect of reality. Hope has a deeper relationship with the third eye, the inner dimension of the real. Hope opens up our vision of this third dimension which has been so undeveloped in recent generations. The shift in meaning in the common use of the word is related to a lack of contemplation and is highly significant: hope has gone from a discovery of a hidden meaning of the present, or of an otherwise invisible aspect of the real, to an expectation of change for the better in the future; from a plunge into the present to a projection into the future. The world in which we live seems to make us believe that the visible and rational universe is the only reality. These lectures aim at communicating an effective hope in the deepest dimension of our world.

There is an urge in the human being toward beauty, truth, and goodness, which entails and demands freedom, joy, and peace. My aim is to point toward that truth that makes us free. Even after experiencing the pluralism of truth, we still strive for growth and wish to cultivate a certain aspiration for wholeness. Some "believe" that this wholeness is embodied in God, others in Being, others in Emptiness, others in humanness, others in "regional truths." We may call this urge the very dynamism of Being, the grace of God, human nature, or just an illusion. At any rate, we all aspire to understand this urge, and we may use the word "truth" to symbolize both the dynamism and its goal. In the western tradition this was called *prōtē philosophia*, the first philosophy, or variously, theology, ontology, or metaphysics (we will not indulge in outlining all the distinctions here in this context).

What I have been saying so far cuts the Gordian knot of our historical intricacies. If Man were only a historical creature, human life would be a tragedy for a vast majority of our fellow beings who do not make it onto the canvas of history. Man is certainly a historical animal, but history does not exhaust his being, and this affirmation does not necessarily say that there is life *after* death. The mystery of human life is not just a temporal phenomenon.

My effort is not directed to a deconstruction of onto-theology or to an overcoming of metaphysics, or even to the question of Being. It is an attempt, rather, at a defense of what in the West still has no better name than philosophy. I am aware of both the ambition of this intention, and its simplicity. The ambition is plain. Thirty to sixty centuries of human experience are involved. The simplicity is equally obvious, for the intention is not (and cannot reasonably or credibly be) to build another more perfect system, but to recover the original insight of Man when confronted by the mystery of the real. *My aim is to present a possible orientation in the* selva oscura, *the dark wood of our present-day situation.*

4. *The Theme*

After this candid declaration of intention, our theme should be simple, although difficult to explain. It purports to deal with the ultimate meaning of human life. We cannot, however, disconnect our particular lives from Life as such. This Life is lived by us human beings on Earth and under Heaven—and this has been the prevalent human consciousness throughout the ages. Heaven, Earth, and Man are three irreducible and inclusive elements of human experience. Because the three are intertwined and correlated, we cannot isolate them, but we shall concentrate on the most neglected of the three in our times: the Divine.

After some introductory remarks on method and on various aspects of the topic I shall approach what I consider the ultimate question of a thinking being, proceeding to criticize the old answers about the Divine, while underscoring the fact that ours is a constructive critique. These preliminaries may make room for a deeper awareness of the divine Mystery. I will try to overcome a rigid monotheism by presenting the intuition of the Trinity as a more accurate representation of the Divine, but without making an explicit christian exegesis of the trinitarian God. A further target of criticism is the extrapolation of modern scientific ways of thinking outside the scientific realm. This will make it possible to sketch some lines of a new vision of the world.

Our theme is the destiny of Man—a "being" that neither actually nor conceivably exists without an Earth below and a Heaven above, ambivalent as the interpretations of these symbols may be. We return to our "All or Nothing."

B. The Method

Caminante, son tus huellas
el camino, y nada más;
caminante, no hay camino,
se hace camino al andar.

—Antonio Machado[12]

Wayfarer, your footsteps are
the way, and nothing more;
Wayfarer, there is no way,
the way is in the walking.

If there is no way, all the more do we need a guide. Who is going to be the Beatrice in this old yet ever-new pilgrimage in our *Divina Commedia*? The question is rhetorical because once love arises there is no hesitation about who is to be the guide. Without love no Goddess will reveal herself, but this love has to be selfless; otherwise the Beloved is only a projection of our desires. Without knowledge we shall not understand the language of the mentor. *Fides oculata*, "enlightened faith," said the ancients, but it has to be faith because this pilgrimage is toward the Unknown. With that I have already confessed that the journey is toward the Infinite—that is, Freedom—because the Infinite is not determined, toward the Ineffable, because we cannot rely on the *Logos* alone. The Goddess has to be a concrete Beatrice who is on the human scale, which demands the concreteness and limitations of Matter, and of our human intellect as well. The question, however, is also biased because Beatrice offers her guidance for the *Paradiso* only. Will that be enough?

The method is not a direct comparative method. It would have been relatively easy to follow a certain fashion and compare different ways of thinking and approaches to reality. A work of such a nature cannot ignore

12 Antonio Machado, *Campos de Castilla* (Madrid: Renacimiento, 1912) "Proverbios y cantares," V.

the radical differences between cultures. The african approach to reality is wildly different from a typical western one, and this view is again radically diverse from the asian one, if we may be allowed a general characterization by reducing the enormous riches of those cultures to certain common traits. In spite of the fact that writing in a western language already implies a substantial limitation, I have tried to integrate certain forms of thinking into my reflections. In this way, instead of comparing, which is ultimately not possible because there is no neutral point of comparison, I have tried to contribute to a mutual fecundation of philosophical traditions.

1. *Humor*

It is customary at the outset, especially in an anglo-saxon milieu, to use the classical *captatio benevolentiae* to gain the sympathy of the audience by cracking an introductory joke. A style too solemn, a countenance too serious, is deemed inelegant and seems almost ridiculous. The speaker plays it all down by saying that, after all, one might be mistaken and the mistake would not be the end of the world. To be too serious is counterproductive; a philosopher who cannot laugh is suspect. Too much involvement makes us lose perspective and forfeit our sense of proportion. "The philosopher is always joyful" (*Philosophus semper est laetus*), wrote that knight of loving wisdom named Ramon Llull.

I agree that authentic humor is a symptom of mental health—although this is not to be confused with bad jokes or with a certain type of irony pressed into service as a dialectical weapon. If I am not attached to my ideas it is because the ideas themselves are somewhat freewheeling with respect to me, and not because I do not care about the opinions I hold. Yet I know that they are opinions and not dogmas. To be ready to die for one's own ideas may be fanaticism, but not living up to one's own convictions is cowardice. The balance is delicate. One dies for one's faith when one lives by it, which is a different matter.

Besides, the deepest sense of humor is based on the awareness that, beyond us and all that we stand for there is a mystery that transcends us all, precisely because it is hidden in our immanence, like *brahman* is hidden in its own qualities.[13] True humor may well be the outcome of a mystical experience which perceives that the abyss between any word and its referent is more than ambiguity or ambivalence, but lies in the mysteriousness of the so-called referent itself. An omniscient God could not laugh. Nothing would be unexpected, no association of ideas funny; there could be no hidden meanings, no ambiguity or distance from the real . . . no surprises.

13 Cf. SU I, 3; etc.

All I shall put forward here are my convictions *secundum quid*, οἷον, *quasi*, *quodammodo*, as approximations, stammerings, provisional and experiential expressions, simulations, provocations, and questions to be further studied and criticized. They are not theses or dogmas, but neither are they hypotheses, because these meditations do not constitute a system or a scientific hypothesis intended to prove something else. I would like to believe that they are truly *philo-sophia*, which is perhaps the only true human *sophia*.

Another disclaimer may be pertinent here. Humor is the art of playing with the freedom of the Infinite by means of words. My words, alas, are without skill and elegance. Writing in the english *koinē* (neither american, nor english, nor indian, nor australian, etc.), my language is bound to be too restrained in its metaphors, too prosaic in its expressions, too wary of not doing justice to the connotations and free associations that give relief to language. *Dhvani* would be the proper word, but *dhvani* belongs to poetry, which, like humor, demands a dialect and not an "academic" language. *Dhvani* in indic poetics stands for the flavor and beauty of words, for their resonance, connotations, and associations. Words have not only meanings; they have also life. Humor is needed to get at what the concepts are too shy or too unable to disclose in a scientific hermeneutic.

Just as an artist sings, recites, draws, sculpts, or paints scores of sketches before the work of art is finally undertaken, I consider all that I have written as sketches for the inexpressible. The true artist realizes, after the work is finished, that it is only another sketch of what one had really (willfully or dreamingly) intended. Similarly, I have to confess that it all remains a sketch, because all that we can "produce" is only a sketch. Or perhaps this is a skewed metaphor that misses the mark by pointing toward a nonexistent ideal reality of which our sketch is supposed to be but an earthly copy. Platonism, vedānta, and idealisms of all sorts are coming to an end. But perhaps this is the most metaphysical joke of all: that the sketches are the reality—which amounts to saying that reality is a sketch we all are trying to make. I find the same humorous awareness in the first meaning of *sophia* in Homer: "skill," a skillful craft.

A metaphysical method without "humor" would be without that "humoral humility" which allows for flexibility, and would be the degradation of metaphysics into an algebra of concepts. The "meta" stands for the distance between measurable entities or concepts and the ultimately ineffable intuitions of the intellect. Concepts cannot put up with humor, since their ideal is to be univocal. Symbols, on the other hand, are polysemic and not only allow manifold interpretation but require a certain nonattachment to the symbol itself lest it become an idea or a concept. We can play with symbols. Symbolic consciousness is irreducible to any algebra.

In addition, humor makes us aware of the relativity of all statements which are meaningful in different ways, according to the diverse backgrounds to which they relate. Humor is at home in metaphor. Any *meta-phora* "carries us beyond" the first meaning of a sentence and allows us to land on unknown shores—and perhaps to get lost in them. Because of its underlying nonattachment humor prevents us from getting drowned in foreign waters.

Humor belongs to the philosophical method of this study for another reason. I will be speaking about serious questions that I consider very important; humor will prevent me from becoming ridiculously solemn. What weight can my opinions have in the light of what has been said by the great sages of human history? Besides, a sense of humor will allow me to express my convictions boldly, without fear. The thoughtful reader will perhaps detect a discreet smile between the lines.

* * *

This does not mean that I am writing as a humorist. I am merely affirming that a sense of humor is essential to my method. Otherwise the "way to" what I am getting at is simply an algebraic operation of induction and deduction, which is the strength of the scientific method: no loopholes consciously allowed—notwithstanding the theorem of Gödel. Extrapolations are to be verified (or falsified) later on, but everything follows a method in which the next step needs to rely on the prior one. This makes for a fascinating trek on the high mountains of a physical world governed by objective laws, while allowing for probabilities and well-tamed degrees of freedom. This is a very serious method indeed. "No jokes allowed" was written in front of the "security" screening machines at an airport I passed through. The obsession with "security" of a technocratic civilization does not allow for humor. A machine follows laws and instructions but does not "understand" humor. A mathematical concept needs to be universal, and the possible variables of a mathematical equation need to follow a certain law, at the very least statistical. Would this be one of the reasons for the lack of spontaneous joy (and unconcern) in modern civilization? Of course, joy should not be confused with entertainment. Our way to approach our problem, our *methodos*, is no less intelligible, though it does not fall into the reductionism of confusing rationality with intelligibility.

The genial intuition of Machado goes further. Perhaps echoing another castilian poet, John of the Cross, who says that in ultimate and vital issues *no hay camino,* "there is no way," because the goal is not a prefabricated construct—not even of our mind or of a supreme Mind, unless we confuse creation with construction. We have already referred to the *creatio continua*, whose implications are literally mind-blowing. Just as, according to the already quoted *Dhammapada*, the birds leave no tracks in the sky,[14] we have no fixed ground beneath our feet. Authentic human life is not a walk over a preconceived territory, lest our freedom be a farce and responsibility be a lie, although we should not confuse freedom with anarchy or responsibility with an absolute law. Reality is not a prefabricated construct.

The humor to which we refer when thinking about method is not what popular wisdom calls "putting the cart before the horse," but rather it is being aware that the cart without the horse is useless (no real cart), that the cart could also have a ox in front, and that sometimes we can do without any cart. . . . Our considerations exclude any prior itinerary; our theme allows no method. I am reminded of Gregory of Nyssa's explanation of Abraham's obedience to God in leaving his ancestral city of Ur: Abraham was certain when facing the desert that it was Yahweh's voice he had heard at home, because he did not know where he was going. No method, no way. If we know beforehand the "destiny of Being," we are not sincere in our search. Nothing is more sincere than humor.

Another more "serious" word for humor, paradoxically enough, is humility. We believe what we say and stand by our convictions, but know well that there are other ways of expressing what we want to say such that all our words (except formal terms) are mere approximations. We know well that all our insights and beliefs are only glimpses of the Real; we do not absolutize ourselves, nor even Knowledge. We realize that the very talk of an *Ab-solutus* is a contradiction the moment that we break its being *solutus* (unloosed) from everything by tying it to our consciousness. Humility is probably the highest intellectual virtue. It is not about despair, but rather about humor. Humor plays with words and so does the philosopher, and no play would be real if it excluded chance, the unexpected, the unknown. Even modern physics dares to confront Einstein about the God who does not play dice, and I repeat, irrationality is the contradiction of, but not the only alternative to, rationality unless we are totalitarian rationalists.

2. *The Holistic Attempt*

To lead us into wholeness (Paradise) is the most arduous task Beatrice has to perform. Even if for an ordinary pilgrimage each pilgrim has to find a personal path, in this ultimate journey to the real there is no way, because

14 *Dham* XVIII, 20.

all the paths already belong to the reality we are searching for. There is no method, no way as it has been said. We are already the method, "on the way," and the real way is precisely the goal, not necessarily the aim. Perhaps real wisdom consists in this experience: that there is no way, not because the summit is far away and has no path, but because there is no further way since there is no-where else to go. We are already there, the way is the goal: *saṁsāra* is *nirvāṇa*, each step is the definitive step, even if afterwards we discover that it has not been the last. When Christ says "I am the Way, the Truth and the Life"[15] he is not saying three different things, but is revealing that the real way is itself the Truth and that this Truth is no other thing than Life.

This is more than affirming that the method is *sui generis*, a proper and unique method. It amounts to saying that our common habits of research and of thinking are not applicable here. No "Discours de la *méthode*" is helpful here. Rather than a way to reach the goal, we should speak of how to open up to that very Whole that permeates us, and not just to a part, but to an image, an icon that reflects the Whole. The proper word would be contemplation in its deepest sense. The only "method" is not to prepare the way, but to prepare ourselves. The sages of all traditions have called it the "purification of the heart," an interior pilgrimage.

Yet I have refrained from discarding the word "method" not simply out of respect for tradition (method has an indispensable role in its proper field), but also because the word is susceptible of another meaning: not that of "going (on) the way" looking for a goal to reach, but that of transcending every way (μετά-ὁδός), because we discover ourselves to be ways of the Whole in its Being, in its Becoming what it is, as will be explained later. If our goal is the Whole, the Whole is already in any of the fragments precisely because it is a fragment of the Whole (subjective genitive). Further, I use the word "method" because from a formal point of view the theoretical statement that "there is no method" is already the proper method for those questions that "have no method."

At any rate, the holistic attempt tries to "reach" the Whole not by a dialectical synthesis but by means of an immediate contact with the Whole, defying the dualistic subject/object epistemology. The modern problematic about pre-understanding and hermeneutical circle is related to what we are saying. We cannot interpret anything without previously knowing that which we are interpreting. We cannot know any part without somewhat knowing the Whole of which it is a part, that is, without knowing it as a part of a whole. Can we, however, understand the Whole without knowing its

15 Jn XIV, 6

parts? It has to be another type of knowledge. To really understand a text we have to know its context, but in order to know the context we need to know the text, etc. I have called all these circles not vicious but *vital circles*. And here advaita offers a clue, as we shall still explain later on.

The simile of the circle is a telling one because the circles can be concentric and also allow for overlapping and disharmony. The more traditional insight on the "specular character" of the universe, however, is more appropriate. A part is a fragment and it can somewhat exist independently and present its own features. In contrast, an image that reflects the Whole expresses the relation between the image and the original in a more accurate way. Each entity is not just a part, but an image or icon of the Whole, as minimal and imperfect as that image may be, or as laden with hidden aspects as it may be if the entity is too small or our eyes too weak.

The holistic attempt to approach Reality as such cannot follow the individualistic method. The Whole is not the sum total of substantial selves, is not an object, and thus is impervious to any *epistēmē* that aims at objective knowledge. Furthermore, it is not the proper field of any exclusive ontology, that is, of any approach to the ὄν (Being) exclusively by means of *logos*. Our attempt requires also the *pneuma*, the spirit, love, not as a second fiddle playing to the echoes of reason, but as a loving knowledge, *reflectens ardor*, symbolized in the trinitarian experience: the *Logos* inseparable from the *Pneuma* (Spirit) and "coming" from the selfsame Source, as we shall see.

In other words, the holistic attempt can only be an insight from the Whole; it is the *svayamprakāśa* (self-refulgence) of vedānta, or the self-illumination of so many spiritual schools in the buddhist, christian, sufi traditions, etc. Not for nothing do all these traditions insist on discipline, initiation, and desire for liberation, in short, on purity of heart, as we are going to elaborate. Our present human condition does not allow us to ignore the factual situation. We do not see the forest for the trees. For too long many cultures have converted the "celestial hierarchy" into a terrestrial caste system. Nobody is excluded, everyone is called, no one is born a *brahmin* (according to some texts). However, not all make it—some due to rough economic or geopolitical impediments, and others for many reasons that we cannot examine here. For too long modern Man has lived in two worlds: a world of scientifically engineered or politically constructed reason, and a world of individually or collectively discovered sentiment. Otherwise useful classifications have been built into cultural apartheids.

a) A Threefold Approach

In order to approach the whole we may attempt to map it out (a) as it appears to us, (b) getting past the appearances to reach the core of the problem, and (c) remaining attentive to the very manifestation of the whole: the phenomenological, the metaphysical, and the sophianic methods respectively.

(1) The Socio-Historical Approach

Man is not *exclusively* a historical being, but certainly we are temporal, whether in the western interpretation, in a more buddhistic sense of the momentariness of unsubstantial moments, in a more karmic understanding of existence, or in cosmic participation in a superhuman destiny, and so on. The past emerges in our present, time is not just an external factor of human existence, and memory (μνήμη) is more than solely remembrance (ἀνάμνησις)—not necessarily in a platonic sense. The human experience of time is extraordinarily rich and complex.

The historical method is necessary today in order to understand ourselves. We all move in a historical context. We cannot approach our problematic *in vacuo* and alone. Our vision of the universe has been conditioned by history, by what other people have done and thought before. The historical method, however, is not sufficient for our undertaking. We cannot be satisfied by reporting other people's ideas or acts. Our being in a world that we have not made and in which we are immersed is, nevertheless, *our* being in the world. Moreover, we could not even *under*-stand the history of our predecessors and contemporaries if in one way or another their narratives did not stand beneath our own being and find a resonance in us. History makes sense only if we are able to rediscover and reinterpret what has been the human experience of our forebears. The Whole is holistically spread into the entire framework of the universe. The holistic attempt should overcome time and space. Is that possible? Or should we reduce the Whole to our individual wholeness?

Limiting ourselves to history, the historical approach tries to reenact the past in the present so as to learn from it. Our historical nature makes this possible. In passing I have referred to the myth of history, but this does not amount to saying that history is unreal. On the contrary, we should remember, commemorate, and reenact our historical past. The very world we live in has been shaped by history. Reality is not only historical reality, but it is indeed also historical. We are, although not exclusively, also historical beings. I repeat, the holistic approach is not obtained by the sum of its parts, but it cannot ignore the existence of the past either.

In sum, sociology and history are important disciplines that help us to get an overview of important fields of the human world, but they do not even claim to cover the entire human experience, let alone the entire reality.

(2) The Philosophical Approach

Which way is the wind blowing? "What are 'they' saying about . . . ?" This is not only a legitimate question but a fruitful one. The sociologist takes the pulse of "what's happening." And what's happening is found to be the result of multiple causes—of which propaganda, fashion, and manipulation are nowadays not negligible factors.

Why does the wind blow the way it does? The philosopher does not *directly* take the pulse of people's opinions the way pollsters do. To ask what "they" are saying about *karma*, democracy, the Trinity, and so on, are certainly important questions, but such asking does not constitute a philosophical inquiry. Nor does the philosopher simply draw deductions. Neither induction nor deduction is the primal philosophical method. Philosophy requires reflection, meditation, and thought, but not specialized knowledge of all the details and all the opinions of our predecessors.

"The study of philosophy does not consist in knowing people's opinions, but in knowing the status of the truth of things," Thomas Aquinas boldly said.[16]

This "truth of things" is the Whole. Yet this "truth of things" is not independent of the knowledge of things (the *sciatur*), and this knowledge is a human knowledge even if it may have a higher source. On one hand, philosophers are bound to be solitaries. The thinking activity requires solitude, nonattachment, distance, and even a certain avoidance of others. One cannot really think if one does not keep one's distance, leave all conformisms behind, and overcome the inertia of the mind. Philosophers have to be ascetics, in the best sense of the word, of course. They have to struggle with reality as Jacob did with the angel, or as Ulysses did with destiny. The thinking activity forges reality somewhat in the way that the smith forges the iron. Thinking shares in the shaping of reality.

On the other hand, philosophers cannot be isolated figures. Such isolation is their great temptation and poses the risk of solipsism. No philosopher is selfsufficient. No one can truly philosophize outside a tradition, even when rejecting that very tradition. Philosophy itself is rooted in history. An authentic "history of philosophy" sooner or later turns into a "philosophy of history." An example of the influence of the historical

16 Thomas Aquinas, *De caelo*, II: "Studium philosophiae non est ad hoc ut sciatur quid homines senserint, sed qualiter se habeat veritas rerum."

Zeitgeist (spirit of the times) in the philosophy of our times is the quasi-"scientific" character of many a "history of philosophy." Such books deal with philosophical ideas as if they were almost algebraic magnitudes linked with one another by mere rules of deduction or induction. It is one thing to realize that Kant is only comprehensible after Hume; it is something quite different to present kantian ideas as an almost logical outcome of british empiricism. A reigning ideology today is called "development," the last bulwark of the myth of progress. Growth, change, and ultimately life are more than just "development." Thinking is neither drawing conclusions nor a whimsical solitary imagination. Philosophical thinking navigates the cosmos by obedience and creativity.

What has given the word "metaphysics" a bad reputation is that all too often this core of philosophy has been taken as if it were atemporal and ahistorical—that is, absolute. Not just the philosopher but philosophy itself is situated in a particular time and space, and relative to the myth out of which it emerges. Philosophers know that in spite of the originality of their thinking, indeed precisely because of it, they stand on other people's shoulders and within a tradition, even if often in dialectical opposition to its main tenets. Authentic philosophers have to be in solidarity with the entire universe. Otherwise, how could they even talk about it? Solitariness and solidarity belong together.

The philosophical method is that of *thinking*, where this word stands for an active and intelligent listening to reality itself—to the Rhythm of Being, as I shall soon be saying. The philosopher does not just take the pulse of the crowd. The philosopher's task is to place one's mind and heart in tune with reality, allowing the very throbbing of Being to pass through one's spirit, and by so doing to change its rhythm. This means that all aspirants to wisdom must strive for purity of heart.

A philosopher's thinking is an active awareness of the "demands" of Being. "Active awareness" means that this awareness shapes (as much as it is shaped by) the very dynamism of Being. A dichotomy between theory and praxis is mortal for both; theory is reduced to barren speculation, and praxis is limited to reshuffling cards.

Each culture has its world and its ways of understanding reality. Indeed, here "world" and "reality" are symbols that cannot be reduced to concepts. Each culture has its own criteria for truth and its proper understanding of what goes under that name. I say truth and not exactitude or correctness. Nevertheless, there are questions, problems, and visions that transcend individual cultures. Philosophy needs a language, and language itself is culturally tinged; there is no supra-cultural language. There may be cross-cultural areas of overlapping affinities and intercultural influences, but anything consciously human is already subservient to a particular culture.

What does a "holistic attempt" mean then?

The great temptation of philosophy understood as *opus rationis*, as an effort of our mind alone, consists in looking for a "common denominator," as if the Whole were what is common to all. This commonality can only be a formal concept abstracted from the immense variety of beings. Again, philosophy cannot be reduced to an algebra of concepts, a juggling with abstractions. Philosophy has to resist, especially today, the trend toward specialization. Philosophy is not an exact science, but rather is a true science (*scientia*, knowledge). Its aim is not to control but to understand by all available means of knowledge. It is therefore a reductionistic view of philosophy to dictate a pre-vision that makes of it a merely rational endeavor. The modern western apartheid between philosophy and "theology," for instance, emasculates the former and destroys the latter. We lose critical touch with the whole.

The Whole is not the totality. The Upanishads are haunted by this holistic search: "What is that knowing by which everything is known?"[17] The answer cannot be a piecemeal cognition of things. The traditional answer is obviously to know *brahman*, God, the Knower of All. Nevertheless, this Knower is unknowable. If it were known it would become the Known, not the Knower. We can only attempt to know with the Knower, to strive to become the Knower. Then "I shall know in the measure that I am known."[18] The process is an existential one, a process of the whole person, which we discuss in our next section.

(3) The Sophianic Approach

This section would not be necessary if we had a more traditional idea of philosophy as wisdom, but the loss of the mystical core of philosophy in the prevalent use of this word behooves this third section. For this reason I have called this third approach "sophianic" instead of "philosophical."

Either we remove the sociological husk or break the ontological shell; in both cases we still need to get to the grain or kernel and "eat" it. Sensual knowledge puts the fruit in our hands, rational knowledge breaks it open and eventually cuts it into pieces so that it may be more understandable, but intellectual or spiritual knowledge eats and assimilates the fruit so that it

17 BU II, 4, 14; etc.

18 1 Cor XIII, 12.

may nurture our lives. This is the threefold structure of human knowledge. Experience means to eat the fruit, but in order to be able to assimilate it we must open and prepare it. What we seek is an experience that transforms our lives and incorporates us into the destiny of the universe. We are looking for an intuition capable of giving us an orientation in life, even if for the time being, for our being in time.

With vital issues we cannot wait until some science gives its final word, which will never come because science is a continuous process. We need another criterion to orient us in life. In other words, our method has to be truly a *met' hodos*, a going on the way, and not simply a marginal digression, an episode (*epi-eis-hodos*). We need to arrive at a simple "vision" of the problematic and come to a conclusion or decision, which is not the result of juggling a practically indefinite number of variables. We may trust our instincts, but human instinct also has an intellectual component. It may well be that *analysis* does not lead to *synthesis*, because the sum of the parts may not yield the whole. Even if analysis should succeed in giving us a synthesis, the whole is more than the result of a synthetic operation. We need the intuition of the Whole, which may not necessarily be a "clear and distinct idea."

Some african languages, aware that there are many perspectives, do not ask how we see the world, which gives preeminence to sight as in greek culture, but rather how we taste the world, since tastes are immediate and not so easily amenable to concepts. Whatever the etymology of *sophia* may be, its immediate meaning points to the ability to orient oneself in any given context, practical or theoretical. A *sophos* is an able and skillful person, a good navigator in Homer, as we have already said.

This ability in the area of ultimate questions consists not in controlling or dominating but in orienting oneself, sailing into harbor despite sociological winds and philosophical waves. A variety of human cultures have called this wisdom the "vision" of the third eye, the power of faith or mystical experience. We are saying, in other words, that the sophianic approach tries to overcome the pretension of both approaches, the historical (piecemeal) and the rational (formal). I should not emphasize that *sophia* is feminine because in many languages it is not, but the attitude behind this approach is certainly not the typical masculine feature of wanting to grasp, apprehend, dominate, and even know, but rather of being grasped, known, assimilated. The underlying problem is that of thinking and Being.

I may start all over again. We find ourselves "thrown" into this world, or simply in the middle of it. We find ourselves not only lost and forlorn, as

Dante put it[19], but also burdened by the very weight of our mind. A profound *śloka* of the Vedas discloses this: "What thing I am I do not know. I wander secluded, burdened by my mind."[20] We have lost confidence in ourselves and in others. The same story tells us that the "Firstborn of Truth" comes to us. The human tragedy, as Saint John's Prologue says, is that we do not receive that very Light which comes to us[21] because our praxis is selfish.[22] Most human traditions argue in a similar vein. In other words, the orientation in our lives comes from Life itself. We simply need a more positive attitude to receive it. This reception, however, does not preclude our freedom and our discernment. There may be false and artificial flashings. We have to use all our faculties for our human pilgrimage.

Now, to be open to the whole requires an attitude other than that of synthesis or analysis. It requires a "new innocence," a "voiding" of ourselves and even of our expectations. The ancients called this attitude *ars vitae*, which was another name for philosophy as a sophianic experience of Life.

b) The Starting Point

Today we stand before a horizon that presumably no other period in human history enjoyed—or at least many people believe so. We "know" about the seas and continents and about past and present. We have access to cultures that until very recently remained isolated, and we have enlarged our physical and physiological horizons as well: atoms, molecular biology, genes, and galaxies, not to mention the psychological forces, libidos, complexes, archetypes and so on.

There is an understandable trend toward the "global village" syndrome. There is much talk about global markets, world government, planetary democracy, universal human rights, world theology, the universality of a neutral science, and so on. Proponents of these ideas are legion in almost all fields. I detect in this new fashion a double force at play. On the one hand, the continuation by sheer inertia of the colonialistic myth which believes that one God, one culture, one science, and the like, is the ideal paradigm for understanding and that makes us believe "we" are representatives of and responsible for this world order. On the other hand, there is the innate human tendency toward unity, universalism, order, intelligibility and the

19 *Divina Commedia*, Canto I.

20 RV I, 164, 37. Cf. R. Panikkar, "Sharing in the Word," *The Vedic Experience* (Berkeley: University of California Press, 1977), 102-3.

21 Jn I, 5-11.

22 Cf. Jn III, 19-20.

like. I link this trend with theistic thinking, especially with monotheism, as we shall explain later on.

I hasten to assure the reader that the "holistic attempt" of this book, while acknowledging that innate human tendency, criticizes the short-circuited interpretation that identifies order, harmony, and concord with unity, homogeneity, and egalitarianism. Here again *advaita* offers the adequate approach. *Advaita* in fact entails a cordial order of intelligibility, of an *intellectus* that does not proceed dialectically.

Our attempt at the Whole is not to be confused with the universalistic ideal of absolutizing human values. Any "universalism," even assuming the whole territory has been mapped out, overlooks one essential thing: the starting point, our necessarily limited perspective, the "window" from which we construct such a universal worldview. No global starting point is possible.

No single person can reasonably claim to master a global point of departure. No individual exhausts the totality of possible human approaches to the real. There is no human perspective of 360 degrees. Even if someone claimed that divine revelation stands as guarantor that a particular perspective is the uniquely valid and universal one, any human understanding of that alleged revelation shares in the inherent limitations of every human being. Furthermore, even if a divine revelation would assure us that our interpretation is the valid one, this assertion would convince only those who have received this sacred revelation, which would make of that system a solipsistic system that is only valid for "insiders."

On the logical plane there are too many irreducible options at the very beginning of any attempt to philosophize. Besides, the very moment we become aware of the existence of other "systems," we cannot avoid trying to understand them by bringing them into relation with our "own" categories of understanding. Perhaps we may succeed in taking "a step back" and finding a new starting point. Or we may come to recognize the irreconcilability of the different starting points, which nevertheless are legitimized by their respective "systems."

A frequent reaction to the difficulty of finding a global starting point consists in saying that, although the points of departure are different, they all lead to the same point of arrival. In such an understanding, "all religions ultimately say the same thing" or "lead to the same goal"; "all systems of philosophy come to similar conclusions from different perspectives"; "human nature is one"; "the universe converges toward an omega point"; "God is the absolute Future"; and the like.

Whether this is pure fancy, wishful thinking, or a fact is not our problem here. My intention is not to create a (doubtful) synthesis of all philosophies or to defend an absolute system. I am simply presenting a plausible "vision" of Reality that, without spurning reason, discovers its proper limits and suggests an *advaitic* order of intelligibility different from rational evidence. The *advaitic* order of intelligibility is intrinsically pluralistic.

Another frequent reaction in face of the differing explanations of reality consists in appealing to higher states of consciousness. The *coincidentia oppositorum*, the harmonization of opposite views, would then be achieved by climbing to a new state of awareness from which Reality may be surveyed. Seen from the perspective of a higher awareness, the cathedrals, the pyramids, the *thankas* and scientific cosmology, all different expressions of apparently divergent worldviews, could then be interpreted as saying the "same" thing.

This legitimate response, however, must constantly be on guard against one of the most insidious dangers that bedevils such endeavors: the totalitarian temptation. My attempt is holistic, not global; I am not offering a system. The pluralism inherent in the *advaïtic* intuition is not a super-system but an attitude. Universality, the whole, metaphysics, and similar notions seem to have an inbuilt claim to encompass the universal range of human experience, the totality of the real. This is a sheer impossibility, unless we enthrone our particular perspective, whether it is called Reason, Revelation, or whatever, as an absolute principle.

The language of the whole is just a language, a manner of speaking. Language is the human way of being in the world, and the plurality of languages shows plainly that there is more than one way to be human. A modicum of cross-cultural exposure is almost sure to cure most of us of any totalitarian tendencies. Our question may be the metaphysical question as such. Bertrand Russell opens one of his essays saying, as if obliquely: "Metaphysics, or the attempt to conceive the world as a whole by means of thought. . . ." Without scrutinizing the meaning of "by means of thought" too closely, I may adopt a plain description of metaphysics as the attempt to speak somewhat meaningfully about the Whole—not about everything. Neither do I need to assume that "the world" is what Russell means. Our problem is this: How can we become critically aware of the Whole? This is a crucial point of philosophy. Three queries arise immediately:

i. How can I pretend to speak about the Whole? Subjective limitation—the *questioner*.
ii. How can we speak about the Whole without knowing all the parts that constitute the Whole? Objective limitation—the *questioned*.

iii. Is the Whole a real question at all? Is it not simply a formal notion that does not even know what it is questioning? Thinking limitation—the *question* itself.

The three queries together should make us aware that if there is to be any approach to the Whole, the method will have to be unique, *sui generis*, not comparable to any other method. Perhaps the *met' hodos* here is just an awareness of being "on the way"—without going anywhere.

In fact, this approach seems to have been constantly attempted by the human mind (and not exclusively by the Nāgārjunas and the Hegels). The μελέτα τὸ πᾶν, "be concerned with or cultivate the Whole" of our motto, the ātman*brahman* of the Upanishads, the *tao* as an empty vessel of the *Tao Te Ching*, the "one needful thing" of the Gospel, or the ἡ ψυχή πάντα πῶς of Aristotle, reflected in Thomas Aquinas's *anima quodammodo omnia*, "the soul is in a way everything," are all examples of this human thirst for the Whole. The desire for God in multifarious traditions could also be interpreted in a similar vein: The human spirit is not satisfied with less than the Whole. Unless the *jīvātman* experiences *ātman*-*brahman*, unless the "individual soul" intuits that its most intimate nature is an aspect of the "ultimate reality," it cannot stop the pilgrimage. The often quoted sentences of Augustine have become classic examples:

> For thou hast made us for thyself and restless is our heart until it comes to rest in thee.[23]
>
> –I desire to know God and the soul.
>
> –Nothing else?
>
> –Nothing else at all.[24]

Perhaps the Serpent understood the ultimate aspiration of Man: "Ye shall be like God."[25] *Nirvāṇa*, *mokṣa*, the *tao*—in a word, the Infinite—is the innate aspiration of Man, and eventually his goal, which may lie in/on the very way. The problem of rhythm looms on the horizon.

I return to the three queries.

---

23 Augustine, *Confessiones* I, 1: "quia fecesti nos ad te et inquietum est cor nostrum donec requiescat in te."

24 Augustine, Soliloquia II (7):
- Deum et animam sciro cupio.
- Nihilne plus?
- Nihil omnino.

25 Gn III, 5.

(1) The Questioner

Let me heuristically call reality what I have so far referred to as the Whole.

Now, who is asking the question about it? If the questioner belongs to reality and that which is questioned is reality itself, this can only be a question that reality is putting to itself. If it were just a question put by one part of reality to another, we would not be questioning the whole Reality. We are not in the field of the so-called natural sciences, in which the subject is left out, or, more accurately, is considered only a measuring subject, an observer with a certain influence on the observed (Heisenberg equations). Here, instead, the questioner about reality is prompted by reality itself. The questioner, nevertheless, is there. He may have no answer, but he is an actual questioner. What is that which the questioner is asking and in which the questioner is also involved? So far as we know, only one being in the world asks such a question: Man. Or, put more carefully: the question appears in and through human consciousness. It is *the* question that occurs to, in, and with consciousness, the question that manifests itself in Man who is the questioner, the *Dasein*.

Now this question about the Whole would not arise if the Whole, in one way or another, were not open to the questioner. We have already cited Aristotle saying that consciousness (as I here translate *psychē*) is in a way everything. We are very close to the universal mind of the christian and muslim scholastic disputes, the *intellectus agens universalis* and the *cit* of a certain vedānta. Reality and consciousness have a *sui generis* relationship. They may not be identical, as some philosophies are tempted to say, but we cannot separate them. Consciousness may not be aware of all individual beings, or even of all that a being may be, but it certainly is aware of the Whole insofar—and only insofar—as the Whole appears in consciousness. The Whole (by definition) cannot "have" or "be" anything "outside" itself but it may "have" or "be" very many "things" "inside" itself not reached or reachable by consciousness. Says the *Tao Te Ching* : "Once the Whole is divided, the parts need names."[26]

What can Man's consciousness "say" about the Whole before putting names to it? Is the Whole a formal concept or has it a reality of its own? Even if it were a mere formal concept, its (conceptual) formality would equally belong to the Whole.

Having realized that consciousness of the Whole is both consciousness

26 *Tao Te Ching*, 32.

of the Whole (not of its parts) and the Whole's consciousness (for there is nothing "outside" the Whole), consciousness is directed toward itself, that is, to introspection, interiority—as Lao Tsu, the Upanishads, Aristotle, Augustine, and so many others remind us. They do not mean intimacy and solipsism, as it is sometimes interpreted. On the contrary, they mean the attempt to overcome the distraction of the parts and to get in touch with the Whole.

In vedic parlance, the Whole is *brahman*, and the questioner is the Self, ātman. Unless and until we have discarded *ahamkāra*, egoism, we cannot even begin to philosophize. Philosophy is not hunting for entities and their links or causes in the critically polished field of consciousness. Philosophy is the opening of our purified conscious being to the self-disclosure of reality—and this finds an obstacle in our ego. Without *mumukṣutva* (ardent aspiration for liberating truth) philosophy is not possible. The culmination of this process is when the ātman realizes *ātman-brahman*.

Says Bhartrhari: "The attainment of Brahman is nothing more than loosing the knot [*granthi*] of the ego-sense in the form of 'me' and 'mine.'"[27]

To renounce one's own ego, however, is to renounce ownership of one's "own" being. No particular being is the Whole; a being is not (the) Whole. Each being may reflect, and refract, the Whole, but only in a certain way, οἷον, *quodammodo*. Each knot of consciousness is not only the ego-sense (*ahamkāra*), it is also the unavoidable perspective which any act of consciousness requires until we reach "that by knowing which all is known,"[28] as the Upanishad says. If to know is to become the known, what is that by becoming which one becomes all? When can we truly say: *aham-brahman*? If only the Whole can exhaustively ask about the Whole, as long as my ego stands in the way the question itself is no proper question. "'Nothing is mine,' means to me, 'I am everything'"[29]—literally, "all"— writes Abhinavagupta, as John of the Cross also said centuries later.[30] Oriental wisdom, Aristotle, and most of the islamic and christian scholastics after him, follow the same line. The question about the Whole haunts the human mind.

The attempt may fail, but it already reveals something about the Whole, which truly or apparently allows such a question. It reveals something not only about the very nature of the Whole but about Man as well, who is prompted to put such a unique question. Who am I? (*ko'ham*) is the vedic

27 Bhartṛhari, *Vākyapadīya*, I, 5.

28 BU II, 4, 14; etc.

29 Abhinavagupta, *Parātrīśika-vivaraṇa*, 5.

30 Juan de la Cruz, *Máximas y sentencias*, 25.

question that a Ramana Maharshi prompts us to ask again in our times. It should be clear that this question about the I is the search for the Whole. We may recall utterances of many mystics who seem to have overcome subjective limitations. Is this possible?

In sum, we can speak meaningfully about the Whole only if the human *psychē* in a certain way, *quodammodo*, is the Whole. It is important to retain this insight. "You would not search for Me if you had not (already) found Me," say many sages East and West. The questioner is a questioner because each of us is also questioned. We know as we are known. The questioner asks about the Whole because it is the very question of the Whole. "*Quaestio mihi factus sum,*" wrote Augustine,[31] which in this context we could translate: "I myself have become (the) question." It is the same reality that questions itself in and through the questioner. Man is such a questioner of the Whole (subjective genitive). But can the questioner coalesce with the questioned?

(2) The Questioned

The second query is: *What* is being questioned? How can a part pretend to know the Whole without knowing all the other parts? I have already referred to the parts of the Whole, but if the Whole is whole it is more than the sum of its parts. The degree of reality of the Whole is different from that of its parts. I am deliberately reversing the nominalistic (and modern-scientific) approach: In a way, the parts are but abstractions of the Whole which, in this very process of ab-straction, lose something irretrievable, something that cannot be recovered by any art or integration. Even if we agree that ab-straction is not necessarily sub-straction (extraction), the abstraction is not the Whole. At its best it could yield only a perspectival vision of the Whole, a formal concept, but the concept of truth does not liberate, just as the concept of water does not quench one's thirst. The realization of truth, on the other hand, truly liberates.

The usual methodology of the natural sciences tends to distract us from our method of approaching the Whole. The Whole is not objective and thus not objectifiable. A wholly objectifiable Whole would leave out the subject. Thought about the Whole belongs to the Whole and in a sense modifies the Whole, since it belongs to the very dynamism of the Whole, but it is not necessarily (identical to) the Whole.

We do not need to wait to know everything in order to think the Whole. At the same time, we cannot know the Whole without knowing about the possible existence of the different dimensions that may constitute it. Hegel

31 Augustine, *Confessiones,* X, 33.

said "truth is the Whole" ("Das Wahre ist das Ganze"). The totality is more than the sum of its parts, but not less. It is necessary to know "something" about the parts if we are to know the Whole. We have to know at least the possible existence of all the parts; not their particularity. If modern science does not know the Whole, nor even claim to know it, it is also true that without modern science philosophy today cannot properly approach the Whole either.

We are not required to know every "part" of the Whole, but we should be scrupulous enough to learn from those who have thought about the Whole. This is not such an impossible task as it would be if a particularized knowledge of everything were necessary, but it is daunting to set sail on a sea in which there have been so many shipwrecks. Already the greeks distinguished between τὸ ὅλον, the Whole, and τὸ πᾶν, the All. The latter often meant the universe as the collection of all things: τὰ πάντα. The Whole, prior to its parts, was already recognized by Plato.

On the other hand, the Whole is not subjective either. That is the idealistic temptation. Because we cannot encompass the Whole from the "outside" we may pretend to imprison it "inside." Since our human consciousness is an inseparable fellow traveler in the human quest for the real, we may be tempted to identify reality and consciousness. If they are certainly inseparable, they are nevertheless distinguishable, and this distinction is real. We cannot reasonably sever epistemology from ontology, but we have no ground either to interpret ontology as the *logos* about the *on* (Being), or even to identify the *on* of the *logos* with the *on* as such, although again we cannot separate them.

If these questions are so difficult and complicated, would it not be better to keep our hands off them? Such a response entails a double fallacy that should be exposed immediately.

(i) Vital and important questions need not—and we might add, should not—be so difficult as to be hidden from people. I shall not adduce the classical examples given by vitalists, organicists, and others on questions hotly debated since the greeks. A simpler case will suffice. Everybody understands that to know Isabel entails knowing Isabel as a concrete person, and yet we do not need to know the entire life of Isabel and her psychosomatic structure nor the whole of humanity in order to know Isabel, although the better I know her the more I shall know humanity—and vice versa. To know Isabel *qua* Isabel I do not need to know the sum total of the qualities. Another (loving-knowing) approach is required. Here is the great challenge.

(ii) Vital questions are seemingly difficult and complicated if we approach them in an improper or "dead" manner. To approach the Whole as a totality or as the integration of all its possible constituents may be a fascinating (and difficult) problem, but this is not our question about the Whole. The Whole is not a thing or an object of thought. It is rather the horizon over against which we experience the Wholeness of every concrete thing. It is that which allows us to relate everything with everything without doing violence to the related things.

In other words, the question about the Whole is neither a cosmological nor an anthropological question. As long as I am not misunderstood as defending a Supreme Being, I would affirm that this is a theological question.

The problem of the Whole has no proper place in the classical discussions East and West about nominalism and realism (along with conceptualisms of all sorts). From real beings we may abstract the concept of Being and reach an empty concept which the scholastics called *ens commune*. The Whole, however, is neither just a name nor a concept nor a thing. Isabel is real and my knowledge of her has a direct approach that is different from all the details I know of her. There is an *advaitic* relationship. Other people may know the same details of her being and form another idea of her. They have integrated all those facts within another horizon of intelligibility.

Our example, however, may be misleading because our problem is not holistic knowledge of an individual but the knowledge of the Whole. Is there such a holistic intuition? This is what I called the great challenge.

In sum, we can speak about the Whole only if in a certain way we can discover the unfolding of the Whole in its particular manifestations, and this is possible only because each of us is a sort of image of the Whole—*quadammodo omnia*. This forces us to recognize that any discourse about the Whole is necessarily provisional because the Whole itself has no extrinsic limits.

(3) The Question

Our third query contains *in nuce* the entire philosophical endeavor. It is the question about the question, the critical awareness of (our consciousness of) Reality. Is it a real question? Is there really such a Whole? Since it is an ultimate query, it has no ulterior basis on which an answer might be grounded.

The most we can do is to show that an answer in the negative tends to contradict itself. If the Whole were merely an abstraction, from where, we may ask, has this abstraction been abstracted? A more careful formulation would ask whether the Whole has any consistency or is merely a mental construct for heuristic or pragmatic purposes. The Whole is not an abstraction, but could it not be a projection, a kind of mental hypothesis?

One thing is clear: the thought of the Whole exists. It is there, in ourselves, and attested by human history. How real is it? For our purposes we need to retain only this much: Talk about the Whole is meaningful even without deciding its degree of reality. All human discourse entails a claim to be understood by others. This implies a sharing of "something" common to us and to others in our universe of discourse. This commonality is not nothing.

When I affirm that talking about the Whole makes sense, I do not imply that this Whole is a thing, an immutable container of everything or a fixed and static entity. I have already insisted that the Whole cannot be approached in the same manner as anything else. I merely affirm that Man has this uncanny power of becoming aware that the Whole is not a meaningless word, even if we come to call it unintelligible, absolute nothingness or by any other "mysterious" name.

We have been saying that our question is about the Whole, and that the Whole by its very nature embraces the questioner, the questioned, and the question all together. The question about the Whole is a proper philosophical question, and some will affirm that it is the philosophical query par excellence. It amounts to asking: What is reality? If we ask about the question, we need to ponder the epistemological status of the question. We may ask about this and that because this and that are objects of and in our consciousness, but the Whole is not an epistemological object of this type.

However, could not the Whole be a phenomenon? Something that appears as a *Gestalt* to our consciousness? In the concrete example of Isabel this seems to be obvious. We see Isabel as a Whole (person), but Isabel is not the Whole. Or is this not the case?

Here we encounter the great challenge to which I referred. Insofar as Isabel (or a pebble for that matter, as we are going to explain) is an individual, a single thing, she is not the Whole indeed. Here is the place and function of the *advaitic* intuition, which precisely harmonizes the Whole and the part (here I prefer to speak of the Whole and the *concrete*—that which has grown together [*concretus* from *con-crescere*], that is, severing itself from the Whole).

The *advaitic* intuition focuses not on the two things (the Whole and the part, in our case) to be related. This is the classical dialectical approach. The *advaitic* intuition intuits the relationship itself. Isabel is not an independent part of humanity and ultimately a piece, an atom of the universe, but the concretion of the universe in her—a spark of the Divine says a certain mystic.

An isolated Isabel does not exist, nor can I know Isabel if I take cognizance of Isabel alone. I have to know also what José Ortega y Gasset called her "circumstance," her world around (*Umwelt* says the german). Then I need to relate both, and this is dialectical thinking—the movements from A to B, Hegel would say. The *advaitic* intuition proceeds differently. It does not look first at Isabel and then at her environment, trying afterward to relate the two. The *advaitic* intuition sees primordially the relationship that "makes" the "two," sees the polarity that makes the poles. It can discover that the poles are neither one nor two. Only by negating the duality (of the poles) without fusing them into one can the relationship appear as constitutive of the poles, which are such only insofar as they are conceptually different and yet existentially or really inseparable. Says William Blake voicing poetically this vision:

> To see the world in a grain of sand
> and heaven in a wild flower
> Hold infinity in the palm of your hand
> and eternity in an hour[32]

To sum up, the Whole as such is just a thought of the human mind, an idea. The reality of this idea is discovered by the *advaitic* intuition, which sees the Whole in the Concrete. This *advaitic* knowledge amounts to a mystical intuition or the vision of the third eye. We do not see the *totum* as such, nor do we mistake the *pars pro toto* (the part for the Whole), but we are aware of the *totum in parte*, of the Whole in the concrete, because we discover the *pars in toto* in the nondualistic intuition. The topic is important enough to insist on it under a slightly different perspective.

c) The Vital Circle

We are attempting to say something about the Whole. We agreed that we cannot wait until we know everything about all its parts. Our method cannot be inductive. Nor can it be deductive, unless we assume that this Whole is a logical mass from which we may draw conclusions. Even then, the wholeness of the Whole would be refracted in terms of the very partial

32 See the poem "Auguries of Innocence," in William Blake, *The Complete Poetry and Prose of William Blake*, ed. David V. Erdman, newly rev. ed. (Garden City, N.Y.: Ancor Books, 1982), 490.

makeup of the part that we are. Three aspects seem to be unavoidable if we want to retain a certain rationality in our discourse.

First, the discourse about the Whole needs to include me, us, the discussants. It cannot therefore be solely objective or exclusively subjective. Neither experiment nor experience will do. The former is too objective; the latter too subjective.

Second, the discourse has to be constantly provisional, never closed, always open. It has to be truly "dis-course"—a running to and fro. Not only can we not put limits on the Whole, but we cannot define it; we cannot have any definitive idea or opinion of it either. We have no criteria for knowing whether we have reached its limits. The Whole can grow. We cannot have any concept of it. If I were to use a word for the proper method, I would have to say observation. Observation does not interfere, as experiment does; nor is it introspective like the experience. But this observation needs to be innocent—a simple insight, ecstatic, without reflection. If we observe the very observation, it should then include the observation of the observer (observing the observation) and thus would lead us to a *regressus in infinitum*. It should be rather an "observant" attitude full of "respect" and "reverence."

Third, the Whole always appears as the all-encompassing horizon within which all the ideas, feelings, and apprehensions we have about it are situated. In other words, the Whole appears only within the corresponding *mythos* about the real in which we happen to believe.

There is an unbreakable circularity between the intellect and the world, between consciousness and the cosmos, between thinking and being. In modern scientific parlance we could also say, between facticity and rationality. The fact is recognized as such only by reason; reason is only actually reason when it encounters facts. Or, in a more philosophical vocabulary, the world is what appears in consciousness, and consciousness is such because it is conscious of the world.

> Nobody is aware that one understands unless he understands something; since first is the understanding of something, and then the understanding that we understand.[33]

This is the aristotelian tradition; platonism would put it differently.

We have here a formulation of the scheme "Thinking/Being," which represents the ultimate paradigm of many a civilization, but I dare to criticize this scheme.

33 Thomas Aquinas, *De veritate*, X, 8: "Nullus autem percipit se intelligere nisi ex hoc quod aliquid intelligit; quia prius est intelligere aliquid quam intelligere se intelligere."

In order not to be unduly hampered by the history of philosophy I have carefully avoided the word Being and instead I have been reflecting on the Whole. But our reflection cannot ignore the weight of tradition. The consecrated word for what we were pondering about the Whole is precisely "Being"—and we shall not avoid this word any longer.

To make my position clear, I assume that thinking is active awareness, whereas pure awareness is passive. Since Aristotle, we have heard about the active and the passive intellect, the νοῦς ποιητικός and the νοῦς παθητικός; chinese sages have taught us about the *yin* and *yang* aspect of reality, the intellect included. *Thinking "thinks Being."* Being begets thinking. One might even risk saying: *Being "beings thinking."* Thinking is thinking (of) something (active thinking), and thinking itself is something (passive thinking). Thinking is such if it is permeated by Being. Thinking is an activity of Being. Being thinks, otherwise thinking would be nothing. The problem is whether thinking is the only activity of Being. Our second sentence, however, calls for a qualification. "Being beings thinking." More simply, Being thinks. Thinking is an activity of Being, but thinking cannot prevent Being from having other activities besides thinking. Certainly, thinking cannot forbid it, but these other activities could not be considered as such unless our thinking were aware of them. That is, thinking cannot be totally absent from those other (possible) activities of Being—insofar as we speak of them. Thinking is a fellow traveler in any of the activities of Being—inasmuch as we are concerned, but thinking is a comrade of Being that knows that its companion (Being) may carry a closed suitcase. Sometimes thinking consoles itself by thinking that in a future time it will succeed in opening the box and exhaust the mysteries of Being. At the same time, thinking well knows that this is only a hypothesis loaded with presuppositions and dependent on a very particular assumption of what time is. It could well be that the box is transparent not to the light of thinking but only to the invisible rays of the *mythos*, of the unthought, which allows thinking to proceed without having constantly to go back in search of its foundations. Nor can thinking dismiss the idea that the box will remain forever closed to the power, menace, or even reduction of consciousness.

In short, the circularity between Thinking and Being can be broken only by the recognition (by thinking, of course) that thinking may not exhaust Being, not only in us, obviously, but theoretically, that is, by pure thinking. Elsewhere I have advanced the hypothesis that Speaking is an activity of Being concomitant with Thinking but not identical with it. For our purposes the *thought* suffices that the approach to the Whole is possible only by breaking the exclusive dominion of the *logos*—both in its peculiar "opposition" to *mythos* and in its no less peculiar "complementarity" to *pneuma*.

I have called this section *The Vital Circle* both to distinguish it from a vicious circle, which is a closed circularity, a *petitio principii*, and to stress the rhythmic aspect of the problem of the relationship between the Whole and the Concrete. The vision of the Concrete in the Whole and the Whole in the Concrete is, in fact, another way of saying that the relationship is rhythmic. Rhythm is not an "eternal return" in a static repetition. It is rather the vital circle in the dance between the Concrete and the Whole in which the Concrete takes an ever-new form of the Whole. The always astonishing Nietzsche wrote:

> Everything goes, everything returns;
> eternally rolls the wheel of Being.
> . . .
> Every moment Being begins
> . . .
> The center is everywhere. Crooked is the path of eternity.[34]

Sharing in the vital circle of the rhythm of life we discover the Whole in the Concrete, we experience everywhere the center of the infinite sphere. A center is not just a dot or a point; a center is center only in (*advaitic*) relationship with a sphere or a circumference. The holistic vision discovers everything as a center and not as an isolated atom. For this vision we need an empty or a pure heart. This leads us directly to the following reflections.

3. *The Purification of the Heart*

My subtlest temptation was to prepare these lectures instead of preparing myself. To search for something to say, instead of aspiring for something to be. The danger was to engage myself gathering "materials" (even "ideas") instead of gathering myself, my Self; to experiment with abstractions, instead of experiencing my-self, and observing reality.[35] The destiny of the universe passes in and through us—once the us, of course, has been purified of all that is "our" private property. We are not isolated beings. Man bears the burden, the responsibility, but also the joy and the beauty of the universe. "He who knows himself knows the Lord"[36] goes a traditional saying of islām that is constantly repeated by sufis. "He who knows himself knows all things";[37] so Meister Eckhart completed the famous injunction of the [Pythia] at Delphi:

34 Nietzsche, *Also sprach Zarathustra*, III, *Der Genesende* 2: "Alles geht, alles kommt zurück; / ewig rollt das Rad des Seins. / . . . In jedem Nu beginnt das Sein; / . . . Die Mitte ist überall. / Krümm ist der Pfad der Ewigkeit." Translation by Thomas Common.

35 This is not an excuse, but perhaps an explanation for this delay of twenty years in publishing these lectures.

36 "Man ʿarafa nafsa-hu ʿarafa rabba-hu."

37 Meister Eckhart, *Vom Edlen Menschen*, DW V, 498.

"Know yourself." The three are here brought together: God, the World, Man. I call this the cosmotheandric experience, but for such an experience we need a pure heart, a heart devoid of all selfishness—an empty *qualb,* the sufi tradition will say, echoed by St. John of the Cross in the company of buddhist and other masters. It is intriguing to know that these three, the "World, the Soul, and God" are the three "realities" off-limits to the kantian "pure reason." "The way to ascend to God is to descend into oneself," said Hugh of St. Victor, echoing Plato, the Upanishads, Śankara, Ibn 'Arabī, and the entire tradition that urges us to cleanse the mirror of the self, the icon of the Deity. Richard of St. Victor seems to complement this thought by recommending, again in tune with the Orient, "let Man ascend through himself above himself."[38]

My preparation for these lectures has been as much a spiritual as an intellectual discipline. If my ambition was to utter words of truth for our present world, how could I pretend first to have, and second to convey, such a vision if my life were not harmonious? *Nemo dat quod non habet*: Nobody gives what they don't have. Wishful thinking is not actually thinking. It is a kind of intellectual cancer, a proliferation of groundless thoughts with no roots.

Anything that does not stem from one's own inner and purified being, from the fullness of life, anything that does not flow from the very wellspring of reality, is tainted, manipulated, deformed, and not authentic, no matter what lofty names may be ascribed to it. There are ontic indigestions and ontological abortions, which give rise to immature thoughts and would-be intuitions. Reality can be twisted and deformed; and yet all is part of the real. The purification of the heart is not a simple moral injunction, but more than an epistemic condition; it is an ontological requirement.

The only relevant advice in this regard is to recall the old sayings about purification of the heart: not to put up obstacles for the Spirit, or barriers to divine Grace, letting the Tao be, becoming transparent, renouncing the fruits of action, and the like.

To say that the solution lies inside is not to assert that it is not outside as well, or that it lies already coiled somewhere within. Indeed, the *kuṇḍalinī* does not even exist before it stretches up, nor does the potency of Aristotle for that matter. The process is one of creation. If we know where we are going we are not really free, but rather are tied to preconceived ideas and bound to a goal.

38 Richard of St. Victor, *De praeparatione animi ad contemplationem,* 83: "ascendat per semetipsum super semetipsum."

For the individual, all this may still make some sense and be possible. I can trust in *Īśvara* (Lord), God, Reality . . . I can be vulnerable, allow things to happen, and attune myself to the spontaneous development of Being. Nonetheless, what can it mean for the collectivity, for the people, for sociological change and historical effectiveness?

My only point here is that we shall not discover the real situation we are in, collectively as well as individually, if our hearts are not pure, if our lives are not in harmony within ourselves, with our surroundings, and ultimately with the universe at large. The conditions for right vision, according to the *Vivekachūdāmaṇi*, concern the aspirant, of course, but they are rooted in the very structure of the real.[39] Christ is born in every one of us only if our heart is pure, echoes Meister Eckhart.[40]

The reason is not only moral; it is ontological. Only when the heart is pure are we in harmony with the real, in tune with reality, able to hear its voice, detect its dynamism, and truly "speak" its truth, having become adequate to the movement of Being, the Rhythm of Being. The *Chung Yung* says, "Only the most absolute sincerity under heaven can effect any change."[41] The spiritual masters of every age agree that only when the waters of our spirit are tranquil can they reflect reality without deforming it.

This implies, of course, that thinking is much more than just concocting thoughts. Thinking discovers the real, and by this uncovering we shape reality, by participating in its rhythm, by "listening" to it, and by being obedient (*ob-audire*) to it. Creative thinking is a genuine creation, a contribution to cosmogony, but in order that our contemplation have this resonance and power, we need to be free from both preconceived ideas (inertia of the mind) and egoistic will. A traditional name for this is sanctity; a more academic name, wisdom. The strongest formulation is perhaps that of the Beatitudes: the pure in heart shall see God,[42] that is, the entire reality.

* * *

In retrospect, my entire life seems to have been led by a passion (a *pathos*) for a truly *saving* knowledge. The names may vary. Perhaps it would be better to say, communion with the real, participatory awareness in reality, wisdom, *philosophia*, or even holiness. They are all approximations of what could also be rendered by the aspiration (not desire) for *sōtēria*, *salus*, *mokṣa*, *nirvāṇa*, and even *gnōsis* and *śūnyatā*.

---

39 Śankara, *Vivekachūdāmaṇi*.

40 Meister Eckhart, Predigt 101.

41 *Chung Yung*, 23 (Ezra Pound's translation).

42 Mt V, 8.

This *pathos* also demands a proper *ethos*: the δαίμων, Heraclitus called it ("The *ethos* of Man is his *daimōn*"[43]). I think I am in the best company in sharing this passion for holiness, perfection, wholeness. The Gospel calls it a thirst for justice, and here I detect a *novum*, a novelty for our times, even if it is at least twenty centuries old. I call it "sacred secularity."[44] Justice (δικαιοσύνη) is as much spiritual justification and righteousness as it is material, social, and even political justice. The "theology of liberation" in the christian West has insisted on that.

Here something relatively new seems to emerge in contemporary consciousness. All the lofty words we have used to denote this aspiration toward salvation have generally been interpreted as the "salvation" of the core of the real, the soul, the spirit by blowing up (*nirvāṇa*) the material, this world, the body.

The contemporary aspiration, however, does not discard anything, does not put anything aside, nor does it despise or eliminate any portion of the real. This *novum* does not take refuge in the highest by neglecting the lowest; it does not make a separation by favoring the spiritual and ignoring the material; it does not search out eternity at the expense of temporality. Should I call it a passion for bringing together the traditional East with the traditional West, as the oversimplified slogan goes? Or the reconciliation between tradition and modernity? Or is it the outer and the inner, the male and the female going together, as the *Gospel of Thomas* says, the *yang* and the *yin* of the chinese tradition?

If not now, at the close of my earthly pilgrimage, when? When shall I gather the broken pieces of specialization—of my many nesting places in the branches of the Tree of Knowledge, and that of Life, of my passing through all the āsh*ramā* of existence? I do not forget, however, that cherubim with whirling and flashing swords guard the way to that tree of Life.[45]

C. Regarding the Title and Subtitle

Tot és com una dansa de la vida i la mort:
hi ha l'home i l'ocell i l'herbeta de l'hort,
l'avet que sembla etern i la margarida,
en el dansar de la mort i la vida.

43 Heraclitus, *Fragm*. 119: ἦθος ἀνθρώπῳ δαίμων, "Man's essence is his *daimōn*."

44 Cf. Panikkar, *El mundanal silencio* (Madrid: Martínez Roca, 1999).

45 Gn III, 24.

Mor algun astre, temps enllà,
i la flor de pereta de quintà,
i la noia daurada s'oblida
en el dansar de la mort i la vida.

All is like a dance of life and death:
there is Man and bird and the sparse grass in the orchard,
the eternal-looking fir-tree and the daisy,
in the dancing of death and life.

A star dies, long ago,
and the little pear-flower in the farmhouse,
and the golden girl forgets
in the dancing of death and life.

—Marià Manent[46]

In these lines we hear echoes of an almost universal experience. Life is a dance. A "serious" thinker like Plotinus writes: "When we regard (only) Him then we reach our end and our rest, [(then) without any displeasure, we dance Him a divine dance]."[47]

This χορεία, this choral dance is the combination of harmony and rhythm, Plato says.[48] It reminds us of the trinitarian *perichōrēsis*, the cosmic and divine dance. Śiva is Nāṭarāja, the dancing God. The dance is his creation. For popular religions dance may be the most genuine human sharing in the miracle of creation.

Were we capable of experiencing the full power of words, as in the *śabdabrahman* philosophy of ancient India, our title would already convey all that is to be said.

Were I to follow the indic tradition I would be expected to explain the *anubandha-catuṣṭaya*, the four necessary ingredients of any *śāstra* or treatise, namely: *prayajana*, purpose (*aim*), *adhikāri*, the competent hearer or reader (*audience*), *abhidheya*, subject matter (*topic*), and *sambandha*, the connection (*relationship*) between them all.

I have already indicated that our *aim* is liberation from the grids that impede our real freedom, that the *audience* consists of those who are engaged in living life to the full, that the *topic* is the gathering of the fragments of human experience throughout the ages in order to participate in the myth

46 Marià Manent, cf. *El Ciervo* XXXVIII, num. 458 (April 1989).

47 Plotinus, *Enneads* VI, 9, 8: τὸ μὴ ἀπάδειν χορεύουσιν ὄντως περὶ αὐτὸν χορείαν ἔντηεον.

48 Plato, *Nomoi,* 665a.

already emerging as the next step in the life of reality, and that the *relationship* among all these is best expressed by the metaphor of rhythm. To sum it up in a single sentence, we all participate in Rhythm, because Rhythm is another name for Being and Being is Trinity.

1. *Rhythm*

In spite of the increasing contemporary consciousness and the permanent voice of traditional cultures, the still-prevalent modern cosmology is that of a mechanical universe in which life is an epiphenomenon and Man a marginal exception. No wonder that the holistic experience of rhythm has been marginalized and reduced to a very restricted notion of music.

The difficulty in experiencing pure rhythm is due to our distracted life, either haunted by the past or worried about the future. In this condition we can hardly experience the present, much less enjoy it. To get rid of the burden of the past we need forgiveness; we need to have eliminated the past *karma*, the burden of our sins. If we are still weighted down with remorse for past deeds (because not forgiven), or the resentment for what others did to us, we shall not be able to dance the dance of life with light heart and unencumbered steps.

We also need a pure heart in order to be freed from the fear of the future. If we are anxious about what time will bring, we shall not be able to experience the present, the presence of ourselves, the presence of the surrounding world and of the Self, the *tempiternal* reality.

The cause and effect of this attitude are our capacity to experience rhythm. Because rhythm does not go anywhere, we are no longer *viatores* (voyagers). We have become *comprehensores* (complete, perfect, all-embracing) in the language of the christian scholastics, *jîvan-mukta* (liberated in life) in the vedāntic philosophy. No longer heading toward a future, we have found our goal while still on the way. We are thereby cured of the malady (should I call it a vice or just cowardice?) of postponing for later (in life or in heaven) what is (already) real in the present. We are cured of the fear of definite issues, excusing ourselves by saying that we are not ready to live life to the full—probably because we idealize and dehumanize this fullness.

a) Universality of Rhythm

For classical greek culture, where the word has its origin, μουσική entails rhythm in sound (what nowadays is called music), movement (not solely reduced to dance), and speech (not limited to poetry). This comprehensive notion of music is what allowed Plato to quote Damon, with approval: "it is not possible to modify the modes of music without unsettling the most basic political and social constitution [of a state]."[49] The education of the citizen, therefore, was centered in "physical exercises for the body" (ἐπὶ σώμασι γυμναστική) and "music for the soul" (ἐπὶ φυχῄ μουσική).[50] Both gymnastics and music are rhythm.

When Kung-fu-tse was asked what he would do to restore order in a certain community, he replied that he would set about putting their music in order. Music is what unites, according to the *Li-ki*, the Book of Rites. Music expresses and reenacts the harmony of the universe. Let us recall that the same chinese character stands for both joy and music. We read in the *Analects*:

> Two things are necessary: the first,
> to bring about an inner harmony of
> the mind. . . . In this pursuit the melodies,
> harmonies and rhythms of music are the great value.[51]

The vedic tradition is more metaphysical. The whole of reality is a splash of the sonorous word represented by the *Gāyatrī*, the holiest of all mantras. It is this singing word that lets all beings come to be.[52]

> The Gāyatrī, indeed, is this whole universe,
> all that has come to be.
> And the Word, indeed, is (the) Gāyatrī
> for the Word sings forth and protects
> this whole universe that has come to be.[53]

For a millennium western education was centered on learning music as one of the four fundamental sciences along with geometry, astronomy, and arithmetic: the famous *quatrivium*. It is important to remark that these four disciplines were supposed to disclose the ultimate structure of the universe, music as much as the other three.

Summing up not only the indic, chinese, jewish, christian, germanic, african, and other traditions, we may say that the ultimate nature of reality is sonorous, a sensible and rhythmic Word. Rhythm is intrinsically connected with any activity of the Gods, Men, and Nature.

---

49 Plato, *Politeia,* 424c: πολιτικῶν νόμων τῶν μεγίστων.

50 Plato, *Politeia,* 376e.

51 *Analects* 15:10.

52 RV III, 62, 10.

53 CU III, 12, 1: "gāyatrī vā idaṁ sarvaṁ bhūtaṁ / yad idaṁ kiṁ ca, / vāg vai gāyatrī, / vāy vā idaṁ sarvaṁ bhūtaṁ / gāyati ca trāyate ca."

Rhythm, as already suggested by the word [from ῥέω, to flow], expresses the very dynamism of reality. This flowing is an ordered flowing. The indic *ṛta*, as well as the greek κόσμος and τάχις or the latin *ordo*, all imply a rhythmical structure. Plato says literally: "The order of movement bears the name rhythm."[54]

The movement of beings is a temporal flowing. Rhythm is the order of things, both in their temporal movement and in our human activity. In the first case, we have rhythm as the natural order of time (φύσει). In the second, rhythm is human acting according to proper behavior (νόμοι). Plato's philosophy is an outstanding example of the central place of rhythm—not only for the education of Man, but also for understanding the nature of the real. Plato almost equates education (παιδεία) with bringing forth the experience of rhythm, to which not only Aristotle but Kung Fu Tze and many others agree.

Playing with a probably "scientifically" wrong etymology of ἀριθμός (number) Augustine, among others, renders the greek ῥυθμός (rhythmic) as *numerus*, whereby number still has a pythagorean flavor. God is the highest number, and the proper field of ἀριθμός is the *ritus*, the ritual, which is closely related to the chinese intuition about the rites as expressed in the *Li-ki*, as well as the vedic idea of ritual.

* * *

Rhythm is essential to christianity. "To be a christian means to participate in the christian rhythm."[55] In fact, most traditional views of reality were rhythmical. Zoroastrian, hindu, greek, and african cosmogonies, as well as the idea of the movement of the universe and of life, *encouraged* rhythmical views. Life on earth—beginning with the stars, the sun, the moon, the seasons, the day, and the body—follows a rhythmic pattern. Archaic traditions and islamic mysticism could provide us with outstanding examples from two extremely different cultures. When the greek Bible speaks of divine Wisdom "arranging all things according to measure [μέτρῳ], number [ἀριθμῷ] and weight [σταθμῷ],"[56] it certainly has in mind this cosmic rhythm of the universe. It may also be pointed out that "number" here, *arithmos*, contains an etymological reference to the latin *ritus*, ritual. Indeed, the vedic *ṛta* (cosmic order) is undoubtedly rhythmical. The roots *sreu* (from ῥέω, to flow) and *ar* (from which come *ordo* and *ritus*) are related.

54 Plato, *Nomoi*, II (664-665 e-a): τῇ δὴ τῆς κινήσεως τάζει ῥυθμὸς ὄνομα εἴη.

55 Pieper (1951), 64, leaning on Pius X.

56 Wis. XI, 20.

It is significant that this most central insight has lately been almost entirely relegated to the specialized field of elementary music. Even one of the few books dedicated to this theme, while stressing the importance of the topic, seems to concentrate exclusively on the human experience of rhythm.[57] More recently, a german philosopher, Albert Stüttgen, has proposed a *return to rhythm*.[58]

b) Phenomenological Approach

In trying to describe the nature of rhythm, our first observation is that as an ultimate human intuition there is no possible definition of rhythm.

Rhythm is neither only dance nor merely movement. Dance offers us a beautiful and profound image: the cosmic dance of creation, the *nāṭarāja* spirituality of shivaism, the purposeless activity of God who has in itself all possible purposes. "All for the sake of himself acts the Lord,"[59] as the judeo-christian-islamic tradition says, because God is moved by love. There is no "why" behind the display of creation as an act of joy, a gratuitous activity with no afterthoughts, projects, or eschatological intentions. "The root *div*, from which the noun *Devī* (Goddess) is derived, means to play," says Abhinavagupta.[60] All this implies rhythm, but we should not identify rhythm with dance. If every dance follows a certain rhythm, not every rhythm is dance.

The simplest definition of dance is to say that it is a rhythmic movement of the body. This is the common phenomenological approach, but it does not help us much to understand the nature of things. It is more helpful to realize, for instance, that in dance we have one of the first manifestations of the passage from the more or less rigid determinisms of nature to the free play of culture. The dance of animals is indeed rhythm, but strictly speaking not a real dance. The conscious awareness of rhythm in the dance is a cultural act—and culture belongs to human nature. To dance is to learn to breathe in the rhythm of the world—said the famous dancer Martha Graham.

There is a fundamental distinction between the series of time-beats (in german *Takt*) and rhythm. The former is pure repetition, and it involves our conscious faculty of reckoning perception. The latter is the return of the similar in a new way. *Taktschlag* is repetition, rhythm is innovation.

---

57 Klages (1944), 23.

58 Albert Stüttgen (1988).

59 Prv XVI, 4 [not in the LXX and susceptible of another translation]: "Universa propter semetipsum operatus est Dominus."

60 Abhinavagupta, *Parātrīśika-vivaraṇa*, 3.

"Tact" in english is not this time-beat, and yet it is related to the (well-timed) opportune time of rhythm. A person who has tact is aware of and respects the rhythms because that person is in "touch" (*tactus*) with the real situation of the particular circumstance.

Repetition succeeds according to a model. Rhythm, however, has no model. A machine generates repetition, not rhythm. A purely mechanical ballet is no longer rhythmic; a real ballet is never a mechanical repetition of the identical. We may call it improvisation or genius in the example. Each performance is good or bad, not in terms of whether it comes closer to an ideal performance but according to an inner harmony inherent in the selfsame ballet. Repetition follows a temporal straight line. If it continues for too long it may be tedious. Rhythm does not follow a line as straight time. When a ballet, for instance, becomes tedious it has degenerated into mechanical repetition, or the spectator has lost the *Takt*, the "touch" with the performing artists. The example of ballet helps us to realize that rhythm is a word expressing a symbol and not denoting exclusively a concept. This latter is objective within an objectifiable field (of concepts). The former includes the participation of the subject for whom the symbol is symbol. Rhythm is a symbol and not merely a concept.

Rhythm is prior to dance. Dance is an appealing image for the Creator in its creative fervor (*tapas*), for God *ad extra*, if we may use this traditional but misleading expression. Rhythm also applies to God *ab intra*, to the very heart of reality. The cosmotheandric order of the universe, the *perichōrēsis* of the radical Trinity is rhythm, as we shall explain later. It is out of this ultimate rhythm that we perceive other rhythms.

* * *

Rhythm is not identical to movement either. Movement can be interpreted as any act or, in a more restricted sense, as any change, mutation, or transition. In this latter meaning it entails space and time and their myriad variations. All things move. Presumably the experience of this universal phenomenon led Aristotle, and following him the scholastics, to consider movement as the transition from potency (capacity to be) to actuality (realization of that capacity). Being is being insofar as it acts, whether it "actualizes" itself or is actualized by another. There is a movement intrinsic to each being. Movement is not only translation from one place to another.

Rhythm is full of movement, but not every movement is rhythm. There can be movement without rhythm: unnatural movements. Nature is rhythmic, but there can be, and there are, unnatural movements. Significantly enough,

Aristotle (in his discussion of the void) calls them violent movements.[61] Ultimately, it is the enigma of evil, which is interference from outside the particular field where each being has its place, its *ontonomy*. Rhythm is the endogenous movement proper to each being. *Omnia appetunt Deum*, "all things move toward their Source," has been the short formulation of the dynamism of Being for over two millennia of western history since the pre-socratics. This movement, whether called *nisus*, *impulsus*, or even the *svadhā* of the Ṛg Veda,[62] is a natural one and belongs to the very nature of things. Rhythm is precisely the dance of Being toward and around an elusive and presumably nonlocalizable Center. Follow your *truly* inner urge, says human wisdom from taoism to christianity and the african traditions. Trust the rhythms of Nature could be another formulation. The fact, however, is that these rhythms can be disturbed and Man needs intelligence and strength (discernment and power) to overcome what in many cultures is called temptation.

Having put dance to the right of rhythm, and movement to the left, let us bring them together once again. I said that every dance is rhythmic, but not every rhythm is a dance; every rhythm is movement, but not every movement is rhythmic. The link is nature, the natural. When the dance is natural, it is rhythmic. When movement is natural, it is rhythmic. The natural flowing of things is rhythmic. The non-rhythmic is not natural. Nature is rhythmic, even though natural rhythms can be disrupted. This is to say that Nature, like rhythm, is neither purely objective, nor merely subjective. Rhythm is only such if we are involved in the rhythmic process. Nature is not just "out there"; we are also nature. Nature is rhythmic because Being is rhythmic, as we shall explain in the next section.

* * *

Here is another example: *poetic rhythm*. The rhythm of poetry is not a mere accident for the poetic text, just something added to the meaning. Poetic rhythm is not a mere device by which one adds beauty to a line or a strophe. It belongs to the full word of the living phrase. Rhythm allows the sentence to reveal itself as what it is, makes it possible for the sentence to flow and be spoken aloud. Rhythm makes the sentence not only palatable but also digestible, that is, easily understandable and memorizable. There is a profound sense in the now almost forgotten practice that every reading was a recitation. Some decades ago one could still hear the murmur of the readers in indian libraries. Today they are "civilized"; at most you hear the whir of computers and the chatting of the *chaprāsīs* (clerks).

61 Aristotle, *Phys.*, IV, 8 (215a ff.).

62 RV X, 129, 2.

Rhythm is intrinsic to the word, the phrase, the sentence. It is not the phoneme alone or any arbitrary succession of them, something we put in once the meaning is clear to our mind, a kind of cosmetics. We need art, we need inspiration, and this means freedom. When our sentences are creations and language is our invention, we discover that rhythm belongs to human words. As with music, it is not produced capriciously; we have to find the proper rhythms. Goethe knew it:

> Stirs them, so rhythmic measure is assured?
> Who calls the One to general ordination,
> Where it may ring in marvellous accord?[63]

Rhythm is not only "rime," although rhyme and rhythm have the same etymology, nor is it mere sound. Rhythm is part of the life of any authentic phrase. Even more, any sentence is literally a rhythm between sound and silence, comprising gesture, mimicry, and life. Living language is also a dance. Scripture, and even writing, is an *Ersatz*, useful as it may be. "The letter killeth."[64] The word needs to be spoken and heard.

In his *Reminiscences*, R. Tagore recalled his first hearing of a bengali rhyme ("the rain patters, the leaf quivers"), and wrote that it is rhyme that makes "words come to an end, and yet . . . not end."

The modern technocratic system threatens both cosmic and human rhythms. Modernity aspires to make everything artificial, including intelligence, precisely in order to escape the natural rhythms of life. Bacon, Galileo, and Descartes speak against Nature because Man is its sovereign lord, and even Kant writes about subduing Nature: *die Natur nötigen*.[65]

c) Rhythmic Quaternity

Modern civilization ignores most rhythms of nature, those of the seasons as well as those of our bodies, the earth, and the forces of nature. We erect cities and construct houses without regard for the rhythms of the earth. We increase speed for its own sake, beyond any acceptable human rhythm. Not only is rhythm rarely mentioned in philosophical works, but most dictionaries and encyclopedias discard the topic altogether, except as it pertains to music.

Rhythm combines in a unique way at least four fundamental elements of human awareness: time, space, objectivity, and subjectivity. If long

63 Goethe, *Faustus*, I 147-49: "Belebend ab, dass sie sich rhythmisch regt? / Wer ruft das Einzelne zur allgemeinen Weihe, / wo es in herrlichen Akkorden schlägt?"

64 2 Cor III, 6.

65 Kant, *Kritik der reinen Vernunft*, Preface to the 2nd edition (B XIII-XIV).

digressions were not required I would be tempted to exemplify it in two basic insights of classical christianity and shivaitic hinduism: *beatitudo* as the joy of human fulfillment in the vision of God, and *rasa* as the human "relish" in the "aesthetic" experience of infinite beauty. Both require total participation in the rhythm of reality that unites the four elements mentioned in a harmonious way.

To be brief, I will elaborate on these four themes simultaneously, since they come together in rhythm and as rhythm. First of all, there is no rhythm without time, but rhythm is the most primordial sort of time; it is natural time, real time. Linear time, the "time" required for techno-science and modern civilization, is not natural time. This is a topic of capital importance that will permeate all the pages of this book.[66]

What is time? The often quoted comment of Augustine, "What then is time? If nobody asks me, I know; if I want to explain it to some one who asks me, I do not know,"[67] may have a deeper explanation than the one commonly given. Augustine's embarrassment comes from a deeper cause than the difficulty of the answer or the inadequacy of the question. It touches a fundamental point, especially for a culture that has achieved revolutionary feats in conceptual thinking, as witnessed by modern science, and notably by mathematics. Augustine senses that he cannot give an answer because time is not an object and that the *concept* of time does not touch the real time he knows (*scio*) by experience.

Time, in fact, defies reduction to a concept. Kant saw this clearly, but, since his philosophy was at the service of the nascent modern science, it went another route, one that would permit calculus with temporal magnitudes. Mere reason attempts to find a concept of time that would allow us to operate with it, and so we have identified it as a measurable relation between distance (called space) and velocity (a concept that already includes time). This may be a scientific concept of time as the measure of a supposed uniform movement within a postulated homogeneous space, but natural time has little to do with that, as the theory of relativity began to suspect. Modern science cannot have a concept of real time, just as it cannot detect the nature of the soul. Modern science does not have the tools for dealing with the experience of time, and such experiences may not need tools.

The time of nature is neither linear nor circular nor spiral. It is

66 Cf. Panikkar, *El concepto de naturaleza: Análisis histórico y metafísico de un concepto* (Madrid: CSIC, 1951; 2nd rev. ed., 1972), 203-32 and passim; (1996/32).

67 Augustine, *Confessiones*, XI, 14, (17): "Quid est ergo tempus? Si nemo ex me quaerat, scio; si quaerenti explicare velim, nescio."

irreducible to scientific geometry or mathematical space, in spite of the heuristic legitimacy of such a reduction. We can extract a concept of tree, train, and eventually even beauty and goodness from trees, trains, and some recurrent ideas of people who call a phenomenon beautiful or some person good. We can also elaborate a concept of mass by observing, or rather measuring, different relationships of bodies with respect to pressures (forces) we put on them. With time, however, where are the "times" from which we can extract the concept of time applicable to all that "perdures" in be-ing, in ek-sistence? Scientific time is either a heuristic and pragmatic postulate or an a priori of our mind.

The temporal processes we observe in ourselves and Nature are all rhythmical times. Rhythm is not the quantitatively regular repetition of beats, sounds, movements, events or the like. Once given a unit, a computer can measure homogeneous intervals of time, but it can never detect rhythm because the time proper to rhythm is qualitative. Rhythm is not simply the repetition of a previous drumbeat. The second beat is different, precisely in time, in spite of the possible equality of pitch. The sound is differently situated; its space is different. Above all, the essential subjective ingredient of rhythm has changed. There is no rhythm without a subject attuned to that rhythm.

As already said, rhythm is never sheer repetition. The second sound, to continue the acoustic example, carries with it something of the first; the listener still remembers the previous stroke. Rhythm is more than the interconnection of things or events; it is their *intra*connection, the indwelling of all in all. The first sound is not just followed by the second; it is still present in the heart of the second. There is resonance in every sense. Just ask a poet, or simply read a verse. The movement of the rhythm needs to be internalized. From afro-american jazz to the rhythms of music in the Middle East and in medieval Europe, to the *japa* and *mantra* spirituality in South and East Asia, the rhythmic *li* of ritual in the farthest East, and the african drums, there is a spiritual and material connection.

Without memory there is no rhythm. Paradoxically enough, however, without the fading away of memory there would be no rhythm either. We do not remember the previous sound, step, or event just as it was. That would be boring, sheer repetition. Yet the previously heard sound, the similar step performed, or the analogous event witnessed, still lingers in our being and is present and somewhat transformed there. We have a sort of memory of a certain discontinuous continuity. Rhythm flows. We remember the flowing, and this flowing is time as such.

Rhythm is not linear. If anything, it could be imagined as somewhat curved. Rhythm is not possible on a plane surface. It needs the curvature of both space and "time." It recoils, but in a peculiar way. The "second" moment is new and yet not new because it is not disconnected, but second. It is the same only as an abstraction, abstracted from its *Sitz im Leben*, its living context. In fact, it is not the same because everything has changed—the situation in time and space, the influence on the subject, and the objectivity of the event—and yet everything belongs together. The rhythm is recollected as equal and yet different. It leaves you unfulfilled in expectation. You were looking for something else, and this is why, as in *The Thousand and One Nights*, you are in suspense, you keep expecting. . . . Maybe a third moment, maybe the very next event will bring you the desired "end," but it never comes. Yet closure is also somewhat there. You know that you are in a way responsible for not putting an end to it, for going on in *epektasis*, looking ahead for the Messiah still to come. All previous manifestations are somewhat disappointing; history has to go on and on. Or the musician has to arrange for a solemn and more or less artificial finale in order to break the spell and let the audience know that this is finally "it." Is this human longing? Is it objective imperfection? Both?

We call it circular space, or perhaps spiral. These are only figures to indicate both regularity and irregularity, the possibility of prediction and unpredictable events, the interplay of pattern and variation. You always expect, but you never really know what to expect. As in an indian musical performance, it all depends on the players, who are themselves attentive to the changing moods of the audience. They do not know how the whole thing is going to end. The end of the world has to be a catastrophe, an overturning, so as to break the rhythm and its spell. A rhythm has no natural ending because it carries time away with it. Ultimately, all spatial metaphors break down.

Rhythm has an "ever more," but it does not have, properly speaking, a future. You expect, you recognize, but you do not exactly foresee. If you were to foresee it all, the rhythm would cease and you would quickly begin to be bored. The sensitive musician would certainly stop.

Rhythm entails movement, and movement implies space. Both demand change, which is not just the "periodic return at regular time intervals" of the formal definitions. This might describe mathematical recurrences but not rhythmical realities. "One would have to wait for the end of history in order to possess the complete material for determining its meaning,"[68] Dilthey

68 Dilthey (1927), VII, 233. See Jürgen Habermas, *On the Logic of the Human Sciences* (Cambridge: Mass.: M.I.T. Press, 1988), 161.

says, seeking to overcome the static character of Being, and thereby paying tribute to the modern scientific mentality by assuming that time is linear. Man is a historical being, but not only that. History evolves alongside linear time, but this is not the Whole of history. Must we really wait until "the end of time" in order to find meaning in our lives?

Once we introduce time into Being, as it has been reintroduced in western metaphysics since Hegel, and this time is considered to proceed forward—as progress, or perhaps only as "process"—we are bound to project the meaning of everything into the future. Christian theology, both catholic and protestant, has to catapult God into a future Omega Point à la Teilhard. All is postponed; "eternal life" runs the danger of being situated in the future. Karl Rahner understands God as "Absolute Future"; Wolfhart Pannenberg says that "God does not yet exist . . . God's being is still in the process of coming to be." "*Gottes Sein ist im Werden*" [God's Being is in Becoming], is the title of Jüngel's spirited defense of Karl Barth's theology. The sovereign shadow of Hegel is, of course, brooding over all these efforts. I said above "reintroduced" time into Being, because the greeks knew and Origenes, Joachim de Fiore, Vico and many others remembered, that Life is the time of being, χρόνος τοῦ εἶναι, as we are going to say later, the very "life of the soul" as Plotinus suggests.[69]

It is within this context that we should understand the power of the Rhythm of Being. We do not need to postpone Life and meaning, and therefore peace and human realization, into a "world without end" at the end of time. One can well understand why James Joyce spoke of the "nightmare" and Mircea Eliade of the "terror" of history in the lives of individuals and peoples. On the other hand, however, I assert that the Rhythm of Being does not mean the circularity of time.

There is still one important feature to be mentioned. Rhythm is always perceived as a Whole. It has no real parts. Any partition would destroy the rhythm, which is not the sum of its components. Each sound, if isolated, would make no rhythm, nor would it do so if each sound were not "inside" its neighbors, so to speak. As we have already hinted, rhythm demands a certain type of *perichōrēsis* (a dancing interpretation—as we are going still to comment upon), being so intertwined that we are not able to decompose the "units" without destroying the true rhythm. If you do not perceive the Whole, there is no rhythm. Μελέτα τὸ πᾶν, as we said before; experience the melody of the Whole, as one may freely translate it.

69 Plotinus, *Enneads* III, 7, 11.

I scarcely need to stress that rhythm is more than just a subjective sensation, but something material and tangible, even if it also demands interiorization. Aristotle, in his *Metaphysics*,[70] speaks of rhythm (proportion) as σκῆμα, *figura*, scheme, structure, the shape of things. The greek verb ῥυθμόω means to shape, to mold.

Rhythm manifests a peculiar relation between rupture and continuity, between the old and the new. It is also intimately related to an essential ingredient of human life: celebration and ritual. Ritual implies a rhythmic reenacting of primordial realities. Seen from the outside, ritual may look like lifeless repetition. This is why many external observers, incapable of detecting the rhythm that is the soul of the ritual, criticize the rites of others. From the inside, any ritual is at least an *anamnesis*, a reminiscence, that represents and thus transforms the past into the present: an actual reenactment. How can a christian understand the Eucharist without this sense of rhythm? In linear time the part is part and cannot come back except as psychological commemoration (μνήμη Plato would say) or by an act of pure magic.

Making allowances for oversimplification, I would say that western Man lives mainly in time. History is then simply the human habitat, and journeying in time becomes the image of personal and collective existence. In contrast, the african Augustine says, "Transcend time in order that you may be."[71]

Here transcendence is specifically temporal transcendence. Eastern Man, on the other hand, lives mainly in space (*ākāśa*). Ātman or *anātman* is the human habitat, and overcoming space the image of human and cosmic fulfillment. *Nirvāṇa* "is" beyond, says buddhism. *Śūnyatā* is the void.

Rhythm is both temporal and spatial; it is the combination of different times in the same (apparent) space and of diverse spaces in the same (apparently repeated) time. Linear time is somewhat defeated; rhythmic time is all in the "timing." Space is also defeated; the *situs* changes but the *locus* remains the same. It seems as if you would expand, and yet you are not displaced.

Rhythm is the marriage of space and time, in the tantric sense that the one is the other: time has become space and space, time. You can distinguish them, but cannot separate them.

---

70 Aristotle, *Met.*, 985b16; 1042b14.

71 Augustine, *In Ioannis Evangelium*, tract. 38, n. 10: "Ut ergo tu sis, transcende tempus."

d) The Experience of Rhythm

In sum, we discover rhythm when we experience the subjective difference of an objective identity (subjective genitive), but we could equally have said: the objective difference of a subjective identity. Identity and difference, subjectivity and objectivity, are overcome. In other words, the experience of rhythm is the experience of the neither-identity-nor-difference of the real. This is precisely the *advaitic* experience: neither monism or identity, nor dualism or difference. Neither the subjective nor the objective views are real. In rhythm we find the (re) conciliation between an objective physical process and a subjective human feeling. The indic *rasa* theory provides an important example of this. Rhythm overcomes the epistemological split between subject and object, the anthropological fissure between knowledge and love, and the metaphysical dualism between the human and the divine.

The tendency of modern civilization to compartmentalize has made it difficult to achieve the holistic experience of rhythm. We need a pure heart to discover the harmony of reality. Here are two examples from West and East.

Pythagoras is reported to have said: "Harmony (is the) Best."[72] According to the belief that "The whole heaven is harmony and number,"[73] where number means more than modern numerals and hendiadys. Or again, the sanskrit notion of *samanvaya* suggests that harmony is the supreme value, the utmost wisdom. "That but because of harmony." [74] This cryptic text, which refers to the internal harmony of the Veda whose only purport is *brahman,* can and has been interpreted as the transcendent reconciliation of all the contraries because of the universal harmony of reality as a whole, because of the rhythmic dance of the universe. In fact, no vedic seer would have dreamt that the bulky corpus of the Veda "says the same." What the *Brahmasûtra* states is that there is a harmony in all the *mantra* and narratives of the vedic revelation. The conclusion of the entire Rig Veda sings this harmony or concord as a cosmic and human ideal:

> Let us be in harmony in our intention,
> in harmony in our hearts
> in harmony in our minds
> that we may live in concord.[75]
>
> —according to the divine and cosmic rhythm of reality.

---

72 Pythagoras, *Fragm*. 58 C 4: κάλλιστον ἅρμονια.

73 Pythagoras, *Fragm*. 58 B 4 (in Aristotle, *Metaph*. I, 5 [98b a]): τὸν ὅλον οὐρανὸν ἁρμονίαν εἶναι καὶ ἀριθμόν.

74 BS I, 1, 4: *tat tu samanvayāt.*

75 RV X, 191, 4.

We adduce these texts, which could be multiplied, just to show that, while the famous *reductio ad unum* or primacy of the One, may be a postulate for rational intelligibility, it is not the only intuition of humanity. Even many of the defenders of Oneness specify that there is a Super-One and that even the One is not a number but a symbol of the harmony we are speaking about. This harmony is neither monism (there is more than one real being) nor dualism (all are intrinsically related entities).

The experience of rhythm makes a me of me, a unique me, liberating me from being just a member of a class, and grants me a certain fellowship with all other fellow beings in their uniqueness. Rhythm, in fact, is not merely objective. I have to feel it in me (subjective), and at the same time outside me (objective). Time flows, but it goes nowhere. Yet it is not sheer repetition. It is at the same time constant novelty, an ever-new experience that is superimposed on the previous one. Rhythm is real growth, overcoming the dualism between continuity and discontinuity; it is new creation, both objective and subjective. Rhythm is outside me; I do not invent it. I have only to listen, to obey (*ob-audire*, listening) the beats of the real, and in order to listen I need to be silent, to silence my egocentrisms, my *ahamkāra*. More, I need to be pure. In addition, rhythm is also inside me. My reception is indispensable, and my identification is a requirement. It is not superimposed on me. I discover it in myself by means of the drums from outside. Serenity, *upekṣa* , *Gelassenheit*, and all these similar virtues consist in discerning the rhythm of life by being attuned to it. Centuries ago we heard the injunction that we should be like children of the Father in heaven who "makes his sun rise on good and bad alike, and sends rain on the just and the unjust."[76] Even before that, the philosopher of rhythm had said: "Before God all things are beautiful [and good and just]."[77] Continuing the thought, he said: "But Men have judged some to be unjust and some others to be just." This is perhaps why he could also declare, as we have already quoted, "The invisible harmony is stronger than the visible."[78]

"Virtue is a harmony, as well as health, goodness as a Whole, and the divine. This is why all (beings) are organized according to harmony (διὸ καὶ καθ' ἁρμονίαν συνεστάναι τὰ ὅλα) and even friendship is a harmonic correspondence (ἰσότητα, equality),"[79] runs a classical text of the third century.

---

76 Mt V, 45: τὸν ἥλιον αὐτοῦ ἀνατέλλει ἐπὶ πονηροὺς καὶ ἀγαθοὺς καὶ βρέχει ἐπὶ δικαίους καὶ ἀδίκους.

77 Heraclitus, *Fragm.* 102: τῷ μὲν θεῷ καλὰ πάντα.

78 Heraclitus, *Fragm.* 54 (cited in I, 1, b).

79 Diogenes Laertius, VIII, 33

This does not at all imply an uncritical optimism blind to the arhythmic processes of Nature. Traditional medicines see illness as a disturbance of the natural rhythms, as a lack of harmony. Disorder is a traditional name for sin. There is a hidden harmony difficult to discover, but Nature is also vulnerable and can be brought to disarray. Evil is rather this disorder than a so-called *privatio*, a deprivation of being.

The experience of Rhythm is a holistic experience; it involves the senses, the mind, and the spirit, the three eyes we mentioned. It requires the *advaitic* intuition. Reason alone (as distinct from intellect) cannot grasp rhythm. Rhythm cannot be brought back to a unity, the *reductio ad absurdum* required for a rational intelligibility is not possible—which is what I have been saying all along. To conclude this section I may share an old note I wrote in 1962:

> Music is an arch between *mythos* and *logos*.
> Music tells, but does not speak. It inspires,
> but has no particular meaning.
>
> The auscultation of Being is Thinking.
> The dancing its Rhythm is living.
> The one doesn't go without the other.

Rhythm is like the mother of time and space. The children do well in being emancipated, but will do even better not to deny their Source.

2. *Being*

Our title contains a much more formidable word still. It speaks of Being, indeed, of the Rhythm of Being, and tries to open that Pandora's box of blessings and ills.

I will not linger on the meaning of Being. We may provisionally agree that the word, as a verb and with all its pronouns, modes, and tenses, encompasses in a unique way all that *is*. In another context I would probably have preferred to use *reality* instead of Being as a word encompassing Being and Non-being, and introduced distinctions in the notion of Being. For our purposes, however, it may suffice to employ the word Being as the overall symbol that encompasses, in one way or another, all to which we may meaningfully say "is," "anything" that enters the "field" of our "awareness" and about which we can speak in one way or another—as we will elaborate in chapter II.

The Rhythm of Being is more than just a metaphor. What kind of attribute can we apply to Being that is not already Being? In this case we cannot speak of a transporting, a carrying over (μετα-φέρειν). Nor can we apply Aristotle's definition: "Metaphor consists in giving (the thing) a name that belongs to something else."[80] The standard latin definition "*translatio est nominis alienis illatio*" is also interesting, but inapplicable. The Rhythm of Being cannot be the rhythm *of* some "thing" called Being. Being is not a thing. There is nothing "outside" Being. The Rhythm of Being can only express the rhythm that Being itself *is*.

We should interpret the word "namc" in a non-nominalistic sense. Names are more than labels. If the Rhythm of Being has any sense, it should be in the subjective genitive: the rhythm that appertains to Being. It is Being's rhythm. The phrase would then spell out a transcendental character of Being itself. Being *is* "in" the beings, and rhythm belongs to Being itself. Could it be the revelation (*aspectus*) of Being to us? The itself (*en soi*) is always a *quoad nos* (according to us).

Material things are temporal, humans are historical, ideal entities are spiritual. Being as such is rhythmic. The Rhythm of Being is the *sui generis* "temporality," "historicity," and "spirituality" of Being. The Rhythm of Being is the very dynamism of Being, its Becoming. Because material things, human beings, and spiritual entities are beings, temporality, historicity, and "ideality" are encompassed in the "rhythmicality" of Being. Being "is" not a genus, and therefore to affirm that "things," "humans," and "spirits" are beings as a plural to Being is not a proper classification of entities. Language is awkward here because our present culture is rather "undeveloped" in this field.

We can be aware of the Rhythm of Being in the same measure that we can become aware of Being. If this is the case, we are very close to a rather general statement—which I propose *cum magno timore et tremula intentione,* "with a great caution and mixed feelings," as I would freely translate this sentence of that extraordinary abbess of the twelfth century.[81]

Rhythm is an aspect, I said, of Being itself. But this "aspect" is neither an accident nor the essence of Being. Rhythm is neither something that befalls Being, a mere accident, nor its essence in the scholastic sense—since there is little point in asking for the essence of Being. What can it be that makes Being Being, if not Being? Aristotle has already warned us: "We should not seek to put limits on [should not delimit, define] everything."[82]

80 Aristotle, *Poet.*, 1457b6: Μεταφορὰ δέ ἐστιν ὀνόματος ἀλλοτρίου ἐπιφορά.

81 Hildegard von Bingen, *Scivias*, 17.

82 Aristotle, *Met.*, X, 1048a36: οὐ δεῖ παντὸς ὅρον ζητεῖν. (*Non oportet cuiuslibet rei quaerere terminum.*)

Nothing ultimate can have any definition.

Interestingly, although much contemporary metaphysics tries to recapture the meaning of Being, the shadow of the *ens commune*, as a pure abstraction, haunts it. The old scholastics considered *motus* (which only with qualifications could be rendered as movement), to be a "post-predicament," that is, a kind of second-class category or "predicament." I would use this insight as a springboard for affirming that rhythm is a *meta-transcendental*—that is, a property that belongs to every being as Being. Rhythm adds nothing to Being, but only expresses a property of Being qua Being. If truth is considered a transcendental because it expresses Being as intelligible, that is, in relation to the intellect, similarly, rhythm belongs to Being considered not in relation to the intelligence or the will, but in relation *to its totality*. Being as such, when considered in its own *wholeness*, appears with that apparent complexity that we may designate as rhythm.

The Rhythm of Being (subjective genitive), therefore, belongs to Being itself—and in that sense I dare to call it a *meta-transcendental*.

Being is not a lifeless reality, an *ens commune*, an abstract common denominator of all that there is. Being presents itself as rhythm. Every being qua Being in relation to one of our human faculties is one, good, true, and beautiful— without now entering into discussion on the nature and number of transcendentals. Every being qua Being in relation to its "Beingness" as it were, inasmuch as we can be "aware" of it, is rhythmic; it presents an apparent complexity that is yet simple, reflecting the Whole with an inner dynamism, or rather energy, for which I do not find a better notion than that of rhythm. This foreshadows the traditional interpretation of the Trinity, but my task now is only to explain the title.

The awareness of Being as rhythm will allow us to think about beings without losing sight of Being, and to pay attention to Being without forgetting beings, to know the particular without abandoning the totality. We do not take the *pars pro toto*, but instead discover the *totum in parte*.

The *advaitic* vision of the Rhythm of Being stands at the "middle way" between a monistic and a dualistic (or pluralistic) view of reality. If Being is a monolithic block, beings have ultimately no freedom and the way to relate to beings is through a pyramidal *heteronomic* order in which every level of beings has to follow the *norms* of *another* superior order: *heteronomy*. Here, beings are mutually dependent, but this mutuality is unequal, since the weaker, smaller, or less perfect will depend on the more powerful ones. Mutual dependency will tend to one-way traffic.

If Being is pluralistic in the classical sense of the word, that is, a conglomerate of atomistic entities in the last instance, then individual freedom will not have internal limits, and the way to relate beings to one another will be through a horizontal *autonomous* order in which every being follows its own (*autos*) norms: *autonomy*, except when it is prevented from doing so by another more powerful entity. Beings are mutually independent, but the mutuality is endangered, since the weaker, smaller, or less perfect entities will have their own independence curtailed by the more powerful ones. Mutual independency will (also) tend to be one-way traffic.

If Being is *rhythmic*, the whole is not divisible into parts, and therefore the sum of the parts does not constitute the whole; each member is an image of the Whole and the Whole is reflected in its members. Each being is unique and indispensable because the Whole is reflected in that being in order to be whole. Reality has inter-in-dependent order. This is the sphere of *ontonomy*.[83] If Being is rhythmic, each entity will enjoy a real freedom according to its nature in relation to the Whole. The way to relate to one another is similar to a rhythmic dance in which I spontaneously create my role in the dance listening to the overall music (which I may also contribute to making). The order is an *ontonomous* order in which every being (*on*) discovers its proper *nomos* within the Whole: *ontonomy*. Each being is mutually inter-in-dependent and obviously according to how I play my score I shall have more or less influence on others, who will be stimulated or disturbed by my melody and will also act or react correspondingly.

If rhythm were not the very Rhythm of Being, the order thus created would become a competitive chaos. If, however, Being itself is Rhythm, the order is ever new and does not follow a preexistent or preordained pattern. It is the *creatio continua* I mentioned several times. The *ontonomy* referred to is not the blind following of an absolute and immutable norm or *nomos* (law), but the discovery of the ever-new or renewed *nomos* of the *on*. The mentioned inter-in-dependence becomes an *intra-in-dependence*.

We may make distinctions, but not separations. Consciousness, for example, is one "thing" and matter another, but the one is not and cannot be without the other. They dance together.

In order to know what Man is, for instance, an isolated anthropology will not suffice. We shall also need both physics and theology, as well as ontology. The being of Man is not independent from Being, but this is equally true for matter and for God. They are all intertwined. Relationship is ultimate. Reality is περιχώρησις, *circumincessio*, the later Patristics would say,

83 Cf. Panikkar, "El átomo de tiempo," *Arbor* (Madrid), 1-32.

resurrecting a word used by Anaxagoras[84] in a sense very close to rhythm. We could perhaps adduce here the vedic notion of the *anyonyayonitā* or "mutual emerging from one another"—as a homeomorphic equivalent.

Theology is not reducible to anthropology, nor physics to theology. The three disciplines are mutually irreducible, yet also inseparable. This may be the *trayī vidyā*, the "triple knowledge" of the indic tradition.[85]

As an expression of this Rhythm of Being I may give two examples from that same tradition:

> That from which beings are born,
> that by which, when born, they live,
> that into which, when dying, they enter,
> that you should desire to know:
> that is Brahman.[86]

This stanza probably inspired the following one, which speaks about *Sarvaṁ* (the all, everything), here translated throughout as Whole:

> In whom the Whole [is], from whom the Whole [comes],
> who [is] Whole and who [is] in Whole [everywhere],
> who, eternal, [is] immanent in the Whole,
> Him the ātman of (the) Whole, I adore.[87]

We find here all the ingredients we discovered in our description of rhythm.

There is a rhythm in each and every being. No being is isolated; each reflects and is reflected by the Whole. The one text speaks of *brahman* and the other of ātman. It is not as if there were one special being, a supreme entity pervading the others, somewhat interfering with the others. Everything is in everything precisely because every being is more than an isolated entity. The vision of the Whole does not blind us to the particulars. It just does not make us shortsighted with respect to the All. The buddhist notion of *pratītyasamutpāda* (radical relativity or dependent origination) is a homeomorphic equivalent of the same insight.

Being is rhythmic, rhythm is harmony, and harmony brings peace and joy. This rhythm, however, is not automatic. It can be disturbed. Evil is real and so is freedom. Destiny is also in our hands.

---

84 Cf. Diels-Kranz, *Die Fragmente der Vorsokratiker,* h. 1.

85 Cf. JaimUB II, 9, 7.

86 TU III, 1.

87 Abhinavagupta, *Paratrisikā,* xviii, translated by the author.

Our human world is not a paradise. The Rhythm of Being is not a panacea against all evils. The different rhythms may interfere with each other and the harmony is not automatically established. *Ontonomy* is not a totalitarian order. The interconnection of all with all is governed neither by heteronomy nor by autonomy. The relation of all with all is not an automatic and one-toone relationship. Things may be prosperous in Europe and rotten in Africa, the conquest of America or the recent Gulf War may have been a great historical success. The rhythm I am trying to describe, however, will sooner or later establish a connection between those apparently so distant facts. The conquest of America by the europeans has repercussions still today, just as the crusades or the more recent Gulf War will be still felt a century from now. It is this Rhythm of Being that interconnects all with all in ways that we do not foresee. The discourse about Being is not just intemporal metaphysics; it also has physical and human aspects.

3. *Trinity*

The subtitle has already been obliquely introduced. We may need not say much more at this stage.

By Trinity, I mean the ultimate triadic structure of reality. By saying unbroken Trinity, I am foreshortening the exposition of the radical relativity of the Divine, the Cosmic, and the Human. The expression theo/anthropo/cosmic trinity may be clear enough to indicate the triad that traditionally goes under the names of God, Man, and World. As I will explain later, it can be said that at least within the horizon of the historical period, Man sees Being as a threefold reality of Heaven, Man, and Earth, or else Gods, Humans, and Nature.

Another, perhaps less cacophonic, phrasing would be to call this *the cosmotheandric trinity*. The word theandric is common in oriental christian spirituality. The neologism is also straightforward. It has the drawback of containing the word *anēr*, which, unlike *anthrōpos*, Man, denotes mainly the male, although there are also enough cases in which *anēr* is used in the feminine and stands for *anthrōpos*. I make a distinction: the theanthropocosmic intuition appertains to human awareness; the cosmotheandric insight is my interpretation of the former—as will be explained in chapter VI.

A complete study of Reality would then entail three parts of a single treatise on the Divine, the Human, and the Cosmic—understanding these words in their utmost general sense. In this book we shall concentrate on one dimension of this threefold distinction: the Divine. The original title, as I said, was *The Dwelling of the Divine in the Contemporary World*.

It would not be adequate to subsume under "natural science" the study of what one may still call Nature and which I have also termed cosmos. The "natural sciences" represent a cluster of very specific disciplines about material reality. They deal with a fascinating and important subject, but they do not fit well with what human consciousness has traditionally held about the material world. This is also the case for the "scientific" disciplines that still use the name of cosmology to designate the idea of the material universe as a whole, under a general "scientific" viewpoint. I will, therefore, have to make a distinction between a modern scientific notion of the cosmos, usually called cosmology, and what I am tempted to call kosmology—as will be explained in chapter VIII.

Something similar might be said concerning anthropology. Unless anthropology is understood as *anthrōpou legein,* as what Man says about himself, anthropology generally means the (modern) science about Man, what the human *logos* has to say about an object "Man"—as if Man were just an object. *Anthropophany*, on the other hand, would be how Man sees and interprets himself throughout his history.[88] We need the *pneuma* besides the *logos* in order to be open to any epiphany of the real.

At any rate, "cosmology" and "anthropology" cannot be dealt with separately and disconnected from "theology" (which also should undergo a change of name). These three branches of human knowledge are part of the tree of Life, and not just of the tree of the knowledge of good and evil.[89]

I have already suggested that one of the main features of modern times is fragmentation and specialization. The "Trinity" has also been interpreted as a specialty of the Divine, locating God in a sublime apartheid. Without plunging into the depths of the christian Trinity, our subtitle wants to point toward a holistic view of the real, for which the Trinity offers us a paradigm. I speak, therefore, of an unbroken Trinity. If the Divine is real and the Trinity is a consecrated word, this Trinity has to pervade everything and be everywhere. It has to be an unbroken Trinity, despite all the distinctions we may be obliged to make.

I am aware that the very name "Trinity" may have disturbing connotations on both sides of the cultural spectrum. Some christian readers may feel uncomfortable that I use a consecrated christian word to speak about something not officially christian. Others may find it irritating that I

88 Cf. Panikkar, "Antropofanía intercultural: Identidad humana y fin de milenio," *Thémata, Revista de Filosofía* (Facultad de Filosofía y CCEE de la Univ. de Sevilla), vol. 23, 19-29.

89 Cf. Gn II, 9.

do not follow common usage and that I insist on employing the same word to connote a "non-christian" doctrine.

My response is threefold. Nobody has a monopoly on names. It would be an abuse of power to "copyright" names. In the second place, "Trinity" is a common name in many cultures, philosophies, and religions. We find trinities everywhere. Third, the dogma of the christian Trinity is not a dead dogma incapable of growth. Furthermore, the christian dogma of the Trinity has been respectfully kept closed under seven keys for almost the last millennium and a half of christian history—some exceptions notwithstanding. It may be all the best for christians to receive some inputs, stimuli, and provocations from an intercultural approach, which is the cultural imperative of our times. My main motive in keeping this name is precisely because I am convinced that, if more fully deepened and unfolded, the traditional christian idea of the Trinity opens immensely fruitful perspectives for our times.

Furthermore, the Trinity, whether the traditional christian idea or a more general one, brings together without confusion the transcendent character of the Deity with its equally immanent aspect, and at the same time overcomes the two-storey worldview in which many theologians have built a comfortable apartment for the Divine that does not interfere in human affairs, thus paying a heavy tribute to the fragmentation both of knowledge and the knower.

It has become a cliché to say that we are taking a new turn in human history, but the tempo of modern life leaves little time and leisure to reflect on the meaning of the radical change and deep conversion (*metanoia*) that humanity needs in order to overcome our present-day predicament. One of the great obstacles to this, besides the inertia of the mind and the laziness of the will, is that we lack an adequate language and intellectual framework. We will have to use eroded words, polish them again, and eventually give them a more complete meaning.

* * *

Let me offer one final reflection to close this introductory chapter. I recall Lord Gifford's injunction to deliver "popular lectures." Unfortunately, the cultural depth of the "popular" readers of our times in philosophical and theological matters is so thin that the context of ancient wisdoms about these ultimate issues of Life is practically unknown, which makes it rather difficult to deal with such topics without banalizing them if one wants to be easily understood.

Certainly the main burden is on the author. I recall Ortega y Gasset's advice that the courtesy of the philosopher is clarity and elegance. But I also recall the frontispiece of the platonic academy twenty-five centuries ago that nobody should enter the premises without knowing geometry, whatever the actual meaning of the sentence might have been. I am not writing for initiates alone, but I trust that the reader will put a certain amount of effort and passion into a theme that ultimately concerns us all.

This study is an effort in this direction.

II
The Destiny of Being

My intention is not to analyze the depths of human subjectivity, on which obviously all depends, as a Kant would half-convincingly put it. Nor do I intend to analyze the heights of cosmological objectivity, also on which all depends, as modern science will unhesitatingly tell us. Indeed, everything depends on our epistemological filters, but everything is equally dependent on what falls upon those filters. Subjectivity and objectivity belong together. Without self-knowledge, we misunderstand everything; without cosmological knowledge, we spin in the air. We are indebted to all our temporal predecessors, and our spatial surroundings. Man is community, Being is solidarity, and our consciousness witnesses to it.

My intention is to approach the Whole as such. If I am to sketch an orientation for my fellow beings entering a new millennium (in spite of the cliché use of the phrase) I cannot wait until all the intricacies of our *psychē* and all the enigmas of our world have been deciphered. One cannot rely on the "last" word of any "science" (natural sciences or humanities) for the simple reason that, come tomorrow, the last word will have changed. The stars leading or inspiring human life cannot be the falling stars in the sky of a summer night of the latest fashion. Since even the pole star moves, we need now and then to revise our compasses. Questions of an existential nature can rely for their answers neither on the shaky ground of our interpretations of the past nor on the hazy mirage of our predictions about the future; the questions demand convincing answers for the present based on personal experience nurtured by the wisdom of history and science.

What are the questions whose answers can orient our lives? I must begin with a reflection on the ultimate questions that may yield some light on our destiny, a word that should be rescued from its connotations of predestination and fate. Perhaps the most popular way to present what I am trying to do is to ask: What is Being all about?

A. The Ultimate Question(s)

> "But dispassion, Lord—for what purpose is it?"
> "Dispassion Rādha, is to get release."
> "But release, Lord—what is it for?"
> "Release, Rādha, means *Nibbāṇa.*"
> "But *Nibbāṇa*, Lord, what is the aim of that?"
> "This question,[1] Rādha, goes too far. You can
> grasp no limits to this question. Rooted
> in *Nibbāṇa*, Rādha, the holy life is
> lived. *Nibbāṇa* is its goal,
> *Nibbāṇa* is its end."[2]

My ultimate question, which is neither rhetorical nor exclusively theoretical, is this: What is the destiny of Being? Nevertheless, I cannot properly approach the ultimate question excluding myself, nor can I properly ask about my destiny without also involving the destiny of the entire human race, the whole earth, and the universe in its totality. Nor can we exclude the Divine in this adventure, or else our personal dignity will become an idle word. Here we understand the Divine as that Power which, while immanent in the cosmos and in us, surpasses all our categories so that it gives us a transcendent point of reference. Without a direct link with that transcendent point we are just one member of a series, replaceable by any other individual of the same species; we lose our uniqueness and with that our dignity. On the other hand, if this ultimate point of reference were exclusively transcendent, besides being unreachable, we could not appeal to it as a safeguard of our dignity. This point of reference must be immanent in this world as well. A common name for this point of reference is the Divine, and this is the aporia that will concern us all along in these pages. In conclusion, we cannot exclude the Divine from sharing in the Destiny of Being. Rigid monotheism wants to save God from Destiny. This may be the reason why "Destiny" has a certain pejorative meaning. To speak of the destiny of the Absolute is either blasphemous or nonsensical. Trinitarian christianity, on the other hand, recognizing the Divine as relationship, does not exclude the Divine from sharing in the Destiny of Being. If Man is *more* than just one other species of an animal genus; if Man is a microcosm and a divine icon, and the destiny of Being is being played out at least "partially" in our destination (and vice versa), what goes on in the universe at large has resonances in us. There is

1 "Accayāsi (assa), Rādha, Panham, nasakkhi panhassa pariyantam gahetu."

2 *Saṁyutta-Nikāya* III, 187/189 (Khandhavagga II, 1).

a universal correlation, *perichōrēsis*, and this connectedness is not governed by the law of causality, which would be magic or sheer mechanicism. The relation of all with all is one of inter-in-dependence. There are, of course, personal tragedies that do not drag down the entire world, and collective or historical blunders that do not burden us personally with an irremediable guilt. There is ample place for what I have called *ontonomy*. Nevertheless, whether or not we can master it intellectually, there seems to be a sort of total solidarity, for which the name of Being may not be the worst word. An individualistic thinking of our destiny is as impossible as a private language.

Common destiny, solidarity, *karma*, *dharma-kāya*, *buddha-kāya*, *ecclesia*, *gahal*, *umma*, the communion of saints, the mystical body of Christ and similar expressions do not mean that the fate of one is the fate of all, that there can be no joy where suffering reigns, or that the radical relativity of everything with everything is an iron chain of strict causality. I will still speak of the inter-in-dependence and intra-in-dependence of all things in which each being has its *ontonomy*, that is, its degree of freedom and responsibility, in their etymological senses and not in an exclusively moral sense. Reality as a living organism is a traditional idea in both East and West; and belief in the *anima mundi* is almost universal.[3]

I have already chastised the fallacy of mistaking the logic of concepts with the real processes of Being. A concept is not the thing, and, physical laws notwithstanding, the real behavior of things does not need to be bound to mathematical calculus with concepts. Yet, the concept, which cannot be of any individual thing, is a powerful symbol for the solidarity of the real. This notwithstanding, the Being we are talking about is not a concept. The so-called *ens commune* is a formal abstraction and the *ens realissimum* just a supreme Entity. The Being I am referring to embraces all that (there) is. If Being applies to all, and to all of us, it means that we are somewhat intrinsically related to one another. This intrinsic relatedness is not a substance and yet it is a real relation (*advaita*). The "Destiny of Being" is not a vain phrase.

I have been hesitating whether I should use this loaded word "Destiny." To forge a neologism should be only a last recourse. On the other hand, we cannot ignore the context of the words and their connotations in past and present times. Learning from the wisdom of words encoded in their etymology, I have decided to keep the word "destiny" as distinct from "fate." Stoic philosophy encouraged yielding to destiny, and a typical example is the emperor Marcus Aurelius, who, drawn toward a more ascetic and retired

3 Cf. Plotinus, *Enneads* IV, 4, 32; etc.

life, did accept all the pressures and stresses of his royal rank and followed his destiny.[4]

The christian spirituality of those first centuries took the opposite view, that of struggling against fate, which included the rebellion against the "social obligations" of the times:[5] "the greatest of all evils is to say that this life is governed by inevitable necessities of fate,"[6] said Thecla, one of the virgins in the Dialogue written by Methodius, a bishop and martyr of the third century defending celibacy as the symbol of christian freedom.

* * *

It is appropriate from the outset to recall the need for intellectual sobriety. It is well and good not to set limits to our quest, but is it proper to undertake an inquiry before checking to see whether we have the appropriate tools? Are we entitled to include the Divine in our intellectual flights? Is the human intellect endowed with such a power? Is the Divine not off human limits by definition?

Such an ambitious topic should be approached with prudence and respect: the prudence of an individual's thought in the face of collective opinion; the respect due to anything superior to us. On the other hand, it would be unhealthy and countereffective to curtail the very thrust of the human intellect and to keep speculation about the Deity off limits. Is not each of us a divine image, as many human traditions proclaim? Furthermore, it is we human beings who speak— or hear—of divine transcendence and by this very fact already transgress such transcendence and incorporate it into the immanence of our being.

Intellectus capax dei ("the human intellect is capable of God"), said the ancients, thereby affirming an openness to infinity. An exclusively transcendent Divinity cannot share the destiny of the universe; it cannot have any relationship with us. If this is the case, then some "devout believers" should not "complain" if modernity in general and modern science in particular breaks off relations with such a God.

It is legitimate, therefore, not to eliminate the Divine when asking for the ultimate question or questions. Here I will (1) give some examples, and then (2) add some considerations, before (3) submitting the whole project to a radical critique.

---

4 See his moving and disarming confidences written in his private Diary: *Meditationes* VIII, 12-23; etc.

5 See a vivid description in Pagels (1988), *passim*, e.g., 78 sq.

6 Methodius, *Symposium on the ten Virgins* VIII, 13, cited in Pagels (1988), 86.

1. *Some Examples*

In the first century BC, Marcus Terentius Varro, *doctissimus Romanorum*, "the most learned of the romans," as Augustine called him,[7] was one of those geniuses whose works have mostly been lost and who nevertheless influenced western civilization as few others have done. While gathering all the available knowledge at his disposal, Varro wrote that in order to organize all human and divine things, the best method was to inscribe them under four headings: *Who? Where? When? What?*

Which is to say:

> *Who* are we? God(s), people, spirit(s), consciousness, animals, matter?
>
> *Where* are we? In which space, place, world, universe?
>
> *When* do we and all things exist? Forever, in time—future, present, past?
>
> *What* are things? Realities, beings, dreams, illusions, essences, existences?[8]

It is inadequate to interpret these questions as pertaining only to psychological or individualistic introspection. Nor are they exclusively political.

Earlier and more concisely than Varro, the indic wisdom reduced the four questions to the first and simply asked in a more ontologically and subjective manner: *ko'ham*? Who am I? The eclectic and practical roman spirit asks four questions in order to do justice to the ultimate human quest. The simplifying and contemplative indic spirit is satisfied with one. The syncretic and metaphysical greek spirit, which is intrigued by the problem of the ἓν καὶ πολλά, "the one and the many," tends to compromise through a theory of emanation, in which some may detect the origin of evolutionist thinking. It is important to note that this dialectical aporia of the "One and the many," which has haunted the western mind since the greeks, does not seem to be a great headache to most of the asian philosophies, perhaps because they do not approach the problem with the head alone.

A fifth query has long intrigued the human mind: *Whence?*

The Upanishads put the (fifth) question by asking: "Whence, truly, are creatures here born?"[9] The answer is the desire of Prajāpati, the Father of

7 Augustine, *De Civitate Dei* XIX, 22.

8 Varro, *Antiquitatum rerum humanarum et divinarum libri XLI.*

9 PrasU I, 3.

all creatures, to have offspring. The query about the origins is not only a cosmological or historical question (origin of the world, the species, etc.); it lies also at the basis of most logical operation: Deductive thinking is concerned "from where" we come to certain conclusions. After reminding us that the vexing question of the ancient philosophers is "How from the One [ἕν] does anything come into being [ὑπόστασις]?," Plotinus repeats the same question: "Why has the Primal [the One] not remained self-gathered so that there be none of this profusion of the manifold which we observe in existence and yet are compelled to trace to that absolute unity?"[10]

We have to stand somewhere in order to ground the answer. Here we can detect the bifurcation between modernity and classical thinking with all its positive and negative connotations. Since the origins are unknown, the modern mind relies on itself for an answer to this ultimate question and, assuming an *ascendant anthropology* (Man being the culmination of an ascendant evolution), tries to organize the available data (to the mind) and come to a plausible answer: the scientific hypothesis interpreted as a metaphysical theory. The traditional mind, aware that the origins are not only unknown but also mysterious, and assuming a *descendent anthropophany* (Man being the result of a descendent emanation), tries to open up to that mystery and organize a sensible answer. The continuation of the quoted text is paradigmatic: "In venturing an answer, we first invoke God Himself, not in a loud voice but in that way of prayer which is always in our power, leaning in soul towards Him by aspiration, alone towards the alone."[11]

We should underscore that here prayer is the highest activity of the intellect, which does not just petition for private favors but connects with the Source of all intelligibility. It is also relevant to note that Justin, a "pagan" philosopher and later a christian martyr of the second century, left his stoic, aristotelian, and platonic masters (in this order) and became a christian because he had not heard from any of them what centuries later another non-christian philosopher did teach: without illumination from above our ultimate questions have no answer.[12]

These ultimate questions in one form or another have haunted the human spirit at all times. A history of humanity could be written by analyzing which questions have been the most fundamental or ultimate. Here are some further examples of the shift from objective interest to focus on the subject. One Upanishad begins with the following questions:

---

10 Plotinus, *Enneads* V, 1, 6.

11 Ibid.

12 Cf. Justin, *Dialogue with Trypho* 2ff.

> What is the Cause? Brahman?
> Whence did we come to be?
> By whom (or what) do we live?
> On what are we established?[13]

Except for the first query, we note that all the questions refer to Man; they are anthropological more than cosmological. Another Upanishad also begins in the same mood:

> By whom projected soars the mind?
> By whom enjoined breathes first the mind?
> By whom impelled do people speak?[14]

This "who" is explicitly mentioned in another text:

In the beginning this was the Self alone, in the form of a Man. Looking around it saw nothing whatever except itself. It said in the beginning: "I am," and thence arose the name "I." So even today, when a Man is addressed, it says in the beginning, "It is I," and then adds any other name it may have.[15]

Here we have an ultimate answer without an explicit last question. The intuition of "I am" is akin to Yahweh's self-disclosure[16]—different interpretations and contexts notwithstanding. All these and similar questions are not prompted by an exclusively objective curiosity. No curiosity or desire can be merely objective. They are prompted by an aspiration to know, because for most cultures real knowledge is saving knowledge. Salvation is understood as the ultimate destiny, at least for Man. The problem, therefore, is to know. To know *what*? To know "God" is the most common answer, which many traditions homologate with knowing oneself, and practically all would equate with knowing the Truth, a Truth that sets us free and liberates us.[17]

The Upanishad asks: "What is that by knowing which all becomes known?"[18]

If the existence of a supreme Knower is accepted, the question turns into: "How can we know the Knower?"[19] The answer obviously transcends the epistemological plane. If we were to succeed in knowing the Knower, the

13 SU I, 1.

14 KenU I, 1.

15 BU, I, 4, 1.

16 Cf. Ex II or III, 14.

17 Jn VIII, 32.

18 MunU I, 1, 3.

19 BU III, 4, 2.

Knower would become the Known, and no longer be the Knower, unless both coalesce and there is identity between to know and to be. Epistemology becomes ontology and perfect onto-logy arrives at the identification between the ὄν and the λόγος, being and thought. This is idealism in its manifold forms. Here an ultimate question turns the very question into the Ultimate and the Answer becomes identified with Being. If to know is to become the known, and God knows the world, God becomes the world and is identified with it. The ideas of creatures in God are God, affirmed Augustine. Another text puts it more simply:

> It is not speech that one should seek to understand; one should know the speaker. . . . It is not joy and suffering that one should seek to understand; one should know the one who experiences joy and suffering. . . . It is not the mind that one should seek to understand; one should know the one who thinks.[20]

The question is here unambiguously directed to the *Whom?*

The three oft-quoted kantian questions could furnish us with another example directed to the *What*. Those questions are:

> What can I know?
> What ought I to do?
> What am I allowed to hope?[21]

The three can be subsumed in one: "What is Man?"

These examples show that an ultimate question can be formulated from any given perspective. There are many perspectives, but human curiosity immediately asks whether there is an ultimate perspective. Ironically, the two questions that have claimed to be the universal ultimate questions are mutually related. One is the question about God, the other about Being.

The ultimate question on which everything depends, it is said, is the question about whether or not God exists. In this context we could describe God as the final point of reference on all levels of being. God is then the cornerstone, the center of all things, all goodness, truth, and beauty. The human mind seems to need a clearinghouse for all human and cosmic operations. The question about God becomes almost by definition the ultimate question.

The question about God would then be the truly "Ultimate Question." It all depends on what the nature of God is, on whether this God exists or

---

20 KausU III, 8.

21 Kant, *Kritik der reinen Vernunft,* A 805 / B 833.

not as a supreme entity, on whether it is the *Hypothesis God*, a postulate for ordering human life and cosmic behavior, or a *Living God*, who is real. The famous "ontological argument" lurks on the horizon. If God is the Source of all things and the very condition for our thinking, then the God question will be the ultimate question indeed, and all ultimate questions will circle about God. If God is described as the Recipient of all the answers, God will of course be the Answer to all our ultimate questions from whatever corner they come. This would be a vicious circle if we were to base on it the so-called proofs for God's existence, but God as an answer to all ultimate questions could be a vital circle only if we take the answer to the ultimate questions to be a description of what the very word God means. In that sense the question about God is a legitimate question. A superfluous God, a God that could or could not be, while the world certainly is, would not fulfill the function God is supposed to play. The once-debated hypothesis: How would the world be and function *etsi Deus non daretur* ("even if there were no God") amounts to a flat negation of the existence of such a God.

The question about God is an ultimate question indeed. The difficulty lies in the fact that God does not give an ultimate answer, not only because this God generally keeps silent or does not give any answer, but also because were God to speak we could not avoid quarreling about the meaning of the answer(s), as the history of religions sufficiently demonstrates.

Even more, God may be an *ultimate Answer*, but an uncalled-for answer is not an answer. Indeed, there are cultures and philosophies that would not consider this question to be the unique ultimate question. Different schools of nihilism, anarchism, and "polytheism," as well as buddhism and jainism, to mention only a few, would not accept the problem about God as the ultimate question. This is because some renounce intelligibility, and others claim that harmony and a certain type of awareness do not require the *reductio ad unum* that a certain monotheism considers necessary to reach rational intelligibility.

Quite different is the buddhist problematic about śūn*yatā*, emptiness. It is not easy for an indo-european mind to reenact the style of thinking that has led to the philosophy of emptiness. It has taken centuries of meditation to come from the *anatta* intuition of Buddha (that there is no ātman, no substance) to the mahāyanic insight that emptiness is the last constituent of reality, or, in the words of Nāgārjuna, that *saṁ sāra* is *nirvāṇa* and vice versa.[22] The ultimate question in this context is not the query about God,

22 Nāgārjuna, Madham, *Mādhyamika-kārikā* XXV, 19.

but the no-question of emptiness. The ultimate answer is that there is no such question—and we leave it at that for the moment.

Our further example is the old and newly debated metaphysical question: "Why are there beings and not rather Nothing?"[23] There is a formal likeness between these two questions (about God and about Being)—they are somewhat circular and beg the question. This is not an objection. It is rather a proof that we have reached a qualified tautology. It has to be a tautology if it claims to be ultimate. Otherwise we could go on and on. Moreover, it has to be "qualified" if the tautology should not be barren. If Being is all that there *is*, the ultimate question, of course, will ask for Being.

The question about Being or Nothingness is the existential counterpart to the ontological argument. If Nothingness is that beyond which no thought can proceed, that empty thought will be the last point of reference and the resting place of every thought. This empty thought, however, is not an answer. If Nothingness were the answer, there would be neither question nor questioner to put the question. I am not going to delve into this metaphysical puzzle, except to remark that the question of a why put to Being implies the double assumption that Nothingness is a real possibility, and that the human mind has a capacity for formal extrapolations (not necessarily false) that need not be sustained by a real state of affairs—*sine fundamento in re* the scholastics would say.

In fact, the question about Nothingness is an outcome of this fundamental question about Being. The question is old—even in the same form. It is a metaphysical, cosmic, and yet profoundly human question, which the young Nachiketas asked in an existential way, while enquiring about the Beyond: "is or is not?,"[24] centuries before Hamlet's question in Shakespeare: "To be or not to be?"

"Why Being?" is an uncanny but not contradictory question. Human reason has the power to ask a why to every-*thing*, whatever the answer may be, but "why No-thing" is a why that rests on itself and asks nothing. The question phrased this way reveals a peculiar form of western thinking. Why is it still a meaningful *why* when we have eliminated any possible answer to the question? "Why is Being?" has its own quandary; but "Why not rather Nothing?" assumes that our power to ask *why* stands above any ontic ground of the question itself. What meaning has a *why* if there is nothing about which

23 Heidegger, *Was ist Metaphysik?* (Frankfurt, 1960), 21, 42: "Warum ist überhaupt Seiendes und nicht vielmehr Nichts?" Cf. Leibniz, *Principes de la nature et de la grace* : "pourquoi il y a plutôt quelque chose que rien?" (Opp. ed. Gerh. tom. VI, 602 n. 7).

24 *astitī nāstitī* (KathU, I, 1, 20).

to ask? The parmenidean balance between Thinking and Being is displaced in favor of the primacy of Thought over Being. Thought can function by itself disregarding whether there is anything besides the sheer formalism of "pure" thought. Pure mathematics functions this way, but mathematics asks no why and functions only on the basis of a set of agreed-upon axioms and rules.

The question persists: Why is there such an autonomy of pure thought independent of any content of thought? Our question could also include formal nothingness. The immediate answer is to say that it is a contradictory question. There is no why to ask a why if the why asks nothing. Ultimately to ask a why amounts to asking for the "reason" of the thing under question. Being may have a reason to be—problematic as this reason may be, but Nothingness does not have any "reason" to "be" what it is not. This may be as far as we can go, at least within a particular metaphysical perspective.

A hebrew psalm, especially in its latin form, has long haunted the christian writers since the gnostics and Irenaeus:[25] "Deep calls to deep."[26] If God has created out of nothing, the proper and ultimate nature of the creature is nothingness—as Thomas explicitly affirms.[27]

We have come full circle. We asked about the objective world; we inquired further about ourselves; we tried to combine objectivity and subjectivity and asked about God; finally we purified the very question from all its adherences (contents) and remained with an empty question that finds the resolution dissolving itself. In our search for the Whole we have encountered Nothingness.

2. *What Is an Ultimate Question?*

Since the first stirrings of humanity one fundamental concern has been: What is it all about? Or, in a more concrete form: *What is the meaning of life?* Hiding in this question is a double doubt. The first is whether life *should* have a meaning at all, and behind this, the deeper doubt whether the very question and the quest for meaning—or for anything that makes sense of reality and of our lives—is not in itself a meaningless search and ultimately countereffective. Perhaps the very method of inquiry is wrong. Perhaps we should not search, much less question, but allow ourselves to be searched

---

25 Cf. the very beginning of Irenaeus, *Adversus haereses*, I, 1, 1.

26 Ps XLI (42), 7 (8). "Abyssus abyssum invocat." Ralph Waldo Emerson translates: "Under every deep a lower deep opens" (*Essays*, "Circles," 1).

27 "sibi autem relicta [creatura] in se considerata nihil est: unde prius naturaliter inest sibi nihil quam esse" (*De aeternitate mundi*).

and questioned—a much more feminine attitude. I will return to this second doubt, but let me try to say a little more about the first.

Has life a meaning? It could well be that meaninglessness is the only "meaning," and the search for anything else is a fatal temptation. The horizon of nihilism, which seems to be a recurrent theme from taoism, buddhism, and christianity to Nietzsche, Sartre, and Heidegger, may well be a human constant, and probably the backdrop for the specifically human question which sets Man apart from being just a species of an animal genus.

Questions such as: What is reality? What is Man? What is God? . . . all assume that there "is" something presupposed in every question. The ultimate question would be that question beyond which there is nothing "else" to ask—which does not question itself, and stops at a *that* without a *why* calling for further interrogation.

There seem to be three attitudes here: (a) *The agnostic*. Since we cannot answer the question about the ultimate meaning of life, reality, or whatever name one chooses, we cultivate an undetached indifference and live without metaphysical qualms—although often with more physical problems. (b) *The pragmatic*. Since the query is too overwhelming for the individual, one relies more or less tentatively on the answers of the respective traditions with which one is more familiar, or which seem more convincing. (c) *The philosophical*. Since Man seems to be a questioning being, we should proceed further in investigating this human character.

Significantly enough, all three attitudes have to stop somewhere, have to take something for granted with or without an explicit foundation. All of which amounts to saying that the ultimate must be always a myth. Myth appears unquestionable simply because it is unquestioned. If something were to be accepted as unquestionable because of some internal necessity, this very necessity (transparency or evidence) would convince us that there is no need to question any further. This would be the myth. Myth can only be explained by transferring it to another wider horizon, even if provisionally or for the time being, and this wider horizon will then serve as our myth. The myth we adhere to is what we take for granted, something so transparent that we do not see it—as myth.

The difference between the unquestioned and the unquestionable is obvious. Something is unquestionable when we see the "reason" why we do not need to question it further. It is evident, transparent, clear, self-luminous, gives reason of itself—it *cannot* be questioned. It is our myth. Yet we have all had the startling experience that what seemed unquestionable to some ("angels do exist"; "reason is the last resort") did not appear so to others.

More importantly, any unquestionability is "based" on absolutizing the last instance on which we ground it, whether God, experience, reason, or logic. . . . However, the consciousness of setting anything as an absolute immediately relativizes it. In other words, the unquestionable, too, has presuppositions. It is not absolute; it is only unquestionable *quad nos*, for "us."

The unquestioned also ceases to be such when it appears to our consciousness as unquestioned. The status of the unquestioned is always the past—and secondarily the future. The simple statement "it is unquestioned" has all the vulnerability of a factual and contingent sentence; it remains unquestioned until *de facto* somebody questions it—even if this somebody is ourselves. We cannot repress the why if something dawns on our consciousness as unquestioned.

In any case, we have to rely on language. As Plotinus ironically puts it: "One should come to terms with names" ("we must be patient with language" [S. Mackenna]).[28] We have to use words in an improper manner (ἀκρίβεια). Language conditions our thinking. Many languages use the verb "to be" in order to ask about whatever is considered the fundamental issue. In this universe of discourse, the question of Being is the fundamental question. What "is" the *is* we use in questioning ourselves about anything? The question is not what is "Being," or what "there is," not even what "exists" or what lives, but what [is] *is*? What or who [is] *is*? We have been so culturally accustomed to objectivity that we hardly realize that this ultimate question "What is Being?" could equally take the form "What or who art Being?" and even "What or who *am* Being?[29]

In asking about Being we should be asking about the *is*, the *art*, and the *am*. Such a question must include all the tenses and pronouns of the verb. I will skip the problem presented by the many languages that do not have the verb "to be." There are indeed homeomorphic equivalents: to exist, to be present, to be real, effective, alive, and so on. Suffice to mention it to make us aware of the relativity of our languages and ways of thinking. I cannot avoid mentioning here incidentally, but not accidentally, one of the greatest genocides of the twentieth century: the linguistic genocide. Over five thousand languages have disappeared in the last hundred years. The "Destiny of Being" is only our ways of speaking and thinking.

We ask questions because we have not reached the ultimate. Questions

---

28 Plotinus, *Enneads* VI, 8, 13: Δεῖ δὲ συγχωρεῖν τοῖς ὀνόμασιν.

29 See Panikkar, "The threefold Linguistic Intra-subjectivity," in *Perspectives in Philosophy, Religion, and Art*, ed. B. Balasubramanian and V. C. Thomas (New Delhi: Indian Council of Philosophical Research), 34-48.

are always penultimate. The ultimate is that which raises no question. The ultimate has no why. It is a supreme innocence—what I have called the "new innocence."[30]

Why should you not eat the forbidden fruit? asks the serpent.[31] The *why* triggers the knowledge of good and evil, but the innocence is lost. Once we start asking *why*, there is no end to it. We cannot stop the flow of whys. The series of "whys" does not stop by itself. The questioner is never totally questioned in the question. If the questioner were totally questioned in the question, that question would destroy the questioner.

Quaestio mihi factus sum,[32] said a Father of western civilization. There is always need of the oblique case because we cannot question ourselves without the split between a subject and a predicate. Even the consciousness of a question implies the awareness that someone (the subject) is asking something (the possible predicate). The most we can do is to ask about ourselves. *Ko'ham*, who [am] I? *Aham-brahman*, answers the Upanishad—but *brahman* neither puts nor answers the question, and vedānta adds that it cannot be self-conscious, otherwise it would be consciousness-of (itself) and not pure consciousness.

In our "sublunar" world, let us assume that our "ultimate" question is the question about reality. I referred to three traditional formulations: What (it) *is* Being? What or who *art* (thou) God? Who *am* (I)? The question about reality entails the awareness that we and our question are also part of reality. It also includes the awareness that we would not be asking if that reality were not, in one way or another, eliciting this very question from us. Further, this selfsame awareness is also aware, though dimly and obliquely, that awareness is not all there is. First, this is because we are conscious that our awareness is not infinite, and is thus limited, and being limited that there may be real things outside or beyond our field of awareness. Second, this is because the entire field of Being does not necessarily coincide with the field of awareness unless *a priori* we identify the two fields, which is what idealism does. Reality does not need to be "reduced" to only *that* of which any awareness may be aware.[33]

Here is the power of theistic religion. They say that there is "Something" in which all questions stop and all answers are dissolved. Says Abhinavagupta:

---

30 See Panikkar, *La nueva inocencia* (Barcelona: Proa, 1998).

31 See Gn III, 1.

32 Augustine, *Conf.* X, 33, 50.

33 See Panikkar, "Das unwissende Bewusstsein," in *Bewusstsein und Person*, ed. G. Rager and A. Holderegger (Freiburg: Universitätsverlag, Paulusdruckerei, 2000), 124-44.

"Even if He (Śiva) is supposed to be obstructed by a cover (e.g., *māyā*), He still shines by His freedom in the form of that cover itself."[34] We may detect an echo of one Upanishad:

> The face of truth is covered over
> by a golden vessel. Uncover it, O Lord,
> that I who love the truth may see.[35]

* * *

There are no absolutely ultimate questions—because any question reposes on (relative) assumptions. There are only provisional answers to whatever is asked. Though this long excursus was necessary, it leaves us on shaky ground.

3. *The Dialectic of Ultimate Questions*

Our formulation expresses a double problem: *Ultimacy* and *Question*. To inquire about the meaning of *Ultimacy* is an incorrect question. Either we call it ultimate because we have not found anything "behind," "beyond," or more basic (until someone comes with a new finding) or it is *a priori*, in which case it is simply a postulate of our mind and not necessarily identical to a real Ultimate (unless one accepts an absolute idealism closed on itself). The question then ceases to be a question and becomes a postulate grounded in itself: we need it in order to think—a thinking that can only think based on itself unable to tell anything about any reality that is not based on the postulate of thinking itself. We are close to the *noēsis noēseōs*, the knowledge of knowledge of Aristotle.

The universe of kashmiri shaivism offers an important approach to the problem. A short text from the tantric *Rudrayāmala* (rendered famous by Abhinavagupta's commentaries), the *Parātrīśikā Vivaraṇa*, and the *Laghuvṛtti*, begins by asking for the *anuttaram*, the ultimate, unsurpassable, supreme, that beyond which one cannot go,[36] "that than which nothing greater can be known."[37] There is an intriguing formal similarity to the so-called ontological argument. Anselm says: "that than which no greater can be thought."[38] Both the *anuttaram* and the *maius* are comparatives—

34 Abhinavagupta, *Parātrīśikā Vivaraṇa*, 79.

35 IsU, XV; *hiraṇmayena pātreṇa satyasa apihitam mukham;* cf. etiam MaitU 6, XXXV.

36 See Panikkar "The Experiential 'Argument' of Abhinavagupta: A Cross-Cultural Consideration," in *L'argomento ontologico*, ed. M. M. Olivetti, Biblioteca dell' Archivo di Filosofia 58, 1/3 (Padua, 1990), 8-19 for comparative study of the two following texts.

37 Abhinavagupta, *Parātrīśikā Vivaraṇa*, 20: "na vidyate uttaram adhikaṁ yataḥ."

38 Anselmus, *Proslogion* I: "id quo maius cogitari nequit."

they express a relation to us who cannot think of anything greater, higher. The comparative form indicates that there are no absolute questions and therefore no absolute answers.

To the traditional phrase *Devī uvāca* ("the Goddess said"), Abhinavagupta adjoins his comments on the importance of the past, since any experience can only be reported in the past tense. Then he adds:

> The Self who is the natural state of all existents, who is Self-luminous, amusing Himself with question-answer which is not different from Himself, and in which both the questioner [as Devī] and the answerer [as Bhairava] are only Himself, reflects thus as I, I myself, being thus desirous of wonderful delight knowing the truth as it is, appear as question and answer (*tathaiva bhavāmi*).[39]

The text reflects another universe of discourse, but we retain here only this: Question and answer belong intrinsically together as the unfolding (divine) Consciousness. As the same text says, "That which is posited [only] as an answer is really no answer."[40]

Any answer implies a question, but any question also entails a possible answer, even if we do not know the answer—otherwise it is only a pseudo-question, because it excludes any possible answer. Either we do not know what the question asks (in this case it is not a question) or it is itself contradictory (and it is not a question at all). The way in which consciousness unfolds is not primarily in terms of subject/object, but rather as question/answer. Both belong together. Every question already covers an answer in potency. Every question is a question because it demands an answer. But every answer contains not only the implicit question of which it is the answer, but also, by the same token (of being an answer), elicits a further question, namely, that of the questioner. "Who's asking?"

This leads us to the second problem of ultimate questions: the *Question*. No metaphysical question can be ultimate, since every question is based on a series of assumptions that are the necessary condition for the meaningfulness of the question.

If the first problem, that of ultimacy, leads to a process *ad infinitum* (we can always question further), the second problem leads to a *vicious circle*. Because questioning is our human way of getting an answer, we cannot recognize an answer as answer if we are not aware of the corresponding question, and we are not aware of the question if it does not appear to our

39 Abhinavagupta, *Parātrīśikā Vivaraṇa*, 5. Singh's translation, 15.

40 Singh translation, 22.

consciousness as the proper question of a set of possible answers which constitute the problem.

Anything we become conscious of appears to our consciousness as an "answer"—literally as a "swearing" conjured up by the implicit question hidden in the reflective act of asking whether what we are conscious of is really so. True questions are not merely impromptus of our curiosity. This is why traditional wisdom both warns us against idle curiosity and makes us responsible for the kind of questions we ask. It is worth invoking the insight that: "You would not seek me if you did not possess me,"[41] in the words of Pascal, who echoes older statements of this kind.[42]

Even Silence and Nothingness do not escape from the field of our consciousness. We are not dealing here with a rhetorical question. To know embraces both question and answer; that is, knowledge encompasses the field where the question has its context and the answer its range of possibilities. Any assertion is an answer to an implicit question, and any question delimits the conditions of possibility for a possible answer. To have an answer without knowing what question it answers is not to know the answer. An answer is an answer if the question remains attached. The moment the answer eliminates the question and stands there alone, it is no longer an answer but a simple affirmation, which by stifling the implicit question will soon turn into an untouchable dogma. An example is the famous *creatio ex nihilo*, so often misunderstood when cited outside its proper context. The "creation out of nothing" is an answer that responds to the question whether creation emerges of "primal-matter" (*prōtē hylē*), or without it. *Ex nihilo nihil* fit: Certainly, "nothing comes out of nothing." The problem is not the *nihil*, but the *ex*. *Creatio ex nihilio* means creation from no primal matter; not *ex Deo*, as an ontological emanation (pantheism), but certainly *a Deo* (by and from God).[43] Without knowing the question, the "answer"—which is then no answer—misfires. To know the question already circumscribes the range of possible answers. If the question is *aufgehoben* (made superfluous, superseded, overcome, integrated—to pay tribute to Hegel) by the answer and disappears as such, it automatically eliminates the answer. The question has to remain forever question, and questionable. This means that no true question can be exhausted by any answer. Both together delimit the range of the problem.

41 Pascal, *Pensées*, VII, 555; cf. VII, 553: "Tu ne me chercherais pas, si tu ne me possédais."

42 Cf. Jn VI, 44; cf. Bernard, *De Diligendo Deo*, VII, 22 (PL 182:987).

43 See "Le mirage de l'avenir," *Convergence* 3-4 (1971), 3-6.

Questioning may well be "the piety of thinking,"[44] but responding is both the icon of that *Frömmigkeit* (piety) and the responsibility of thinking itself.

Lurking behind these apparently abstract reflections is the political problem of power. The questions we ask will trigger an entire culture in one direction or another. To spell out the questions is more powerful, and often more dangerous, than to find the convincing answers. It is more difficult and delicate to challenge the questions than the answers. In the paneconomic world today, for instance, the liberal capitalist answers or the socialist answers fade into insignificance in front of the powerful scheme of the set of questions that trigger the disparate answers—"how do we make a living" or "maximize profit," for instance. We touch, once again, the issue of the myth. We ask what we see as "fragwürdig," as demanding an answer out of the mythical horizon that lets the question appear.

In the West, since God ceased to be the unquestioned myth, that is, the unquestionable symbol, philosophy has asked for a *fundamentum inconcussum*, an indisputable ground. Names like Descartes, Natorp, Dingler, Husserl, Maréchal, and scores of others could be brought to witness to that search for *le point de départ de la métaphysique*. All searched for "something" that could be the epistemological answer to all starting points. If one is to avoid a *recursus ad infinitum,* one has to find a *principium non principiatum* ("a principle without a beginning"). The only logical outcome has to be the circularity of all in all (*a* rests on *b*, *b* on *c*, . . . until we come back and close the series). Only the free act of positing a beginning can be the foundation for all that follows. This is the strength of a monotheistic God. The problem of the question is not an epistemological problem. It is a matter of Being.

The motto at the beginning of this chapter introduces the traditional buddhist dialectic. If we do not know the limits of the question, how can we expect an answer? The silence of the Buddha is not an epistemological twist, but rather a metaphysical stance. It is not that Buddha uses another logic; he simply offers another insight into human life.[45]

We are beings endowed not only with *logos*, but also inspired by *pneuma*. *Pneuma,* or the spirit, is neither above nor below the *logos*. *Logos* and *pneuma* are not two separate "faculties" through which we enter into contact with reality—and therefore they are not subordinated to one another. Neither are they indistinguishable, the same "thing." We need to distinguish them, but they are inseparable. If the senses are the first eye and reason is the second,

44 Heidegger, *The Question Concerning Technology,* 1954, Vol. I, 36.

45 See Panikkar, *L'esperienza* filosofica *dell' India* (Assisi: Cittadella, 2000).

then the spirit is the third eye, but the integral vision is only one, the synthesis of the three eyes.

All in all, I am saying that the dialectic question/answer, important and indispensable as it is, is not the only method to reach the real.

B. Reality and Being

1. *The Sense of the Real*

The typical residents of the modern city are struggling to "progress" in a world converted into a supermarket and to succeed in the cold war of a competitive society, with not much more "intellectual" input than that of the popular "mass media," and the equally typical "residents" on the fringes of the "First Class" society are the hungry, displaced, and terrorized human majority with hardly a realistic possibility to live a human life. Both such residents must feel a sense of estrangement if they happen to hear philosophers talking about reality. What strange world of lifeless abstractions is being discussed? Our contemporaries may not understand Einstein or Heisenberg, but with physics the results are at least tangible. In contrast, the prestige and credibility of philosophy have never been lower. It seems irrelevant and often incomprehensible. Most of the words philosophy uses have become either obsolete or confiscated by a popularized techno-scientific language. Hospital, information, and contact are accepted words; hospitality, formation, and contingency may require explanatory footnotes.

Of course, the average peasant or burgher of earlier times had equally little inclination to mull over philosophical topics. Nonetheless, the experiences of nature, life, birth, death, suffering, and even of eating were, so to speak, "saturated" with metaphysics, and discussions around the hearth, in the plazas, or in the pub often took a cosmic or theological turn. Despite long hours of toil, the absence of our modern distractions left plenty of time to those inclined to speculate about the meaning of life and to sense the weight of the real. Practically all celebrations and festivities were positively and negatively saturated with a sense of the sacred.

Nowadays the vital issues are taken to be simply scientific or technical problems, or occasions for witty reactions to the "news" purveyed by the mass media. It was not accidental that the prestige—and, at least indirectly, the power—of thinkers and theologians, *brahmins* and priests, was once so high. Even fifty years ago a *Herr Professor*, a "Reverend Father," an *acharya* or a *svāmi* had an aura that—for better or worse—has today faded away. Rather than feel pity for philosophers, the important concern is to recognize that all this marks a change in our understanding of reality. Our sense of the real is shrinking to the immediate *Wirklichkeit* (that is, to what "works"), to the effective and the efficient, and all too often to the expedient.

What is undermined is our *sense of the real*. Is the Being of the philosophers something real? Isn't Plato just a poetic dreamer with an inflated reputation? Is the world of the Desert Fathers a habitable universe? Aren't Śankara and Rāmānuja basically talking about some nonexistent superreality? Shouldn't we realize that Hegel is an unreadable and uninteresting exercise in futility, and Heidegger nothing but wordplays and empty speculation?

In order to know what colors are, we need eyes and some understanding of what a color is. In order to know what justice is, we need a certain sense of justice and fair play. Similarly, in order to know what is real, what that overall "something" is that we call reality, we need a "sense" of the real. Not so very long ago our ancestors believed that angels and demons were real—real beings, as other cultures still do. However, few people today among the "First Class" citizens of the world are ready to believe that angels are real, and so-called theologians will turn exegetical somersaults trying to demythologize that traditional belief. Since angels are no longer taken for granted as part of the universe, their existence will have to be proved or disproved in accordance with today's accepted norms of what is real.

What does it mean for us today, when a John of the Cross says, "A single spiritual thought is worth more than the entire material world"?[46] Or when a more contemporary thinker like Nicolai Berdiaev writes that "the spiritual life is the most real"?[47] Or when we hear the traditional idea repeated that "the human soul is more valuable than all the kingdoms of the world, for it encompasses the infinite . . ."?[48]

All this is at loggerheads with the predominant modern worldview and even seems incomprehensible, despite the increasing number of people turning to all forms of exotic spirituality that have little relevance for the functioning of a world that still spends about three billion dollars a day for armaments.[49] All those metaphysical expressions are bound to sound like exaggerations, at the very least, to the majority of the citizens in our technocratic civilization. The reality of human life today is gauged by the

46 "Un solo pensamiento del hombre vale más que que todo el mundo" (Juan de la Cruz, *Dichos de luz y amor* [*Avisos y sentencias espirituales*]).

47 Berdiaev (1984), 32, 33.

48 Ibid., 219. Cf. "What does a man gain by winning the whole world at the cost of his true self?" (Mk VIII, 36).

49 US Department of State: World Military Expenditures and Arms Transfers 2005.

needs of the species, which is considered a species of the animal realm: a rational species. It is the regression from *homo sapiens* to *animal habilis*. Paradoxically enough, the classification of Man as just another animal species living on the planet fosters the desire to escape from this earth.

What, then, do we understand by reality? Common language distinguishes something real both from something merely possible and from something purely illusory. In a more problematic way, ordinary language also distinguishes the real (as something) from the non-real (as nothing). The common understanding is to equate reality with existence. All these expressions, however, are full of ambiguities that require careful and extensive qualifications.

I am not directly concerned here with the idealism/realism problem, nor with the related epistemological question of the "reality" of our knowledge, nor indeed with whether we can prove or be certain that an external world exists, and the like. Our concern, instead, goes to the very roots of these questions, to something that touches the deepest recesses of the human being. Our sense of the real is linked with our identity, with the conviction that something matters in our lives and that this "something" is not a totally private affair, that it somehow extends into a sphere that transcends our egos, that we have a sort of biography or destiny because we belong to a larger Whole that has at least as much reality as we have. It may be through a *cogito*, or common sense, sentiment, certainty, experience, suffering, *Angst*, desire, or whatever, that we realize that there is a "me" and something else besides me, perhaps even beyond and above me, that is as real as I am. I may easily go beyond this and affirm that my life is real because I share in a universe in which I am not alone. I mention love last, but stress that it occupies the first place among the factors that give us a sense of the real. Pure reason can doubt that there is something real; authentic love cannot.

To cut a long story short, I shall limit myself to using the word "reality" in the ordinary way it has been used in many traditions, without digressing into many legitimate philosophical distinctions. We give only *two examples* of two different cultures.

In the first example, the greek and latin traditions used the words φύσις (*physis*) and *rerum natura*, respectively. These words indicate *what* we are and *that* in which we are—namely, everything that may be the subject matter of an actual or possible experience. Anything is natural when it is alive—this is what the two words connote. Something is alive when it changes, moves, grows, comes, and goes, when it stands independently, although inter-dependently, "outside its causes" (*extra causas sistere*), when it exists. Both the greek *physis* and the latin *natura* imply movement, generation, life, and therefore a certain inner harmony, an *ordo*, that is, a rhythm that makes it a *kosmos*, a *mundus*, an entire universe.

The word "reality" not only expresses the sum total of existing things but also presents a certain unity; it implies a *kosmos*, a world, a uni-verse. Reality is the life, the space, the where, which encompasses all these things, πράγματα (*pragmata*), *res*, *Sachen*. (Kant still translates *realitas* with *Sachheit*.[50]) Reality is the realm of the *Tatsachen*, weakly rendered as "facts." The indo-european root of "reality" is *re* (*rei*), with the meaning of possession (*r*ām, *r*ās means riches in vedic sanskrit—and *rayi* a blessing of abundance). *Res* (from which comes "reality" and "thing," "property," "affair") suggests that that which I have, what is present and on which I can count, is (handy) because it is real. Reality is what stands present at least in front of (our) Consciousness.

For our *second example* I introduce three expressions from the indic tradition. One comes from the śruti or sacred "revelation"; the others have a more general philosophical use. We often find in the Veda the phrase *idaṁ sarvaṁ* , literally "this all," generally translated as "world" or "universe." *Idaṁ sarvaṁ* is "this all" to which one might say, imagine as, refer to, or think of as *this*. Anything that falls under *this*: this tree, this idea, this God, feeling, woman, number, color, sky, symbol, myth.[51] *Idaṁ sarvaṁ* is not only "all this" that we actually perceive. It is also "this all," but not as a notion or idea *of* the "All." It has to be *this* All. Not "this (is) all," or "this (is the) All." And much less "all (is) this." The two words are placed together without a verb. *Idaṁ sarvaṁ* denotes *All* that can be *this*, because *this* can be *all*. Reality is *all* that can be addressed as *this*. Real is anything to which a *this* may be applied—the *this* together with the *all*.

Idaṁ sarvaṁ is the All inasmuch as we can say "this" to the All and not just to the sum total of "things." Nothingness, which escapes perception and thought, can still be addressed as *this* provided we do not interject any verb in between. The *this* of nothingness is not a "this is not." It would be a contradiction and would make no sense: This *this* which *is* (this) *is not* (this). Grammatical english has to say: "(it) is not," "*this* is an *it* that is not." The negation has to negate something. The *this* of nothingness cannot be the negation of "anything." Nothingness has no *this*. A different matter would be the experience of Emptiness or vacuity. There is no *this* for the son of a barren woman, to use the traditional indic example, but there is the experience of the empty womb of the barren woman. We leave it without

50 Kant, *Kritik der reinen Vernunft*, A143, B182.

51 See I, C, 2 above.

pursuing the problem further. We conclude saying that "*Idaṁ* is anything that can fall within the range of any possible experience."[52] This is the real.

"In the beginning *this* (was) water,"[53] asserts a cosmological text; "In the beginning *this* was the ātman alone in the form of a Man"[54] says another foundational text. A little later, it tells us that *this* (*idaṁ*) was only *brahman.*[55] Abhinavagupta comments pertinently that once the *this* enters into our consciousness, it becomes part of us and yet conserves its diversity. I, Thou, It would be the triad of *Śiva*, *śakti*, *nara* (God, Power, Man—an approximate translation): "That which appears even as 'this,' when addressed, becomes completely enveloped with the I-feeling (*ahambhāva*) of the addresser."[56] A little earlier he explicitly affirmed that "all this (the entire universe) has the threefold form,"[57] the famous *trika* or triad of kashmiri shaivism: *nara-śakti-śivam-ātmakaṁ trikaṁ*.

There is still another set of texts that will tell us: "In the beginning (all) *this* was Non-being only."[58] For our purposes here, we will retain only this much: *idaṁ* : "this" is all that we may, in one way or another, be able to indicate by whatever human operation.

The sanskrit word *tattva* also illuminates what I am saying. So many philosophical works have this word in the title that in modern times *tattva-vidyā* or *tattva-jñāna* are used as synonymous with "philosophy." Usually the word is translated as "essence," sometimes as "truth." Literally, it means "that-ness," but it could also be rendered as "thus-ness," and stands for reality. Reality is all that has the character of *thatness*. It signals an immediate presence of things.

Tad-ekam (this one) is often used in the Veda.[59]

Another expression is *eka-tattva* (the one or sole entity), used, for instance, in Yoga,[60] whether it is understood as only one truth, Īśvara (God), as Vācaspati Miśra and others think, or as any entity apt for yogic meditation.

---

52 See Panikkar, *The Vedic Experience: Mantramañjarī, An Anthology of the Vedas for Modern Man and Contemporary Celebration* (Berkeley: University of California Press,1977), 656.

53 SB XI, 1, 6, 1: "āpo ha vā-idaṁ agre."

54 BU I, 4, 1: "ātmā-eva-idam agra āsīt purusa-vidhaḥ."

55 BU I, 4, 11.

56 Abhinavagupta, *Parātrīśikā Vivaraṇa*, 70.

57 Ibid.: "idaṁ sarvaṁ trika-rūpam-eva."

58 TU II, 7, etc. "āsad vā idam agra āsīt."

59 RV X, 129, 2 and 3; etc.

60 YS I, 32.

Within sanskrit grammar itself, therefore, one can detect the two main thrusts of indic philosophy. What is real is *this* (*idam*), or *that* (*tat*). The mādhyamika, for example, will emphatically say that the real is *tattva*, *that* not *this*, precisely because it is beyond thought.[61] The Kathopanishad, on the other hand, emphatically declares as the acme of wisdom: "This (is) truly that."[62] Or, as a coptic Gospel puts it: "When the inner is the outer and the outer is the inner. . . ."[63]

The third expression for reality is *satyam* translated both as "truth" and as "reality." Literally *sat-yam* means "being-ness." There are scores of scriptural texts on the notion of *satyam.*[64] This third expression for reality is close to the scholastic tradition identifying truth and reality, which tallies with the statement of Jesus: "Truth shall make you free."[65]

We are free when we are real, when we are in harmony with reality. The sanskrit word for untruth or a lie implies division or disorder: *anṛta*, something that disturbs *ṛta*, the cosmic order. A cryptic Upanishadic text says:

> He asks him: "Who am I?"
>
> "Reality" (*satyam,* truth) he replied.
>
> "What is this reality (*satyam*)"?
>
> "Whatever is different from the *deva* (senses, divinities) and the *prāṇa* (vital breaths), that is *sat* (real, Being), but the *deva* and the *prāṇa* are *tyam* (*'that'-ity*) [to match the sanskrit pun]. Therefore it is expressed by the word *sat-yam* (real-ity) which comprises all this. *Idaṃsarvam asiti* (you are this all/all this)."[66]

"I am" insofar as I am real, insofar as I am truthful. This reality is more than what is disclosed by my senses and my rational life, it is Being (disclosed by the third eye).

I have digressed on this *second cultural example* for a vital reason. Modern western languages approach reality by means of the verb "to be" up to the point that intelligibility is expressed according to the scheme "S is P." Many

61 Shāntideva, *Bodhicaryāvatāra*, IX, 2.

62 KathU IV, 3ff. *etad vai tat.*

63 *Gospel of Thomas*, 22.

64 See Panikkar, "Die existentielle Phänomenologie der Wahrheit," in *Philosophisches Jahrbuch der Görresgesellschaft* 64 (1956), 27-54.

65 Jn VIII, 32.

66 KausU I, 6.

other languages reach intelligibility simply by juxtaposition. Chinese and japanese could be adduced as examples. Sanskrit takes a middle position, and thus it can help to bridge both extremes. We have had to say "this (is) that," reality (is) "this all," where the verbal form "is" becomes an intermediary, the copula. It is the philosophical problem of "mediation." Our contact with reality cannot be mediated by anything other than reality itself. The insight into reality can be only an immediate experience. In the logical formula "S is P," the Subject is the Predicate, the identity can never be total as long as the Subject (Gopal, Triangle, Beauty) remains subject and the Predicate ([is] a Man, a geometrical figure, a quality) predicate. The copula unites, but our consciousness of it separates. In a word, although our language obliges us to speak of Being and say "is," the experience of the real has to transcend all "is-ness."

A few characteristics emerge clearly. The real is something immediately given, but given not just by ourselves. It is a given that constitutes us. The real is not pliable to our whims. It offers resistance to our intelligence, will, and all our faculties. We are not its masters. The real is irreducible to the subject. These caveats are important because, of course, all these statements would require further qualifications. It may be worthwhile to recall Descartes' sarcastic comment that there are some people so stupid they do not even know what real things mean.[67] Apparently one cannot get very far with only pure ideas. Even Kant recognized that the idea of a hundred possible thalers is different from a hundred real thalers.[68] And the mīmāmsaka says that even if a hundred scriptural texts assure us that fire does not burn, we would not believe them. Reality takes primacy over any idea or theoretical statement.

A unique feature of reality is that its immediate givenness excludes any criteria for its own reality. Concrete events or things can be tested to tell whether they are real according to previously accepted criteria, but we cannot ask for the criteria of reality itself as such, since we cannot ask for the criteria that give validity to our criteria without proceeding *ad infinitum*. If the criterion for reality is some kind of correspondence between subject and object, we will be entangled forever. If we, our mind, feelings, sense of ego, or whatever, ask for ways to discern reality, we are already "outside" reality on what we take to be a firmer ground than reality itself. By doing this, we have already decided that we, the human subjects, are real and thereby split "reality" in two: our-selves (or our minds) and all the rest. And this split is

67 Descartes, *Principia* I, 10 (in his own french translation although not in the original latin).

68 Kant, *Kritik der reinen Vernunft,* II, 3. 4.

unbridgeable, because the pillars are not real, Thomas says. "Being [Existence] is more intimately and profoundly interior to things than anything else."[69]

To sum up. We all are conscious that we live in a universe (cosmos, world, space, time, . . .) in which we breathe, move, dream, think, suffer, enjoy, prior to any interpretations of this primordial awareness. This is what leads me to speak of *mythos*. Paradoxically enough (or should we say it is the irony of history?), it is the *mythos* in which we live that gives us the sense of the real. The *mythos*, in fact, is the "world" in which we believe we live. Real is what has a place in the world in and from which we live.

* * *

The sense of the real dawns upon us when we really live. We live authentically when we experience Life purified from all its accidents. Modern civilization with its acceleration and its success in bringing about external comfort without effort makes it difficult to experience such moments in which we sense the real in that inexpressible way, transcending ideas, sentiments, time, space, and all egoistic individualism (*ahamkāra*). Our sense of the real seems to shrink only to those moments of so-called peak experiences, like the awakening of reflexive awareness when coming of age, falling in love, witnessing a disgrace, a death, or other special times of contemplation and of joy. In short, we experience the real when we live Life and are not distracted by its operations. One can understand the great masters who do not write and hardly speak, as well as that selfcontradictory statement: "Those who know do not speak; those who speak do not know."[70] Long ago Irenaeus said that Silence gives birth to the Logos and the Logos takes flesh in each of us when suffused by Love. Might this be "the discovery of Being"?

2. *The Discovery of Being*

Until now I have been speaking about reality. But as I said, the title includes an even more forbidding word, "Being." All too familiar is the nominalist attack against the meaningless use of an empty concept, an open box that says nothing in particular to anyone about anything and contains nothing for which such a box would even be necessary. One need only recall the names of Hume, Carnap, Russell, and Ayer.

On the other hand, offering the most divergent interpretations, there is the impressive array of philosophers, eastern and western, who have

---

69 Thomas Aquinas, *Summ Theol.* I, q. 8, a. 1: "Esse autem est illud quod est magis intimum cuilibet, et quod profundius omnibus inest."

70 Cf. *Tao Te Ching,* 56.

taken Being seriously since the remotest antiquity. Yet some epigones of the metaphysical traditions have reduced Being to a concept that has little to do with life and reality. Words may hide either a vital symbol or a useless and disorienting sign.

I would like to offer some reflections that spring from an original encounter with the problem, after having passed through the multiple filters offered by the history of human thought. Only what has been totally assimilated and comes from the overflowing of one's heart is worth writing down for others. I confess that, despite the great minds I have encountered on the way, I often feel lost in the jungle of opinions. Should I keep silent or perhaps sing my song without a text? The music still remains in me and this is what I offer, hoping that the reader will become a listener and fill the music with an original text.

Here is a partial score for this unfinished symphony in twenty-four points.

1. A thing is a given. A gift to us. Here we touch a fundamental and yet neglected human attitude of opening ourselves to what is given, of being aware that everything that comes to us is a gift. The attitude of receiving everything as a grace, as something gratuitous and often agreeable and gratifying, elicits in us a sentiment of gratitude and joy (χάρα). The root-metaphor of śruti (hearing) is closer to this attitude than the corresponding greek metaphor of seeing, but since I am expressing myself within the western tradition, I will work with the visual metaphor.

2. Things are "complexes" that "show" a threefold character: a sort of existence (stability), a certain essence (intelligibility), and a kind of intraconnectedness with everything (mystery). Things make a "claim" to exist outside us. They speak to us from a certain transcendence, and we hear them. This claim is perceived only through our own operations (of the senses, mind, spirit), in our consciousness, which is the field where all "things" meet.

3. We order things in clusters of similar things and situate them on a plane that confers a certain unity on them. Here is a stone. All stones are "stone." This ordering is not arbitrary. Somehow we find this order in our perception of the things themselves. We do not confuse stones with plants. We detect the mutual likeness of all stones. Stone is a concept. The concept appears in our mind when we conceive a formal unity out of an individual diversity. The concept is the transfer of the thing perceived by the senses to the thing apprehended by the mind. The very awareness of a thing through the senses already entails an act of the mind—and of the spirit, as we shall see.

4. Things therefore are both sensible and conceptual entities. There are things predominantly of the senses (bodies of all types), and entities that are predominantly of the mind (concepts of all sorts). We can further extrapolate in time and space and speak of things past or future and even "outside" the spatio-temporal realm. Pulling all these things together, we may obtain the most general concept, a genus that includes all species and subspecies of things.

5. What we apprehend with our senses is a stone. What we apprehend with our mind is "stone." What we in fact apprehend is both a stone as "stone" and "stone" as stone: the thing and its concept in mutual relationship. There is a transcendental relation between the two: "stone" is real in a stone—independently of whether "stone" (the essence of stone) has a degree of reality of its own. We have arrived at the hotly debated problem of the universals, in East and West. Whatever the reality of the concept "stone," it has a different degree of reality than a concrete stone. With the help of the concept, we may construct a science of stones—which was, incidentally, a classical definition of architecture. With concrete stones we may build a temple—for which the science of "stones" will also be needed. All stones are "stone," although stones are more than "stone"—and perhaps "stone" is also more than stones. The concept has also a certain degree of reality of its own.

6. A temple is not a stone, but is not a non-stone either. It is "stony," made of stones; it is the stones of a temple, the "stone" as a temple. This third vision of the stone-temple is not the vision of the curious onlooker, nor that of the analytic thinker. It is the vision of the master builder, of the artist, and of the worshiper.

This is the contemplative vision of the *oculus* fidei (eye of faith), the *intellectus* fidei (intellect of faith) in the sense of the subjective genitive, which sees both the temple in the stone (for the worshiper) and the stone in the temple (for the artist). A stone as a stone is what the senses perceive; stone as "stone" is what the mind discovers, the "stone" as a temple is what the spirit (intellect) sees. Such is the contemplative vision of mystics, poets, and (seeing faith or faith full of eyes) some latin philosophers called it. I recall that hymn which christian generations sang for centuries without worrying in the least that it could be labeled as pantheism by the two eyed vision:

Quem terra, pontus, sidera
Colunt, adorant, praedicant
Trivam regentem machinam
Claustrum Mariae baiulat.
Cui luna, sol et omnia

Deserviunt per tempora,
Perfusa caeli gratia,
Gestant puellae viscera.

The God whom earth, and sea, and sky
adore, and laud, and magnify,
who o'er their threefold fabric reigns,
the Virgin's spotless womb contains.
The God whose will by moon, and sun,
and all things in due course is done,
is borne upon a Maiden's breast,
by fullest heavenly grace possessed.

This is truly a holistic insight. The hymn is directed to a young woman whom the christian tradition called begetter of God, *Dei Genetrix*, θεότοκος—Mother of God (the compromise title of Mother of Christ having been considered insufficient for the Mother of Jesus in the hotly debated sessions of the Council of Ephesus in 431). Heavens, Earth, Humanity, and Divinity all seem to be present in just a woman. The senses perceive a jewish woman; the reason sees (the concept of) womanhood (eventually idealized to the utmost); the third eye discovers the entire universe, a symbol of the Whole.

7. A stone is a thing. "Stone" is not a thing (except in a stone) but it is something—it is (also) an entity. The "stone"-temple is not a thing (except that the temple is made of stones and without them it would not exist), but it is something—it is (also) a being. We can climb in the porphyrian tree from stone to material entities and higher up to spiritual beings, but we cannot reach the "stone temple," say, of Konarak, by way of abstraction. This is not the way, the method to arrive at the notion of Being. When we transcend all *genera* by the same process of abstraction we reach a pseudo-concept of Being. As Aristotle already recognized, "Being is not a genus."[71]

Being, therefore, is not a concept. By a double abstraction we may arrive at a formal common denominator of all things. This is precisely what allows us to call them beings: *ens commune*. All "stones" are "stone," but stone is not a thing. It is a concept (first degree of abstraction). All entities are "Entity," but this "Entity" is just another formal concept (second degree of abstraction). Being, however, is more than that, more than the *eńs commune*, which I called Entity.

Properly speaking, the second degree of abstraction is more than a

71 Aristotle, *Met.* III, 92b13: οὐ γὰρ γένος τὸ ὄν ("ens autem non est genus").

degree of a higher order. It is formal jump based on a vicious but useful circle. All stones show something similar, which we can detect by our senses in order to reach the concept "stone." In the porphyrian tree we could also detect similarities by our reason between all "living beings" which share "materiality" with inert things, and then climb to a higher concept. More doubtful indeed is the effort to include something like beauty and injustice. One is forced to classify them as human feelings or human conceptions, but they have little in common with material things. Even more difficult was to include angels and spirits in the classification, but a certain worldview could put them all together as "created beings." We abstract specific features and something common still remains. But when we intend to find a homogeneous category to all, we invent the empty notion of being, because there is nothing in common except this "being," which we cannot detect by our knowing faculties. It is a formal postulate of the mind. This is the "common being" which is an empty concept. But this *ens commune*, this formal pseudo-concept of Entity, is not (yet) the Being we are looking for. For this we need another method, another jump, the integration of symbolic thinking by the third eye, which does not abide by the principle of abstraction. Being is not the remnant of the porphyrian classification. It is totally present in each entity inasmuch as it *is*.

What (is) that *is*?

In the western tradition, Boethius,[72] inspired by Aristotle, said that "Being (*esse*) is different from that which is (*id quod est*)"—he recognized what Heidegger called the ontological difference between Being and beings (entities). In other words, Being (*esse*) is not a being (entity, *ens*), and abstraction is not the proper method to arrive at the awareness of Being.

8. In order to reach Being, therefore, we do not need to climb the hierarchy of beings and get to the top of this ladder. This top is the *ens realissimum*, the Supreme Entity, what Eckhart called the *hoechste und oberste dinc* ("the highest and supreme being"), which in many a system is interpreted as prime cause and source of all things and is called God. There is a certain ambiguity in the words, the *dinc* of Eckhart's phrase, for it could be interpreted as *esse* as well as *ens*.

The terminology is ambiguous and the question of vocabulary is paramount here. Even among the greeks there was a certain ambiguity between ὄν and οὐσία, just as for the latins between *ens* and *esse*. English has had to introduce the relatively awkward name of *entity* in order to spell out the distinction between *Sein/Seiende* or *Être/étants*, *Ser/entidades* (for which

72 Boethius, *De hebdomadibus*, PL, 64:1311.

I would prefer *Ser / enseres*—which makes the point beautifully that the *enser* is *en-Ser*). Sanskrit makes use of two different roots. Being, *Esse*, is *sat* from the same root. On the other hand, entity is *bhūta*, related to *physis*, fieri. Being would then be that which *stands*. Beings, *bhūtani*, are those which have become (τὰ φυσικά). This would be an example of the "inter-in-dependence" between language and thought (or philosophy).

This ambiguity extends also to many other philosophical notions. Words are polysemic. *Dharma* in hinduism is not the same as in māhāyana buddhism, and this again differs from its theravada understanding. A sometimes disturbing ambivalence is the unclear english use of reason (*ratio*) and intellect (*intellectus*), like that of understanding (*Verstand*) and reason (*Vernunft*). I am inclined to use reason as the overall activity of the second eye, the mind, and the intellect for that of the third eye, the spirit. Although it is an urgent philosophical task, we cannot discuss it further without aspiring to a univocal language. Words are multivalent and polysemic symbols.[73]

9. We called Being a pseudo-concept in order to stress that the operation needed to climb the porphyrian tree is of a different order. Since we abstract hetero-*geneous* entities in order to reach the would-be concept of Entity, Being is then, at the least, a different class of concept, what I would call a quasiconcept. In this way we reach the *ens commune* and the *ens realissimum*, but we have not yet reached the *Esse*, that Being which is more than existence and more than essence. To become aware of that Being, in which we also really participate, we need more than an aggressive method of abstraction. In Being there is no *quantité négligeable* that we can discard, as Leibniz wrote when he had the genial idea of mathematical calculus. That infinitesimal residue is also Being. What is needed is a more feminine attitude of openness and readiness than the active epistemology of the hunter searching for an object to apprehend. We began by saying that a thing is a gift. This gift is a gift of Being (subjective genitive)

10. The point at issue is of capital importance, and has been rather neglected by the predominant western mind, perhaps with the exception of the poet-philosophers and intellectual mystics. Socrates is supposed to have discovered the concept, a marvelous discovery that has both enlightened and darkened the western mind. The enlightenment made possible the conceptual thinking that has nurtured most of western philosophy and almost all modern science. The darkening has led to the neglect, followed by

73 Cf. Panikkar, "Words and Terms," in *Freedom Progress and Society* (Delhi: Motilal Banarsidass), 330-50.

an atrophy, of symbolic thinking, as well as to many a misunderstanding in the interpretation of oriental philosophers.[74]

It should be said in defense of Xanthippe's husband that the conceptualism of his successors is not what he practiced or intended. His maieutic method is itself a proof that he thought and taught that the concepts are valid only where they have been conceived, where the umbilical cord uniting the conceiver with the concept has not been cut. He did not believe in objective concepts—but only in conceived concepts. Another proof of this is that he did not write or dictate a single line. If we do not beget our own concepts, we end up dealing with corpses—and most often, the fruit of abortions. Should I recall that Xanthippe was a midwife? In more academic language, anything that is not fruit of our experience is dead conceptualism. Philosophical thinking is not an algebra of concepts.

We may be now a little more precise. A stone is a thing, "stone" is a concept, but the "stone" is a symbol. A stone is an individual (thing), "stone" is a "universal" (concept), and its ideal is to be universal. The "stone" is a symbol and its ideal is to be polysemic. Strictly speaking, the "stone" of symbolic awareness is not just an entity but (a) Being. It is Being in the form of "stone"; it is a symbol of the entire universe, a symbol of Being. There is no physics or chemistry of the "stone." After having discovered the "stone" as a temple it is easier to discover it as Being. I would invite the reader to contemplate the Sun-temple of Konarak in Orissa—or, simpler for many, the Parthenon in Athens, a cathedral in medieval Europe, the Taj Mahal in India, or the Pyramids in Egypt. I could have mentioned, of course, statues, paintings, and symphonies. . . .

11. Supreme entities (or Entity) received the names of God (or God). Some philosophers (also called theologians), however, called God not the Supreme Entity but the supreme Being, or rather the proper Being, *esse a se*, Being in itself—perhaps with properties of an *Ens* at the summit of the ladder of beings—although, to use this language, there is a jump from the highest angel to that supreme Entity.

This homologation between Being and God, which was not too difficult in the indic tradition, represented a revolution in the abrahamic world. It was the metaphysical interpretation of a historical text that led christian scholastics to consider Being the self-revealed name of God.[75]

12. We have, first, the *entia* (τὰ ὄντα, *bhūtani*), all the beings of our

74 Cf. Panikkar, *L'esperienza* filosofica *dell'India*, 61ff.

75 Gn II, 14.

perception; then, with a formal jump the *ens commune*, as an empty concept; then, with another ontological jump into transcendence, the *ens realissimum*, the most real or the highest in the hierarchy of beings; and finally, with a plunge back into immanence, the symbol Being. The *ens* is a thing, the *entia* are concepts, the *ens commune* is a pseudo-concept, the *ens realissimum* is a unique Entity, supreme in the hierarchy of beings. And Being is the symbol of "beingness" of everything.

What is this Being? The stone, the concept, the temple?

Thomas Aquinas has a profound sentence: "being is the first that enters into the intellect" (primum quod in intellectu cadit est ens).

It is ambiguous whether *ens* here refers to a particular entity or to Being as such. In the first case the human intellect would be put in action, "actualized" when knowing something, any thing. Here, Aristotle sets the paradigm, followed by Thomas and most moderns. Knowledge comes from the very power of the thing that impresses our senses and from there it reaches to our reason and from there to our intellect. This opinion tallies with the evolutionistic way of thinking and what I have called the modern ascending anthropology[76] and the mirage of the future.[77] There is a dynamism from below, from the origins toward higher and more developed beings, states of consciousness, and the like. The classical formula is the thomistic one, following Aristotle: "Nothing is in the intellect which was not first in the senses."[78] The statement was complemented and somewhat corrected by Leibniz: everything is in the senses prior to being in the intellect, "save the intellect itself."[79]

This problem stands at the crossroads between the ancient and the modern theories of knowledge, and ultimately between tradition and modernity. Modern science, for instance, is a corollary of strict thomistic interpretation: the sensual observation of phenomena offers the starting point to insert those sense data into a mathematical pattern that will allow us to predict material behaviors; from there it leads us to the alleged knowledge of the structure of material reality and from there to the at least partial knowledge of reality as such.

---

76 See Panikkar, "Anthropofania intercultural: identidad human y fin de milenio," in *Thémata: Revista del Filosofia* 23 (1999), 19-29.

77 See Panikkar, "Secularization and Worship: A Bibliography," in *Worship and Secularization*, ed. W. Vos (Bossum: Paul Brand, 1970), 131-41.

78 Aristotle: "nihil est in intellectu quod non prius fuerit in sensu."

79 Leibniz, *Nouveaux Essais sur l'entendement humain*, Livre II, chap. I: "Nihil est in intellectu, quod non fuerit in sensu, excipe: nisi ipse intellectus."

The fact that modernity does not feel the need for any extra power to help make the jump from sensible to intellectual knowledge implies that the second possible interpretation of *ens* as Being in the cited sentence from Thomas is felt unnecessary or stigmatized as "ontologism," which interprets Being as God, the Supreme Being, which then becomes the first and immediate object of human knowledge. If what falls into the intellect is Being, what the sentence says is that our intellect is not only open to Being as reality, but also that the relationship is inverted: the human intellect is open and attuned to receive the illumination from Being: *capax dei* said the scholastic. Nonetheless, I should proceed in my pilgrimage toward Being.

13. Thomas Aquinas, after stating the quoted principle, adds: "but the second is the negation of being."[80] The second character of our intellect, after the first capacity of being open to Being, is the power of negation. This power also appertains to the intellect, but where does it come from? The intellect "receives" beings, but what makes it negate them? This negation by the *logos* is much more than a moral denying (they should not be) or a nonrecognition of existence (they do not exist). It amounts to removing the ontological carpet on which they stand (they are not). Can our intellect also negate Being? We can negate the existence, even the reality of a thing (although this is more problematic), but what can it mean that the intellect can put a *no* to Being and still make sense?

At any rate, Being is certainly no (other) thing. Is it then No-thing? To be sure, Nothing is-not a thing, an entity, but *is* it a no thing, a non-entity? It is an abuse of language to say that it *is* Nothing. Or is language the only obstacle? The *logos* seems to correspond to beings, entities, but *logos* has still another function. It is the *logos* that allows us to meaningfully perform the act of negation and ultimately reach Nothingness. It is as if this *logos*, thanks to which we can know and handle things, were ruling over things and could deny all of them.

Heidegger says: "The nothing is more original [*ursprunglicher*] than the 'not' and negation."[81] Without dismissing the importance and consequences of this insight, one might say that it is our intellect that makes us aware of this astounding power of acknowledging Nothingness as a possible reality since the idea of it (empty as it is) is not contradictory. One is reminded of an astounding intuition of Goethe's *Faustus*, which could be interpreted in this context as saying more than Mephistopheles meant: "I am the Spirit which constantly denies."[82] The power to put a *no* to any being, to say no

80 Thomas Aquinas, *De potentia* IX, 7 ad 15: "Secundum vero est negatio entis."

81 Heidegger (1929), *What Is Metaphysics?*, 29.

82 Goethe, *Faust*, Erster Teil v. 1338: "Ich bin der Geist, der stets verneint!"

to destiny, to "deny" a free act, the capacity of negation seems to belong to a superhuman power embodied in our carnal existence.

14. If Non-being is the fruit of an operation of our intellect, we may say that in a certain sense Being also embraces Non-being inasmuch as that idea enters also into the field of our consciousness. Taking into account the wisdom of many traditions I would distinguish three spheres of reality while remaining well aware of the metaphorical and symbolical power of words:

a) The reality of *Being*, in the above indicated sense, as that which enters in one way or another into the field of our consciousness, which we may eventually extrapolate to consciousness in general.

b) The realm of *Non-being*, which lies in the fringes of our consciousness. Non-being is not Being, and yet we speak meaningfully about it marginally as it were. Mystical traditions speak frequently of this. Non-being can be interpreted in two different ways: *dialectically* as the contradictory to Being and *dialogically* as that which pierces our logos (διὰ τὸν λόγον), as it were, and yet the *logos* still keeps a certain remembrance (ἀνάμνησις) of it. This is what I meant saying that Non-being lingers on the fringes of our consciousness. We can speak about it, but only from the outside, so to speak.

c) The realm of *Silence* or *turīya*, which we can denote only by saying that it is "neither-nor." This has little to do with a polyvalent or any other kind of logic. It is "beyond" any logic and thus neither contradicts nor non-contradicts any logic. We can speak of it only through a second-degree metaphor, so to speak. The proper metaphor "translates" us to the other river. The second-degree metaphor simply catapults us into no other river, which, only in an improper way, we could call the infinite ocean of emptiness. Yet for those who have had that (mystical) experience it is non-sense. In fact, the talk about Non-being seems to be present in practically all cultures. I give two examples:

> At first was neither Being nor Nonbeing.
> . . .
> there was no death nor deathlessness;
> . . .
> A crosswise line cut Being from Nonbeing.
> . . .
> Who really knows? Who can presume to tell it?
> . . .
> He who surveys it in the highest heaven,
> He surely knows—or maybe he does not![83]

83 RV X, 129.

When this experience dawns it remains in the twilight of an expecting awareness before coming into the light of consciousness. "Darkness was there, all wrapped around by darkness."[84]

The fourth state, which the same tradition calls *turīya*, is described thus:

> That which is neither internal consciousness
> nor external consciousness nor both together, . . .
> which is neither conscious nor unconscious
> . . . which is unthinkable, unnameable,
> whose very essence consists of the
> experience of its own self, . . .[85]

The problem remains: how can we speak about this? To take refuge in the mystical experience is a legitimate move, but it is not enough if we have to avoid the pitfall of irrationality.

15. The scheme of Being-Speaking-Thinking may perhaps help us here albeit with one important qualification. The parmenidean schema I am trying to overcome plays with the dual paradigm Being-Non-being, where the former *is* and the latter *is-not*. If we accept it as point of departure there is not much to add, but then an almost universal human experience which "speaks" about the "unspeakable" is sheer contradiction and makes no sense at all. If we do not presuppose that parmenidean framework at the very outset we do not need to reduce our paradigm to the dilemma of Being or Non-Being, and could take Being to stand for the whole reality that overflows the caged enclosure under the surveillance of thinking, in the sense we have already described. The paradigm would then be:

Being (Reality)–Speech (Language)–Thinking (Rationality)[86]

In fact there is a speech as a primal manifestation of Being which oversteps the realm of thinking, as so many traditions witness. The speaking field of Being is wider than its thinking field. Thinking reveals Being as at least potentially intelligible. Speech is the revelation of Being as Silence. It is through the door of speech that we enter into that silence which is neither Being nor Non-being.[87] We should, however, return to our concrete topic.

---

84 Ibid.

85 MandU 7.

86 See Panikkar, "Identity and Non-Contradiction: Two Schemes of Intelligibility," in *Murti and Indian Philosophical Tradition* (Varanasi: Banaras Hindu University, 1989), 207-15.

87 See Panikkar, "The Silence of the Word: Non-Dualistic Polarities," *Cross-Currents* XXIV (1974), 154-71.

16. In perceiving a stone we apprehend more than a stone (with our senses), "stone" (with our mind or reason), and *the* "stone" with our symbolic knowledge. We also perceive that all those perceptions are situated in a horizon that is not "stones" and makes possible for us to distinguish the "stones" from all that is not "stones." Generalizing, we can say that we perceive things in a horizon of nothingness. This nothingness is certainly nothing, it is not a thing, but in a certain way it *is*, since this makes it possible for us to perceive things as things. Ever since the greeks we distinguish μὴ ὄν (a relative negation for something) from οὐκ ὄν (nothingness). The question is, do we become aware of Being against the background of Nothingness?

Yes, inasmuch as the human intellect can exert the function of negation on the same level as the affirmation. To any *ens* we can meaningfully say *no-ens* including the *ens commune* (nihilism) and the *ens realissimum* (atheism). This is the power of dialectics. This *no-ens* is what we call No-thingness.

No, inasmuch as Being is not a concept and does not offer any target to dialectical negation. Yet we are somewhat aware that Being, in its dynamism or life (imperfect similes), seems to make room for what we may call Emptiness. The confusion between Nothingness and Emptiness has had dire consequences in the history of human thought.

17. Nothingness is still an object of our consciousness; it appertains to the realm of the *logos*. Now, if knowledge is a total human activity and not just an epistemological function of a disincarnated mind, it is an assimilation of the being known, a personal embrace in which love is as necessary as cognition.

In such a case, when apprehending a stone in the horizon of our sensitivity, we not only apprehend "stone" in the horizon of our intelligibility and become conscious of the "non-stone" in the horizon of nothingness, but also perform a fourth act. We experience the stone in the horizon of Emptiness or śūn*yatā*. Unlike Nothingness, which still belongs to our logical thinking, Emptiness is not the negation of any affirmation. Emptiness does not negate; it offers a blank horizon beyond the possible or the impossible. Learning from the Kyoto school, one could call the former "relative nothingness" and the latter "absolute emptiness." To the question "What is this Emptiness?" the obvious answer is: Nothing! Since the question is inadequate, however, it elicits a wrong answer. Silence exists, but we cannot speak about it without breaking it. It is often said that silence is the negation of sound because we are aware that when we speak (or make a sound) we break "something," but this some-thing is no-thing. We cannot hear silence. Yet silence is not nothing; it is not nothingness. To say that silence is the negation of sound is a mere formal statement, an operation of the mind that does not yield the experience of silence.

Silence "is," rather, that Emptiness from which sound emerges as sound. It is not so much the negation as the absence of sound, the concomitant absence of the presence of sound. The absence that accompanies every presence could be a way of making indirect room for a description of Emptiness.

18. The place of the *pneuma*, the spirit, is silence, not as a repressed or suffocated *logos*, but a silence that does not contra-dict the *logos*. Silence is empty, it has nothing to say—and when there is something to say out of silence the word is born (as Irenaeus said when describing the christian Trinity).

There are many types of silence. One corresponds to Nothingness, but there is another silence that may correspond to Emptiness, *śūnyatā*. Can we say that Being and *śūnyatā* "are" correlative? We are not speaking of the formal Emptiness of conceptual contents proper to the *ens commune* that can receive any and every determination. Being and Nothingness (Non-being) are dialectically correlated. An extraordinary book that came to public light in the second half of the twelfth century, without explicitly assuming the identity between God and Being, states that "God is the opposite to Nothingness through the mediation of the entity."[88]

Beings (entities) are in between Nothingness and God, intermediaries between the two, on the middle way between God and Nothingness, with both possibilities (divinization or annihilation) open to them.[89] Being and Emptiness, however, are not in such dialectical relationship. We do not have to negate Being in order to have "access" to Emptiness. Whatever Being may "be," it is different from and irreducible to beings. We may call it Emptiness, or Being (*Esse sive vacuitas*, one is tempted to say).[90] At any rate, the experience of Being belongs to this field of Emptiness.

19. I already said that Emptiness is not the fruit of an active negation of the human intellect, and *śūnyatā* is not the result of a dialectical movement. Zero as a mathematical sign may be the result of $a - a = 0$, as indic mathematics discovered (although the word used was *śūnya*), but Emptiness is not the

88 *Liber XXIV philosophorum* XIV: "Deus est oppositio nihil mediatione entis."

89 See Panikkar, *El concepto de naturaleza: análisis historico y metafisico de un concepto* (Madrid: CSIC, 1951).

90 Cf. Nishitani, *Religion and Nothingness* (1982), who speaks in Jan Van Bragt's translation of "being *sive* nothingness."

conclusion of any syllogism. We cannot reach *nirvāṇa* by any operation of the will or the intellect, or of heaven for that matter. Emptiness is not Non-being. Being/ Non-Being, *sat/asat* operate within the principle of non-contradiction, and their relationship is dialectical. The field of Emptiness is outside dialectics—I do not say "beyond." Here is where *logos* and *pneuma* are two powerful and traditional symbols. Nevertheless, we should return to our stone.

20. This awareness of the stone endowed with a character beyond its individuality and generality is the fruit of the symbolic knowledge that lurks behind any complete act of knowing. The symbol stone is not exclusively an objective thing or a formal reality. Since the symbol discovered in symbolical awareness has as much objective reality as subjective participation, it overcomes the subjective/objective split. A symbol is only symbol for those who "see" it as a symbol. This is why there is no possible hermeneutic of a symbol. That by means of which we interpret the symbol would be the real symbol. To say that Being is a symbol is to affirm that Being is neither merely objective nor purely subjective. To say that a symbol is symbol only for those who discover it as a symbol is to affirm that symbol is such only over against a horizon of Emptiness. Otherwise, we interpret the symbol and it disappears as such, yielding its place to the interpretation of the symbol by means of another symbol, which for us does not require further interpretation.

21. On one extreme of the spectrum, when we only pay heed to a stone (or stones), there is crude empiricism and/or materialism, since ultimately they are only stones—or similar material things, of course. On the other extreme, by concentrating only on what some may call the ultimate horizon of Nothingness, we are left with a crude nihilism, since everything is only a mode of that horizon. We have here again the excruciating dialectic between monism and dualism. If the stone is real and the ultimate reality is also real, either there are *real* degrees of reality or all is one single reality with only modal differences. We have monism in the latter case, and pluralism in the first one. This traditional "pluralism" should not be confused with the pluralistic attitude of the contemporary discussion about the truth claims of different religions, and because many a pluralism in the traditional sense can be reduced to dualism, we shall use the word "dualism" in order to avoid confusion.

Within this rigid scheme of either monism or dualism one can understand the neglect and suspicion with which human reason has met the utterances of mystical insight and the expressions of symbolic knowledge. They are certainly not dualistic (in our example, the stone is the symbol of the temple and the temple is the symbol of the Divinity); therefore, it is assumed that they have to be monistic. We have forgotten the wisdom of *advaita*, which is at the heart of this study and is found in almost every culture that has not stifled all mystical insight. Between monism and dualism there is a middle way that is neither the one nor the other.

22. Here may be the place to spell out what was implicit since the beginning of this point: the nature and function of the "third eye," which is what opens us up to the *advaitic* intuition.

The *advaitic* insight is certainly not rational. Our reason cannot understand unless it reaches the *reductio ad unum*, unless it reduces the multiplicity to unity. In the face of an "either-or," pure reason cannot say: both. Dialectics is the rational device to overcome those contradictions by striving toward a synthesis between the thesis and the antithesis. The synthesis may be dynamic and a totally unreacheable ideal, but a rational approach cannot sacrifice rational intelligibility. Our reason functions *componendo et dividendo* ("by synthesis and analysis") said the scholastics.

The *advaitic* intuition, on the contrary, says "as well as," without indulging in weakening the rational challenge of the dilemma "either-or" by introducing perspectivisms of all sorts (looking for loopholes in the contradiction) or falling into irrationalism.

Here is the place for the function of the third eye in the mystical intellect. If an aristotelian epistemology offers the basis for empirical and rational knowledge, the *advaitic* vision requires an illumination from a superior source of knowledge. This third degree of knowledge comes into being not when we see or know, but when we are conscious that we are seen or known. It is neither sense knowledge nor rational knowledge, and yet it is inseparable from both. It is not irrationalism. It emerges when the dynamism of knowledge inverts its direction, as it were: we are aware that in touching we are touched, in knowing we are known. It is conscious that there is an illumination from "above." I know a thing fully not when the thing is sensible that I may sense it, or intelligible that I may understand it, but when both the subject and the object are illumined by a light that comes neither from me nor from the object. Then it produces an "understanding" that is more than sense or rational experience; it creates a union between subject and object that is of an order other than a sensuous touch or a rational contact. It is a more holistic participation, which produces a conviction that is more than physical or rational.

I should not close this brief description without warning of the dangers of the reductionism of the third eye as if we could experience reality with exclusion of the two other "organs" we possess to enter in contact with reality. A thing is a given, a gift we said at the beginning. To discover the thing as given we need first of all to know the thing as real by our intellect—otherwise no thing is really given to us.

23. The *advaitic* experience, inasmuch as it needs the *logos* to express itself, does not reduce Man to an object of anthropo-logy. It needs an *anthropophany* in which the spirit is equally present but not subordinated to the *logos.*[91] By *anthropophany* I understand not the object *anthrōpos* studied by the *logos* but the *epiphany* of Man as it appears, as it manifests to all the "organs" Man has in order to be in contact with reality. How Man "sees" himself in the light of all organs of knowledge, he believes he has and is able to submit then to the scrutiny of his fellow-beings—whereby the acceptance of a divine or super human illumination is not *a priori* excluded. Besides the *logos* (and the senses) there is the spirit to disclose to us what we are.

The relationship between the *logos* and the *pneuma* is not dialectic but *advaitic.* One does not exist without the other. They are neither one nor two; they are linked by an inter-in-dependent relation. Between Being and Non-being (Nothingness) there is a powerful and important dialectic; but not between Being and Emptiness. The latter relationship has no place in a competitive world. This is a metaphysical and not merely a sociological statement. Under the aegis of the present-day dominant anthropology, it is illusory to want to eliminate a competitive society without recourse to violence (dictatorship). We insert this remark just to show that these reflections are not alienating us from "real" life.

24. My final question is the meaning of reality. My approach is to look at the sense of the real in a very realistic way. I started with a pebble in my hand and I have taken all these steps trying to discover if that stone could be a Revelation of Reality. The intermediary steps have led us to Being and even to Non-being and Emptiness. In other words: Being is the metaphysical interpretation of reality. Non-being is the way of handling Reality dialectically; and Emptiness, mystically. We are in that reality and we cannot avoid asking: What is happening to us? Where have we landed? What is our destiny? The issue is not how to save our private and individualistic souls; but it is also more than just saving our planet; a purely ecological concern is still an extrapolation of that individualistic view. The question, to put it in the strongest possible terms, is the salvation of Being. Thus, we land at our initial query: *What is Being?*

A final Upanishadic consideration may perhaps be in order. One of the most straightforward answers to the question of what Being is comes

91 See Panikkar, "Anthropofania intercultural" (n. 76 above).

from a central passage of the Chāndogya Upanishad, prefacing the *parama-mahāvākya* (the *tat tvam asi*), the greatest of the traditional great utterances: "All these (beings) have Being as their root, have Being [*sat*] as their habitat (abode, resting place), have Being as their basis (support)."[92] In sum: Being is the root, the dwelling place and the foundation of everything. The text continues: "This ultimate (indivisible) essence, by which all is animated (enlivened, ensouled, endowed with a self), that is truth (reality, beingness), that is the ātman, that art thou."[93]

As for the cosmic description of Being, the same Upanishad says:

> In the beginning, my dear, this was Being alone, one only without duality. Some people say in the beginning only Non-being was one without duality, and that from this Non-being Being was born.[94]
>
> But my dear, how could this be?, said he, How could Being be born from Non-being? Truly, my dear, it was Being alone that was this in the beginning, one only without duality.[95]

This *sat* does not need to come out of Nothingness because being non-dual does not demand a dialectical relationship (out of Non-being, Being). This Being indwells, enlivens, and supports everything that is. It has a core, as it were, which is the beingness (*satyam*) or truth of everything, the ātman, of which we are its *Thou* in a personalistic relationship.

* * *

Being, in short, is that symbol that embraces the whole of reality in all the possible aspects we are able to detect, and in whose Destiny we are involved as cospectators, actors, and co-authors.

C. Becoming and Destiny

"He is all Becoming and He is the One by
Whose Becoming I become . . ."[96]

—Ibn 'Arabī

1. *Becoming*

Using Heraclitus more as a banner than as a teacher, and oversimplifying

92 CU VI, 8, 6: "San mūlaḥ, (saumya), imāḥ prajāḥ, sad-āyatanāḥ, sat-pratiṣṭnāḥ."

93 CU VI, 8, 7: "sa ya eṣo'ṇimā, aitad ātmyam idaṁ sarvaṁ , tat satyaṁ , sa ātmā: tat tvam

94 CU VI, 2, 1.

95 CU VI, 2, 2.

96 Ibn 'Arabī, *Fusūṣal-ḥikām* X (R. W. J. Austin's translation).

traditional metaphysics, modern philosophy has developed a visceral antipathy for anything static or immutable. Hegel, Nietzsche, Bergson, and Whitehead are clear examples. Becoming is winning over Being; ontology is temporalized. The sociology of knowledge becomes paramount, and time as ontological dynamism reigns supreme. Movement, and even more, rapid movement is perhaps the most important category of technology.

My thesis is simple and not new: Being is Becoming, and Becoming is Being. What is relatively new is the *advaitic* interpretation of that polarity. Being is an act that, seen from the perspective of a temporal observer, is a constant coming to be. Being is be-ing, a verb, an activity, an act, a *Zeitwort*, says the german language, where the time (*Zeit*) is intrinsic to Being as verb, a temporal act that does not run along an external time because it is timeful in itself.

To claim that Being has to be permanent already implies an underlying idea of time either as a Superbeing or as a metaphysical infrastructure of reality, like a riverbed on which Being flows (away). The self-identity of Being is then interpreted as a dimly temporal continuity. To be sure, A needs to "remain" A "when" for a "second time" we refer to A—otherwise all speech is meaningless. This argument, which may be valid for our concepts, does not apply to Being. The temporality underlying beings can in no way be superimposed on Being. Being does not admit anything "besides" it except Non-being by the negative power of our mind, and śūn*yatā,* which is nonrepresentational. Being does not move on an external superhighway of time. Nor does Becoming need to travel on a "beingless" time in order to reach Being. By the same token, it is already a very particular idea of Becoming to assume that it is the opposite of permanence. This assumption presupposes a static sub-stance whose function is to "permit" us to affirm that it is the same "something" that changes.

A parenthetical observation is pertinent here. It is too readily accepted that A has to remain unchanged if we have to say anything about A at a second moment. This is certainly the case for any concept A. This is the logic of concepts, but not necessarily the order of reality. When we are actually speaking to each other (not just repeating concepts learned in the past), when we exchange living ideas, our A varies depending on the moment, the context, and the person we are speaking to. Human speech is living dialogue, not an algebraic game with fixed concepts and well-defined variables. Not only connotations and resonances, not only the *dvani* of indic poetics is constantly changing, but also denotations and their interpretations inevitably vary. A capital and oftentimes tragic example is the so-called immutability of the dogmas of some religions. If the dogma is identified with a concept A, the A has to remain the same when we speak of it. If the dogma is the living orthodox belief, however, the panorama changes. *Doxa* means glory and held opinion—not an algebric and abstract concept. A dogma, strictly speaking, cannot be written down; it has to be confessed—in a concrete time, place, and language by a living person.

The problem of Becoming is a major headache of a certain type of mind. After nearly three millennia of philosophical reflection, it should be possible to learn from the *aporias* of our ancestors. I am here approaching the problem of Being and Becoming outside the dialectical mind-set. To begin, we should distinguish Becoming from the four related human experiences with which it has been generally identified.

a) Movement

We distinguish Becoming from *movement*. I understand movement here as a quantitative magnitude, as local movement or transposition, a change of place. One may, of course, also understand movement as covering the wider meaning of the scholastic *motus* and further interpret this latter as any action or operation. Understanding (*intelligere*) is then a movement, and this movement occurs also in God. The intratrinitarian life is also movement. This is close to the understanding of Being as Becoming and vice versa. But I am restricting the meaning of movement to any transit in space or variation in time.

There is still a middle notion of movement, described by Aristotle as "The latent power of potential Being (the act of Being in potency inasmuch as it is in potency)."[97] I will give also the traditional latin translation because of its clarity and the fact that many reflections on the theme were based on this text: "actus entis in potentia prout in potentia." In this case, of course, God cannot move because this would imply that God is not perfectly and completely Being, but still retains an unfulfilled capacity to be (potency). This definition has caused no little consternation right up to our own day, especially in theology, but we should distinguish this concept of movement from the notion of Becoming.

It is instructive to observe how the uncritical acceptance of an apollonian idea of perfection (*per-factum*, τελείωσις, achieved, arrived, already made) has influenced most of the monotheistic christian theology. A perfect God, therefore, should be immutable—an idea that is incompatible with a trinitarian and incarnational notion of the Divine.

97 Aristotle, *Phys.* III, 1, 201a1: ἡ τοῦ δυνάμει ὄντος ἐντελέχεια, ᾗ τοιοῦτον κίνησις ἐστιν.

b) Change

Becoming should also be distinguished from *change*. Change, understood as a qualitative modification of Being, like the change of color in a material thing: "I have become pale." This "turning pale," this change, is not the "essence" of Becoming I am trying to find out. Change can also be understood as a substantial change and not an accidental modification. "Generation and corruption" was the classical expression. It is the vital circle: butterfly-egg-caterpillar-chrysalisbutterfly. When we see different entities, we also observe that one comes from the other. We call it change because of a habit of our mind that supposes a temporal continuity. We assume that one entity *becomes* the other, because we are outside that dynamism and see them as different. No doubt we are aware of change, but we are not sure that the same thing has "changed" into another. We "simply" see another thing.

c) Growth

Becoming is not identical to mere development or *growth*. There is an important distinction between becoming and evolution. Development and evolution happen *in* time, that is, along an extrinsic temporal riverbed, so to speak, that allows things and events to flow within its banks. Becoming is not necessarily temporal in this sense. In growth there is continuity and discontinuity. We cannot deny that it is we ourselves who grow; we become what we are not. Growth is certainly Becoming but not all Becoming is growth.

d) History

Finally, Becoming should not be equated with *history*. History is here understood as a process of temporal events or as the accumulation of the past in the present, as well as the temporal unfolding of Man individually and collectively—leaving aside the question whether other beings may also be historical. History is a becoming, but Becoming does not need to be historical.

All four of these "eventualities" of Being are certainly *forms* of Becoming, but they do not reach the core of what Becoming is. They touch space, time, qualities, modes of Being, but they do not constitute the very essence of Becoming. There is no intrinsic necessity for Becoming to move, or change, or grow, or even be historical—although each of these cases may deeply manifest some aspects of Becoming.

What, then, is Becoming?

Ever since the pre-socratics, the problem of Becoming in the West has been approached dialectically as the outcome of the opposition between Being and Non-being. If Becoming is a name that expresses the process of things "coming to be," it means that "before" they were not. The concrete thing comes to be from another thing. But the other thing has disappeared and indeed a new thing has come to be—through modification or transformation of the former; but nevertheless "something" new, *previously* nonexistent has appeared. What is this? Or, rather better, what has happened? Things that become did not exist before they came to be, and most probably they shall cease to be. The greek name is γίγνεσθαι (*gignesthai*). They come and go—come into being and go into nothingness. They are not consistent, they are contingent—mortal if they are living things. The simplest theoretical expedient is to deny ultimate reality to the things that become: they are labeled as unreal, illusory, appearance (*māyā*), impermanent (*anitya*), mortal. A disincarnated intellect, self-appointed arbiter of the real, tends to deny reality to what it cannot master. All human reason cannot master all those fleeting things. Zeno of Elea, as a good disciple of Parmenides, will deny movement (and ultimately Becoming) because our mind cannot comprehend it.

Human experience and common sense, however, resist this purely dialectic deduction. The strongest argument, besides the personal experience of our own becoming, seems to be our innate resistance to considering ourselves mere appearances, unreal entities. In order to maintain the reality of the things given in our sensible experience, we have to accept the existence of an invisible power (act, energy, entelechy, . . .) which "causes" this Becoming. This power in the most common experience of the generation of things seems to lie in the beings themselves. It cannot but be Being itself. Being "causes" Becoming.

The hypothesis of Aristotle accounts for it. Becoming is a coming into Being by dint of a hidden inner energy inside or outside every being. Becoming, therefore, is identified with movement. The system is coherent. Every being, except the supreme Being, is movable, it becomes insofar as it realizes, "actualizes its potentiality." A genial theory, no doubt, relying on the prior hypothesis of act and potency. Since no potency can "actualize" itself, we need a "Prime Mover," which the scholastics replaced by *actus purus*, pure Act, identified with God, moving absolutely every being.

In dealing with material things this is a plausible explanation as far as it goes. A major difficulty arises when this Prime Mover, identified with God as infinite and omnipotent Goodness, has to move all free and even criminal acts of human beings. The depth and subtleties of the scholastic and later traditions are breathtaking and admirable, but the inability to admit the *advaitic* intuition (because of the understandable fear of falling into an undiscriminated and undiscriminating monism) has meant that the western mind has by and large accepted the dualistic answer: Being is one reality and beings another. Being is immutable, it is not Becoming; beings (entities) are mutable, they are Becoming.

I submit that Being and Becoming stand in a nondualistic relationship. They should neither be identified nor separated. Being *is* Becoming, and in an analogous manner Becoming is Being—whereby the *is* does not mean ontological identity, as the "equality" of the "persons" in the christian Trinity does not mean total undifferentiation. For Being to be Being "it" has simply to be. Being *is* and this *is* we see as Becoming. Becoming is the subjective aspect of Being, and the latter is the objective aspect of the same "reality"—where both "subjective" and "objective" are "categories" of the human intellect.

Becoming (which is Being) does not appear as Becoming within Being itself, "seen" from the interior of Being, as the earth does not appear in movement to the inhabitants of the planet if they do not look outside it. The moon is called moon in english because with it we measure (*mesura*) the movement (of the "months" of time). In this sense, Being (which is Becoming) does not appear as Being within Becoming itself, "seen" from the interior of Becoming, as the earth does not appear to be still to the astronauts seeing the planet from the moon.

In other words, Becoming belongs to the very essence of Being. An entity is not an entity because it persists "in" Being. Becoming is the very act of Being, and Being is only Being when it becomes (Being). *Being has no inertia*. It has energy, ἐνέργεια, Aristotle would say: Being is *act*. An entity is an entity insofar as it *is* Being. If an entity is, it is. This *is*, the *is* of Being and Becoming is neither merely temporal nor solely eternal; it is *tempiternal*. Time seems to be intrinsic to Becoming and eternity to Being. If Being and Becoming belong together in an *advaitic* relationship, this entails that time and eternity are the two faces, as it were, of what I call *tempiternity*. At present, suffice to say that were an entity not to become what it is each moment that it is, it would cease to be. The entity exists and this existence is its Becoming. When the scholastics, Descartes, Malebranche, Spinoza, and others wrote about continuous creation, *creatio continua*, this was their latent problem. Every being is be-coming; not becoming another being, but becoming what it is, because Being is Becoming. If the creation, in this hypothesis, happened *in illo tempore* (once upon a time), it is still continually happening. Creation did not happen in time, but brought about time along with it. Creation is not a temporal event. It is the very event of time. It has nothing to do with any "Big Bang" at the beginning of time. Creation is Becoming, the continuous Becoming of the creature. In such a perspective, if God created once, he has to "go on" creating constantly. Creation is neither a temporal act, nor is it a gigantic work of an all-powerful Engineer. Creation is the constant Becoming of Being.

It has often been noted that, in the work of Zeno of Elea, Becoming is unthinkable, that we cannot catch Becoming with our mind because the moment we are there that being has already become something else. To become, however, is not to become something else; becoming is not synonymous with transformation, metamorphosis. Becoming is the *coming to be* of the being that *is*—precisely *becoming*. Paradoxically enough, Becoming is the "permanence" of being in Being. If thinking were merely a calculus of fixed patterns, or if thinking were no more than modern scientific investigation, it would indeed be true that we can never catch up with Becoming. However, if thinking can apprehend the intellectual manifestation of what Being is, then this impossibility of thinking Becoming need not be the case, because being is in each case the "result" of the actual Becoming. It is a common observation that thinking is not remembering past thoughts, that when we truly think, we think anew about that being which is becoming what it is when we make it the object of our thinking. In this sense prayer could be said to be creative thinking, and contemplation an active sharing in the adventure of the real (a participation in the creative activity of God, in a theistic perspective). If Becoming is becoming the being that it is now, our thinking is also becoming the actual thinking that it is now.

Most philosophical reflection has been directed to distinguishing between a fixed, unchangeable, immutable base, a substance, a ὑποκείμενον and some accidents that move, change, and give the appearance of Becoming. When the substance changes, one speaks of generation or corruption.

In the final analysis, the difficulty lies not with Becoming or Being, but with our thinking about reality within mental schemas that can only discover fixed patterns—sometimes called mathematics, physical laws, or even first principles—in order not exactly to know, but to foresee, calculate, and dominate the subject matter of our investigation. The difficulty resides in the kind of thinking we do, or rather, in the kind of calculating we deem thinking to be. The authentic philosophers of East and West knew that thinking is a contemplative act. Later, I will return to this dominant paradigm of thinking and Being, which has expelled Becoming from the bosom of Being and relegated it to more or less external eventualities.

Until now, I have deliberately avoided thematic treatment of another of those intimidating words: *time*. I will only repeat this much. Being is a verb, I have written it as be-ing. Becoming is its translation. We may even transpose the word and explain it as coming to be. To be is to come to be. This coming to be is, properly speaking, time, "the life of Being." This life is rhythmic. "The Rhythm of Being" we already said, like the "Life of Being" is a subjective genitive.

Time is not a neutral and external track—linear, circular, or whatever—on which beings proceed as if on rails. Time is intrinsic to things. Each thing has its own time, as it has its own space, as it has its own being. Yet this does not prevent us from speculating meaningfully about the meaning of time, space, and being—provided we do not identify them with mere concepts.

I do not have any public power to enter into the politics of words. Should we reserve the word "time" for the modern mathematical, or rather physico-mathematical, notion of it? Should philosophy strategically retreat and introduce the word "temporicity" for the specific time of beings, reserving "temporality" for the human mode of existence?

Although words are important, they should not deter us from further thinking by clinging to them. Whether we call it time or temporicity, there is in every being, by the very fact of its being, a constitutive "element" that makes it "timely," or indeed, "time-full." This time-fullness or being ripe and laden with time is what makes beings real, as the Atharvaveda suggests.[98] Soon we shall have the opportunity to see some consequences of this vision.

* * *

The western difficulty of relating Being and Becoming in a nondualistic way proceeds, among other causes, from the fact that western philosophy began mainly from a wonder (θαυμάζω) about the world, about objectifiable things, and about objects. In contrast, Upanishadic reflection gives priority to introspection, to the subject, the interior. If we reflect on an objective Being and the model is the *is*, its becoming is problematic. If we reflect on the subjective aspect of Being and its model is the *am*, its becoming is rather obvious. I am, just becoming. I am not what I was, but what I have now become. I will only expound on one of the famous utterances of the Upanishad: *aham-brahmāsmi*, "I am brahman." This *mahāvākya* (great liberation-bringing utterance) does not say that my ego, as the *ahamkāra* or *asmitā* (individual ego or "I-am-ness"), is *brahman*, but that *brahman* is "*I am*." When rid of all selfish individuality, we also are able to experience

98 CF. AV XIX, 53 and 54.

"I am" in a way, however dimly, in which our *being* identical with ourselves does not exclude our *becoming* identical with ourselves, in which Being and Becoming coalesce. *Bhana*, from the root *bhu*, to become (fieri) is even an epithet of Śiva, the absolute God who *is Becoming*.

2. *Destiny*

As already mentioned, the conflict of worldviews is one of the main causes of the crisis of our times, but the dominant present-day worldview is itself in crisis. This becomes evident from a simple embarrassing fact: we do not have convincing answers to give to our children.

a) Sociological Interlude

At one extreme there lurks fanaticism and dogmatism: to give apodictic answers, to condemn those who do not think as we do to hell—the so-called niggers, mlecchas, kafirs, goyïm, infidels, barbarians, unbelievers, undeveloped, immigrants, and the like. At the other extreme there floats the amorphous—more indifferent or cynical than truly skeptical—attitude of the defeated or resigned person who no longer cares anything about life or the meaning of life.

I said that the fundamental questions are the most elementary. Today we do not know what answers to offer not only to our children but to ourselves. We have lost the underlying, and unifying, *mythos*. When asked, we try to convert the hidden *mythos* into *logos*, and it hardly works. It hardly convinces any child, for instance, to be told that if she disobeys her parents she is going to be punished by bad luck or even by hell. It is equally unconvincing and unacceptable, however, for parents to appeal to raw power, whether physical or not.

To postpone answers to the fundamental questions initially thwarts and eventually destroys the child—and the adult as well. Many of the traditional answers, which shift the solution for all these legitimate and fundamental human questions to some other life, work well enough until the moment in which they are found to be merely diplomatic delaying tactics on the part of the parents—or the powers that be. For half a century, for instance, we have been bombarded by official and nonofficial talk about the eradication of poverty when poverty in fact has been increasing every year. We have eliminated the ideal of heavenly paradise, and now the idea of an earthly paradise is equally disappearing, which is not an altogether bad symptom.

It is a symptom of crisis when parents and teachers have no wisdom to propose, but only scientific hypotheses that will change tomorrow and which camouflage the really fundamental questions. When a child asks why grandmother has died, or why the sun does not fall, or what the toy is made of, or who made the fields, the child is not making scientific inquiries about heart attacks, the law of gravitation, the nature of atoms, or geological epochs. Nor will today's child be satisfied with standard "religious" or "old" answers in which the parents do not believe. The child is asking what is this world we live in, and whether everything does or does not fit together. She is looking for a myth and is more attracted by grandfather's little stories than by the pedagogical explanations of the teacher. We adults can give no convincing answers; we have only a broken myth and a bundle of half-scientific explanations. We have nothing but *hows*, which only suffocates all the child's *whys*.

If we do not believe in metaphysical or religious answers, we cannot give them. To say that "Man is created to serve and glorify God in this life and to enjoy Him eternally in the next" is a complete and magnificent answer. The fact, however, is that the innocence of that answer is lost—and probably rightly so—for most parents. Our lives do not look as if we believe in what that sentence says. We have lost our myth.

My point is not to conjure up an answer for the children, but rather to prepare the ground for an understanding of our situation. Only then will it be possible to trace the emergence of a new mythos that would both heal the wounds left by the past and gather up the valuable bits and pieces of modernity. My point is to rescue these ultimate questions from the exclusive domain of priests, pundits, intellectuals, and other elites, and, imitating that Rabbi of Nazareth, make things plain for the common people—which we all are—plain.

I began by asking Who? Where? When? What? And now, like children, Why? Here is the painful dilemma. To give the traditional answers to such questions is hardly possible anymore. Yet to say that we do not know implies not only defeat but also that while we know we do not have the answers, we still feel we can go on living. This in turn implies that for us those questions were not really questions of life and death. Have we resigned ourselves to living without answers, or have we stifled all our questions until a disgrace falls upon us as death approaches? Do all metaphysical questions simply operate to distract people from the labor market?

Such an attitude already provides a sad answer. We are saying that those questions are not really fundamental; that religion, metaphysics, and human thinking ultimately do not matter. We can live without them. This is a serious situation. It amounts to an abdication of personal humanness.

No wonder that the strongest become workaholics, the most sensible depressed, and the rest resigned. This failure explains the sociological power of fundamentalisms today. They do not postpone the answers. "The guru, the prophet, my church, the scientific community, tradition, or party . . . , they know." Their followers believe them, even if told to risk their lives in blind faith or uncritical hope.

There is yet another important "reason" why we cannot give convincing answers to the most basic questions of our children. Their questions are innocent. No adult answer in our times can be innocent, and probably no answer could be so innocent as to suppose that there can be an ultimate question, let alone an ultimate answer. This is the danger of all ideologies, and also of a certain type of totalitarian metaphysics. In a word, the *logos* cannot, not even logically, construct a complete system of anything.

In this sense the question of the temporal or historical destiny of Being is a fallacious question—because, as Lord Buddha long ago warned us, we do not know the limits of our question, we do not really know what we are asking. Our question presupposes that the Being whose temporal destiny we are asking about needs to have a destiny qua Being—that is, we are including a teleological *a priori* in the question. Once again, we cannot do without the *mythos*. The *mythos* makes the *logos* possible and the answer convincing. Yet neither is reducible to the other. Can we come up with another story? Or are we really trying for a meta-story? Who will tell the tale of what we really believe? The song is in the singing, life is in the living, Being is in be-ing.

b) Etymological Excursus

The indo-european root for destiny is *sta,* from which we get *stare,* stand, stability and even sub-stance, ek-sistence, rest, and a hundred more related words. The phrase "destiny of Being" "stands" for its "destination," its dynamic "steadfastness," its "standing" over against all temptations of robbing Being of its "status" of serving as the ultimate "standard" for what is real. The destiny of Being is neither purely "static" nor "ecstatic" or "enstatic." Some of the greek Fathers of the christian Church called it *epektasis*, especially when referring to our human destiny destined to become divinized. There is more to it. Etymologies are not prescriptive; they are suggestive.

"De-stiny" suggests both *stare,* to stand, have a strong stance, and at the same time *de-stanare,* which means a destabilizing of our stand, a loss of our stance, our standards. Instead of the intensive *de* in the common meaning of the prefix, *de-stanare* could mean not a fixed or known destination, but an awareness of the shaky stand that is our destiny. It recalls the "wheel of becoming," to speak with James, the brother of Jesus, with echoes of the orphic mysteries—ὁ τροχὸς τῆς γενέσεως, which the Vulgate translates as *rota nativitatis*, the wheel of birth.[99]

This ever-new birth may be our destiny. The New Year's festivals of practically all cultures celebrate and commemorate an ever-new birth of the world. In order to celebrate the resurrection of the earth and new hope for cohesion and prosperity of the country the "divine" emperor in ancient Japan used to drink the first new rice wine every year after the harvest along with his subjects. The feast of Christmas as the ever-new birth of Christ, and of us along with him, has become so popular because it is a clear symbol that deep down in human consciousness there is an *aspiration*, a *svadhā*, an *energeia*, *actus*, a *śakti*, *nixus*, *Drang*, élan, *impetus*, *urge*—each word opens up an entire worldview—toward . . . an *end*, an *eschaton*, a *telos*, a fulfillment, a fin*ality*. . . . Some possible names are God, *nirvāṇa*, Nothingness, Future, Justice, Annihilation. . . .

Our question consists in asking what is this *destiny*, and here, in using the common word of destiny, we employ it in the sense of *de-stanare*, destabilizing. If the latin world would have translated εἱμαρμένη not as "destiny" but differently (say, participation in the dynamism of the universe), the english word would have had different connotations. In greek δύστηνος (δύς-στα-νος) means unhappy because one has lost one's stand, and thus is in a bad situation.

The greek notion of *moira* has usually also been translated as "destiny," although sometimes one also reads "fate" (latin *fatum*, that which has been spoken and thus determined). The english word "doom" contains the root *sta*, present also in destiny, and the old anglo-saxon "Weird" (*Wyrd*) is the uncanny destiny of each human being (we may remember the "Weird Sisters" of *Macbeth*). The german *Geschick* and *Schicksal* (*Geschehen*, *Geschichte*) would invite us into yet another world.

We have a destiny, not if we have a fixed destination, but if we have no fixed stand at the end of the pilgrimage, because this end, our stand, is freedom. We have a fate if everything is predestined. We are doomed if the inexorable law has fallen upon us and we lose our stand.

Moira, on the other hand, suggests, first of all, a part or a portion over against the whole. We have our part. *Kata moira* means what is just and according to order, rightly so. *Moira* in her guise as Goddess of Death also may be our portion in the destiny of all livings things, that is, our death.

99 Jas. III, 6.

Something similar occurs with *heimarmenē* (from μείρομαι, receiving our share), which also conveys the idea of participation and, as the latin *mereor* suggests, of meriting or conquering that part which is due to us.

The whole cannot have *moira*; it is different from its parts. Can Being have a destiny? If it has, this could be only Non-being. Otherwise the destiny of Being would still be (the same) Being. What is the *sthānam* (state, position) of Being? Either itself or *asat*, Non-being, as the Upanishad says, echoing the Rig Veda.[100]

If our destiny is not to have a predetermined destination, because our share is freedom, if the *telos* is not fixed, is perhaps rhythm the answer? It may well be that the *destiny of Being* is its very *rhythm of Becoming*. The *destinatio* of Being may also be its σταυρός, its stake, its *crux*, its cross—following etymological hints. We should still consider a few more aspects of our overall topic.

c) The Destiny of Being

The destiny of Being cannot be deduced from an extrapolation of the diverse worldviews that people have held over the ages. It is a free destiny and not a predetermined destination. It does not need to follow any kind of necessity, or any sort of rule. It is not bound to obey logical thinking. Hegel writes in the last page of his *Philosophy of History* that "the history of the world is nothing but the development of the idea of freedom." Our free destiny, our *fatum*, εἱμαρμένη, *Schicksal* (should I add our *karma*?) is precisely played in the role that appertains to us in the cosmic adventure of the universe—what the greek Fathers of the Church called περιχώρησις—without restricting it now to the Trinity *ad intra*. Our role, portion (μοῖρα) is played out in freedom.

If we call the "omega point" the destiny of Being and Being has "not yet" reached it, we shall have to say that this omega point is Being only in potency. What is the nature of this "not yet"? It "is" an emptiness that we "discover" in Being and makes possible for Being to become what it shall be when Being reaches the omega point. That emptiness is present in Being.

Being cannot have any other prior or outside activity to which Being would be subservient and which would thereby contradict the very nature of Being. "The destiny of all things is to 'rest and be quiet' in God," says W. R. Inge, commenting on John Scotus Eriugena's ideas.[101] The destiny of "creatures" as creatures may be what this line suggests, but the destiny

100 RV X, 129, 5.

101 See W. R. Inge, *Christian Mysticism* (New York: Meridian, 1956).

of reality, the destiny of Being, with which we are inextricably linked, is just to Be, to Become. As we shall see, this destiny also, to a certain extent, depends on us. This is our human dignity, and our responsibility. According not only to Eriugena but to many a tradition, the only logical alternative is Nothingness, which is indistinguishable from Being. Nishitani uses the leitmotif of "Being *sive* śūn*yatā*," as we have already said.

If our hypothesis about the Rhythm of Being is correct, what prompts us to ask about this—and about the meaning of reality—is the rhythmic oscillation of that very Being. We stand at a precarious moment in the very destiny of Being. The dream of an everlasting progress has lost its plausibility, just as long ago in the West the dream of a *regressus* unto God lost credibility. It is the *inertia of the mind* that continues to demand progress or recurrent return, but Being has no inertia. The new question derives from Being itself, and the new question is not absolutely novel, but prompted by the failure or at least the inadequacy of the old problematic. The new is new only over against the old.

The destiny of Being also concerns human history, concerns us, concerns me. What happens in a galaxy millions of light-years distant from the earth (assuming it is a fact) may or may not influence this planet and we may or may not know it, but it belongs to the destiny of Being, and the destiny of Being is our destiny; we are involved in it. It is not a barren or frivolous speculation. Our effort at thinking the destiny of Being belongs also to this destiny, configures and shapes it along with all the other forces of Being itself. It belongs to the nexus, the aspiration, the very dynamism of Being.

What we are saying would be ridiculous if we were to subscribe to a merely quantitative vision of the universe in which Man is an insignificant factor among billions of galaxies that have been moving around for billions of years. To replace an infinite Deity, living and loving, with an infinite universe that is mechanical and dead does not represent real progress, besides the fact that it is a surrender of our dignity and responsibility.

My reflection is neither induction by extrapolation nor mere deduction from more or less postulated premises. Nor is it sheer guesswork or pure reflection. It is a passive/active conscious involvement in that selfsame destiny. Passive, because we have to listen, to obey, to open it to the "voice" of Being. Active, because by so doing this passive "activity" discovers, shapes, transforms, even steers Being itself. "Real history is pregnant with destiny," wrote Oswald Spengler, "but it has no law."[102]

102 Oswald Spengler, *Der Untergang des Abendlandes* (Vienna, 1918), vol. 1, 156.

This is what I have been calling contemplation, the active/passive co-involvement in the destiny of Being, which in christian parlance is the building of the Body of Christ, or which finds homeomorphic equivalents in the sharing in the *dharmakāya* of buddhist spirituality, the elimination of all negative *karma* for a certain hinduism, the life of the Spirit, the sharing with the Gods, the intratrinitarian life, etc. There is something grand in the simple belief of the old illiterate woman, a belief so easily dismissed as superstition, that were she the only human being, Christ, the Son of God, would have died for her sins and given her the hope of the resurrection. In other words, she believes that the entire universe has been so arranged so as to bestow eternal Life on a single poor peasant woman. Her faith steers the Destiny of Being.

Our assumption here is that Man has a unique position in the whole of reality. Man is not a thing, not just a product of the blind forces of cosmic evolution, but is rather the author of the very problematic we are talking about. It all still belongs to the *idaṁ sarvaṁ* , the "all this" ("this all") of which we are aware. The notion of Being may not be implied here, but the notion of consciousness is needed to give any meaning to the sentence. The *sarvaṁ* (all) puts no restrictions on the *idaṁ* (this), but the *idaṁ* has a meaning only if it implies a consciousness for which it makes sense. "This" is an act of awareness, whether it is empirical, noetic, or metaphysical. Some are aware only of the sensitible "this," others with a second eye also see noetic realities, while still others with a third eye are aware of a spiritual or divine aspect of the real. It is the "this" of my finger and also of the moon to which my finger points, including its dark side or invisible face to which both finger and moon jointly refer when they disclose the third dimension of the earthly satellite.

The Rhythm of Being is not an automatic or a merely cosmic process; it is not something left to what once was called divine providence, nor to what was later envisioned as laws of nature. Both Cosmos and Deity are involved, but Man also plays a crucial role: it is our human responsibility. This responsibility is Man's response to the destiny of Being. It is not a question of just reasoning, of just theorizing, but of Man's "own" being. We are not the masters of Being, but neither are we its slaves. We have this mysterious power to effectively participate in the free destiny of Being. Being is not a neutral (and neuter) reality but the very Life we also share.

To share in that rhythm is our destiny and our responsibility. For this we need that purity of heart which will allow us to be attentive to the real rhythms of Being, detectable, first, in the revelation that comes to us from the others, the joys as much as the sufferings of humanity and Nature. It is a dance that is as much ethical as it is metaphysical and cosmic. I am not saying that the Deity plays the tune, but I am reminded of the Gospel's parable of the children playing the flute both joyfully and mournfully, and the people not reacting, not being responsive, not being responsible.[103] If we take the hint of the parable, we, children all, are invited to play and to dance. We are players and chorus, actors, spectators, and co-authors in the rhythm of the real. Paradoxically enough, this openness to the other and the exterior requires a concentration on our interiority, as the Upanishads[104] (*antar*ātman, inner self) and Plotinus[105] (ἄναγε ἐπὶ σαυτοῦ, "go down deep into yourself"), among many others, advised us.

* * *

This is how the panorama appears to me. I have already said that the destiny of Being is freedom. Though our freedom as limited beings is indeed limited, the freedom of Being cannot be limited. A traditional and illustrious name for this is God, and I would like to rescue the word from two great traps into which that name has fallen—the one is historical, the other theological. The historical pit is obvious. After at least six thousand years of God's "dominion," humanity is painfully aware that in this name, in addition to the most sublime actions, the most hideous acts of inhumanity have been perpetrated. *Corruptio optimi pessima* (the corruption of the best is the worst). Furthermore, and related to what has been just said, all too often God has been made the private property of particular groups of "believers" who thereby convert the others into "unbelievers," who are called by many names, and not always gentle ones.

The theological snare is more subtle. If the first trap is due to the fact that certain people fall victim to a certain type of God intoxication, this second is the fruit of the human intoxication with our rational powers. We have believed it possible and even a duty to elaborate a theo-*logy*, a human science of God to entrap God in our categories.

To be sure, the best spirits, the most powerful minds as well as the simplest people have always surmised that if God is what God is supposed to be, no human *logos* is empowered to speculate on that Mystery. "Theology" could be redeemed as a subjective genitive, as the very divine *logos* to which

103 Cf. Mt XI, 17.

104 KathU V, 9-12, etc; MunU II, 1, 9; etc.

105 Plotinus, *Enneads* I, 6, 9.

we may be able to listen, but certainly not univocally interpret. Our present-day historical and intellectual experience makes us surmise that the until-now-standard traditional answers need a careful but radical examination, and perhaps a prudent but daring transformation.

Imitating the Pythia at Delphi, we can do no more than suggest some traces of this turning point.

I
Ancient Answers

... ὅτι τὰ πρῶτα ἀπῆλθαν. ...
ἰδοὺ καινὰ ποιῶ πάντα

... *quia prima abierunt, ...*
Ecce nova facio omnia

... since the former events are gone, ...
See, I make all (things) new.

—Rv XXI, 5

We began by inquiring into the ultimate concerns of human consciousness when confronted with the mystery of reality. Sooner or later, after experiencing the world around and in us we land in the question of human identity. Whatever the world may be, it all depends on our vision of it: who are we? This "we" surpasses the ego and even the human race. We are linked to the world. Our destinies are tied together, but somehow Man resists being swallowed into the destiny of the earth. Our intellect has discovered something other or even "bigger" than the material universe. One of its names is Being. This Being, so our thinking leads us to say, "beings" beings, lets beings be, but in order to do this, Being has to be other and probably more than beings. It has to be a very special kind of "being." The "being" of Being is not that of a mere entity. Either it is a Supreme Entity or it is of a different order, which we call precisely Being.

Crossing millennia of human reflection and overlooking many aspects of such a stupendous human adventure, we may say that humanity has almost unanimously believed that either above, besides, or identified with Being there is a kind of Source, Power, or Energy, one of whose names is God. This ultimate Being or God becomes a last point of reference, whether for negating its existence, qualifying its meaning, or accepting its presence. In order to focus our inquiry to a less bewildering panorama, we shall look at a simplified scheme of the western problematic. After all, it is an acutely western problem—although I will occasionally insert reminders from oriental traditions.

I said earlier that there is an intriguing consensus today that humanity is facing a turning point in its destiny, and it is becoming clearer each day that the great challenge is a change from a culture of war (even if called competitiveness and progress) to a culture of peace. Sociological investigations, historical studies, and phenomenological analyses are of little avail without a metaphysical basis on which it all may be grounded. The time of *reformations* of ancient habits is over, and *deformations* of the present-day system are countereffective. The needed *transformation* calls for a radical reexamination of fundamental problems. New situations and new ways of living require new ways of thinking. New wine needs new wineskins.[1] It is no wonder that the human question about the Divine, which has been a central preoccupation of *homo sapiens* for millennia, is now in crisis. The present-day worldview has radically changed, but our perception of the Divine has either undergone only cosmetic changes or practically been relegated to a private corner of life for a decreasing number of people. God may be immutable, but we are not, and our problem is how we envision that Mystery which for many still bears the name of God.

1. Immutability

The notion of destiny suggests that anything subjected to destiny stands in the flux of a certain becoming. If Being is intrinsically Becoming, we cannot avoid asking whether Being too has a destiny. I do not find a basis for excluding anything from this destiny—even Being itself. In this case, the destiny cannot be caused by an external Factor, but must be inbuilt, as it were, in the very nature of Being. Nature, *physis,* implies already *phyomai*, fieri, becoming.

An ancient answer says that everything is in the state of Becoming, everything is in flux, with one exception—Being, which *is* "outside" that stream: immutable, unmoved, "always" the same, static. Becoming is contingent, Being is necessary. I already hinted at the surreptitious introduction of a temporal *a priori* in the very formulation of the problem—as evident in the "always" used in the very presentation of the case. Immutability means atemporality. Anything immutable is timeless. Time implies movement and movement is "always" a long time.

I also suggested that the dichotomy of Being/Becoming, which asserts Being to be static and Becoming dynamic, leads to an unbridgeable dualism:

1 Mt IX, 17.

Being could not Become and Becoming could not come to be (Being). Theologically speaking, divinization, becoming *brahman*, *nirvāṇa*, perfect (as the heavenly Father) would then all be the undue projections of wishful thinking. Vedānta, for instance, will coherently affirm that we do not become *brahman*; we are (already) *brahman*—only that we (generally) do not know it. Where *avidyā* (our ignorance of being *brahman* even though we are it) comes from remains a problem.

The abyss between divine immutability and cosmic/human mutability has been a constant irritant in the history of human thought. It is this immutability that requires the transcendence of God, since the entire world is mutable. God's transcendence is what makes it "Wholly Other" according to modern christian theology. Nevertheless, it is significant to remark that a study on Karl Barth, the great protestant champion of God as the Wholly Other, written by one of his followers, carries the challenging title *Gottes Sein ist im Werden* (The Being of God is in Becoming).[2] It is also significant that a great catholic theologian made a qualified defense of Barth, pointing out the difference between the title sentence and statements like "Gottes Sein ist Werden" (the Being of God is Becoming) or "Gottes Sein wird im Werden" (the Being of God becomes in Becoming).[3]

I give this one example among many just to show how even orthodox theologies are changing. I could, of course, also have quoted "process theologians," although most of them remain under the spell of Aristotle. In the spirit of the Gifford Lectures, however, I now proceed to describe the still-popular belief in God as an immutable Being.

There is little need to remind the reader that there are other conceptions of reality. In the buddhist tradition, for instance, consistent with its *anātmanic* character (belief in the insubstantiality and impermanence of all), that ultimate icon is not God. Here we will leave aside the question of whether *śūnyatā* and *nirvāṇa* are homeomorphic equivalents.

In this discussion I will concentrate on the God symbol as a representative symbol for our problematic. Scores of civilizations have turned around that symbol, either affirming, qualifying, modifying, or denying it. I give this attitude the generic name of theism, with *theos* being the point of reference.

---

2 E. Jüngel, *Gottes Sein ist im Werden* (Tübingen: Mohr Siebeck, 1986), 116: ". . . den Satz 'Gottes Sein ist im Werden' nicht verwechseln dürfen mit Sätzen wie: 'Gottes Sein ist Werden.' Oder: 'Gottes Sein wird im Werden.'" ("The Being of God is in Becoming" should not be mistaken as saying "God's Being is Becoming" or "God's Being comes to be in Becoming.")

3 K. Rahner *Schiften zur Theologie* IV, 147.

2. *Respect for Tradition*

When a certain view of reality has persisted for millennia under the most diverse conditions, it carries a great weight and value. Hence, if I suspect that the days of unqualified theisms are not going to be bright, there must be powerful reasons for such a suspicion. Ours, I believe, is the proper moment (the *kairos*) for struggling with this weighty issue, and for overcoming the superficial reactions which only erode the old view and make more difficult the discovery of a viable alternative. Perhaps J. Huxley's flippant remark that "one of the major results" of Comparative Religion is that God "is now proving to be an inadequate hypothesis" needs to be qualified both historically and philosophically: historically, because a majority of humankind still believes in God, notwithstanding different interpretations; and philosophically, because if God means something, that something cannot be a "hypothesis." Indeed, any "God hypothesis" is contradictory to the traditional idea of God or makes of him an ungodly caricature. The title "Ancient Answers" is not meant to be derogatory; the elders have a vital function in any healthy society, but life continues, both biologically and culturally. The old images also need to be qualified. As the saying goes, the sages of antiquity pointed to the moon with their fingers. They themselves, however, tell us that we should not scrutinize their fingers, but only look in the direction they point. Yet there is more. In following the direction of those fingers, our predecessors may have found the moon, but if we just do the same, we may not discover the reflected bright light of the sun that we look for in our neighbor, the moon, because the moon itself has moved in the meantime.

The requisite materials for dealing with this subject are simply staggering. There is both the jungle of the history of religions, and the equally dense forest of the history of philosophy. A third perspective, which also should not be ignored, is the psychological view, which affects every human thought and action.

To cut across these three perspectives would be presumptuous, and ultimately impossible. We need to be aware of this impossibility and approach the problematic with great respect, but also without evasion. After all, only the impossible is worth the effort of trying.

This is more than a rhetorical sentence. The realm of the possible/impossible belongs to logic, ultimately to the *logos*. We may recall that "nothing is impossible to God," or that the "yes" of a young woman triggered twenty centuries of christian spirituality because she realized that the *pneuma* (πνεῦμα ἅγιον) is not subordinated to the *logos*, and thus performs impossible things.[4] I have made and shall also make repeated reference to the *creatio continua*.

Our problem is a case in point. The problem of the Deity cannot be adequately dealt with by a mere dialectical method. If I dare to approach what the human race has considered the most important, illuminating, and disturbing problem of the ages, I must attempt to reenact in my own way this ancient experience of humanity when confronted with the ultimate Mystery of life and death, time and timelessness, Being and Nothingness, sense and senselessness, . . . one of whose symbols is God.

The awareness of this human situation has not only prompted a jungle of theories about the Divine, but has also elicited love and hatred, passion and serenity, fear and confidence, war and peace, sublime actions and atrocious deeds. It would be wrong to approach the question of God by simply mapping the human ideas about the Divine. We must somehow sense, I would say experience, what the human mind has glimpsed and the human heart has felt. Only if we are touched by similar sentiments can we set our conscience at peace that we are not intruding on foreign grounds with violent means. Two classical words are appropriate here. The fact that their current meanings have become so eroded that I hesitate to use them shows the difficulty of the problem. The two words, of course, are *reverence* and *devotion*.

This *reverence* is not merely a moral attitude; it has to be built into our method, it also has to impregnate the interpretation of the philosophical ideas our ancestors have had about what we call God. This methodical respect allows me to criticize many of these ideas without saying that those who expressed them were wrong in their belief. Not only is each belief contextual; it is also personal. Each idea comes from and expresses an ideal, and one of the arches of the bridge of truth is such an existential relationship between idea and ideal. Therefore, I am not going to be judgmental of persons or historical periods. I am analyzing ideas.

Devotion is the other word. Devotion is not only a moral attitude. It is also an intellectual virtue. The investigation of living things is radically different from experiments with mechanical devices. Their very methods are distinct. If elementary particles are sensitive to our approaching them (Heisenberg) how much more will living entities react to our methods of approach! The very subject matter "God" demands devotion as part of our intellectual approach. Devotion means our consecration to our topic and our surrender to its dignity. For good and for ill the subject "God" has raised

4 Cf. Lk I, 34ff.

the hottest passions: love and hate, resentment and adoration . . . I might recall here that oxymoron of the women departing from the empty tomb "with fear and great joy"[5] as the proper sentiments when dealing with the subject of God.

3. *Classification of Religions*

It is tempting to build a basic typology that would make for a certain order and clarity. This is the current "scientific" method, but I have my doubts about such a neatly objective typology of beliefs. My contention is, in spite of the undoubtedly practical usefulness of such classifications, that they are not an appropriate method for understanding a human phenomenon. The classification of religious beliefs betrays the beliefs of the classifiers as much as it does the different beliefs of the classified. The *metron* of such a classification in our case would be a general notion of God as a Supreme Being. This notion, of course, gets stretched and opened so as to admit a plurality of such Superior Beings, their non-substantiality, a concentration in One or diffusion in many or even All. The extreme case would be the negation of such a Being.

This is an example of the reductionism implied in reducing human understanding to conceptual cognition and identifying the latter with a kind of algebra that permits inductions, deductions, and even probabilities and calculus, as computers do. For a "modern-scientific" method, such classifications are indeed a useful tool, but even leaving aside other critical considerations, classification, important as it is in "physics," cannot be an adequate method in metaphysics. Any classification has to leave outside the classification at least two essential constituents of reality: the criterion of the classification and the human classifier.

In the particular case of classifying beliefs, such a classification cannot be "objective": It depends on the particular assumptions of the classifiers, and it may not represent the beliefs of the respective believers—since "beliefs" are not necessarily homogeneous (a condition for the validity of any classification). The classification needs to practice a sort of reductionism to a certain type of conceptual and universal language that is unfit to convey the unobjectifiable and often non-homogeneous beliefs of the respective believers. True "polytheists," for instance, do not recognize themselves when classified as polytheists. Their beliefs are translated in the language of others (anthropologists, intellectuals, sociologists, monotheists, etc.), but the soul of their beliefs escapes those descriptions. We cannot obtain an accurate objective description of subjective convictions or states of consciousness.

5 Mt XXVIII, 8.

I am saying that in such subject matter there is no possible objectivity. I have introduced the notion of *pisteuma* in religious phenomenology as a substitute for the *noēma*.[6] The belief of the believer (*pisteuma*) is what religious phenimenology attempts to describe. It is a question of "the belief of the believer" and not of the belief of the observer (in spite of all sympathy and empathy). The observer cannot put in *epochē* (brackets) the very means of observation. Classical phenomenology, of course, claims to observe with "pure reason," and the universality and adequacy of *that* reason is assumed uncritically or taken as a postulate. Heraclitus is reported to have said long ago: "Most divine things (Gods) escape our knowledge because of lack of faith."[7]

At least since Aristotle it has been accepted that Being is not a genus. Kant, too, has said very unambiguously that "Sein ist offenbar kein reales Prädikat"[8] ("Being is obviously not a real predicate"). In brief, existences cannot be classified; they defy classification. We may classify mental constructs, concepts, abstract entities, but not real things as such. We can put "real things" in groups, but groups *qua* groups are abstract entities. Science is bound to classify; that is its strength. The only thing it cannot classify is real things. That there is no science of the individual was clear already to the ancients. Single events (singularity phenomena) are not a proper object of modern science. Peoples and their beliefs cannot be treated as abstract entities.

Although a classification into different theisms is only the classification of our mental schemes, it undoubtedly has a certain pragmatic value. Part of that value is that classifications are helpful in unearthing the assumptions of the classifiers. I already mentioned the assumption of the objectifiability of reality, at least to a certain extent. A second assumption is that of the universal character of a certain conception of reason. A third is that a single point of reference is capable of furnishing an explanation of a complex human reality. Such a classification of religions assumes that the *reductio ad unum* does no violence to reality, as if the beliefs of believers were sufficiently homogeneous that they could be put under one group without distorting them. A fourth assumption is that human reality at this most profound level can be an object of phenomenology—that is, that the *phainomenon* of the observer, is an adequate icon of the *noumenon* of the "observed" (classified).

---

6 See Panikkar, "On the Importance of Faith," *Hinduism Today* (September-October 2002), 17, among many other writings.

7 Heraclitus, *Fragm.* 86 (116): μὲν θείων τὰ πολλά ἀπιστίῃ διαφυγγάνει μὴ γιγνώσκεσθαι.

8 See Kant, *Kritik der reinen Vernunft*, A 598 / B 627.

My suspicion is that classification very often amounts to a superimposition of categories, which, while plausible for the classifiers, are not very pertinent to an understanding of the religious phenomena in any depth, let alone to those being classified. I am only saying that not all "atheists," "pantheists," and "polytheists" are really what they are classified to be, for the simple reason that their classification is not proper. Here again the paradigm of modern science proves decisive. The logical divisions plainly do not fit when the "object" is the belief of the believers in non-objectifiable "realities."

What has complicated the picture is that we are already accustomed to seeing the panorama of the world's religions in the light of the scholarly myth of our times. This is not a criticism but a critique. We all think within a given *mythos*. All this means that we need to exercise extreme caution in order to differentiate current understandings from the self-understanding of the movements that are being considered. I must also recognize that I, too, operate under yet another mythic horizon, so that at best my descriptions will be valid only as long as the myth stands. Inasmuch as the descriptions appear convincing, they presuppose the same horizon that renders them plausible.

I should further qualify this last affirmation. I am not operating totally under another myth, but from a horizon that permits me to perform a radical critique at the level of the myth I am uncovering, without being able to entirely extricate myself from that very myth. Indeed, I do not even know exactly the shape and scope of the new horizon which is not yet fully in sight. Put another way, the new horizon will be effective only when we see things clearly under a new light. Paradoxically enough, we shall see that horizon only when we have already begun to leave it behind. The process of human understanding is a constant passage from *mythos* to *logos*, and from *logos* to *mythos*—a kind of permanent transmythicization.[9]

I will therefore refrain from classifying religions or religious doctrines. For heuristic reasons, however, I will try to describe general traits of several religious attitudes of so-called theism. It will be clear from my description, however, that many of the traits overlap. I am describing attitudes more than classifying doctrines.

* * *

Before embarking on our topic, another important proviso is needed. I

9 See Panikkar, "Die Unmythologisierung in der Begegnung des Christentums mit dem Hinduismus," *Kerygma und Mythos* VI (1963), 211-35.

am not dealing with religion as a social institution, but with *religiousness* as a human dimension. This human dimension, however, should not be severed from its insertion in the complex canvas of human existence, nor separated from the political connections of historical religions. We should not forget, for instance, that the Enlightenment, despite all its simplifications, blindness, and reductionism, was on the whole a healthy reaction against the obscurantism and misuse of power of the religious institutions of the times. If the Goddess Reason is an exaggeration, the *Pantokratōr* of the times was a blasphemy. If atheism is an oversimplification, to say the least, its antitheism is a purification of an Ideal that supposed itself to be divine. To continue with these delicate examples, we cannot separate the idea of monotheism from its origins in the political empires and monarchies of the time, but we can and should distinguish between them, as we will elaborate.

A. The Theistic Mythos

In the current science of religions, theism is classified over against the background of western culture according to the different conceptions of God. In this sense theism is characterized as the belief in a personal God who governs the world. Therefore theism accepts "providence" and "revelation." From an intercultural perspective things are seen differently, and I shall adopt this latter view, focusing on ways of thinking more than on beliefs—without, of course, forgetting doctrinal contents.

Theism assumes a general scheme concerning the ultimate structure of reality, which takes its purest form in monotheism and presents itself with modifications in other like forms which present a similar pattern. Some of these forms are clearly reactions against monotheism, but as reactions they still move within the same overall scheme of theism, while other forms are qualifications or modifications of the same theistic pattern. Here I leave out of consideration other secularized aspects of theism as the different modern offshoots of colonialism (globalism, globalization). In saying this, I am not lumping all those forms together. The scholarly distinctions remain. Polytheism, for instance, is different from monotheism. I am also trying to avoid the danger of reductionism that is caused by uncritically accepting an abstract common denominator. Instead, I am trying to discover different myths that have prevailed in shaping the experience of reality—a reality that will appear, and perhaps be, quite different each time around. On this level, all theisms belong to what one might call the theistic *mythos*, which is what I am trying to narrate here.

As the conclusion to his *Patterns in Comparative Religion*, Mircea Eliade says he would "like simply to declare that almost all the religious attitudes man has, he has had from the most primitive times."[10] He states further that "from one point of view there has been no break in continuity from the 'primitives' to Christianity."[11] From the mythical point of view there has been, certainly, no break in continuity, although perhaps the modern techno-scientific world may be beginning to cause some cracks in the overall canvas. In any case, theism is not the unique category of *homo religiosus*. The universal *mythos* of *homo religiosus* (the acknowledgment of a sort of ungraspable "transcendence" and mysterious "immanence") is not identical with the theistic *mythos*. In fact, theism represents a particular *forma mentis* (mode of thinking) which has produced a certain type of worldview, and developed its own specific variety of theology.

1. *The Principle of Reasonableness*

Paradoxical as it may first sound, the way of thinking that has led to theism and helps characterize it is the Principle of Reasonableness. Something is reasonable when it is amenable to reason without having to be intrinsically rational. The God of theism makes reasonable the existence of the world and all its enigmas by throwing upon him all unresolved problems. Even the antitheistic attitudes will argue that it is more reasonable to dispense with such a "superfluous hypothesis" than to accept it. The theistic God does not shun rational proof of his existence. *Fides quaerens intellectum* (faith looking for understanding) and *intellectus* fidei (understanding of the faith one professes) are technical expressions of christian theology. The famous hebrew psalm: "Said the fool in his heart, there is no God"[12] is another classical expression of the same.

The world of theism is, first of all, a world in which all the many principles of life are felt to be in need of a unified coordination. There is a Supreme Instance and a hierarchy among all beings. It may be that the Entity who sits on the top is idle or has left the throne empty, or perhaps there are many thrones, or we know nothing about the entire issue, since it may be all an illusion. At any rate, the pattern is the same in all these cases: the ultimate thinking. There is one single transcendent Principle that gives or should give cohesion to the entire Reality. This Principle may succeed in giving cohesion, but it may also fail, in which case we discover the lack of that Principle—a *privatio*, a positive absence of something that must have

10 M. Eliade, *Patterns in Comparative Religion* (New York: Sheed & Ward, 1958), 463.

11 Ibid.

12

been there. The cohesion may be rational comprehension, just practical coexistence, or merely factual juxtaposition. All in all, the *theistic mythos* is a genial attempt at rationalizing Reality—at finding it at least reasonable. This is the strength and weakness of the bundle of civilizations which we call the West.

When metaphysical thinking sets in, God becomes the Supreme Being, the highest Entity, the Ultimate Person—and at the same time problematic. When moral thinking comes to the fore, this Supreme Being becomes good, the Good Lord responsible for the Kingdom. When anthropomorphic thinking takes the upper hand, the Deity acquires personal character, which gives rise to a personalized and personalistic cult. Ritual, prayer, worship, entreaty, all have a personal aspect.

The world of theism demands a universe in which there is a Supreme Ruler and Lawgiver, whether this is called Nature, Reason, the Market, or even Democracy. Today's "global thinking" is another hidden and not so subtle form of theism. Indeed, there have been numerous adaptations of theism to scientific cosmology and to a more modern mentality. They may be no "God," but a "unified field theory" or an ultimate Law is still assumed to operate in the universe. Most of the problems discussed in terms of "religion and science" and "reason and belief" since the nineteenth century have been efforts to reconcile theism with modern science. The present-day discussions about "evolutionism," "entropic principle," "big bang" (significantly enough, written as "Big Bang!") and the like are examples of controversies within the framework of theism, and in most cases, monotheism. The normal "humus" of theism is the old realistic world order common to all those cultures in which theism has flourished.

It is important to note the profound and paradoxical affinity between theism and rationalism—to the point that Reason has dethroned God and taken its place in many offshoots of modern culture. What is "according to reason" amounts to "the will of God." Reason demands the *reductio ad unum*, the concurrence of thoughts to a certain unity—otherwise there would be no possible understanding of anything. Reason as God reigns supreme and is the source of truth, morality, and law. Reason, like God, is the principle of order. The reign of Reason is all the more universal and pervasive the less she has lost the aura of the Goddess with which she was naively and revealingly endowed a couple of centuries ago in middle Europe. Scientific atheism could be cursorily described as the replacement of the God Principle by the Principle of Reason.

Perhaps we could use a single word to describe the essence of theism:

proto-archeia. Theism is a protoarchy. One Principle, of whatever nature, even if unknown, unknowable, or pluriform stands at the top. There is a world of *archai*, and among these principles or beginnings there is a *proto-archē*, there is an ἀρχή—which will be identified with the principle of order: "All things emerge out of one principle,"[13] wrote Cicero over a millennium and a half ago before Leibniz's principle of "sufficient reason." This *proto-archeia* can, if the need arises, be somewhat shared out or distributed in pantheons and henotheisms of all sorts. Obviously, depending on the different theisms, this point of reference may be visible or invisible, transcendent or immanent, or a merely pragmatic hypothesis that does not appear in the final process, etc. The strength of theism is this *archē*, this principle.

The *forma mentis* of all theisms is the projection of the Mystery of reality into a reasonable One. Reasonable does not mean rational. The *theos* of theism is not necessarily or even primarily rational. Our mind cannot grasp the Mystery; but it strives to show that it is reasonable that such an ultimate point of reference exists (is real). This point of reference may be a substance, an idea, a nothingness or simply an epistemological postulate, or even a hypothesis necessary for our mind. It is reasonable that such an ultimate point of intelligibility "exists." This principle is an offshoot of the particular *forma mentis*, or peculiar "mindset" proper to theism. Let us examine three mutually related traits of this ἀρχή.

2. *The Axiom of Non-Contradiction*

One distinctive feature is the practically absolute *primacy of the principle of non-contradiction*—which Thomas Aquinas calls *sacrosanctum*, which even the supreme Deity has to respect. Not even God can do anything that breaks this principle.[14] This principle of thinking reigns supreme, and it is even considered to be the "condition for the *possibility*" of thinking. Having said "possibility," we have already indicated the vicious circle of the principle which grounds itself by saying that it is *not possible* to contradict this principle without applying, viz., presupposing, it.

This argument is feeble on two accounts. First, the proof is a vicious circle; it is a tautology. It is a postulate of the mind postulated by the same mind. Possibility means non-contradiction. Something is intrinsically possible when it is not self-contradictory. To affirm that it is not "possible"

13 Cicero, *Tuscul.* 7, 54: "A principio oriri omnia."

14 Thinkers like Tertullian, Peter Damian, and Lev Chestov, to draw on three different epochs of the same monotheistic tradition, are scandalous exceptions in the western theistic world.

to contradict the principle without applying it means that it is not "non-contradictory" to contradict the principle—that is, it is contradictory to contradict it—which is a tautology that makes sense only by virtue of the principle of identity.

Second, there is no need for a holistic consciousness to contradict the principle and function properly. Thinking is more than calculating reason. Such a calculating reason certainly needs the principle, but we can proceed non-dialectically with our thinking without contradicting the principle. To retort that not contradicting the principle amounts to abiding by it, is only a conclusion of the same principle, which cannot be forced on those who do not apply it. Properly speaking, it is an axiom.

Here is where the strength and the limitation of the principle appear. The principle does not simply affirm that what is contra-dictory cannot be *said* (a contra-diction), but goes further to deduce that it cannot be *thought*—and even cannot *be*. In other words, we convert a logical axiom into a *principium cognitionis* (a principle of knowing).

"What cannot be said," of course, means "what cannot be meaningfully said"—which is fair enough. A contra-diction is the "non-diction" of the same "diction." If there is "diction" there is not [cannot be] a non-diction—a "contra-diction" of the "diction." Our principle is a logical axiom which postulates itself in order to be a logical principle. We need such an axiom for any diction. The first trait of the principle leads quite logically to the conclusion that not all *can* be said—and therefore that not all is said. There is a realm of silence: apophatism.

The primacy of the principle of non-contradiction extends itself not only to "diction," but also to thinking. It affirms that something contradictory cannot be thought because thinking is non-contradictory thinking and contradictory thinking is not thinking. The axiom of contra-diction extends to the realm of thinking. It is a principle of "not-contra-thinking"—which may be valid only insofar as thinking is a logical operation. The second trait concludes that not all can be logically thought—and even that not all is thought. There is the realm of mysticism: the ungraspable.

But there is still a third trait of the same axiom. It upgrades itself to a *principium essendi*, a principle of Being. The possibility of saying is extended to the possibility of thinking, and this latter possibility of thinking is identified with the possibility of Being. What cannot be thought (because it cannot be said— being contra-dictory) simply cannot be. The principle of (non-contradictory) thinking is identified with the principle of (non-contradictory) Being.

The insight of Parmenides is the basic paradigm of theism. Thinking and Being correspond to Being and Thinking. Being is Thinking, that is, Intelligibility—not certainly for an individual mind, but as such. Here is the ultimate basis for the famous ontological proof of God's existence. A supreme thought would lead to a Supreme Being. Philosophers and theologians are in dispute as to whether this supreme thought is possible (*id quo maius cogitari nequit,* "that more than which cannot be thought"), but agree that if this "Supreme Thought" were possible, it would lead to a "Supreme Being." If this identification between Thinking and Being were not the case, we would be open to the realm of Emptiness, to a Being empty of Thought. I have argued that the scheme of Parmenides (with all its qualifications) is not the only philosophical paradigm.[15] Our question here is limited to showing a particular *forma mentis* of theism, and not to discussing the force and value of all those arguments or whether Parmenides has always been correctly interpreted.[16]

It is rightly argued that without accepting the validity of such a principle we would be condemned to solipsism and human communication would be not possible. Human communication, however, is not only logical. There is also the communication of the senses and the communion of the spirit, which do not need to be irrational or "contradict" reason. Conceptual communication is based on that principle, but not symbolic understanding. As I have repeatedly stressed, for instance, philosophy does not need to be limited to an algebra of concepts.

The strength of theism is that it offers one single center for the whole of reality. This center fulfills a triple function: (1) it vouches for the unity of the uni-verse; (2) it provides us with an ultimate point of reference, which allows us not only to be able to dialogue with one another, but to appease our thirst for intelligibility, the *reductio ad unum*; and (3) the fact that this center is transcendent or unknown/unknowable/inexistent makes room for human freedom and is the principle of moral order. The weakness of theism consists in the fact that it tends to believe that it is a universal paradigm, and that its only alternative is total disorder, irrationalism, and a total loss of coherence.

3. *Non-Theistic Mythoi*

It may seem far-fetched to include under the same word so many

15 See the interview with me, "A Centre for Intercultural Studies" in *Intercultural Horizon* [Montreal] (February 1989), 11.

16 See Hanspeter Padutt, *Und sie bewegt sich doch nicht: Parmenides im epochalen Winter* (Zurich: Diogenes, 1992); see also Arthur Berriedale Keith, *The Religion and Philosophy of the Veda and Upanishads* (repr., Delhi: Motilal, 1970), Appendix G, 634ff.

different beliefs. I do so on purpose in order to emphasize the importance of a crosscultural approach that does not reduce human experience to a single paradigm. Though the beliefs of all those theisms are different and even incompatible, they reflect a certain thinking pattern and underlying vision of reality. We have to recognize that the world of theism is not the only religious world. Everybody accepts today that there are different cosmologies, worldviews that belong to other cultures, but fewer people reflect on the fact that those visions of the world are the fruit of different ways of thinking. Modern science is not universally useful and powerful until we accept its axioms and assumptions.

I have already mentioned the triple assumption of the so-called principle of non-contradiction. Dialectical thinking is not the only existing way to reach intelligibility. The "Principle of Reasonableness" is viewed in some cultures as dealing with the lowest degree of reality. The western effort to force reality to follow the exigencies of logical thought is seen by some highly developed cultures as a preposterous human hubris, in spite of some spectacular material achievements. God or Non-god is not seen as an ultimate dilemma by cultures outside the theistic realm. Neither the *tao* nor *brahman* is God or Gods. To require them to be either substances or accidents, either individualizable beings or Being in general, is simply to project one set of categories onto another field of human experience. Suffice to mention *kami*, the *tao*, *brahman*, or the universe of buddhism, to immediately perceive the difference. *Kami*, says one expert, "can be regarded as the spiritual nature of each individual existence." Yet, according to shinto tradition, there are eight hundred thousand of them. The word *kami* phonetically means resplendent and the shinto tradition says in the words of a sage of the fourteenth century: "*Kami* is real, it is that Light which in heaven is called God, in Man Sincerity and in Nature Spirit."[17] This is not theism, or animism. It comes from another way of thinking and from a different worldview.

We are all children of our times, although to acknowledge ourselves also as grand-children may give us more freedom. For centuries, especially in the West, not only theism but also monotheism was considered the superior form of culture. For centuries western culture has considered itself to be superior, when not the only truly "developed" culture. It is no wonder that Ananda Coomaraswamy, a master of both indic and western wisdom, in order that the Veda not be dismissed as "orieņtal gibberish," developed the misconception of "Vedic monotheism": How could the Veda

17 Imbe no Masamichi (apud J. López-Gay, "El shintoismo japonés," in *Historia de la Epiritualidad* [Barcelona: Flors, 1969], vol. 4, 663).

be so "crude" as to defend "polytheism"? The only alternative left was either polytheism or monotheism. In fact, Coomaraswamy's arguments are simply the interpretation of many texts in the light of Śankara's philosophy. The different Gods are simply manifestations of the higher reality of *brahman*, the many names are nothing but labels:

> They call him Indra, Mitra, Varuṇa,
> Agni or the heavenly sunbird Garutmat.
> The seers call in many ways that which is One;
> they speak of Agni, Yama, Mātariśvan.[18]

The "fault," however, is not with the Veda, but with (western) monotheism as applied to the Veda. They are two different worlds. The identity of the Gods is not based on the principle of non-contradiction, according to which the Gods would be either many (polytheism) or different names of the "same" (monotheism). In fact, there are number of texts that say without any qualm: "I Varuṇa am Indra"[19] or identify Agni with Mitra or with Varuṇa, etc. No doubt, the Upanishads have a unifying idea of the many Deities[20]—although the *devaḥ* of the Upanishad may not be properly translated as Gods in a monotheistic sense. Max Müller's hypothesis of "kathohenotheism" or "henotheism," which explains that the texts speak each time of one God according to context and function, is a well-intentioned effort to make the vedic world understandable to the West. I do not deny a certain type of monotheism in the Gītā and later indic philosophies. What I contest is the dilemma monotheism-polytheism, or in more general terms, theism as the only "high-cultural" way of dealing with the divine reality. The Veda, I submit, are not theistic—and thus neither monotheistic nor polytheist, much less atheist. The universe can have meaning and harmony, order, *ṛta* without having to accept a theistic worldview. Even calling later vedāntic doctrine on *brahman* (mono)theistic is stretching the meaning of this word beyond its limits. What I am contesting here is an excessively monocultural method of interpreting other cultures. Because most forms of theism are reactions against monotheism, as noted above, we may continue our description by bearing in mind thẹ general theistic framework.

---

18 RV I, 164, 46.

19 RV IV, 42, 3.

20 Cf. BU III, 9, 1-9; etc.

B. Monotheism

Hear O Israel, the Lord is our God, one
Lord, and you must love the Lord your God
with all your heart and soul and strength.
These commandments which I give this
day are to be kept in your heart; you shall repeat them.

—Dt VI, 4ff.

1. *Description*

Whatever one thinks of Wilhelm Schmidt's once widely accepted hypothesis of an *Urmonotheismus*, the fact is that monotheism is one of the most developed and extended forms of religious belief. The word has had many interpretations. We may understand the word to say that there is but a single *theos*, and take *theos* to stand for an ultimate agency. Here the *monos* does not need to be a numerical category, nor the *theos* a particular entity. In this sense, Plotinus's *hen*, eighteenth-century european *deism*, and Max Müller's *kathenotheism* (often simplified as *henotheism*) are all forms of monotheism. There are many possible and actual forms of monotheism. Hellenic monotheism, for instance, is not the same as the muslim scholastic notion of it. We do not need to go into all the scholarly discussions regarding monotheism, or to describe the force of Schmidt's argument for a "primordial monotheism." We can likewise leave aside the famous monotheistic innovation of the pharaoh Amenhotep IV (Ikhnaton) in the fourteenth century BC, about which Freud wrote his last essay, *Moses und das Problem des Monotheismus*. Instead of attacking or defending monotheism, we would like to understand it in its depth.

To begin, a distinction imposes itself between monotheism and monism. The latter affirms that there is ultimately only a single reality, which, however, does not need to be interpreted as an undifferentiated reality. Within the *monos* there may well be a legitimate place for diversity of "modes," provided these differentiations do not impinge upon the absolute purity of the unique Monad. One difference between monotheism and monism is that the former is not satisfied with distinctions and demands a radical separation between God and all the rest. Monotheism recognizes the existence of a privileged Being. Let me cite a highly poetic and profound philosophical passage of the Holy Qur'an: "When the night grew dark upon him [Abraham], he beheld a star. He said: This is my Lord. But when it set, he said: I love not things that set." [21]

21 Qur'an VI, 77 (M. M. Pickthall translation).

Monotheism is a special form of theism that affirms that this One Supreme Being, which does not "set," is the Source of all things. This Source is different from that multiplicity of things which it originates. Strict monotheism is the belief in a self-sufficient (solitary) and transcendent Supreme Being. God has no counselor; nobody stands at his side. This Being is a Substance, a self-subsistent Entity called God. It is the Agent ultimately responsible for all things and all actions. God is the Highest Entity among all existing things.

> The mark of [hebrew] monotheism is not the concept of a god who is creator, eternal, benign, or even all-powerful; these notions are found everywhere in the pagan world. It is, rather, the idea of a god who is the source of all being, not subject to a cosmic order, and not emergent from a pre-existent realm; a god free of the limitations of magic and mythology.[22]

This is strict jewish monotheism. Yet the notion can be widened.

In most types of monotheism, God occupies such a higher position that his transcendence is situated not just above all beings, but beyond the very scale of beings, so that God is not a mere thing among things. The difference is not only of genus but of "being." It is transcendent. This God may be Creator, Demiurge, Origin, Source, Shaper, or Controller; he may exercise all power alone or associate himself with his own "emanations" of many sorts, that may be called *śakti*, Goddess, or even Word.

This God may "allow" many manifestations of himself, to the point that these manifestations may themselves appear to our human view as very nearly absolute within the horizon of the particular culture, tribe, or time in which they flourish. This God may equally allow a certain cultic plurality of forms, so that each form is believed to be unique for the particular worshiper. God may delegate some powers to the freedom of creatures, or to the laws of nature, or even to an apparently blind evolutionary process, but there is ultimately only one Source of Being. I mention these many possibilities because of the protean nature of monotheism, which leaves room for many explanations of the divine mystery.

The entire first book of the second volume of F. W. J. Schelling's *Philosophy of Mythology* is dedicated to monotheism.[23] While theism is a purely rational discovery, he says, monotheism is a fact. If monotheism

22 Yehezkel Kaufmann, *The Religion of Israel: From Its Beginnings to the Babylonian Exile* (Chicago/London: University of Chicago Press, 1960), 29.

23 See Schelling, *Philosophie der Mythologie* (Darmstadt: Wissenschaftliche Buchgesellschaft, 1986), 2:24-48.

merely affirmed that God is One, it would be a simple tautology. There cannot be many Gods, Schelling writes. Polytheism, in this sense, would be a contradiction. Abrahamic monotheism is thus not so much opposed to polytheism as it is to pantheism. Monotheism is not just a logical proposition but a fact that implies history, and possibly revelation. Monotheisms are founded religions, a point I shall return to. I will not follow Schelling's reflections now, tempting as they are. I merely stress one thing most monotheisms underscore: that God is a Person. In this sense, monotheisms foster personal relations with God, as Person, a subsistent person, that is, in the words of one indic tradition: *icchā* (will), *jñāna* (knowledge), and *kriyā* (activity).[24] Prayer and worship belong to monotheism in a very special way. This is in line with most classical descriptions, although polytheism, for instance, shows a similar feature, perhaps even in a stronger form.

We have to recognize—and perhaps islām is a paradigm for this grandeur—that monotheism is the simplest solution to all the riddles of the human heart and mind. If God did not exist, one would have to invent it, so the saying goes. Monotheism is probably the simplest solution. This does not prove that monotheism is either false or true—nor that it is easy to believe and follow. Monotheism projects onto one mysterious Being all the ultimate human problems: time, space, matter, evil, life, death, tragedy, chance, causality, intelligibility. . . . We cannot solve these riddles; indeed, we have known all too well and all too long that humanity has not resolved them. Although we go on questioning, we are resigned to the fact that some things are beyond us. This very fact suggests that there is, or might be, another Being in which not only the *coincidentia oppositorum* may occur, but the universe may come to rest, as it were, and become intelligible.

Monotheism thus understood is a source of optimism. It overcomes the resignation and depression of having to live without finding an ultimate meaning for life and existence by believing in (or projecting onto) a living and loving God who takes care of everything so that all may end well.[25] Monotheism offers a certain peace and serenity, encourages humility without humiliation, and gives a sense of the real and a sense of proportion without despondency. This God may pose insoluble difficulties for our minds, but we fear its radical elimination would be worse. We do not discover the meaning of the universe, or find lasting answers to the ultimate problems, but we believe there is a Being which, so to speak, takes care of them on our behalf.

Perhaps the best example of the force of monotheism is *bhakti* mysticism.

---

24 Abhinavagupta, *Parātrīśikā Vivaraṇa* 6.

25 Cf. 1 Cor XV, 28.

God is discovered as the Beloved, but soon becomes the Lover. The infinite desires of Man rest in God, and Man's mind trusts in the divine Intellect. The Universe has a Creator, a Lover, a Providence. Human souls encounter the hidden presence of Love in their own hearts. Everything else here on earth is disappointing and fails to satisfy the infinite longings of the children of God.

I should emphasize this point, which is perhaps the strongest and the weakest facet of monotheism. In fact, without a loving relationship with God monotheism is on the brink of becoming a dangerous ideology. The real God is a loving God. It would be a tremendous mistake to interpret our effort to overcome monotheism as a sort of "intellectualizing" or, even worse, "rationalizing," the divine symbol and converting it into a lifeless Being or a metaphysical entity. We need human access to the divine. This means that this access has to be, if fully human, a truly personal relationship. God needs an iconic face if it is to be a God for us. My only caution is not to absolutize the icon. The monotheistic God is a living and loving divine Icon.

At the same time, the "love of God" is a weak facet of strict monotheism. One can understand that the sufis are felt as a danger to orthodox islām, and christian mystics are treated with suspicion in monotheistic christianity. In fact, divine love (from both sides) seems to do away with the pure divine transcendence. Between the lover and the beloved there is distinction, but there cannot be such a distance as to make the embrace between the lovers impossible. Paradoxically enough, the greatest difficulty about accepting monotheism is not the presence of evil but the existence of love—in spite of all the theological subtleties that have been used to explain these two human experiences. Indeed, most monotheisms are qualified monotheisms. The experience of love tarnishes if not destroys divine transcendence (the lover does not love a shadow), but it equally makes impossible divine immanence (the Beloved has to remain an *alter*, an other, to be loved by the lover).

The very idea of the reality of God is so powerful, however, that its simple acceptance makes it undefeatable. It is so all-embracing that there is nothing left outside it from which we could criticize it. We may here translate the wager of Pascal, not as the fear of losing eternal life, but as the fear of falling into chaos if we do not accept the "God hypothesis."[26] Elsewhere we will criticize the weakness of the argument that subordinates God to rational common sense.

God is a self-supported or rather self-contained hypothesis, a challenge to all or nothing, the manifestation or revelation of something totally different

26 Pascal, *Pensées* (ed. Brunchvicg), 233

from anything else in our experience. Monotheistic belief puts the stakes so high that it can neither be verified nor falsified. These two criteria cannot be applied to something that does not claim to be subservient to our reason. If there were a convincing mathematical proof of the existence of God, God would be a mathematical object, not the living God of the believer.

I have used the phrase "God hypothesis" several times with a certain irony, because the monotheistic God, according to his formal description, cannot be a hypo-thesis, since God is the ultimate *hypo keimenon*, the ultimate basis of everything, including our knowledge. A scientific hypothesis is something that we set up as a tentative explanation to verify if it yields a satisfactory answer to our means of establishing the pragmatic validity of the hypothesis. However, there is a difference with a "God hypothesis." The ether hypothesis was accepted as long as it helped to explain the propagation of waves through space; it was abandoned when a more plausible explanation was found. The "God hypothesis" does not leave untouched any nook or cranny of our being: not even the principle of non-contradiction is an archimedean point from which we may show a kind of internal coherence of the belief in such a God. Here again we confront the "all or nothing" of our introduction. The belief in God, traditional theology says, is pure grace.

The arguments that have usually been presented against monotheism ever since the most remote antiquity tend to miss the point in familiar ways. For example, the fact that we have an anthropomorphic idea of God, so that for horses God would be the Great Horse (as already the ancients said), only shows that we need an image of the Divine. At the same time it indicates that the image is precisely nothing but an image adapted to our means of perception. The tone of many of these objections is well known: If God permits evil, God cannot be at the same time good and omnipotent. There is a contradiction between human freedom and predestination, between providence and the tragic end of those trusting in providence, etc. Such logical impasses or even contradictions do not touch monotheism in the least. To accept them as valid objections implies that one has already abandoned monotheism. Here monotheism makes a giant's stride above theism. Nicholas of Cusa, among others, has already warned us that the *coincidentia oppositorum* is characteristic of the infinite intelligence. There is, however, something more. The God of monotheism stands above all human principles and requirements of the human mind.

It is against these and other difficulties that the function and locus of monotheism appear most clearly. If God is that which it is supposed to be, it is absolute Lord over our minds and feelings. If we find something repugnant to our reason or ethical sense, God overrules it. God is the very ground of our awareness and moral sense. The attitude of an Abraham ready to sacrifice his own son was not, from this point of view, anything extraordinary; it was simply the believer's act of accepting monotheism. If such a God exists, it is absolute Lord—not only of my actions but of the very ground of all my actions, thoughts, and feelings. If Yahweh appears to me as a monster for demanding the sacrifice of my son, and I believe that Yahweh is the *absolute* God, my very moral repugnance has been given to me by that God. Now the same God is asking me to overcome the moral nausea it has given me. So I acquiesce—in such a scheme of things, I *must* acquiesce. In other words, God does not descend to the round table of logical, mathematical, philosophical, or even ethical discussions. God is infinitely far above all this. Otherwise, we are degrading monotheism and using it to justify our own beliefs and judgments. The monotheistic God is neither a "stamp God" to certify our own certainties nor a "gap God" to cover our uncertainties and ignorance.

People are free, of course, to say that they do not believe in such a Being, but then they ought to be clear that they prefer to believe in their own sense of truth and goodness than in any Existence that absolutely transcends all creatureliness. If we put conditions on the existence of God, the problem is already solved. In that case, we are just unbelievers, playing with words. We believe in God insofar as this God suits our judgments—and, after further reflection, we are clever enough to convince ourselves that God has to be truthful, good, and beautiful according to our standards, which we then turn around and pretend that God has given us. Such an approach shows that we have not overcome anthropocentric humanism. We still harbor the secret desire to make God in our own image and likeness, instead of surrendering ourselves to God without conditions.

To be sure, all theologies, inasmuch as they are human *logoi*, will try to soften this discourse and assure us that the God they are talking about is "humane," logical, good, and all the rest. This may be true, but we should be clear about where we place our priorities. We believe then in ourselves and our criteria, and find the "God hypothesis" quite reasonable and profitable. Fair enough. But this is not monotheism. Instead, the epistemological status of such a rational and reasonable claim has been given priority as regards statements that purport to reveal the unique status of God's revelation. We cannot ever transcend our homocentrism in this way.

Historians of religion usually affirm that monotheistic religions have a founder. This is not just a historical fact but also an anthropological fact, a fact of human experience. We should recall here what was said before about religious experience in a discreet and almost veiled way. Monotheistic faith can be explained only in terms of a personal encounter with a monotheistic God. Monotheism is understandable only out of a "burning bush" experience, a "fall from a horse," a "desert vision," a sense of being "taken up to the heavens," or just an intellectual insight. For believers, love, surrender, total consecration, and dedication to this Godhead are real if the initiative comes from above, the other shore, the living God, and not from us. Such a monotheism is not a matter of "we humans looking for God," but "we mortals overwhelmed by the visitation of the divine"—with the accompanying possibilities of subjective hallucinations and fanaticism. Neither dangers nor possible abuses are enough to dismiss the fact of a possible encounter with what we called a Founder—through whom we may be able to reenact the decisive experience. In that sense monotheism is the fruit of a Revelation, or in other words, a matter of faith.

God cannot be an expediency for a rational or plausible explanation of the world. God is not a pragmatic hypothesis. If there is a monotheistic God, it cannot be at our service, or at the service of our reason. I said at the outset that discourse about God is *sui generis*.

2. Genesis

Such a powerful and widespread belief, especially if one responsibly dares to raise some doubts about its validity for our changing times, triggers the unavoidable question about its origins. Man is not only history; he is also a historical being. The monotheistic God might have revealed himself to Man, but apparently Man did not hear or understand his voice before a few millennia ago. It is therefore legitimate to inquire into the genesis of that belief.

I shall make only two comments on that complex and delicate problem.

a) Political

Since at least the writings of Max Scheler, western scholarship has become increasingly aware of what he called *Soziologie des Wissens*, translated as "sociology of knowledge." It amounts to the insight that all our human knowledge does not come only from above (God, illumination, world of ideas, reason, *intellectus agens*, . . .), but that it also needs an apt receptacle from below. I mean that our ideas are also rooted on earth, they germinate in time and space; our knowledge also depends on history and geography.

To come directly to our case: the political times and concrete places when and where monotheism flourished were those places and times in which societies were ruled by emperors and kings. The political society offered at least its language to monotheism. No other language was better suited. God was called King of kings, Lord of lords and Emperor of the universe. When only a few years had passed after Constantine's edict allowing freedom of worship to christians and protection to christianity, emperor Theodosius went a step further, substituting the earthly emperor by a heavenly one so that if earlier it was a crime not to worship Caesar, now it was a higher crime not to worship the celestial Emperor whom the christians adored. Here we may see the power of the monotheistic *mythos*. We have already made several hints at an analogous transfer from religious monotheism to its secularized forms, like colonialism, capitalism, and globalization, and I also detect a similar rigidity among the functionaries of the new monotheisms. The old dictum "outside the church there is no salvation" takes today the form of *extra scientiam nulla salus* ("outside science there is no salvation").

I have already made reference to the *proto-archeia* of theism. The most powerful example of this *proto-archeia* is the *monarchia* of monotheism, of course. Historically speaking, monotheism flourished along with the great political monarchies. Theism recognizes a supreme point of reference. Theism is against *anarchia*, which in a theistic world is revealingly translated as disorder and chaos. Why should the absence of a commanding ἀρχή or dominating principle mean such an absence of harmony and concord? Apparently, without a boss—God, Reason, Führer, King, President, Police, or Army—we would be killing each other, as the old adage would have it: *Homo homini lupus* ("man is a wolf toward his fellow man").[27] It seems that we need a "Grand Inquisitor," perhaps a changeable one every four or six years. To be fair, and with fewer innuendos, there were also absolute monarchies in the East that did not subscribe to monotheism—China and India, for example.

Although monotheism was not born in Israel, it was there that it took its most powerful form. We cannot affirm categorically that monotheism was the useful outcome of a political ideology nor that religious monotheism was at the origin of political monarchies in spite of the undeniable fact of a holy and/or unholy Alliance between the two.

b) Philosophical

We have been asking why monotheism has had such an appeal and success. To adduce mere political reasons is not enough. One could equally retort: Why did monarchies wane in the twentieth century? Even

27 This crucial sentence of Thomas Hobbes was said already by Titus Maccius Plautus (cf. *Asinaria* 495) in the third century BC: "Lupus est homo homini."

if one were to answer that it was because of sheer force or abuse of power, nothing forbids us from asking a further why. Why did both monarchy and monotheism become so powerful and convincing? After the fall of the (absolute) political monarchies, are monotheisms a thing of the past? Or, on the contrary, do they offer an effective remedy to the "anarchies" of modern times? A philosophical reflection seems to be required. Philosophy must investigate whether there is something in human nature which justifies political monarchies and religious monotheisms.

I have also given an implicit answer to the philosophical aspect of the question. All theisms in general and monotheism in particular operate on the principle of reasonableness. Once monotheism has liberated us from the anguish that we cannot so quickly find all the vital answers for our existence, we can dedicate ourselves freely to a more serene investigation of all those problems, as well as to all those other problems that are perhaps secondary, but are more immediate and eventually more practical. In fact, the modern world lives under the spell of the "scientific" discoveries. This state of affairs is more than sociological. The human thirst for understanding and the human desire for certainty are authentic and powerful. Monotheism provides a remedy for both, at least for the insiders.

c) Theological

One cannot discard a third reason. If the divine is real, even if it is a divine dimension, it is active. We cannot exclude that the perdurance of monotheism may be due to the selfsame revelation of God. God reveals himself as such. This *schema* is probably one of the most powerful expressions: "Hear, O Israel, the Lord is our God, one Lord [or the only or one Yahweh]."[28] Although one could have another exegesis, namely, that this is the revelation of God to Israel: "our God," "our Lord."

At any rate, if the Yahweh of the historical books of the hebrew Testament was a tribal God in battle with other Gods, the Yahweh of the Prophets soon became a monotheistic and universal God. This monotheistic God revealing himself in history makes history the framework of his manifestation, and human life on earth a pilgrimage. It is understandable that this is the God fitting to the victors, who rely on the protection of God. In fact the victims of history can rely little on that God who intervenes in human history. One can understand the crisis of orthodox judaism after Auschwitz.

3. *Critique*

Monotheism is invincible on its own terms. It is a perfect system. It

28 Dt VI, 4.

is selfsufficient, closed, though the enclosure is said to be infinite. Once an omniscient, all-powerful, and eternal God is introduced, not only is there absolutely nothing outside the reach of its knowledge and power, but it has the key to all our own problems and interpretations as well. The Supreme Being has absolute and immediate jurisdiction—moral, ontic, ontological—over any notion, thought, feeling, or being. The early christians (Hilary, Irenaeus, and others), who stood at the confluence of the hebrew notion of Yahweh and a hellenic idea of *theos*, saw rightly that only God knows God. As I have already stressed, only in and through God can we know about God. A lapidary sentence sums it all up: "The Lord taught us that nobody can know God unless He Himself teaches us."[29]

The monotheistic system is absolutely coherent, and we are deprived *a priori* of any means of rejecting it with any cogent argument. There is no point in believing in God if we are free to dictate what God has to be or how he has to behave. The case is all the more unassailable when the only Achilles' heel of monotheism, namely, that it is we who introduce the belief in God, is countered by the affirmation, or rather the experience, that monotheism is revealed. Indeed, a coherent monotheism cannot but be revealed. Only God can say what he is, and if he says so, we have only to listen. As Schelling said, it is a fact in which we believe, because it imposes itself on us.

If we want to submit monotheism to criticism, we cannot do it from the "outside," which by definition does not exist. The God of monotheism has absolute immunity. There is no tribunal, and surely not our reason, which can summon him to judgment. As soon as we do so, we have already rejected monotheism. Hence, there is nothing to discuss. A critique from "inside" has to use the very tools that monotheism has furnished. There are indeed internal difficulties, and millennia of theological thinking have attempted to solve them by refining the notion of God.

a) Internal

Critique in its philosophical sense (and not in the accepted sense of criticism) may help to understand better the strength and weakness of monotheism. We may cite three examples of this critical approach.

(1) Understanding Faith

The first critical method is expressed in the classical dictum, "Faith searching for understanding."[30] This adage speaks of a faith striving,

29 Irenaeus, *Adversus haereses* IV, 6, 4 (PG 7:988): Θεὸν εἰδέναι οὐδεὶς δύναται μὴ οὐχὶ Θεοῦ διδάξαντος, which latins translated "Edocuit autem Dominus, quoniam Deum scire nemo potest nisi Deo docente."

30 See Panikkar, "La foi dimension constitutive de l'homme," in *Mythe et foi*, ed. E. Castelli

searching, and even praying to understand, not to prove or justify, but just to implore intelligibility. This belief in God is a gift, a grace, and can eventually turn out to be an experience: it is ultimate and supreme. Faith itself implies an awareness that it is neither inhuman nor irrational; it is possible to understand that faith does not demean our faculties but enhances them. Faith itself searches for intelligibility. We could quote here Thomas Aquinas again.[31] Another representative author could be Moshe ben Maimon when he begins one of his books by exclaiming, "We know the Name!" It is only out of this knowing experience that he can "Guide the Perplexed." In both cases, we divine a powerful personal experience.

The anselmian dictum should not be interpreted as fides *inveniens intellectum*, faith finding intelligibility, but *quaerens*, searching for understanding by dint of an internal and constitutive dynamism without any assurance of finding it—which is also the case for our intellect as it searches for intelligibility. We have to rely on the *mythos* that we accept. As I already said, there are no ultimate answers.

This first critique softens the irritating *Absolutheitsanspruch* of monotheism (its "claim to be absolute" and the last instance of everything), helping us see that the human effort at making sense of reality has to stop somewhere—whether at evidence, reason, common sense, indifference, conscious trust, or nihilism, and that this last Foundation is precisely the *mythos* in which we ultimately believe without further "foundation"—unless we are to fall into a *regressus in infinitum*. Faith itself is looking for understanding both of its own nature and of what faith believes.

We may also read the classical latin phrase as fides *petens intellectum*, faith asking, praying for insight. Monotheistic faith is a gift, I said. We accept it, we receive it. However, we are also thinking beings and have difficulties with understanding what faith means, and with many of the claims of monotheism. We are conscious of our frailty and contingency. Even though we search, we often do not find satisfying solutions; therefore we pray for the gift of intelligence, for an illumination of our minds. This faith then becomes a prayer and turns out to be a hope, a companion on our pilgrimage who spurs us to go on and not to stop. This faith is humble and trusts in the very God which one does not understand—and is aware that one cannot understand. Faith is this intellectual openness toward the infinite.[32]

(Paris: Aubier, 1966), 17-63.

31 Cf. *Summ. Theol.* I, q. 32, a. I ad 2.

32 See "Faith as a Constitutive Human Dimension," in Panikkar, *Myth, Faith, and Hermeneutics* (New York: Paulist Press, 1979), 187-229.

This first internal critique of monotheism leads to an understanding of faith in the sense of *intellectus* fidei, this time as subjective genitive—that is, as faith understands itself. This faith opens us up to the divine Mystery, but as long as we are on our earthly pilgrimage—*viatores* says the christian tradition—we cannot see God as an object of our knowing powers. Faith is not the "beatific vision"; it is existentially directed toward God but not toward God as an object. On the other hand, faith is not directed toward other beings. Faith, therefore, has no object; it is an existential openness to the Mystery.

This implies that from the strict standpoint of monotheistic faith we cannot draw any doctrinal conclusion. Faith is not belief, and since ancient times a distinction has been made between the act of faith and the articles of faith. This means that from the standpoint of monotheistic faith we can say very little about monotheism as a doctrine—which fits in with our second critique.

(2) An Unknown God

A second example goes under the dictum of *theologia negativa*. This approach is not directed, like the first, to refining and deepening our notion of faith, but instead tries to purify our notion of God by stressing the "infinite *agnōsia*" (unlimited ignorance), the "beam of darkness," "learned ignorance," the "cloud of Unknowing," the *nescire,* the *toda sciencia transcendiendo* and many other expressions which indicate that the thinking and language about God transcend all our "normal" categories. Our only adequate approach to the mystery of the Divine is the silence of all our faculties, not by a violent act of the will but by an experience of the utter emptiness of that God. We cannot say anything about it because in itself it is ineffable. To use any notion of God, therefore, as an ideology for dominion or any other purpose is an abuse of power, and ultimately a blasphemy.

This second critique also softens the absolute claims of monotheism by taking the "Absolute" ab-solutely—that is, by disolving all its *kataphatic*, affirmative assertions in utter silence and discovering the very Emptiness of the Absolute— otherwise it would not be Ab-solute. Paradoxically, the monotheistic affirmations are thus relativized as human ways of speaking and representing reality. Absolute transcendence has to lose its absolute transcendence when entering into relation with us. Again, paradoxically, the often persecuted *apophatic* and mystical interpretations of monotheism remain its last defense. As the Upanishad sings, God survives hidden in the "cave of the heart."[33]

33 SU 3, 20; see CU 8, 3, 3; BU 5, 3, 1; KathU 2, 20; etc.

The problem remains how to combine an *apophatic* with a *kataphatic* monotheism. Neither extreme by itself is convincing, as history shows and the intellect confirms. *Apophatic* mystics write and certainly speak. *Kataphatic* thinkers contradict one another and their own affirmations become obsolete or are even proved to be wrong with the passing of time. As a matter of fact, there is coexistence between the two with greater or lesser tensions in between.

The positive result of the symbiosis is the relativization of both. There is always a silence behind any affirmation that makes room for other possible formulations. There is always an implicit word behind any silence that does not permit pure nihilism or utter indifference.

The problem remains and is not solved dialectically, because silence is not the negation of the word nor is word the negation of silence. Their relation is nondualistic. They are neither one nor two, but it is not enough to keep silent in order to be in the truth, and to use words does not necessarily mean to fall into error. What concerns our inquiry is this: Monotheism is not an absolute truth but a human reaction in the face of the mystery of the Deity, which is legitimate although not unique, genial although not without loopholes. It is needless to stress that this relativity is not relativism.

(3) The Historical Touchstone

Our third example is the more historical approach which consists in applying the maxim "by their fruits ye shall know [them],"[34] and in criticizing the particularly virulent interpretations of the monotheistic spirit that have led into totalitarianisms of all sorts. This critique is pertinent because, unlike other religious worldviews, monotheism takes history, as well as providence, very seriously. This world is not an illusion and history matters. Indeed, we cannot dump on monotheism all the historical horrors committed under its banners nor make of divine Providence a ferocious guardian of Law and Order. Nonetheless, after millennia of blunders, many of them religiously "justified" as punishment, will of God, or what not, it is more than legitimate to ask whether there is not something weak or even wrong in the monotheistic belief.

Without necessarily subscribing to any materialistic analysis of reality, it is opportune to note the congruence between the framework in which the idea of God as Supreme Being is meaningful, and a certain sociological and political order. The titles of King and Lord fit the monotheistic God quite well, and, conversely, the human king could easily be the representative

34 Mt VII, 16.

of the God, and his retinue a copy of the heavenly hierarchies. "Authority [ἐχουσία] comes from God."[35] Political theocracies may be either cause or effect, but the correspondence is there. For starters, God is not a democrat because God does not belong to the *dēmos*.

This is the crux of the discussion, rekindled by Erik Peterson, that has lately been drawn out in detail by many others.[36] Instead of retelling and emphasizing the dangers and abuses of monotheism, this last critique asks for causes and whether these aberrations are built into its very idea. Monotheism has been the justification of conquests, crusades, empires, and colonialist exploitations since times immemorial. Nowadays monotheism is no longer inspiring political empires or monarchies, but it remains the paradigm for the dominant ideology of our times: globalization. It is the same monotheism in more or less disguised and disfigured forms—one Global Market, one Democracy, one World Government, one Technocracy, and so on—which are flexible enough to allow for varieties of colors and shapes within the overall monotheistic tableau. Significantly enough, all these newer forms retain the most precious attribute of monotheism: transcendence. There are many mansions in the Father's palace. The "World Order" also pretends to be transcendent. Nobody in good faith today wants to impose a fascist uniformity, although the real danger is there. A positive result of this critique is that it unveils the danger involved in any powerful idea, ideology, or system. *Corruptio optimi pessima* (the corruption of the best is the worst), as the ancients said. The abuses cannot condemn the uses, but should put us on our guard.

We are dealing with a criticism from within, not from the outside. If, for instance, somebody should say that fascism belongs to the essence of christianity or that the elimination of the palestinians from the land of Israel is a divine right of judaism, we might not have any way to argue against the will of a monotheistic God. However, we take exception to the two examples by virtue of the internal norms of those particular religions. Regardless of certain forms of fundamentalism, christianity and judaism clearly show that human freedom and love of neighbor belong to the kernel of their message.

This is a critique from (the only) standpoint that an allegedly revealed monotheism must legitimately allow: its human reception. There is no doubt that monotheism is either an almost satanic idea that postulates an Absolute unreachable to any argument, feeling, and human power, or a fruit of the

35 Cf. Rm XIII, 1.

36 Erik Peterson, *Der Monotheismus als politisches Problem* (Munich: Kösel, 1951; 1st ed., Leipzig, 1935).

experience of a direct revelation of that selfsame God. This reminds me of the profound and ironical statement of that great muslim saint Al-Hallaj: "There never has been among the denizens of heaven any other monotheist [*muwaḥḥid*] comparable to Satan."[37]

The fact that the monotheistic belief has been spread all over the world for millennia makes the first horn of the dilemma somewhat improbable. It is, however, a cunning pitfall worthy of Lucifer to undermine the "reign of God" by whispering to human ears a belief that is so impossible to follow that the human race will voluntarily surrender to the "prince of this world." While this argument is worthy of *Iblis*, it may be too foreign for a secularized modern mentality. We might as well assume that monotheism is the outcome of the belief in a "divine revelation," thereby taking monotheistic belief very seriously. We leave unexamined what this revelation may be and take it at its face value.

This "divine revelation," of course, has to fall on human grounds in order to be a belief for humans. This belief may be the fruit of a personal, or even collective, experience of a speaking Deity, or a divine self-disclosure, but in any case it is a human experience, humanly interpreted, and humanly received into the collective consciousness of a culture at a given time. Here again the insights of the "sociology of knowledge" are appropriate. It is understandable that in periods of absolute monarchies and other absolutisms the idea of the Divine takes the form of a monotheistic God. After all, a divine Monarch may be more kind (more human, one is tempted to say) than an absolute ruler on earth. We have no grounds to doubt the authenticity of so many monotheistic witnesses, but we have to understand them within the context from which they proceed.

Even as an actual revelation of God monotheism needs to be interpreted. It is a particular interpretation of a genuine experience: that of being overwhelmed by a divine presence—already making use of words that are not neutral (neutral words do not exist). This divine presence Man has experienced as the revelation of a Supreme Being. This is the Achilles' heel for any critique of monotheism. The experience of the theophany is interpreted with and within the light of our human context: God is the celestial King, the divine Emperor, the supreme Ruler. This critique targets not the possible authenticity of a divine revelation (which is a different problem), but its interpretation. This gives us a respectful way to reinterpret the theophanic experience within a different framework both as it concerns us, because we live in a different context from our predecessors, and as it concerns God,

37 Mansur Al-Hallaj *Kitab al Tawasin*, VI.

precisely because this God is a living God—we need not assume that he has to repeat himself.

Because monotheism is taken to be the archetype of all theisms, the critique of monotheism, when radical enough, is not satisfied with leaning toward other types of theisms but will tend to eliminate God altogether from the human scene. Furthermore, because God is considered to be the only or at least the best archetype of that other dimension of reality which is called the Divine, many of those criticisms throw out the baby with the bathwater and chop off the Divine from the real, and certainly from all human affairs.

My position, on the contrary, is neither naively iconoclastic nor satisfied with a reformed monotheism. It recognizes the valid insight of belief in God, but at the same time it acknowledges that God is not the only symbol for that third dimension that we call the Divine, and it attempts to deepen the human experience of the Divine by formulating it more convincingly for our times.

This middle way criticizes what I term "Ancient Answers" without eliminating that third dimension about whose nature we may disagree but which nevertheless is a real "factor" in the universe—one of whose names is precisely God. It may be healthy and prudent to retain that name, at least in certain parts of the world.

b) Philosophical

I come now to three traditional attributes of the monotheistic God—substantiality, omnipotence, and omniscience—and will try to show that they do not necessarily belong to monotheism. First, they are not part of divine revelation; as their very name says, they are attributes. If I succeed I may pave the way for a radical transformation of monotheism without spoiling the deepest insight of monotheism.

I could eliminate the following pages by saying that even in the unlikely event that God were to reveal doctrines, they would have to be interpreted and thus understood by human minds. Furthermore, even if, in accordance with a divine promise, there were some infallible interpreters, their interpretations should not contradict each other, and much less within a single tradition over the ages—which is not the case among the many monotheisms. Besides, the infallible interpreters should in turn be infallibly interpreted by the believers of that tradition, which is hardly the case. All those thirdhand interpretations certainly cannot claim to have received a direct divine revelation. In view of the following part, however, and skipping any technical philosophical discussion, I prefer to raise a few more concrete considerations.

(1) Substantiality

The genesis of the western notion of monotheism constitutes an intriguing chapter in the history of philosophy. The hypothesis I would advance is that western, mainly christian and later muslim monotheism, is a blend of biblical monotheism and the hellenic mind represented mainly by Plotinus—although later jewish thought has also played an active and passive role in the formation of our present-day syncretistic monotheism. Neither Plato nor Aristotle (with apologies to high scholasticism) was a strict monotheist. It was Plotinus who articulated the monotheistic worldview that has served as the basis for western monotheism. It is interesting to know that Plotinus, unlike his beloved disciple Porphyrius, never criticized christianity. Is it perhaps too far-fetched to surmise that Plotinus's silence concerning christianity is due to the fact that he drew from it his inspiration for a monotheistic worldview?

Monotheism introduces us to a Supreme Being, an individual Supreme Being, so individual that the very notion of another is contradictory. There can be only one Supreme Being. Otherwise, how could it be absolutely Supreme? God is the Supreme Individual, which possesses to an eminent degree all the characteristics of the highest individuality to be encountered here on earth—the human person. What precisely makes Man a human person is a non-transferable individuality. God is absolutely Supreme and beyond all genus. God is Person, that is, Intellect, Will, and Action; as we saw, God is the unique Individual par excellence. This uniqueness is grounded in the absolute character of God's individuality.

The birth of individuality is a much-discussed topic both in the West and in other cultures as a result of western influence. Although the problems are complex and ambivalent, one thing emerges unmistakably: monotheism is no interloper on the scene but figures prominently from the start. The monotheistic God plays a decisive role in the birth of modern western individualism. If God is an individual, the ideal for Man will be to become a perfect individual in its genus. This idea also makes sense the other way round, that is, we make God the Supreme Individual because we discover ourselves as individuals. "I am the Lord your God . . . you shall have no other Gods besides me."[38] Is this individuality or uniqueness? In point of fact, we may understand uniqueness in two ways. We may detect the uniqueness of a flower by noticing its difference (from everything else and from all the other flowers). We then apply the principle of non-contradiction to reach the uniqueness of the individual flower: it is not like any other flower; no other

38 Ex XX, 2-3; cf. Dt V, 6.

flower has that (unique) fragrance. Among the many flavors, the fragrance of our flower is different.

Or we may detect the uniqueness of a flower by not noticing anything else but that flower. Its identity in being flower is so total that we cannot see any "other" flower outside of or independently of "our" flower. We have eyes and senses only for the Beloved and for nothing else. We cannot find other flowers. We apply the principle of identity to penetrate the real being (essence) of that (unique) flower. That individual flower is *the* flower (for us).

In the first case, uniqueness implies difference: there is no other flower like this flower; it is different, and this difference makes its uniqueness. In the second case, uniqueness implies incomparability: we cannot compare because we cannot differentiate it from anything (we see God everywhere). There is only the flower and that flower is simply Flower. We are so taken by the fragance, form, color, or overall beauty of our flower that no comparison is possible; we find that beauty everywhere. That beauty which we cannot really extricate from anything is unique. These are two different worldviews, or ways of apprehending reality.[39]

In the first case, uniqueness is somewhat quantifiable. It is an individual unity in a series. In the second case, uniqueness is such precisely because it is not quantifiable—it is not a number of a series. The unique being is so identical with itself that it does not leave room for any comparison. In the first case, all beings are unique because different. According to the second case, all beings are unique because no difference is detectable. In the first case, uniqueness is individuality. In the second, uniqueness is the totality. In the first case, if we eliminate a member of the human race, we suppress a number in the series; in the second, we wound or transform the whole series. In the first understanding, we are individual monads. In the second understanding, we are individual reflections or images of the whole. From the second point of view, differences are detectable only against a common background (or common denominator). This means that individual differences are not unique since they share that commonality. Something is absolutely unique if there is no common background to share.

These two different worldviews entail two different anthropologies: Man as an individual versus Man as a microcosm. Knowledge as an individual affair versus knowledge considered as an aspect or quality of the real in which we share in different degrees. The soul that is a living atom, or the soul that in a certain way is all things—as we are going to say. In sum, there are two different ways of experiencing reality.

39 See Panikkar, *Le mystère du culte dans l'hindouisme et le christianisme* (Paris: Cerf, 1970), 37-39.

We are here in the presence of a truly cross-cultural paradox. The prevalent quantitative (mathematical) sensitivity (our first case) will defend the dignity of the individual because of the different singularity of each member of the series. Each number has to affirm its personality by being different, by creating or doing something that the others do not do—by being useful, in a word. We may imprison or even eliminate harmful members in order to keep the series healthy. Should I mention the contemporary discussions on the death penalty?

The prevalent qualitative (emotional or aesthetic?) sensitivity will equally defend the dignity of the person because a person is an image, an icon of the whole. Each member is—re-presents—the series. Each member embodies the entire species, as each angel in the vision of the scholastics is a species in and by itself. Each member has to affirm its personality by being an undistorted image of the whole by being pure—that is, purely itself. We have to eliminate the dust or dirt that has tarnished a particular image, which also may need forceful polishing (but not by throwing away the dust in the air). I am the more myself the more the self is not "my" self, but the Self—in a unique way

The cross-cultural paradox lies in the fact that those cultures that seem to be more sensitive to the individual seem to give priority to the greater efficiency of some members, thus neglecting most individuals. On the other hand, those cultures which seem to be more sensitive to the whole seem to concentrate on those few who may reflect the whole better, thus neglecting the great mass of individuals. This example shows that those two thought paradigms and their two different visions of the world need a thorough revision. Neither individualism nor collectivism seems convincing. We have mentioned several times that we are at a turning point in history.

Uniqueness implies incommensurability and incomparability. God is not only One; it is also Unique; there is no other One. Its uniqueness has generally been seen in light of its incommensurability with any other being. It is unique because it is transcendent, beyond any possible measure with others. On the other hand, Brahman is also unique—to make a long story short by means of an example—not because it is different, but because it is the absolute self-identity, indistinguishable from anything else, and thus abides with perfect immanence (not some kind of negative transcendence) inside every being. From this standpoint the uniqueness of Brahman does not mean the same as the uniqueness of Yahweh.

The unique God of monotheism demands difference, transcendence, and superiority. The uniqueness of *Brahman* demands in-difference, immanence, and interiority—to use foreign categories for "brahmanism." That is what led me to say that "Vedic Monotheism" is a misleading phrase.

Now this sense of individuality by differentiation, complex and ambivalent as it is, is far from being a common human heritage. Atomism in its widest and also deepest sense is not the only framework for human life. Besides the individual God there is the irretrievable *brahman*; besides the world order formed by individuals—whether subatomic particles, things, Men, or angels—there is another type of universe that is more kaleidoscopic, as if the differing manifestations of reality were without individual consistency. In such a universe everything is a part of everything else, so that any attempt to isolate things is already methodologically flawed. The factors of the real are not isolatable, but flashes of reality that share, reflect, refract, and shape the Whole in "moments" of time, space, and spirit. In short, there are other worldviews, which have succeeded in providing a cultural habitat for entire civilizations, that do not subscribe to the premises of monotheism. The challenge of our times is the creation of a "culture of peace," which extends especially to this religious domain.

* * *

This long preface is meant to introduce the word that we have not yet mentioned, although announced in the title: the substantiality of God. God as Being is often considered synonymous with God as individual substance. God is the only one and unique individual substance. This is another key word with many meanings. To be sure, from the *ousia* and *hypostasis* of Aristotle, the *hypokeimenon* of christian theologians, to the *substance* of modern philosophers, there is an immense gamut of opinions even among those who are believing monotheists. We could venture (a great venture indeed) to sum up all these diverse notions saying that *substance* stands formally for a sort of *subject*: an ontological, epistemological, pragmatic, empirical, psychological, synthetic, or dialectical subject. The word "subject" stands for an ultimate point of reference according to different philosophical conceptions.

There is no doubt that the classical monotheistic idea of substantiality is close to the aristotelian *substance* as the standing support of all the different accidents. The already quoted symposium of philosophers to discuss the nature of God says, "God is that in the face of which the substance is an accident, and the accident nothing."[40] All substances, all substantial things are just qualifications, aspects, contingencies, accidents ("parasites" I am tempted to translate) for that unique Ground, Basis, Support, Foundation,

40 *Liber XXIV philosophorum*, VI: "Deus est cuius comparatione substantia est accidens, et accidens nihil."

and Substance which is God. Substance is what is in itself and by itself: *ens a se*.

Monotheism is therefore almost forced to say that, properly speaking, there is only one substance, the divine Substance. The classical doctrine of creation affirms that there is only one single individual substance, God, but at the same time an indefinite number of created substances, knots of a second degree, sustaining the different accidents that inhere in those secondary substances—since they are not *a se* (in themselves), but *ab alio* (from another), not in-dependent, but depending on the only Substance.

It is not necessary here to explain or criticize the concept of substance. My only point is to show that the notion of substance is not essential to the monotheistic idea of God—and is certainly not revealed. To begin with, no attribute is revealed. An attribute is a product of our intellectual operation. *We* attribute a quality to a certain being because *we* see it directly linked with the being in question. It is a human idea, not a divine revelation. Now, any encounter with the Divine, in as far as it is a real encounter, will convince us that God is a reality. We may say that the Divine reveals itself as real, as a reality. Our mental habits tend to let us think that something really existent is not only independent of our mind, but a center of activity—that is, a substance. It is a widespread way of thinking and a very legitimate idea, but it is our construction, not a revelation, not something immediately given—unless substance is identified with reality—which would present other philosophical difficulties. In other words, to affirm that God is not a substance or that it does not need to be a substance is not to deny the reality of God, nor its existence (in the common sense of the word).

Ultimately the oneness of anything is a tautology—a transcendental, as the scholastics called it. The oneness of God, however, is a double-edged sword. On the one hand, it stands for *unicity* so that its non-numerical oneness makes it impossible to discriminate this "one" from another "one" God. If they were two monotheistic Gods, they would coalesce. On the other hand, one stands for *universality*: "Our" God is the one unique God, because it is the universal God. The historical consequences of this are demonstrated by the innumerable wars waged in the name of God.

In this framework, if other peoples adore other Entities which they call Gods, they are not the true and the only unique God. They have to be, if at all, minor Gods, lower beings when not false Gods. Despite a few contemporary thinkers for whom space and time are more than physical coordinates or kantian categories, for the average modern mentality today the statement that truth is one seems glaringly obvious. We tend to believe that if something is true it has to be universal, because the claim to universality belongs to the very nature of truth. Moreover, this universality is taken to be the very criterion of truth: if we can universalize our code of conduct, it must be the supreme ethical rule; mathematics are true, so they must be neutral and universal. Monotheism belongs to the same family, or rather, monotheism is the *pater familias* of that way of thinking. Monotheism has built into it the claim to be universal. If there is a single God, a Supreme Being, this can only be a God of All, and for All. Now a totally apophatic Deity without attributes, a *nirguṇa brahman*, an Unknown Divinity, a pure śūn*yatā*, may claim to be universal because there is nothing in the claim that can be contradicted, except eventually the claim itself—which will only reinforce the *apophatic* position. But if God is also *kataphatic*, he will have attributes. And those attributes will also have to be universal.

The only monotheistic explanation for those who are not (yet) monotheists is that they have not yet realized its truth and are still entangled in provincialisms of one sort or another. The revealed monotheisms assert this in so many words: No salvation without the one God—regardless of various theological subtleties (e.g., invincible ignorance, *in voto*, eschatological salvation . . .). This amounts to saying that the revealed monotheisms are universal because they recognize only a single way to reach salvation.

Revelational monotheisms—here the abrahamic religions are the paradigm—imply a God who speaks Something to Somebody, Sometime. This Something ("you are my people," "you are my Son," here is the Book, . . .). This Somebody (Moses, the Prophet . . .) and this Sometime (*anno Domini*, *Hegira*, Common Era, . . .) are privileged contents and moments immediately elevated to the level of God. I refer in passing to the monotheistic and even colonialist flavor of the incipient north american habit of using the phrase "Common Era" that imposes on other chronologies a qualitative judgment. Everything has to be structured in a congruent manner by an organization sanctioned as of divine origin, above all the others. Before or after Christ is not judgmental (and not even an historical truth) whereas to call "common" a time reckoning which was not common at all betrays the modern blindness of monotheistic globalization.

All this may be a fact, but it cannot sustain the claim to a genuine universality. It entails a very particular concept of universality, which is linked to what a particular group thinks or believes universality to be. In order to understand monotheism, for instance, one has to accept history as the paramount arena of God's revelation, time as really divided into a time before and a time after the Event, some spaces not just sacred but unique places, and some particular institutions existing by divine right. To be sure, the human pilgrimage may still follow a wide road, and lanes of different dimensions and qualities will be allowed, but it is all a march down a single avenue; the valley is one, the peak is single, the Omega Point is unique.

There is equally no doubt that there have long been multisecular societies, traditions, and civilizations that have lived under very different assumptions. It all hangs together. Neither the idea of universality nor the notion of individuality would appear convincing if they were not linked by the overall string of linear time. By linear I do not mean straight, but following a continuous line. In a word, *evolution*: the revelation of historical evolution to begin with, and the discovery of biological evolution that followed on its heels. Even today, it is evident that not all people agree with this idea of universality, just as it is obvious that monotheism still has not convinced everyone either. The common western assumption is that some peoples and cultures have not "yet" arrived at "our" stage of evolution. There has undoubtedly been wandering and even regression but on the whole, monotheism believes that we are proceeding toward a single goal—"development" is inevitable. In this always tantalizingly "imminent" *eschaton*, the universality is finally going to be—is already being—realized. The anticipated universality is only a function of time; all that is needed is a little patience. This is the monotheistic mentality visibly straining to put up with the obvious fact that its expected universalization never quite comes to pass. So it plays for time—even offering a prophetic eschatology, if need be, in economic or scientific or technological terms.

The evolutionist frame of mind is simple enough. It tends to consider everything a function of its subsequent evolution. In such a framework, we have passed from a rude conception of Deity, even a polytheistic one, to the more refined monotheistic belief. It should be added in passing that atheism repays monotheism in its own coin, considering it a progress compared with polytheism, but still immature and "undeveloped" compared to atheism. In terms of a certain temporal conception, *homo sapiens* has no doubt made some relative progress since first learning to walk upright. Nevertheless, Thomas Aquinas reveals an equally dynamic vision of reality, without linear evolution: "All things, by desiring their own perfection, desire God Himself, inasmuch as the perfections of all things are so many similitudes of the divine being." [41]

---

41 Thomas Aquinas, *Summ. Theol.* I, q. 6, a.1 ad 2: "Omnia, appetendo proprias perfectiones, appetunt ipsum Deum, inquantum perfectiones omnium rerum sunt quaedam similitudines divini esse."

This progress, however, has been neither straight, nor linear, nor without points of discontinuity, nor absolute. Once physical and linear time is taken as a pattern for understanding Man, there is no difficulty in accepting ups and downs, or even temporary regressions and "recessions." There might also have been diachronical lines of evolution: Africa may have gone one way, Asia another. The question is deeper than finding data for or against a certain idea of progress. The question, to which I shall return, has to do with time and history. For the moment, I will only say that here, as hardly anywhere else, it becomes patent that one finds *what* one is looking for—and *where* one looks for it. What self-awareness underlies this type of search? I am not criticizing here the socalled theory of evolution, or proposing another cosmology, or accepting any of the traditional ones along the lines of the *philosophia perennis*. It has recently been done by S. H. Nasr in his Gifford Lectures.[42] Nor will I spend time on the points where evolution is most feeble—logical inconsistencies, inadequate empirical verification, unwarranted social extrapolations, and the like—even on its own terms. My concern here is rather with the *forma mentis* that gives rise to all this. My approach is simply cross-cultural and centers on a criticism of the most uncritically accepted definitions of Man: the rational animal.

Leaving aside the original Aristotelian formula (*zōor echon logon*), which says that Man is a living being through which the logos transits, I still find fault with Aristotle not for his fascinating statement (*legein*) about the *logos* in the best hellenic tradition, but precisely for the classificatory genius of the western mind which he exhibits in such a genial way. We shall never come to understand what Man really is unless we do away with the biased and, ultimately, erroneous starting point of an objective classification of a porphyrian tree. We shall never find Man in this way, even if afterwards we try to enhance the specific difference with something higher, and affirm that Man's rationality has been infused by God, or comes from some other source. Similarly, we blind ourselves to what a plant is, to take another example from further down the line of development, if we define it as "living organic matter," or if we consider the Moses of Michelangelo a "sculptured block of marble." I criticize such a starting point as well as the assumption behind it. The former obliges us to look in the wrong direction. The only thing one may be able to find is an animal endowed with language, thought, and some other marvelous qualities, which at great pains can afterwards be glued together with the underlying common animality. No matter how Man's specific difference is separated and flattered, it remains forever stuck in

42 Seyyed Hossein Nasr, *Knowledge & the Sacred* (New York: Crossroad, 1981).

the biological chain of beings. Once started on this path, the most plausible outcome is indeed the evolution of species.

A more important problem is the assumption behind this method. The assumption is that in order to know what Man is we have to look back and not on high, to analyze and decompose without recourse to a more synthetic human power which may reflect what we truly are instead of just what we are made of. The assumption I am criticizing is the apparent poverty of ontological introspection, which is not the same thing as psychological analysis. In order to know what Man is, one looks at attributes like speech or bipedalism (or else investigates how an individual feels), instead of discovering in the deepest recesses of the human being the entire universe, the microcosm, the true ātman, the *tao*, the *logos*, the uncreated *Fünklein*, the trinity, I would say, or the like.

This tallies again with the individualism mentioned already: Man appears to be an individual of a species belonging to a genus, and then to a zoological phylum, differentiated from a wider series of objects called vegetables, these latter emerging from alleged minerals, and so on down to the molecular and atomic and subatomic levels. No wonder we have such a low opinion of ourselves—and of everything else—since we seem unable to come up with a better theory than the evolution of species by random natural selection. Why do those stubborn theologians still insist on trying to make Man an exception? This is anathema to the modern mentality. If reality is really made of such elements, and evolution a "fact," as is so often reiterated, what kind of troublemaker is this human being that, after being placed in its niche, seems so restless, stirs so uncomfortably, and even tries to break out? After all, Nobel laureate James Watson has recently assured us that the Human Genome Project—a vast multi-national research program to "decipher" the entire three-billion-letter sequence of DNA in the chromosomes of a human cell—contemporary biology's "Holy Grail"—is the definitive quest "to find out what being human is." Should we not be content simply to await the answer? Perhaps I need only say that, all in all, the universality of monotheism, even when smoothed over by an evolutionary process, has not turned out to be a very universal way of seeing either the divine Mystery or the entire reality.

* * *

All in all monotheism affirms that God is a substance because it wants to say that God is real; he is not an accident, therefore he is a substance. Furthermore monotheism affirms that God is One, and although this oneness is not a number, the combination of the two affirmations has led monotheism to affirm that God is the One Substance, the one substantial Being. This brings monotheism into the Scylla of pantheism (one single [divine] Substance) or the Charybdis of idealism (all the rest is not real—since there is no room for anything else).

(2) Omnipotence

Another unmistakable and popular claim of monotheism is that God is allpowerful. I am not going to elaborate the in-house tension within the christian tradition when trying to blend the hebrew notion of a historical God of a particular people (although creator of heaven and earth) with a metaphysical God of greek influence. Nor am I going to criticize the later interpretation of the *pantokratôr* of the first christian creeds as meaning an omnipotent absolute Being. *Omnia-potens* and not *omni-potens* was the first translation. The "omnipotence" of the primitive christian creed did not mean the absolute power of a super-demiurge, but the relatively "absolute" power of a monarch in the fashion of a roman emperor. The *pantokratōr* has power (*kratos*) over all (*pantos*) his people and even over all (*pan*) the cosmos, power *over* all, but not an absolute Power. This is, incidentally, what the christian creed says. It does not say: "I believe in an omnipotent God (or Being, or divine Omnipotence)." It confesses: "I believe in an almighty Father" (not even in an almighty tyrant, who would by the same token cease to be Father).

My point is that if the oneness of the monotheistic God is just a tautology interpreted in a very particular way, the omnipotence of the same God is diplomatic court language applied to a divine monarch. Outside of this context, the omnipotence of God needs a radical reinterpretation. The *theos* of the three abrahamic monotheisms was not the Being of later scholasticism. In other words, theological fullness of power has little to do with metaphysical omnipotence. One may retort that the creation of heaven and earth or the creation of Man entails more than the enhanced political power of a *pantokratōr*. Certainly. The power to let a flower blossom out of a small seed, an animal appear out of the conjunction of two cells, or even the universe be out of nothing prior to it, is more than a moral power. It is undoubtedly a divine power inherent in the nature of things, but different from the alleged omnipotence of the will of a monotheistic God who, despite being all-powerful and good, "permits" the existence of evil. This is the strength of evolutionism, that there is an immanent power in Nature that transcends the so-called natural sciences.

Divine power, as in the examples of nature, is immanent in the nature of things themselves, which brings us much closer to the trinity of the cosmotheandric insight I shall present later. Divine full-power is not disconnected from the (divine) potency inherent in the very nature of beings. It is not the omnipotence of a separated God, commanding from the outside. It is not the omnipotence of the will.

This question, since ancient times, has been a conundrum to monotheistic minds. How can there be a Most Blessed Supreme Just, Good, and Omnipotent Being if we are still languishing in a most unblessed, unjust, and wretched state? How can we affirm that this God loves us, and even more, has made us? Being omnipotent, could God not have created us better? That in order to create us free God was bound to allow our free will to go against his Will and choose evil is a very weak argument—besides the fact that to put on our shoulders the burden of the entire evil of the world does not explain either how a just and omnipotent God allows that we have to suffer from the bad *karma* of our ancestors. The suffering of the innocent may be explained by *karma*, but not by an omnipotent and good God. The argument of freedom is weak on three mutually related accounts at least.

First of all, if freedom entails the capacity of doing evil, God is not free, since being absolute Goodness he cannot do evil. To retort that he does not do evil because he does not want is not convincing. Why does he not want it? Can he or can he not? If he cannot, he is not free. If he can and does not do it, it is meaningless, because whatever an infinite good God would do would be good— unless we postulate a moral code above God himself which he is obliged to obey, whereby his omnipotence fades away. If our human will can overrule divine will, his will is not almighty. Already Saint Augustine (whose concern was predestination) distinguished between freedom (*libertas*) and free will (*liberum arbitrium*). God is free; but he does not need free will.

Second, the conception of freedom used in the argument is not really freedom, but whim. Freedom is not caprice. Freedom is precisely the contrary of desire. Without delving into the buddhist analysis of desire, a desire is the opposite of freedom. A desire entails precisely the captivity of our will, which finds itself conditioned and determined by the desired object. If we yield, we are thereby free *from*, but not necessarily free *to*. We may conclude that we do not possess free will, but then the argument collapses and reverts to the problem of evil.

Third, the very assumption that there is a will of God who could have created us so or so, happy or unhappy, with free will or without it is a crude anthropomorphism. We have free will, because our freedom is not almighty; it is both limited by our finite power and conditioned by the object we will. A divine free will has no such restrictions, not even the restriction of having to have a will in order to do anything. A will has to will something. If this something either does not exist or is created by the same will, a free will makes no sense at all. In short, an omnipotent Will is an anthropomorphic extrapolation where such an extrapolation does not belong. The will of God is his own nature, which, when we become aware of his action, we interpret anthropomorphically as will. The "Thy will be done" of the "Our Father" is a powerful prayer to surrender our will to an inscrutable Power which liberates us from our selfish desires. The aspiration of our inmost being to happiness, peace, and perfection is not the (selfish) desire to realize ourselves, to reach heaven or to acquire perfection. The very desire to *nirvāṇa* is the greatest obstacle to reach it, says the Buddha; the very desire to enjoy the result of our good works tarnishes the purity of the action, teaches the *Bhagavad-gītā*; if our left hand knows the good deed of our right, the action is of no avail, proclaims Jesus; anything not done gratuitously by pure love has no value whatsoever, teach practically all traditions. This attitude could be summed up as: all is grace.

The truly formidable problem for monotheism lies elsewhere: in the existence and nature of evil. How can an omnipotent God condone evil? It would take us too far afield to deal with this question here. My only point at this juncture is to sketch the difficulties of monotheism. "Either an omnipotent God or I (we)!" was (and still is, but more subdued) the desperate cry of atheistic existentialism. Many different attempts have been made to resolve the dilemma. They reduce themselves to reforming either the notion (*a*) of God, or (*b*) of Man.

(a) God

1. Such a Deity does not exist. It is all either a projection of human impotence and dreams, or else a remnant of primitive magical thinking, or both— which is then exploited by the powers that be in order to maintain a political and social status quo. The Deity is an imaginary one, perhaps heuristically needed as a theoretical point of epistemic convergence.
2. The Deity is not in such a blessed state, but is itself involved in the struggles of the World in general, and of Man in particular. We have to change our vision of the Divine. God also suffers, or becomes incarnate, or descends, and is part and parcel of what we call the universe. Evil is also a mysterious aspect of the Deity.
3. The Deity, on the contrary, is so utterly transcendent that it does not mingle in human or cosmic affairs. It is eventually the only reality and the rest is mere appearance. Or if we are the real beings and the Divine is utter Nothingness.

4. God is not such a Supreme Being, but just a shall-be God at the end of the entire cosmic struggle. God is the absolute Future that gives us hope to continue on our pilgrimage.

(b) Man

5. Real Man does not exist in such a miserable state. Suffering and disorder are only apparent and certainly not ultimate. Our ignorance is the result of a cosmic process. Such a belief in the aberrant reality of the world is either a projection of our conceit and ambitions, or else a remnant of immature or uncritical thinking that cannot yet distinguish the real from the unreal.
6. Man is not in such a desperate situation. Man is also involved in the divine reality, and all that we have to struggle with here and now is only the means or the occasion for developing our potential divinity. Involved in the divine destiny, we partake of the divine nature, and we shall eventually ascend to that blessed state. Our suffering is provisional and a springboard to real life.
7. Man is so utterly corrupt that what we complain about is only the desperate cry of our conceit or our hubris. Such is reality and it is of no use to deceive ourselves by sugarcoating it.
8. Man is the great illusion. Such a being does not exist. What exists is a world in a state of flux and fermentation so that it is pointless to concoct theories before the eschatological finale, whether glorious or catastrophic.

To sum up: omnipotence is not an absolute attribute of God.

(3) Omniscience

This is another *strong* and *weak* point of monotheism. The *strength* of an all-knowing Being is clear: all the mystery of the world is concentrated in a single point and is eminently resolved there. The assumption is that God is infinite. This infinity is equivalent to immateriality (spirit) and/or knowledge. Knowledge, the *esse intentionale* of the scholastics, is assumed to be infinite because it is not limited by matter.

Intelligence is our highest gift. Man awakens as Man by an act of consciousness. Consciousness is the ultimate and irreducible bulwark of our openness to reality, the inseparable companion of Man. We know things because things are knowable; they are knowable because between things and our intellect there is a primordial relationship, which we have not established. It is precisely this relationship, as we noted earlier, which led Aristotle to affirm: ἡ ψυχὴ πάντα πῶς, and after him Thomas, *Anima quodammodo omnia*, that is, "the soul is somewhat all things." There is an air of identity between all things via the mediation of the intellect. The *pōs* or *quodammodo*, the "somewhat," or "in a certain way," has generally been interpreted in the restrictive sense of the *esse creatum,* the created being. A finite being, even if immaterial, is only everything or all "in a certain way." But within this universe of discourse it is assumed that a perfect intellect, a divine immaterial being—knows all, absolutely everything: it is omniscient—by reason of being present everywhere, in every being, it knows everything. All things are transparent to the Supreme Intelligence. The traditional doctrine says that God *is* everywhere because He *knows* everything—and knowledge implies presence.

We may stretch the meaning of the "certain way," the *quodammodo* in two ways. One way is traditionally used to differentiate God from creatures. The Creator, knowing all beings, is *quodammodo* all of them. The *quodammodo* of the infinite Intellect, however, preserves the distinction between Creator and created. God knows the creatures as creatures, in Itself but not as Itself. Here we have also a close connection with the theory of the *visio beatifica* (the vision of God in heaven), and with the traditional (often forgotten) notion of the divinization of Man, and of the whole cosmos: God becomes flesh so that the flesh may become God. God knows everything, because *in a certain way* he is everything.

The other way of interpreting the *quodammodo* is more rarely employed. The divine Intellect is "in a certain way" all things. In fact, it knows all things, and thus it is "in a certain way" all things. This *quodammodo* is that from the side of the Intellect. The Intellect knows all and therefore it is all—since perfect knowledge entails identification. It knows obviously all knowable beings, or rather, the fact that God knows them makes then knowable. Nothing of all that can be known escapes the divine Intelligence. It is all things insofar as it knows them, but this identity is only *quodammodo*—otherwise we would have pure pantheism. In other words, reality does not need to be totally transparent to the Intellect. Things are insofar as they are knowable, and there is no thing which is not knowable. The *quodammodo*, however, makes room for non-identity from the other side. Things do not need to be totally transparent to the Intellect, they may have an opaque side, a mystery of their own. It may be argued that God, having created everything, by this very fact knows them and is identified with them. Unless this identification is qualified, however, we have strict pantheism: God *is* all things and all things are God. The traditional answer, as we have already affirmed, consists in saying that God knows things as things and not as He, himself. There is therefore a difference: the divine ideas, the godly archetypes may be God, but not the incarnated or created archetypes. There is an ontological degradation, which is the creatureliness of the created reality. This difference may be the opaqueness suggested above. We are not claiming here that this opacity is identical to matter or to evil. We are simply saying that when monotheistic thinking affirms that there is only one God, that one divine Intellect knows everything and thus that everything can be reduced to a divine Unity, it is thinking in a circle.

Let me try to make this a little clearer. In order to understand anything, this anything has to be understandable, and it is only exhaustively understandable by the divine Intellect. I am not constructing an argument for the existence of God, but only saying that we have to postulate a further irreducible principle if we are to understand anything. It could very well be that this principle is only a heuristic device and does not exist. I am not discussing the ontological argument. I am saying that the intelligibility of the World, or of things, presupposes an Intelligence at least equal to the World itself. If we examine our own knowledge, we may have to add that this Intelligence has to be superior to the World it knows, for otherwise it would have to refer, as we do, to some other principle *et sic ad infinitum*. It will thus have to be a νόησις νοήσεως, a perfect self-consciousness, in Aristotle's phrase, or as monotheism will assert, an infinite Intelligence. God is omniscient, all-knowing.

God knows all, to be sure. God knows all that is knowable, and beings are knowable because they are known by the divine Intellect. Nonetheless, from here to inferring that God knows All, all Being and beings in their totality, implies that All is knowable, which is precisely what is under discussion, namely, whether Being is totally knowable, pure knowability, whether Being is consciousness, or conscious Being. So we identify the two, and again come round to equating thinking and Being. Perhaps thinking does not exhaust Being, perhaps Being has a dimension opaque to the Intellect. Perhaps not everything can be reduced to oneness. Being may not even be utterly reducible to consciousness, and consciousness may not be a faculty capable of reducing multiplicity to unity. The unity of the idea stone does not do away with the multiplicity of stones. I would add that, from the point of view of Being, this "reduction" does not need to be total. There is of course a difference between the stones and the idea of the stone but there is also a difference between the divine archetype stone and the created one. The monotheist may say that this difference (opacity) is still willed by God, but nevertheless it remains opaque. The traditional elucubrations boil down to simply offering a foundation for human confidence that the world makes sense. Although we may not understand it, it is transparent and understood by a divine Intelligence. This Intelligence is the foundation of our knowledge and our trust.

So far so good. But we mentioned a subtle circle. I do not call it a vicious circle, unless it is recognized. It is a constitutively unbreakable circle, once the problem is stated in this way. Here is where monotheism has a *weak* point. In fact, we may assume that there is such an infinite Intelligence that knows everything, and this by virtue of the postulate itself. We may even concede that this Intelligence exists, a divine omniscient Supreme Being who knows All.

Now this Intelligence can be identical with the monotheistic God under only one assumption: the identity between consciousness and reality, which for our purposes comes to the same as the identity between thinking and Being. Without this conscious identification we move in a vicious circle: It is all knowable because God knows it all, and God knows it all because it is all knowable.

In fact, an infinite Consciousness will know all, and by this act convert that all into the knowable. The divine Intellect scrutinizes everything, there is no way to hide from It. It knows all. All what? All that is knowable—even if it is made knowable by knowing it. Moreover, all that is knowable is all that there is. How do we "know" this? Only because we know, believe, or assume that God knows it all. Yet unless we independently and *a priori* identify all that is knowable with reality, we cannot say that the infinite Intelligence knows all reality. We will have to say that this Intelligence knows all knowable reality and that reality is knowable, but we have no guarantee, except our own postulate, that reality does not have an opaque side, as it were, something that is not transparent to Intelligence, something irreducible to the knowable/unknowable dilemma.

In brief, unless we subscribe to the classical interpretation of Parmenides ("It is the same to think and to be"[43]), we cannot assert that divine omniscience extends to the whole of reality. Omniscience knows no limits to itself. It knows all about anything that can be known; it knows all the knowable things and may even be infinitely making all things knowable. Irrespective of this, nothing would impinge upon its infinite Intelligence if reality had a dimension that is not covered by knowledge, or is not knowledge, unless *to know* and *to be* coalesce.

This is not an argument. I do not affirm that reality has an unknowable "side"—I cannot know it. I simply affirm that it could. Nonetheless, the

43 Parmenides, *Fragm.* 3: τὸ γὰρ αὐτὸ νοεῖν ἔστιν τε καὶ εἶναι. Cf. Plotinus, *Enneads* V, 1, 8.

purvapakṣin, the objector of indic philosophy, the *advocatus diaboli* of the western world (more juridically minded) will retort that this "could" entails again the same confidence in our logical mind which *thinks* the possibility of such a possibility. By so doing we have not yet broken the parmenidian bind between Thinking and Being. It is our thinking that "allows" Being to trespass that identity. Thinking sacrifices itself, as it were, on the altar of Being, but does so while still respecting its own principle of non-contradiction. This self-sacrifice of thinking is the highest tribute to thinking itself. It is the resurrection of thinking, its victory over Being. It is not for nothing that Saint Thomas calls the principle of non-contradiction a "holy" principle.

Our answer cannot be a dialectic *sic et non*, yes and no; that would still be within the domain of thinking—as the use of "cannot" already proves. Our answer leads us to swear (as the word "answer" suggests) that there is the realm of the mystical word which is silent, perhaps poetic and metaphysical—a word uttered by Being, which is the mediator to Thinking but which is not (yet?) thinking. An entire human tradition East and West "speaks" of Silence, Emptiness, Nothingness, the third eye, Ignorance, Unknowing, and the like. This *speaking*, this *logos* is the mediator between Thinking and Being, and we are aware of it with an awareness that is not (yet?) understanding.

The *yet* we have parenthetically interjected connotes the dynamic aspect of this process. We cannot stop at silence, or at non-thinking, and remain in nothingness or emptiness. The equilibrium is unstable. A bicycle stands while it runs; if it stops it falls to one side or the other. The third eye requires the other two.

What I am hinting at, returning to our subject, is that we may very well identify knowledge with Reality, but when we do so monotheism will have been transformed into an idealistic system—in favor of God as ultimate Knower, of course. Augustine interprets the platonic ideas as the divine archetypes. The Middle Ages wanted to reconcile platonic ontology with aristotelean epistemology; its failure opened the way to a constant irritant to monotheism—and ultimately to the Modern Age. In sum, the problem of monotheism lurks behind (and sometimes beyond) the history of the whole of western thought, which is not the case with the Orient.

4. *God and Being*

The just-mentioned difficulties, along with many others, have led to a slow transformation of monotheism. It is the passage from the notion of God as Supreme Being to God as Being, from *ens realissimum* to *ipsum esse* (*subsistens*). This implies a passage from a strict and rigid monotheism to a qualified monotheism, due mainly to the contribution of the mystics. One example is sufficient: if we compare the God of the orthodox islamic believer Abū Bakr Muḥammad ibn al-ʿArabī and the God of a literal reading of the Holy Qur'an.

Owing to what I have called the *inertia of the mind*, the word monotheism has remained, along with the congruent practices inherent to monotheism, while another notion has penetrated into the consciousness of many people, which is incompatible with strict monotheism, and yet *de facto* coexists with it. This coexistence, however, explicitly for some and implicitly for many, creates a climate of crisis from which we still suffer today. Contemporary studies of so-called popular religion are highly instructive: the cult of the saints is newly explained, apparent superstitions are reinterpreted, processions are justified psychologically, miracles are unraveled, and even demons are given an archetypal function. "Theologians" know very well that the "real" God smiles at all this, understands, even condones, but is not involved in it all. It takes Gulags, Auschwitzes, Hiroshimas, and massive earthquakes to call forth new theodicies. Either God is the Supreme Being above the contingencies of all those events, and this is monotheism; or God is Pure Being involved in the fate of beings, and this is not traditional monotheism.

* * *

Three words in the western world have sustained the struggle for primacy over the longest period: Being, Reality, and God. God, in this arena of ultimacy, was perhaps the latest comer among the contenders.[44] God came in, if not by the back door, then certainly through the gaping hole left by Being. Being, in fact, was too general, too vague, too polysemic, as Aristotle already saw: "Being is said in a manifold way."[45]

Man is interested in the real, but the real, once-raw empiricism is overcome, is also invisible, mathematical, ideational, and so forth. We may discuss the criteria for the real, but one criterion is incontrovertible: *Wirklichkeit*. The real is what works, what affects something. Some may call it, rightly understood, pragmatism.

Where does reality lie, in what does it consist, once we discover that it has to stretch from past to future, from visible to invisible, from material to spiritual, from rationality to things or events we cannot rationally account for, and yet are still real? What is the reality of the real, or the *satyasya satyam*,

44 See Panikkar, *The Silence of God* (Maryknoll, N.Y.: Orbis Books, 1989), 210ff.

45 Aristotle, *Met.* V, 7: τὸ ὂν πολλαχῶς λέγεται.

the truth of truth or the being of Being, as the sanskrit tradition will put it? Reality may be what works, *Wirklichkeit*, but, in a more subtle and humane way, reality may also be *res*, our property, our riches, and also, by a highly interesting formal and material concurrence, that which can be said, spoken, the *rhēma*. In both cases we have hints regarding the criteria for reality: that which works and/or that which can be spoken about.

What is "that which works"? Not how do we recognize or test it, but what *is* (it)? What *name* has it? Here is where the two competitors begin a truly epochmaking history. In so many words: Is the true name for reality ultimately Being, or God?

Being is flexible and will not yield easily. Being can be matter, but also spirit. Being would perhaps even be ready to camouflage itself as Non-being, knowing full well that when silence passes and we open our mouths, or even our conscious minds, Being will take over, at least as the only lawful representative of Non-being. Being is indeed so flexible that it was even amenable to being called God. Relatively late in the christian tradition, as (good or bad?) luck would have it, some theologians happened to come across a biblical text that lent its authority to calling God Being, *the* Being. *Yahweh*, "I am who I am"[46]—or, "I am who I shall be." God is Being and Being is God, and there's an end to the struggle—or so it seemed. After Creation, Cajetan said, there are more beings but there is no more Being. A scale for Being would not show the slightest variation.

God was going to be enthroned as Being; except that three disturbances of a very different order appeared on the scene; a threefold "obstacle," which is one of the original meanings of the word problem. The first was religious, the second cultural, and the third philosophical.

The *first problem* was that Being, as *ipsum esse*, as *esse a se* ("Being as such," "Being in itself"), could hardly perform some of the divine tasks ascribed to it: God had to speak, to be worshiped, to act in history, and eventually even to create or give the first impulse (the *chiquenaude* of Descartes) to the world. In brief, it had to be *ens realissimum* besides and above being *esse absolutum*. How could it play both roles? Could it be Being, *the* Being, and thus the soul of all beings, the ground of all entities, the all-pervading reality, could it be *brahman*, and at the same time be *Īśvara*, the Lord, the Beloved, the Person, the Provident, the Creator, and the one invoked (which is one of the roots of the name "God" in indo-european)?

Certainly, the identification of God with Being solves most of the

46 Ex II, 14.

endemic problems of monotheism, but it also transforms strict monotheism and generates other types of quandaries. You do not worship Being; you do not have personal relationships with an *ipsum esse*, foundation and source of everything, manifested in every being. In short, could it be at once Absolute Being and the Supreme Entity? Could it be *das Sein* and *das höchste Seiende*? Philosophers and theologians went on treating God as Being, but believers within the three abrahamic communities related to it as the Supreme Being (Entity). Being as such is not going to deliver you from the hands of your enemies, or lead you through the desert; Being does not descend from on high and become flesh in a single Man; Being does not dictate a Book and send it through its Messenger to the Prophet. The difficulties are not minor. Pascal's anguished cry is well known: "God of Abraham, Isaac, Jacob and not the God of the philosophers."[47]

The *second problem* was cultural. The western tradition has increasingly come to know other traditions which seem to challenge this neat compromise between Being and God. Sinic and indic religions in general, and taoism and buddhism in particular, proceed along different lines. God and Being are not in competition; theology and philosophy are not split. It is enough for now that we recognize the crisis.

The *third problem* is philosophical and has stood since the beginnings of western philosophy. Martin Heidegger has reopened old wounds by his colossal effort to disentangle Being from God without necessarily denying the latter altogether. This marks his difference from the post-hegelian inheritance of marxisms, neo-marxisms, and the so-called postmodern movements that eliminate God as a remnant of past unenlightened ages.

I recall a personal souvenir from the early fifties, my first encounter with Heidegger. For more than three hours we debated, sometimes vehemently. He defending the position that God cannot be Being, I, supported by Dean Max Müller, asserting that the christian God cannot but be Being. With the hindsight of nearly half a century I see now that we both were implicitly accepting that the monotheist conception of God—perhaps the *Monototheismus* of Nietzsche—was no longer tenable from a certain philosophical standpoint. He might have been wrong in his almost postulatory *epochē* regarding God when speaking of Being. Gilson is on firm ground when he points out that scholasticism is simply not understandable without this belief. There are things that by their very nature do not admit of being "bracketed." I may have been wrong in defending a monotheistic position while giving up belief in a Supreme Being. I remember sketching out to him

47 Pascal, *Memorial*: "Dieu d'Abraham, d'Isaac, de Jacob et non Dieu des philosophes."

my trinitarian interpretation, but he was interested in *De Deo Uno* as the living christian God. My conception may be the trinitarian God of some theologians, he kept saying, but not the real God of christians. This is the real God of the christians, I kept insisting. I confess that I had not read his opinion on the matter. That might have made the discussion more vivid. We both were *zur Sache* and not interested in academic scholarship.

Heidegger will not discuss God, will even refrain methodologically from doing so. In this he already betrays his position: his Being has nothing to do with (his) God. He is not concerned with a Supreme Entity. This appertains, he says, to theology. He is concerned with Being and worried by the oblivion of Being since the beginning of western metaphysics. He will interpret this fact, not as a fault of metaphysics, but as a revelation of the very history of Being for whose unconcealement (*alētheia*) his thinking is one of the instruments, since he explicates what the poets had already envisaged but not thematically formulated. The *pathos* of Heidegger's approach, whether it is right or wrong, lies in the fact that he believes he is dealing not with some mental construct or theoretical subtlety, but with the very future of Man and the destiny of the World. His *pathos* is religious, and, without quibbling over words, theological.

While many contemporary thinkers welcome his deepening of the notion of Being, they try to maintain that this Being is the Being of Thomas Aquinas, for instance, who would agree with the analyses of Heidegger along the following lines: Being *qua* Being does not exist. It is indistinguishable from Nothingness. From Dionysius onward, we can cite any number of mystics from the three abrahamic traditions concurring on this *apophatic* character of God. I limit myself to Thomas to maintain the parallelism of one to one. After all, the most quoted author in the *Summa Theologiae* is Dionysius the Areopagite.

In the Beginning was Being. In the Beginning was God. Being is in beings. God is in beings. The way in which Being comes to be in beings is truth. We do not possess truth, but truth possesses us, as Thomas says *verbatim*. Among the many beings, one being in the sublunar world is uniquely capable of detecting this epiphany of truth. This is Man, *Dasein*. Properly speaking, only Man is *capax Dei*, capable of the "beatific vision." Only Man is the "shepherd of Being." The bridge between Man and Being is the intellect. The human intellect is capable of reaching the existence of God. Thinking is the human deciphering of the language of Being. The human intellect reflects the divine *logos*, because it stands between the corporal world and the *psychē*. We have in Plato the triad of Intellect, Soul (of the world), and Body (of the world).[48]

Through thinking, Man discovers that Being is letting beings be in that they are and in what they are: Existence and essence, *prōtē ousia* and *deutera ousia* ("first and second substance"). Existence is *energeia* and was also called *actualitas, causa,* and God (as the Supreme Entity), which could not but be identical to its own essence. Essence was called idea, representation. This split was the beginning of metaphysics and led directly to the loss of Being, its oblivion. The history of Being is Being; the history of the oblivion of Being is metaphysics.

Reality is the autonomy of beings. Entities are real. Being is concealed. Being *is* not, it is not another being, insists Heidegger. *Esse non est ens*, says Thomas. *Being is only in beings*, Heidegger repeats. *Beings exist only through Being*, says Thomas: "It is necessary to affirm that any entity which in whatever way is [exists], is [comes] from God."[49] Being is what lets beings be (Heidegger). Thomas says: "Because it is not proper to say that Being is, but that through Being something is."[50]

Many a page of Heidegger, freighted with the responsibility he feels for the "oblivion of Being" (*Seinsvergessenheit*) of the modern age, sounds in style and prophetic mood similar to the writings of many religious thinkers describing the God-forsakenness of modern society. Heidegger's new introduction to the 1949 edition of *What Is Metaphysics*[51] reminds me of the writings of Pius XII, his contemporary. If we moderns have forgotten Being and modern Man has forgotten God, this is due not exactly to our individual guilt, but to something much deeper inscribed in the very destiny of western history. In this sense there is also a similarity between Heidegger and many representations of the *philosophia perennis* in spite of the personal antipathy of some of its representatives and the philosophers of Freiburg.

Be this as it may, the upshot of this ancient but also contemporary discussion, as in so many other similar cases (grace and predestination, for example, knowledge and will, etc.), may be that once we become aware of the shaky ground on which it stands or falls, we discover it as a pseudo-problem. If successful, this study would like to show that the problem of the Divine

48 Plato, *Sophista* 248e; *Timaeus*, etc.

49 Thomas Aquinas, *Summ. theol.* I, q. 44, a. 1: "Necesse est enim dicere omne ens quod quocumque modo est, a Deo esse."

50 Dionysus, *De divinis nominibus* VIII, I, 1: "Quia non sic proprie dicitur quod esse sit, sed quod per esse aliquid sit."

51 Cf. Heidegger, *Was ist Metaphysik?* (Frankfurt a. M.: Klostermann, 1975), 12.

is centered not on theisms but on the very nature of Reality as a whole, and that theocentrism is as inadequate as anthropocentrism, or for that matter cosmocentrism. The question of the Deity is not a specific theological, anthropological, or cosmological question. It concerns the very nature of the real.

I will try to sum up. On the one hand, if we are in quest of monotheism, the living God, the Supreme Person, the Creator, Origin, Source, or Father, we shall not find Being on the way—unless we deviate and become distracted by *thoughts* instead of being led by that existential urge, *nixus*, aspiration, *svadhā, kṣobha*. We are in quest of Somebody, an Existence, a Source of Life. We are not on an intellectual "trip," even if our intellect may be a fellow traveler (on a ticket paid by the entire human pilgrim). If we are on such a quest, it is only from the side of that Existence that the answer can come, perhaps because the very quest has been prompted by that "other shore." Either we stumble across It or we do not; either It speaks, manifests, reveals Itself to us, or we are not going to find It. The quest for God is a pilgrimage of the whole Self guided by the hidden attraction of that Something, or that Void we feel in ourselves, or that mirage by which we have been deluded. We may look inside, or outside, or both, but we do not keep still, we are on the move, we turn anxiously this way and that, we search—ἐρόμενον is the happy phrase of Aristotle: the Prime Cause pulls us on "as a loving thing."

Phenomenologically speaking, God is what we are searching for, not necessarily what we find. The finding is authentic only if we can say that it is God who has erupted into our lives, if we are forced to admit that, without our knowing it, God was mysteriously preparing us. Augustine writes in his *Confessions*: "You made us for you and restless is our heart until it rests in you."[52] How we figure that out, how we formulate our findings or reformulate what we have been taught, is obviously an outcome dependent on the culture in which we live and many other factors.

On the other hand, if we are "interested" in Being, it is thinking that set us on this course. Our thinking will also be conditioned by the Invisible, the Silent, Elusive, and yet perhaps (already) Present (Being). The philosophical journey has religious connotations, but here the intellect takes the lead and our whole being is the fellow traveler. We are not in search of Somebody, we are not looking for a Person, or directly interested in finding an answer in any presumed direction. Even if we surmised that hell and not heaven was the outcome of the journey, we would not cease in our exploration.

---

52 *Confessions* 1.1.1.

The philosopher's search for Being is a search for intelligibility, a passion for truth, whatever the outcome may be. It is a search for the totality. I am not looking for Somebody or Something. I am looking for the Whole, for Being. Yet the similarities are also intriguing. In both cases we do not know what we are looking for; in both cases we feel an urge to find . . . whom? what? We do not know. We have only a negative criterion: *neti, neti* ("not this, not this"). If on our search for God we find something that still smacks of our creatureliness, we shall not be convinced and will proceed further. We are looking for the Infinite, even if we come to the discovery that there is no such Entity, that heaven is empty, and the Void is its name. If in our search for Being we find an Entity, even the highest one, we shall not be satisfied. We were looking for something different, perhaps a fantasy, an abstraction, but certainly we were not looking for an Entity. Perhaps we were attracted by the possible Ground of existence or the Source of all entities, but not for Something or Somebody. In both cases we are looking for a Presence that presents itself to us and is not our projection.

It is in taking this step outside and inside, beyond and within, that the two movements coincide. Nothing could be more plausible than to unify that "x-factor," that Mystery, by saying that the Ground of all existences is both Being *and* God.

It is when reflection intervenes that there appear insurmountable difficulties in accepting either God as an Entity or Being as devoid of Divinity. A Supreme Entity (be it Prime Mover, Absolute Master of History, *Pantokratōr*, Maker of everything, whatever) as *Supreme* Entity has to have an essence different from the essences of all other entities—that is, a supreme essence. What makes an entity an entity is its essence. That which makes the Supreme Entity be what It is (Its essence) cannot be anything superior to Itself. Its essence is that It *is*. The essence of the Supreme Entity has to be Its own existence. What does this mean? It means that It is no longer an entity with an essence. This Entity, in a sense, has no essence, no entity. There is nothing that can be said of It, except that It exists, and even this in a radically different sense than that of all the other existences. There is no *ex* out of which It stands (ek-sists). It is pure *sistence*. It simply *is*. The Supreme Entity comes very close to Being. It reinforces Being; It gives to Being a sort of divine power, It saves Being from being degraded to an *ens commune*. Being also has no essence. The essence of Being is in each case the particular essence of the entity (in) which Being is, in which it is be-ing.

This is straight scholasticism. God is Being as *actus purus*. As Supreme Being, It has no essence to make of It an entity. It is pure Being. But then . . . we have abandoned monotheism. As a matter of fact, many theological "monotheisms" are not properly so-called. As Söderblom said, "Neither 'monos' nor 'theism' are proper ways of characterizing the beliefs in a Supreme God." Perhaps the most glaring example of this metamorphosis is the case of islām, traditionally the perfect monotheism. We may adduce the analyses of Henry Corbin as an example. He defends monotheism, even more vigorously than traditional christians, but he makes it quite explicit that he is speaking of true monotheism, which is a *monothéisme esotérique*. This is the line taken by Guénon, as well as by S. H. Nasr and many others, in alliance not only with the great mystics like Ibn 'Arabī or Rumi, but also with the great muslim scholastics, Ibn Rushd and Ibn Sina (Averroes and Avicenna) as well. Christians, of course, have the loophole of the Trinity, although they have been "prudent" enough not to make use of it, at least in the way in which I am proposing to do. Just as circumcision of the body was abrogated at the First Council of Jerusalem, perhaps in its third millennium christian self-consciousness may overcome the circumcision of the mind, and overcome monotheism.

* * *

It should have become clear by now that qualified monotheism may be one of the least imperfect historical ways to confront ourselves with that real Mystery one of whose names is God. It should be equally clear that we cannot go back to ancient traditions which for a multiplicity of reasons have lost hold of presentday humanity. Yet we must connect with them and take a giant stride across Modernity (in a way that has little to do with what is called postmodernity). Third, it should be clear that religions themselves are in dire need of "conversion." This *metanoia* is something more, not less, than repentance and change of mind; it demands an overcoming of the mental—without denying it.

C. Other Forms of Theism

I have already said that all theisms, in spite of differences, display a relatively homogeneous mode of thinking. All could be distinguished according to whether they recognize a God, and as to what kind of Entity it is: one, many, all-pervading, sovereignly transcendent, intervening in the affairs of this world, not existing, unknowable, or irrelevant. The problem is with the classification. Real people may not consider themselves polytheists or pantheists, but find themselves classified as such. I shall describe attitudes more than doctrines. The discussion will be extremely brief since we should concentrate on the central topic of our theme.

1. *Deism*

After recent studies situating the contemporary (mainly anglo-saxon) context of deism, and the ironic quotations of the *Encyclopedia Universalis* to the effect that a deist is somebody who does not have the time to become an atheist (Louis de Bonald), with the retort that a deist is somebody who did not want to become an atheist (Paul Hazard), we may be spared dealing at length with the subject. According to its origins and its own formulations, deism has been an offshoot of monotheism since its inception, flourishing in the seventeenth and eighteenth centuries under this name, in its british and french versions. Dictionaries attribute the word to Pierre Viret, a Calvinist theologian who in 1564 wrote that he had heard the word as a self-denomination of those who refuted atheism and refused to believe in Christ, while still believing in God. Deism makes its appearance as a reaction against intolerance, fanaticism, shortsightedness, and supernaturalism—all alleged sins of monotheism. Deism does not want to accept dogmas, religious authorities, or any sort of divine interventionism on the part of a gap-filling Supreme Being who seems to repent of having allowed the world to go its own way and still wants now and then to exhibit Its divine power. The question of miracles is thus paramount here.

The history of deism is conceptually unoriginal but historically important. It has contributed to establishing in the West a regime of religious freedom, and has certainly curtailed many religious abuses of monotheism—in spite of its philosophical weakness and religious superficiality. Perhaps it was a sign of those times.

We shall retain only one feature. Deism believes in a God compatible with modern science, or rather a God tailored to the needs of modern science. God is a non-interventionist power which will not impede the momentum of science. It may seem necessary to some, and superfluous to others. At any rate, it will not make trouble. It is what the history of religions describes as a *Deus otiosus*. It is flexible enough to help some not to become atheists, while it will help others avoid the trauma of having to declare themselves atheists. If modern science still needs a Divine Being, it has to be a docile God devoid of any embarrassing attributes of power, no longer intent on proving that he has still a grip on the world. Science now has this power and may allow a God, provided he behaves as a "good God" should behave. Deism is the God of science. Once it has set forth the premises under which discourse about God is to take place, and has assigned our scientific reason (*ratio*) to ferret out the role God has to play, there is not much more deism can do than console those for whom a God is still needed. No harm is done by a harmless God.

Kant is less ironic and makes the following distinction between the deist and the theist:

> The person who believes in a transcendental theology alone, is termed a *deist*; he who acknowledges the possibility of a *natural* theology also, a *theist*. The former admits that we can cognize by pure reason alone the existence of a Supreme (primordial) Being [*eines Urwesens*], but at the same time maintains that our conception of this being [*Wesen*] is purely transcendental, and that all we can say of it is that it possesses all reality, without being able to define it more closely.[53]

God is the Cause of the World for the deist, while God is the Author of the world for the theist. "The deist believes in a God, the theist in a living God" (*summa intelligentia*). Yet the name is very vague. There have been, in fact, christian deists, and anti-christian deists, deists who admit personhood in God and others who deny it. Deism is not an explicit doctrine. It has ceased to be controversial and popular today because, by and large, it has already obtained its desired effect and secured the advantages it sought. It suffices to mention Voltaire to make our point. Many if not most of his "revolutionary" thoughts for his time sound obvious if not trite to a contemporary monotheist.

We should not minimize the importance of deism because, as I have indicated, it often survives under the cloak of reformed monotheism. The inroads deism has made into popularly accepted monotheism have not only restricted the "living God" to sacristies, churches, private pieties, and religious institutions; they have also given free conscience, and with that free rein to the creation of the "artificial" world of technocratic civilization. Deism has convinced many believing monotheists that we can no longer rely on God to protect us from the outbursts of Nature; nor have confidence any longer in God for our human relations. We have to overcome both floods and "feudalisms" by our own efforts. The wars triggered by monotheistic beliefs have left a lasting trauma in world history and the human psyche. We have to construct our own world, the total habitat, and proclaim democratic rules of order and behavior. We have to take history, and all of Nature, into our own hands. The deist God has given us a free hand. It is up to us to construct a technocratic world in which we may feel secure. Deism is a fruit of the technocratic impulse, and has given religious sanction to it.

For a couple of centuries, and in a special way since Marx, this has been the driving force of the western civilization, which has now spread over the

53 Kant, *Kritik der reinen Vernunft*, B 659.

entire world. There is no doubt that it has been a powerful and creative force. Yet there must have been a hidden poison in it somewhere, for what we see today in consequence are ecological disasters and historical monstrosities without precedent. The creation of our "artificial" fourth world—besides and above the worlds of the Gods, of Man, and of Nature—has not yielded the expected results; it has not delivered the goods. In its own very practical and materialistic terms, the dominant pan-economic and technocratic regime has been a disheartening failure. Should we just try harder for more of the same? Or should we consider a radical *metanoia*? These lectures are an attempt to explore the latter possibility.

2. *Pantheism*

There are many types of pantheism. Dean Inge distinguishes five varieties of pantheism, but we shall follow a simpler route. Without further analysis I shall mention three types that are quite different. One could be said to belong to a "pre-pantheistic" phase, the second type has emerged from within the theistic universe as a reaction against it and fits neatly into the classification. Another type would include all those who never dreamed of being pantheists, but to whom the label has been attached for classificatory reasons. The three types present similar features, of course, but their contexts and concerns are very different.

The very fact that the label "pantheism" stems from the early eigthteenth century in Europe raises the suspicion that many of the so-called pantheistic systems are, if at all, pre-pantheistic and are somewhat forced into the classification. A case in point is the example of the so-called pre-socratic philosophers. Although it would amount to an oversimplification to classify all of them as belonging to the "cosmological epoch" of western philosophy, it seems to be a fact that one of the main concerns of most philosophies was the problem of φύσις, nature, that is, the reflection about the cosmos. What is the universe in which we live? What are the things of this world? What are things? Many of them, however, did not forget to ask for the place and function of Man in the Cosmos.

Their main philosophical query was: What is this Cosmos as a Whole? Now, because of their close connection with what some histories of ideas call the "mythological period," the reality of the God was the prevalent *mythos* of those times. We have already quoted that phrase attributed to Thales of Miletos, whom phoenicians of the seventh century BC considered the "Father of greek Philosophy," that the universe is full of Gods. In brief, the κόσμος (*kosmos*) of the pre-socratics was considered divine almost as a matter of fact. To call them "pantheist" is perhaps too far-fetched.

The second type begins with an existential critique of monotheism; it is a sort of anti-monotheistic pantheism. One of the functions of the *monos* of monotheism, this critique suspects, is to "control," as it were, the overall intrusion of God into other domains of the real. Monotheism, these pantheists feel, is afraid of God and want to tame him. Monotheism introduces the *monos* so that there will also be space for Man and World. Our second type of pantheism is a thoroughgoing rejection of this attitude, which is looked upon as a trick in order to both "have" an infinite God, and to "rescue" the independence (autonomy) of Man and World.

This type of pantheism takes the absoluteness of God very seriously and says that if God is the infinite Being, we cannot be satisfied with the tautology that God is one and unique only on his own level. All levels belong (also) to God. Pantheism is not content simply to accept God's functions: sovereignty, cause, or whatever. God not only reigns or acts, creates or judges; God also— and mainly—*is*. This *is* includes and exhausts all the rest. God *is*. It is the only true Being. This, of course, explains the visceral reaction of the abrahamic religions against pantheism. For them pantheism would deprive the things of this world of existence and reality, and sap both human dignity and the intrinsic value of the person.

It is out of fear of pantheism that a substantial part of christian theology has fallen into dualism. "True monotheism is perhaps nothing else than the overcoming of pantheism," Schelling says.[54] The principle behind pantheism, he explains, is the immediate potency of existence, *potentia existendi*. This principle is incontrovertible. He has Spinoza in mind, obviously. God is absolute Substance. God is, in Schelling's language, *das unendlich seyn Könnende*. But in order to pass from potency to act God needs the actuality of the Will. This Will is the difference between a blind and deaf pantheism and a living monotheism, he says: "the will itself is act."[55] Without it, God would amount only to the potency of its own Being. Pantheism has no freedom: it is sheer passivity, pure potency; so Schelling affirms. There is an interesting link between Schelling and the nietzschean "will to power": "Between Non-being and Being there is nothing in the middle except pure Will (of the power to exist of Being)."[56]

Pantheism is not satisfied with God as Supreme Entity. It needs God as Being, and if this Being "produces" beings, God has also to "be" those beings

54 Schelling, II, 40.

55 "Das Wollen selbst ist Actus."

56 Schelling, II, 37: "Zwischen dem Nichtseyn und Seyn steht ihr [der potentia existendi des Seins] nichts in der Mitte als eben das blosse Wollen."

inasmuch as they are (beings). One subtle form of pantheism, of course, is absolute idealism. God is All, because All is the Idea and the idea is God. We have already observed that if God knows all with absolute knowledge it is because He is all. From Plato to Hegel there is a common undercurrent, which emerges with more virulent force in Nietzsche and Marx.

* * *

The word "pantheism" indicates that we are dealing with a doctrine that defends that All (*pan*) is God, and God (*theos*) is All. In other words, the All constitutes a real Unity, and this Unity is God. We should stress that this Unity has to be a real Unity. The logical unity at which our thinking arrives has to be raised still further to an ontological status. God is the absolute reality in whatever way this reality may be interpreted: matter, spirit, thought . . .

Pantheism, however, should be differentiated from monism due to the residuum of God. A monist is not necessarily a pantheist. To identify the two is again an extrapolation of the theistic mindset, which needs a God and, finding no place for it in monism, concludes by identifying God with monistic "stuff." I could spell out the distinction in a more phenomenological manner: Pantheism identifies God with the World and/or the World with God. Monism does not identify anything; it does not say that they are one. If at all it would defend that they are zero. Monism does not even recognize the split in order to bring the two together. It simply affirms the absolute Oneness of all that there is. The pantheist is concerned with God and calls it Unique Being, which is what many medieval scholastics also defended. The scholastics admitted that this Being "emanated" beings (creation was the technical term) which, without impinging on Being—that is, without multiplying, affecting, or modifying it in any way— would be real beings—and yet not Being. Thomas does not shy away from introducing the topic of creation with the title: *De modo emanationis rerum a primo principio*[57] ("Concerning the way that things emanate from the first principle"). The so-called doctrine of participation arose in this way.

The theory of creation is the monotheistic key to maintaining the absoluteness of God and the reality of the (created) world in order to avoid pantheism (we will not now enter into the discussion of the meaning of the ontological degradation from Being into beings). The famous formula *creatio ex nihilio* should not be confused with a *creatio ex Deo*, which would be pantheism. *Ex nihilio*, as I have explained, means *ex nulla* (*praevia*) *substantia*.

57 Thomas Aquinas, *Summ. Theol.* I, sq. 45.

Scholasticism identifies God and Being. This is qualified *monotheism*. *Pantheism* identifies God and beings. *Monism*, on the other hand, identifies Being and beings (*Sein* and *Seiende*). They are three distinct attitudes. Oversimplifying we could summarize these two types of pantheisms saying that the first affirms that "the World is divine," while the second maintains that "the Divinity is the World."

I have also spoken of a third type of would-be pantheists, the "'associate' pantheists," those who are included in the classification although they never asked to join the club. For instance, to call many forms of upanishadic spirituality "pantheistic" shows an absence of what I have called "diatopical hermeneutics."

Neither *ātman-brahman*, nor much less *tat tvam asi* ("that thou art"), has anything much to do with the affirmation that God is All or All is God. First of all, the hellenic/abrahamic idea of God is simply not present. *Brahman* is, at most a homeomorphic equivalent of God, certainly not even analogous to the concept of God, as I have taken pains to explain elsewhere. The affirmation that all is a manifestation of *brahman* is not an epistemological statement of an underlying ontological identity. The manifestation itself is ontological. Most of the time, *avidyā* (ignorance) is not an epistemological notion. It may sometimes be monistic, but not pantheistic. *Theos* and *brahman* are not interchangeable. "Pan-*brahmanism*" makes no sense; pantheism is merely a cultural extrapolation. Whether pantheism or not, there is a passage of the *Gītā* that has created difficult problems of interpretation. I cite it here only to stress a different way of thinking:

> By Me, in My unmanifested form, this entire universe is pervaded. All beings are in Me, but I am not in them.
>
> And yet everything that is created does not rest in Me. Behold My mystic opulence! Although I am the maintainer of all living entities, and although I am everywhere, still My Self is the very source of creation.[58]

* * *

A still more recent word that should be distinguished from pantheism is the so-called *panentheism*, which is intended to be a reaction against certain monotheistic doctrines, but not against its main thrust. Panentheism affirms that "All things are in God," which a qualified monotheism would also

58 BG IX, 4-5: "mayā tatam idam\ sarvam\ jagad avyaktamūrtinā / matsthāni sarvabhūtāni na cāham\ teṣv\ avasthitaḥ / na ca matsthāni bhūtāni paśya me yogam aiśvaram / bhūtabhṛn na ca bhūtastho mamātmā bhūtabhāvanaḥ."

accept, adding, however, that God is not exhausted in them. God is "more," not less, than "all things." This "more" remains a problem. "God is in all things" should complement the prior sentence, whereby the subject (God) is not exhausted in the predicate (World). The panentheism of Krause, who allegedly introduced the word panentheism, may be closer to pantheism, whereas in Bulgakov and many other christian thinkers the word may be closer to monotheism. In both cases, it is a form of theism.

3. *Polytheism*

It is significant to remark that most studies on "polytheism" are either anthropological or historical; by and large, they avoid philosophical reflection. It is almost taken for granted that "polytheism" is either an aberration, a fall from an earlier monotheism, or else a "primitive" stage in the evolution toward a more perfect form of religion or belief. At best, there is a condescending sympathy for polytheism and sometimes even a patronizing justification for the "polytheists": Better "that" than nothing. Many dictionaries of philosophy that have entries on the other forms of theism do not even bother to mention "polytheism." When a more philosophical approach is ventured, we read sentences like the opening of the RGG in the corresponding entry: "Der Begriff Monotheismus setzt den Polytheismus voraus." ("The concept [of] monotheism presupposes polytheism.")

I wonder if there has ever been a polytheist who imagined as *many* what the monotheist believes to be *One*. The monotheist has such an idea of *theos* that a multiplicity of monotheistic *theoi* would be contradictory, as we noted earlier. The true "polytheist" does not fall into such a crass contradiction. For this reason I write "polytheism" in quotation marks, because it is only a pseudo-polytheism, a creation of theists. I am saying that the *theos*, when affirmed as *monos* is not the same *theos* when affirmed as *polys*, since even formally, *theos* does not represent the same notion in each case. I must add that here *monos* and *polys* do not express the relationship between the (numerically) singular and the plural (number). Most monotheists will agree that the *monos* of monotheism is not a number; it is rather a reminiscence of the platonic and neoplatonic One. "God is one without [number] one and above number" says Meister Eckhart.[59] Most modern scholars of religion would not even consider the possibility that the *poly* of "polytheism" may not represent a quantity or a number, but rather expresses a quality. The true polytheist does not count the Gods, does not quantify divine "objects." "Polytheism" simply belongs to another universe of discourse, and of life. I

59 Eckhart, *Proa. Cof* II (Nr. 107): "Deus est unus sive uno et supra numerum."

even wonder if that attitude wrongly called "polytheism" really belongs to theism. Once again we encounter, in an even more acute way, the same case as with pantheism. A classificatory scheme is superimposed that does not fit the "things" so classified.

This state of affairs is significant because it betrays the evolutionist framework through which the modern history of religions views what it terms polytheism, namely, a cultic approach to the Divine under many names and forms, without these scholars being aware of a double cosmological and epistemological extrapolation. For the traditional "polytheist," forms, names, time, and places have other meanings or rather other degrees of reality than the western nominalistic interpretation found in most scholarly works on the subject. The world of "polytheism" is not an epistemological world in which knowledge, let alone worship, accepts the dichotomy between subject and object. To know and to worship, for the "polytheist" are two human acts in which that dualism is overcome.

Monotheism may have come before or after polytheism, but the "concept" of monotheism is certainly not a "refinement" of polytheism unless the latter is defined as merely an imperfect and primitive form of monotheism. In that case, however, one is simply affirming what one should prove. Here is an example of a monocultural approach to an intercultural problem. From a certain point of view, the only way to understand "polytheism" is to see it in relation to monotheism. The latter is the model and offers the measure to explain, if not to judge, all other beliefs. The example of Schelling is telling. Although he wants to present "polytheism" as somewhat adequate for those "primitive" people, he says, "originally God is at the very basis of polytheism."[60]

If we want to understand the "polytheistic" attitude we have to divest ourselves of all those modern interpretations that have been unable to overcome their "monotheistic" background. Polytheism is manifold because there are "many" divine Names, and many notions of a not individualizable God. From a substantial point of view, God is an individual, but it is not individualizable; we cannot pinpoint God and delimit its boundaries. As Hermes Trismegistus says: "God is an infinite sphere whose center is everywhere and circumference no-where."[61]

---

60 Schelling, I, 75.

61 *Liber XXIV philosophorum*, II: "Deus est sphera infinita, cuius centrum est ubique, circumferentia nusquam." It is interesting to realize that Saint Bonaventura instead of *sphera infinita* writes *sphera intelligibilis* in his *Itinerarium* V, 8, and that Alanus ab Insulis (de Lille) in *Theolg. regul* (regula VII) was his source.

God is everywhere, and the polytheist discovers in each point a center of the entire Divinity. This discovery has to be a personal discovery—otherwise we are talking about an ideology. The image is powerful. The superficial critics of "polytheism," and of pantheism as well, say that there is a divine point everywhere. The positive insight of those two forms of theism, however, is not the vision of many or infinite points, but the vision of an infinite numbers of centers. In order that a point be a center it has to be more than a dot. If we are unable to see the circumference everywhere, the aura of everything, I am tempted to say we shall not see the centers, we are missing the experience of the divine. We may not see the required circumference of every center, yet we may see the point as a center when we somewhat discover the center of everything and not just circumferences.

"Polytheism" does not need to recognize a Super-God hidden or transcendent, silent or absent from this world. When not a westernized interpretation, the relation between the so-called High God and the worshiped Gods of many african religions is rather an *advaitic* relationship. Indeed, iconolatry is not idolatry—to use two words to make a fundamental distinction. The idol is an identification of the Divinity and one generally material object. When the idolater has many such idols, he could be called a polytheist. The icon is the real re-presentation of the Divinity. If this presence is taken as a psychological device, we have a holy image. When it is experienced as a real presence, we have the basis for iconolatry. If the icon is always the same, even if the act of worship is repeated, we cannot speak of polytheism—just as the adoration of the Eucharist in many consecrated breads is not polytheism. If the icons differ, we cannot decide apart from the experience of the worshiper. A christian will not confuse the Body of Christ with the Blood of Christ but does not believe that there are two Christs.

The polytheistic idea of the Divinity is certainly not that of a substance in the monotheistic world. The Gods, like the humans, are all denizens of the universe, along with the living cosmos. The universe is just a name to designate the fundamental structure of reality. The Gods are not necessarily the creators of the universe, nor does one of them even need to be the Creator. Creation is a monotheistic belief. Neither does polytheistic belief say that the universe is God presided over by a Super-Godhead. The Gods are not inferior to the universe, just as humans are not. They all are in the universe; together they all form the universe. It is only from a monotheistic viewpoint that, if no single God were found to be absolute Master, the universe could be called a chaos, or the whole universe would be made divine in a more or less pantheistic sense.

When, speaking of monotheism, I said that "polytheism" could be described as the strongest form of personal relationship with the Divinity. In order to be brief and concrete, I will try to reenact the sentiment behind so-called "polytheistic" worship. First, I do not worship (a) God because it is an obligation. I do so because I feel the need to express my gratitude, pain, frustration, love, prayer, adoration, and so forth in the face of a concrete icon re-presenting the Divine, although routine or custom may also play its part here. In the face of Divinity I forget myself. I am in sober *exstasis* (sometimes not so sober) and have eyes only for the divine presence. The entire Divinity is there. When at a second moment at another occasion, and in a different form I happen to worship, I will not make comparisons and eventually may not even remember the previous act—like an act of love, it is ever new or it is not love, ever spontaneous or it is not authentic. I shall not ask whether that icon is the same as or different from the first. Such a thought does not apply. It would even appear blasphemous. Although I am fully conscious that the icon is not the same, neither are the ritual and many other concerns identical. Seen from the outside I may be labeled as a polytheist. For myself, I am simply a sincere worshiper. Should I recall that we are speaking about the sacred and not about a *divertissement*, to use Pascal's word? Respect is always in order when dealing with the entire problematic of Man in the face of the Mystery.

* * *

I mentioned above that a certain form of deism arose as a reaction to the alleged abuses of monotheism. Similarly, a contemporary "new polytheism" is emerging as a reaction against the monarchic principle inherent in monotheism. Polytheism here will stand for polyarchy, for overcoming the need to reduce everything to a single principle. In this sense the "new polytheism" is also a reaction against the larval monotheistic attitude of modern science whenever it seeks universal principles and unified field theories, or attempts to formulate a "Grand Theory of Everything," to use the current lingo, in a single equation.

As we have seen, none of the forms of theism is able to overcome its general horizon, and yet most of these theistic forms feel in their own ways the strictures of that grid and try to break out of it. The "new polytheism" is an example. It grows out of an awareness that if God is an ultimate point of reference and a single principle of intelligibility, there are many such Gods. In contrast with the more traditional forms of "polytheism," which do not, properly speaking, have doctrinal underpinnings, the new polytheism is indeed more intellectual. There are many centers, but each center is a center of a unique circumference—if we disregard the circles.

These brief descriptions of those different theisms, besides being simple sketches, do not intend to criticize them; on the contrary, my intention has been to emphasize the positive aspects of all those ideas about the Divine, which will help us to proceed toward our constructive part. The same should apply to the following sections.

* * *

For anybody living in a cultural world different from the dominant one today, it is obvious that the three following sections apply both to forms of theism and to non-theistic systems. Western scholarship has indeed found forms of atheism, agnosticism, and skepticism in other cultures. They are certainly homeomorphic equivalents, but do not fit the western pattern in which these three words have their origin and their proper meaning. We have already noted how we tend to reduce everything to our own parameters of understanding; indeed, there is no other way to proceed if we want to understand. Yet we should be aware that these parameters belong to a particular culture. The misunderstanding begins when for whatever reason, usually political power, we take those parameters as universal.

There are, no doubt, forms of "atheism" in Asia, for instance, but it is improper to classify them as such when they are neither anti-theisms, or rather anti-monotheisms, nor reactions against any form of theism. To call mīmāmsā or the jaina atheistic is another example in my critique of classifications. The three forms I am going to discuss below are reactions against the underlying monotheistic *mythos*, even if the context is often secularized.

4. *Atheism*

The most formidable reaction against monotheism comes from atheism, of course. The literature today is overwhelming. Gone are the days when the atheist was the only enlightened citizen or, at the other extreme, an untrustworthy and immoral person. We should distinguish also the main thrust of atheism from what is called nihilism. To be sure, there is a nihilistic atheism as well as there exists a metaphysical nihilism. In fact, all the notions of our list are polyvalent and polysemic. We cite them only by way of examples. It remains true that most so-called atheisms are practical atheisms and anti-monotheisms. In both cases it is mainly a negative attitude. A God, whether in the sense of a Supreme Being or the ultimate key to the riddle of human existence, does not exist.

I said that atheism still belongs within the world of theism, for perhaps nowhere is the thirst for an ultimate point of reference stronger than in the modern atheist. It is a serious desire for rationality and intelligibility. Reason is all that remains, we have to hold to it as the only rope of salvation. If dialectical reason collapses, chaos invades everything. There is no *theos*, but reason is his heir, more humble indeed (it does not know everything), more patient (it has to reckon with time), less demanding (it is not absolute), but nevertheless the ultimate guiding principle. Modern science is the best example. It leaves as much room as the individual scientist desires for private beliefs, but the scientific method excludes *a priori* any external interference. Science has to proceed as if God were nonexistent. The "angels" should not interfere with the Second Principle of Thermodynamics.

The positive atheist will say that we do not need God, that its existence does not matter and that everything would follow the same course anyway. God is a superfluous hypothesis, and an encumbering one. A healthy scholastic and scientific principle tells us that elegance and simplicity are attributes of truth. "Entia non sunt multiplicanda praeter necessitatem"[62]— "entities are not to be multiplied without necessity." This carries the paradoxical result that, for all practical and theoretical purposes, the alleged "Necessary Being" becomes unnecessary. The argument is existentially cogent in our technocratic civilization. The proof is in the day-to-day life of modern society. When the death of God was proclaimed, "business-as-usual" was the order of the day. "No problem." Not so the day that someone dares to write a novel insulting the Name of the Prophet; or the day that a small brother challenges the Big Brother by invading a territory that is rich in oil!

Atheism is much too vital an attitude to be satisfied with attacking the metaphysical notion of God. It simply refuses to believe in the personal or anthropomorphic conception of God. The entire history of the western world is full of *Atheismusstreiten* à la Fichte. The very notion of God could probably serve as the best leading thread for a history of philosophy. Atheism would fill up an important chapter.

I have already mentioned how deism, pantheism, and polytheism make sense only in dialogue with, and opposition to, monotheism. Atheism is our fourth case in point, and probably the most important for our contemporary age. It has so nearly won the battle that it has caused a thorough revision of the monotheistic attitude. The reaction of many monotheistic believers to the arguments of Feuerbach and Russell, to cite just two names, is simply to say that they miss the point because "true" monotheism has long since overcome that crude stage of its "evolution." The tension is not entirely

62 Sentence attributed to William of Ockham although not found verbatim in his works.

dissipated, however, for many monotheists will still rally to defend the Supreme Entity. Only the hiatus now is no longer between "believers" and atheists, but between a certain type of believer and a second type, who share their destiny with the "theists." The name of Ernst Bloch may be a symbol to express what I have in mind.

It could very well be that one of the historical reasons for modern western atheism was the general liberation from christian dogmas once they were felt as an imposition, as something one had to stick with in order to reach salvation. "Thank God we are atheists" was the phrase one often heard shortly before and after the theological trauma of the spanish Civil war of 1936-1939. The moment a dogma is taken in isolation from all the others and is severed from the living Source from which it is an intellectual and authoritative expression, it becomes the "letter that killeth,"[63] but the moment you liberate yourself from the burden of an imposed doctrine that promises eternal salvation, you need to establish some other norms, rules, or grounds for truth. This is the step taken by Descartes: replacement of theological monotheism with philosophical monotheism. The ego, the subject, the doubt, the subjectivity, will become the *fundamentum absolutum inconcussum* of truth. If we have ultimately to trust solely in ourselves, in our thinking—even if dialectically we still need God to guarantee the truthfulness of our mind's inner workings—we become something Protagoras had never imagined: the measure of *all* things, even the final arbiters of whether God exists or not. Those believers, in fact, will seriously attempt to prove his existence, and not just to show the reasonableness of his existence. Monotheism becomes absolute subjectivism and subjectivism turns either to absolute idealism or into the pragmatic atheism of our plurality of egos that do not need any other foundation.

Atheism may be right in its critique of a certain monotheism. It may succeed in eliminating an anthropomorphic God considered as a Supreme Entity, but it remains a fact that even within the atheistic world Man needs a guide, some principles, a foundation for morals. Man needs a substitute for the monotheistic God, and there is no other candidate than reason. Yet contemporary Man has had quite enough negative experiences with reason and reason alone not to be suspicious that the "remedy" might turn out to be worse than the "disease." Only the "Will to Power" of a capitalistic ideology remains, or perhaps a radical *metanoia* of the sort these pages attempt to describe.

63 2 Cor III, 6.

5. *Agnosticism*

Monotheism believes that in the end all shall be well and all riddles will be solved. For this we need that patience or tolerance which will save our lives.[64]

Agnosticism lacks such endurance and is concerned with our concrete situations without eschatological promises (hallucinations or mirages). God may know all, but we are not God and certainly do not know all, not even the most elementary things. We have to confess ourselves a-gnostics because we do not have the divine *gnōsis*, the knowledge of things that really matter. The reference here, of course, is monotheism. No doubt we know many things, but we do not know anything exhaustively, as God is supposed to know. Therefore, we have to confess ourselves agnostics, if we may adopt this name of recent coinage.

The agnosticism of Thomas Huxley, who introduced the name in the last century, simply negates any knowledge beyond so-called scientific knowledge. In order to defend itself, this form of agnosticism has to negate the possibility of any non-scientific knowledge and in so doing somewhat trespasses the proper limits of its name. Because many theisms affirm that God exists, the agnostic position will be one of denying the possibility of such knowledge. The word made fortune not only because of its simplicity, but also because it did touch a central point of theistic religions: the *apophatism* of the Divine. In view of sentences like this: "This is the ultimate human knowledge about God: that it knows that it does not know God [*quod sciat se Deum nescire*],"[65] one could well defend a religious agnosticism. This is once again an example of the dazzling, not to say blinding, effect of the scientific *mythos*—which we should also take as a warning for all myths. This religious "agnosticism" is a common trait of almost all mystical traditions, and it does not for that matter fall into irrationalism. There are endless examples, including the agnosticism of the *Cloud of Unknowing*, the *docta ignorantia*, the "new innocence," the socratic knowledge of our ignorance, or the upanishadic innocence of our own ignorance. We may recall the *agnosia* of the greek Fathers of the Church. Evagrius Ponticus equates it to blessedness: "Blessed are those who have reached infinite ignorance." It is obvious that these agnosticisms do not fit our classification. Modern agnosticism knows that we do not and cannot know God, which once again betrays the monotheistic background.

---

64 Lk XXI, 19.

65 Thomas Aquinas, *De potentia Dei* VII, 5 ad 14. Cf. among many parallel statements, *Summ. Theol.* I, a. 3; *Contra Gentiles*, I, 5; etc.

6. Skepticism

Unlike agnosticism, the name of skepticism is an ancient one—although it has undergone a change of meaning. The ancient skeptics were the seekers, which is what the name means. Skeptics are always skeptical of ever having found anything final, because they go on and on constantly seeking. No opinion is absolutely certain. We doubt. How could we be sure to have found *the* truth without a criterion of truth? God is supposed to be the truth, but how can we be sure of our criterion of truth without another criterion? Thus, there is no end to the search. We cannot be absolutely sure of anything. I include skepticism in our list because in spite of the numerous varieties of skepticism, here again the point of reference is the monotheistic God, or the philosophical monotheism of Descartes.

We could not doubt having found any truth if truth were a meaningless word.

* * *

To sum up, theisms, considered as a whole, teach a lesson:

- Monotheism teaches us that reality has an ever-transcendent dimension.
- Deism strives to harmonize God and Reason.
- Pantheism stresses the all-pervading nature of this divine dimension.
- Polytheism reminds us that the Divine is irreducible to any singularity, of whatever type—intellectual, ontic, etc.
- Atheism draws our attention to the fact that Man is an adult who, coming of age, has to confront himself with the *apophatic* character of the Ultimate.
- Agnosticism reminds us that only God is omniscient—and we are not God.
- Skepticism makes us aware that we cannot be absolutely certain of anything. The ground of our certainty could only be God and we are not it.

These seven traits are ultimately understandable only within the framework of theism. Monotheism is their appropriate horizon.

Let me say this in a different way. Monotheism, on one hand, and all other forms of theism, on the other, have so modified the theistic *mythos* or horizon that it has today become practically unbelievable—at least for a considerable part of the world. A *mythos*, however, can neither be thrown away nor replaced at will. We cannot change our beliefs and replace them with others just by an operation of the mind. Even if we find something unbelievable, it is because we have discovered a new ground, *in which we believe*, that makes our former beliefs unbelievable. The alternative is neither theism nor despair, but the realization that what needs to be changed is not so much the answers as the question itself. In these vitally ultimate matters this ground cannot be a pragmatic postulate or a rational axiom. No postulated principle has enough force to sustain the burden of our conscious existence. We cannot pretend to believe, to be convinced, or to be certain of anything, if we are not. Plotinus advised us to pray in facing such momentous questions, and it is with this prayerful attitude that we should now proceed in our quest.

IV
The Dwelling of the Divine

A. The Divine Mystery

For lack of a better word, or rather because all words are inadequate, I have chosen the word *Mystery* in order to symbolize that element, factor, being, dimension, ultimate, abyss . . . that in one form or another is present in human consciousness. A traditional name for that Mystery has been God. I call it the divine Mystery or simply the Divine without at the outset assuming the degree of reality of its "attributes." One thing seems to be undisputed: the human being *qua* human being is aware of "it." This "it" may be the unknown, the infinite, the void, the space that allows for growth, hope, or despair. Man is conscious of Man's finitude, and the very awareness of these limits provokes a confrontation with the infinite. This is the "space" of the Divine, the object of this chapter.

I have been saying that theisms are inadequate, that they often contradict each other, although they may also be mutually complementary if we enlarge the horizon from which they emerge. I have also been suggesting that theisms as such do not exhaust the human ways to encounter the divine Mystery. The world of theisms has been a domain of great power. Theism has persisted for millennia and will no doubt continue to survive in some form. "Right" or "wrong" are inapplicable epithets here. The world of theism is a universe in itself, which selects its own criteria for judging what is right and wrong. Yet theisms no longer seem able to satisfy the most profound urges of the contemporary sensibilities both in the civilizations that first nurtured these theisms, and in others as well. The world of theism is not alone in facing religious problems, as well as vital metaphysical issues. In short, the divine Mystery remains a mystery.

We cannot deal with this subject as we are accustomed to treating most other topics of inquiry. In this chapter I will describe the pitfalls of theology when it claims to be a science like the others, even when called "sacred." The Divine, whether real or not, has existed in human history as an integrating and/or disintegrating factor. The Divine is unique, and thus incomparable, irreducible to any other experience. It is *sui generis*, a special case that calls for awe, respect, and humility, and elicits from us a sense of inadequacy and mystery. I do not say fear or love, since this depends on the notion we may have of the Divine, but certainly the epiphany of this mystery demands reverence and has elicited from us the most extraordinary responses, both sublime and atrocious. It belongs to the realm of the sacred, the ancients said, and the sacred terrifies as much as it attracts, repels even as it appeals; it allures and assures at the same time, both irritates and enamors, and may demand surrender or command flight.

We do not all have the same notion of the Divine. There are people for whom the whole thing is a hoax. Even so, if we respect our ancestors and have a minimal sense of hierarchy and of history, if we have any sensitivity for language, then the discourse about the Divine is a religious discourse in the best sense of the word, for it deals with ultimate things. We are dealing with the most dangerous and lofty topic, at once most clear and most elusive, inspiring both the greatest love and the greatest hate or utter indifference. It requires a unique attitude. Otherwise, we are flatly untrue to the subject matter. If the Divine exists, human lives have a radically different meaning than if the Divine does not exist. Any approach that does not take this risk into account is simply not an approach to the Divine Mystery, but only a private whim (positive or negative) without any roots in human soil.

I am not insisting on any particular belief but simply asking that we be in conformity with the topic. It is a methodological requirement. In our desacralized climate it is especially appropriate to highlight this attitude. The Divine stands here for any ultimate value, even if indicating the "monotheism of the market." Adopting this attitude of awe, I submit that the most prevalent conceptions of the Divine today, which could be encompassed by the name *theism*, are no longer convincing, not just to a few skeptical intellectuals, but to vast and increasing numbers of people. I also propose that this lack of convincement may have come about for a "reason" that belongs to the very "Destiny of Being."

This is not a sociological thesis based on some demographic poll. I submit that the felt inadequacy of most forms of theism represents a profound change in our understanding of ourselves and the world. I am not passing judgment on times past, but we should squarely face up to what could be called the greatest challenge to the destiny of reality in our day. All of this implies, obviously, that the Divine is not just an objective "thing," nor is it solely a subjective image. The challenge to theism does not come from modern science alone. It also, and perhaps mainly, comes from other visions of reality, which the predominant and victorious western culture does not (yet) take very seriously. Cultures are not mere folklore, and have a vital role to play in the emergence of the new myth to which we alluded earlier.

It is a very positive sign of our times to hear more and more about intercultural philosophy, cross-cultural studies, interdisciplinary approaches, and the like. Nonetheless, in many influential circles the problem of the Divine still seems by and large taboo—perhaps because for many the Divine connotes the God or the No-God of theisms. Significantly enough, although it has been claimed that the Divine is everywhere and permeates every field,[1] such a claim has not been refuted but either carefully ignored or zealously marginalized to the preserve of God-specialists. Physics can be taught on all levels in any educational curriculum, but not so religion. God continues to be seen as a sectarian notion when not plainly viewed as an intruder in the allegedly "neutral" field of education. This trend has permeated most of the current curricula of Africa and Asia as well. Needless to repeat, I understand "religion" to be that which "re-links" us with the three worlds.

My contention is that, without an awareness of the divine Mystery, we cannot deal seriously with either education or life. That Mystery, however, is not identical with the theistic Being. It is a "dimension" of Reality as a whole, commingled with all of us and with the entire World in the cosmotheandric adventure, and yet, as the *Gītā* says,[2] neither reducible to nor identical with anything else. I do not postulate at the outset the degree of reality of such a "dimension."

It is not a question of just reforming technocracy, or of returning to a pre-technological lifestyle, or even of finding a convenient escape hatch. Nor is it merely a question of wresting the reins of the historical process from the powers that be and taking them into our own hands. Rather, it is a matter of attuning ourselves once again to the rhythms of Reality, of learning to cooperate in synergetic symbiosis with the entire universe in and around us for the very survival of Being. If this seems to be too much for the human person, then the first task of religion, I submit, would be to instill in the human being the consciousness of the dignity of that person, who is never a means for something else.

The chinese were once acutely aware of what it means to be a true Man.

---

1 Cf. IsU 6; Acts XVII, 28; *Tao Te Ching* 22, 25, 34. These are not pious sentences but repre sent the very core of the last six to eight thousand years of human civilization, except the last three hundred years of our technological world.

2 BG IX, 4-5.

It is to be gentle, high-minded, truly aware that we are more than selfish bodies or reasoning brains. Man is the link between Heaven and Earth. The Upanishads, as well, tell us that realization of the ātman-b*rahman* identity is not an escape from the World. Man is not truly Man, really human, without this realization of the ātman. Aristotle reminds us that the ancients called Man a microcosm. Man shares in the life of the *logos*, and this *logos* pervades everything. The scholastics speak of the "specular" nature of the human being, which is the image of God and thus the image of the Whole. After saying that the world is threefold (*triplex mundus*): the small (Man), the greatest (God), and the great (the cosmos), Nicholas of Cusa adds that "in each part shines the whole."[3]

Rather than the rich, the powerful, or the famous, the saint, the sage, the realized person, even the gentleman was held up as the human ideal. There is a fascinating homeomorphic equivalence between the *zhenren* of Chuang Tzu, the gnostic God Man of Clement of Alexandria, and the *al-hakim* of Ibn 'Arabī. Theology was the "science of God," not out of people's curiosity to have detailed information on what the divine Being looks like, but out of a need for a mirror showing how Man may attain perfection and fulfill destiny.

Luther speaks of the *Gedritt*, and if he takes his stand on faith alone (*sola* fides), it is because faith is what elevates Man to all that Man is called upon to become. Kant may place limits on human reason, but it is in order to make room for faith, since he is always sensitive to the dignity of Man. Heidegger also tells us that the *humanum* is called upon to shepherd the totality of Being.

In all these cases, instead of a compartmentalized picture of the universe, we find a World where neither "God" nor Man is isolated, and where matter is no longer completely impenetrable. Everything is permeated by everything else in a kind of total *perichōrēsis*, in the way the early Church Fathers envisioned the Godhead, and as most traditional cultures understood the entire universe. In all these cases, Man is "more" than just an individual being, the Divine "different" from a Supreme Lord, and the World "other" than raw material to be plundered for utility or profit.

* * *

In calling this part IV the "Dwelling" of the Divine, I am conscious of the ironic and significant shift that has taken place in this english word, from a dynamic and rather pejorative meaning to a more static and positive one. The original meaning of dwelling, akin to erring, connotes going

3 Cusa, *De ludo globi* I (ed. Gabriel III, 260): "In omnibus autem partibus relucet totum."

astray or wandering off; and its sense gradually changed to being stunned and perplexed, and thus staying, abiding, inhabiting. The two meanings are highly significant here. The Divine passes, transits, errs, goes somewhat astray, in a disorienting and upsetting way, always somehow escaping, eluding, disappearing. Yet, on the other hand, it is also remaining, resting, staying, abiding, inhabiting, indwelling, being present, effective. This ambivalence and ambiguity could scarcely correlate more closely with the contemporary situation. God is both a reassuring and a disturbing word. We may recall here the verse of the latin poet, directing it this time not to human love but to the presence-absence of the Divine: "Neither with you nor without you can I live."[4]

Let us now sketch the three dwellings of the Divine that we have mentioned.

1. *The Transcendent Plane*

In the technocratic civilization in which so much of humanity is obliged to live today, any discourse about the Divine situates it in the Beyond, in the transcendent plane, because we do not normally encounter it here below.

We all easily discover the referents of the two words: World and Man—they are ever around us. The referent of the Divine, on the other hand, is not so obvious for many of our contemporaries. It can be described first negatively and then positively. Negatively, the Divine, whatever degree of reality we may ascribe to it, is that which is neither Man nor World. Now, if God is an entity, this entity is radically different from any other. If God has no peer and is unique, we cannot have any concept of God. Thus, the positive approach can come only from a sort of direct disclosure of the Divine itself. In the words of christian tradition: "God cannot be apprehended except through Himself."[5]

This patristic source of such experience resonates with the johannine assertion: Nobody has ever seen (ἑώρακεν) God.[6] With Jesus we are in a jewish milieu and with Irenaeus in a jewish-hellenistic world. The prevalent

4 "Nec cum te nec sine te vivere possum," Catullus said of his mistress, echoed by Ovid, Martial, et al.

5 Hilary, *De trinitate* V, 20. Irenaeus also said it in a slightly different way: "Edocuit autem Dominus, quoniam Deum scire nemo potest nisi Deo docente"; "The Lord taught us that nobody can know God unless God himself teaches (it to) us." Cf. Irenaeus, *Adversus haereses* IV, 6, 4.

6 Jn I, 18. Christ's words: "No one knows [γινώσκει, ἐπιγινώσκει] the Son except the Father, and [no one knows] the Father except the Son, and those to whom the Son wishes to disclose [ἀποκαλύψαι] him" (Mt XI, 27; and Lk X, 22).

scheme is the divine transcendence. Thus, we need to do something more than look around in order to discover a transcendent God. We need a divine descent. That is, in the worldview of a transcendent God, if the divine Mystery is to be more than simply wishful thinking and an empty projection of human desire, then to reach the Transcendent, Man needs a descent of the Divine. To be open to that descent, a "feminine" attitude is required, an awareness that receiving is as important and positive as giving, that to know is not just to find out or apprehend but also to recognize, to be fecundated by the message, to be open to the descending stream of an illuminating light, a descending voice. This does not, however, necessarily mean abandoning our discerning (critical) faculties.

This descent of the Divine seems to be a general conviction of most monotheisms. An idea of the Divine is not immediately given to us by the senses nor is it directly perceived by the mind. It has to come from the Divine itself, or be transmitted by tradition. This is precisely what makes tradition sacred, and probably lies at the origin of the need for revelations in order to have a proper knowledge of God. Pure reason cannot leap from a cosmological Prime Cause to a living God.

We know because our minds are illumined by the very light of what is to be known. *Svayamprakāśa*, the self-luminous, is one of the names of the Divine in indic classical philosophy. Between the platonic theory of knowledge (*anamnēsis* or remembrance of our previous dwelling in the world of the ideas) and the aristotelian-thomistic theory that all our knowledge begins with the senses, there is a middle way in which the active and passive roles of our spirit find an equilibrium. More broadly, between "rationalism" and "sensism," on one hand, and "angelism" and "fideism," on the other, there is a *via media*—which undergirds everything I would like to say.

At any rate, the way to the Divine is different from all the other human ways to anything else. Whatever degree of reality the Divine may have, it does not have a referent disclosed to our senses or to our reason. Or at least its alleged referent would be completely different from any other, a referent open only to our intellect illumined by the Divine itself, some traditions would say. Simply stated, revelation is the main category (*pramāṇa*) here. God dwells in an inaccessible place, and if God is to call us up to Him, He has to reveal Himself to us, or at least His voice has to come down to us.

2. *The Immanent Locus*

What makes present-day religious dialogue so painfully difficult is the fundamentally different referent of the Godhead, and the lack of an adequate western language, despite western languages being permeated by theistic, especially monotheistic, ways of thinking. The notion of divine immanence is not foreign to western culture, although by and large it is a mitigated one in which immanence is interpreted as a kind of negative transcendence: God as a guest of our souls, a welcome or disturbing visitor, but nevertheless a foreigner, lest we lose our individuality. This is another example of the primacy of the principle of non-contradiction over the principle of identity, as mentioned in the previous chapter. If I have to be myself, this self has to be other (different) than the immanent Divinity dwelling in me. This divinity has to be somewhat transcendent even if with a negative transcendence, as it were. Applying the primacy of the principle of identity, on the other hand, I do not need to separate myself from the immanent Divinity in order to be myself. I will come back to this point.

This divine immanence does not need mediation; otherwise, it would not be immanent. To assume that the Divine is not experienced as a *datum* pays tribute to the modern mentality, since in other times and cultures the problem did not appear in this way; the problem was the World, not God. The Divine was obvious. Although there was a difference between "sensible," "rational," and "sacred" realities, all were perceived as *data*. Spirits, ghosts, *apsaras*, demons, and angels all were citizens of this universe—not excluding the Gods. Traditional Man understood himself to be living in three worlds, for example, the *triloka* of the indic tradition.

We have just said that the Divine has no referent like other things because the Divine is not a thing. God has no referent only when we accept an independent epistemology, one disconnected from any ontology (to use accepted words), only when we assume that all our knowledge starts with the senses and that our *empeira* (experience) can come only from the senses, elaborated *a posteriori* by "reason." It is only in that case that the Divine has no referent and we have to make inferences or deductions in order to include the Divine in the field of our consciousness. It is highly significant that the western tradition, at a certain moment, abandoning Plato and following Aristotle, forged the so-called proofs for the existence of God. Thus, the Divine was made subservient to our reason: God's existence followed as the conclusion of a syllogism. Incidentally, we should remember here that the thomistic "proofs" were not scientific demonstrations, but "ways" to show the reasonableness of the existence of "that which all call God."

In practically all traditions except the modern one, and this only up to a certain extent, Man has believed it possible to "detect" a third dimension in addition to those disclosed by the senses and the mind, which is accomplished by means of a sort of faculty sometimes called the *third eye*.

In spite of the shining witnesses of saints and sages, there is no denying that the vision of this third dimension has often been blurred and sometimes kept captive by a minority of shamans, brahmans, priests, mullas, and rabbis. It is also known, however, that once a minority becomes institutionally established, there is a great temptation to monopolize the power that this vision gives, and thereby cause that vision to atrophy among the common people. As early as the first millennium BC this intuition about the Divine, beautifully voiced by poets, critically described by philosophers, and sincerely believed by the people, began to be challenged by some "intellectuals" in concert with those political leaders who wanted to preserve "Law and Order." Perhaps neither brute thinking nor blind submission to institutional powers, be they political or religious, is the best way to approach the Divine. The condemnation of Socrates is a paradigm of this conflict: the political status quo condemned him because his idea of the Divine was too unorthodox. Buddha had to break with the *astik* (vedic) and ātmic (substantialistic) tradition of his times because it did not agree with his ultimate experience under a bodhi tree. The sentence against Jesus had also to do with another experience of the Divine. How could someone who was just a Man affirm that he was "son of God"? For an immense number of people, the divine referent on its own level was just as present and powerful as the two other data. The same was true in the times of the Buddha, although the language was different. As I have said, whatever our opinion about the Divine, one thing is sure: the Divine is not an object among others, it is not something trivial, no matter how opinions about it may differ.

Immanence entails that the immediate awareness of the Divine be given not to the senses or reason, but to that third organ of perception, the third eye, which may also be called *intellectus* in distinction to *ratio*. This perception, however, needs the complement and interpretation of the two other organs of knowledge, as I will try to explain in part V. Thales of Miletus, the acknowledged father of greek philosophy (although he was a phoenician) is supposed to have said:[7] "All things are full of Gods."[8]

There is an apparent paradox here. *On the one hand*, divine immanence is a perception of our third eye. "The heavens narrate the glory of God, and

7 Aristotle, *De anima* I, 5 (411a8). The reason Aristotle gives for this belief is interesting. Because the soul, he says, is intermingled with the entire cosmos and the universe is ensouled, that is, has a *psychē* which makes it a living creature and because Life is the highest symbol, all things (because they are alive) are full of Gods: The Gods are everywhere, the Divine is all-pervading. Augustine, the acknowledged father of christian theology, although he was an African, called God *intimor intimo meo*.

8 πάντα πλήρη θεῶν, quoted by Plato in *Laws*, 899b9 (R. P. 14 b).

the universe proclaims the works of his hands," sings one of the many hebrew psalms expressing the same connection.[9] A simple and beautiful chant to that common belief is expressed in the last complete kosmology of the west:

> The glory of Him who all things moves
> through the entire universe penetrates,
> and shines in one part more
> and less in another.[10]

On the other hand, this very Divinity in all things seems to be veiled to the ordinary eye. *De deo abscondito* ("On the hidden God") is not only a precious jewel of Nicholas of Cusa but a recurrent theme of world literature.[11] The "Kingdom of God" does not arrive with fanfare. Religious "triumphalism" does not fit well with the Divine. Nevertheless, the divine referent is not absent. "The greatest mystery is that 'it' is not hidden at all," Abhinavagupta cryptically says. "The Lord is hidden in his own qualities," the *Gītā* had already said.

The paradox may be easily explained in terms of a common understanding in most traditions: only the pure of heart shall see God. The third eye is blurred, if not blinded, by an impure heart. In such a case one needs "proofs" for the existence of God. "The face of truth is covered over by a golden vessel."[12]

Like a beautiful veil over the face of a beautiful woman, there is something covering truth, and at the same time spurring our imagination to see the invisible. *Satyam*, truth, like the *lēthē* ("concealment," "oblivion"), which needs to become *a-lētheia* ("unconcealed," "discovered"), has to be uncovered, unveiled, revealed, as the second distich of the same text says: "Uncover it, O *Pūṣan*, that I, who hold to truth, may see it."[13] It is also significant that this is a prayer directed to divine providence (*Pūṣan*), which alone has the power to remove the veil, because this veil is plaited with gold, and the temptation of gold is an ancient one: power, riches, lustre, fame, beauty, ductility, endurance. Even at this early stage the difference between

9 Ps XVIII, 1.

10 Dante, *Divina Commedia, Paradiso*: "La gloria di colui che tutto move / per l'universo penetra, e risplende / in una parte più, e meno altrone." I may add that Dante's *gloria* is closer to the splendorous Power and uncreated Light (*doxa, exousia*, etc.) of the christian Scripture and the hindu Upanishad than to the "fame, prestige, glamor and greatness" of modern dictionaries.

11 See Panikkar, *Humanismo y Cruz* (Madrid: Rialp, 1963).

12 IsU 15; cf. BU V, 15, 1-3; MaitU VI, 35. hiraṇmayena pātreṇa satyasya-apihitaṁ mukham.

13 BU V, 15: tat tvam, pūsan, apāvṛṇu, satya-dharmāya dṛṣṭaye.

the greek and indic approaches reflects the distinctive spirit of the two traditions. For Thales, the Gods are powers, living beings, free agents whom Man can contact, entreat, and even quarrel with or struggle against. The Upanishads stress the more entitative presence of the Divine in things—or rather of things in the womb of the Divine.

3. *The Adualistic space*

For heuristic reasons I have emphasized the cliff between transcendence and immanence; in real life, however, as in authentic thought, the transcendent God-head is discovered both outside ourselves and within our hearts and minds. We speak of it because we sense its presence to some degree. Similarly, the immanent Godhead does not simply remain always elusive and ungraspable; its own presence discloses an ever more mysterious absence.

In point of fact, we cannot even think of transcendence without implying its immanence (in us)—otherwise we could neither speak it nor think of it. Viceversa, we can only think of divine immanence if we distinguish the Godhead from ourselves, if we recognize a certain transcendence in its immanence—otherwise we might confuse it with our empiric selves. In short, the divine Mystery is neither there, outside, nor here, inside. What, then, is its space?

* * *

Where does the Divine dwell? Using the word "space," I have in mind something more like the greek *chōra* and the sanskrit *ākaśa* than physical or merely psychic space. The scholastics also made fine distinctions between spatial referents such as *ubi, situ, locus,* and *spatium* in order to show that God is *everywhere*. To avoid another digression on *chōra*, *ākaśa*, space, and the void, we will simply say that God's space is not just a particular kind of space where God "lives" (the "space" of God), but God's space (subjective genitive)—although not in the manner of the newtonian *sensorium Dei*. An upanishadic dialogue on the last foundation of everything ends with the affirmation that "space is the final goal."[14] This space (*ākaśa*) is identified with *brahman* and is situated outside and inside Man (*puruṣa*). This ā*kaśa* lies within the heart of Man (*antar-hṛ dayam-ākaśaḥ*) and constitutes his fullness (*purṇam*).[15]

Recalling our earlier citations from Protagoras and Plato, I would say that the space of Man is in God in much the same way as the space of God

14 CU I, 9, 1: ākāśaḥ pārāyaḥam̃.

15 Cf. CU III, 12, 7, 7-9.

is in Man. Man and God are not two separable entities, two independent substances. Man and God are not two. There is no real *two* encompassing Man and God (the "two" would then be a Super-god), but they are not one either. Man and God are neither one nor two. We cannot assimilate this statement with mere logical reason; that is, we cannot find any rational sense in it. The statement, however, is not contradictory. "1" is contradictory to "not 1" and "2" is contradictory to "not 2" but "not 2" does not contradict "1," unless if we assume that "not 2" equals "not 1." Moreover, what holds in the case of the series of whole numbers is not necessarily so in reality. Reality is not reducible to algebra, to formal calculation, to thinking. Even if one assumes the galilean-cartesian dogma that nature is "written" in mathematical figures, nature is not identical with the scripture in which it may be written. The *advaitic* intuition is not an attack on logical thinking, but simply demonstrates an awareness of the limits of logic and does not subscribe to the parmenidian principle of identifying Thinking and Being.

Here again we see the "violence" of the question. Where does the Divine dwell? I am tempted to repeat the answer of Jesus: "Come and see!"[16] Only a direct personal experience is the answer. The bias of the question is that it lets us assume that the Divine must be "somewhere" within a "space" that embraces both God and Man, which is certainly not the case. To employ an english pun: God is "nowhere," that is, "now-here," although this is misleading if we do not note that time and space are more than epistemological categories. The mutual indwelling of God and Man makes it impossible that both God and Man be substances. Substances are mutually impenetrable; they cannot occupy the same space, or else space is something different from what we assume it to be.

What then is the "space" of the Divine? Where can we find it? Where does it dwell? Here the ambivalence of this word helps us to realize that the language about the Divine requires a language different from our talk about "things," as I indicated at the beginning. To ask when or where the "Kingdom of God" will appear has no meaning whatever said Jesus, as the angel said to the women at the tomb: "He is risen, he is not *here*,"[17] not in any newtonian here.

We may vary our language, but the question remains. Yet the answer also remains elusive, because if we were to put the question in the most general way: "What is the Divine?" we would have to say that the Divine *is* not in any of the ways we use this word when dealing with all the other objects of our

16 Jn I, 39.

17 Lk XXIV, 6.

experience. Thus, we cannot escape the quandary by taking this statement as an answer. We cannot avoid our human limits by dialectical subtleties. If the answer were that the Divine *is* not, we would begin all over again when affirming that the Divine is (an) *is* not. This is why we hear everywhere that the *tao* that can be spoken about *is* not the *tao*, that the *nirvâṇa* we think is not the real one, that the God we see or imagine is not God, and the like.

The question remains, and I may venture an answer that transfers it to the region of Ultimacy I have tried to describe. *The Divine dwells where Man dwells*. If we try to escape from God, writes Augustine, following the Bible, God is there. If we want to liberate ourselves from the Divine, sings Rabindranath Tagore, following the Upanishads, we need God's selfsame power, which will tie us up with our own freedom. I am only repeating the common opinion that God is everywhere, trying to rescue the answer from a categorical and even independent metaphysical interpretation of the "where."

We do not have to undertake painful pilgrimages to distant places to find the Divine, say jewish, persian, hindu, and christian legends. The treasure lies underneath our own house, just in our family, in ordinary life, in our beloved, ultimately in our own heart when our interiority has been cleansed of any particle of selfish dust. Immanence and transcendence are spatial symbols. To continue with the same symbol, I have written "adualistic" space. I can touch upon this capital problem only very briefly.

It means that space is neither a purely objective nor a purely subjective reality. There are no things without space and there is no space without things. If we consider only physical space we are making the common scientific statement that there are no bodies without space and no space without bodies. If we enlarge the notion to cover spiritual spaces we would say something similar. What we have to add in all cases is that they (thing and space) are not the same: body is not space and space is not body. This is the *advaitic* relationship as we are going to explain later.

Coming back to our question, where does the Divine dwell? The answer is unambiguous: inside and outside; the Divine is immanent and transcendent. Many mystics will say God wanders between us, inside and outside, goes in and out, appears and disappears, strays, dwells.

B. Theology

The divine mystery dwells in the heart of Man; thus the divine presence is also a fact of history. Man as a thinking being feels an urge to scrutinize the nature of that mystery. "Theology" is a consecrated word that connotes this problematic. Nowadays it has taken on a very specialized meaning because of the reductionistic understanding of both *theos* and *logos*, and ultimately because of a very reductionistic "anthropology." Yet this has not always been the case. Moreover, in dialogue with some other cultures, like the jaina, the buddhist and the atheistic, I would be ready to drop the word altogether and replace it with "philosophy." Nevertheless, the word "theology" is of venerable greek heritage, and although it has acquired a restricted meaning at present, we cannot use a series of vague synonyms each time we refer to this field. I therefore opt for keeping the name while qualifying and enlarging its meaning. In so doing I shall translate the *theos* (of theology) as God and understand "God" as that ultimate Mystery that is called by many names, one of which is God.

1. *Philosophy and Theology*

At this juncture, I am obliged to recall what has already been alluded to, namely, the artificial and lethal dichotomy between philosophy and theology.[18] Skipping the long history of the relations between these two notions, and attentive to the quaternity of their basic components (*philia, sophia, theos,* and *logos*), we may say that both words stand for the holistic approach to reality and attempt to orient us in our conscious pilgrimage on earth. The "love of wisdom" (philosophy) embraces all that is seen as necessary for the fullness of life, just as the "word of God" (theology) is seen as the authentic key opening us to the true reality of the universe and ourselves.

Western civilization has introduced fundamental distinctions that have ended in a lethal separation between philosophy and theology, leading to the fragmentation both of knowledge and subsequently of the knower.

There is a manifest distinction between the senses, reason, and the intellect (as will be explained in the next part). There also exists a patent difference between the cosmos, humanity, and the divine. The moment that reason is enthroned as the supreme arbiter, rational distinctions tend to become ontological separations. Philosophy then deals with reality as it is seen by reason; it becomes *opus rationis* and theology is given a special "object," God (and no longer the entire reality), which object is supposed to be better known by a special form of knowledge often called faith. This separation is a rather modern phenomenon, although it was already

18 See Panikkar, *L'esperienza* filosofica *de la India* (Madrid: Trotta, 1997), 25-37.

prepared by the scission between the natural and the supernatural.[19] This dichotomy is not the original christian insight, nor does it exist in most traditional cultures. Once the epistemic dualism is accepted, it becomes an anthropological split and in the cosmological arena leads to an ontological two-story building. The holistic approach of the whole Man to the entire reality then loses all meaning. "Theology" without "philosophy" cannot rely on reason and becomes a special field for those who claim to have another source of knowledge. Theology is then often reduced to mere exegesis of alleged "Sacred texts" or degenerates into superstition. Philosophy without theology is reduced to mental analyses with practically no relation to real life.

The entire approach of this book contests both assumptions: the three human "faculties" (sense, mind, and consciousness) belong together; and the three referents of our awareness (World, Man, and God) are also inseparable. Reality is their relationship.

* * *

Theology is a pretentious word. This is another reason why I prefer the equally traditional word, "philosophy," which does not restrict the notion of *theos* to the theistic understanding. Abiding by the cross-cultural nature of this study I make a short incursion into another culture, which will help to deepen and enlarge the meaning of the word (theology) that, out of respect for tradition, I try to rescue.

The dwelling of the Divine is not a matter of our making a place for it or deciphering its language. It might better be understood as becoming conscious of our aspiration toward the Mystery, because it already somehow (potentially some will say) dwells in us. In the indic world of the Upanishads, despite all the good will implied by *kathenotheistic* and other interpretive subtleties, the usual classifications of theism do not do justice to the deepest insights of human experience, or to the way(s) in which the divine disclosure has been received in this culture (I think for instance of *mīmāmsā*, which has been labeled "atheistic").

---

19 The longer treatise on the Trinity of Thomas Aquinas is found in the *Summa contra gentiles*, which was supposed to be mere philosophy, and not in the *Summa theologiae* (which is his longer theological work). We can see what idea of philosophy was assumed in the long title of the compilation of Saint Nikodimo of the Holy Mountain (1748-1809) which Makarios of Corinth published in Venice in 1782: *The Philokalia of the Neptic Saints gathered from our Holy Theophoric Fathers, through which, by means of the philosophy of ascetic practice and contemplation, the intellect is purified, illuminated and made perfect.* (*Neptic* comes from *nepsis*, which means watchfulness, alertness, awakening). Cf. P. Sherrard, *Christianity: Lineaments of a Sacred Tradition* (Edinburgh: T&T Clark, 1998), 256, for an enlightening commentary.

Among the over thirty sanskrit names (and notions) that could legitimately render the meaning of the greek words "philosophy" and "theology" I choose here only one: *Brahmajijñāsa*.[20] Āthato *Brahma jijñāsa* begins one of the most important texts of the vedantic tradition.[21] "Now the aspiration (effort, investigation, existential pilgrimage) to know *brahman*." The classical exegesis of the first word (āthato) consists in stressing that this "desire to know *brahman*" comes as the fruit of a strenuous preparation having purified ourselves of all selfish desires and being ready to consecrate ourselves to find the hidden pearl, the philosopher's stone, the elixir of life, the true reality.[22]

The word, *brahmajijñāsa,* a compound of *brahman* and the optative form of the verb to know (*jñāna*), means the aspiration to know *brahman*, a homeomorphic equivalent to God. There is in Man an urge, an aspiration to know the source of all knowledge, and by knowing this, all becomes known. This aspiration from without meets an inspiration from within. The meeting of the two forms the "space" where the Divine dwells.

The primacy here is given to this existential urge, *nexus*, *élan*, *Drang*, *svadhā*. By becoming conscious of this aspiration, we reach the divine Mystery (*brahman*). Delving into ourselves, we find the presence of this Mystery in our dynamism toward it. This aspiration is a total movement of our being; and becoming conscious of it, we reach an awareness of the reality of *brahman*.

Instead of "philosophizing" further, I will be descriptive, choosing a single, fragmentary example. Kena Upanishad begins:

> Impelled by whom does the mind [*manas*] dart forth?
> Directed by whom does life [*prāṇa*] start on its way?
> Incited by whom is the word [*vāc*] we speak?
> Who is the God [*deva*] who directs eye and ear?[23]

The starting point is not just any arbitrary question, it is *the* question. In fact, the title of this Upanishad indicates that it is posing the central question. *Kena* is the interrogative pronoun in its instrumental form: *By whom?* (or *By what*?).

---

20 See Panikkar, *La esperienza* filosofic*a de la India*, 25-37, where those thirty notions are given.

21 *Vedānta Sutra*, 1, 1, 1.

22 See Panikkar, *The Unknown Christ of Hinduism* (Maryknoll, N.Y.: Orbis Books, 1981).

23 KenU I, 1: "kenesitaṁ patati presitaṁ manaḥ / kena prāṇaḥ prathamaḥ praiti yuktaḥ / kenesitāṁ vācam imāṁ vadanti / caksuḥ śrotraṁ ka u devo yunakti."

The birth of consciousness, human consciousness, most certainly begins with a question, and this question is personalized because we are people who perform personal acts.

What is this question?

It is double. It is posed three times by means of the instrumental pronoun (*kena*), and once by the nominative case (*ka*). The instrumental questions are directed to the three immediate data of consciousness: our mind, our physical breath (or rather, our psycho-physical life), and our words, or language. We are mind, a living body,[24] and language. The questions are about the force, the energy by which our mind, body, and speech are impelled, directed, and incited. It is not so much asking what is "behind" it all, or where it comes from, but rather *who* or *what* makes it work? By what sort of energy are our vital processes enlivened? It is not asking what "it" consists of, but *by whom* or *what* it all functions? It is a question about the "life" of all these lively activities, as it were.

The fourth question asks about the Power that prompts vision and hearing. Although it would be misleading to translate *deva* as "God," without qualifications, the Upanishad is surely pursuing here the question of God.

The four questions do not proceed toward an object: *What* is mind, body, speech, God? They direct us to the agent, but not to an external agent acting from afar, nor to a unique Prime Mover. They ask about the ear of the ear, the mind of the mind, the word of the word. Yet the hearing of the ear, the wording of the word, and the minding of the mind cannot be another ear, word, or mind. The wording of the word is unwordable, ineffable, inexpressible. Otherwise we go on and on, *ad infinitum*.

> That which cannot be thought by thought,
> but by which the thought is thought.[25]

Or again, from another Upanishad: "It is not the mind that one should seek to understand; one should know the thinker."[26] We are not asking here about a substance, a supreme Entity. In the final analysis we are asking about "other than the known and beyond the unknown."[27]

---

24 Life and body are etymologically related; see, for example, the german word *leben* ("live") and *Leib* ("a living body").

25 KenU I, 6. "yan manasā na manute, yenāhur mano matam," or "that which is not minded by the mind, but by which, they say, the mind is minded."

26 KausU III, 8: "na mano vijijñāsīta mantaraṁ vidyāt." Or more literally: "not the mind one should strive to know, / one should know the 'minder.'"

27 KenU I, 3: "Anyad eva tad viditād / atho aviditād adhi."

The indic tradition gives it a name: *Brahman*. Nonetheless, we should refrain from calling this God, or even another conception of God. It is a *homeomorphic equivalent*, a third degree analogy. *Brahman* is not an object of thought. It is not an object at all. "It is not what is worshiped here as such," the same text underscores,[28] and soon becomes highly ironic about all the Gods— whose existence, be it noted, is never contested. Upanishadic Man is looking for something else.

Another Upanishad insists time and again on "That by which everything is known."[29] This is the scope of indic theology: the saving knowledge, that knowing by which we will know everything worth knowing. This liberating knowledge can be interpreted in many ways: escape from *saṁ sāra*, from this world and the circle of transmigrations, contribution to keeping the world together, *loka-samgraha*,[30] illuminating knowledge that merges with *brahman*, and so on. At any rate, the theological activity is a contemplative action sharing in that supreme mystery called *brahman.*

* * *

Summing up, I would say that philosophy and theology are two names that stand for the human effort to make sense of life and understand reality as far as possible, and to attain salvation, liberation, truth, peace of spirit, clarity, or even sanity. If the existential way to Man's end (liberation, realization, *nirvāṇa*, nothingness, God, . . .) could be called religion, philosophy or theology would be the name for the concomitant awareness and critical knowledge of that way—as far as it is given to us to be conscious of it.

The division between philosophy and theology by virtue of the different methods used (reason, intuition, faith, revelation, . . .) could justify a distinction, but not a separation. Most traditions, however, do not exclude from philosophy or its equivalents any of the means supposed to help Man in this pilgrimage. Judging *a priori* that belief, the senses, feelings, or revelation are unreliable means, and accepting only reason as the proper instrument is already an un-philosophical decision or a pragmatic postulate.

2. *Theology and Kosmology*

Theology is a consecrated word, with a pedigree of over two and a half millennia. The *theos* that the human *logos* wanted to investigate was not just the God of monotheism, but that mysterious "dimension" that intrigues and

---

28 KenU I, 8.

29 BU II, 4, 14.

30 Cf. BG III, 20; III, 25; etc.

fascinates the human spirit. The word "theology" is probably more ancient and a little more encompassing than "philosophy," although the separation of the two is a fairly recent phenomenon.

Until well into the Middle Ages theology was called the "Queen of the Sciences," *regina scientiarum*. In spite of the abuses to which it led, the phrase meant that the knowledge of God (theology) embraced everything in heaven and on earth, since the knowledge of God included the knowledge of God's creation—as we see in the famous *Summae Theologiae* of those times. Later on with the specialization of the new "sciences," theology also aspired to become a specialized "science" about a peculiar object. This was not its original meaning, and the shift led to the abusive interpretation that one particular science was the queen of all the others.

Our topic could be introduced through the backdoor, as it were, by remarking that the conception of God has always been intimately connected with the reigning worldview of a particular epoch. Cosmology was a part of theology as long as the cosmos was believed to be God's creation or the Divine intrinsically related to the universe. In a parallel manner, anthropology was a theological chapter studying "the image and likeness of God," while cosmology was another chapter studying the divine *energeia* in the universe. The moment that the link is broken, the "natural sciences" are converted into a cluster of very specific notions about material reality with a specific method of approaching nature, which has nothing to do with theology. The study of the material world is a fascinating and important subject, but it does not include what human consciousness has traditionally held about nature. This is also the case for the scientific disciplines that still use the name of cosmology to designate the idea of the universe as a whole, under a very specific perspective. One should distinguish between the scientific notion of the cosmos, which usually goes under the name of cosmology, and what I shall style as kosmology with a *k*.

I understand by kosmology not a calculating *logos* about the *cosmos*, as in current "cosmological" doctrines that attempt to decipher the intriguing enigmas of the universe by a specifically "scientific" method. By kosmology I understand the *kosmos-legein*—that is, the self-disclosure of the cosmos as human consciousness "hears" or "sees" the cosmos "speak" or "manifest" itself in every culture that has developed such a sensitivity. It is, in other words, how Man feels, understands, suffers, and knows the cosmos when receiving, as it were, the revelation of the cosmos. Kosmology is that which discloses itself when Man is attentive to the disclosure of the cosmos, and deciphers, surmises, or understands what the cosmos is saying. Mythology can be interpreted in two ways: (a) our *logos* about the myths, our study of the myths, the "science" of the myths, or (b) as the *mythos-legein*, the telling of the myths, the listening to and enjoyment of them, the understanding of the myths not as objects of scrutiny but as part and parcel of human life and experience, which in no way excludes critical awareness, analysis, and reflection.

God is always God for a World, and if the conception of the World has changed so radically in our times, there is little wonder that the ancient notions of God do not appear convincing. To believe that one might retain a traditional idea of God while changing the underlying kosmology implies giving up the traditional notion of God and substituting an abstraction for it, a *Deus otiosus*. One cannot go on simply repeating "God creator of the world," if the word "world" has changed its meaning since that phrase was first uttered—and the word "creator," as well.

An instructive and dramatic example in western history was the encounter between Galileo Galilei and Roberto Bellarmino around 1615. Bellarmino is usually held up to ridicule as an obscurantist enemy of progress, but he was right: you cannot propose a new scientific theory as truth without taking into account the underlying kosmology that offers the basis for the "new" truth. In the emerging cosmology of that time there was no dwelling place for the Divine. Of course, I am not defending the old worldview, but I am asserting that any statement about anything in the world is a function of the *mythos* "world" that we consciously or unconsciously hold. Bellarmino was wrong in believing that the old kosmology was still applicable. This permitted Laplace later to proudly announce that his telescope had never shown him a trace of "the Old Man" in the heavens.

Theism is linked with the kosmology that Dante unfolded, perhaps for the last time since Pythagoras. It is not just the mathematics of Ptolemy but the pythagorean kosmological vision that began to collapse around the time of Galileo, though it was still alive even after Newton. Since then theism has been trying to adapt itself to this changing worldview, with singularly little success. Stephen Hawking's simplistic view of God could be adduced as a popular and almost pathetic example of such an encounter. His significance is no greater than the astronaut Gagarin's alleged declaration that he did not find God on the first manned space flight! "Thank God" they did not find "Him"! Each kosmology demands a corresponding theology—and vice versa. Now, here again the relationship is not dialectical but *advaitic*. Neither does theology have a right to dictate what kosmology has to say, nor has kosmology any authority to demand that theology adapt to its findings. They have to interact together in dialogical dialogue.

There have been several basic changes in the relationship between God and the World, a fascinating subject that remains relatively unexplored. Yahweh is certainly not Zeus; the Prime Mover of Aristotle cannot be reconciled with the christian God, nor can the christian God be equated, without some violence, with the God of the hebrew Bible. Brahman is not Allah; nor *kami*, Quetzalcoatl. Similarly, the vision of the World today is not the world of the incas, jainas, or the christian Middle Ages. Bellarmino was right to suspect that kosmology and theology are so intimately connected that a change in kosmology would entail a change in theology. Creation, much less *creatio continua*, has no place in a modern scientific conception of the universe. The "coexistence" of two such "universal" worldviews can only be superficial, and pathetically so, as the recent discussion between "creationists" and "evolutionists" demonstrates. Each vision may be sovereign in its domain, but who delimits the boundaries, and who decrees that there should be boundaries at all?

Modern sciences deal with "natural objects" that form part of the world. This world in turn forms part of the universe at large, which is the ultimate background of that particular science. Interpretations of the findings of that science have to take into account the context in which they are integrated. The relationship between theology and kosmology is of a still more intimate nature, because theology, like philosophy, is not a particular science. It is related to the whole. This is to say that the very name of God is a kosmological notion. God is God for the world, the Creator is creator of the creation, and the Lord is Lord over somebody. As I will expound later, God has a kosmological dimension, just as the cosmos has a divine aspect. In short, a theology without kosmology is a mere abstraction of a non-existent God; and a cosmology without theology is just a mirage. Kosmology and theology are intrinsically knit together.

I have already said that theology should not uncritically yield to modern science as if the scientific cosmology were an apodictic and established fact. Theology should not adapt itself to the demands of "science" before examining the claims of science, something many contemporary studies seem to do when discussing the so-called problem of "reason and faith." Nor should modern science be the point of reference in the dialogue. I am saying that the old solution of the two truths (natural and supernatural, *saṁvṛti-satya* [concealing or enwrapped truth] and *paramārtha-satya* [supreme or highest truth] or the like) only deepens the fragmentation of knowledge and thus of the knower. If there is no cosmos without God, neither is there God without cosmos. A cosmology that a priori excludes the Divine from its understanding of the cosmos is, to say the least, a lopsided and ultimately wrong cosmology. In a similar manner, a theology that severs itself from the world where believing people believe will stagnate in its own cloistered tower. Just as a scientific cosmology that denies the divine dimension is not convincing, a world-denying theology or a *fuga mundi* ("flee the world") spirituality is not valid.

We are touching here on the delicate problem that goes under the confusing name of "reason and belief" or "religion and science." I hope that this entire study may shed some light on those vexing questions by changing the premises on which the problem is based and the method employed to reach some harmony.

3. *The Word of and about God*

Before the fragmentation of knowledge due to the myth of pure objectivity, knowing meant the ontological activity of Man through which the human being came into communion with the rest of reality and reached salvation. The indic wisdom affirms that *jñāna* is for the sake of *mokṣa*; knowledge is undertaken as a path to liberation. Christian theology was saving knowledge and implied prayer, contemplation, and holiness as much as information about doctrines.[31]

Such knowledge could not ignore the knower and thus entailed selfknowledge. Self-knowledge, at least since the famous dictum of the Sibyl of Delphi, *γνῶθι σαυτόν*, "know thyself" was the vestibule to God's knowledge—as Socrates, Plato, Plotinus, and the Middle Ages, as well as the jewish, christian, islamic, hindu, and buddhist traditions most explicitly affirm. It is not only in India that there is an intimate bond between the Self and God. Plato's *Alkibiadēs* is a powerful example. A common but less known saying in islām affirms the same. Centuries later, on the entrance of the great temple of Harrān the same inscription was written: "He who knows himself knows Allah"[32]—that Corbin translates as "becomes divinized (θέωσις)." Meister Eckhart goes so far as to say that "he who knows himself knows all things." The topic has been widely studied, and yet forgotten.

This knowledge of God (theology) is undoubtedly a human knowledge of God, but who is Man, the knower? Can there be "knowledge of God" without "self-knowledge"? Posed the other way round: Can there be self-knowledge without knowledge of the "Self"? Here we reach a critical moment. Is Man only a *logos*-endowed being or also a *pneuma*-laden reality?

31 See Panikkar, *Misterio y revelación: Hinduismo y cristianismo, encuentro de dos culturas* (Madrid: Marova, 1971).

32 Man "*'arafa nafsahu ta'allaha*" (=θέωσις).

In spite of the tripartite notion of Man (body-soul-spirit) in the jewish and primitive christian traditions, the prevailing western culture opted for a bi-partite anthropology (body-soul), a choice that has had momentous consequences. Indeed, although the greek *logos* is not identical to the later european understanding of reason, anthropological dualism permeates the greatest part of today's dominant culture. Even when the spirit is acknowledged, it is generally made subservient to the *logos*, which is what the first christians called the heresy of "subordinationism."

This oblivion of the *pneuma* had a double consequence. On the one hand, theology became less and less the human reception of the self-disclosure of God, and more and more our critical reflection on the mystery of God, on his revelation, and eventually on a revelation of doctrinal statements down to the lowest degree of deductive "theology" (*Konklusionentheologie*). Theology and contemplative prayer were intrinsically linked until the late Middle Ages. Later, the dwelling of the Divine was submitted to critical scrutiny. By whom? Obviously, by the human *logos* reduced to *ratio*. Theology came more and more to mean the human *logos* about the *theos* rather than the very *logos* of the *theos* to which Man used to listen. In brief, it was the victory of *theology* as an objective genitive (our *logos* about the *theos*) over the subjective genitive (the *logos*-of-*thetheos*). To be sure, the *logos* can also be interpreted in many different ways—and we cannot do away with reason, much less with language. Furthermore, the relationship *logos-pneuma* is adualistic, and certainly not dialectical. We cannot reduce Man to *logos* nor separate *logos* from *pneuma*; we cannot sever the "word" from its "breath."

The complete meaning of theology would then be a blend between the subjective and the objective genitives: the proper divine *logos* (the *logos* of God) as well as our *logos* about God. In spite of the danger of anthropomorphism, we cannot *a priori* exclude the possibility that God can also speak—albeit in a peculiar way. Nonetheless, this is not enough. What is needed is certainly not a theo-logy of the Spirit, a "pneumatology." This would be subordinationism. The Spirit is not subservient to the *logos*—nor the *logos* to the *pneuma*. The relationship, I repeat, is not dialectical but *advaitic*. If one understands spirit as the spirit-of-the-*logos* and *logos* as the *logos*-of-the-spirit, the word theology could be "saved." That is not, however, our direct concern here.

Modern scientific research experimenting with matter, for example, learns to be attentive to the changes of energy in any physical interaction and discovers the laws of energy. In a certain way matter "speaks" to us through its behavior, that is, tells us if not its essence certainly something of its ways of action and reaction. The scientist "listens" to matter through measurable experiments. The philosopher listens to Being, and to what Being manifests of its structure, or its "whims." For this we need ears attentive to the language of Being. When philosophy does not exclude *a priori* the possibility of a divine reality, it will become theology. For this we need the ears of faith and attention to the language of the Divine. In this way theology is the human effort to understand the *logos* of the *theos* and to use our *logos* to "translate," as it were, what the divine *logos says*. At any rate, whether we speak about God or listen to God's word, it is we who speak and listen. This is theological language.

4. *Theological Language*

The Divine, to be sure, is not the Lord God who condescends or graciously takes the form of a slave. This was a powerful and beautiful metaphor, but it became an obsolete image once the glamour and grandeur of the absolute monarchy was no longer compelling. The Divine is humble by nature, and not by condescension—although it is only fair to understand the context of patristic theology when it spoke of "divine condescension." It is significant that the *kenōsis*,[33] or self-emptying of Christ, understood today in an ontological sense, is one of the key themes for buddhist–christian dialogue.

The Divine is never "alone," never in or by "itself." It has, paradoxically enough, no "itself," although some would like to call "it" the real Self. It is a dimension of the Whole, but once again, this is not demeaning the Divine. It does not make the Logos less divine to affirm that it is one person of the Trinity, nor does it undermine the divinity of Jesus Christ to affirm that he was totally human.

As I have stressed time and again, we cannot properly speak of the Divine in the third person as if it were a thing, an object.[34] We are obliged by language to use the word "it." Properly speaking, the Divine *is* not. The Divine, if at all, can only be said to be an *am* and not an *is*. The *is* points only indirectly to the Divine, converting "it" into a predicate. The *art* refers to the Divine when we speak to "it" in prayer or otherwise. Only the *am* belongs directly to the Divine. Which human being would dare say, responsibly, (I) *am*? Simone Weil wrote: "qui dis *je,* ment" ("whoever says I, lies"). We can

33 Phil II, 9.

34 See Panikkar, "The Threefold Linguistic Intrasubjectivity," in M. M. Olivetti, ed., *Intersoggettività, socialità, religione: Colloquio internazionale (Rome 4-7 Gennaio 1986),* Archivio di filosofia 54/1-3 (Rome: CEDAM, 1986), 593-606.

only listen to the *ahambrahman*—perhaps, at first, resounding in us, and eventually, co-involving us. This is why Man *is* not God, because God *is* not. God ("is") *am*. The Divine Mystery is the ultimate *am*—of everything. Yet we also experience the *art* and the *is*. This is the cosmotheandric experience: the undivided experience of the three pronouns simultaneously. Without the Divine, we cannot say *I*; without Consciousness we cannot say *Thou*; and without the World, we cannot say *It*. The "three" pronouns, however, are not three; they belong together. They are pro-nouns, or rather pro-noun; they stand for the same (unnameable) noun. The noun "is" only in the pronouns. God is unnameable—or, as Meister Eckhart says, God is *innominabile* and *omninominabile*, all-nameable. He stands at the "end" of any authentic invocation. Any name will do, provided we do not fix the names as labels on substances or as signs pointing toward univocally isolable entities. Centuries before Eckhart the eclectic *Corpus hermeticum*, repeating a common intuition, says: "All names are names of Him."[35]

Any name names the Divine, provided it is a real name and is used in the vocative, and provided that it names and does not just signify. It has to name, to call, to invoke, and thus evoke, and not only designate or signify. A name names when Man, like Adam, uncovers in the name the deepest nature of every thing. Each name ultimately names the Divine, as Thomas Aquinas affirmed, going so far as to say that any desire, and not just a human desire, is a desire of God.[36]

One might shake one's head in passing over the stupendous grammatical incongruity of the christian liturgy, which begins "In the Name of the Father, and of the Son, and of the Holy Spirit"—not in the "Names" of the three persons or of the Father. Nor does it say "in the Name of God." It says in the Name of the one noun which *is* not. There are not three Names. It is only one Name in three pro-nouns. The noun is in its pronouns. Each pronoun is the whole noun in its pronominal way. One could speak here of three dimensions which totally interand intra-penetrate each other. This is the *perichōrēsis* repeatedly referred to.

Theisms generally move in pendular oscillation between apophatism and kataphatism, and both languages make sense. The difficulty lies in combining both languages and discerning whether we are really talking about the same "thing." My contention is not sufficiently answered by affirming that "there is no adequate talk about God." *Prima facie*, this seems to be just a friendly amendment to monotheism, about which one could easily agree. On a deeper level, however, there is a pitfall we should avoid.

35 *Corpus hermeticum* V, 10.

36 Thomas Aquinas, *De veritate* q. *22* a. 2.

That we speak of inadequate talk about God implies either that adequate talk is possible (we just have not talked it yet), or that we have come to discover the intrinsic inadequacy of our talk. In this latter case we can affirm that there is inadequate talk about practically anything: love, justice, a friend, or even a lowly fly. We cannot know anything adequately. "God," in this case, would simply be another of the "objects" of inadequate human talk. We discover our own inadequacy in talking about any thing. Nevertheless, painting God with the same broad brushstrokes degrades the Divine to the status of an object. If any talk is inadequate, so that there is no adequate talk of anything, then we change the meaning of the word. Inadequacy here stands for the fact that no language exhausts the meaning or the essence of anything it talks about.

We may agree that there is no adequate talk of any object, but if God is not an object, the query remains and the dilemma stands. Is there an adequate talk about God hidden away somewhere that is reserved for saints, mystics, or some special people, or is there an adequate talk about God that belongs to God alone? It is difficult to accept the first "solution," because, aside from other intrinsic difficulties, the mystics themselves are the first to tell us that they can only stammer about the Divine, and many would prefer silence to any talk.

This God "dwells in an inaccessible light"[37] (*φῶς οἰκῶν ἀπρόσιτον* [*α-πρόσι-τον*—not-toward-go-capable, "unapproachable"], an exquisite expression). Should we dare to approach this divine light, we would be blinded by it.

There remains the response that God can speak adequately about itself because it is itself Language, Word, Logos. God has an adequate language about itself which is itself. This is a trinitarian response that gives language its divine dignity and at the same time explains the inadequacy of our language as long as we are not united with the divine Logos.

Within christian orthodoxy we may say that the "divine" talk about God— the Word of God, the Logos—adequately expresses the Divine Mystery only, as it were, on the part of the Logos. The Logos says everything that God is; it is, so to speak, the "fallibility" of God. It is the Name of God. There is, however, still the Spirit, and the Spirit is not the Logos. It is infinitely different, according to classical christian theology. There is nothing finite in the Trinity. We cannot and should not separate the Spirit from the Logos, but we should not confuse them either. The Spirit *qua* Spirit (a sentence that we cannot pronounce outside the Logos) is unintelligible,

37 1 Tim VI, 16.

since intelligibility is the Logos. There is adequate talk about God, but even this adequate talk (the Logos) is not exhaustive because the Divine Mystery is "more" than Word alone.

I should now qualify my affirmation. There is an adequate talk about God as far as it goes—that is, as far as there can be an adequate language about God; it is the divine Word. While the Word is God, however, the Divine is not exclusively Word, Logos. Or again: God may be *said* to be Logos, and the Logos, God. But God is "more" than what can be *said*, even by itself. There is "something" that cannot be said, thought, spoken. As Gustave Thibon says, "The infinite retreats indefinitely before he who rushes to conquer it, and gives itself to he who watches it without advancing."[38]

The Logos *qua* Logos is divine, inferior neither to the Spirit nor even to the Father. The equality of the Logos with God is absolute *a parte rei*. There is no other *logos* that is not included in the divine Logos, the Second Person. All that can be said about God, all talk about God, all the intelligibility of God is (in) the Logos, and this intelligibility is infinite. This Logos is what many a tradition calls the intelligible world, the divine Intellect, the first manifestation or emanation of the One. I am not propounding a particular doctrine but describing a problem, the gist of which is the following.

Language about the divine is different language altogether from the so-called ordinary language of a desacralized civilization. This point must be emphasized especially in an age that has lost the sense for hierarchy (sacred order). The questions are so momentous that I am obliged to present some comments in an overcondensed form lest the harmony of the whole be distorted. Theology is certainly a language, understanding language as the most general form of communication and communion. Language is more than what is commonly identified with the *logos*. Language is also mythos, as the word itself reveals and as many traditions affirm.

In an effort to deepen and enlarge the meaning of theology, we could rescue the word if we go back to the vedic *vāc*, the biblical *dābār*, the heraclitean and johannine *logos*, along with the understanding of the word in so many african religions. We could then maintain that theology is an existential urge toward the fullest possible human realization, which demands awareness of our real situation and actualization of all our potentialities precisely by listening to and sharing in that Word which is more than a merely human construct. Theology entails the sacredness of the Word—Θεός-λόγος and not only Θεοῦ-λόγος.

38 G. Thibon, *L'ignorance étoilée* (Paris: Fayard, 1974), 28-29: "L'infini recule indéfiniment devant celui qui marche à sa conquête, il se donne à celui qui le regarde sans avancer."

a) Theology as an Activity of the Logos

Even a "*pneuma*-tic" theology has to use the *logos,* that is, words. Words, of course, are spoken as signs, concepts, symbols, and gestures. Confusion among these four uses of words lies at the origin of tragic misunderstandings of historical proportions. All are words. We speak words.

(1) We have words at the tip of our senses: a house, a stone, a sound, a scent, a banner—these are primarily *signs*, signaling a particular thing.

(2) We also conceive words at the tip of our minds, abstracting from particular things or events: numbers, geometrical figures, gravitation, entropy—these are *concepts*, conceived as expressing specific commonalities.

(3) We also speak words that express areas of human experience shared by a group of people (of a particular time or culture): beauty, goodness, time, God— these are *symbols*, viewed as such by a particular cultural group.

(4) We also use words to encourage, threaten, praise, pray, command, or trigger some activity—these are *gestures*, understood within a specific context.

Theological words can be understood on those four levels.

(1) Theology as a Construct of Signs

Signs are very useful. They orient us, but give us little information about the thing. They point in a direction and serve to discriminate one thing from another. To say that God is transcendent is more a sign pointing to an ever beyond than a concept. A sign explicitly announces that it is not the thing: it is only a label. To employ the terms of the divine as signs is not idolatry, for no label is ever confused with the thing it signifies. It becomes idolatry only if we take the sign for the reality. A sign claims that the thing is such that it permits a label through which we can identify the "object." The Divine, however, is not an object. If we make it one, that is idolatry, but an idol is not what most human traditions understand by the name of the Divine. Theology aspires to more.

Theology as a science of signs is legitimate and useful inasmuch as it expresses divine transcendence. Becoming a specialized science, however, incurs the danger of being an empty science, or perhaps an esoteric science into which only a few experts (theologians) know how to enter. "Our Father in Heaven." "Father" is a metaphor, "heaven" is a sign—although both names could also be symbols for certain people. No name is purely objective or exclusively subjective.

The "sign of the Cross," a "holy picture," and a religious image may be mere signs for some or may turn into symbols for others; a sacred *icon* is a consecrated *mūrti*, for instance. History reports many martyrs who chose to die rather than to trample on a holy image or offer incense to a mere human being. Signs are important, even if they are only signs. A Theology of the Temple, for instance, is an important theological chapter in some religions.

(2) Theology as a Conceptual System

Signs are only indicators. The Divine is transcendent and signs are helpful, but the Divine is also immanent and signs are not enough. Something of the Godhead has to strike our mind which allows us to have a certain knowledge of it by interpreting some positive attributes of our experience of reality in an eminent way. This involves concepts.

A concept is a *medium quo* (a means through which), a device that lies between the sign and the thing, which is obtained *through* a rational operation *to* get at the "essence" of the intended thing. Concepts belong to the world of mental intentionality. The concept is undoubtedly not the thing, but makes it possible to understand the thing to a large extent. Most modern theology is conceptual theology, and it has made important strides in the knowledge of God.

Conceptual theology, however, has a gigantic drawback. The concept is surely not the thing, and in spite of its possible analogy with the thing, the concept itself is fixed, it is a mental object. Once we have applied concepts like immutability or omniscience to God, for instance, it is extremely difficult to criticize one of them without preventing the entire conceptual system from collapsing. If a christian criticizes the "Virgin Birth," for instance, since this concept is linked with Jesus being free from original sin (supposedly transmitted by male semen), and since original sin is connected with the very meaning of Redemption, which in turn is connected with creation and the latter with the Creator, the denial of one single dogma entails the denial of all of them—unless the tight conceptual scaffolding is replaced by another one.[39]

In addition, concepts are human constructs dependent on the collective historical womb that conceived them. We apply, for instance, the concept of justice to God. God is certainly a just God, but what is justice? To wage war against the enemy? To condone slavery? To "predestine" some and condemn others? Is there any objective justice? Aristotle seems to distance

39 See Panikkar, "Pensamiento científico y pensamiento cristiano," *Cuadernos Fe y Secularidad* 25 (Madrid: Sal Terrae, 1994).

himself from platonic Socrates when affirming that justice is what the just Man does, and not the Man who fulfills the abstract concept of justice. What could a non-objective justice be? The idiosyncrasies of Indra? The whims of a *Pantocratōr*? If relativism would destroy any rationality, theology as an immutable castle of concepts would destroy any human and divine freedom.

Man is much more than a rational animal, but he cannot dispense with rationality, and the main instrument of reason is the concept. Theology as the human effort to make sense of the *Theos* by means of the *logos* is bound to build a conceptual system. Yet this indispensable conceptual system, which remains a kind of infrastructure in many theologies, has tended to get the upper hand in western intellectual history. Among other possible explanations I venture the following.

The destiny of western theology has been greatly influenced by a genial philosophical discovery: the concept, which is due mainly to the no less genial figure of Socrates. Since Socrates the meaning of a language—and theology certainly needs a language—has tended to be more and more identified with its conceptual contents. Since concepts have proved themselves to be so rich and useful, the *sophia* intended by philosophy and theology has been overshadowed by the *epistēmē* of concepts, specifically, of general concepts. Theology then slowly becomes a conceptual system, and once the concept has emancipated itself from all its emotional constituents, theology can dispense with love as a constitutive ingredient. The concept does not need love to be a clear and distinct concept. Love becomes relegated to piety or devotion and no longer to theology, which increasingly grows into a conceptual science.

To be sure, theology needs to use language and language needs words, and words are words because they have *meaning*. "Meaning," however, is a rich and polysemic word of which conceptual meaning is only one of its senses. The meaning of a word is that which hits the "mind" (from the root *men*) inciting us to think and to love (cf. the old german *Minna*, "love," which is from the same root). The meaning of a word is its intention (cf. the german *Meinung*, "opinion").[40] To get the meaning of a word, let alone of language, we need to catch its intentionality. Now, the intentionality of a word is not primarily its conceptual content, but its referent. When we say "beautiful music," a "sacred space," or "life," we may have as referents Beethoven, the mosque of Cordoba, or God, and not a problematic concept of beauty applied to music, a "scientific" concept of space with a specific quality, or a physiochemical concept of life applied to God. The referents are

40 Consider the expressions "I mean to say" and "You know what I mean?" "Saying" and "knowing" are only such when we get the meaning.

symbols and not necessarily concepts. Many misunderstandings of historic proportions have their origin in this confusion. We could distinguish scientific "terms," which are concepts, from spoken "words," which are symbols.[41]

(3) Theology as a Symbolic Knowledge

Traditional theologies were more concerned with symbols and praxis than with concepts. Language was more symbolic communication and existential communion than conceptual information. This use of symbolic language was most prominent in theology, since there is no possible concept about God. It is understandable that all theologies have a mystical component, and mystical language is hardly conceptual. Yet language is language and not just a conglomeration of sounds, because it has a meaning, and meaning needs a referent, not necessarily a concept, as I have tried to explain. This referent is the symbol God (or equivalent) and/or its "effect," that is, praxis. I should recall the importance of symbolic awareness and the nature of the symbolic difference.[42]

God is not an object of the senses, nor is God a concept of the mind. Yet God is neither a meaningless nor a superfluous word. On the contrary, in the majority of cultures it is one of the most important words. As a word, it stood and still stands for "something." We realize, however, that the sense of this word has varied enormously throughout the ages, among a variety of cultures and peoples. It is a non-objectifiable word because its referent is essentially linked with the knowing subject, and therefore cannot be negated by an appeal to a merely objective instance. This is not to be understood individualistically, but as a function of the horizon of intelligibility of a given culture, which we have called a *mythos*. In a word, God is a symbol, the highest symbol. God is open to the symbolic awareness that many relate to what has been called the third eye.

It is a fact that there are many symbols of the Divine. This plurality of different symbols is not necessarily contradictory, since symbols may not belong to a common epistemic field where they could come into confrontation. The symbol is symbol when it symbolizes, and it symbolizes when it speaks immediately to us, that is, without any further mediation. Symbolic knowledge overcomes the excruciating problem of modern western philosophy: the subject/object dichotomy. A symbol is such when

41 See Panikkar, "Words and Terms," in M. M. Olivetti, ed., *Esistenza, Mito, Ermeneutica,* Archivo di Filosofia (Padua: CEDAM, 1980), 117-30.

42 See Panikkar, "Introduction," *Myth, Faith, and Hermeneutics* (New York: Paulist Press, 1979).

it is a symbol for someone, when there is a subjective participation in the symbolizing power of the symbol. This "someone" cannot be an isolated individual. The symbol is such when there is a community for which the symbol symbolizes. An example may substitute for a long excursus. If Sarasvatī (the Goddess of wisdom) is for me a symbol of the Divine, and for somebody else just an exotic image pretending to be divine, then we are not on the same *noetic* field since my *pisteuma* is only the other person's *noēma*.[43] In such a case, we cannot discuss "Sarasvatī" because we would not be talking about the same "phenomenon." We may discuss whether the concept of Sarasvatī sufficiently represents our respective conceptions of the Divine, but not about that symbol, which is not a symbol of the divine for my partner. Is there then no way of communicating? As already suggested, dialogue is possible when it assumes a common *mythos* or when it creates a new one. This commonality is not an abstract common denominator, but a common horizon as in the *Horizontsverschmelzung* (fusion of horizons) explicated by Gadamer.[44]

I have just said that the symbol requires a community for which the symbol is such. This is the key for understanding a feature of theology that has often been misunderstood by the modern mind, and that has been dropped or not taken sufficiently into account by some contemporary theological works: the role of initiation in the study of theology. Hindu theology requires an ardent thirst for liberation and an ascetic practice; buddhist theology (allowing for the name) demands a teacher and some formal initiation; christian theology was meant for those who had received the initiation of baptism, and faith was a requirement; and so on. In spite of possible and actual abuses, the reason is that without some sort of initiation the student will not discover the symbolic power of the words and will mistake them for mere concepts. The concept demands understanding, the symbol participation.

(4) Theology as Theopraxis

Theopraxis is an indispensable aspect of theology, just as orthopraxis is one of faith. Both of these words should not supplant, but rather complement and eventually deepen the "meanings" of theology and faith. Faith without works is dead. Theology without praxis is barren.

Theology also speaks a language of praxis. I said at the outset that

43 See Panikkar, "The Ambiguity of the Science of Comparative Religions: Noêma and Pisteuma," in S. Painadath and L. Fernando, eds., *Co-Worker for Your Joy* (Delih: ISPCK), 25-36.

44 H. G. Gadamer, *Philosophical Hermeneutics,* trans. and ed. by David E. Linge, 30th Anniversary Edition (Berkeley/Los Angeles: University of California Press, 2008).

language uses signs, concepts, symbols, and gestures. Theology is also gesture. We read of saints who could not utter the name of God without bursting into tears, dancing, or experiencing melancholy or joy. More needs to be written and learned about those who speak by dedicating themselves to doing what they believe to be God's work, an activity not so much entrusted as "intrusted" to them, for "God" always acts from the innermost recesses of our own intimate being.

The winds that have burst open the pods and carried away the seeds of spirituality from the grounds of "systematic theology" have left those grounds barren earth. This is another example of the dualistic split between theory and praxis, contemplation and action, a split that often extends unto the very heart of the *logos*, understood as word on one side, and as reason on the other.

We should not confuse different fields. Distinctions are necessary, but separations are lethal. Praxis without theory is blind and ineffective, when not countereffective. At the same time, theory without praxis is barren, thus fruitless, when not destructive. A certain distinction between theory and praxis is healthy for both when dealing with ordinary matters, just as any division of work can be. In the case of theology, the issue is more delicate because we are not dealing here with specialized science or specialized action. The whole requires a holistic approach. Not for nothing, I repeat, did the ancients insist on initiation before beginning the *studium* of theology. Initiation is required in order to understand some aspects of reality and to have the strength to put our insights into practice. I have used the word *studium* in its classical sense of total consecration to understand a subject matter and to be worthy of its exacting demands. Cicero says, "Study is an enduring and intense activity of the spirit directed to something with a great resolve."[45]

We are far away here from what is usually understood by theory as captured in the adage: *Grün ist das Baum des Lebens, grau ist alle Theorien* ("Green is the tree of Life; gray is all theory"), wrote Goethe, who needed all his theoretical knowledge to see and enjoy the tree of life. He was obviously using the words in the already modern dualistic sense.

The present-day Theology of Liberation is an example of this theopraxis. I would say more: praxis is a *locus theologicus* in the classical sense of being one of the starting points of theological activity. Utilizing two gestures, Hans Urs von Balthasar spoke of a *kniende* and *sitzende* theology (kneeling and sitting). We should add *handelnde*, an active theology.

45 Cicero, *De inventione* I, 36: "[Studium] est autem animi assidua et vehementer ad aliquam rem adplicata magna cum voluptate occupatio."

Living language is also gesture. A gesture is an outcome of an inner attitude; it is the praxis that results from contemplation. This praxis has a double aspect, an inner and an outer manifestation. Authentic theology has a transformative power, and it changes our lives. Spirituality is the inner aspect of theology. The contact with the Divine challenges us to live a divine life. Theology has a mystical kernel, as it were. There is no knowledge without love and there is no love without an aspiration to union. Authentic theology leads to a divine union. It is a conscious sharing in the trinitarian life.

The theological gesture also has an outer aspect: it is involvement in the world. It is, first of all, a communitarian activity; it builds communion. "Church" would be the christian word for this. Moreover, it is a praxis, an action of love for justice, peace, harmony.

There is still another reason explaining the contemporary move to re-link theology and spirituality. Conceptual theology has reached its limits, especially in the West, where it has mostly flourished. After millennia of conceptual thinking, pure speculative theology has not found a rational explanation for some pressing problems insoluble by the human mind. Let us take a single one: the problem of evil. All our rational speculation finishes by recognizing that it is an enigma, which obviously remains a scandal for a rational theology. A spiritual theology leads us to experience evil in ourselves and how we are able to overcome and redeem it, how a curse may become a blessing and how evil is part of our own personal existence, which we nevertheless consider good. This does not undo the intellectual problem but introduces us into another dimension of the quandary; we discover that reason alone is not the only instrument to live meaningfully in the universe. In addition, experience introduces us to a dimension of reality that is impervious to reason, and to the fact that thinking alone is not the ultimate judge of reality. We are reminded again of Parmenides. The experience of our union with God, which only love makes plausible, does not throw all responsibility on an omnipotent Divinity, but helps us to realize that we also are involved in the adventure of reality.

* * *

It should be obvious to the reader that this book, which criticizes overspecializations, will stand for the harmonization of these four aspects of theology. Some may object that this is an idealized notion of theology very distant from the current one. If this be the case, it may show how far away we have moved from a holistic vision of reality. It is one thing to say that our human limitations and fragility make it difficult to fulfill this ideal, another thing to abandon the effort at a holistic approach to reality.

b) Theology as a Work of the Mythos

Theology is more than merely rational activity. It requires faith, and more than simply faith in reason. There is a profound relation between *mythos* and faith.[46] Both are accepted as truth, and are neither rational nor irrational. The truth of *mythos* can be expressed only in a narrative and the truth of faith in a belief. A *mythos* is not such if we do not believe in it. Otherwise it is only mythology. A symbol is not a symbol if it does not symbolize for us, as a song is not a song if it is not sung. I use *mythos* as that which offers to us each time a corresponding horizon of intelligibility. Otherwise it is just a "myth" in the vulgar sense of the word. Theology is also a mythic language.

I may spell it out by describing another set of four features.

(1) Aesthetic

God may be pure spirit, but we are not. The *logos* may be an intellectual word conscious of itself, but *mythos* is the complete story that engages more than just our intellect. In christianity in an eminent way, but in other religions as well, the Divine is not bodiless. Theology as "God-talk" encompasses all our senses. In some traditions beauty is the most important attribute of God, and beauty is perceived by the senses and enlivened by the intellectual and the mystical eyes. Our approach to the Divine Mystery takes hold of our entire being. The theological language is also a sensuous language, the language of the heart some would prefer to say, an aesthetic language. In other words, sentiments also belong to theology. Sentiments are essential "ingredients" of Man.[47]

Man is not reason alone. There is a "factor" in us which we may call sentiment, feeling, and love that cannot be ignored in the human enterprise of theology. Human sentiments are part and parcel of theological speculations, not mainly as "proofs" or "ways" to God, but as essential elements to understand who we are and what or who this other dimension is. If the Divine dwells in the human heart and the heart is a symbol of the whole Man, theological language cannot spurn those aspects of the human being. In point of fact, there may be more genuine theology in literary works and in art in general than in many modern theological manuals.

Theological language should be as much as possible poetical language. Theology is not algebra and does not deal with lifeless concepts. The

46 Panikkar, *Myth, Faith, and Hermeneutics,* 4-6, 17-64, 213-18.

47 Panikkar, "El sentido cristiano de la vida – III," *Revista Española de Pedogogia* 5 (1948), 1-18.

metaphor and especially the parable are theological tools. The dictum of the late thomists— *formalissime semper loquitur divus Thomas* ("Saint Thomas always speaks a formal language")—besides not being true, already represents the decline of thomism and all of the scholastic tradition. How dare we encapsulate in clear and distinct ideas what deals with the ineffable mystery of the real?

Just as any material thing has color although it is more than its color, analogously any word about the Divine Mystery is pregnant with sentiment. This is one of the many reasons why there cannot be a pure phenomenology of God. The way a word connotes a bundle of sentiments that color the concept makes impossible any phenomenological *epochê*.[48] God is not a value-free concept, and even those who would claim that God is a value-free concept would do so because they feel that that attitude is the most "valuable" one. Even skeptics will take the skeptical approach as being the most appropriate, that is, the most "valuable."

This is not to defend a purely sentimental language of theology. It is to say that theological language is human and humane language and as such is not without sentiment. It all depends, of course, on what we understand by that word. Without indulging in any theory about feelings, we may conceive that a sentiment is a participation of the senses in the intellectual operations of our mind, the αἴσθησις concomitant to the νόησις. The poetics of theology, thus, has still another function: it prevents theology from becoming a mere conceptual and exact "science."

(2) Apophatic

An apophatic feature is different from an unknown aspect. Any object of knowledge has an unknown aspect, since no human knowledge can claim to exhaust its object. We do not have exhaustive knowledge of anything. We do not know all the properties of a triangle or the complete nature of a stone or the total beauty of a symphony, let alone the nature of Man, God, or Reality. There are, furthermore, things we simply do not know. Although we cannot say without contradiction, "I understand that I do not understand," we can say, "I am aware that I do not understand." The field of awareness is broader than the field of understanding. Apophatism lies on those fringes of consciousness. Apophatism is aware of the non-said and does not say it. Silence is also a language. Although it says nothing, we are aware of the "nothingness" of silence.

48 Panikkar, "Progresso scientifico e contesto culturale," *Civiltà delle macchine* [Rome] 5 (1963), 3-13.

The apophatic factor of theology discloses not only an unknown or even unknowable feature of the Divine Mystery, but makes us aware that there remains a factor that cannot be put into words. A geometry of a triangle, a physics of a stone or an astrophysics of the material universe will make it plain to us that we cannot know everything about those "objects." A theological reflection, on the other hand, will make us aware that those very "objects" have, as it were, an ingredient of silence, that their "essence" (all words fail) is untranslatable into concepts, ideas, and words. The unknown things in our scientific knowledge are on the same ontological level as the known facts; these unknown things have to be "scientific truths." They are enigmas belonging to the epistemic order; they are un-known. On the other hand, the "referents" of apophatic theology are not modifications or even transformations of kataphatic statements; these referents transcend the ontological order. They are mysteries—the *logos* stands at the threshold. In spite of its name, theology transcends the *logos* dimension of everything. The ineffable is different from the unknown.

We should not be overly clever about apophatism and dismiss it saying that "of what one can say nothing, one must keep silent."[49] First of all, perhaps that which eludes our language may be the most important thing to try to spell out, lest we fall into utter passivity in the face of reality's resistance to being incarnated in language. Second, language itself has not only a revealing but also a concealing character. Serious esotericism is not a matter of private secrecy, but rather the hidden core of language itself is only revealed to those "who have ears to hear," and there is no need to conceal it from others.

Moreover, language is much more than conceptual language. Language is also symbolic language, which amounts to much more, not less, than metaphorical and practical language. The *symbolon* catapults us not only to the other shore (*metaphora*) and from there back to ourselves (*parabola*), but throws us to the mysterious core of that which the symbol symbolizes in its deeper self. Here we are already in the antechamber of apophatic theology. The Cloud of Unknowing, beam of darkness, *docta ignorantia*, and the like are all the linguistic tools of apophatic theology.

Finally and mainly, apophatic theology is not limited to saying nothing, but tries to unveil the vacuity that accompanies all linguistic statements. It does not tell us that the Mystery cannot be told—that much we know from the very outset. It tells us that the *logos* is not everything, but that we cannot dispense with it. It tells us further that language is not everything,

49 Wittgenstein, *Tractatus Logico-philosophicus*: "Wovon man nicht sprechen kann, darüber muss man schweigen."

but awareness of the void, which is beyond, behind, beneath, and/or above all that language can say, requires us to undergo an abolishing or cleansing of ourselves. Emptiness is not nothingness. Emptiness, like an infinitesimal calculus in an opposite direction, is that which "remains" once we have emptied ourselves from all our thoughts, representations, the mind itself, our very egos. The indic theology is emphatic about this. I have already mentioned the thirst for the knowledge by which everything (else) is known.[50] The Upanishad continues: "With what (*kena*) can one know it? / With what should one know the knower?"[51]

And the same Upanishad provides a first answer:

> You cannot hear the hearer of hearing;
> you cannot think the thinker of thinking;
> you cannot know the knower of knowing.[52]

The Kena Upanishad, which carries all this to its utmost consequence states: "It is not known by those who know; it is known by those who do not know."[53]

Brahman is not known by those who know, because it is not knowable; it is not an object and, therefore, cannot be an object of knowledge. It transcends knowledge. It is present to those who do not know, because those who do not know have no power of abstraction, and *brahman* is not an abstract reality. There is "something" besides or beyond knowledge. If knowledge is a sort of identification of the knower with the known, there is no subject here (knower) to identify itself with something else (known) called *brahman*.

We touch here a fundamental difference between indic and western intellectual approaches to the ultimate cognitive problem. Husserl sums it up, saying that any consciousness is consciousness *of*. The upanishadic wisdom affirms, on the contrary, and vedānta thematically concurs, that pure consciousness is so pure that it is not consciousness of anything, not even of itself—it is not consciousness *of*. Paradoxically enough, pure knowledge does not know that it knows; pure knowledge does not know *is*. This is what the following verse states:

---

50 BU II, 4, 14.

51 Ibid.

52 BU III, 4, 2.

53 KenU II, 3: "avijñātaṁ vijānātāṁ / vijñātam avijānatām."

> When it [*brahman*] is known through (in) every
> act of knowledge it is verily known;
> Then one attains immortality.[54]

One does not know *brahman* directly; *brahman* is not an object of knowledge. One knows *brahman* in every act of cognition, when it is a flash of awakening or illumination (*prati-bodha*). Authentic knowledge is not an epistemological activity but an ontological state. The Divine Mystery is a question not of knowledge but of Being. We cannot know the knower, for then the knower would become the known. Nonetheless, we can be it; that is, we can become the knower. The true knower is an unknowing knower. When we truly know something, we know *brahman*; when we truly know a being, we know Being. The *Corpus hermeticum* puts it forcefully: "Mind is seen in its thinking, and God in his working."[55]

One classical indic example is that of the mother-of-pearl (while it is really silver). There are those who know only the mother-of-pearl. These know only the appearance without even knowing that it is an appearance. They do not know silver; they do not know *brahman*. There are also those who, upon seeing mother-of-pearl recognize it is as "silver." These take cognizance of appearances and know them to be appearances of the real. In truth, they do not know the real; they only infer it—they have *parokṣa jñāna*, a mediated knowledge. There are, finally, those who truly know the silver (in the mother-of-pearl). Although they can know it only "through" what to others appears to be mother-of-pearl, these do know *brahman*. Nonetheless, since they have no other point of reference, they do not know how to distinguish it from the appearance that they do not see. They do not really "know" silver, or *brahman*; they know the "true" mother-of-pearl which is silver, and which is *brahman*. They know "it"—the "it" being neither what people call mother-of-pearl nor what the pundits call *brahman*. "That truly *Brahman* thou knowest!"[56] This short Upanishad speaks several times of reaching immortality. It symbolizes the existential way of "knowing" *brahman*, of transcending inauthenticity, *saṁ sāra*. It is a flash of awakening—like lightning!—as the text says. Realization is not of the order of knowledge, but of presence, of Being.

(3) Mystical

The mystical character of theology could have been included in the

54 Ken U II, 4. The text is difficult to translate: "pratibodha-viditam matam . . ." means that [*Brahman*] is rightly known when known in every actual act of knowing.

55 Hermes Trismegistus, *Corpus Hermeticum* XI, 22.

56 KenU I, 6, 7, 8, 9, repeated refrain: "tad eva brahma tvaṁ viddhi."

formulation of the apophatic aspect. By introducing a new section I would now like to stress another important aspect of theology, that of experiential science. It need hardly be stressed that I take mysticism to be the study neither of parapsychological phenomena nor of the exceptional insights of a privileged few, but rather the immediate awareness of reality that can be awakened to a greater or lesser extent in any human being by means of the third eye, as I will describe more fully in the next part.

This experience in no way excludes critical awareness and the discernment of the intellect. Theology is not merely rational, but it is by no means irrational. The dialectical dilemma of either rational or irrational presupposes an almost totalitarian idea of rationality in both the epistemic and metaphysical spheres. It assumes that the only form of knowledge is rational knowledge, which is an assumption that only can be accepted as a postulate. It assumes, further, that Reality or at least humanity, is rational or irrational, the latter being unworthy of the "rational animal."

Again, theology is not merely rational, without thereby being irrational. This is a very traditional thesis of most theologies: *theology belongs to the domain of faith*. It is a science that unfolds the vision of the *oculus* fidei; it is the product of an *anubhava*, an insight into the nature of reality; as many vedantic texts tell us, it is the fruit of the ardent urge to attain realization and be liberated from a world of bondage. The language about the divine can only be a mystical language. Some would prefer to say a poetic language, others a mythic one, and still others will, less poetically, speak of a religious language.

In any case, it has to be a language of its own kind, for the referent (whether personal, entity, Being, or emptiness) is elusive, silent, transcendent, hidden, and immanent, and only the third eye detects it.

Since this is the case, it cannot be a language of mere information. We cannot use language as an instrument to link a subject (Man) to an object (God). Such a bridge would either destroy God or destroy itself before reaching the other shore. The practice of poets and lovers may help us understand this. You have to use a courteous language in which you dance around, suggest, run away, play hide and seek, make advances and retreats, say things you do not intend, do not mean, and do not understand. You have to say that all you say is fiction, is merely straw, was not really said but something that just escaped from you without your really meaning or wanting to say it. All you can do is to use a metaphor to make a retraction and add that you really did not want to say that, since you do not want to say "it." You mean "another thing," which is neither other nor a thing. Finally, you fall into silence. When they force you to speak, you begin to utter strange phrases: about being and non-being, name and no name, good and evil, here and there, begotten and unbegotten, Father and Son, Spirit and Matter. And when they say that you do not know what you are talking about, you begin to feel that they have finally understood what you wanted to say.

It is not only poetry and art that require inspiration; authentic theology, too, calls for it in the highest degree. In-spiration is the breath of the spirit inside, the inner Breath that gives us life. I am reminded of a nineteenth-century spanish poet, who is not very well known, and who dreams not of theology but of love:

> These humble songs that I do offer,
> in my mind are born through no small wonder.
> Stripped of the garb that art presents,
> my will is in them totally absent.
> I can not resist nor evoke them,
> neither understand when I sing them.
> . . .
> thoughts and words from thee receive
> you speak in silence, I write in need.[57]

I am not saying that language about the Divine has to be an ecstatic language. The *ecstasis* is often a way of giving up, of covering and concealing that which you cannot speak *about*. If at all, you would like to speak *with* the Divine. It is always a language in the vocative, either openly or implicitly. Adoration, love, worship, submission, and a peculiar form of daring—peculiar because humble. It is a language of the body as much as of the mind and the heart. You sing or cry, shed tears, or smile—or keep quiet (*hēsychia*).

This language of love and worship is the field of *theology* we enter when we take the word *theos* for ultimate reality and *logos* for everything about which we can be aware. Otherwise the word *philosophy* (as the "wisdom of love") may be more appropriate. Yet theology should not neglect the utmost discipline and strenuous effort of authentic thinking, *die Anstrengung des Begriffes*, as I may interpret the laconic phrase of Hegel—the *sobria ebritas* ("sober drunkenness") of the christian liturgy.

57 Federico Balart (1831-1905) "Restitución," *Las mejores poesías de la lengua castellana* (Madrid: M.E. Editores, 1997), 470: "Estas pobres canciones que te consagro, / en mi mente han nacido por un milagro. / Desnudas de las galas que presta el arte, / mi voluntad en ellas no tiene parte; / yo no sé resistirlas ni suscitarlas; yo ni aun sé comprenderlas al formularlas; . . . / pensamiento y palabras de ti recibo, / tú en silencio las dictas, yo las escribo."

Let us now try to repeat in a little more experiential way what was said in the previous section when describing the immanence of God. If I do not experience the Divine, all my theological statements will be lifeless concepts and not descriptions of a living symbol. If I do not experience God within, I will not be able to experience God without, in my neighbor, in things, and in any religious language. The implications are simple and far-reaching. If God were a solely transcendent Substance we would never be able to experience God. So many mystics have been accused of blasphemy because of a strict monotheistic interpretation within a framework of substance. The execution of Al-Hallaj for heresy because of his declarations of God as the beloved is paradigmatic here.

A later text of the kashmiri shaivism, the *Parātrīśikā*, begins: "How, O God, [can] the Unsurpassable [be realized]?"[58] Abhinavagupta's commentary on that first word (*anuttaram*) quotes another *āgama* that says: "There is no one to whom the *anuttamam* [Highest Reality] is unknown." *Anuttaram* is comparative, *anuttamam* superlative. The epistemic act is conscious that nothing is *higher*; the "ontic" act of consciousness is simply installed on the *highest*. The text clearly says that ultimate reality, the Divine, is not unknown to anybody. This is not ontologism. It is the direct awareness of the true reality (*satasya satyam*), which is not a *brahman* behind or underneath, but *brahman*—in its concrete form (*saguṇa brahman*). We do not see Being, we see being(s) as (in) Being—and Being as (in) beings.

We should not interpret these and other texts as simply abstract metaphysical reflections on Being. Here we have a more basic approach, more existential and practical. The questions are prompted not by a merely rational inquiry, but by an aspiration to break all bonds, overcome all limitations, and attain *mokṣa*, liberation. The Upanishad speaks not of intellectual curiosity, but rather of the longing for liberation from it. This is mystical experience.

In short, there are different names for the Deity, which is represented by different symbols of different values. One might nevertheless make an approximate description of where the different symbols of the Deity find a common arena. This is the field of the *mythos*.

(4) The Mythological Character

I have been using the word *mythos* throughout as the ultimate horizon against which all our reflexive states of consciousness are situated, that background we no longer question, because we no longer feel the need to question. The *mythos* gives us an undisputed horizon where we can situate the

58 "Anuttaraṁ kathaṁ deva?"

insights of the *logos*—"undisputed" precisely because the direct light of the *logos* does not reach there. I have qualified my statement by saying "direct," because indirectly the *logos* has dimly arrived at the *mythos*, which is why we can speak about it. *Mythos* and *logos* stand in an *advaitic* relationship.[59]

This is the place for dialogical (non-dialectical) dialogue as a necessary instrument for any cross-cultural encounter. It is the function of this dialogue to disclose or eventually create the field in which a symbolic consciousness can operate. If theology is a language about or of an Ultimate, it cannot have an ulterior point of reference—no other proof based on something else. This explains the well-known *furor theologicus* (theological rage). The worst wars are religious wars. It is not to demean the importance of theology that I stress its mythological character. On the contrary, only when we believe wholeheartedly in our own theology can we be creative and feel free. As someone once said: With dogmas one can construct cathedrals, with opinions one can only build a new road—to the same place. To absolutize one's own beliefs, however, is fatal and leads to dogmatism in its pejorative sense. Here it is crucial for the awareness to dawn that our theology is based on our *mythos* and that there are other *mythoi* in the human community.

It is this awareness that permits us to be fair with other cultures and helps us to overcome the temptation of double standards when we deal with our own culture and those of other peoples. Our wars are just wars of liberation, while those of the enemies are invasions and terrorist campaigns. Have "we" discovered or conquered America? Have "we" colonized or exploited? Is God only on our side? Or to put another recent and more academic example, we could look at the famous *Entmythologisierung* (demythologization) of christian theology. We demythicize ancient narratives having discovered their underlying myths, which we no longer accept. This is a healthy and necessary step for our understanding. Nevertheless, we deem that we have reached a real explanation once we have translated those myths into our acceptable conceptual system, unaware that our system is another myth that we accept as plausible and convincing. We do not demythicize; we simply transmythicize. The *Entmythologisierung* is simply an *Ummythologisierung*, a remythologization.[60] Theology, like philosophy, rests on a particular worldview that is our ultimate myth.

---

59 See Panikkar, "Mythos und Logos: mythologisce und rationale Weltsichten," in H. P. Dürr and W. Ch. Zimmerli, eds., *Geist und Natur* (Bern: Scherz, 1989), 206-20.

60 See Panikkar, "Die Unmythologisierung in der Begegnung des Christentums mit dem Hinduismus," *Kerygma und Mythos* VI (1963), 211-35.

(5) Theology as Divine Life

Theology and philosophy are not merely speculative sciences; they are art as much as science, praxis as well as theory. We encounter here again intellectual distinction converted into lethal separation, which is what an adualistic vision of reality hopes to heal. In this sense, and in accordance with most sacred traditions of humanity, theology is a conscious and responsible sharing in divine life. I speak of divine life because of the connotation of the word theology. For an atheist, I would delete "divine" and write Life with a capital letter to shift the discussions about content to another level.

In almost all traditions there has been something considered to be the highest and most comprehensive human activity by which the human being reaches Freedom, Happiness, Realization, Salvation, Peace, or any other name such as Heaven, *nirvāṇa*, or God. If theology is one of the names of this human activity, philosophy, wisdom, *dharma, nijñāna, budhi, tao,* and many others could be considered homeomorphic equivalents.

Earlier I referred to the fragmentation of knowledge and present-day cultural schizophrenia. I also said that there is a human need to have an ultimate point of reference, but this point does not need to be a monolithic point. We need a center of harmony where our aspirations find an outlet, a living symbol of our inner peace, a resting place for our thirst for knowledge and our longing for love. Our intellectual and spiritual nature is not appeased by an individualistic solution to this need, nor is it convinced by totalitarian and universalistic ideals. The *via media* I am trying to describe is that human activity which is sometimes called Wisdom and theology.

Adopting a concrete theological language, we can say that the ultimate aim of theology is working out that consciousness of our fellowship with the entire reality, symbolized by the word *Theos*, which accompanies us in our life toward its destiny. The theologian is not alone in this pilgrimage. I do not mean, of course, the professional theologian, but any *sadhaka*, anyone concentrating in living life (human, and thus also intellectual, life) to the full. God is the fellow traveler of the theologian. Theology is the effort to share in God's life and to live in harmony with the whole by assuming the responsibility of finishing the divine icon that everyone of us is. *Philosophus semper est laetus*, "the philosopher is always joyful," said a mystical "theologian" of the Mediterranean shores centuries ago.[61] The theological method, therefore, is not demonstration. Demonstration is a rational method that proceeds from accepted principles to less immediately known "truths." The proper theological method is not demonstration but

61 Ramon Llull, *Liber proverbiorum* VI, 5, 122.

"monstration" to show the splendor of the "truth" by polishing both the view and the viewer.

Summing up a long tradition, which has continued after him, Dionysius the Areopagite said that theology "does not demonstrate the truth, but exposes it nakedly, in symbols, so that the soul, changed by holiness and light, penetrates without reason into it,"[62] implying that the view and the viewer share in that Light which permeates the Universe.

* * *

We should be careful here to avoid the pitfall of a certain type of intellectual totalitarianism or cultural colonialism without falling into the trap of an even more pretentious and encompassing system. If there is the danger of a "logomonism," there is also the temptation of despising the *logos* and accepting an equally pernicious "*pneuma*-monism."

There is still another danger, although of another order: the misinterpretation of language. Most of the words I have used to hint at overcoming theism have their proper place and function within the theistic world. I must therefore try to offer a new language that can express what humanity has already experienced, albeit sometimes only dimly. We are trying to "uncover" (*vivaraṇa*) the overall experience covered by the history of humanity, to "catch" or "glimpse" this particular moment in the rhythm of reality over against a more cross-cultural horizon. We hope to include the spiritual connotations of the words in a special way, in their "pneumatic" sense. After all, the four classical senses of Scripture (literal, anagogical, allegorical, and spiritual) also belong to theology.

The dwelling of the Divine is not only in heaven, nor exclusively in the deepest recesses of the human soul. It is there, too, but its primary "dwelling" is in the whole Man and Man's world, in the midst of human life and earthly existence, among everyday things (like the famous "pots" of Saint Teresa's *entre los pucheros anda Dios*). The body, too, is a theological category. The dwelling of the Divine is everywhere, not as a more or less welcome guest, but as a constitutive element of every being. In that sense theology has the existential character of a companion of Man. If religion is the *way* to the goal of life, philosophy or theology is the conscious fellow traveler on this pilgrimage. I am not advocating the *heteronomic* dominion of "theology" over the particular "sciences," but neither am I defending the autonomy of every branch of knowledge. I am aiming at the recovery of the *ontonomic* harmony of all the branches of the one tree of knowledge, which requires the *inter-in-dependence* of the entire order of the real.

62 Dionysius, *Epistula* IX, 1 (PG 3:1105 CD).

C. Ultimate Answers?

I will now sum up what I have been saying so far: What, in the final analysis, are we asking about? What is "it" all about? There is no single ultimate answer, because there is no single ultimate question. I have referred to a variety of them. This plurality of questions and answers does not imply that all answers are correct or all questions well put. It does imply, however, that unless we work out a common ground in a dialogical dialogue we have no neutral basis on which we may evaluate either the questions or the answers if we want to compare them. This is one of the foundations of pluralism, which should not be equated with "anything goes." Pluralism entails relativity, not relativism. One can understand that a rigid monotheism cannot accept pluralism on that ultimate level.[63] A monotheistic God cannot be a symbol for pluralism; the Trinity may.

Theism is but one possible form used to frame the question. Seeing that there are problems, riddles, and events we cannot explain to ourselves, we could ask whether or not a Supreme Being might (at least) concentrate in itself all the answers. We are prompted by a peculiar thirst for coherence, assuming that reality is endowed with a rational coherence, to accept monotheism as the most plausible explanation. Armed with our rationality, we discover an inner dialectic that leads us up the ladder to the thought of a Supreme Being. This God will then be either the absolute solution, or else the scapegoat for all our frustrations. It will remain the ultimate point of reference even if we eventually qualify it, divide it into many, negate it, reinterpret it, or whatever. All in all, the existential cry of the human being still is: "Is Anybody there?"

This is a cry of human nature in front of an inexplicable "feeling" of absence—which no psychological theory succeeds in quieting. Modern literature is full of variations on this question. My contention is that the question about the Deity, important and vast as it is, already assumes a certain *mythos* about reality, and this assumption inevitably conditions the way we frame the question. In its classical form, it becomes the question about the transcendent— God, for instance.

Close to this question is the related one about the character of such transcendence—the future, for instance. In turn this raises the next question, about immanence—the ātman, for instance. Then there is the question about the very nature of Reality, which can be asked without specifying a cause, ground, consciousness, etc.—the simple acceptance of Life, for instance. We also encounter the question about identity, the true identity

63 See Panikkar, "The Pluralism of Truth," *World Faiths Insight* 26 (October 1990), 7-16.

of ourselves and of things—the problem of *brahman*, for instance. There is also the attitude that refrains from questioning, well aware that searching for something already distends and distorts both the searcher and whatever is sought—the *tao*, for instance. We could easily multiply the number of such basic questions. The shortest rhymed poem in english, for instance, is said to be only these two words:

I
Why?

The poem is also said to be anonymous in the western sense, but it has the unmistakable stamp not only of the english language but also of the author. Only a staunch individualist could have written it, and only a believing rationalist could have put the interrogation mark at the end. It is not an ultimate question for everybody. India, for instance, would say that an authentic I would never dream of asking why. The I that asks for a Why is not an authentic I.

Undoubtedly Man is a questioning being, a being in search of intelligibility. We question because we are not satisfied with what we have at hand. We question because we feel the need to do so. We question because all these "questions" emerge from a basic attitude prior to the questioning mind. The questions are already pre-formed, indeed pre-formulated, by the kosmological environment of the people(s) who frame the questions. They occur to human awareness against a particular horizon in which the questions make sense.

We are entering mythic terrain. . . . In other words, we are reaching the limits of the *logos* and of the secondary sense of theology. Perhaps, in spite of its high-sounding name, God cannot be reduced to being an object of theology. The *logos* seems incapable of encompassing the Divine.

These samples cannot be reduced to a single coherent pattern. They are examples at random, and this randomness should be respected, lest we produce again another super-system of worldviews, or some metaphilosophy of philosophies, in purely formalistic terms. To imagine that a merely formal structure is a real image of Reality would mean falling back into the monocultural presumption that "we" possess, at the very least, a formal key for truly re-presenting reality.

Yet we cannot renounce altogether the effort to make sense of human experience, at least insofar as we are able to enter the world of *homo literatus*. Pluralism does not mean non-intelligibility within the respective worldviews. It only entails accepting that there may be a mutual incommensurability between various existing parameters for understanding the real, and that there may be some irreducibility of the attitudes fundamental to these understandings because no single human being or culture can pretend to embrace the universal range of human experience.

I have repeatedly hinted at the fact that rational understanding or even intelligibility is not synonymous with awareness. We may not understand a set of affirmations or convictions of people of another culture, and yet we may be fully aware that we do not understand them.

* * *

In our quest for a basic human attitude, we found within the framework of theism a place for the question about the Deity. We also found that some peoples, also our kith and kin, adopt other attitudes or start with implicitly different assumptions (or, more exactly, presuppositions). Among the many words we might have used to hint at this quest, we chose the name Mystery—in spite of its many hellenic and post-hellenic connotations. The words *noumen*, sacred, holy, and the like seem more biased than Mystery, a word whose etymology (μύω, "to close, to mouth," cf. english "mute") already invites us to silence, putting aside any pretense of dominion, even on the part of the intellect or of the *logos*. For the sake of clarity I have called it the Divine Mystery, with the intention of including the homeomorphic equivalents of God.

In this quest some minimal presuppositions are unavoidable. These would seem to be the following: We are each of us conscious that we are not alone, that we do not know everything, and that around us there are other "egos" and "thous" in a similar situation. We are further aware that this situation is extended in time and space, and suspect that this very situation has conditioned us, so that any queries we may put to ourselves will also be conditioned by all sorts of geographic, cultural, and anthropological factors.

In sum, any and every Man is inextricably linked with a world. However, there seems to be a third element, inseparable but also irreducible to the other two. One of its traditional names has been the Divine, the Deity, the Godhead, or perhaps the holy or the sacred, purposely avoiding now any names from other traditions. I do not want to quibble over the politics of names. Even if all this were an illusion, it has been a powerful, pervasive, and effective illusion—a very real one, for good or for ill.

It may be proper in western languages to retain the name of God, even if we do not consider this name synonymous with monotheism and/or theism. After all, the english word God, like the latin and greek words *deus* and *theos*, is a common and not a proper name, as the arabic Allah and the hebrew Yahweh have become.[64] The upshot is that God may indeed be a sufficiently "non-sectarian" word to serve its purpose.

I have also introduced the same topic from the viewpoint of a sociology of knowledge. Having so radically changed our vision and experience of the World and of ourselves, it is not surprising that our notions of the Deity may change accordingly. Besides the shifting kosmological picture, one of the most prominent of these changes is that described as modern individualism. To dare say that God may not be an individual, let alone a substance, will sound blasphemous to many of my contemporaries. My obligation is not only to be respectful, but to be clear and persuasive when expounding other ideas.

64 The etymologies, uncertain as some may be, relate God to the Sanskrit *-huta* (*ghūta*) from the root *hū*, "to invoke." God is the much invoked, the one who is called upon (cf. old irish, *guth*, "voice, guttural"; and latin *guttur*, *glutus*, "throat"—although this may be another root). We may also remember the common roots of *Deus, theos, dyaus*: day, light, sky, etc.

V
The Triadic Myth

Sa tredhā ātmānaṁ vyakuruta[1]
He revealed Himself in a trinitarian way.

Until now I have been descriptive and critical. From here on I shall be offering my own experience of the Divine Mystery, basing its exposition both on the preceding considerations and, as much as possible, on the religious or simply ultimate experience of humanity during its historical period, that is, during the last six to eight millennia.

Needless to say, when having such an ambitious aim we should be well aware not only of the subjective limitations of the author, of any author ultimately, but also of the objective impossibility of encompassing the universal range of the human experience. Yet, even if no single individual can claim to embrace the Whole, we can be aware that the Whole embraces us and that as a microcosm we are an icon of the entire reality even if we cannot eliminate our limited perspective.

The *kairos* of our present human situation, independently of the artificial third millennium and the less artificial Aquarian age, represents a turning point in the adventure of reality. I say reality and not just humanity because Man is not an epiphenomenon in the universe and the "Destiny of Being" is intrinsically connected with our human existence. If we have criticized any sort of theocentrism and have overcome an anthropocentric view of reality, we should not fall then into any cosmocentrism. There is no doubt that the scientific and technological discoveries of Man form a unique development in human civilization and demand a radical change in our ways of living and thinking, but this does not necessitate or justify a total break with the past.

As already suggested several times, the *advaitic* intuition, which implies

1 BU I, 2, 3.

symbolic knowledge and an overcoming (not denying) of rationality, offers a key to opening us up as much as possible to the mystery of reality. After a brief description of this intuition, which is intimately linked with the almost universal trinitarian insight of humanity, I shall attempt to describe its repercussions in human self-consciousness. Finally, as the Trinity seems to have been revered in the christian vision, I shall end this chapter with a christian reflection.

A. *Advaita* and Trinity

It is intriguing to observe that, during the high tide of monotheism, christian theologians did not (or did not dare to) "see" the revolutionary character of the Trinity, and, with few exceptions, interpreted the Trinity as a mild qualification of monotheism with practically no major importance for christian life. It is also ironic to note that "non-confessional" historians and philosophers downplayed, if not overlooked, the trinitarian aspects of the religions they studied. Furthermore, it is instructive to recognize that an increasing number of people today are becoming aware of the amazing ubiquity of the trinitarian pattern. This triadic structure seems to be reflected in the very constitution of our minds as well as in manifestations of nature and culture. It may be found in East and West alike, in the most highly sophisticated cultures as well as in the most primordial. It seems to dominate both the conscious and the unconscious psyche, in literature, as well as in the graphic and plastic arts.

It is indeed striking to discover the presence of this triadic *mythos* at the ultimate level in most human conceptions of reality: Reality is trinitarian because the structure of the mind is trinitarian, or the other way round, our mind discovers the trinitarian pattern because the very constitution of reality is triadic. To be sure, we are still accustomed to encountering monistic and dualistic conceptions of reality, but the trinitarian vision is gaining momentum probably because of the crisis of monotheisms and the decline of substantialistic visions due partly to the influence of the functional thinking of modern science.

1. *Monism and Dualism*

The words "monism" and "dualism" have a variety of meanings. I use them here following Christian Wolff, who introduced them in the eighteenth century to refer to metaphysical doctrines concerning the existence of one or two types of ultimately irreducible substances in the universe.

Monism believes it discovers an ultimately real oneness not only beyond or above everything but constituting the ultimate "essence" of everything. The oneness of monism is not a formal abstraction but the ultimate reality. If oneness is an idea, then this idea is the Absolute. If the oneness is material, matter will be the Absolute. We shall have other corresponding forms of monism depending on whether the real oneness is identified with God, Consciousness, Thinking (identified with Being), Energy, Spirit, and so on. Monism does not recognize ultimately real distinctions between entities, because it admits these only as modes (or moods) of the one reality. If the distinctions between things are not ultimately real but only modal or functional, we have to postulate a modal plane, that of the appearances, upon which such distinctions "appear" to be real. This modal plane where the appearance makes its appearance, however, cannot be real in itself, or else monism collapses and we fall into dualism. In other words, appearances are only apparent modifications of the unique reality, and if the appearance of the appearances is only apparent, it is not even a "real" appearance. It is all a dream, but a dream dreamt by no one, as Śankara is supposed to have said, and as the ficciones of Borges so often reiterate. Error itself has no basis, no *pratiṣṭhā*, except as a mode of Being itself. *Saṁsāra* may well be *nirvāṇa*, and *nirvāṇa saṁsāra*, but in a monistic view the two words are merely a tautology.

For those who do not know that appearances are only appearances, their ignorance (*avidyā*) is very real, unless it is affirmed that the subjects of *avidyā* are not real, and thus that ignorance itself is only apparent, in which case there is no ignorance. Monism either turns into dualism, or else collapses in a totally apophatic system—logical as it may be. In fact, it can only be pure logic. Monism is ultimately idealism or idealistic materialism. I am reminded of that ironic and profound confession of the devil to one of the damned in hell in Dante's *Divina Commedia*: "You did not think that I was logical?"[2] The strength of monism is its logical consistency. Once we accept the premises of monism (the *more geometrico* of Spinoza), it cannot be proved wrong. To which one can retort: it may not be *proved* inconsistent, but neither can it be proved that reality has to be consistent. . . . Such a discourse ends by recognizing two different kosmologies, and shifts to the problematic of the *mythos*.

In point of fact, most monisms are mitigated monisms, which makes room for a certain degree of reality of the modes of the One. Most absolute monotheisms could be said to be mitigated monisms. There is one Absolute, one absolute Reality, but because of its absolute freedom it may "create,"

2 Dante, *l'inferno,* canto XXVII: "Tu non pensavi ch'io loico fossi?"

"emanate," "produce," "generate" entities that are modes of Itself, although "seen" from "our" finite perspective they may appear as more or less independent substances. The world "is real" from our (ignorant) point of view. In God entities are God as Thomas Aquinas says. We are in front of one of the ultimate options of the human mind. It would be immature, to say the least, to want to refute a longstanding worldview with a couple of arguments. The premises of monism are clear. Logic is ontology. The laws of logic are ontological laws. The shadow of Parmenides spreads over practically all monisms. Monism is absolute logical coherence once logic dominates metaphysics.

In order to truly understand anything, we need to be able to reduce it to the formula "A is B," whereby A and B need to be as univocal as possible. A needs to be A and not A_1, A_2 . . . and the same for B. The statements "*Las Meninas* is a beautiful painting" and "The Vietnam War was an unjust war" need to identify the subject and, in our example, not mistake it for another painting of Velázquez or the french occupation of Vietnam. The predicate needs also to be understood univocally so that "beautiful" and "unjust" mean the same to those who use those sentences. Some may judge Velázquez kitsch and justify the Vietnam War depending on the meanings of our words and the interpretation of facts. Monism is a case in point. *Monas* means unity, but we know, for instance that the One (ἕν) of Plotinus is not a number and is in no way quantifiable. That everything has one Source does not need to be monism, if it does not imply that all is one single substance.

Dualism is another ultimate option. Logic is only one "ingredient" of reality. Once an ontological separation is accepted between two ultimate realms of reality, there is going to be a fight to the bitter end. The war cannot be waged on logical grounds because logical coherence does not need to be metaphysically binding. It will have to be fought in the field of praxis, with the will to power being its theoretical ally. It is clear that the dualism between God and the world is a glaring example of this. That dualistic God will lose the battle in spite of good intellectual reasons in its favor, or it will have to retreat into irrationality. Our reason cannot admit two Ultimate and Absolute principles because we could not then distinguish them. The very formulation of ultimate dualism presupposes at least an epistemological link between the "two." If this link were real in both realms (*pāramārthika/ vyāvahārika*, absolute/relative, God/World, Reality/Appearance), neither of the realms could be absolute since each one would be really related to the other. Ultimately dualism would collapse. In order to maintain the absoluteness of the two realms, platonic dialectic was born: the ascension from the sensible to the intelligible. The dialectical game, however, introduces a third factor: the mediatorship of dialectics, and with that dualism falls into a logic-monism, which becomes the supreme judge. If we want to save at least one term of the dualism, the relation of this term with the other side cannot be real. This is the so-called *relatio vel distinctio rationis* (distinction of our mind, but not objective or real). It was the opinion of Śankara, Thomas Aquinas, and others that the link is only real from our side so that the Absolute is absolutely unrelated—while we are related to the Absolute without impinging on its Absoluteness. This puts the human mind under a dilemma: either the "real" side utterly disappears into an unspeakable, unthinkable transcendence with no real relation to us, or we take refuge in our finitude, and having dispensed with that radical apophatism, we absolutize this world, and so turn dualism into monsim.

Indeed, what is generally described as dualism in the history of religions is only a kind of provisional or temporal dualism—"for the time being," so to speak. Zoroastrianism would be the classic example. In the end, a single principle triumphs. We can say that dualism is only provisional and not definitive or that it is essentially dynamic, dialectical, and eschatological. Because it cannot be rationally proved, it is faith that maintains the transcendent side in existence. In fact, most dualisms, like the majority of monisms, are not pure, but strike a compromise. Human thought has been seesawing for its entire history between these two extremes, although, in the final analysis, the best minds in the many human traditions have always been striving to find a *via media*, a *mādhyama*— between rationality and irrationality. I submit that the Trinity and *advaita* are simply two names for this middle way.

2. *Advaita*

Advaita overcomes the strictures of positing the *logos* to integrate the *pneuma* (spirit) in our approach to reality. This is the task of love, not as second fiddle to knowledge, but as the firstborn of the gods.[3] Or, as a western classic that echoes the indic insight says: rebounding love [*reflectens ardor*] belongs to the ultimate nature of the Whole.[4] *Advaita* is spiritual knowledge that does not need rational evidence in order to gain an insight into the nature of things. In fact, the attempt to master the just-mentioned polarity by reason alone is at the origin of the dialectical method: *sic et non*. Reason demands (rational) evidence, and this is only possible focusing on one object at a time.

3 AV IX, 2, 19: "Love is the firstborn, loftier than the gods."

4 *Liber XXIV philosophorum*, I: "Deus est monas monadem gignens, in se unum reflectens ardorem" ("God is a monad begetting a monad and rebounding in itself a blazing love").

This is the *reductio ad unum* if we want to understand something. Reason cannot handle the ambivalence and relativity of symbols. *Advaita* amounts to the overcoming of dualistic dialectics by means of introducing love at the ultimate level of reality.[5] Let us make three observations concerning *advaita*.

Reason alone cannot reach the *advaitic* intuition because the adualistic structure of reality opens up only to a loving knowledge or a knowing love for which we lack a proper word since the divorce between *gnōsis* and *eros* (or *agapē*, or for that matter, even *philia*). When love is set aside, only the dialectical method is open to us, and this brings us to a second observation.

A-dvaita was usually translated as "nonduality," because the dialectical mind of the european indologists who first rendered the word into european languages a couple of centuries ago interpreted the *a* as a negative particle. In fact the *a* of the *advaita* intuition does not connote a dialectical negation, rather, here the *a* is a primitive prefix pointing to an "absence of duality." "A-rational" does not necessarily mean "irrational" (non-rational), but rather indicates something outside the rational order. *A-bhaya* does not mean "non-fear" but the absence of fear (fearlessness—which is also a name of Śiva). Now, the "absence of duality" is not perceived if we ban love from our knowledge—as any lover knows. Only loving knowledge has this overall vision, which is more than the rational awareness of *privatio*. I propose, therefore, to render *advaita* as "aduality" (or "adualism").

Having translated *advaita* as nonduality has had deleterious consequences in the encounter of cultures. The dialectical method is based on the principle of non-contradiction. If *advaita* is "nondualism" and at the same time claims to be non-monism, then *advaita* is pure contradiction. Excluding any other plurality, we cannot escape the dilemma of either one or two without falling into contradiction. We cannot *deny* both one (not two) and two (not one) at the same time. It would amount to negating two and non-two. The only dialectical escape is simply monism, which is the great pitfall into which many interpreters have fallen when they interpret *advaita* rationally, that is, dialectically. *Advaita* cannot be reduced to a concept. This leads us to our third observation.

Adualism qualifies the one (*ekam*) so much that it negates the very essence of oneness, namely, that one allows for a second. Otherwise, why is it one? From the *advaitic* perspective, uniqueness is not a number. Any quantification of reality destroys uniqueness and constitutes an abuse of our mind. Yet *advaita* affirms that the "one" reality reveals the absence of any

---

5 See "Advaita and Bhakti. A Hindu-Christian Dialogue," in R. Panikkar, *Myth, Faith, and Hermeneutics*, 277-89.

duality; that reality has absence adhering to the one so as to disallow any numeric "one" lest we fall into a mere formal abstraction.

Albeit crystallized in a doctrine, *advaita* represents that experience of the real which, when articulated, asserts that the ultimate character of the real cannot be breached by reason even though our intellect discovers the inner light of that supra-rational insight. The formulation of *advaita* consists in two negations: *neti, neti*, (*na-iti, na-iti*) "not this, not this." Reality is-not one; reality isnot two (*a-dvaita*). This famous formula *neti neti* refers to the description of the ātman, which is "not this, not this"—incomprehensible, indestructible, unattached, unfettered, impassible, the highest, and the real of the real (the truth of truth).[6] This double negation does not allow conversion into an affirmation, except a formal one, like affirming: reality is nondual. This is a merely formal or logical sentence and cannot be used as a principle from which one may draw conclusions or make deductions. From "reality is nondual" we cannot deduce therefore "it is one"; it could equally be triadic, quaternary, etc.

Monism is logically intelligible. "Reality is One" is an intelligible sentence. Dualism, on the other hand, renounces linking the "two" together in any intelligible way (otherwise dualism disappears) or shifts intelligibility only to one side of the real. The other side is then darkness, evil, or at least unintelligible. "Reality is two" is also a logically intelligible sentence. The monistic sentence can shift from the logical order (of a formal sentence) to a metaphysical sentence assuming that the "one" reality is intelligible, which amounts to the idealistic postulate. The dualistic sentence, however, cannot be shifted from the logical (formal) order to the metaphysical without contradicting itself. "Two" is an intelligible concept, but not an intelligible "thing." "Two" may refer to two intelligible things. In such case the two intelligible substances are linked by a third factor, our intellect, which would destroy dualism unless this intellect is one of the "two." In this instance we have introduced a hierarchy within dualism that makes the non-intellect (non-intelligent) part subordinated or inferior to the intellect (intelligent) one. This relative dualism is in fact the most common one.

Advaita denies both that "reality is one" and that "reality is two" precisely because it discovers that the real is not reducible to intelligibility. The intellect is neither "cornered," as it were, on one side of the real (this would be dualism), nor is it identified with reality forcing the other "side" to disappear (this would be monism). Reason cannot understand without bringing the knower and the known into some kind of "union." If knowledge

6 See BU II, 3, 6; III, 9, 26; IV, 2, 4; IV, 4, 22; IV, 5, 15.

is to be true, that is, real, this implies that, because it cannot be "embraced" in a single act of intelligibility, reality ultimately transcends knowledge. It implies that to be is "more" than to know. *Advaita* denies the absolute identification of knowing (thinking) with Being not because the intellect is weak, but because reality is stronger. Thus, adualism asserts that Being is irreducible to *cit*, *intelligere*, *percipi*, or intelligibility in whatever form.

Nonetheless, this does not imply irrationalism precisely because it is the intellect that discovers that it *is* not all (of) reality. Adualism simply implies an avoidance of rationalism—that is, rational monism or absolute idealism. It amounts to overcoming absolute monotheism. Intellect is the supreme arbiter, but it is an arbiter, not the "thing." The intellect is a highly qualified arbiter indeed, since it will not blink for a moment in its vigilance over Being. Thinking accompanies Being all the way, but Being may have a secret, a *guhyam māhāguhyam* (to paraphrase the *Gītā*, Abhinavagupta, and many other classical works[7]), a "secret, a great secret" precisely because this secret is impenetrable to rational consciousness.

* * *

Common philosophical language regarding the mind is very vague, not only in the West but also in India (*jñāna, budhi, cit*). For the sake of clarity and leaning on the latin tradition, which is not always consistent, I shall use reason as discursive reason, and intellect both as that which leads us to the rational evidence of reason (rational intelligibility) and as that (organ of) knowledge which lets us reach an awareness (and thus is not irrational) irreducible to rational evidence and/or to merely psychological convictions. I shall call such awareness spiritual knowledge since it stems from a spiritual experience belonging mainly to the third eye. In this sense we may say that the human *intellect* in its wider sense of spiritual knowledge, unlike pure *reason*, does not require the *reductio ad unum* to understand an object as one single object, but rather can grasp the relation that has produced the object (*objectum*) and be aware of the relation "prior" to the things related. This is the *advaitic* intuition: the awareness of the relation without which the two poles of the relation would not be poles. To be aware of a thing as a pole we need to know "previously" the relation that makes the thing be pole. The relation is neither one (it needs the poles) nor two (it is not two relations). It is a-dual.

We have here two possible approaches: we can focus our attention on the poles or on their relation. Reason perceives ones thing, which generally

7 God (Reality) "is hidden, yet most manifest, . . . all names are his names" (*Corpus hermeticum*, V, 10; etc., etc.).

is considered to be a substance, and is aware that this thing tends, demands, entails, etc., another thing. Looking into the thing, as it were, reason discovers the relation of one thing with another. There are many sorts of relation, of course. We deal here with constitutive relationships that make the things dependent on each other. We call them poles, and the relationship depends on the poles. Reason considers first the things and second the relation that links them; it sees the things *in themselves*, in their own consistency (substance). The loving intellect, however, sees that the object is lacking something without its constitutive links and sees the relation as relation and the poles subsidiarily. Our analytical thinking introduces lethal dichotomies in our thinking and our lives: we say "Man" and exclude woman, World and eliminate God, spirit and excommunicate matter. We lose sight of constitutive relationships and reify reality. The other extreme, of course, would be the elimination of differences: a male is not a female, nor is God the world, nor is spirit matter, but there is not the one without the other. The relation is neither a thing nor a substance; it is not strictly one, since any relation needs at least two poles; but it is not strictly two either, since there are not two relations. The relation is real and yet is not in itself. This is the key to one of the central buddhist insights: *pratītyasamutpāda*, the radical relativity or dependent origination of all, the universal net of relationships. This is not the hellenic atomistic theory because the buddhist "atoms" are not substances. The net is the real, the atoms have no "self," no ātman, and they are not substances.

We may still ask what prompts the intellect to overcome the dialectic between monism and dualism. I may insert here a philosophical reflection, since *advaita* has been misunderstood and is of crucial importance for our topic and for our civilization. I have already indicated the movement of our intellect from thinking about substances to being directly aware of relationships. This may be a very positive side effect of the functional thinking of modern science.[8] If we direct our intellectual attention not to individual "things" (substances or substantialized "things") but to their relations, we do not see first one object and then another one, but become directly conscious of the relation itself by a special kind of awareness. This awareness does not make the strenuous effort to simultaneously understand the two substances—by means of a quick dialectical movement from the one to the other. It is an awareness different from rational evidence. This understanding is the awareness that we stand-under the spell, the light, of the

8 Cf. Panikkar (1962/15), "El pensar sustantivo y el pensar functional en Ciencia y en Filosopfia," *Actas del Segundo congreso Extraordinario Interamericano de Filosofía, San José, Costa Rica, 22-26 de julio 1961* (San José: Imprenta Nacional, 1963), 133-36.

reality so understood. It is not that we dominate reality by our reason. There was a crucial turning point in modern science when it renounced declaring anything about reality and concentrated on calculating how it functions. The tradeoff was giving up the claim to say anything about real substances and concentrating on a formal description of the phenomena trusting that "nature was written in mathematical language."[9] This shift from metaphysics to logic was the price it had to pay for not abandoning rational evidence.

This is a critical change that took place after a long period of preparation. "Clear and distinct ideas" can claim rational evidence. Rational evidence belongs to the epistemological order. No metaphysical statement can claim rational evidence unless previously translated into a logical language. This assumes that the logical order is a correct image of the original reality. If after some epistemic operations (on the logical plane) we want to make valid ontological affirmations about reality, we have to further assume that the correspondence between the two planes is biunivocal so that reality is subservient to our logical thinking. This assumption of correspondence is not made by pure modern science, although some scientific cosmologists actually attempt this by (unscientific) extrapolation. Modern science has maintained itself in the field of formal epistemic statements. Yet the spectacular success of techno-science has tended to make us believe that it discloses the reality of things. Here we find the momentum of *advaita,* which does not renounce saying something about the "reality of the real" (*satyasya satyam*). *Advaita* is not a formal statement that can claim rational evidence; it is a metaphysical insight that claims to be illumined (justified) by the light of consciousness emerging from a spiritual experience of an ontological character. The price paid is to abandon rationality as the ultimate criterion of reality. In order not to fall into irrationality, we then need to become aware that the field of spiritual experience is larger than rational evidence. We need a third eye, as we shall explain later.

This awareness is not the rational evidence of an *individual mind* intellectually grasping an *individual object*. The *object* is not a thing but a relationship. The correlations of the Upanishads offer us an extreme example.[10] Such correlations or correspondences are totally un-understandable if we exclude this *advaitic* awareness. Otherwise, they are interpreted as sheer magic, as has often been done, sometimes not without some truth. Earth is not water, nor water plant, nor plant Man, nor Man word, to quote one

9 Galileo: "Il libro della natura è *scritto in* lingua matematica."

10 Cf., for instance BU I, 2; II, 5; III, 9; V, 5; VI, 1; CU I; III, 13; V, 18ff.; VIII, 6; AU I; KausU III, 3; etc.

Upanishad.[11] Yet there are correlations that are neither necessarily causal nor genetic. The entire universe is such a net of cosmic correlations. This is also the vision of the buddhist *pratītyasamutpāda,* or radical relativity (relatedness) of all with all. This is also the background, *mutatis mutandis,* for the law of *karma*, the *buddha-kāya* (body of Buddha), the mystical body of Christ, etc. *Sarvam sarvātmakam,* said Abhinavagupta, *quodlibet* in *quolibet,* wrote Nicholas of Cusa and so many others expressing the same insight. This inter-relatedness is what I call the *ontonomic* relatedness of a universal *interindependence,* which is another way of explaining the *advaitic* insight. Otherwise we have monistic dependence (heteronomy) or dualistic independence (autonomy).

In sum, the object of this awareness is not the individual thing but the net itself, the whole of consciousness, the Whole as such.[12] In other words, the *object* of the *advaitic* experience is not an individual thing but a field of consciousness, as it were. As already hinted, there is still more: the *subject* of the *advaitic* experience is not an individual mind. The *advaitic* experience is not that of an individual subject apprehending an individual object. As long as there is ego-consciousness the adualistic awareness will not emerge.

As long as I am aware that I, as an individual, know A and B, I will individualize A and B and see their relatedness as subsidiary to A and B. In this view, A and B are entities by themselves and not *ab alio,* not utterly depending on "another" entity. There is, however, another way to view the relationship between entities. This alternative vision sees that this "other" entity is not an *aliud*, but an *altera*; not an other and alien thing but rather the other part, aspect, or dimension of the thing. Here we touch a vital point. We cannot understand that something is contingent (has its entity reposing on another) unless we grasp also its relation to the other entity on which it depends without alienating the *forma* of the thing. This amounts to saying that the object cannot be individualized by abstracting from all the rest if the knowledge of that thing is to be complete and thus accurate. Moreover, the net extends also to the subjects having the experience. There is no private *advaitic* experience in the way that there is a private sensual experience. To be sure, any actual experience is personal, but like rational experience, the *advaitic* intuition claims to touch the real. In fewer words: it is a spiritual experience, which requires a pure heart, just as there are rational insights that demand a clear and acute mind. Just as there is a rationality in which we all

11 Cf. CU I, 1ff.

12 "The one spreading his net [over all the worlds]" is one of the names of God (Rudra) in SU III, 1.

share, there is a spiritual awareness (sometimes called *intellectus* as distinct from *ratio*) in which we equally all share albeit in different degrees.

The *advaitic* knowledge is knowledge *of* reality and not the abstract knowledge of a formal pattern of reality. This is why I spoke of *advaitic* spiritual experience: the awareness of relationship is not a secondary knowledge derived from the knowledge of individual things. It is a primary knowledge, a spiritual knowledge indeed, but knowledge after all. It belongs to the third eye. Yet, as we shall say later, all knowledge, inasmuch as we are conscious of it, "knows" the real in the field of that knowledge, that is, in the field of consciousness. Now, when we identify consciousness with reality (as so many philosophical systems East and West have done), we cannot maintain that *advaitic* knowledge as such yields the real. As the mystics have witnessed, we need mystical experience in order to break into the level of consciousness that is to be grasped by the *advaitic* nature of reality.

An example may help to describe not the experience but the intellectual (spiritual) aspect of it. I do not try to know the mother as an individual substance that has a special relation to another entity that she has begotten: the son. I do not try to understand first the mother, then the son, and thirdly to establish a link between the two entities, one of which happens to have given birth to the other. I try to focus my awareness not on the mother and her maternity, nor on the son and his filiation. The relationship is neither one (there is maternity and filiation) nor two (there are not two relations). Actual maternity (without offspring) does not exist. Mere sonship without the parents is equally an abstraction. There is not the one without the other. The relationship is neither one nor two: motherhood demands filiation and vice versa. We shall not understand the mother, and much less the son, simply by examining the mother as an individual substance. In order to understand, we cannot reduce the two poles to a unity; the relation would disappear. I need to discover a sort of dynamic field of intelligibility that is not directed to an individual substance and is not a one-directional relationship either. Maternity and filiation go together; they are inseparable and yet are not one. This knowledge is not a subject-object knowledge. I know what maternity is only by knowing what filiation is, but if I substantialize both into a mother and a son, I will not be able to bring the two together in a single act of my spirit.

Furthermore, the *advaitic* intuition does not stem from an inductive act emerging from the fact that both monism and dualism are unconvincing. Such thinking could equally lead to an absolute pluralism or an absolute nihilism for example. *Advaita* is an experience. One cannot adduce it from any strict proof. One can bear witness to it and show that it is not irrational. If *advaita* were not an experience, it would turn into its logical consequence: monism. If reality is not two then it is one. The authentic *advaitic* insight does not play a dialectical game in order to prove the experience. If at all, we use the acumen of the mind to rebuke the arguments of the adversaries, as did Nāgārjuna.

It is important to stress the fundamental difference between *advaita* and monism, especially since a good number of so-called *advaitins* ancient and modern are in fact monists. Here, it is of little interest to discuss whether Śankara was a monist or an *advaitin*, or whether Rāmānuja's or Abhinavagupta's nondualism is a more perfect form of *advaita* than the buddhist *advaita* or the jaina *advaya*. *Advaita* would not have taken pains to keep its name if it were a mere monism, *ekatva* (*māyā* as an illusion, the world as non-real, etc.). Indeed, the dialectical interpretation of *advaita* yields a more or less strict monism, but I repeat that *advaita* is a spiritual experience which challenges the primacy of rationality over both intellect, on the one hand, and reality, on the other.

Furthermore, be it *cit*, *nous*, or *intellectus*, our awareness can still do something crucial. It can become aware of its proper limits. Only jokingly would I mimic Heidegger and say that our thinking is *bound* (directed) to *bound* (leap) within the *bounds* (boundaries), which both keeps that thinking *bound* (tied) and allows it to re-*bound* (bounce) from a reality which, not being *bound* to ourselves, releases us from *bondage*. This does, however, come fairly close to expressing what I would like to say. This awareness is implied in the very fact of reflection. Reflection means that as subjects we bounce back, recoil from a wall, from an *objectum* that is not ourselves. We encounter a *Gegen-stand* (an object), which shows itself by offering resistance to our intellect. Without this stumbling on a wall as a limit, there is no bouncing back, no reflexive awareness. If the intellect reflects on itself, it is because it has bumped into a wall beyond which it cannot go, and so turns to itself. This is why I said that the intellect discovers that there is something behind the wall that is not intellect. We discover our limits. This fact implies that the intellect transcends itself without at the same time destroying itself, that is, without ceasing to be intelligent. It sees that it can see all that there is to be seen, but it "sees" also that it has no guarantee, no assurance, that beyond the "barrier" of what it sees there may not still be Being, reality, or perhaps emptiness. The intellect sees this because it becomes conscious of its proper limits—precisely in the reflexive act.

These limits are the very limits of Being only inasmuch as Being is assimilable, that is, cognizable by the intellect. Unless the intellect postulates its own absolute dominion over Being, however, it cannot know anything outside its own field (of knowledge) (which is a tautology), and cannot therefore proscribe reality from having some dimension that is off limits to knowledge, as I already indicated when discussing the "omniscience" of God. These limits are the very limits of the intellect, but once the intellect is aware of its limits it cannot reflect on itself with a total reflection. Absolute self-reflection is self-contradictory or a tautology. It is contradictory because total reflection would be a total bending back on something that is itself (the subject) and not itself (the object). No act of knowledge can itself be object and subject exhaustively in the same act. We would then have nothing to reflect upon, because everything is already "flexed," "bent" all the way around (in) the "bend," so that the bending-back (the re-flection proper) does not bring back anything more or different. Or, it is a tautology. Absolute self-reflection would be pure consciousness that does not reflect on anything. Pure consciousness, if reflexive, is not reflexive of anything different from itself, pure consciousness. That is, it is not conscious *of* anything since the *of* itself is not absolutely identical with the itself and would have to be an object, and thus not be pure. This is what I have called the "consciouslessness" of pure consciousness. In some vedāntic schools *brahman* as pure consciousness has no consciousness *of*, no consciousness of anything, not even of itself. *Brahman* does not know that it is *brahman*. It is *Īśvara* who knows that he is *brahman*. The *jīva* or individual atman is also *brahman*, but inasmuch as the *jīva* does not know it is *brahman*, it is suffused in *avidyā*, ignorance.

This awareness of its own limits allows *advaitic* consciousness to deny that reality is either one or two, and in so doing, it reaches the limits of intelligibility. *Advaita* does not renounce the intellect, but it does not enthrone the intellect as the unique reality. The intellect must keep an eye on the complexity of the real where evil, error, and ignorance are possible. For this reason, *advaitic* writers will insist on *ātman-anātma-viveka*, discrimination between *ātman* and *anātman*, or *sadāsatvastuviveka*, discrimination between things that are and things that are not, or between the eternal and the non-eternal (*nityā*nit*ya*), as the Prince of the *advaitins* repeatedly says.[13]

Advaita also tries to avoid dualism. It does not renounce making sense of things, but recognizes that reality is not split asunder into two irreconcilable fields of good and evil, Being and Non-being, subject and object, rational and irrational, spiritual and material, or the like. This is the product of the

13 Śankara, *Vivekacūdāṁ ani*, 2.

dialectical mind, which also belongs to the real. By dint of its own experience of the real, *advaita* will try to give a coherent vision of reality by recognizing constitutive polarities within the very structure of the real such as God and the World, for instance, or in the more religious context of the words of Abhinavagupta, *nara-śakti-śivatmakaṁ trikam*, the triad of *Śiva*, *śakti*, and *nara* (God, its Power, and Man).

3. *Trinity*

Formally speaking, Trinity amounts to *advaita*. From different perspectives, both attempt to overcome the inadequacies of dualism without falling into monism. It should be clear that I do not intend to mix up christian Trinity and vedāntic *advaita* as theological belief systems. Each belongs to a distinct universe. However, just as Trinity is not a christian monopoly, so *advaita* is not an exclusively indic insight. In order to be brief, and also because there is a longstanding and well-chiseled christian language, I shall use that language with the proviso that it represents a human experience and not a specifically christian doctrine, as we will elaborate later.

The formal structure of the Trinity is analogous to the *advaitic* vision. If we look into the heart of the christian trinitarian controversies, we wonder at the otherwise inexplicable stubbornness of the Fathers of the Church in maintaining the trinitarian dogma against "milder" interpretations. It came neither from a logical deduction nor from clear exegetical interpretations but rather from an insight into the ultimate character of reality. We may also ascribe it, of course, to a *sensus ecclesiae* and *instinctus* fidei (a communitarian sense of Church and a faith instinct), but even then, *gratia non tollit naturam* (grace does not abolish nature). Christian orthodoxy consists in avoiding tritheism, on one hand, and strict monotheism, on the other. This is all the more surprising because the christian trinitarian dogma is not "revealed" *expressis verbis* in any sacred text. This focus of the early christian thinkers is particularly remarkable because the hellenic background posed a standing temptation to fall into monism, while the hebrew background was a powerful invitation to dualism.

A quick glance at the sociology of knowledge helps to explain the eclipse of the doctrine of the Trinity in spite of its being proclaimed the central christian dogma. During the early christian centuries the doctrine of the Trinity could grow and come to a maturity by a pure reflection on christian faith. The christians of the first centuries were a "counter-culture" and were afraid of nothing. They clearly saw that without the Trinity the Incarnation made no sense, and they would be forced to accept docetism or admit a second God. After Constantine, allowing for sociological delays, christianity became a political force for which a too explicit Trinity was not "politically correct" on two accounts: it would be felt as a threat to the imperial policy of monotheism, and it would add fuel to their increasingly strained relations with judaism. The result was that with the major exception of the orthodox liturgy, the doctrine of the Trinity remained in abeyance up to the present times. The Trinity is an irritant to any monarchic ideology, be it religious (monotheism), political (imperialism and colonialism), economic (global market), academic (*pensée unique*), or even of lifestyle (technocracy). In the Trinity the difference between the persons is infinite. The Trinity, furthermore, is another irritant to the historical cradle of christianity (judaism), and one can well understand that in order to appease anti-semitic trends of political, economic, and cultural nature a certain type of shortsighted prudence tended to downplay the dogma of the Trinity. Even today, to affirm that judaism is an independent and respectable religion, as is islām or hinduism, seems too much for many christians who want to heal the shame of anti-semitism by insisting that the mother of christianity is judaism, by neglecting the father, and by forgetting that a grown-up daughter may have better relations with her parents if she leaves the parental house. The sociology of knowledge, however, is not everything.

The main insight of the doctrine of the Trinity is simple. Ultimate reality is neither One (Being, or anything real) with three modes, nor Three (substances, beings) within a single abstract oneness—*neti neti*. The Trinity is pure relationship, and here lies the great challenge and the profound transformation. If the Divine were a substance we would have three Gods; if the Divine is infinite relationship, this relationship also enters all creatures and Man in a special way.

Using christian language, the *aporia* here is also resolved by overcoming the latent dualisms of Father-Son, Begetter-Begotten, Being-Intelligence, etc. by means of the Spirit, which is not subordinated to the Logos (intelligibility) and is no more separable from the Source than the Logos. The Father is as much totally in the Spirit as in the Son, yet in a different manner, precisely because reality is not identical with its *logos* character, with intelligibility. So the indwelling of the Father in the Son is an exhaustively intelligible indwelling. Because intelligence is not all that there is to reality, the Father can also indwell totally in the Spirit without diminishing the fullness of that first indwelling. There is obviously more, because that indwelling is mutual, otherwise the so-called three Persons would not be "equal."

The trinitarian insight sees reality as nondual and irreducible to intelligibility alone because alongside the very principle of intelligibility, or the Logos, there is the Spirit "who" as such cannot be confused with the Logos. At the same time, neither is reality reducible to a single Being, such that all is the same. The genial Plotinus, who had such an influence on the formation of christian self-understanding, was nevertheless constantly rebuked because his Trinity, emanating from a single principle, remained monistic or at least monarchic.

Here the difference is clear. The Trinity is not some sort of monarchianism; it is not an emanation from the plotinean One or a certain vedāntic *ekam*. Understandably enough, such interpretations have been the refuge of a certain mitigated conception of the christian Trinity lest it be expelled from the monotheistic fold. Nonetheless, the christian Father is certainly source, but there is no source without what flows from it and without being constantly "refilled" with what returns to it. In the dogma of creation, what comes from the source suffers an ontological degradation. Not so in the begetting of the Son. There is a Begetter only because there is a Begotten. The Begotten is not inferior to the Begetter. Without Son, there is no Father, but this Son is not only *ab intra*. This is the christian challenge of the Incarnation.

In brief, the challenge for us is to rescue the traditional doctrine of the Trinity from the *topos ouranios* of an atemporal, eternal realm and allow it to descend into the *palestra* of the whole of reality, which is also temporal—or rather tempiternal. In christian words, to take the Incarnation seriously as a divine act and not exclusively as a historical event.

If the Trinity belongs to the very structure of Being, and there is an uncanny relationship between Being and time, one may also inquire into the relation between eternity and time, which is also the relation between Trinity and "creation." Using the language of monotheism, I could say that the traditional, although often forgotten, doctrine of the *creatio continua*, is the link between time and eternity. The eternal God continuously creates the temporal world. Each temporal moment is created by an eternal act. Still in traditional language, the temporal flow is constituted by tempiternal moments. The temporal being is sustained in existence by an eternal Being. Eternity is the very ground of temporality. The Creator is not "outside." Eternity is co-eternal with time, just as time is co-temporal with eternity. Time is temporal—it exists because it has its "backing" in eternity. Eternity is eternal; it exists because it is (and not only manifests itself) in time. The structure of the Whole is tempiternal from moment to moment, the continuous creation of the rhythm of the dance of Nāṭarāja, which is an indic symbol for creation as divine play.[14] Here again, time and eternity are neither two nor one.

The immanent Trinity reveals something about the Trinity *ad extra*, which is the World, but the Trinity *ad extra* also reveals something about the Trinity *ad intra*, which is the Divine.

We have brought together *advaita* and Trinity because the two manifest a similar structure of human thinking and an analogous vision of reality. Being is not a lifeless monolithic unity. The *tad ekam*, "that One" of the Upanishad, is *ekam evādvitīyam,* "one only without a second," or literally, "one only nonduality."[15] This non-dual-One or One-non-duality does not, as it were, exclude any being and does not suffocate Being in the embrace of the One. Only a second "One" would destroy the first. It has not a "second One" because that selfsame One is itself *advitīyam*, adual. This is not a tautology like "the One is One," or an identity like "the One is not Two." It asserts that in the very heart of the One there is a nonduality which makes the One a living, fecund, and truly real One—a dynamic relationship (*perichôrêsis*), not a substance.

The Trinity qualifies this Oneness, telling us that this nondual Oneness embraces the whole of Reality and is completed in itself. It returns to the Source, gathering in its return all the scattered temporal fragments originating in the primal outburst of the Source.

Both intuitions address in a nondialectical way the *aporia* of the greek mind, "the One and the Many." The always problematic "and" is not resolved by an ontological pluralism ("only many"), by a rigid monism ("only one"), by a mitigated one ("one as many"), by a renunciation of intelligibility ("one as well as many"), or even by a dialectical device ("one turning into many, many turning into one"). The hindu and christian intuitions deny both elements of the *aporia* ("neither one nor many"). The dilemma of our two first organs of perception is overcome by the more holistic vision of the third eye. The senses perceive the "many": we see many things. The mind perceives the "one": we can understand only by finding, reducing, or abstracting the "one" (underneath or above the "many"). Our discursive mind is able to discover the One in the many (as we have indicated), but cannot see the many in the One (once the One is reached, all differences disappear)—and the mind drags us unto absolute idealism.

14 See Panikkar, "El presente tempiterno: una apostilla a la historia de la salvación y a la teología de la liberación," in A. Vargas-Machuca, ed., *Teología y mundo contemporáno* (Madrid: Ediciones Cristiandad), 133-75.

15 CU VI, 2, 1.

Advaita and Trinity degrade both the One and the many as ontological categories. Reality is neither One (as our mind postulates) nor Many (as our senses perceive). Reality is neither what our senses alone perceive nor what our mind alone discovers. Reality transcends us and we are aware of it. Furthermore, we complete these two perceptions by a third faculty, as I will elaborate later. Reality is *advaita*; it is trinitarian.

The christian insight was that the "structure" (to use a more neutral word) of God is trinitarian. The emphasis was on God as the Supreme Being, and mainly as transcendent and therefore with minor repercussions on the "created" world. Once the immanence of God is stressed as much as his transcendence, and his infinity as much as his goodness, the trinitarian structure of the Divinity percolates, as it were, through all His creation. The classical *vestigium trinitatis* becomes *imago trinitatis* without diminishing the special case of Man.

I am not concerned here with vedāntic *advaita* or the christian Trinity as much as with the depth of human experience, as exemplified in both these traditions. I will also give enough hints from other traditions to render at least plausible the observation that there must be something universal in this most human experience of reality. Neither am I directly concerned here with the important problem as to whether this intuition stems from a special divine revelation or is arrived at by human intellect alone. This does not pertain to our problem because of the cosmotheandric *perichōr*ēsis, as we are going to explain later. The intellect is never "alone."

4. *Some Examples from History*

This introduction to the triadic *mythos* has so far been rather theoretical. I should now complement and eventually correct this by a more historical presentation. The Trinity is not something generated by thinking alone, nor is it merely a convenient frame to be superimposed upon phenomena. From totally different backgrounds, and thus also with diverse meanings, we find triadic conceptions both of the Divine and of reality from the remotest ages to the most modern times.[16] We know, of course, that "every perfect thing is threefold," as the Mahābhārata says directly,[17] and the Latin dictum repeats: *omne trium perfectum*. "The Father's Intellect said that all things be divided into three," stated the *Chaldean Oracles.*[18]

16 Recently, for example, there has been talk about "the significance of the triune patterns of ultimate reality," and of an axiological "metaTrinity of values" represented by the good, the beautiful, and the holy. Cf. Mountcastle (1978), 5, 115-33. The literature today is overwhelming.

17 MB XIV, 39, 21.

18 *Chaldean Oracles*, 22.

The triad seems to be the universal symbol for the perfect unity: World, Man, and the Divine. Again, within the World: earth, air, and sky; in Man: body, soul, spirit; and in the Divinity: many examples, some of which we are going to cite below. In one way or another we seem to be aware of a threefold field of reality, be it *triloka, trikāya, trividham brahman*, Trinity, Man-Heaven-Earth, the One-the Intellect-the Soul, *wu-yu-t'ai*, or the like. There seems to be a universal human awareness that the triad is something that pertains to reality as a whole. Here are a few examples.

From Egypt: "One is Bait, one is Hathor, one is Akori—to them belongs one Force. Salutations to you, Father of the World, salutations to you trimorphic God."[19] The Air, Chou, is an egyptian divinity precisely because it both separates and unites Heaven and Earth.[20] The egyptian Trinity is explicit: "Three are all the Gods: Amun, Ra, Ptah." The most common names are: Ptah, Sokaris, Osiris.[21] I am not competent to enter into the discussion about the possible egyptian influence on the christian Trinity. I simply point out that the problem of the three-unity is already present in Egypt.

The vedic revelation is forthright in this respect, as are the sayings of the Upanishads, which seem to recognize theological, cosmic, and eschatological trinities.[22] As in an immense number of kosmologies, the universe is considered to be of three regions: sky, air, earth.[23] The Atharvaveda speaks of Agni, the King of the Gods,[24] as "one energy whose process is threefold."[25] "He revealed himself threefold," say several texts that deal directly with the foundation of the world or the meaning of *Aum*. [26]

The same Upanishad further elaborates this idea: "The entire reality [*idaṁ*] is a triad of name, form, and act."[27] This serves to qualify the following verses:

25

19 Morenz (1960), 270. Τρίμορφος θεός, of which Bait is masculine and the other two are feminine.

20 Bonnefoy (1981), II, 326.

21 Cf. Morenz (1960), 150ff. and 270, etc.

22 Cf. Koch, which tries to show similarities with the christian tradition and how its translation could be perfect.

23 RV X, 158, 1.

24 Coomaraswamy, *Axis mundi*, 63.

25 AV VII, 9, 26: "ekam ojas tredhā vicakrama."

26 BU I, 2, 3; MaitU VI, 3: "sa tredātmānam vyakuruta" (Some translators take the more immediate and crude meaning of the verb to say that he divided himself in three ways).

27 BU I, 6, 1: "trayaṁ vā idaṁ nāma rūpaṁ karma."

"This triad is one, this ātman; the one ātman is that triad."[28] Hume gives this translation: "Although it is that triad, this Soul is one. Although it is one, it is that triad." The sense is nevertheless clear: Reality is one, yet works in a threefold way. It is all one and three, for they work and are together: *A-u-m*![29]

One well-known trinitarian formula has been commented upon since time immemorial as the most perfect description of Brahman: "Brahman is truth, knowledge, infinity."[30] An enlightening comment on Śankara's interpretation is worth citing. The *sat*, *cit*, ānanda: being, consciousness, joy "are not concepts or predicates. . . . Each is a *sui generis* Self. Each is identical with Brahman, substantially, not conceptually. . . . Brahman is triunal."[31] Another text explicitly states: "This has been praised as the supreme *brahman*: the triad (*trayam*)."[32]

The ubiquitous *triloka* or three-worlds doctrine should also be mentioned, as well as the śaiva-siddhānta doctrine of the *pati, paśu, pāśa*—the Creator, the creature, and its bond. Indeed, there could be no end to the indic triads: the three *guṇa*,[33] the threefold meaning of Aum,[34] the Trimūrti, etc. "The real Trinity in the vedānta is the Brahman, the finite ātman, and the material world."[35]

Neither should one neglect the buddhist *trikāya*, the three manifestations of the Buddhas: *dharmakāya* (the teaching of the doctrine transmitted to the Community), *nirmaṇākāya* (manifestation on earth in a human body to ordinary people and animals), and *sambhogakāya* (mystical communion with the *bodhisattvas*); or the three jewels or *triratna*: Buddha, Dharma, and Sangha (or Buddha, Justice [Law, Order], and Community). In the long course of its tradition, the *triratna* has also become *bodhisattva, mahāsthāma,* and *Buddha*, or, as in indian, tibetan, and chinese buddhism,

---

28 BU I, 6, 3: "tad etat trayaṁ sad ekam ayam ātmā, ātmā ekaḥ sann etad trayam."

29 CU III, 17, 6. This is the reason why another Upanishad adds: "In the last hour Man should take refuge in these three: You are imperishable, You are immovable, You are firm in life."

30 TU II, 1, 1: "satyaṁ jñānam anantaṁ brahman." Other texts say ānanda (joy) instead of *ananta*.

31 T. R. V. Murti, *Studies in Indian Thought* (2nd ed.; Delhi: Motilal Banarsidass, 1996), 147-48. One might also compare Lipner's exegesis of this text according to Rāmānuja. While for Śankara the text reveals an undifferentiated *brahman*, for Rāmānuja it provides a possible kataphatic approach to the Divine.

32 SU I, 7, which is repeated and explained in the following stanzas. In I, 12 it is called the "threefold Brahman": *Tri-vidhaṁ brahman*.

33 BG XIV.

34 MaitU, VI, 3.

35 Raju (1985), 526.

the past, present, and future Buddha: Śākyamuni, Avalokiteśvara, and Maitreya. To the three jewels, the Mantrayāna will add the three roots, and so forth. We also encounter the *ratnatraya,* or three jewels, in the jaina *dharma* represented by the *samyak-darśana, samyak-jñāna,* and *samyak-cāritra*: right vision (faith), right knowledge, and right conduct, respectively. The three together form the *mokṣa-mārga*, the path to liberation.[36]

In Greece, Parmenides begins with three hypostases, while Numenius of Apamea (second century AD) speaks of three Gods. Plato speaks of the Trinity of the Intellect, the Soul, and the Body (of the world).[37] Plotinus, of course, is the systematic thinker of the three hypostases—the One, the Intellect, and the Soul,[38] presumably elaborating on Numenius. The *Chaldean Oracles* formulated it as a common belief: "For in each world shineth the Triad, governed by the Monad."[39]

In Rome, Valentinus elaborates his system of the three divine hypostases— the transcendent, the intellect, and the soul (or wisdom)—with their three corresponding metaphysical principles, *Deus, forma, materia.*[40] Esoteric judaism and esoteric islām also know the triadic structure of the divine. Philo of Alexandria interprets the vision of Abraham and his three "visitors" in a trinitarian fashion:[41] "To those who have discernment, Moses presents it as a plain thing that one can be three and three one, because, in fact, according to a higher intellect they are one."[42]

Henry Corbin describes *une triple théophanie primordiale*: first, the Essence itself, Unity; second, that of the Names and Attributes, pluralizable unity; and third, the theophany of the Manifestation of Being as Light, the theophany proper.[43]

Ibn 'Arabī is even more explicit:

My beloved is Three—
Three yet only one;
Many things appear as three,
Which are no more than one.[44]

36 Cf. Shāntā (1985), 209ff.

37 Plato, *Timaeus*, *Sophist,* etc.

38 Plotinus, *Enneads*, V, 1, 3.

39 *Chaldean Oracles*, 27.

40 Montserrat (1983), I, 40.

41 Gn XVIII, 1-22.

42 Philo, *Quaestiones et solutiones in Genesin* VI, 2.

43 Cf. Corbin (1981), 27.

44 Apud R. Graves in his Introduction to I. Shah, *The Sufis* (Garden City, N.Y.: Doubleday, 1964), ix.

For Lao Tzu, the entire notion of reality is built on three principles: eternal Non-being (*wu*), eternal Being (*yu*), and the Great Oneness (*t'ai i*).[45] "The three produced the ten thousand things," the text says, after having declared the origin of the One and the Two,[46] which is echoed by an Upanishad that explains the threefold unfolding of everything.[47] In general, taoist ideas about Man and the Universe all seem to be trinitarian. Heaven, Earth, and Man would be the familiar confucian formulation in China. Yang Hsiung's (53 BC-18 AD) fundamental work, *The Great Mystery*, spells out how the Mystery (*Hsüan*) constitutes the way (*Tao*) of Heaven, the way of Earth, and the way of Man—and then goes on to develop groups of threes for the entire universe.[48]

A traditional christian approach is that of the *vestigium trinitatis*, conserved in an obscure and often distorted way from the primordial revelation. It is the well-known idea of a *praeparatio evangelica* and a cosmic testament. The Fathers of the Church see many of those examples as a proof of a primitive revelation that they called Divine Condescendence.

The *Evangelium Thomae* (13) speaks of the triple Christ, and the entire gnostic tradition is in agreement about the tri-corporeal Christ,[49] as well as the three human natures: spiritual, animal, and material.[50] Purified of most of the overtones of a superiority complex, this theory is still found in our times.[51]

Richard of Saint Victor, voicing a general belief, speaks of a threefold realm: the immortal, the incorruptible, and the eternal,[52] pointing out that we may ascend to the three realms *actualiter, virtualiter, intellectualiter*. As a citizen of this earth, Man is capable of ascending to the angelic and divine worlds, since we are more than earthlings.[53]

One might also refer to the hypothesis of the archetypes as C. G. Jung interprets them. Although Jung tended to see the human psyche as a

45 Fung Yu-Lan, *A History of Chinese Philosophy* (1934), I, 173.

46 Ibid., 42.

47 CU VI, 3-6.

48 Fung Yu-Lan, *History of Chinese Philosophy*, II, 140.

49 Orbe (1976), I, 10.

50 Ibid., II, 629.

51 Cf. Daniélou (1967) and Seifert (1954).

52 Richard of Saint Victor, *De Trinitate*, Prologus (PL 196:890A-C): "triplex regio immortalitatis [the human], incorruptibilitatis [the angelic], aeternitatis [the divine]."

53 The belief that man's real home is not the earth but heaven was common in the first christian generation; cf. Heb XIII, 14; etc.

quaternitas because of its apparent "balance," he freely concedes that the Trinity appears and reappears in such a variety of forms and over such an enormous span of time that it represents one of the most fundamental human archetypes. From quite another, almost neo-pythagorean angle, R. Buckminster Fuller's (re)discovery of "Nature's Coordinate System" as an "omniintertriangulated" matrix may turn out to be a more daring sort of archetype or *vestigium*. "Triangle is structure," says Fuller, and any structural engineer (or any spider, for that matter) would have to agree.[54]

What I draw from all this is that theisms as such do not exhaust the richness of the religious phenomenon, not even that of the christian Trinity.[55] From a predominantly christian perspective we have the impressive thirty titles of the *Bibliotheca trinitariorum,* International Bibliography of Trinitarian Literature.[56]

All the examples show a certain *Urphänomen*—divine triads, metaphysical triads, anthropological and psychological triads, kosmological, chronological, ethical, and also liturgical triads, as well as legendary ones.[57] Indeed, one can also find dyads, quaternities, and other holy numbers around which the number of divinities crystallize.[58] No hurried conclusions should be drawn from such vast materials. One is led to think, however, that a certain trinitarian pattern seems to have occurred spontaneously to human consciousness since the beginnings of historical memory. While admitting the force of subjective explanations, namely, that the Trinity belongs to our mental or psychological makeup, the question remains whether this is because reality as such exhibits a trinitarian structure. Where do these archetypes come from?

Both objective and subjective explanations have their drawbacks. A merely subjective explanation is one-sided, since it then has to claim objective validity for the subject (by creating a "science" of psychology, for example). On the other hand, a merely objective explanation is equally inadequate, since many of the data are not objectively verifiable, and not even in

---

54 Fuller, *Synergetics* (1975), 610.

55 Moltmann (1980), 33, 34. Suffice to quote one of Jürgen Moltmann's leitmotifs: "Auslösung der Trinitätslehre in abstrakten Monotheismus" or "Reduktion der Trinitätslehre auf Monotheismus." The idea that classical theism has given rise to modern atheism has also been revived (Willis 1987 passim; cf. Bracken review in *Theological Studies*, 49/3 [Sept. 88], 549-50).

56 E. Schadel, ed., *Bibliotheca trinitariorum* (Munich/New York: Saur, 1984-88).

57 Heiler (1961).

58 Berner (1980), 111; and Heiler (1961).

agreement with one another. We shall now look at this knotty problem from an anthropological perspective, and in Part VI from a more cosmic point of view.

B. The Anthropophanic Factor

Divine light may be glaring; it illumines everything, but if it is to illumine us we cannot be completely transparent, and thus we have to reckon with our shadow. Even if we were to succeed in reflecting that divine light, the image may be somewhat distorted, and at any rate it is a divine image on a human screen. In other words, the human factor cannot be eliminated. Even if we were puppets in the hands of a divine Power, it is we, the puppets, who play our role more or less consciously. Whoever pulls the strings in this scenario, it is all a *Humana Commedia*; whoever may have written the libretto and however the show might have been organized, we are the actors. If we are not puppets but rather free persons, then our own diversity and different understandings of the Divine make the human factor indispensable in everything we do, think, and even are. Our experience need not be anthropocentric; we must avoid uncritical anthropomorphisms, but we cannot escape the *humanum*.

The word *anthropophany* stresses the fact that whatever our notion of Man may be, the basis of any anthropology is how we see the epiphany of that peculiar being that we believe ourselves to be. Although Man is not the center of the universe, anything we think and do bears the human stamp. Anthropology is the *logos* about Man. In the same way that theology can be understood as meaning an objective or a subjective genitive, anthropology can refer to our (natural) science about Man or as the word of Man about himself, as his self-understanding, as Man appears to himself. This latter is what can be designated as anthropophany. This self-understanding is not independent from how Man understands the world.

1. *The Human Approach to Reality*

I am not alone in the world—calling "world" everything that is around me. Before, or along with the consciousness of "I am," we are aware that "thou art," and even that "it is." Later on we are aware that we, you, and they are in the dual and plural.[59] The child's awakening to human consciousness probably begins with the *art* followed by the *is* and ends with the *am*—all

59 It is significant that most european languages have subsumed the dual into the plural, and that the english language has eliminated any verbal differentiation for the plural: we, you, they—all "are" (not *somos, sois, son* as in spanish).

in an intertwined manner.[60] At any rate, we are conscious beings. Although we are not simply consciousness, consciousness of one type or another is inextricably linked with ourselves. We may not know what we are, but we are conscious that we are. What we call reality is the ultimate referent of that awareness. As noted earlier, the scholastics said that this ultimate referent is the first that falls on the intellect.

Reality, we said, is all that there is, all that *is* in whatever form—*idaṁ sarvaṁ* (all this, this all). We are not only aware of it; we are aware of our awareness. It is a reflective awareness built into our awareness. We know (reality), knowing that we know (reality). That is why we have human speech, which is more than an instrument for information. It is the affirmation of our humanness. This prompts the question about such knowing of reality, which allows us to speak (about it). We are conscious of it because in one way or another we share in that reality about which we are conscious. This is a first and fundamental step, which has often been overlooked by concentrating on the second: the means, organs, faculties, or windows that allow us to see, perceive, do, or enter in conscious contact with reality. What we say about reality depends on how we perceive it, but we would not perceive it if in one way or another we were not "part" of it.

"We know inasmuch as we are known"[61] is a traditional way of describing this first step. "Every gift . . . springs from above coming down from the Father of all lights."[62] "The light of all things"[63] is the source of all knowledge descending from "the Storehouse of the Great Light"[64] with no need now to quote Plato, Augustine, Bonaventure, and scores of other thinkers defending the illumination theory of knowledge. In brief, we know because we are suffused in light, in knowledge. We see because there is a light that allows us to see.

This implies that the subject/object epistemology does not cover the entire field of knowledge; even though there is no denying both the heuristic value of such an epistemology, and the fact that it has been prevalent in an

60 Here we have another example of the difference between the prevalent western psychological analysis and the indian metaphysical speculation. "Thou art" is said to be the first conscious act of the child—I have just said. "I am" is the first utterance of Man writes the *Upanishad* (cf. BU I, 4, 1; etc.). Consciousness of the other (thou) versus self-consciousness, a "self" that is probably not only the individual.

61 1 Cor XIII, 12.

62 Jas I, 18.

63 Nishitani (1982) 167.

64 *The Sutra of Perfect Enlightenment* (apud Nishitani, ibid.).

important part of many human cultures. Yet, before our epistemological (subject-object) knowledge there is ontological awareness. This latter may be the task of the *intellectus*, νοῦς, or spirit in contradistinction with the *ratio*, διάνοια, or mind— although the vocabulary here remains very fluid and ambivalent.

* * *

In modern times, the threefold vision of a tripartite anthropology (body, soul, spirit), has been superseded by a dualist anthropological model (soul and body), corresponding to a cosmological scheme (Man and the universe, or spirit and matter). Modern Man, caught in the vise of technocracy, appears to accept uncritically the dual paradigm of two fields of reality, the theological or metaphysical realm and the realm disturbingly called "real" or ordinary. Many people may still pay lip service to religious values, and philosophers to metaphysical queries, but in every country under the sway of technocracy life is lived out mainly on two levels, the sensible and the rational. The third element has been "privatized." No wonder islām and buddhism appeal so powerfully to people living in this desacralized, two-dimensional world.

We have here a typical example from the "sociology of knowledge." Modern science with its undeniable pragmatic success presents an implicit cosmology which supersedes all the others, and subsequently forms the context (the myth) in which human thought thrives. In spite of the good intentions of Descartes to revere theology and his desire to *gagner le ciel* like anyone else,[65] in spite of the sincere effort of Kant to restrain the power of reason "in order to make room for faith,"[66] modern culture has constructed a civilization in which the Divine is ousted from the actual life of the *civitas*. The *fanum* has been practically tamed by the *profanum* and reduced to a private enclosure outside the *polis* (and politics). We may recall that with the main exception of the so-called Enlightenment, most traditional cultures have considered the universe in general and the earth in particular as a temple of the Divine. Once the sacred (the divine or God) has become a superfluous hypothesis for the running of civic life, the sacred suffers social atrophy, and talk about the Divine is reduced to a more or less odd specialty for some people who are removed from "real" life. Religious faith is sociologically irrelevant; it becomes an indifferent matter whether to believe or not to believe. We can be tolerant; the trains run and the computers work, whether we believe in God or not—provided there is adequate energy.

---

65 Descartes, *Discours de la mèthode*, I.

66 Cf. Kant, *Kritik der reinen Vernunft*, Introduction to the second edition, B,XXX: "Ich musste also das Wissen aufheben, um zum Glauben Platz zu bekommen."

This oversimplified description should not overlook the responsibility of religious institutions which felt (with allegedly good intentions) that the privilege of managing the sacred was theirs. The religious elite thereby gave apparent justification to all those who, chafed by the institutional monopoly on the sacred, imagined they could dispense with religion altogether and become the builders of the profane city. This does not mean that we should be nostalgic for past theocracies whether of the right or of the left.

If many traditional cultures suffered under the reign of an other-worldly supernaturalism, the modern state of affairs is ultimately the outcome of rationalism. I understand by this word, not that reason can explain everything (which reason herself knows she cannot), but the conviction that we are *essentially* rational beings. There is no denying that we are *rational*, but that is quite different from considering *animal rationale* as the essential definition of Man. Or in less anthropological and more metaphysical terms, rationalism is the belief that reality is essentially dialectical—precisely because the essence of reason is dialectical.

* * *

With a bipartite anthropological vision, we have only the senses and our reason to put us in contact with reality. This converts the problem of mediation into a central philosophical problem. Knowledge is mediation; modern culture is a civilization of mediations, generally called instruments or "services." The spirit of Hegel reigns supreme in spite of his *unmittelbare Vermittlung* (immediate mediation), and Knowledge remains fundamentally instrumental and dialectical.

In short, modern civilization seems to reduce our organs of perception to two, barely tolerating the third power in less-developed stages of human maturity—or banishing it to parapsychological states. Yet it is not only sorcerers, esoterics, and charlatans but also wise people, artists, and thinkers, as well as common folk, who all seem to be saying that above and beyond what the senses and our reason tell us there is something else. *Homo religiosus* buries the dead, prays, sings, and dances to an invisible reality, believes in something above him, a heaven within or without, or has a longing for the unknown and a fascination (and dread) for risk, as Nietzsche says.[67]

---

67 Nietzsche, *Ecce Homo* (1898):
Ja, ich weiß, woher ich stamme,
Ungesättigt gleich der Flamme
Glühe und verzehr' ich mich.
Licht wird alles was ich fasse,
Kohle alles, was ich lasse,
Flamme bin ich sicherlich.

The greatest prophet of the *Tôrāh*, Moses, is described as: "one seeing the invisible."[68]

Although it may not be a proper definition of the human being to affirm that Man aspires to become seer of the invisible, it might well serve as an accurate description of humanity's most enduring ideal. *Homo religiosus* refers to the deepest aspect of Man. We should not, however, confuse religion with morality. The *homo religiosus* can be not only a fanatic, but even evil, or as the christian Scripture says, the peaks of religion do not exclude the depths of Satan.[69] To be succinct, the human approach to reality, in one way or another, cannot dispense with encountering "the divine Mystery."

2. *The Three Eyes*

"How is it," Dionysius the Areopagite asks, "that we know God when he is neither *noēton*, nor *aisthēton*, nor any particular being?" How is it possible, since God is not an object of the senses, or of reason?[70] God is not any being among the beings (τῶν ὄντων ὄντα), "none absolutely of the beings that are." God is not a being, not even the Supreme Being (Entity). What allows us to speak about God if God is not to be found among beings? God is only to be "seen" "by the heart alone" says the *Corpus hermeticum,*[71] which echoes the upanishadic "with senses and mind entering into the heart,"[72] wherein "heart" is the seat of our complete knowledge. The "inner heart of Man," smaller than the kernel of a grain of millet and yet greater than the sky, is *brahman* says another Upanishad.[73] Mary kept in her heart all the words and deeds of her son says one Gospel.[74] In the very beginning of *De mystica theologia* Dionysius repeats this theme even more emphatically:

> For this I pray; and, Timothy, my friend, my advice to you as you look for a sight of the mysterious things, is to leave behind you

68 Heb XI, 27: τὸν γὰρ ἀόρατον ὡς ὁρῶν ἐκαρτέρησεν. ("Seeing the unseen").

69 It is significant that the greek βαθύς (the deep) is rendered by the Vulgate as *altitudines* (the height) of the devil.

70 Dionysius the Areopagite, *De divinis nominibus* VII, 3 (PG 3:869). Literally: ζητῆσαι χρή, πῶς ἡμεῖς θεὸν γινώσκομεν οὐδὲ νοητὸν οὐδὲ αἰσθητὸν οὐδε τι καθόλου τῶν οντων ὄντα. Or as the latin translation puts it, tellingly inverting the order: "Praeterea quaerendum est quomodo Deum cognoscamus, qui neque sensu percipitur nec intellectu, et nihil omnino est ex iis quae sunt."

71 Hermes Trismegistus, *Hermetica* VII, 2.

72 SU II, 8.

73 Cf. CU III, 14, 3: "esa ma ātma-antar hṛdaye etad brahma," a very extended notion known as *śāndilya vidyā.*

74 Lk II, 51.

> everything perceived and understood, everything perceptible and understandable, all that is not and all that is, and, with your understanding laid aside, to strive upward as much as you can toward union with him who is beyond all being and knowledge.[75]

The injunction to leave behind the sensible and intelligible worlds is not in order to cling to a supernatural world, thereby escaping from what we call the World.

The spiritual experience that many call "mystical" does not put us in touch with a third world, but lets us experience the third dimension of the one and same World, opening us up to a more real union with reality. It may be of interest to taste the somewhat different flavor of a less "up-to-date" translation:

> Such be my prayer, and thee, dear Timothy, I counsel that, in the earnest exercise of mystic contemplation, thou leave the senses and the activities of the intellect, and all things that the senses or the intellect can perceive, and all things in this world of nothingness, or in that world of being, and that, thine understanding being laid to rest, thou strain (so far as thou mayest) towards an union with Him whom neither being nor understanding can contain.[76]

Centuries later Richard of Saint Victor expresses the same idea: "If I am not mistaken, we have a threefold way to knowing things: Some by experience, some by reasoning, and certain others by believing."[77] There is a similar tripartite discussion of reality in a good number of cultures, which say that we should remember the three dimensions of Earth, Man, Heaven, or, according to the common indic schema, between the *ādhibhautika, ādhyātmika, ādhidaivika*, referring to things worldly, human, and divine. Yet it is not that each eye sees only its "proper" field, but rather that the three organs complement each other in putting us in contact with reality. I cannot repeat sufficiently that it would be wrong to fall into specialization, whether

75 Luibheid (1987), 135: τῇ περὶ τὰ μυστικὰ θεαματα συντόνῳ διατριβῇ καὶ τὰς αἰσθήσεις ἀπολεῖτε καὶ τὰς νοεράς ἐνεργείας καὶ παντα αἰσθητὰ καὶ νοετὰ καὶ πάντα ὄυκ ὄντα καὶ ὄντα. "Tu vero, o care Timothee, intenta mysticarum contemplationum exercitatione et sensus relinque et intellectuales operationes atque omnia sensibilia et intelligibilia, et universa quae non sunt aut sunt, (et quantum fieri potest erige te ratione arcana ad unionem [πρὸς τὴν ἕνωσιν] eius qui super omnem est essentiam et scientiam)."

76 Rolt (1972).

77 Richard of Saint Victor, *De Trinitate* I, 1 (PL 196:891A); "Rerum itaque notitia, ni fallor, modo triplici apprehendimus. Nam alia experiendo probamus, alia ratiocinando colligimus, aliorum certitudinem credendo tenemus." Cf. Hugh of Saint Victor, *De Sacramentis* I, 10, 2 (PL 176:327-29), who elaborated the same idea.

on the part of the subject or that of the object. Each "organ" apprehends (the total) reality under a perspective which lets it "see" one aspect of the real more clearly than the others. The "three" form an indivisible triad and are involved albeit in different degrees in any human experience. In fact, reality is not compartmentalized and consists of all its dimensions together.

I have already said that each word entails its proper context and that the ambivalence of words at once shows the riches of those words and makes confusion over them possible. Yet we should not mistake clarity for univocal rational evidence. Words, like symbols, are polyvalent, and too sharp a distinction may create artificial borders in the bountiful territory of the human world. A couple of examples may help to situate attempts at putting some order into this field. The academic world became excited when a great hellenistic scholar, Anders Nygren, made the distinction between *erōs* (human sentimental love) and *agapē* (more spiritual and divine love). Likewise modern exegesis will not confuse *chronos* (chronological time) with *kairos* (opportune or appointed time). I myself insist on the distinction between *bios* and *zōē*, or individual and person. Yet we should not exaggerate. The living languages past and present are often not consistent with such clear-cut distinctions. Here as well, it is wise to chart a middle way.

After such a proviso, I may venture an attempt at clarity based on both etymology and tradition by adopting the following language, which leans on greek words, which have been the starting point of western philosophical language. It would be pretentious to offer a definitive vocabulary for such a complex issue.

I use *experience*, ἐμπειρία, as the general word embracing all forms of immediate or ultimate knowledge; that is, those forms irreducible to any other prior sources. *Empeiria* stands for a perception that does not admit any doubt in the subject having that experience. Being immediate, no mediation is required. *Esse est percipi*[78] is the short formulation of british empiricism. I will not try to elucidate how this *empeiria* works or originates. Most medieval and indic systems, for instance, say that the divine light passes through body and matter, producing the *aisthēsis*, passes through the mind and the *noēta* emerges, and beyond these two media *ta pneumatika*, the spiritual, shines forth. I remain at the more phenomenological level by observing that it is a single "light" that diffracts in a threefold manner, and insist that the three are inseparable, although one sense may be more acute than the others. This experience is threefold and corresponds to the traditional tripartite "anthropophany" of body, soul, and spirit.

78 George Berkeley: "To be is to be perceived."

a) The Senses

Sensual experience is the experience of our senses in their widest acceptation, including sentiments as well as sensibility. The greek word (αἴσθησις) embraces also the aesthetic experience. We cannot doubt those experiences that are linked to a subject and refer to a particular object. We cannot deny our sensations of cold, pain, pleasure, beauty, sadness, joy . . .

Quite a different thing is our interpretation of those experiences.

Ta aisthēta (τὰ αἰσθητά) stands for all that is open to us through the senses. *Aisthēsis* (αἴσθησις) is the faculty of perceiving. Interestingly enough, the same faculties are called "discrimination" by the Upanishads.[79] When some philosophical schools teach that all our knowledge begins with the senses, they do not necessarily subscribe to a crude materialism (sensism) or deny that the senses know thanks to a superior illumination. They affirm that the testimony of the senses is true knowledge, and therefore that the material world is real in its own right, as it were, and not because human reason proves it. Human knowledge is first of all sensual knowledge, which is even called *jñāna* (knowledge) by one Upanishad in contrast to the general tendency of a certain Vedānta.[80]

The crux of the epistemology of the Enlightenment, with its enthusiasm about the power of reason, was precisely how to prove (rationally, of course) the real existence of the material world, specifically, how the knowing subject can prove the real existence of the known object. How do we justify that jump? All the more, since our reason all too often discovers the fallacies of the senses, how can we trust them?

My reason can doubt the existence of all objects outside the mind that are in the field of its perception, but my reason cannot doubt the existence of the reasoning subject whose bodily reality is witnessed precisely by my senses. The senses are the very basis on which my reason stands. My reason can doubt all that the senses present to my mind except the senses themselves. Sensual knowledge is the fundamental human knowledge, and acceptance of the body counters extreme rationalisms and spiritualisms. The christian dogma of the Incarnation and one of its corollaries, the Assumption of Mary into heaven with her whole corporality, are telling examples. The new contemporary awareness of the ultimate importance of secularity, which implies the importance of the body, also goes in this direction.

---

79 Cf., e.g., MandU III, 2, 7, etc.

80 Cf. KathU VI, 10, cited also in MaitU VI, 30.

b) Reason

Rational experience is the experience of our mind, also in its widest acceptation. The senses know, ecstatically, as it were. They do not know that they know. The mind knows what the senses know, and it is conscious too of what the mind knows. This knowledge of the mind culminates in rational evidence, that is, that light which does not allow us to doubt our rational vision. If the locus of sensual evidence is the singular object of a singular subject, here the locus is the universal (idea, concept, notion . . .), which has an inbuilt claim to be valid within the parameters of some objective conditions. The greek word is *noēsis* (νόησις), which is variously called intuition, understanding, simple apprehension, and so on. We may reach toward rational vision by a simple act of the mind or by a long process of our reasoning reason following what is commonly called logic. Rational evidence is more often than not formal evidence, that is, an immediate intellectual vision based on agreed-upon postulates or principles. Reasoning reason arrives at evidence from what was initially opaque to reason without this rational operation of the mind. In order to justify itself, however, reason has to recur to a higher instance like a divine light or a universal consensus.

Ta noēta (τὰ νοητά) stands for all that is open to the mind, that which we perceive mentally with the *nous*, our mind. The ideal is the construction of what the greeks called the *kosmos noētos* (κόσμος νοητός), the intelligible world. Quite a different thing is the conflict of interpretations between those diverse allegedly rational visions of the world.

Reason is a broad notion. It has tended, especially since the european Enlightenment, to embrace all the operations of the intellect. Up to a certain extent this is a semantic question, but, following an almost universal tradition, it proves meaningful to distinguish the reasoning reason from the intellectual intuition, although here as elsewhere we cannot draw rigid boundaries.[81] The two main functions of reason are the capacity of reasoning, which is a passing from one thought to another by becoming aware of certain coherences, mainly along the lines of induction and deduction. The second function is connected with the first and constitutes the power of discovering evidence. Reason flashes, as it were, under the light of evidence, but this light is not visible at first sight.

In most cases, what modern reason calls evidence follows a geometrical

81 Samkhya and kashmiri shaivism, for instance, expound *ashuddha* or impure *tattvas* (material, senses, organs of action, the mind, and the ego) that represent a different way of distinguishing the mind and intellect.

model. We see that when a circle is divided into two parts, one part alone is smaller than the two parts together. We see that if every Man is mortal, a particular member of that class is a part of the class, and what applies for the entire class applies to a part of it. I see with my reason that seven is bigger than five (7 = 5 + 2); and when seven defend an opinion against five, I see the seven have more power, and that it may be prudent to yield to the majority. It is not evident, however, that the opinion of the seven is right and that of the five wrong. What evidence do I have for the truth of the opinion of the majority? Is there any other evidence? Or is evidence the only criterion?

c) Spirit

Spiritual experience is the experience of our spirit, also in its widest acceptation, and some use the name intellectual enlightenment for what we see as truth without intermediaries in this experience, while others call it spiritual realization, mystical insight, the inner sense of the spirit, or many other names. It produces an existential confidence that convinces us of the truth of what we see without reducing it to rational certainty.

Spiritual knowledge is based neither on any postulate nor on any logical operation derived from other principles. It is immediate self-refulgent luminosity (*svayamprakaśa*), which is not based on any ulterior principle (such as that of non-contradiction). *Cogito ergo sum* ([I] think, therefore [I] am) is a paradigm of rational evidence, which lies in the *ergo*. The *ergo* is the power of reason. Spiritual knowledge is not of this kind; it is not derived.[82] Indeed, *spiritual* has many meanings, and the word *intellectual* has its contours vaguely mixed with the *rational* experience, but I venture the word *spiritual* trying to rescue it from both its specialized use and its pejorative connotations.

Ta pneumatika (τὰ πνευματικά) stands for that knowledge of reality which cannot properly be rationally proved. Unlike rational perception, spiritual knowledge-perception does not refer to anything else "beyond." This is why it cannot be proved by appealing to a higher instance. If such an appeal were possible, then there would be no end to it. There is a certain claim to objectivity in rational knowledge, even if it is difficult to prove it rationally. Spiritual knowledge, like sensual knowledge, simply witnesses, but with a difference. The senses express themselves with signs, which need to be interpreted by the intellectual language of reason. Reason uses concepts. Spiritual knowledge uses symbols. Its language is not conceptual; it is symbolic. The intentionality of the mystical symbol does not refer to

82 We know that Descartes played down the role of the *ergo*, but he had to rely on it to overcome his methodical doubt.

anything objectifiable outside the symbol itself and yet is not identical with the symbol.

The *symbolic difference*, that is, the difference between the symbol and the symbolized, lies in the very relation between the three: the symbol (which implies itself), the symbolized (which is the selfsame symbol), and the "symbolizer" (who is the "subject" for whom the symbol is real symbol). The symbol has no external referent. Through the symbol, spiritual knowledge touches the fringes of the mystery.

The witness of the third eye, being an ultimate organ that makes us aware of reality, cannot have a further ground outside itself. This constitutes its power and its weakness. The sensual and the rational faculties are also ultimate in their respective fields: each experience is ultimate as experience. However, there is a hierarchy among the three fields. Hierarchy does not mean that a "superior" form of knowledge has to interfere with another one by dictating the rules or the limits of that knowledge from the outside. Hierarchy does not mean superiority or inferiority; it means order, specifically, sacred order. It is *ontonomic* order in which the inter-independence of the "degrees of knowledge" cooperate toward the knowledge of the whole, each by virtue of its own nature. In other words, the ontonomy of the diverse "levels" of Being is not competitive.

The so-called *oculus* fidei is to be confused neither with belief nor with an insight into what is sometimes called "objects of faith" or "statements of faith." Faith, unlike belief, has no object. Faith is pure awareness, a conscious openness before it closes itself on an object by dint of sensual, rational, or spiritual knowledge. The eye of faith is generally reserved for the third kind of knowledge and more specifically to religious faith. To assume that faith can define what God is amounts to idolatry. Likewise, to assume that reason can define what the world is amounts to rationalism; and to assume that what our senses tell us is reality amounts to materialism. The three eyes together allow us to penetrate into the mystery of the real without exhausting reality

Three leading threads emerge from what I have said:

1. Reality is not exhausted by what the senses and the mind disclose. *Ta aisthēta* and *ta noēta* are not enough.
2. That which is disclosed in *ta pneumatika* is disclosed by union (*henōsis*), and demands the preparation of our entire being. It is not just cognition, but embraces all our being, and thus is beyond dialectics. "Neither Being nor Non-being," as almost all traditions say.

3. The threefold knowledge lets us surmise that "there is" a realm "beyond" knowledge in *advaitic* relationship with consciousness, which is the ultimate "seat" of reality.

3. *The Threefold Experience*

The three organs that open us to reality are, in fact, neither "three" nor "organs"—unless we take the word to mean that which "actualizes" or "energizes" us. They are not "three," for none of them can be isolated from the others and continue to function as an activity of our truly whole being. In any sensation there is a rational perception and something more. In any rational intuition there is a basic sensory perception and a residue, a void that testifies that there is something still more. In any spiritual experience there is also a *sensorium* and a rational component. There is not a single human act in which the entire human microcosm does not participate. We may feel sometimes that the spiritual aspect is absent when in fact it is only latent or in potency. The three "powers" are always there together, though the predominance will often go to one or the other.

Furthermore, this amounts to saying that not only are there not "three" organs, but that they are not "organs" at all. We need no special "faculties" to enter into contact with the real. We are as much part of reality as reality is part of us. We do not need some special organ to open up a closed monad to a reality from which we are not excluded. We exist and live because we *really* do exist and live. We are because we are *real*. Reality is not an object thrown before us by a special faculty we possess. We do not need special keys to enter that which we ourselves already are. Where there is no lock, no key is needed. Knowledge is part of reality, matter is part of us, divinity is part of what we are. We are not some sort of strangers, intruding invaders making forays into some foreign territory by grasping, apprehending, comprehending—all "prehensile" tactics. Knowledge is not a conquest; the world is not our enemy. The entire perspective that seeks to achieve awareness of reality by such dichotomized procedures is radically flawed. If we take this wrongheaded tack, there will be no way to disentangle ourselves from the mass of pseudo-problems it inevitably spawns.

Only a mutual and harmonious interplay between and among the "members" of the triad will yield a satisfying experience of reality. In this way the material is not degraded to an inferior level, but its foundational character is recognized. Neither is the intellectual dimension reduced to a "mental" reckoning or abstract calculation, but is understood in its middle and mediating function—so that without it there is no possibility of saying anything at all. By the same token, the spiritual ingredient will not be left as an unassimilated remnant, or a humiliating reminder of our contingency, but will be experientially accepted as a third element irreducible to the empirical or the rational.

Indeed, when our talk is real, that is, when it is not an algebraic abstraction, we can eliminate none of the three, not even in talking about any one of them. A word is more than its conceptual meaning. Real matter is already intellectual and spiritual. Real mind is both material and spiritual, as well as being intellectual. Real spirit is never devoid of matter and consciousness. Reality is irreducible to any of its constituents, and any abstraction is just an abstraction (when not an extraction) from reality, which *qua* reality is indivisible.

The experience of beauty, music, or architecture, for instance, unmistakably shows the involvement of the three eyes. Without the senses there is no artistic experience, but neither is there without the rational awareness of it. The artistic experience is sensual, rational, and something more. We may call this "more" a third element, which together with the other two constitutes the artistic experience. We are aware of it and a probably appropriate word may be *sentiment*. A sentiment of beauty is more than a sensation and a concept. A sentiment is an ecstatic experience. The "memory" of a music conductor knowing by heart scores of lengthy symphonies is not a mechanical association. Without the inner hearing of the music no physiological organism could "remember" the sequences of thousands of groups of simultaneous sounds.

I could have also adduced the experience of goodness as an example of the vision of the third eye. A good act is not just an action according to a norm; a good act implies a good person and a good person is not just somebody acting according to ethical syllogisms. To be aware of the goodness of a person we require more than rational judgment.

We cannot sense, think, and experience without matter, *logos*, and spirit. Thought and spiritual awareness are not possible without matter, indeed, without the body. All our thoughts, words, states of consciousness, and the like are also material and have a material basis. Likewise, our mind would not have life, initiative, freedom, and indefinite scope (all metaphors) unless the spirit were lurking, as it were, behind or above, and matter were hiding underneath.

It is impossible to let matter stand alone; it is always accompanied by the *logos*. It is equally impossible to let the spirit manifest itself alone; it is always "co-extensive" with the *logos*. They are different, but inseparable. We can indeed think that once upon a time there was the solar system without humans; we can also think that there was a God without the World. This thinking tells us much about our intellectual power, but perhaps not enough. This thinking tells us also that the essence of World and of God includes that World and God can *be thought* as independent of the existence of Man, which is not the case with Man. It is our thinking that brings us to understand that World or God *can* exist without Man, but Man cannot exist without Man. Furthermore, it is also our thinking that makes us aware that the intelligibility of our statements about World and God presupposes the myth of linear time. Under the myth of the Rhythm of Being the whole panorama changes. It shows the interconnectedness between these three dimensions of reality, and many of our *aporias* turn into smoke.

Surely, as two distinct notions, matter and spirit make sense only to our mind. Were it not for the mind, we could not even speak of difference and separation—we could not speak at all. This is equally true of the senses and the spirit. None exists without the others. This fact has a profound significance because it manifests the correlation between the three dimensions of the real. We can come in contact with material things because we are also material. We can know the intelligible world because we are also intelligence. We can speak about God because we are also divine. Now this sense of the Divine, the *toque substancial* of John of the Cross, the *scientia infusa* of the scholastics, the *anubhava* of vedānta, is more than touch, science, and experience. The expressions *toque, scientia, anubhava* cannot dispense with being metaphors of the sensible and mental realm. The third sense is irreducible to, although not disconnected from, the other two. Beauty is more than sensible pleasure, and yet not totally independent of it. Divine *agapē* is more than mental *philia*, and sensible *erōs* (to use different words without pretending they have such exclusive meanings), and yet they all belong together. The sacred, or the numinous, points to a reality quite as real as the other two "realms."

The three corresponding transcendentals should still be mentioned: beauty corresponds to the senses, truth to reason, and goodness to spiritual awareness. Perhaps this gives suitable pretext to comment on contemporary discussions regarding the importance of justice, goodness, and beauty. Something is good not because it is beautiful or true, but because it is good; being good, it houses those other, equally irreducible dimensions. Goodness cannot have a subordinate role or an inferior place, vis-à-vis truth, for instance. Goodness does not arise from a mass of pragmatic evidence, nor does it flow from the intelligibility of truth. Pragmatism is a powerful doctrine as long as we leave aside the metaphysical dimension. Goodness is more than usefulness. It is not a "useful" means for something else, but has its own proper "subsistence." When evil prevails in us or around us, individually or collectively, it is not because we are in error, nor because we are not intelligent enough. It is because we suffer from an atrophy of the sense of the sacred, because our spiritual awareness has been obscured. Similarly, something is true not merely because it agrees with the mind (*adaequatio rei et intellectus*), but because it stands in intrinsic harmony with the good and the beautiful. We may, of course, abstract and cut the real into pieces, but then our language is not about the real, it has become a formal language, an algebra of abstractions.

To sum up, Man is a triad of senses, reason, and spirit in correlation with matter, thought, and freedom.

4. *The Mystical*

I am not going to open the Pandora's box of mysticism, simply because I do not believe that it is a box, a closed box of esoteric treasures. Indeed, the word *mysticism* is one of the words that has been interpreted in the most divergent ways—the understanding of it being dependent on the particular worldview of the user. Consistent with the holistic vision of this entire study, I understand mysticism as the experiential awareness of the Whole and/or the study thereof.

The depth experience of beauty is an experience involving the third eye, but it is not, strictly speaking, a mystical experience. The mystical experience claims to touch Reality and not only one aspect of it—although I may enter into that holistic touch through the door of, for example, musical experience. To "touch Reality" does not mean to experientially know all the aspects of the real. The mystic is not omniscient. Even more, his knowledge of the Whole is not analytical knowledge. He knows "*That* by knowing which everything is known."[83]

a) Its Locus

We have said so far that our approach to reality is a conscious approach. We are open to reality by means of the threefold knowledge we have described. If there were any other form of knowledge, one could easily subsume it under one of the forms described so far. We cannot speak about something of which we have no knowledge. We take knowledge in its widest sense of field *of consciousness*. We have even described reality as "anything" that in one way or another falls into that field so that we are aware of it. In that sense even Emptiness and Nothingness appear in the field of consciousness.

83 CU, VI, 1, 4.

This is clear enough, but the unquenchable thirst of the human spirit pushes it to ask whether there is "something" transcending the field of consciousness. Even if we were to answer that the hypothetical "something" outside the field of consciousness is "nothing," we have already included the "something" and the "nothing" within a "field" outside the field of consciousness. Some philosophies, especially a certain oriental one, will affirm that this is the "field of emptiness," which, following the spatial metaphor of the field, would be an empty field, about which, nevertheless, we are aware. It seems that we cannot escape the net of our consciousness.

We can know the limits of our knowledge, but we cannot trespass them with our own knowledge. Granting, for the sake of the argument, that we could cross to the other shore of knowledge, we would not *know* what is on it. We do not even know if there is another shore; it is the shore of the unknown, but we are aware that this classical metaphor has a meaning: the unknown is not known, but inasmuch as we speak about it, we are aware that the other shore could be populated by "something" unknown to us. That unknown "something" is still in our field of consciousness as unknown or as only a possible entity. Here is the next question: Does that "something" leave any "trace" of transcendence in its very appearance in the field of consciousness? Simply put, are the entities present in the field of consciousness *presentations* of what they are in *representations* of a reality beyond or behind? Twenty-five centuries ago Plato put the question in the still powerful and simple myth of the cave.[84] Do we see reality or do we just see shadows of that reality? For Plato it was easy to recognize the shadows as shadows because he had been outside the cave, but how do people jump from their subjective consciousness to the "real" world? This has been the main problem of any epistemology severed from ontology. To identify epistemology and ontology might not be a satisfactory solution either. Ultimately it comes down to asking whether consciousness is identical to reality or whether reality transcend consciousness?

There are two possibilities here. The first says that things are objects of consciousness (subjective genitive). That is, Being is consciousness, and consciousness is Being. The second claims that things are only objects of consciousness (objective genitive). Being is consciousness, but consciousness does not cover the whole of Being. We may discover an intentionality of things to transcend the field of consciousness, but it is always within that very field of consciousness that we discover such intentionality. Based on such premises, the problem is difficult to solve. The two options are open

84 *Republic* 507b–509c.

and do not transgress the canons of rationality and intelligibility. This, it seems to me, brings us to the proper locus of the mystical.

b) The Field of Emptiness

The mystical is still an anthropophanic factor; it is a human phenomenon, but it does not belong to the field of consciousness. Here lie its importance and its difficulty. The importance is universally recognized. If the word "mystical" stands for something true, then it touches the deepest stratum of the real, the groundless ground, *Ungrund*, on which everything stands and finds its support (*pratistha*), and therefore a truly human life depends on it. The mystical liberates us from the thick net of consciousness. If what the word stands for is not true, it is the biggest mistake and main obstacle to a full human life. We had better get rid of all that "opium." In sum, the mystical is not a luxus for a few or an idle speculation about a superfluous problem, but rather a vital question for humanity.

The difficulties, which are cultural and philosophical, are also patent. For western culture, by and large, the mystical is supposed to be an exceptional and odd phenomenon of human existence. For eastern cultures, on the whole, it is something so taken for granted that it can easily become uncritical. My attempt here faces an intercultural challenge. It is for this reason that my description of the mystical does not follow the usual western reflections on the topic, although the writings usually considered to be mystical documents seem to support my interpretation. The greatest difficulty is of a strictly philosophical order: while we can speak of the three doors of "understanding" (the three eyes), we cannot properly speak of the mystical because the claim that the mystical lies "beyond" the field of consciousness means that there is no proper eye to see it and therefore no proper language to express it. If we do not identify consciousness with Being, doubtlessly any experience is an immediate touch with reality and thus beyond the field of consciousness. Nevertheless, while the threefold experience I described by the metaphor of the three eyes struggles to find a language landing in the field of consciousness, the mystical keeps silent, or rather, remains in Silence, and silence does not speak. It has nothing to say.

Practically all classical reflections on the mystical will stress that "mysticism is ineffable." Now mystical ineffability is due not to the imperfection of the human intellect but to the "nature" of reality itself. Reality is ineffable because it is beyond thinking, and thought is the normal origin of language. To affirm that reality is beyond thinking implies the transgression of the parmenidean principle of the identity between thinking and Being. The unthinkable aspect of Being in the substantialist traditions from india to greece has a dialectical name: Non-being, *asat*, *mē-on*, and the like. Non-substantialist philosophies have used other names such as emptiness or *śunyatā*, as in the *anātmavada* of buddhism, or *nada* (which is not nihilism) as in spanish mysticism. The home-ground of this emptiness is the mystical.

In the christian tradition I could say that reality is not only Logos, or more accurately, that the *is* represents only the Logos dimension of reality. Yet the Father and the Spirit are also real and irreducible to the Logos. The mystical does not belong directly to the Logos and thus it has no proper words. The mystical touches the real. The silence or emptiness of the Father and the love or activity of the Spirit, if "they" speak at all, do so through the Logos.[85] Without the Trinity, the mystical is in danger of irrationalism. Not without cause does rigid monotheism regard all mysticism as suspect. I may say the same in more philosophical words. Reality, as we have said, is not a concept. Any concept we may have about it is real, as a real concept, but it is not necessisarily identical with reality unless we postulate it so (as a postulate of our thinking). When we *speak* of reality we are already within the field of consciousness; such speech is just a representation of reality. Can reality present itself to us, who are a part of it, as it "really" is? This is one of the main concerns of mysticism and a central problem of almost all philosophies when they encounter the ultimate, be it called Absolute, *nirvāṇa*, *tathatā* (suchness), emptiness, God, *brahman*, Nothingness, and the like, in spite of the divergent interpretations of that mystery. Or, to use a historical metaphor, the "tree of the *knowledge* of good and evil"[86] gives us the *knowledge* of reality, and knowledge belongs to consciousness. The "tree of knowledge" is powerful enough (up to the point of having "triggered" original sin), but it is not the "tree of life" that stands in the middle of Paradise. All things share in the "tree of life" with their life, and not just through consciousness. Life is life and not necessarily thinking.

The Upanishads say it clearly:

> Into blind darkness enter those who revere ignorance [*avidya*].
> Into blinder darkness enter those who find satisfaction in knowledge.[87]

Knowledge is not all.

---

85 See Panikkar, *The Trinity and the Religious Experience of Man* (Maryknoll, N.Y.: Orbis Books, 1975).

86 Cf. Gn II, 9.

87 BU IV, 4, 10 and IsU IX, 12.

This touch with the real without the mediation of consciousness is precisely the mystical. We described the three forms of knowledge symbolized by the three eyes, and did not include the mystical. I spoke of the sensual, rational, and spiritual experiences. The mystical is certainly also an experience, but it is not knowledge. I said that experience has no intermediaries and puts us in immediate contact with reality, but the moment that we become conscious of that experience, so that we speak of it, we enter into the field of consciousness and abandon the mystical.

A common notion of mysticism would be the experiential awareness of the three eyes together when directed not to particular entities but to the entire reality. If this reality is identified with God we have the classical definition of *cognitio Dei experimentalis,* "experiential knowledge of God," or the knowledge of *brahman* (*brahma-jñāna*), illumination (enlightenment), and so on. This type of description puts the mystical within the field of consciousness, that is, knowledge under the assumption that to know is to become the thing known, but neither God nor reality is a thing. What I am defending is that the locus of the mystical is not knowledge, not even knowledge of Being, but the realm of *śunyatā*, of emptiness. Only there does nothing interfere between ourselves and the real, ātman and *brahman*.

An already quoted Upanishad asks: "What is that by knowing which everything is known?" "That" is the "knower" of all things; and the immediate question follows: "How can I know the knower?" If I were to "*know* the knower," first of all, this would not be the mystical because it would be knowledge; but, second, it would not answer the question because the "knower" would become the "known" of my act of knowing, and not the knower. I cannot know the knower, and this is the greatness of mysticism. In fact, most mystics have been active people, they do not sever action from contemplation. Even if to know is to become the known, if I know it, it becomes the known. Here again lurks the idealistic temptation: the knower is the known. Being is intelligible. What is not (in principle) intelligible "is-not." The mystical resists the reduction of the knower to the known. The knower of mysticism is the knower and not the known. It is unknowable inasmuch as it is knower. It is beyond knowledge.

The knower that the Upanishad is asking for is not the knower of one or another object. It is the knower of the All ("That by knowing which everything becomes known"). The All is not an object; it is not a knowing determined by its object. The object does not exist. It is a creative knowing, out of nothing, since it springs from emptiness.

A classical text describes this "beyond the field of consciousness," *turīya*.

> [*Turīya* is] not that which cognizes the internal, not that which cognizes the external, not that which cognizes both of them, not a mass of cognition, not cognitive, not non-cognitive. Unseen, incapable of being spoken of, ungraspable, without any distinctive marks, unthinkable, unnameable, the essence of the knowledge of the one self, that into which the world is resolved, the peaceful, the benign, the non-dual, such, they think is the fourth (*turīya*) quarter. He is the self (ātman); He is to be known.[88]

I repeat: How can this be said at all? Actually, it is not truly said (because the saying is all wrong and contradictory). It can only be heard by those who have ears to hear.[89] The others will hear and not understand.[90] Those who really hear (śruti) will have their lives transformed.

c) The Mystical Translation

We know reality by means of that triple knowledge received in the field of consciousness. Consciousness is the mediator, and this is why we can speak of those three experiences; but the translation of the experience into language is no longer the pure experience. Yet it is an "authorized" translation, as it were. This is the difference between the threefold experience and the mystical. The experience of the three eyes can be translated into the field of our consciousness, allowing for all the margins of inexactness of any translation. The mystical experience, on the other hand, is not translatable into the field of consciousness. As we said, most mystics speak about nothingness, *nada*, *agnosia*, *śunyatā*, . . . which simply means nothing in the field of consciousness.

One can understand the resistance of all intellectualisms (in the widest sense of the word) to accept any reality beyond or behind the field of consciousness: a no-man's-land outside any control of knowledge. This is the great temptation of all idealisms East and West, ultimately of all monisms and eventually of a certain monotheism. The real is identified with what appears in the field of consciousness, be this consciousness sensual, rational, or spiritual, or any combination of the three. This is the principle of Parmenides to which we have made allusion several times. Being is intelligible, so that what does not fall into the field of consciousness "is" Non-being; it does not exist, utter Nothingness.

It is a great irony, or rather a highly significant fact, that the apparently

88 MandU 7.

89 Mt XI, 15.

90 Mk IV, 12.

most unworldly attitude (of mysticism) is the most powerful witness for the reality of the material universe. Matter, in fact, is impervious to intellectual knowledge; we can only know its behavior. Because of this, many gnostic and some idealistic systems see matter as evil or illusion. Matter indeed offers resistance to knowledge; it is opaque to the light of the intellect. Were it not for the mystic insisting that the mystical is real and yet not representable in the field of consciousness, matter would be dismissed as unreal by all idealisms. The mystical discloses to us precisely that not all can be reduced to consciousness, that there is a dimension of the real irreducible to the *logos*. This is the "reason" why the mystical as such is untranslatable while the other experiences can be translated into the field of consciousness.

* * *

All this may be well and good, but the unavoidable objection arises immediately. How is it then that we speak of the unspeakable? We have already hinted at the Trinity as a way out of the apparent *aporia*. Reality cannot be reduced to *logos* and the *logos* does not stand above. It is the *logos* of the Father (objective genitive) and of the Spirit (subjective genitive). The mystical does not enlarge the field of consciousness, but liberates it, as it were, from its own limits; the mystical discloses to us the freedom of Being which is not limited to the structures of logic, but which does not have to contradict them.

The question about the unspeakable touches the very core of mysticism. The mystical, as the very word betrays, does not speak, does not even know: "And I remained without knowing, all knowledge surpassing."[91] The "supreme experience," if we still use human language, is no experience at all.[92] Every mystical language is a translation, a transfer from the field of emptiness, as it were, into the realm of consciousness. While the other experiences translate from the reality of the *logos*, the mystical is at home in the field of emptiness, and this field is empty; it is *nada*, unborn (into Being). Mystical language comes, as it were, out of "nothing." This is why true language of the mystical is like an act of creation, out of "nothing." Emptiness is not language and is not *logos*, and mystical language has no model. It does not allow any "verification"; we cannot check with the original, which does not exist. Mystical language does not signify. It has, as such, no meaning in the field of consciousness. The hearer of the mystical, if having an empty heart, will *under*-stand in the measure that that hearer has gone *under*, into the

91 John of the Cross: "Y me quedé no sabiendo, toda sciencia transcendiendo."

92 Cf. Panikkar, "The Supreme Experience: The Ways of West and East," in *Myth, Faith, and Hermeneutics*, 290-317.

abyss (of the mystery) and *stands* there. Only the "initiated" were allowed into the "mysteries" because, as many a tradition has said, only they could understand.

I have said "translation," but it might have been better to say "transfer." The mystical is properly transferred from master to disciple, from those who from the "other shore" give hints only understood by those to whom it "is given" to understand. "We played the flute for you, and you did not dance; we sang a dirge and you did not mourn."[93]

d) Its Existential Character

The mystical is irreducible to the field of consciousness, and therefore all our speech about it is a translation, or rather a creation from the field of emptiness that is received only by those who have understood the transfer and are able to decipher its reality. This is the grandeur and the weakness of mysticism. It has no language of its own; it uses a borrowed language which is foreign to the mystical. Mystical language has no referent. Emptiness cannot be a point of reference. In that sense, mystical language is ultimate, but having no further criterion, it could all be a hoax.

The mystical traditions unanimously say that in the mystical pilgrmage there is no way and therefore the mystic needs a guide, a guru, the internal and/or external guidance of the spirit. A *magisterium* is needed. "No Man is an island." It is a paradox for the modern individualistic mentality that the most personal act, the mystical experience by which we enter into immediate contact with the real, is the most cosmic experience. Its subject is not the individual, and thus the single person needs a human communion, a true community of some sort, be it of love, friendship or a concrete human entrance into the "mystical body," *buddhakāya*, communion of saints, *paramparā*, *samgham*, *synagoge*, *qāhāl*, *umma*, *ekklesia*, etc., which serves also as an initial point of reference. This is the value of an authentic tradition.

The mystical way, the most personal and unique way, is also the least individualistic. Because it does not belong to the ego, the mystical experience belongs to humanity at large, and what goes on, or rather in, within the heart of the mystic, has immediate repercussions in the mystical body of the real. I, Adam, the whole cosmos, have sinned. In Christ the entire universe is redeemed. In Buddha the karma of all living beings has changed. The prayer of the saint is powerful. The destiny of the village depends on the *mahātma*. All these examples of that mystical connection explain the vicarious satisfaction found in some spiritualities, notwithstanding the potential for exaggerations, abuses, and distortions.

93 Mt XI, 17.

The mystic goes the way alone, but not isolated. A *kaivalya* spirituality can easily lose the balance. The mystical way is dangerous, and a "master" can be a fake, and even a tradition can degenerate. Hardly any need to stress that one of the crises of our times is a crisis of truly spiritual masters, to which one may add, as cause and effect, a crisis of disciples who are ready to undergo spiritual discipline. From the *guru* is required wisdom, and wisdom is more than science; and from the *sadhaka* (aspirant), faith is needed, and faith is more than knowledge. Faith is empty; it has no object; it cannot be conceptualized. Faith is not belief. The mystic cannot have sufficient faith as long as the mystic is encumbered by the ego. Humility, which is the death of the ego, is the first mystical virtue. If this is the case, however, the risk of going astray cannot be checked by the ego. If "my" experience is final, what criterion do I have that it is authentic? Here is where the ego is a two-edged sword. "My" experience can be wrong as long as it is "mine," and it is mine as long as there is an ego that "senses" it as "mine." Otherwise, I can only witness to the experience without any value attached to it in the field of consciousness. Joan of Arc comes to mind as a typical and tragic instance.

I have said faith, not trust. Latin christian theology distinguished between *credere Deum* (trust God exists), *credere Deo* (trust what He has revealed) and *credere in Deum* (have faith in that mystery which surpasses all understanding). Only this latter is faith. When some indic schools affirm that the *cela* should worship the *guru* as a God, they do not divinize the master so much as attempt to purify the eye of the disciple so that the *si\ sy\ a* (disciple) may discover the divine mystery through and in the person of the teacher. This does not mean "blind faith." Faith can never be blind because faith does not see, does not need to see. It does not belong to the field of consciousness. This means that the way to cross the barrier of consciousness is through love of a real person. In christian language this is the mystery of the Incarnation, it is Being as christophany. That is not, however, our topic.

Our concrete topic is that the master could also be spurious, and the *magisterium* degenerate. Are we then at a loss? Not at all. The "discernment of spirit," *viveka*, is not only an inalienable right but also a non-transferable duty. If there is no internal criterion to mystical language, there are a number of external criteria: "By their fruits you shall know them."[94] if something is authentic or not, and we are those who have to see whether the fruits are good or bad. In a word, the three eyes are indispensable.

94 Mt VII, 16.

e) Its Fragility

I would like to underscore the issue hinted at in the beginning, namely, that precisely because the mystical belongs to the *humanum*, it has all the fragility of everything human. It would be out of place, and a proof that I have explained myself wrongly, if we were to imagine that the mystical is superior to the threefold knowledge, or that the field of emptiness is more important than the field of consciousness. The mystical witness is immediate, but so is the testimony of the senses, and we cannot draw any conclusion from those facts. I have several times alluded to the possible abuses and degenerations of anything human. We should not play the dialectical game in these fields.

Perhaps a *tao* spirituality is closer to what I have been trying to describe: "The spoken *tao* is not the *tao*." "Those who know do not speak, those who speak do not know." The mystical sage sees nothing, says nothing, does nothing, demands nothing, judges nothing, . . . and yet those sages maintain the cosmic order. We have here instances of the reality of the third eye. But there is more, we need to take cognizance of the near universal claim that "mystical" experience exists, and that sensory, mental, and intellectual experiences are not the only human avenues to reality. Even more, the human mind itself discovers that by itself it can neither explain nor harmonize contradictory "ultimate" human attitudes.

Too many attempts have failed. Even if one accepts the hypothetical success of an *Ethica ordine geometrico demonstrata*, the human world would not necessarily become more moral. The true thinker "sees," "suffers," and "experiences" the shifting of this mystery, the changing of this *mythos*, but is not only unable to touch a *terra firma*, a Ground, but is not even able to lay hands on a firm rudder to steer the human pilgrimage.

We may return now to the query whether we cannot appeal to a fourth, higher "court" in the same manner as the tribunal of reason passed its verdict on the testimony of the senses? The "case" would then never be closed. Either reason furnishes sufficient "precedent," or the spiritual experience (*cit*) will pass sentence on grounds other than sheer rationality. The fact that there is no superior criterion is what renders such "judgments" so dangerous. Nevertheless, this would not be a proper explanation. In that case we could equally stop at reason and adopt a merely pragmatic stance. This is what I hinted at when saying that the mystical insight has no referent outside itself and is, therefore, ineffable and final. When we speak, language itself is the mediation. In contrast, the mystical experience is immediate, it has no mediator. The referent of reason, except in absolute idealism, lies outside itself. Reason has therefore to justify itself before a tribunal somewhat independent from reason in spite of the fact that the tribunal has been appointed by reason itself, like the legislative judges of a democracy appointed by the government. This is not the case with the mystical experience. It has no superior instance.

Mystical texts are full of such final statements. I shall quote only a pair of sentences from christian Scripture: "The Spirit scrutinizes everything, even the depths of God."[95] Or still more forcefully: "The spiritual Man discerns (ἀνακρίνει, judges) everything and it is not judged (ἀνακρίνεται) by anybody else."[96]

We cannot, however, contravene the demands of the mind either, just as the latter cannot overrule the testimony of the senses. Irrationalism is just as wrong as anti-empiricism. The *aisthēta* and the *noēta* must also be respected. Yet we cannot remain on these two levels alone if we are to hear the affirmations made by so many traditions and if we are to understand the testimony of so many people to the most intimate personal experience of Man in face of the groundless abyss.

C. A Christian Reflection

It may legitimately be asked whether this study is a christian one. Am I speaking about the christian Trinity, or what kind of relationship is there? First, it is important to realize that the notion of God is not specifically christian. I have even argued that the notion of the Trinity is not exclusively christian. I intend to present now the concrete vision of the christian vision of the Trinity continuing that very tradition by a personal interpretation.

In a nutshell, it makes no sense to speak about God without the Trinity. There is no point in speaking about the Trinity without Christ. It is meaningless to speak about Christ without Jesus. There is no sense in speaking about Jesus without Christ. These four statements could be said to contain the "christian revelation," the christian unfolding of reality. Of course, there are many religious languages, and one language does not necessarily exclude the other. It is further open to discussion which language comes closer to the mystery. This is not our point now.

Before attempting an answer, I may insert a cross-cultural remark. Although the spirit of the greek Fathers was of another type, the prevalent christian selfunderstanding during one and a half millennia was couched

95 1 Cor II, 10.

96 1 Cor II, 15. The entire passage vv. 10-16 is central for a christian interpretation of what we are saying here.

within the forms of thinking of semitic culture, which was and is keenly aware of its differences from other self-understandings.[97] Following this semitic cultural paradigm, christian doctrine was interpreted as specifically christian, and thus its truth criterion was interpreted to be its difference from all the other doctrines. *Christentum als Neuheitserlebnis*[98] was the telling title of a book overshadowed by the political events of the last "world war." Today's winds are slowly changing. The fact that a doctrine like that of the Trinity is found in most cultures is now coming to be seen rather as a positive argument for christianity which deepens in a concrete way and by means of a specific language that generic truth. The neglect of a cross-cultural philosophy has led and still leads to tragic misunderstandings. Commonalities between christianity and other religions in no way demean christianity. On the contrary, they enhance its verisimilitude. A monopolistic truth, in this other way of thinking, would be rather suspect.

The question whether what I write is christian or not, is synonymous for me with whether I believe that what I write is true or not, authentic or not. To *be* christian is, for me, not a superstructure, an *adhy*āsa, a superimposition, but my concrete way of being authentically what I am. There is a transcendental relationship between the two. I am too much a hindu to believe that to be a christian is a matter of being a member of a respectable club, and I am too much of a philosopher to accept that my identity is simply a sum-total of mere accidents. I have interiorized my christian identity, as I have assimilated my priesthood, so that all I do is for me a priestly activity, and all that I think a christian thinking, which does not mean, of course, that my thinking is infallible. The question, however, entails more than whether I have the private intention to write as a christian.

It already implies a certain understanding of the christic fact. If with the best intentions of being a Scot, I try to behave accordingly, you may appreciate my idealism or my innocence, but nobody is going to take me seriously. The accepted and public criteria are not met. There is need of an agreed-upon criterion for christian identity.[99] This is not a moot issue. There are groups in India, for instance, who confess themselves to be christian without accepting baptism. I shall not elaborate now on such questions. I will simply try to answer the legitimate question regarding the relationship

97 See "Secularism and Worship: A Bibliography," in Panikkar, *Worship and Secular Man* (Maryknoll, N.Y.: Orbis Books, 1973), 94-109.

98 K. Prumm ("Christianity as an Experience of Newness")(1939).

99 See Panikkar, "La diversidad como presupuesta para la armonia entre los pueblos," in *Antolgía sobre cultura popular e indigena: Lecturas del seminario Diélogos en acción, Primera etapa* (San Angel, Mexico: Culturas Populares e Indigenas), 105-13.

between this study and christian philosophy or theology. At the beginning I said that these lectures were intended to meet Lord Gifford's requirement to be natural theology, and at the same time I acknowledged the eroding and/or purifying power of the century that has elapsed since his bequest.

This study is certainly not along the lines of the usual christian exegesis, nor is it an idiosyncratic interpretation of already formulated christian dogmas. It claims to spring from a personal (not individualistic) experience that has assimilated some of the human traditions of (mainly) the indo-european world with which I am conversant, and to which I belong. It takes these traditions into account insofar as I am conscious that they have shaped and influenced my approach to reality and given me the language with which to express what I have to say. The christian tradition here is paramount, but not exclusive. This attitude of tolerance and not exclusivity corresponds to the christian spirit— historical instances of christian fanaticism notwithstanding. If christians should not quench the smoking wick, much less should they blow out the living flame. "Whoever is not against you is for you."[100]

I do not propose, as some writers do, "to reflect on the central concepts of christianity." I do not believe in "concepts" fallen from heaven, nor is reflection on concepts my present task. The subject matter of this study is reality, as I see it and hope others see it too. In this "seeing" there lies hidden the problem of truth. My seeing is conditioned by the christian tradition but, at the same time, by others as well.

Yes, I do believe that this vision is compatible with the tenets of christian tradition, especially the central dogma of Incarnation. Incarnation of Whom? For what? Only a trinitarian notion of the Divine allows for a divine Incarnation. Incarnation is for Man (and the cosmos), so that Man (and the cosmos) may reach the goal. God becomes Man, said the christian Fathers, so that Man may become God.[101] The "christian revelation" is that disclosure of the Divine which says that the distance between the Human and the Divine is zero in Christ and may become zero in us. Here we leave aside the question of whether other religions may agree with that insight, albeit using a different language. This is the christological revelation, which at the same time does not blur the differences between the Human and the Divine. The difference between the Son and the Father in the Trinity is infinite and both are God. This simple sentence makes clear that the christian notion of God

100 Mk IX, 40.

101 See Panikkar, *Christophany: The Fullness of Man* (Maryknoll, N.Y.: Orbis Books, 2004).

cannot be understood in terms of substance. This would be tritheism. "God is not an *ousia*," says Maximus the Confessor.[102]

My concern here, however, is not to offer an exclusively christian view, or a buddhist or hindu view, for that matter. My hope is to share an experience that may be enriching for all these traditions, and eventually may offer a point of crystallization in the supersaturated climate of today's religious ideologies. It searches for truth, a "truth that makes us free." This study is neither purely exegetical nor individualistically hermeneutical.

There is a christian doctrine about the Trinity, "revealed," "inspired," "formed" by tradition and promulgated by the Church. There are thousands of articles and books trying to make sense of that dogma for our times. They study christian Scripture and the greek and latin Fathers, interpret and correct them, follow the scholastics or depart from them, are inspired by more modern thinkers, use process theology, secular methods, or a liberation paradigm, and so on. Such works, of orthodox, catholic, and/or protestant inspiration, perform an invaluable service for the christian community, and again make credible and effective that central dogma of christianity.

The import of these Gifford Lectures, however, is different. I do not intend to superimpose the framework of the christian Trinity in order to understand something about reality; my surmise is, rather, that it is reality itself that discloses itself as Trinity—at least to me, and I am inclined to add to christians and to an immense number of people seriously concerned with the problem of the Divine.

I am ready to concede that were it not for the christian doctrine I might not have the experience of the Divine in the form that I have come to. I may also confess that without the vedāntic *sat-cit-ānanda* I might not have deepened the same experience in the way that I have. Nevertheless, whatever the intellectual preparation might have been, I have to add that I "received" the intellectual awareness of the truth of the Trinity in and through the experiential knowledge of Christ. I am making this sort of confession not by any desire to be autobiographical but for the purpose of philosophical clarification.

* * *

However this may be, I hear the same question put to me: Am I approaching the problematic as a christian, or am I not? Am I putting my christian convictions (of the so-called articles of faith) in parentheses (*epochē*), or am I not? I suspect that this question is not a totally innocent

102 Maximus Conf., *Gnostica Centuria*, I, 4 (PG 90:1083-84): Οὐκ ἔστιν ὁ θεὸς οὐσία.

one. In this regard I contest the possibility of *epochē*. We cannot put our most intimate convictions into brackets when making a sincere approach to real problems.[103] I speak as what I am. I speak my convictions. I write what I believe I have intellectually experienced. I am aware that what I am saying is influenced by my life, and I do not deny my christian fidelity as I understand it. Yet I do not speak an exclusively christian language. I do not presume to speak in the name of official christian doctrine, nor do I start from specifically "christian" assumptions. Indeed, I am convinced that most so-called christian doctrines are not essentially, but only culturally, christian.[104] Much of what is called a "christian position" is only a certain cultural interpretation of some fundamental experiences believed to be christian. I claim the same privilege, although I am convinced that naked experience (before its reflexive consciousness) admits no qualifications.

One thing is clear: I am not speaking to christians alone or trying to explain the christian position to non-christians. Nevertheless, one may still insist on knowing whether what I am doing is christian philosophy. I submit that this modern separation between philosophy and theology is based on assumptions no longer tenable today, and that it blurs the real issues.

Christian philosophy would be a "square circle," as Heidegger once put it, if—and only if—philosophy were a circle with a fixed radius (postulating once and for all what philosophy is, and what its instruments are), and christianity were so "square" as to be unable to accept as christian anything that has not appeared as such until now, generally in textbooks.

The most startling novelty for historical christianity may be the effort of this study to disentangle "christian faith," which is the belief of christians, from the until-now-accepted monotheism. Outsiders may see it more clearly. I wonder if Martin Heidegger knew the following passage when writing the phrase that I have just cited above. Spinoza wrote in a letter to Oldenburg:

> Si certaines églises ajoutent que Dieu a pris la nature humaine, je ne comprends pas bien le sens des ces mots, ainsi que je l'ai franchement exposé: à vrai dire, cela ne me paraît pas moins étrange que si l'on disait qu'un cercle avait pris la nature du carré.[105]

---

103 Panikkar, "Epoché in the Religious Encounter," *The Intrareligious Dialogue* (New York: Paulist Press, 1999), 73-83.

104 See Panikkar, "Indic Christian Theology of Religious Pluralism from the Perspective of Interculturation," in Kuncheria Pathil, ed., *Religious Pluralism: An Indian Perspective* (Delhi: ISPCK, 1991).

105 Spinoza, *Lettre LXXIII* à *Oldenburg* (1675).

He would be right if "God" were not Trinity. The Incarnation is incompatible with monotheism. What the Incarnation does is to upset the monotheistic idea of Divinity. The Incarnation is either reduced to pure docetism or breaks with such a monotheistic idea of the Divinity. Here is where I see the acid test, and so invert the question put to me: Are you christian if you stick to hebrew monotheism? To exclude those who respond yes would, of course, be against the pluralism I defend, since there are many ways of being christian, although I am nonetheless free philosophically to challenge such positions.

My argument is somewhat like this: There is a doctrinal incompatibility between a strict monotheistic belief and the traditionally orthodox christological belief (Christ fully Man and fully God). Either God is not one God or Christ is not (that one) God. We have to sacrifice one horn of the dilemma. Because of my christic experience I opt for sacrificing monotheism. Others may prefer to qualify christology. For this they will have to renounce experiential theology, since, while one can have an experience of Christ, one cannot experience a monotheistic God.

In sum, in order to answer whether this study is christian or not, we must assume that we know where the limits of christianness lie. It is generally those on the outside, the so-called non-christians, who dictate to christians (or, as they say, remind them of) what they are supposed to believe. This freezes christianness. Who decides what is christian?[106] I will not claim my thoughts as christian unless and until they are recognized as such by an acknowledged christian body. A christian is not a solitary. For such acknowledgment, however, I may have to wait. *Die Wahrheit kann warten*, wrote Hegel. Or as Heidegger said in a more poetic vein, it is a process of coming into the light of the manifest. It is easier to recognize what is not christian, and ecclesiastical condemnations generally proceed on this basis. They do not, however, prescribe what is christian; they only proscribe or condemn a certain doctrine (always within a particular context) as non-christian. This does not preclude the transformation of christian self-consciousness. After twenty centuries of christian theology, that should be sufficiently clear.

Furthermore, the first function of christian theology is not the clarification of the "data of Revelation." There are no such data. If there is a *datum* at all, it is revelation itself, which has to be humanly received and understood. Such an understanding needs to take a human spirit. Even

106 See Panikkar, "On Christian Identity—Who Is Christian?" in Catherine Cornille, ed., *Many Mansions? Multiple Religious Belonging and Christian Identity* (Maryknoll, N.Y.: Orbis Books, 2002), 121-44.

assuming that Revelation provides us with the means of understanding, there is no possible communication if this understanding, *qua* understanding, is not communicable.

To be sure, there is an impressive body of doctrines and disciplines that are called respectively theology and philosophy, and we should not ignore tradition, it is part of the *depositum*. No text, however, is independent of its context, and our contemporary context has undergone changes that we cannot ignore.

* * *

I have every right to say Trinity, but I do not have the same right to speak about the christian understanding of the Trinity without explaining how my interpretation fits into that tradition. I will say only this much:

1. My interpretation is not a lifeless copy of today's popular understanding.
2. It does not intend to describe the mystery of God, as christian tradition has interpreted it in recent centuries, as a progressive deduction of what was implicitly "revealed" or inspired. My effort does not belong to what germans call *Konklusionentheologie*.
3. In order that this interpretation may be an enlarging and deepening of the traditional christian doctrine, it needs to fulfill a threefold condition:
    a. Not to stand in contradiction with what is called the "deposit of faith" (although that would not be my expression);
    b. Allow a certain integration into the general christian vision; and
    c. Be accepted by a recognized christian community. It cannot be a one-Man-show. It has to be an ecclesial, communitarian affair.

In order to do justice to the query about the christian character of this text, I have to introduce two other disciplines that will give a more complete picture of this already complex problem. Besides "theology" and philosophy, the third pertinent discipline, generally forgotten in such discussions, is the science of religions or *Religionswissenschaft*. In today's world we can no longer reflect on such problems within the exclusive limits of a single culture or tradition. The issues at stake concern and deeply involve all of us, hindus as well as christians, people of the West as much as those of the South, etc. It is only fair that, as far as possible, we also take into account these human wisdoms and their diverse expressions.

The fourth relevant discipline is the set of the so-called secular sciences, those modern sciences, both humanistic and scientific, which have today attained an unprecedented degree of sophistication and development. One does not need to be an expert in astronomy and atomic physics, medicine and neuroscience, or psychology and history, but without a certain knowledge of all those *aṅga*, or branches of the tree of knowledge, our vision of reality, even if it does not have to be the integral of those particular sciences, would be somewhat faulty and partial.

* * *

For the sake of establishing a link with christian tradition, I may formulate this insight of the *radical Trinity* as follows. Christian tradition has elaborated not only a profound and subtle, but also theoretically beautiful, doctrine of the socalled *immanent Trinity*. God is Life. Life is communication, donation, love, expansion. God is all this. This is the immanent Trinity. There is Life within the Godhead. Such a Trinity renders thinkable the historical fact of the Incarnation with all its consequences. This then leads to the so-called *economic Trinity*, which is the action of the Trinity *ad extra*, the saving action of the Trinity. This Trinity is a doctrine concerning mainly the salvation of Man—and I would add, divinization of the cosmos. Contemporary theological thinking has united these two dimensions and declared that the immanent and the economic Trinities are not only one and the same, but that the one reveals the nature of the other. Karl Rahner is credited with this insight, but one could equally have cited Thomas Aquinas affirming, from a very monotheistic perspective in a trinitarian setting, that the one and same act by which the Father begets the Son creates the world.

The trinitarian dogma needs to be put in intimate contact with the equally christian dogma of creation. There is not a Trinity over there, and a creation over here . . . created, dependent, contingent, separated. One can understand the fear of monism and pantheism—all the more because the christian "novelty" is Christ in whom "all fullness of the Godhead dwells," and who is at the same time Man, *totus homo*. "*La* vérité *est la Trinité*,"[107] reads the first paragraph of Margerie's book, citing and commenting on the inverse sentence by Daniélou, "la Trinité est la verité"[108] and approving as well Daniélou's forceful statement:

"Le fond de la réalité n'est pas la composition nucléaire de la matière, mais la Trinité."[109]

107 Margerie (1975), 11.

108 Daniélou (1966), 88-89.

109 Ibid., 89.

I could not agree more, but in spite of such daring formulations both authors restrict the Trinity to the nature of God, while accepting only a certain trinitarian presence of God in creation. The immanent processions of the Logos and the Spirit are the exemplary causes of Creation, Saint Thomas said.[110] But thinking in terms of cause and effect weakens Thomas's position, since he had affirmed in a much more theological way only a few questions earlier:

> Word implies relation to creatures. For God by knowing Himself, knows every creature. . . . And as the knowledge of God is only cognitive as regards God, whereas as regards creatures, it is both cognitive and operative, so the Word of God is only expressive of what is in God the Father, but is both expressive and operative of creatures; and therefore it is said: "He spake, and they were made"; because in the Word is implied the operative idea of what God makes.[111]

The radical Trinity I am advocating will not blur the distinction between Creator and creature—to use these names—but would, as it were, extend the privilege of the divine Trinity to the whole of reality. Reality is not only "trinitarian"; it is the true and ultimate Trinity. The Trinity is not the privilege of the Godhead but the character of reality as a whole. The universe is Father, Christ, and Holy Spirit, as I tried to formulate it over half a century ago, taking Christ, the *Christus totus* of Augustine, to its eschatological culmination in connection with 1 Cor XV, 28. In this sense the christian complement to Genesis I, 1 ("In the Beginning God created heaven and earth") should be John I, 3 ("all has come to be through me"—the Logos, inseparable from the incarnated Logos). This leads me to a follow-up of the *creatio continua* by an *incarnatio continua*, of which Christ is the head following christian Scripture. This is not the direct concern of this study, but it may be a hermeneutical key to it. The entire destiny of reality is a christic adventure.

* * *

In order to explicate a little more how I see the christian Trinity, I may add a few more considerations. The constitutive relations of the Trinity are not different from each other—and this applies to the radical Trinity as well. If they were different, they should share in something identical in relation to which they differ. This something identical is the idea of the *Quaternitas* which is bound to haunt the notion of the christian Trinity once we forget to think directly of relationships and focus on substances.

---

110 Thomas Aquinas, *Summ. Theol.*, I, q. 45, a. 6.

111 Thomas Aquinas, *Summ. Theol.*, I, q. 34, a. 3 (cf. Margerie, 260).

The constitutive relations are differently different. The difference is not in relation to something that makes them different, but it is only a relative difference precisely in relation to each other. They are different only seen from each other. Seen from outside, by a presumptive (and nonexistent) "objective" observer, they would not be seen as different. The constitutive relations would be indistinguishable, identical. Such an observer would see the unique divine act of a God begetting Man and creating Cosmos. From a nonexisting outside platform, Father, Son, and Spirit could not be distinguished. Father and Son are only different as Father and Son. The Father is Father-of-the-Son, the Father "fathers," begets the Son. The Son is begotten. The begetting and the begotten are different, but this is all. There is no other difference. The "result," as it were, is indistinguishable. There *is* not something like a being called Father and another being which has gotten its being from the Father and thus it is another being. The "things" that we call Father and Son are not "things."

The same could be said between Man and God (or God and Cosmos). If seen from our human point of view, then we make the distinction between us and God (and us and Cosmos). It is obvious. We are neither God nor Cosmos, the same as the Father can say I am not the Son. Seen from the outside, however, that hypothetical observer would not discover any difference. He would only see Begetting/being begotten; Creating/being created. This "objective" view may be what explains monotheism.

We could express it in more theoretical terms. Let us take Man and God. We make the difference. From the outside there is no difference because there is no such independent and outside platform on which the distinction could be based. We carry with us our necessary perspective for the distinction. Thus we will have to say that ontological distinctions always presuppose two allegedly different entities and a third independent entity from where the distinction is made. We see ourselves and we are aware that we do not come out of ourselves, that we are contingent. We then assume, infer, discover, or believe (or whatever pertinent verb you prefer) another Being, cause, source, or origin of ourselves. We distinguish begetter/begotten, creator/created, cause/effect or the like. "Seen" from the outside, however, there is only one process: *creatio continua*.

* * *

I may add here something of capital importance for the third christian millennium. The *kairos* of christianity in this new period of the world consists not only in overcoming monotheism but also in overcoming the myth of history. Here "overcoming" does not mean denying God or historical reality. It has been rightly said that the historical sense of the jewish religion has been continued and enlarged by christianity, which has transformed the "chosen people of Israel" into the "people of God of the Church," which includes all humanity. Understandable as all this may be within the premises of an abrahamic mentality and as a corrective of the Middle Eastern and hellenic-roman surroundings of those times, the dilemma of christianity for the third millennium consists in maintaining its identity. This can be done either by difference, that is, by christianity being a historical religion besides many others, which logically are labeled as false or at least imperfect, or by christianity itself becoming a leaven to human religiousness. If history is the only reality (and here lies the myth of history), the second horn of the dilemma makes no sense and is bound to be condemned as heretical. Within the myths of other cultures, however, a leaven to human religiousness does makes sense and constitutes the challenge of realizing the claim to universality of christian faith without the sting of colonialism.

The key that opens the door to christianity for its third millennium is precisely the Trinity, which overcomes the myth of history. Here we offer only a few broad brushstrokes.

Jesus is a historical figure, but not Christ. We cannot identify the two and yet we cannot separate them either. Here again, the *advaitic* intuition offers an intellectual clue, and the experience of the Trinity is of paramount importance. Within the myth of history, that is, within the belief that history is the only canvas of reality, an historical event is interpreted as the only real event. It is enough to compare the greek sense of reality, let alone the indian one, in order to grasp the difference. In those cultures, time is not linear, and progress has hardly any meaning. The judeo-christian-islamic sense of history is a specific trait of the monotheistic tradition of abrahamic vintage, replete with its advantages and drawbacks.

The idea of the Trinity rescues christianity from the sense of historical time that is so crucial for the jewish and islamic traditions and so essential for christendom. This trinitarian awareness must come to the fore in the encounter of christianity with other cultures. Here we may also find the relevance of the Rhythm of Being for christian life.

VI
The Theanthropocosmic Invariant

A. The Invisibility of the Obvious

I thank you, Father, Lord of heaven
and earth, for hiding (*because* you hide
[ὅτι ἐκρυψας ταῦτα]) these things from the
wise and prudent [συνετῶν] and revealing
them to the children [νηπίοις].[1]

1. The Open Secret

I feel like uttering that profound prayer of the kashmiri *shaivite* tradition: "Tell me, O my Lord this great truth [*mahā aguhyam*] which still remains concealed [*guhyam*]."[2] This could also be read thus: "Tell me, O Lord, this secret [*guhyam*] which is the great non-secret [*mahā-aguyam*]." Or even more plainly: "Tell me that which being unhidden yet seems hidden"—"the hidden great unhiddenness—the great unabsconded secret." The secret is that there is no secret: The *guhya* is a *mahā-aguhya*.

Guhā literally means "cave," and in the literature stands for concealment, secret (known only to few), or even, mystery (unknowable). One could relate it to the greek λήθη, forgetfulness, oblivion, the lower world, and then undertake a heideggerian exegesis.[3] One might also recall the *Gītā*, where Krishna is going to reveal the *guhyatamam*, the most secret experiential wisdom (*jñāna vijñāna*).[4]

---

1 Mt XI, 25. The "simple" (instead of children) say some translators.

2 Abhinavagupta, *Parā*triśikā 1, 18: "etad guhyaṁ mahāguhyaṁ kathaya-sva mama prabho." Another possible reading is worth recalling: "Tell me this secret, this greatest secret [*mahāguhyam*], O Lord, you who are my very Self [*mama sva*]."

3 Heidegger, "The Origin of the Work of Art," *Poetry, Language, Thought* (New York: Harper & Row, 1971).

4 BG IX, 1. Cf. also the *Tripura rahasya*.

A-guhya, a-lētheia, un-concealed, patent, un-veiled, revealed, discovered, not secret. The greek *alētheia* (ἀλήθεια) is morally contrary to the lie, but ontologically opposite to the appearances. *Aguhya* is the non-apparent, the truth.

This plain truth, this "open" secret, is a *mahāguhya*, a mystery still greater than the *guhya*, the secret, the concealment. *Enfoncer des portes ouvertes.* You open the open doors. You reveal what is plain and patent to everyone. You tell a secret that is no secret, but is the most obvious and immediate thing of all: *Un secreto a voces.* "I was a hidden treasure and loved to be known," says a *hadith* quoted by Ibn 'Arabī,[5] explaining in this way the fact of creation.

Commenting on this "shining of reality in the heart of all, and yet not intimately assimilated; although (for many) it is present, as if non-present," Abhinavagupta uses a telling simile, which our automobile-driven civilization should find even more striking. We overlook the real "just as the grass and leaves on the path (are overlooked by) someone who passes on in a chariot."[6] The drivers of cars and chariots alike do not enjoy, or even see the ever-present "shining" beauty, the very reality of the grass and leaves along the way—or of the "lilies of the field,"[7] for that matter.

My prayer is clear. What I would like to say is not a secret, not something hidden that I have found, not a new philosophy or revelation. It is not something buried deep in the cave of the centuries, or of the human heart. To the contrary, it is the great "unconcealed," *mahā-aguhya*, the most obvious thing, which practically everybody is already experiencing, which the simple people intuitively live by, and which already proffers hope and love to all humanity. It transcends ideologies; it is the patent reality here in front of us all, a wide-open secret.

"That which is non-determinate [*avikalpitam*] and intrinsically inherent in everything [*avinābhāvi*], that is truly Supreme [Consciousness] *anuttara*,"[8] the same indian sage says. Likewise, the Master of Nazareth, echoing the great jewish Prophet, called out, "Who has ears may hear, who has eyes may see."[9] I would like to be truly original—that is, in touch with the Origins, indeed, with the Source where "living waters" well up for everybody, always, at no charge to anybody. The Origins do not lie back in the past of

5 Ibn 'Arabī, *Kernel of the Kernel* I (p. 3).

6 *Laghuvṛtti*; in J. Singh, ed., Parātrīśikā-vivaraṇa: The Secret of Tantric Mysticism (Delhi: Motilal Baharsidass, 1988), 58.

7 Lk XII, 27.

8 Abhinavagupta, *Tūśikā*, 22.

9 Mk IV, 9, 23; Mt XI, 15; XIII, 9; Lk VIII, 8; etc.

a linear time, but spring forth at the emergence of any original experience. "The *hūd* [straight path] to God is not secret, but universally revealed,"[10] says Ibn 'Arabī, who declares elsewhere that the "great secret" (*sirr kabir*) is hidden in (apparently) trivial sentences.

When the real moments come to us, when we throw away our masks, or are stripped of them, and stand naked before all because there is nothing to lose or gain, each of us instinctively deconstructs all *vikalpas*, all the mental constructs and belief systems, and dis-covers exactly what we *are* (Being, real), which for far too long has been split into egos and non-egos, subjects and objects, believers and unbelievers, and all the rest.

Reality is threefold, as we have already heard from all corners of the human world. Śiva reveals himself "in a threefold manner": "The Self whose body is Light, Śiva . . . hides his own nature by the . . . play of his freedom, and again reveals himself fully, either successively or immediately, or in a threefold manner."[11]

Elsewhere we find: "All has a triadic form."[12] Moreover, the universe is threefold, says Nicholas of Cusa:

> . . . we may agree that the world is threefold: a small [world, which is] Man, the greatest [world, which is] God [and], the great [world which] is called the universe. The small [world] is the likeness of the great [world, and] the great a likeness of the greatest. . . . In all the parts shines the whole, then a part is part of the whole.[13]

The use of the three adjectives indicates the interconnectedness of the three worlds. There is the greatest world, the *maximus*, God; the great world, *magnus*, which is called the universe; and the small world, *parvus*, Man. This small world bears a likeness to the great, and the great to the greatest. Curiously enough, although Man here has not the middle position but the inferior one, Cusa commences the list with Man. We stand at the beginning and the end.

The great difficulty in expounding this insight may well lie in the discursive character of our language, especially of our academic language.

---

10 Ibn 'Arabī, *Fusus al-hikām* (*Kernel of the Kernel*) X, trans. R. W. J. Austin (New York: Paulist Press, 1980).

11 Abhinavagupta, *Tantrasāra* I, 7.

12 Abhinavagupta, *Sarvaṁ trikarūpam eva* (ed. B. Bäumer, XVI).

13 Nicholas of Cusa, *De ludo globi* I: ". . . concedi potest, quod triplex est mundus: Parvus, qui homo; maximus, qui est Deus; magnus, qui universum dicitur. Parvus est similitudo magni, magnus similitudo maximi. . . . In omnibus autem partibus relucet totum, cum pars sit pars totius."

Spoken language, especially sung and danced languages, cannot be reduced to abstract meanings and lineal-sequential thoughts. The often-denigrated oral traditions know that "The word that was at the beginning"[14] is not meaning alone. "The word [of God] is alive"[15] christian Scriptures declare. To sing or shout AUM! would say it all, for those who understand.

The *oṁ kāra* is *idaṁ sarvaṁ* ,
the Oṁ is all this,
the entire universe.[16]

"Om is both the higher and the lower *brahman*."[17] This indeed is the holistic insight. As Abhinavagupta says, calling it a universal principle, "Everything is an epitome of all."[18]

L'écriture is not superior to the word. However, if one writes not simply to convey information, but in order to share insights and help them crystallize in simple and transparent forms, the reader is invited to share in the systole and diastole of the Rhythm of Being.

Perhaps I need to spell out this intuition if only to get "in" to it. This ex-plication and im-plication is not just a weakness or lack of depth, but inherent in the very nature of reality which loves "to hide itself" (κρύπτεσθαι), as Heraclitus already said.[19] It is another instance of the primordial insight concerning the Rhythm of Being. Just exclaiming AUM! will not suffice. The *oṁ* must resound, reverberate, live, and expand. "Not everyone who calls 'Lord, Lord' will enter the kingdom of Heaven, but only those who do the will of my heavenly Father."[20] Sim-plicity and com-plexity go hand in hand. To understand is not just to get the meaning but to stand-under the spell of the "thing" so understood.

It is the spell of the Whole that allows this spelling out, if we carefully trace the contours of that selfsame holistic insight. This can be conveyed analytically, in a descending process, or synthetically, in an ascending manner. Heraclitus again comes to our aid: "The way up and the way down is one and the same."[21] Both ways are required, because they belong together, and

14 TMB XX, 14, 2; Jn. I, 1; etc.

15 ζῶν γὰρ ὁ λόγος (Heb IV, 12; cf. Jn I, 4).

16 CU II, 23, 3.

17 MaitU VI, 5.

18 Abhinavagupta (ed. Bäumer, 42, 72, etc.).

19 Heraclitus, *Fragm.* 123.

20 Mt VII, 21.

21 Heraclitus, *Fragm.* 60.

together are part of the very dynamism of the real. In neither case should we forget, however, that while the Whole does not exist without its constituents, the parts as such do not form the Whole as whole. It is again Muhyiddin Ibn 'Arabī who said in the preface of his *Fusūs al ḥikām* (Jewels of Wisdom): "Then with understanding see the details in the whole / And also see them as part of the whole."[22] The same idea is expressed paradoxically in the old indic tradition, with the words of Śrī Krishna:

> All beings subsist in me,
> I do not reside in them.
> And [yet] the beings do not subsist in me . . .
> My self sustains the beings.[23]

In calling this chapter "the invisibility of the obvious" I play with the ambivalence of the word. Although the obvious is generally understood as that which is visible because it stands in the way (*ob-viam*), it can also mean what stands in the way as an obstacle. Thus, the obvious is both what we see and what prevents us from seeing—if we do not stop on the way. This is contemplation.

I might mention here how the prevalently rational mind of western christianity has interpreted the so-called theological virtue of faith as a belief in particular doctrines whereas Scripture explicitly states that faith is in the invisible.[24] Without faith the obvious is invisible.

The cosmotheandric vision is the most obvious human experience, so obvious that it becomes an obstacle to see it once we begin to specialize in our knowledge and forget the whole. It is this fragmentation of knowledge that has brought about the fragmentation of the knower. The secret is not "secretum," separated, but perhaps lost in the obvious, hiding in plain sight. "Blessed are the pure of heart, for they shall see God,"[25] I understand this to mean that a pure heart, a naked heart stripped of pre-judices and after-thoughts, *because* it is innocent, because it does not even harm itself (*in-nocens*) through self-reflection, shall enter into immediate contact with reality. The pure of heart shall be real, shall live life to the full and not just feel or think about it, notwithstanding the human condition which can only reach that purity after forgiveness, purification, redemption, illumination, or realization.

---

22 Ibn 'Arabī, *Fusūs al-hikam*

23 BG IX, 4-5.

24 Cf. Heb XI, 1-3.

25 Mt V, 8.

In a word, the "secret" is no secret, it is obvious for the pure of heart. They do not need to dis-cover reality, to un-cover the truth, to prove God. They are and live truly, in truth, in God. . . . The way, however, may be arduous and may require the asceticism of the full person. Only an enlightened person enjoys *advaitic* vision, says the nondual school of vedānta.

2. *Human Invariants and Cultural Universals*

I already alluded to the current debate in philosophical circles about cultural universals. Without entering now into all the complexities of the problem, we should draw a fundamental distinction between *human invariants* and *cultural universals*. Concerning our issue, I submit that the question of God (in the theistic sense) is not a cultural universal, while the question of the Divine (in the sense of Mystery) could fairly be called a human invariant.

The difference should be clear. A *cultural universal* is "something" that has universal value, because it crosses all cultural boundaries. I am inclined to think that while there are cross-cultural values at a given time and limited space, there are not cultural universals. A cultural universal presumes a common basic human culture that does not actually exist. It is again an example of the modern myth of the "theory of evolution," which makes us believe that we are the most developed culture that has evolved until now and can embrace all that is positive in "less developed" and more "primitive" cultures. Unless we reduce cultures to folklore, each language or group of languages represents a universe in itself. To be sure, all people are born and die, eat and drink, speak and sleep, reason and believe. These are *human invariants*, but not cultural universals. Death and eating, speaking and sleeping, reasoning and believing are practiced and understood very differently in different cultural and anthropological constellations of meaning. The *human invariants* are invested with widely diverse cultural interpretations. Death, love, eating, reasoning, and believing are not the same for a naga, an eskimo, an ibo, and a modern city dweller. Another example, more to our point, would be the recognition of a third factor in reality that differs from both Man and World. This third element, which I have been calling the Divine Mystery, is a human invariant. God, however, is not a cultural universal.

As a complement to the Divine as a human invariant, I go a step further and speak of the *theanthropocosmic invariant*. All of us are aware that we have to eat, that we speak, love, and the like. Furthermore, we are aware that we do not know everything, that there is a Mystery in life. We are also aware that this Mystery embraces something we call World, something we call Man, and something that many cultures call the Divine. The awareness of this triad belongs to our very nature, though the names and conceptions of the three differ widely.

There is some sort of connection between the three. We are together with other Men, on a common Earth, under the same Sky, and enveloped by the Unknown. There is an interconnectedness among the three. The triad is a Trinity. I call this Trinity, the *theanthropocosmic* invariant. Man as Man is conscious of this Trinity.

I said earlier that there are human invariants, but no cultural universals, no totally cross-cultural concrete values. There are, of course, purely formal invariants. These are either tautological affirmations or axiomatic sentences. An example of such a tautology is the universal statement: we should do good and avoid evil, since good is what we should do and evil is what we should avoid. Everything, however, depends on what we understand by good and evil—and even on what we mean by doing. Is a lustful thought or a tranquil meditation a doing? Some cultures will say yes, and others will say no. Axiomatic sentences, like mathematical ones, are those statements which derive from the setting of certain postulates and the acceptance of some logical rules for combining them. Reality, however, does not need to be mathematical, and a mathematical sentence has no validity outside the fields that comply with the mathematical universe. $2 + 2 = 4$ here and always by dint of a postulate, but 2 flowers and 2 thoughts do not yield any 4 equal to 2 elephants plus 2 clouds. Mathematical science has created a widely accepted *artificial universal* which should be distinguished from a cultural universal, which would be a statement univocally recognized as valid in all cultures.

Of course, there are some *cross-cultural universals*, within a culture or within a particular set of cultures. These are limited *cross-cultural universals,* not truly cultural universals. The ambition of these Lectures is to present the *cosmotheandric intuition* as such a cross-cultural universal for our times. The distinction should be clear: The *theanthropocosmic invariant* belongs to human consciousness. We are all aware that, besides our own existence and that of our similar fellow beings, there exist Nature or the World and an invisible and/or unknown third factor, one of whose names is the Divine. The *cosmotheandric intuition* is the hermeneutic of this experience expressed in some parameters that I believe could become a fairly widespread cross-cultural universal—open, of course, to diverse interpretations of the overall hermeneutic.

This is the experience I would like to share. Man as Man is aware of the three realms. This is the *theanthropocosmic invariant*. This study presents the *cosmotheandric intuition* as an adequate *cross-cultural universal* for the majority of cultures of our time. It is a cross-cultural interpretation of the invariant. The christian Trinity is considered to be an "inspired" disclosure of the triadic myths interpreted within a particular context. My conviction is that the "radical Trinity" of the cosmotheandric intuition belongs to a mature understanding of the christian insight and of most human traditions.

B. The Primacy of Life

In this dance [the soul] sees the source of Life,
the source of the Intellect [νοῦς],
the principle of Being [ἀρχὴν ὄντος]
the cause of Goodness [ἀγαθοῦ αἰτίαν],
the root of [the] Soul [ῥίζαν ψυχῆς].[26]

1. *The Being of Life*

The vision of primordial Man, and I suspect our first vision as children as well, is an undiscriminated view of the whole. To see parts as parts presupposes already the view of a certain totality of which the parts are parts. One of the most common data of which humanity is aware is not the notion of Being but the experience of Life. We experience ourselves as living, and we see life everywhere. Reality is not a dead thing.

The belief in the *anima mundi* may well be one of the most widespread convictions of Man. By different names and in diverse forms this seems to have been a common *mythos* until the incipient technocratic civilization obliged us to live in a mechanical world. One example is the shock the western world received when Pasteur "discovered" that spontaneous generation did not occur. That life did not come forth from matter seemed a mortal blow to the view that life pervaded the whole of reality. All sorts of later vitalisms were reactions against the ensuing lopsided scientific reductionism, but in general the holistic vision was not recovered. A particularly blatant example would be the long article (thirty-six columns) on "Life" of the 1974 *Encyclopedia Britannica*. In it, life is a purely scientific subject matter—that is, a physiological, metabolic, biochemical, genetic, and thermodynamic affair. Indeed, the very motto of the entire *Encyclopedia* is a monument to the spirit of the times: "Let knowledge grow *from more to more* and thus be human life *enriched*" (emphasis added). Not deeper and deeper, not simpler and simpler, not truer and truer, each time better and better. . . . This is

26 Plotinus, *Enneads* VI, 9, 9: Ἐν δὲ ταύτηι τῆι χορείαι καθορᾶι πηγὴν μὲν ζωῆς, πηγὴν δὲ νοῦ, ἀρχὴν ὄντος, ἀγαθοῦ αἰτίαν, ῥίζαν ψυχῆς.

more than a change of metaphors. Given the contemporary saturation of unassimilable information, we may justifiably begin to fear the cancer represented by this type of so-called more-to-more knowledge.

Neither from the fact "proven" by Pasteur that *omne vivum e vivo*, nor from the opinion of modern science that life is no more than a very complex organization amenable to being "created" by the scientist, does it follow that the universe may not be a living thing, or even that Being may not be alive. Similarly, the Church's condemnation of the assertion that the Soul of the world is the Holy Spirit does not mean that the Church claimed that the world has no soul.[27] The Church was concerned with avoiding pantheism, not with denying the general belief that the creation of the living God was also alive.

The fundamental insight of the belief in the *anima mundi* is neither a scientific discovery that the earth presents regularities of self-organization, as do plants and animals, nor a theological formulation of pantheism. Nor can it be reduced to the idea of the sublunary world as a living thing. The traditional insight sees the entire universe, and not the earth alone, as a living organism that constitutes a Whole of which human life is the root metaphor. From the *puruṣa sūkta* of the Rig Veda[28] and the several metaphors of Saint Paul regarding the mystical body of redeemed Reality,[29] and passing through the chinese, buddhist, african, and native american traditions, one could give innumerable examples.

Once modern science is interested in life exclusively as a phenomenon of individuals, and investigates its bio-molecular manifestations, it becomes nearly impossible to reenact the primordial and almost universal human experience of Life as the very nature of reality. The word *nature* itself suggests nativity, generation, power of procreation, spontaneity. Reality is *nature*, φύσις. This does not primarily convey the idea that all is material, or a particular bio-molecular phenomenon, but that all is Life, or rather, that *the All is alive.*

Some linguistic reflection may put us on the track I want to explore.[30] "Life," which is related to the german *Leib* ("body"), and probably also to the english "liver," contains a much-discussed indo-european root *libh* (*laibh*), which connotes the idea of remaining, being sticky, sticking, surviving. The

27 Cf. Denzinger-Schönmetzer, *Enchiridion Symbolorum,* 722.

28 RV X, 90.

29 Cf. 1 Cor XII, 12ff.

30 It would be illuminating to extend this reflection outside the indo-european languages, but that would distract us from the main thread of our considerations.

latin languages with *vita* and *vivere* are related to the greek *bios* (βίος) and *zōē* (ζωή), to sanskrit *jīva* and to the indo-european root *gwei* (with variations). "Soul" is probably connected with the greek *aiolos* (αἰόλος), with the meaning of quickness, swift movement. It translates the latin *anima* and the greek *psychē* (ψυχή), which, along with the sanskrit *prāṇa*, all connote breath, air, wind, vital breaths (cf. greek *anemos* [ἄνεμος]).

In european languages, we still call animals those beings endowed with *anima*, soul. For the greeks animals have *bios* but plants do not, except when a special character has to be stressed. A plant has *physis*, not *bios*. The hellenic world makes a basic distinction between *bios* and *zōē*. The former is individual, characterized, mortal life. The latter is Life in general, the very "time of Being," as Hesychius said. The increasing western belief in "reincarnation" amounts to a belief in zōē, but because of our entrenched individualism people interpret it as one individual *bios* moving unto another *bios*. What perdures is *zōē*, not *bios*—life, not individual life.

I would like to re-introduce the word "Life" at the level of Being, as a human experience of the Whole, because the modern notion of nature has been reduced to a dead essence of things. Life is not only *anima*, animal life, but *physis, natura, prakṛti*; it is reality as a Whole. I already referred to Aristotle saying that the *psychē* is in a certain way all things because it shares in all aspects of reality. Our starting point, of course, is human consciousness. When this consciousness turns back onto itself, we discover ourselves as a living being. Man has this *sui generis* consciousness of self-consciousness, of being alive, of being the bearer of something we identify with ourselves and which we call (our) Life. This Life is Man's Being. Following Aristotle, the medievals used to say, "Life for living beings is their Being" (*vita viventibus est esse*). Life is not an accident that adheres to matter.

Before the distinction between *natura naturans* and *natura naturata* there is the realization of *natura*. This *natura* is the undivided (but not necessarily undifferentiated) reality, inasmuch as it is dynamic, as it moves and reproduces itself. We still speak today of the new birth of stars. The vision of the universe as *natura* does not need to be monistic pantheism, nor does the distinction between uncreated and created *natura* need to be dualism.

Here we encounter a semantic problem. If we decide to ascribe life only to one particular class of beings, we feel automatically compelled to call the others lifeless or dead, since we pose life as the opposite of death. I will not enter into the tricky question of what kind of movement is the essential feature of life, in case elementary particles are also alive. Nor am I discussing what sort of reproduction is proper to living things, in case crystals are also alive. These are valid distinctions, of course, but I would like to recover the fundamental meaning of Life as a correlate to Being, but I will have to abstain from citing such "authorities" as Plotinus, Proclus, Dionysius, the scholastics, the philosophers of the Renaissance, and after Descartes' break with that tradition, the reactions of Bergson, Scheler, Ortega, and many others. I am also refraining from comment on the clauses of John's Prologue that say, "what came to be through him was life (*zōē*)."[31]

We are conscious of things (the "external" world), and at the same time conscious that this light of consciousness is within and without ourselves. *Within*: if we were not somewhat lightsome, we would not be aware of that consciousness as our own and use it to recognize aspects of things unknown at first sight. It is enough to think of the astonishing fact that outer reality seems to obey our inductions and deductions (calculus). At the same time, this light of consciousness falls on us, as it were, from *without*, so that we discover that real things impose themselves on us and we cannot manipulate them at will. We have to obey not only the external things but also the structure of our own thinking, which has been given to us. Our very consciousness is a given, a gift. Nevertheless, the fact that we are the bearers of that consciousness makes all the difference with regard to everything else. Human life is not just what we detect with our experiments. It is the "we" which is alive, which makes the experiments and endures the experiences.

Human life is what allows us to see and to conduct the experiments. Contemplation, as I will say later on, is not in order to see new things or to view old things differently; it is to see with the seeing of the Seer. This is what makes life human. We quickly discover that we also share some common traits with other beings: animals, plants, and apparently non–self-moving things. It is significant that modern civilization, instead of focusing on our high distinction (pun intended), is more interested in the lowest common denominator, namely, that all living beings move and somehow reproduce themselves. I mean both distinction and the distinctiveness—that is, that we are unclassifiable. We cannot classify ourselves without reducing ourselves to objects.

Human life is the human being. We cannot divide them without killing both. Without the body, for instance, human consciousness is neither human nor conscious. More than an aggregate of properties, be these material or spiritual, Man is also the self-consciousness that discerns and embodies such

---

31 Jn I, 3-4: πάντα δἰ αυτοῦ εγένετο, καὶ χωρὶς αυτοῦ ἐγένετο ουδὲ ἕν ὃ γέγονεν εν αυτῷ ζωὴ ἦν, καὶ η ζωὴ ἦν τὸ φῶς τῶν ανθρώπων.

properties. Human life is embodied consciousness, corporeal intelligence, and incarnated will. Life in the individual *bios* (not *zōē*) is a fleeting phenomenon. The individual is mortal. We have the evidence in the death of others. We do not have, nor can we have, the experience of our own death. We can perform any and all sorts of self-reflections; we can experience love, pain, hope, fear, understanding, beauty, whatever. We can, apparently, even have "near-death" experiences, but we cannot have any reflexive knowledge of our own physical death.

Singular life, *bios*, has an end. Life as such, *zōē*, does not (need to) have an end. "Within death there is immortality," says the śruti.[32] "Life does not die" another text affirms.[33] After telling us that the soul (life, the *jīva*) does not die, this *mahāvākya* goes on to say: "It is by this subtle principle (essence) that the whole universe is enlivened; this is the real (the truth); this is the ātman; this art thou." This are we, living beings, Life. This is our ultimate identity, the experience of Being, the experience of Life. This is why we cannot experience death.

We can imagine our own death on the model of what we see happen to others. I may assume that the individual ego, the *me* (not the "I" that thinks) disappears, dies. I may have the experience of the "me" dying. I cannot have any kind of experiential thought of the death of the "I," if that "I" also disappears. Life, inasmuch as it *is*, is Life, the very contradiction of non-life, death. We cannot understand contradictions. My ego can "think" the concept *of* death in the abstract, but it cannot think real death. The dead ego can no longer think. How is it, then, that death is a real concern for the human mind? We touch here on a momentous problem, understanding which could help us to overcome modern individualism. The person is more than the individual ego. The I is more than the *ego*. Is the I, then, more than the person? We leave this problem aside for the moment.

My *ego* cannot think its own death, but I can experience the death of a beloved person. The I really knows something, the death of the other that the ego cannot know. Death touches my I because "part" of my I was/is the beloved person. Love trespasses the ego-boundaries. Something of my I dies when I experience the death of a beloved one, and yet I remain alive. In this sense I can experience death. Death becomes known to the mother who has lost her son, to the lover whose beloved has been killed. . . . This experiential knowledge transcends my *ego*, because I am also in the beloved Thou. The boundaries of my ego are not the frontiers of my I. My I, or rather the I, is

32 SB 5, 2, 4: "Antaraµ mṛtyor amṛtam."

33 CU VI, 11, 3: "Najīvo mriyata iti."

not limited to the ego. A *mahātma* is a person whose ego has transcended the frontiers of kith and kin. A *jīvan-mukta*, an enlightened or a risen Man, is a person whose limits have been superseded by an I that does not die. We are not elaborating an argument for immortality. We are trying to recapture the experience of Life as the correlate of Being.

When we become conscious of ourselves, we become aware of movement, change, and growth, of aspiration, suffering, and joy, of an inner principle of becoming. Life is that Being of ours that makes us bearers (but not necessarily "substances") of our own existence. We may call this Being *puruṣa* , *psychē*, "soul" when we think of it as the principle of Life. This soul, the Life of a living being is not an accident or an attribute. Life is the very "stuff" of the living being—it is its Being: *Vita viventibus est esse*!

Human Life is conscious Life, but this consciousness is not any individual "thing." Consciousness is trans-individual. As persons, we share in that consciousness. With that consciousness we discover that all beings have traits in common with us. We discover certain peculiarities of self-movement, self-regulation, reproduction, and the like, and we draw the well-known division between animate and inanimate things, that is, between those that breathe and those that do not. *Anima* is related to the greek *anemos* and sanskrit *aniti* (he breathes), which means breath, as does *spiritus*, which translates *pneuma*, all with the same meaning. In short, animals and plants also have Life insofar as they participate in Being in their own way. Their Life is also supra-individual. Material things share in Being differently, but unless we make that division between animate and inanimate things into an ontological one and reserve Life for a certain class of beings, we shall have to say that material things also have a particular type of Life.

2. *Life of Being*

If we enforce this split between animate and inanimate, we have divorced Life from Being, even in ourselves. Life is then degraded to a mere property of some beings. Life is seen then as an accident to Being. Life becomes a peculiarity of some beings that happen to show certain special features. Life becomes a property of some individual beings, and by the same token we introduce individual death. We have then departed drastically from the traditional insight of the *anima mundi*, which is not just a sum-total of a multitude of individuals. In short, we have "killed" Life itself, and reduced it to certain properties of some beings which enable us to call them "living."

Many traditions have not limited Life to Men, animals, plants, and things. The earth is a living being; the universe is a living being; the whole cosmos is alive; it has an inner dynamism, a *nexus*, a movement, and perhaps even its own growth. There may also be superior sorts of living beings, and even a supreme Being, the bearer of pure Life.[34] Or, as the *Gītā* says: "my superior nature enfolds into life by which this universe is sustained."[35] In short, reality is alive. Life is coextensive with Being, with reality. Life is not a mere quality of some beings; it is another name for Being, for the whole of reality.

In fact, many traditions have considered God as the soul of the Universe, and even as the soul of Man. We may recall Saint Augustine's exuberant exclamation: *anima animae meae*, "soul of my soul," referring to God. He walks here in the footsteps of Paul's: "to me, to live is Christ."[36] We are still describing a traditional belief. As for the asian distinction between sentient and non-sentient beings, it is not the same thing as the division between living and non-living.

This solidarity of all beings is not anything artificial or esoteric. It is not something to which only the saint, the *bodhisattva* (the being on the way to enlightenment), or the *jīvan-mukta* (liberated while alive) has access. It is the law of *karma* in an eminent sense, the very constitution of the real. Of course, not everything has the same degree of life. The life of a stone or a nail is different from that of a Man or an angel.

This is not an apology for a so-called primitive animistic worldview. I am not saying, for instance, that each thing has an individual soul. Plato, Rāmānuja, Origen, and Augustine were not animists, nor for that matter was Newton, in spite of his belief that the planets were moved by angels.

As we have already seen, one word that has found wide acceptance in many languages and cultures, besides the formal concept of reality, is the word and verb *Being*. I submit that Being and Life are homeomorphic equivalents, and that Life corresponds to a more widespread vision of the real. It seems as if modern western culture is afraid to recognize the homeomorphic equivalence of Life and Being. Truth, goodness, unity, and beauty are freely called transcendentals, but Life seems to be reserved for a rather small proportion of beings. This leaves us abandoned in a lifeless universe. No wonder that Pascal, already living in the incipient modern period, could exclaim, "Le silence éternel de ces espaces infinis m'effraie."[37] My comment, of course, is that *those* spaces do not exist. "In space I am the

34 Cf. Aristotle, *Met.* XII, 7 (1072b28).

35 BG VII, 5.

36 Phil I, 21: Ἐμοὶ γὰρ τὸ ζῆν Χριστός, "mihi enim vivere Christus."

37 Pascal, *Pensées* §206.

sound," says the Lord in the *Gītā*. This is the opposite of the frightening silence and is much closer to the music of the spheres of the pre-socratics.

Modern Man feels a demeaning sense of insignificance before the immensity of the astronomical time and space and loses all notion of self-esteem and human dignity as well as any sense of proportion when confronted with the innumerable galaxies and clusters of galaxies in which, to use the phrase of Leibniz from another context, Man is a "quantité négligeable." The modern "vision" is nothing but the quantification of the universe sweetened by some minor qualifications. There is a difference between a sentiment of respect and even awe that does not exclude responsibility, and a sense of despondency and the feeling of impotency. The grandeur and magnificence of the universe can trigger praise and glory, as in the hebrew psalms, or depression and an envious sense of inferiority, as modern psychiatry so often detects. The "thought" of Pascal is highly significant. It shows the pervading myth of the modern western spirit beyond doctrinal differences. Pascal is almost the opposite of his contemporary conational Descartes, and yet both seem to accept the same scientific "kosmology": "space" as a "big box" (not *ākāśa*), "silence" as absence of sound (not *tusṇ im*), "eternity" as a long, never-ending time (not *ākala*), for instance.

The equivalence of Being and Life is not to be mistaken for any so-called vitalism. The new vitalist theories (Driesch and, with some differences, Bertalanffy, Haldane, et al.) insist precisely on reinforcing the divide between organic or vital beings and inorganic or non-living matter. These theories may be correct within their own scientific precincts; my assertion here belongs to quite another level. I am not speaking about vital forces, or about a vital principle irreducible to physico-chemical energies. What I have in mind is a holistic vision of reality, for which Life may be an appropriate symbol.

Here is another field where the modern western divorce between philosophy and theology shows its deleterious side-effects. To affirm that God is Life, that God has an internal energy, *actio immanens*, even without a specific trinitarian structure, appears plausible. On the other hand, to affirm that Being is Life, movement—or as I am saying, that Being is rhythm—seems in need of an extra explanation. The Being of philosophy has become lifeless Being, an *ens commune*, a flat abstraction—perhaps akin to Pascal's "God of philosophers"— which is no longer the "living God." In spite of the good intentions of Pascal's famous "Memorial," if the God of Abraham, Isaac, and Jacob has nothing to do with the "God of philosophers," then the just mentioned divorce has been sanctioned and the fight between "faith and reason" will be fought to the bitter end. How can there be a "living God" of dead things?

If Life is our Being and conscious life our most primordial activity, our most important concern should be what the ancients called contemplation, but with a momentous novelty. Here, contemplation stands not for a mere theoretical or intellectual life (βίος θεωρητικός), disconnected from practical existence and social solidarity. Contemplation includes the novelty that I have described as "sacred secularity."[38] Contemplation of Being includes the act of merging with, or rather becoming Being—a Being that is itself Becoming, pure Act.

Without contesting the eschatological destiny of Man, the primacy of Life entails much more than a projection of a real life into a future life, whether after our terrestrial existence or in the near or distant future of the collective human pilgrimage. The *eschaton* is the Ultimate, the Finality, but not necessarily the final point of a lineal time. Certainly, human life is not lived all at once. Our past and our future also shape our life. In other words, human life is historical life, but it is not only history, and I would add, not even primarily history. If the *Kurukṣetra* is historical, the *dharmakṣetra* is not—to play with the first words of the so-called fifth Veda.[39] Life flows on the historical fields of all sorts of human struggles, the plains of the *Kurus* of all times, but life also enlivens the human being in the tempiternal grounds of the *dharma*. To live is not to live for the future; to live is more than a drive, whether short or long, slow or quick, on the "highway" of lineal time. That sentence of the Son of Mary, "I came so that they may have Life and Life abundantly,"[40] is not the promise of a successful existence or a happy dwelling in the hereafter but the "good news" about the real possibility of piercing the surface of the *chronos* and reaching the fullness of Life for everybody.

Man is a microcosm, a mirror (*speculum*) of the entire reality. Each "member" of reality reflects the Whole, and contemplation is the human act of reenacting the Whole in Man as a microcosm.

C. The Triple Interindependence: The Cosmotheandric Intuition

"Triple Interindependence" is a philosophical expression inspired by the christian trinitarian *perichōrēsis*, the buddhist *pratītyasamutpāda* and the hindu cosmic *karma*. All these notions are *homeomorphic equivalents* relating to the corresponding insights underlying the equivalent problematic. It would be a mistake to interpret these holistic worldviews either with a

38 See Panikkar, *El mundanal silencio* (Barcelona: Circulo de Lectores, 2000).

39 BG I, 1.

40 Jn X, 10.

monistic or a dualistic scheme. Reality is not the sum of independent parts interacting among themselves following an external force like an atomistic system, nor is it a monolithic block of interdependent forces.

Although our first dim intuition is that of Being, our first mature reflective intuition is that of ourselves. We are conscious of many things external to us, but we soon become aware that it is we who are conscious of them. I say "we," because in this "we" the consciousness of "thou" has perhaps a certain priority over the ego. At any rate, Man is that being that knows that it knows, which presumably may not be said of any other animal. Moreover, as I have said, we are aware of the tripartite division common to cultures everywhere: Earth, Heaven, and Man; matter, spirit, and mind; or any of many other homeomorphic equivalents that we may find for this triad. The three belong together, but cannot be "handled" indiscriminately, nor should we confuse the one with the other.

Modern scientific thinking has deontologized the notion of cause. For modern science the notion of ontological cause becomes an unnecessary burden. A *post hoc* is enough without having to assume a *propter hoc*. For all practical purposes it is enough to know that B follows A without assuming that A causes B. Mathematical reasoning is the model here. If by logical deduction B follows from A, this is enough for a strict calculus. An effect can have a certain degree of freedom in relation to its cause, whereas a logical deduction either does not allow freedom or admits only a certain degree of ambiguity—allowing for statistical conclusions and equations of indeterminacy. The correlations I am referring to, however, are connected neither by logical deductions nor by a strict law of causality. Here we cannot analyze the many theories about the notion of cause or about mathematical deduction, but in these cases the logical conclusions depend on the premises and the physical effects depend on the causes.

Inter-in-dependence, on the other hand, may appear as a quandary to a merely rational mind: either dependence or independence, but not both. Yet we are not trespassing the principle of non-contradiction when defending the inter-in-dependence of the three dimensions of the real. The *inter* is neither a causal nor a logical link. This is why we spoke of *ontonomy*, which is neither heteronomy nor autonomy, but "order of Being," the *nomos* of the *on,* which is not identical to the "law of the logos"—unless we subscribe to the parmenidean equation between *being* and *thought,* and this is why we preceded this section with the section on "the Primacy of Life."

In short, the cosmotheandric "structure" of reality is neither a monarchic constitution laid down by a supreme *theos* nor an anarchic disorder of the three disconnected dimensions of the real. The three are connected by an ontonomic connection that is neither causal nor logical but constitutive of the very order of the real—of Being. This is the very Rhythm of Being, as we are trying to describe all along.

The inter-in-dependence of the three dimensions of reality is essential to the cosmotheandric experience. Otherwise we have only a mental construct. Matter, Man, and God are interrelated and connected, but the nexus is not determined by any of the three "factors" independently of the others. The connection is a free connection, the fruit of the spontaneous response to the free actions of the others. Perhaps I could venture the second-degree metaphor of human resonance. The repercussions are mutual.

The first degree of the metaphor is the musical resonance, which still follows physical laws. The second degree of the metaphor introduces human resonance.

Here we may draw on the powerful notion of *dhvani* of classical indic aesthetics. Each word has more than grammatical connotations; it has also a suggestive power, which varies in every hearer of the word. When Jesus utters that cryptic sentence "If you have ears to hear, then hear,"[41] he may be saying that the resonance of his word in the hearts of the hearers makes all the difference. A pure heart will understand; not so a selfish person. All is inter-related. The same words trigger different reactions. The relation is one of interindependence. Each hearer has an inter-in-dependent reaction. We are free agents and yet mutually connected.

I may give as an approximate example a system of equations with more variables than needed for a logical solution. Normal equations are systems of interdependence. Once a certain value (or function) is assigned to a variable, we may find out the value of the incognita. However, if the number of variables is superior to the number of equations and we assume each variable to represent a degree of freedom, the system as such will have no fixed solution because of the interindependence of the variables, which amounts to saying that, if there is freedom in the world, the riddle of the universe is not soluble by rational calculus.

I offer still another metaphor from a different field: classical jazz. Each musician has a degree of freedom. All are attuned to the music. The rhythm is paramount. If one instrument improvises a new sound or a new compass the others follow and vice-versa. Each musician is independent and all are

41 Mk IV, 23. Jesus is quoting from Is VI, 9-10, but there is a difference. Cf. Mt XIII, 14; Jn XII, 40; Act. XXVIII, 26-27; Proust. IV, 12.

inter-independent. There is no conductor, one is attentive to one's own instrument and to the sound of all the others.

The Divine, the Human, and the Cosmic are correlated and interconnected, but each is independent in an interindependent way. For an exclusively rational mind this is difficult to grasp. In fact, it cannot be com-prehended by reason. This is also the challenge of *advaita*. I said at the outset that the destiny of Being is also in our hands. The Cosmos and God have their role to play, but we also have our freedom and our responsibility.

* * *

I will now attempt a description of the cosmotheandric insight from its triple perspective: (1) *Kosmos*, (2) *Anthrōpos*, (3) *Theos*.

1. *Kosmos*

a) A Stone *qua* Real Stone

I use the more academic adverb *qua* instead of *as* in order to avoid the possible restrictive interpretation ("the stone only as 'stone'") instead of the constitutive meaning (of the stone in its total reality). This simple example may permit us to be brief.

Are stones alive? Are they divine? Or is consciousness material and divine? Is the Divine conscious and corporeal? We have to distinguish two levels: *First*, the level of the stone in its *singularity*. The stone "itself" is alive with a life of its own, which is not, of course, the life of an animal. We have already said that life can have a broader meaning than the one reserved to the so-called living beings only. The stone shows or contains a sort of consciousness. Here we encounter again the politics of words. What does consciousness mean? Where are its boundaries? The stone is subjected, we say, to the law of gravitation, and this law is called the law of "attraction" and "repulsion" of bodies, two anthropomorphic words. The stone is "attracted" by the earth. In one way or another the stone is conscious of that "attraction" since it reacts to it. Consciousness, unlike self-consciousness, does not entail freedom.

Obviously, this consciousness is not like human self-awareness. The stone shows a kind of memory, a sort of growth and degeneration, an internal movement. Matter presents, in its atomic and subatomic structures, practically all the features of traditional living beings. Furthermore, the stone is divine inasmuch as we are able to detect in the stone phenomena that are more than material and somewhat infinite. The stone possesses a mysterious, unlimited, infinite character that is irreducible to pure "materiality." An exhaustive knowledge of the stone is not possible, since pure matter is more than a "physical" mass.

It may be convenient to stress again why I am saying that the stone is also human and divine. The immediate answer is to say that it is that way because the stone presents features that we habitually reserve for Man and for God. We are also so accustomed to divinizing language that we find it awkward and even confusing to break the boundaries of those artificial constituencies on which we base "Law and Order." We may, however, still need reason as a policeman to enforce that law and order.

If by awareness we mean self-reflexive awareness, a prerogative of Man, then a stone indeed has no awareness. If by freedom and infinity we understand free will, it would be plainly false to attribute those features to a stone. The other way around, if by human and divine we refer exclusively to substance, Man and a transcendent Highest Entity, we could not sustain our prior statements. Precisely here lies the cross-cultural challenge and the importance of language. This entire study aims at meeting this challenge and at liberating human language from the structures of a particular worldview without falling into irrationalism or whimsical anarchy.

It may be retorted that I am anthropomorphizing, that is, attributing to stones qualities that do not belong to matter. This objection is the fruit of the epistemological twist which slowly won the cultural main scene of the west. What are we? Developed apes or fallen angels? What is our knowledge? A refined empiricism or a blurred spiritual vision? Is knowledge a sharing of divine knowledge or a refined perfection of animal consciousness? Is Plato or Aristotle the paradigm?

Is the human sexual force a sublimated animal instinct or an expression of the divine polarity between Śiva and Śakti? Is gravitational attraction a particular case of sexual attraction and divine love or the other way around? Where is the point of reference? Is Man a small God or God an immense Man? Or should we also interpret in this way the cryptic four words of Heraclitus saying that the "immortal [Gods are] mortal [and] mortal [Men] immortal"?[42] Or, coming to our starting point, is the pebble a miniaturization of God and his attitudes or is God the most perfect stone? Is the attraction of the stone to its ground sensitivity, love, or just weight? But why is not weight the love of the stone to go to where it belongs and can rest?

Following the spirit of these Lectures I would say that we need to make distinctions, a stone is certainly not an angel, but we should avoid ruptures of the warp and weft of the real. In summary, I am saying that isolated matter

---

42 Heraclitus, *Fragm*. 62: ἀθάνατοι θνητοί θνητοὶ ἀθάνατοι.

does not exist and that in matter are also present those two other features, freedom and consciousness, which we ascribe to God and Man, so that "pure materiality" is only an abstraction. This takes us to the second level.

Second, the level of the stone's real *individuality*. There *is* no isolated stone. An isolated stone simply does not exist. A stone "alone," by itself or in itself, would be merely an abstraction. A "stone *qua* stone" may mean an isolated and quite abstracted concept of "stone," or it may mean a stone *qua* real. In this latter sense a stone is stone *qua* all that the stone *is*—and this *is* includes the human and the divine. The stone that actually exists *is* not without Man and God, and this is the case not only *de facto*, as a matter of fact, but also *de iure*, as belonging to the very nature of a stone. A stone not in principle visible to our senses and capable of being experienced by the human mind would not be a real stone. As we shall explain, a stone totally outside of or impervious to the divine reality (as we are describing it) would not be a real stone either.

Without Man and God the stone does not "actually" exist. The reverse is also true, "Man" and "God" are not separated from the stone but rather coexist with it. Only as abstract concepts are they separated. Man and God belong to the stone. Man *qua* real Man is also matter, and the same may be said for God.

The problem would not have appeared in this form if in our cultural unfolding we had included and cultivated *symbolic knowledge* in addition to a conceptual epistemology. Conceptual epistemology is needed. It is the basis of abstract thinking and modern scientific knowledge, but perhaps due to its glamorous feats it has practically superseded all other types of knowledge. As a sociological example I may cite the neglect of artistic education in the dominant culture of our time. Artists are benignly tolerated in modern society—and the law of the jungle (survival of the fittest) explains the fact that not every one is considered an artist, but only the outstanding specimens that have survived and whose existence is "justified" by being recognized as marketable or as entertainment for the people.

Be this as it may, symbolic knowledge is a direct knowledge through participation in the power (revelation, light, . . .) of the symbol. A symbol is only such for those who recognize it as a symbol without any mediation. Symbolic knowledge overcomes the subject-object epistemological split. The symbol is neither merely objective nor purely subjective. We discover a symbol as symbol only within an accepted *mythos*.[43]

43 See Panikkar, "Introduction," *Myth, Faith, and Hermeneutics* (New York: Paulist Press, 1979); see also Panikkar, "Per una lettura transculturale del simbolo," *Quaderni di psicoterapia infantile* [Roma: Borla], vols. 5, 53-91 and dibattito, 113-23.

Why do I include Man and God when I say stone? Why do I say that Man and God also belong to the stone *qua* stone? In other words, why should the holistic vision be prior to the particular aspects of reality? Does it not bring us to utter confusion and impossibility of discernment? This would be the case if we were to discard conceptual knowledge altogether. My plea is for a recovery of nondualistic experience as manifested in a symbolic approach to reality. Symbolic knowledge is what prompts the mystical literature of practically all traditions to see the world as the Body of God, to discover in the universe the image of the Divine, to say that the heavens sing the glory of the Creator, to experience the Buddha nature in everything and to enjoy the Presence of God in every creature. This is neither conceptual knowledge nor sheer hallucination. It is real knowledge of another type. I could elaborate now on the just mentioned symbolic thinking, but we shall remain on the current common track so as not to complicate matters unnecessarily.

What *is* a stone? Is it that which a stone *is*, its *identity* without which it cannot be, or is it that which *differentiates* the stone from all the rest and marks the specificity of the stone? How do we come to know the stone? By *identifying* the stone with itself or by *differentiating* it from all that the stone is not? By looking at its identity, or by analyzing its differences? I submit that both methods are required and that they are complementary, so that the one without the other is an insufficient method to approach reality.

What do we mean when we say stone? We mean, first of all, this sensible object that I hold in my hand and see with my eyes. What, however, does "*qua stone*" mean? It means *all* that makes the stone stone.

What, more precisely, is that? I hold the stone in my hand. I perceive its weight. Is the stone really its weight? Does weight belong to the essence of the stone? Does the stone cease to be stone in a vacuum or outside the atmosphere? There, it has no weight. Beyond the pull of the earth's gravity, we could prove to my senses that the stone is still stone by its hardness, color, and temperature, although we could not convince my double beam balance. There, outside the gravitational field of the earth, the stone is still within the solar system. Could a stone "be" outside every galaxy existing as a single, isolated stone with absolutely no weight, beyond all gravitational fields? No, it could not so exist. We do not affirm this, however, because of our scientific knowledge about gravitation, astrophysics, and elementary particles. We affirm it because it is an impossible thing to think.

A stone *qua* stone brings with it its own space; it occupies a certain place, and it forms a certain distance between its points and its relations to the universe. The stone I have in my hand may have no weight; it could at the utmost perhaps be colorless, but it cannot be "spaceless." An isolated stone outside, or rather without, space is a sheer contradiction. It cannot be space and no space. We cannot isolate the stone from its space. Space belongs to the very nature of the stone. In brief, we cannot, in thought, separate the stone from the surrounding universe, which equally belongs to the stone qua stone, for without it our stone would not and could not be.

In addition, the stone *qua* stone implies our thinking about it as well. We can certainly imagine a stone on earth without any human hand to hold it. I am sure this pebble I have on my desk existed millions of years before any human being arrived to take hold of it. This brings us to an argument about time, basically similar to the one we have just sketched about space.

Because *this* pebble exists now, as I hold it in my hand, I can say that it existed millions of years ago. But also, if *this* pebble did not exist now, it could not have existed before. I mean precisely *this* pebble—not another one. I picked it up, from the hill nearby; it has not come out of nothing. The argument works in both directions: its presence now assures me of its existence then; its existence then reassures me of its presence now. *This* pebble in fact exists along with my consciousness of it, although my consciousness is bound to admit that the pebble did exist *before*. But this *before* only has meaning together with the *now* that makes the *before* meaningful, and, in fact, without the *now* of *this* pebble there would not be this pebble *before*. A similar argumentation might be made regarding *later*. *This* pebble may exist later because it exists now.

The same argument applies directly to *this* our earth. We are living *in* the same earth (I won't say merely *on*), which existed before us. This earth in fact *is* not without the human consciousness for which it is earth, and if I were to say that the earth *was* before our human consciousness, the *was* refers already to the *is* of our consciousness. But I return to the stone for the sake of clarity. It is not my consciousness, or my hand holding the stone, that makes the stone stone, yet *this* stone, without my hand or consciousness laying hold of it, is not this stone, but rather an abstraction. It would be only my thought about "that" stone which was, will be, or could have been in my hand, a possible stone, but not a real stone.

This stone, the real stone, and this earth, the real earth, imply our human consciousness of them. I am saying that the link between consciousness and stone is constitutive. A consciousness that could not be conscious of stones would not be consciousness; and a stone of which no consciousness could be aware would not be a stone. The stone *qua* stone implies the (human) consciousness for which it is a stone. We cannot prove the contrary. Indeed, this is a reversal of the ordinary way of speaking, which is a one-directional way. Realists will say that because the stone is there we are conscious of it; the strict idealist will defend, on the contrary, that the stone is there because we are conscious of it.

In truth there is a two-way traffic in a nondualistic relationship without causal links in either direction. This is *ontonomic* order.

We can have a concept of stone in our mind, and our mind projects the (conceptual) stone onto the outer world, helped in this case by the testimony of our senses, a testimony that is validated by our mind, by our awareness of it. A vicious circle? At any rate we distinguish it from an imaginary stone. Yet a real stone does not *really* exist without a constitutive link with the human mind, but nevertheless is not a product of the mind. The reality of the stone and the human mind belong together. We cannot "think" of a single exception.

* * *

I proceed to the divine dimension in a similar way. This real stone that I hold in my hand and have just now deposited on my other sheets of paper in order to go on writing, this real stone that is constitutively linked with the human mind, shows a depth and an independence that are not reducible to my limited knowledge of that particular stone, or even to any of our mental constructions or deductions about the nature of matter. We may analyze the stone up to its finest and ultimate elements, but the "core" of the stone, its ultimate "essence," so to speak, escapes us. We speak and are aware of the stone because in a certain way it offers resistance to our knowledge of it; it is not totally transparent.

The stone is vulnerable. I can destroy it. It can also cease to exist as this stone. In this sense one could say that it can die. We may "console" ourselves by saying that a transformation of energy has taken place, but the stone is no longer here, even if no energy has been lost—although perhaps part of it is no longer available (entropy increases). That "amount of energy," however, *is not* the stone. The stone *is* as if it were hiding a mystery.

The stone has something uncanny about it. It not only embodies weight and color, space and time, shape and content in a unique way but also demonstrates a mysterious stubbornness and independence. Modern science may have pursued this in the most scrupulous detail, but always balks at the irreducible question of *why* the laws of nature (whether those of the stone, those of its elementary constituents or those of our mind), behave the way they do. Chance is as mysterious as necessity, and probability just as unintelligible as fixed behavior. *Why* are matter, time, space, our mind the way they *are*? Why do they display and *have* the nature they have?

We could go even further by applying the same question to our own minds and asking about the "why" of intellectual evidence. Why do I see that 2 + 3 = 5?—even if we have postulated it to be so. Why do the postulates we postulate hold? What makes the pythagorean theorem so seemingly evident? What does reality, or our mind, for that matter, have that makes it the way it is? The evidence is ultimately as mysterious as the enigma of an unsolved problem.

The only real answer to an ultimate question is to say *amen*. It is so because it is so, because there is no "because" behind it, because our own "why" appears meaningless, and we do not even know *why* we ask "why," let alone *what* we are asking with our "why." Silence is just a word, or rather, real silence is not even a word, no *logos* at all.

The stone I held in my hand encodes the whole universe, but its own "code" has to be taken as a given—indeed, as a gift. There is something in the stone that makes it stone, and that "something" is irreducible, inexhaustible, in some way infinite and inexplicable. That stone *qua* stone "enstones" (incarnates if we prefer) the very mystery of reality. The stone *qua* stone is a groundless abyss. Many human traditions have called this the Deity. The stone qua stone is also divine.

It all hangs together. All are pointers to the infinite. Without a tripartite anthropology, without a theory of knowledge that starts from above (the Divine) and not from below (the senses), without an adualistic vision which intuits that God and the world are not two substances, we cannot understand this *perichōrēsis* of Reality itself; the ultimate *pratītyasamutpāda* of all that exists, and in short, we cannot penetrate into the mystery of reality. However, this is not all. A more suitable anthropology, a better ontology, a more refined and comprehensive philosophy may convince us more and help us to decipher the code of the real, but the final mystery persists, the ultimate question remains unanswered and the ultimate answer keeps its secret. We cannot eliminate the Mystery. Paradoxically and significantly enough, if we could, we would eliminate ourselves. We, even in our corporeality, are parts of the Mystery. Plato ends his *Timaeus* speaking of "a sensible God made in the image of the Intelligible, which is the only begotten [μονογενής] of heaven,"[44] and we could adduce similar quotation from practically all traditional wisdoms.[45]

---

44 Plato, *Timaeus* 92c: εἰκὼν τοῦ νοητοῦ θεὸς αἰσθητός.

45 The christian Patristics are not afraid to speak of a "divine sensibility" (αἴσθησις θεα) and sensibility above the senses (αἰσθάνεσθαι ὑπὲρ αἴσθησιν). Cf. Balthasar (1961), 283ff.

In a poetic and more immediate way, a sufi proverb simply states:

> God sleeps in the stones,
> He breathes in the plants,
> Dreams in the animals,
> And awakens in Man.

We could have expressed it in one single word: Mystery. Reality is Mystery, and this Mystery is in the stone as much as in us—if we but awaken to it.

It may not be too far-fetched to recall here the buddhist and the christian insight about "living stones." Saint Peter says:

> As you come to him, the living Stone—rejected by men but chosen by God and precious to him, you also, like living stones, are being built into a spiritual house to be a holy priesthood, offering spiritual sacrifices acceptable to God through Jesus Christ. For in Scripture it says: "See, I lay a stone in Zion, a chosen and precious cornerstone, and the one who trusts in it will never be put to shame."
>
> Now to you who believe, this stone is precious. But to those who do not believe, "the stone the builders rejected has become the capstone," and, "A stone that causes men to stumble and a rock that makes them fall."[46]

b) The World *qua* Real World

I will now take leave of pebbles and try to describe the status of the question in a more general way. I have been saying with the example of the stone that matter is co-extensive with the Divine, and also contemporal with it, that there is an interindependent penetration between the three dimensions of the real, that the full reality of each "thing" implies the dynamic presence of this radical trinity. For the sake of clarity, let us use a creational language as an example without necessarily subscribing to any creationist theory. After all, at this ultimate level we only have metaphysical options open to our intellect, none of which can lay claim to absolute truth without condemning itself to absolute silence. This does not prevent us from defending some options in the human arena, or from defending even only one as the most complete and satisfactory. For this, however, we must descend to the human *agora* of dialogue and make our point.

Adopting the ancient creationist language, I may venture the following, perhaps overcondensed comments. If creation is contemporal with the

46 I Peter II, 4-8.

Creator, we have a *creatio continua ab initio*. God creates continuously since the beginning (of time). There is no time "before" creation, but even more, there is no Creator "before" creation. There is no such "before." Creation and Creator are contemporal, and therefore coexisting. Existence is also a temporal word. We may think that creation had a beginning. This beginning of creation is also the beginning of time. Therefore we cannot think of any "before" before time. Eternity is certainly both "before" and "after" the beginning of time, which is a contradiction. In this context time is another word for creation. Time would simply express the *ek-sistence* of the world in its adventure "outside" its Source, be that going away from or returning to the Source.

In order to maintain the difference between God and the cosmos, it is commonly said that their relationship is asymmetrical inasmuch as the World is temporal and God eternal, that the world has had a beginning but not God. The world is co-temporal with God, but God is not covered, as it were, by the temporality of the World. God is "more" and "other." God in "Himself" is not temporal; He has no real relation with time. He is eternal.

A subtle and double fallacy lurks behind these statements. The relation is asymmetrical indeed. It has no common *metron*, no common measure. Under this mental scheme, to maintain such asymmetry, which would "safeguard" the transcendence, immutability, and thus perfection of God, the human mind is bound to defend that the relation between God and his creation, is real from the side of the creature, but is unreal for God. Otherwise, if there were a twoway relationship, God would then be "dependent" on his creatures. The link, therefore, is only from the side of the creature. This is the *relatio rationis* of Thomas Aquinas and the illusory link of Śankarācarya. The exclusive absoluteness of God demands the total relativization of the creature—a *relatio quaedam* (a "certain relation") says the medieval world.

The cosmotheandric vision, on the other hand, affirms that there is a real relationship from both sides. Yet not all relations need to be measurable by our mind—like the relationship between the hypotenuse of a right-angle isosceles triangle with its two other sides: the relation is real and yet we cannot measure it. It is rational to assume that if our mind can find (or postulate) a sufficiently small unit we should be capable of expressing numerically such a relationship. Yet such a number does not exist; nevertheless, we are aware of their mutual incommensurability in spite of the fact that the triangle is a measurable figure. Something similar occurs with time and eternity. Between time and eternity there is no common measure, and yet they belong together as the two sides of Reality.

The other fallacy is to think of eternity as a never-ending time. God's *eternity* is neither co-temporal nor non-co-temporal with the temporal World. Time and eternity are incommensurable, and yet they belong together, as do the sides of the isosceles triangle. This contemporaneity between Creator and creation has sometimes been mistakenly called *creatio ab aeterno*, which is a contradiction in terms. Whatever *creatio* may be, *ab* (i.e., "from") is here a temporal particle. *Eternity* is intemporal and not a never-ending or never beginning time. *Creatio ab aeterno* cannot mean *creatio sine initio* ("creation without beginning"), since, the world being temporal, this would amount to creation having no beginning and thus it could never reach the present moment. The phrase is an awkward way of saying *creatio continua*, a continuous and thus ever-new creation—although "new" and "continuous" should also be "purged" of their spatio-temporal connotations. Yet this is ultimately not possible without transcending the spatio-temporal structure of our thinking. We leave this problematic for our next part.

From the side of the creature, creation is contemporal and coextensive with the creator because time and space are created in the very act of creation. Or rather time and space are not created, they are not creatures; rather it is the creatures that are temporal and spatial. From the side of God, so to speak, creation is coeternal, continuous with (*con-tinere*, "hang together") and contiguous to (*con-tingere*, "contact on all sides") God. This would be another way to introduce the notion of *tempiternity*.

All this directly concerns our cosmotheandric intuition. Undoubtedly "God in 'Himself'" is not temporal, but such a God in "Himself," an isolated God, does not exist. God is not without Man and World, although our mind discovers that there is a difference between God and Creation: God "could be" without us, while we "could not be" without "Him." Nonetheless, we are speaking about reality, and thus about a real God, not a conceptual description of the Divine. A concept God is just that: a concept, an abstraction, useful and necessary as it may be, assuming that such a concept is possible.

There is an essential difference between matter and God. Matter is contingent, temporal. The Divine is necessary, eternal. Within a hindu world-myth one could say that matter is the Spouse of the Deity, its feminine counterpart, but we should not mix different worldviews without first delimiting their respective parameters.

Many hindu kosmologies speak, therefore, of an ever-recurrent or never-ending process of creation, dissolution, and "new" creation. This is often misunderstood, notwithstanding neo-hinduistic, and of course legitimate, interpretations influenced by the western myth of history. The classical ever-recurring process is not temporal, and undoubtedly not historical. It is not a "worldly" process, as it were. A universe is not just another world, another species of the genus "universe." The universe of the indic "kosmology" collapses, disappears, ceases to be. The "new" universe is so new that it is not a second, or an "*nth*" universe. There is no series: 1, 2, 3, . . . *n* universes. This is so for two "reasons."

First, an infinite series from minus infinite to plus infinite would never reach the present point of the actual universe. There would be an infinite time needed to reach the actual universe. Were we still to affirm such a series, the only coherent position would then be the unreal character of our universe—because that infinite time past that would have been needed for crossing that infinite temporal distance could not be real time. This is, in fact, a thesis that a certain type of monism consistently holds.

Second, the series of universes is not temporal because each universe segregates, as it were, its own time. When there is no universe, there is no time. Or, in traditional hindu terms, the universe lasts as long as the God that gave birth to it. Each universe is incommensurable with every other. Time is not an independent riverbed through which a finite or infinite number of universes flow. There is neither a meta-history nor a meta-time that would permit us to number the universes.

It is this insight that opens the door to transcendence. Each universe is unique, and yet we "know" that this uniqueness somehow breaks down—or rather up. There are not *many* universes, since the set of all the universes is not a homogeneous set. That set would be a purely formal concept, which does not allow any conclusion or application to any real universe since there is not an homogeneous time linking all the universes, and an algebraic algorithm connecting all of them could not have any foothold on a universe diverse from the one from which the algorithm has been abstracted. There may be many physical worlds, but then we abandon the metaphysical sphere to land on a physical (cosmological) plane. Indeed, there may be many "worlds" like our own following more or less analogous laws to those of our world. This implies an anthropomorphic and "kosmomorphic" idea of reality, as well as a simplistic idea of an Engineer God. This is not our metaphysical and truly theological question. Our problem is not "science-fiction." All these considerations are meant to show that the *is* of which we can be aware is something "more" than a material universe— otherwise we would not be able to think like this.

In this sense, our consciousness, which is not separate from matter, transcends the material universe. Matter transcends itself insofar as we, material and conscious beings, are aware of this transcendence. Our transcendence is not, however, an individualistic privilege but a feature of "our" Being. We are "more" and "other" than our isolated singularities. Reality is "more" and is not exhausted by what falls on the field of our senses and intelligence. Consciousness may not be all, but it is the bridge. It makes us aware that we are "eternal," "infinite," and yet also temporal and belonging to this world. This is consciousness of *tempiternity*.[47]

The main thrust of these considerations should be clear by now. The challenge to the human intellect is how to keep both the unity of Being and the diversity of beings without "injuring" either. At the dawn of greek philosophy it was expressed as the problem of "the one and the many" (ἓν καὶ πολλά). At the peak of the upanishadic reflection it was formulated as "the one without duality" (*ekam eva advitīyam*).[48] At the acme of taoist wisdom it was said:

> The Tao begot one.
> One begot two.
> Two begot three.
> And the three begot the ten thousand things.[49]

If oneness absorbs all diversity, monism is the outcome. If the many take the upper hand, pluralism wins.[50] This study is an effort at maintaining a harmonious polarity overcoming the tensions of either of the two extremes. Our main symbols are rhythm and harmony, the metaphysical question, *advaita* and trinity.

What I have been saying in this section is that the world is the real world when it is not severed from the entire reality, which is also symbolized as Man and God. The world abstracted from Man and God is not the real world. I could adduce here an aphorism probably hermetic in origin that was accepted by the monotheistic religions: "God is that in comparison with whom substances are accidents and accidents nothing."[51]

Leaving aside more critical comments concerning the second part and the very notion of substance and accident, we retain here only this much. Things are different from God; they are his accidents. Their reality stems

47 See Panikkar, "Le temps circulaire: temporization et temporalité," in E Castelli, ed. *Temporalité et alienation* (Paris: Aubier, 1975), 207-46.

48 Cf. CU VI, 2, 2.

49 Lao Tsu, *Tao Te Ching,* 42.

50 This cosmological pluralism should be distinguished from the pluralism used in the context of belief systems.

51 *Liber XXIV philosophorum*, prop. VI: "Deus est cujus comparatione substantia est accidens, et accidens nihil."

from the fact that they fall into (*ad-cadere*) divine reality. They are not nothing, but they are real inasmuch as they adhere to (befall into) God as an accident falls on a substance and subsists in it. This is the traditional idea of contingency as *esse ab alio*, a being dependent on another. Furthermore, one might amplify this and say that a substance without any attribute would not even be substance, would not sustain (*substare*) anything. It would be sheer nothingness. In a word, we should describe the properties of any being, of the entire world as well, without forgetting that being itself is accidental—contingent, we may translate.

The importance of this intuition is also directly related to our personal lives. Our creativity, our urges and desires, all have a certain ingredient of transcendence. If this transcendence is not rooted in our immanence, that is, if transcendence (future eternity or Deity) is not linked with our contingent existence, we open the door to anxieties and alienations of all sorts. We would live then, as it were, thrown forward, always running ahead, trying to go higher, further, to get more, go beyond, and the like. This is the cause of anxiety, fear, and discontent.

Retire when you have done your work; He who knows he has enough is rich; He will always have enough.[52]

We do not want to be mortal; we fear death and are convinced it will come. We hurry to finish what we may not have time to achieve. Death is the enemy because it disrupts our flow of life on the riverbed of linear time and the grid of merely material space. If, however, the meaning of my life does not come from prolonging my individual *bios* into an uncertain future of this temporal universe, then the very sense of my existence changes. I am then no longer a traveler rushing and scurrying and eventually competing with others to reach a goal or get a prize. Once I experience that time is the other side of eternity, I do not need to treat time as a scarce commodity. In order to be, said Saint Augustine, we need to transcend time.

2. *Anthrōpos*

Around the same time that the discussions about humanism began to proliferate (Heidegger, Sartre, Maritain), on a much humbler scale I was trying to elaborate what at that time I called "an integral anthropology." One of the insights basic to that conception was that Man is not a rational animal, a species of the genus animal. I already touched on this in our discussion of monotheism. I tried to apply this insight to the study of "patriotism" and to defend the opinion, unpopular at the time, that "christianity is not

52 Lao Tsu, *Tao Te Ching*, 9, 33, 46, respectively.

a humanism."[53] Without now delving into that problematic or further elaborating a tripartite anthropology (body, soul, spirit), I would like to offer some considerations within the general contours of our present study.

I have already hinted at the fact that anthropology is a peculiar science inasmuch as its study includes the studying subject as much as the studied object. The studying subject is not simply the anthropologist, let alone merely presentday Man, but Man throughout the ages as a self-understanding being, along with what Man has understood, since any knowledge modifies the knower and thus his self-understanding.[54] Now, I will simply draw a few sketches from this perspective, which sees Man in relation to the World and the Divine.

a) Caturloka

Triloka (three-worlds) is a classical sanskrit word, one of whose meanings is precisely the divine, the human, and the material worlds. I include a fourth world in the list. The relationship of Man to Nature offers us a point of reference for examining the relations of Man with the Divine. It is common today to affirm that the relation between Man and Nature has gone through three periods:

- *Submission* of Man to Nature. Man and Nature form one indiscriminate Whole. Man is in and under Nature. Man is one among the living beings. *Animism*.
- *Liberation* of Man from the forces of Nature (magic, demons); discovery of interiority. Two examples in the West are the early greek philosophers' criticism of mythopoetic literature and christian demythologization of Nature. *Humanism*.
- *Domination* of Nature by Man. The human mind decodes the enigmas of the material universe. Man believes himself to be the Lord over Nature. Culture becomes civilization. *Illuminism*.

This scheme is no longer complete today. We are proud to have achieved "independence" from the three worlds. *Techniculture*.

The three worlds that Man has confronted, at least during the historical period, are the following:

53 See Panikkar, *Patriotismo y cristiandad* (Madrid: Rialp, 1961); and Panikkar, *Humanismo y Cruz* (Madrid: Rialp, 1963).

54 Panikkar, "Antropofania intercultural: Identidad human y fin de milenio," *Thémata Revista de Filosofía* 23 (1999), 19-29.

(1) The World of the Gods

The Gods are everywhere. Thales and Heraclitus are often quoted in this regard, as we have seen. One could also cite african and oriental sources. Man has to reckon with the world of the *numina*, the sacred, which is powerful, dangerous, and awe-inspiring. The *numen* is *tremendum*, although *fascinans*; and the *mana* is all-pervading. Man has to learn how to "cope" with the Gods. They are often whimsical, if not outright cruel. Religions, from this viewpoint, can be envisaged as different ways for taming that world, as various forms for instructing Men on how to cope with the Gods. Sacrifice, rituals, and the like, can all be seen as means to appease and praise the Gods and by so doing to reach salvation.

(2) The World of Nature

Nature is not just the sweet mother. She is also whimsical, cruel, and unpredictable. She is often in connivance with the Gods, and perhaps undifferentiated from them, but Nature shows its power and autonomy even in the face of the Gods. Man has to deal with Nature on her own terms, and learns slowly her ways, tricks, and laws. A lighting rod is more efficacious than a prayer. The so-called *natural* sciences today believe they contribute to Man's salvation by liberating humans from the grip of nature. Natural sciences worship nature. Their ritual is called Research.

(3) The World of History

Fellow humans have not been notably kind to one another. We may escape the wrath of the Gods or the menaces of nature and still fall victim to our fellow beings. Senseless violence, absolute monarchies, slaveries of all sorts, exploitations, and dominations are daily events, grist for the mill of history. To be sure, there have always been rebellions of slaves and oppressed people. Resignation is no longer a virtue, and an awareness that history must be taken into our own hands is slowly dawning on the human mind. Marxism is only one of its most recent expressions—and democracy today's prevalent *mythos*.

The results are not very encouraging. Human life on earth has never been easy. Harmony among the three worlds is difficult to achieve, but there have been noble efforts everywhere. Religions were humanized; science discovered the habits of Nature; cultures increasingly recognized the rights of individuals and the duty to respect other traditions. All these ups and downs, breakthroughs and setbacks, prophets and profiteers, are still very much with us. Human life has been a constant struggle on the three fronts.

This unstable balance has been broken by the complex phenomenon of modernity. It starts with the nominalistic onslaught on language, followed inevitably by the fragmentation of knowledge, then the divorce we have discussed of theology (philosophy) from kosmology, and finally the complete rupture of equilibrium caused by the tremendous proliferation of the modern sciences. Technoscience has produced a technocratic civilization.

(4) The World of Technocracy

Technocracy has, in fact, created a *fourth* world, which is quite different from the three we have discussed. It is an *artificial* world of dialectical struggle and challenging tensions. This fourth world—which entails, obviously, its own ways of thinking about and viewing the world, and its own particular way of life—is the global fruit of that "artificial intelligence" so long dreamed of and still actively sought. Its very name already reveals the intention behind it. "Artificial flowers are only paper, not flowers at all. . . . But artificial light is light and it does illuminate. It is fabricated as a substitute for natural light," a modern scientist says candidly.[55] The threefold world, which has been dominant for at least eight thousand years, has been dispensed with. Today "we" believe "we" are able to live in an artificial world, from habitat to clothing and eating to the rest of our (once) human activities. We begin to wonder what happens to cows and pigs fed artificial food, to hens raised under artificial light and to people conducting their lives under artificial living conditions.

Artificial intelligence is the mechanical device aimed at by artificial Man in order to complete the fabrication of an artificial Nature which may even provide us with an artificial God—if the latter is needed by the designers of "AI" so that they may continue their work on the project undisturbed.

I may give another example of the anthropological change brought about by the technocratic civilization: the monetary social imbalance produced by the rupture of the human and natural rhythms caused by the industrial and neoindustrial revolutions. To put it succintly: "salary" has become "livelihood." The salary was the extra salt, otherwise difficult to find, to compensate those, mainly soldiers, who could not subsist from a self-sufficient economy (the order of the household). Today the salary has turned into "livelihood," means of living. Technology has not produced riches; it has produced means of earning money to increase the salary of those chained to the market so that they can "live" out of that salary. Technology does not multiply gadgets only; it multiplies money and makes us totally dependent on it. The traditional *otium* has been substituted with

55 Sokolowsky (1988), 45.

the *negotium*, creative leisure by labor. Man is simply another piece of the technocratic megamachine. I submit that there is a regression from *homo sapiens* to *homo technologicus*, and that this qualitative change has called for a qualitative restructuring of our existence. Here is where our earlier discourse on the destiny of Being becomes crucial, and obviously this is far more than an academic exercise.

It is easy to see that the dynamics of the three worlds are today no longer feasible; our innocence is lost. The Gods have externally withdrawn, Nature is acting out an ecological vendetta, and history has become a tool in the hands of technocrats and financial tycoons free to operate within an increasingly irrelevant political system. All this is a lopsided and rather negative description of the human predicament, but it may help to trigger a healthy reaction, which has to strike at the root of the problem and not be satisfied with merely moral or political reforms—needed as they also are. I shall concentrate on a single item as an example.

b) A Rational Animal?

Although the phrase is an inadequate translation of Aristotle, this "definition" of Man has become popular and extremely influential for contemporary human self-understanding,[56] No doubt such a definition has been qualified and complemented, but the belief in rationality as the nature of Man remains a widespread one. My criticism of the conception of Man as a rational animal is assuredly not a criticism of reason or a facile attack on rationalism. My aim is rather a defense of Man's integrity and a critique of any reductionism, including rationalism. I should also add that the following reflections deal with a cosmotheandric vision of Man and do not touch upon the modern scientific hypothesis of evolution. Whatever the temporal origins of Man may be, the biological genesis of a thing does not disclose the essence of the thing. *How* an entity has come to be following a linear temporal sequence does not disclose *what* that entity is. The fact that water comes out of hydrogen and oxygen does not reveal to us *what* water is. A second preamble draws our attention to the temptation to fall into a mere tautology. The rationality of Man has penetrated so deeply into our present western culture that we are prone to include under rationality anything that we take to be specifically human. Undoubtedly, human reason is more than strict rationalism, and more than scientific rationality or the power of rational evidence; nonetheless, no matter how broadly you stretch reason, not all essential human features can be absorbed into rationality. Even if we

56 Cf. Aristotle, *Pol.* I, 2 (1253a9).

were to identify reason with awareness, which I would reject, Man could not be reduced to mere awareness—not even to *logos* alone.

My critique is threefold:

(1) Formal

I have already alluded to the unwarranted assumption that everything is classifiable. First of all, only objects are classifiable and not the entire reality—which is not objectifiable. Second, objects may be classified only if we have a classifier and an independent or neutral criterion for classification. To begin with, Man cannot be totally identified as an object; human beings are also subjects. Ultimately, what Man *is* escapes a subject/object epistemology. To make matters worse, in this definition Man is also the classifier. To be the classifier is different from being one member of the classification. I can classify the citizens of Edinburgh according to age or income, and still be one of them. This is not a classification of the citizens but of their age or income. I can classify classifiers of human definitions according to the different criteria they use for their classifications, and I can even classify my own classification. I cannot, however, classify myself *qua* classifier. That is, I cannot make any classification in which I enter as both classified and classifier—*qua* classifier. I can classify myself—that is, place myself in a class, according to whatever criterion I use for my classification. In this case, I am classifying objects, not myself. The latter would be a class with only a single member, and serves no purpose. I cannot classify myself; the thing defined cannot form part of the definition. I am saying that there is no possible total definition of Man given by Man.

In short, to classify implies a classifier, a criterion of classification distinct from the classification itself and the actual entities to be classified. Man *qua* Man is not such an entity. Classification implies a belief in the possible formalization of real things *qua* real. Without entering into the present-day discussion concerning the nature of mathematics, it is enough to say that, at best, what we could classify is not Man but certain objectifiable aspects of the "human being." This operation of our mind presents undeniable heuristic and pragmatic advantages, but the cognition of such aspects is certainly not equivalent to knowing what Man is, which is our question.

Such a classification already has to suppose that observation of certain material features will tell us what Man *is*. Man *has* a body with features similar to those of an animal—and among these, of primates. We also notice that Man exhibits some difference from them, and we call this rationality. We then define Man as an animal with a difference. Ever since Porphyry, the

West seems to accept the idea that the specific difference constitutes the very identity of the species. We take the "specific difference" for the essence of a thing. In this case, we are saying that the specific difference (essence) of Man is his rationality. The "animality" of Man, so to speak, is specifically his rationality. The classification is not so imperfect as to affirm (by juxtaposition) that we are animals who are endowed, above and beyond our animality, with something other animals do not possess, namely, rationality. It duly recognizes that our entire animality is permeated by rationality, so that the very concept of animality differs in Man and in beast, although modern pragmatism seems to have forgotten the traditional idea of classification.

Such a conception presents an insurmountable difficulty. If the specific difference is the "specific" manner in which a genus exists, how is it that we still classify by generic commonalties (animality, etc.) even though we realize that those common features are not common—that is, they are not generic but only specific? Why do we call both a Man and a cat animals, while knowing that our "animality" is not the same? Why do we call digestion both what the cat does and what we do, although we know that the cat will never have a gastric disturbance because it cannot solve the question of whether or not platonic idealism or the resurrection of Christ is meaningful? If we affirm that my love is of the same nature as the desire of the male cat for the female, our classification turns out to be nothing but a crude juxtaposition of externally similar features. Yet this is a widespread myth. Modern medicine, for instance, seems to operate under this belief. The animality common to a cat and a Man is just an abstract and empty concept, since the "animality" of a cat, its felinity, is not the "animality" of a Man, his rationality. To classify cats and Men as animals is a merely formal and external classification which does not allow us to classify the feelings of a cat and of a Man as animal feelings. A feline feeling is not a rational feeling—unless we make of rationality a mere accidental feature of Man. In that case rationality is not the essence of a Man, but just an attribute.

This is one of the most momentous side-effects of biological evolutionism: our intelligence becomes a mere accident. In this case, what we really *are*, our essence, is sheer animality common to snakes and even amoebae. The so-called genomae are our identity. We are a particular configuration of biological genes. Freedom and responsibility are gone—and we cannot sweeten the pill with external interventions of a *Deus ex machina* or with equally extrinsic moral laws. In short, this anthropology pretends to "resolve" the problem by telling us that what Man apparently *has* defines what Man really *is*. Are human beings simply the sum of their attributes?

(2) Cultural

More important than the formal criticism alone is the particular *forma mentis* that claims to be able to give a universal definition of Man. Since it is a formal definition, it "generously" leaves open the interpretation of both animality and rationality. Nevertheless, it is a straitjacket that will prevent us from ever finding out what, or rather who we are. If the concept of water does not quench our thirst, the concept of Man does not tell us what Man *is*—unless we reduce "telling" to mere labeling (nominalism), the "is" to a formal concept, and Being to an abstract *ens commune*.

I pass over the deformation of Aristotle's famous dictum from "a living being through which the logos transits" (ζῷον λόγον ἔχων)[57] to a "logical living [being]," a "living (being endowed with) [logical] *logos*" (ζῷον λογικόν), and from there to *animal rationale*, where the *logos* has turned into *ratio* and the *ratio* has shifted its meaning from *ratio entis* to *ratio mentis*, to *ratio nominis* and finally to flatus *vocis*: from "rationality" of being to "rationality" of the mind, to rationality of the name(s), and to mere sound—eventually pointing to something.[58] The very shift of meaning is significant: *logos* is more than *ratio* and *ratio* more than *reason*.

This way of viewing the question itself betrays a particular cultural bias that cannot claim to provide us with a cross-cultural notion of what Man is. *Homo sapiens* turns into a *machina technologica*.

To begin by asking what distinguishes Man from all other beings is to use the modern "scientific" method to approach reality. This assumes that reality is an observable field in front of us, even though we have come to recognize that our observations modify that very field, something that any Man of prayer already knew. Observing human beings in front of us, we discover they are endowed with capacities similar to the animals, plus a definite capacity of reflection. The latter allows us to take cognizance of facts other beings do not. Consequently, we behave in ways "special" to the human species. This is fair enough as a method that yields unexpected and fascinating views regarding the behavior of the human species. Nevertheless, in so doing we shall never touch what Man really is; indeed, we deny ourselves access to that reality which Man is.

Let us return to ordinary language and unearth its presuppositions. It is common today, in order to overcome patriarchal usage, to eschew the english word for *anthrōpos*, which is Man, and which males have unjustly

57 Aristotle, *Pol.* I, 2 (1253a9).

58 See Panikkar, *Christophany: The Fullness of Man* (Maryknoll, N.Y.: Orbis Books, 1979).

monopolized—as I have said in the preface. Instead, we are asked to use "human being," but in avoiding the pitfall of sexism, we fall smack into dehumanization. If things are beings, to be called a "human being" is to fall prey to the classificatory mania. There are many beings; among these there is a special class, humans. Human beings are more or less special beings among all the others. We are one class among many: the human, a special class of animals—and each individual only a mere member of that class, with a specific number, be it of passport, identity card, or the particular order of three billion genes. I simply refuse to be tossed into the same basket with all other beings, losing my uniqueness, even if I am to be considered some sort of superior being in this homogeneous scale of beings, the "highest" form of animal—until, of course, we are all superseded by the *Übermensch*!

This is the form of thinking I am trying to leave behind. The genus of "beings" is understood according to the model of material "things," and "human" becomes the specific difference. This is another example of the solely spatial imagination of the objectifying scientific mentality: here is this interesting object, Man, among the many beings we are keen to investigate. I am not, however, a member of a class of beings. If we want to be called "beings" at all, we are *humane* beings, beings in which the *humanum* is not a class, but the essence of every such "being."

This method of looking for "specific differences" is so built into the modern mentality that one wonders whether there can be any other. Yet it leads directly to many basic misinterpretations of other cultures. When, for instance, many people read in ancient books of wisdom about interiorization, introspection, and even contemplation, they interpret such sayings as merely types of psychological analysis—with all the attendant dangers of narcissism, escapism, and the like. Of course, such degradations are always possible, as can often be seen in many contemporary "gurus," eastern and western. Not without reason did the authentic masters warn constantly against the dangers of psychologizing, subjectivizing, *ahamkāra*, *curiositas*, *vanitas*, and selfishness, or the need for a preparatory purification of the heart, indeed of the whole being, before embarking on the path of the spirit. The *gnostikoi* are to be carefully distinguished from the *pneumatikoi*, western sages reminded us. The aspirant to wisdom, *mukti*, or liberation needs to be initiated; indeed, despite superstitions and abuses, this was the traditional custom. There has to be a second birth (*dvija*, baptism, puberty initiations . . .) for one to be truly Man. It is misleading to consider Man only as a special type of animal.

In order to approach the anthropological question, a philosophical indic tradition, for instance, does not begin by asking what Man *is*, but rather who I *am*. We are thereby searching out our identity, not our *differentia specifica*.

I have already mentioned two methods Man has used to reach intelligibility: the way of the principle of non-contradiction, and that of the principle of identity. In order to know "What is A?," the first method uses comparisons and distinctions. Because "A is not non-A," in order to know A, we distinguish it from all possible non-A(s). We look for differences in order to locate the identity. The difference "identifies" the thing! We are ourselves, insofar as we are different, and we are all the more what we are the more distinct we are. We even aspire to be people "of distinction." In such a mental world, the sacred will be the segregated, that which is separated, set apart, the different. God is "Wholly Other," supremely transcendent, totally different.

"What is A?" The other method gives primacy to the principle of identity, and says "A is A." There is no other A than A, no better way to identify A than to find that which is so truly A that we cannot distinguish it from A. The identity of A is that which severed from A destroys A, reduces it to nil. No wonder the indic mind discovered the zero: A – A = 0—which was called śūn*ya*, an empty figure. Only if we succeed in "reaching" the total identity of a thing, its fullness, shall we be able to attain the pure vacuity by performing that subtraction.

To know is to identify myself with the thing known, not to observe it from a certain distance, no matter how conscious I may and should be of my perspectival angle (critique). In such a mental world, the sacred will be the inseparable, that which cannot be set apart, the truly identical (with itself). Brahman is the Wholly One, utterly immanent, totally identical (in itself).

What is Man? His specific difference!, the first method declares: rationality. What is Man? Be it!, the second method says, and you will know it.

If method means way, the first method is a path into analysis, the second a pilgrimage to synthesis. The first divides and distinguishes; the second unites and identifies. If the first asks what thing (Man) *is*, the second asks what thing (Man) I *am*.

It would probably be wrong to reduce any approach to Reality to a single method. Because the first method is sufficiently known and frequently applied, I shall comment only on the second. In order to know, "What *is* Man?," I also have to ask "What *are* You?," and end up by appropriately asking "What *am* I?" Or, forcing grammar: "What Man is (it)? What Man art (thou)? What Man am (I)?" The question, again, is not what *kind* of thing we are—that is, our specific difference. We are not inquiring about the difference between a Man and a beast or between you and me. We are asking about Man: "What Man is/art/am?" It should also be obvious that unless

I have attained knowledge by identification with the known, unless I have realized *aham-brahman*, my asking "What am I?" would only be asking what my ego is. To really ask what "I am" is to inquire about the *Am*, about Man, about Being—since it is the I who is asking.

It is here that the experience of Man's nature may dawn, and another dimension of the real may disclose itself to us. This dimension is not *specifically* human, and yet it is truly human. It is not the human difference, but the humane identity. It may be extended everywhere, shared by everybody and everything. It is nobody's monopoly. We are not envious. It is a dimension of reality and thus has to be wherever reality is. But it is markedly human. We share in the *humanum* in a predominant, but not exclusive way. I called it awareness, or rather selfawareness, which at least since Plato has meant God-awareness.[59] "Who knows himself knows the Lord"[60] a famous islamic saying sums it up.

That self-knowledge is knowledge of God has been the deeper understanding of the "revelation" at Delphi. We understand knowledge of God here in the double, but not dualistic, sense of the "genitive" (that which begets): the objective and the subjective. The knowledge of God is both our knowledge of God, of Reality, of (our) true Self, and knowledge of God as divine knowledge, as the "own" knowledge that the Self has.

Cutting across millennia from that "Gift of the Gods,"[61] we retain only the insight that our human knowledge, especially the knowledge of ourselves, is a sharing of divine knowledge. We are far away from the "rational animal." "What is Man that You are mindful of him!," sings a hebrew psalm.[62] To be a Man is more than to be a God, says the vedic tradition.

(3) Experiential

The third critique of the hypothesis that Man is an animal species could be called experiential. This is something difficult to convey to the scientifically trained citizen of a technocratic society who is obliged to keep up with the breakneck accelerations of modern civilization. It is the awareness of Man as bearer of the human experience. It may almost be enough to say self-consciousness, but because of the cultural atrophy I alluded to, this notion

---

59 Cf. Plato, *Alcibiades* I, 129ff. especially 133c and ff. Significantly enough, in this dialogue Socrates asks: "What is then Man?" (Τί ποτ' οὖν ὁ ἄνθρωπος).

60 "Man 'arafa nafsa-hu 'arafa rabba-hu."

61 Juvenal, XI, 27: "E coelo descendit gnosi se auton" ["From heaven came down 'know yourself'"].

62 Ps VII, 4.

may not convey the experience. If I refer to beauty or aesthetic experience, I may also fall short of what I wish to convey; if I speak of it as a mystical experience, I will probably be misunderstood. Since I am not describing any sort of elitist experience I will try to describe it in plain words. I call intellectual experience that immediate touch with the thing that makes the concept of it superfluous; we do not need then to objectify in order to know.

I cannot resist quoting from a christian mystic philosopher of the seventh century:

> The immediate experience of a thing eliminates the concept which means that thing; and the intuition of the same thing makes it impossible to objectify it when we reflect on it. I call experience the perfect knowledge which appears once we overcome the concept of the thing. Intuition is the participation in the object which appears when thinking disappears.[63]

There are moments in human life, and I am convinced they are more numerous than we think (even if we do not reflect on them too often), in which we experience to some degree the totality of Being and the universe becomes something we touch with our lives. In such moments we discover what we truly are: simply that we *are*—and not just that we do, think, have, or desire. It may take many different forms: love, pain, imminent death, waiting for a bus, reading a book, listening to music, seeing children play, praying, whatever. There are moments in which we are aware of being, of living not quite grasping the meaning of existence or deciphering the mystery of life, and yet we experience naked existence, a transparency in and outside ourselves, a "something" we do not even care to describe or get into clearer conceptual focus. We do not necessarily think of transcendence or any "religious" phenomenon. Such experiences are too down-to-earth for such reflective thoughts. There is no pretense whatsoever of revealing to us anything more than the immediately given—but in that immediacy is everything.

It may be described as the awareness of uniqueness, of the unrepeatability of moments that are not exclusively temporal, though fleeting and unobtrusive, without pretensions. It is something that illumines our dignity, that shows us we are, after all, "something" we would not like to exchange with anybody or for anything else. We may desire the beauty of one, the intelligence of another, the youth of a third, and so on, but we always seek those values for ourselves, for us. Yet we feel somehow this is not just selfishness.

63 Maximus Confessor, *Quaestiones ad Thalassium* 60 (PG 90:624 A).

I am describing this awareness in a low key and not referring to any sort of peak experiences. It happens when a mother catches her daughter looking at her in a certain way, or on a few minutes' walk somewhere, sometimes in solitude or in company. I am not claiming that time stands still, or that the entire world concentrates itself in me, or that we touch the timeless. I am only saying that all these numerous moments in our daily lives make most unlikely the belief that we are just passing and interchangeable things, simple thinking and feeling devices in the gigantic machinery of a material universe in evolution. It is beautiful to see the universe in slow motion on a videotape, but we feel somehow that something has been left out of the picture, and that this remnant is not just the cameraman or a selfish ego who fears death but, on the contrary, something in us that does not fear death and yet does not hanker for an afterlife, but simply resists believing that all we are about is just a chain of time, space, thoughts, feelings, and the like. It all defies rationality, but it is not sheer irrationality. I am not describing a feeling. The feeling may come later. I am not saying it is a profound thought. The thought may come later, or we may reconstruct it from memory. I am not talking of love. A sense of love may be an aftermath. "And I remained not-knowing / all knowledge overcoming," says a poet not necessarily describing a high mystical experience.[64]

There is something inhuman in the belief that we are only another class of animal, one of the most evolved mammals, a stupendous evolution of the primate brain, just another number in the staggering multitude of elementary particles that constitute the universe. Although we enjoy being spectators and actors in the great cosmic play, we resist being completely swallowed up. We feel that we are authors too—co-authors, to be sure—and not just actors and spectators. There is something demeaning in the belief that each of us is simply a number, even if a "different" number in the great army of beings, even if we can fall into ecstasy contemplating the complexities revealed by microscopes and telescopes. It is written that to give a glass of water may be enough to enjoy eternal life. The hunch that this may not, after all, be an exaggeration smolders somewhere in every one of us. There is infinite value in the simple act of satisfying someone's thirst.

I can make it even simpler. It is the experience of a small child discovering all of a sudden that she has a proper name, a name that is hers alone, and perhaps the vague sentiment that when she grows up this uniqueness may be rediscovered by someone who loves her. Rational and scientific explanations somehow seem to miss that point. They do not touch that human core that

64 John of the Cross, "Y me quedé no sabiendo / toda sciencia transcendiendo."

refuses to believe that the individual is only a complex conglomeration of forces, or even spiritual energies, on the way toward an omega point—whether heaven, hell, or nothingness. Neither the past, nor the future, nor even the thought of eternity is paramount here, but just that moment, or simply, my life. A being with such an experience feels instinctively that philosophy, theology, and science may be all right, but that there is still something else. *Individuum ineffabile*, as the ancients said—Man is not classifiable.

There is a traditional islamic saying that is marvelously ambivalent: "All men are asleep, they wake up only when they die." It may lead an Ibn 'Arabī to pledge for the imaginary character of the ordinary world, or a sensible preacher to instill a ray of hope in people who have dissipated their lives. It may also mean that all our rational dreams in the world are of little value for our true humanness.

At any rate, the human experience witnesses that we are endowed with reason, but that this reason is not the motor of our lives, that is, not what drives us to act and do good as well as evil actions. Reason has a veto power in our lives so that we should abstain from falling into irrationality, but it is not our driving force. The alternative is neither irrationality nor falling into a kind of sentimentality governed by "passions" of whatever kind. The alternative lies in finding out by our Selves who we are.

We spoke of self-knowledge, but the phrase may sound too academic and conceptual. We said also that who knows oneself knows God, but again this is simply not the case if knowledge means conceptual knowledge and "self" is the object of our knowledge.

I may not need to elaborate further, since it was all indirectly said in the previous chapter when we spoke of "Primacy of Life." The simple experience of Life is at loggerheads with an exclusively rational anthropology. We quoted there Saint John's Prologue saying that "the all that was made by him, in him was Life."[65] This experience of Life, the Life of all that has been made, insofar as it has been made by him, is to experience the Source and Light of reality, is to experience the Divine.

c) A Trinitarian Mystery

If Man is not an animal, although both share in corporeality, what is Man? A trinitarian mystery. This would be the interpretation of my inner experience. By saying interpretation, I am already introducing all the

---

65 According to where we put the comma the text reads differently: "Without him nothing has been made [of] what has been made. In him was life" or ". . . what has been made in him was life."

contingent parameters of reference, which I have received from my culture in spite of my efforts at making them as cross-cultural as possible.

To say that Man is a fallen angel, an incarnated spirit or a manifestation of the Divine may need important qualifications because one cannot abolish straightaway the positive contributions of an ascendant anthropology. We may descend from heaven, but nevertheless we are now here on earth and it is from here that we have to start. The rain falls from the sky, but it is from the earth that we enjoy and suffer it.

I have already tried to describe the cosmotheandric vision.[66] It qualifies both the ascendant and the descendant anthropologies. I shall insist now on a "strictly" human perspective.[67] A pebble is more than a pebble, as Gelsomina discovered in Fellini's *La strada,* and as Pascal said, Man "is more than Man": "L'homme passe infiniment l'homme."[68] This *dépassement* is neither a quantitative "more" nor, as some theologians would maintain, something that is not natural to us because it is supernatural "grace." It is certainly a gift, but such a real and constitutive gift that without this "grace" Man is not Man. Without this gift, Man does not fulfill his task, his destiny, his very being.

The relatively modern distinction between the natural and the supernatural in christian theology was the result of accepting an unfortunate anthropological hypothesis in order to avoid pantheism and to interpret the saving act of Christ as a free act of God because the mere "will" of our "fallen nature" is incapable of reaching the "supernatural" end to which Man has been "elevated." There are other ways to understand christian orthodoxy without reducing human nature to rational animality and "original sin" to a total depravity of our nature so that we are now simply brutes. The problem arose once christian theology became rigidly monotheistic neglecting its trinitarian insight, which sees in Man and in the entire cosmos a participation in the "Son" by whom all has been made.[69]

A merely rational human nature surely needs some extra grace or gift, but this "nature" does not exist—even according to christian theology. Yet this is not of our direct incumbency here.[70]

---

66 See Panikkar, *The Cosmotheandric Experience: Emerging Religious Consciousness,* ed. S. Eastham (Maryknoll, N.Y.: Orbis Books, 1993).

67 See Panikkar, *A Dwelling Place for Wisdom* (Louisville: Westminster John Knox, 1993); and Panikkar, *The Trinity and the Religious Experience of Man* (Maryknoll, N.Y.: Orbis Books, 1975).

68 Pascal, *Pensées* §258.

69 Cf. Jn I, 3.

70 Juan Martinez de Ripalda, M. de la Taille, Henri de Lubac, Baron d'Holbach, Louis Alonso Schökel, etc.

What is a Man? Ultimately we have to ask ourselves this even while keeping ourselves open to all the revelations and teachings we are aware of and believe in. I am able then to say that I embody in my limited way the awareness that I am part and parcel, an icon rather, of a Whole that we may call reality about which we cannot have any objective knowledge since we are part of it. This awareness of the real pervades all human acts, and each of us shares and shapes it in a unique way. I have shifted from the first to the third person, because "my" consciousness is not a solipsistic ego-consciousness. My consciousness embraces in the same act a *thou* and a *it*. "My" consciousness is not a grated window that bars me from the "wide" universe—provided, of course, that I do not make of that consciousness my private property, provided that I do not stick my own ego on the glass of my own window. I can experience this consciousness that transits in me, this *logos*, Heraclitus would probably say, this ātman the Upanishads would suggest. This consciousness, however, is not my own. I am not the master of the consciousness. I cannot command my consciousness to be conscious of what I want, unconscious psychological factors notwithstanding. The colors of this consciousness may be my own colors. The intellectual interpretation of reality is, no doubt, cultural and time-bound, and I am unable to see reality without my (our) particular colors. Nevertheless, I am aware that the colors make reality "visible" (intelligible) for me and that without them I would not see reality. At the same time I am aware that they are colors, accidents the already cited *Book of the XXIV Philosophers* would say.

This is to say that we can experience this consciousness as a cosmic light in which we share. Here is the locus of the once so hotly debated universal *intellectus organs,* which, inspired by Aristotle, Ibn Rushdi reintroduced among muslim and christian scholastics. Many human traditions indeed have interpreted this light as a divine light or as a something that is more than "human nature."

This is a crucial point in human self-understanding:[71] Does our knowledge of things and even of ourselves stand with the senses, or does this knowledge come from a light from above, from the "Father of [all] light"[72] as christian scholastics[73] liked to quote, or in the same spirit, from the "Brother of the Lord" as in the Prologue of John?[74]

There is no doubt that everything Man does, thinks, receives, . . . has

71 Cf. Philip Sherrard, just to cite a modern author dealing with this multisecular problem.

72 Jas I, 17.

73 Cf., e.g., Bonaventure, *Itinerarium.*

74 Jn I, 4-5.

a human touch and even a particular color, as I said. Everything has to be somewhat homogeneous, that is, assimilable to human nature, which is what medieval philosophers called the *potentia obedientialis*. Here we also have a semantic problem, which reveals a fundamental turn in the unfolding of human awareness. Does human nature belong to the nature of animals as the (for the moment) last item of an ascendant anthropology, or is Man an offspring of a nature that many cultures would call Divine Nature? In the first case we may speak of a "supernature" bestowed on Man. In the second case we may speak of an undistorted nature that Man is called upon to attain, to realize. In either case the very notion of nature is at stake. What is *natura*: something produced out of mechanical evolution (whose driving force remains mysterious), or something born from a Begetter, one of whose names is "Father"? The only difference is that in one case to be a perfect Man is to be a spotless animal, eventually with an indefinite perfection, and in the other, an offspring of an infinite Being.

In many books of western vintage regarding the so-called history of ideas, or simply "history of philosophy," it is common to speak of anthropocentric and theocentric worldviews. The beginning of the "modern age" boasted about the "copernican revolution" overcoming the anthropocentrism of the medieval ages. It was called the conquest by critical awareness. Whatever the cosmological shift of that time, anthropocentrism did not disappear. On the contrary, it increased with the marginalization of the Divinity. I insist that human knowledge is involved in all that it knows. We cannot jump over our shadows. Any reflection on what Man is cannot disentangle itself from Man's consciousness.

To be sure, this indispensable human factor does not depend on the knowledge of a single individual. An individual (psychological) element is present in all our dealings, but human consciousness is trans-individualistic. My ego is not the center of the universe, but human consciousness is the center of the universe. It is a universe that Man can measure, imagine, or think. This center is not a temporal or spatial center. Man is not at the center of the astronomical universe. Modern astronomy is almost sadistically insisting on making us feel the insignificant particle of "dust" that we humans represent in the vast astronomical world.

Modern tendencies to destabilize Man fall again on their human feet. Critical awareness tells us that we should be aware of our own pre-conditions, prejudices, perspectives, *a prioris*, and so on. But nevertheless it is we who overcome them. Materialism may be a grand construction putting Matter at the center of everything, but it is Man as a *pontifex maximus* who enthrones

Matter. Theocentrism is another, perhaps even greater, vision of reality, but it is always Man who almost condescendingly—we say critically—allows God to take his place. We even dare to "prove" his existence.

Now the cosmotheandric insight does not displace the center from Man back to God (or "ahead" to Matter). It eliminates the center altogether. This, it may be said, is still an operation of human consciousness. To which one may reply that it is an operation of consciousness, but not necessarily "human" consciousness. We do not need to assume that the fact that we *have* consciousness proves that consciousness *is* exclusively "human"—although we cannot escape the fact that it is our notion of consciousness. I can only hear the echo of transcendence as a resonance in my spirit; but I know it is an echo since I do not hear the original sound nor did I produce it. Our knowledge that we are not the center, however, does not allow us to postulate the center elsewhere.

Human history shows us that there is a strong human tendency to rely on something, which generally is seen as Source, Ground, or, as I say here, Center. This Center has been believed to be either in the Cosmos (Man as part of the world or even a *microcosmos*), or in the Divinity (Man as an emanation or creature of God or even as a *microtheos*), or finally the Center is Man himself (Man as an ultimate reality: naked *humanism*—in spite of the many acceptations of the word). Whatever the critical comments on these three attitudes, a cosmotheandric vision of Man is aware of a threefold horizon when describing Man, that Mediator between Heaven and Earth. This is the trinitarian mystery I referred to at the beginning of this subsection. In one way or another Man seems to be at the crossroads of the entire reality inasmuch as we can think, feel, and say anything about reality. We are aware of that triad no matter what degree of reality we attribute to any of those three dimensions.

Without necessarily having to subscribe to a christian interpretation, one of the most powerful symbols of Man is the figure of Jesus Christ encompassing (not to say incarnating) in himself corporeality (matter), humanity (consciousness), and divinity (infinitude). From the presentation of Pilate, *Ecce homo!* ("See the Man"),[75] to the definition of Christ in the first Council as "full Man," the christian tradition has seen in Man, represented in Christ as head of the entire "mystical body," the icon of the entire reality. The notion of Trinity allows for the necessary distinctions without lumping it all together in monism or pantheism.[76] Man shares in this trinitarian

75 Jn XIX, 5.

76 See Panikkar, *Cosmotheandric Experience.*

Mystery in fieri, becoming, imperfectly, in potency, on the way or however one might express it. The simplest and indeed shortest way of formulating this insight is that "Being is a Christophany."[77]

Coming back to our anthropology I may still say the following. Man may not *be* the center of reality, but we *stand* at the crossroads of all we are able to do, think, and say. The three realms of which we are aware meet in Man, but we are not the center—and are aware of it. We are a meeting point of those three dimensions, which we discover above, within, and below us: the spiritual, the intellectual, and the material—as we shall still see. But we must still try to sketch the third dimension of reality—stressing once again that distinctions do not mean separations.

3. Theos

To project all unsolved problems of a personal as well as intellectual nature onto a Supreme Being, whose traces may be discerned everywhere, seems to have been an age-old human necessity and a nearly universal phenomenon.

To overcome the need for an anthropomorphic God is no easy spiritual discipline. To project onto a Supreme Being our dreams, fears, and ignorance, even our love, is one of the most spontaneous human instincts. It is visible already in the child's first gropings toward the mother. On the other hand, the opposite attitude might with equal justice be compared to the reaction of the adolescent striving to get rid of parental protection—and throw away the Divine altogether.

The mature attitude I am proposing would be neither projection nor rejection (much less repression)—neither theism, nor atheism. One "thing" seems to remain as a human invariant. Whatever name we may use and whatever conception we may have, Man cannot get rid of the consciousness that there is "more" than what meets the eye and falls within the range of his intellect. One of the words for this "more," "above," "other," "Being" and the like is undoubtedly "Deity."[78] I use here the word *theos* in order to keep the expression I have been using throughout. The *theos* of the *theanthropocosmic* invariant should be not confused with its more concrete interpretation in the *cosmotheandric* intuition, as we discussed earlier.

77 See Panikkar, *Christophany.*

78 See Panikkar, "The Invisible Harmony: A Universal Theory of Religion or a Cosmic Confidence in Reality," in Leonard Swidler, ed., *Toward a Universal Theology of Religion* (Maryknoll, N.Y.: Orbis Books, 1987).

Before describing some *Features of the Divine* I shall make an important distinction and an essential epistemological observation.

a) Faith and Belief

There is a fundamental distinction to be made between faith and belief.[79]

The distinction has sometimes been blurred because the two substantives make use of the same verb "to believe," and some languages do not have even two substantives, such as german for instance.[80] This confusion has had dire consequences in the history of humanity, including religious wars, for instance. Faith belongs to human nature, so that the "infidel" is like an animal, while belief as "our" intellectual articulation of faith is susceptible to other interpretations, wrong as "we" may consider them. To fight an "unbeliever" would not then be the same as to "eliminate" an infidel.

(1) Faith

Faith is not an epistemic category; it has an ontological nature, or rather, an ontologic-pneumatic character. Faith has no object and cannot have one. It would be idolatry. An object is *ob-jectum*, something "thrown before" our thinking mind for it to assimilate. Thinking requires an object, we think something, and generally about something. The object is an object of thinking. Something we think about is not faith. Faith, if at all, requires another organ or faculty different from that which is generally called reason. It belongs to another level. The latins made a distinction, although all too often a blurred one, between *ratio* and *intellectus*, and we see similar distinctions in the greek (διάνοια, νοῦς, λόγος, and even φρόνησις, etc.) and the sanskrit (*cit, buddhi, manas, etc.*). Our language in this field is not differentiated enough and has been the cause and effect of many confusions and misunderstandings. In fact, different philosophical "systems" have different interpretations of our organs of knowledge, if "knowledge" is here the right word.

Faith is pure awareness, the awareness of a virgin field, as it were, before that awareness is articulated into different beliefs, which afterwards are sorted out by the power of thinking. We cannot and should not repress thinking. We are aware that we have faith as our fundamental human attitude. This faith is prior to thought. We are aware that we are not closed into ourselves, not finished or per-fect, that we are open to "what" we do not know. Yet we are also aware of our ignorance. Faith is this openness that makes it possible for us to receive the *datum*, that which comes to us as a given. We are aware

79 See Panikkar, *Myth, Faith, and Hermeneutics.*

80 One is obliged to say *Glauben* and *Glaubesatz*—which has other advantages.

that something is given to us, that ultimately we ourselves are a gift. We have not given our existence to ourselves. We are aware that our thinking itself is given to us not as an object of thinking but as the thinking itself. Before the *noēsis noēseōs*, the pure reflection of Aristotle, there is naked νόησις. I am not saying that we should necessarily conclude that there is a giver. This would already be the result of a thinking process that is expressed in a belief.

Faith is a constitutive dimension of our being: an openness to the more, the unknown, transcendence, the infinite: openness to the given. Faith is an awareness that we are still on the way, incomplete, unfulfilled, not yet *totally* realized, divinized, liberated, human—and, playing with words, the awareness that we are in-finite: *capax Dei*, the christian tradition used to say, capable of receiving the Divine.

(2) Belief

Man, as a conscious being, is aware of this constitutive openness and tries to understand it. Here our thinking sets in. This is the place of belief. Now this belief splits into two, and this is again a momentous distinction. The distinction is important, but its separation lethal. There is "rational belief" and "religious belief."

Rational Belief. We are aware that we have taken something as a given, something as the basis of all our thinking. We believe in our senses and we may examine afterwards how much we should rely on them. We believe in our mind and submit its findings to critique; but first we need to believe in its existence and power. These beliefs belong to what I have called rational belief, the indispensable *mythos* on which we base all our rational lives. It is *trust*. We trust we have a body, a mind, and senses, and, with all the necessary cautions, we must somehow trust in their reliability. We believe that the world exists as do other fellow beings, and we believe that it all may or may not make sense. I have called this "cosmic confidence."[81]

In this sense everybody is a believer, but what and whom do we believe? This is precisely the misleading question if disconnected from our thinking. Believing is not a respite from the process of thinking, as if to believe what we have not thought through gives us a momentary foothold on life. When thinking comes to displace belief, such belief systems do indeed collapse. The so-called scientific victories have always been followed by "strategic" retreats in the field of beliefs. This has triggered, mainly in the monotheistic cultures, the so-called conflicts between "reason and faith," while in fact these conflicts are part of the dialectic between reason and belief.

81 See Panikkar, *Invisible Harmony: Essays on Contemporary Responsibility*, ed. Harry James Cargas (Minneapolis: Fortress, 1990).

However, I am not using the word "belief" in this way. This needs to be emphasized because that is the manner in which "belief" has most often been used. This is another example of the lethal dilemma of either monism (believing is only a weakness of thinking and is progressively displaced by the latter) or dualism (believing has an independent hotline to the "supranatural" realm and thinking remains for the sublunar world). The *advaitic* insight relates the two in a mutual interindependence.

Belief is the intellectual articulation of faith, and faith corresponds to myth and to *ta mystika*. Belief is not a substitute for thinking; it is neither "soft" nor "hard" thinking. Belief is concomitant with thinking, inseparable from thinking. There is no thinking without believing: believing that it may make sense, that I may find something out, that this is a proper human activity, that thinking is an instrument of knowledge, and so on. Likewise, there is no believing without thinking: thinking that this may be the case, that not everything can be thought out, that we have assumptions, presuppositions, and the like. We believe, for instance, in the value of rational evidence, we believe that our words have a certain meaning that other people can somehow grasp. Believing is neither a respite nor a weakness of thinking. Believing is the starting point of thinking, the *mythos*, which the *logos* takes as its basis. The conflict starts when we are unaware of this and for one cause or another the *mythos* changes.

Religious Belief. When our thinking moves on a field with empirically or rationally verifiable (or falsifiable) referents, although we believe in them, we do not generally speak of beliefs. Rather, we speak of axioms, postulates, assumptions of different sorts. When our thinking moves outside that field, we generally speak of beliefs, religious beliefs. We are aware that we believe, but we cannot put this belief into ordinary concepts. Such beliefs fit into symbols that are intelligible only to those who also believe, to those who already share in the same myth, the myth that there is more than the empirical. Those sharing a myth have a set of intellectual answers that a particular religion or culture has elaborated or has received from tradition. These answers are beliefs, articles, or symbols of faith; that is, such answers comprise the intellectual articulation of faith. Beliefs are concrete cultural translations or interpretations of faith. This human mediation is inescapable. Monotheism is a belief, a legitimate, profound, and widespread belief, but not to be confused with faith. We try then to put this awareness into words. These words are the articulation of our faith, the symbols of our beliefs.

This distinction between faith and belief also addresses the legitimate query of a monotheistic believer as to whether, prior to all our disquisition from below, we should not include the fact (or at least the possibility) that it is God speaking to Man from above. Certainly, we cannot exclude, and should rather include, the fact that the human race has believed and still believes that the Divine has talked and continues to talk to Man. The recipient of the divine discourse, the receiver of God's self-disclosure is faith, not belief; otherwise, we would be anthropomorphizing the Divine in a crude way. The Divine makes itself "known" to faith, to the third eye, to a human awareness prior to the crystallization of that disclosure in belief, into particular words of a particular culture capable of being understood by the people of that culture. For centuries jews and christians believed that hebrew was God's language.

The most common and *sui generis* referent for these specific beliefs is (the) Deity. The situation most current in the West today seems to be either a more or less qualified monotheism or a practical atheism. Either there is a personal God, a Supreme Being to whom we direct our prayers, or such a thing does not exist, and *tertium non datur*. My entire effort has been to show that there is such a *madhyama*, such a *tertium*. It would be enough to throw a glance at the non-monotheistic religions, especially jainism and buddhism to convince us that such a possibility exists.

I take the word *theos* as a symbol for that Mystery about which we are aware because of our faith and which Man formulates in a variety of beliefs. This symbol is not a concept and is not within the range of human rational understanding, and yet the symbol is still in the field of the human consciousness. The *theos* is ineffable.

The Divine (*theos*) is not a thing, not an entity among other things. We cannot deal with the Divine using the same "categories" with which we deal with other beings. Either the Divine is not existent, it has no reality, or it has a *sui generis* character about which we are aware by means of another type of awareness, be it through a special faculty or whatever. Faith is the name for that awareness, which, of course, may have different degrees, and obviously may have a variety of beliefs.

b) Apophatism

Nicholas of Cusa's short jewel *De Deo abscondito* begins with the following dialogue:

> I see you prostrated most devoutly and with a profusion of tears of love, . . . who are you?
> I am christian.
> What are you adoring?

God.
Who is [the] God whom you adore?
I do not know.
How can you so earnestly adore that which you do not know?
[Precisely] because I do not know, I adore.[82]

One may call it apophatism. One might also say it is the affirmation that the Divine is not an object of knowledge, that there is another approach to the most sublime dimension of the real, by a path other than knowing.

If we are to avoid turning God into an idol, we should take seriously this quotation from Nicholas of Cusa, which simply reflects a universal tradition. God is unknowable. Its essence is unknown. We know only its existence. God is just a symbol for *that* which may be so different from all other beings that it may not even deserve the name of "being." We do not really know anything about it, except that once we accept its existence, reason assures us that this is a very reasonable attitude. The so-called proofs for the existence of God only prove that "that" which everyone already acknowledges as the Divine (*quod omnes appelant Deum,* as Saint Thomas says[83]) is a reasonable belief.

Indeed, *what* this belief believes is a reasonable belief, but it is not rational. Something is reasonable when it "makes sense," that is, when we can insert it into a coherent vision without contradiction. God may be a reasonable hypothesis, but this belief might have been the door to modern practical and theoretical atheism. A reasonable hypothesis depends on what the hypothesis tries to explain. It depends both on the "thesis" which the hypothesis "sustains" and on the (rational) power of our explanation. In this case the hypothesis ceases to be what the divine Mystery, the thesis, purports to be. God is not rational, and thus it cannot be reasonable—in spite of all our reasonable explanations. This does not mean, however, that the divine Mystery is irrational.

Irrational is a polysemic word that could include supra-, infra-, meta-, non-, trans-, a-, and ir-rational. Sometimes irrational is equated to

82 Nicholas of Cusa, *De Deo abscondito, Opera Omnia*, IV, 1-10.
Video te devotissime prostratum et fundere amoris lacrimas . . . quis es?
Christianus sum.
Quid adoras?
Deum.
Quis est deus quem adoras?
Ignoro.
Quomodo tanto serio adoras quod ignoras?
Quia ignoro, adoro.

83 Thomas Aquinas, *Summ. Theol.*, I.

with nonlogical. Here I take it strictly to mean something that does not "necessarily" abide by the principle of non-contradiction. By saying "not abiding" I do not mean negating it. God lies outside the jurisdiction of that principle, as it were. Whatever this may be, it is a historical fact that practically all cultures speak about the "unspeakable," think about the "unthinkable," and speculate about the "unknown." What does it mean? Is it plain contradiction? Irrationalism?

Three main attitudes have been present in human history. I limit myself to the problem of Deity, although one could easily apply these attitudes to other fields.

1. The *irrational*. Speech, thought, and all intellectual operations when applied to the Deity lose their meanings so that it is indifferent whatever we say, think, or speculate, since affirmation and negation do not apply or have the same value. Apophatism does not claim to have a special meaning in the kataphatic field. It is equally synonymous with kataphatism. The talk about God is sheer irrationality. It has no sense, not necessarily because there is no such referent, but because any talk about it is meaningless.
2. *Dialectical*. We may affirm and negate anything about the Deity, because its reality can best be described by paradoxically affirming and negating any attribute or predicate. We cannot say that the statements about the Deity lie in between, because this would be plain contradiction, since between A and non-A (by an identical A) there is no in between by definition. Most modern western talk about God has been such. Once the mythical awareness has been "demythologized" and the parmenidean principle reigns supreme, God can only be approached dialectically: is and is-not.
3. *Dialogical*. The Deity is not "intended" by any concept because it lies "above" or "outside" any logical concept. No *logos* alone can speak of or understand God. Silence may come closer, but silence may mean absence of noise or absence of the word. The very expression "absence" already implies a relation to something else. The silence of any word about God does not mean a total lack of "intelligibility." It means that an isolated *logos* cannot "word" the Divine. It requires the *pneuma*, the spirit in an *advaitic* "union" with the word. "Dialogical" means here "dia-logical," *dia ton logon*, "through the *logos*," leading the spirit by the impulse of the same spirit and together with it. This is in accordance with what has been previously said about faith, which has no object.

I have not used the traditional word apophatism in the usual sense of "negation." This translation betrays already the dialectical interpretation of "negative philosophy"—or theology. Ἀποφασία (*apophasia*) may mean negation by a common understanding of the contrary of ἀπόφημι (*apophēmi*), "to speak," "to declare." The same word, however, also comes from ἀπόφαίνω (*apophainō*) which means "to show forth," "to make known, reveal, and even proclaim, affirm."[84] Apophatism does not need to mean negation (of the word). It can also mean absence (of speech), silence.

The dialectical trend has often interpreted the apophatic approach to God, such as the *neti neti* of the Upanishads or the negation of christian (apophatic) theology as one of negating all our possible affirmations. There is also, however, what could be called the mystical trend which does not make an enigma of God but rather acknowledges a positive awareness of the Divine such as the eyes of the heart of the christian tradition.[85] Indeed, we cannot have a conceptual and rational knowledge of God; all our categories need to be transcended. Yet we are aware of that limit to rational knowledge.

By way of example, I may turn to the christian catholic tradition as formulated in the Fourth Lateran Council. After having affirmed that there is "one supreme thing, incomprehensible and unspeakable"[86] the formulation goes on to say that "one cannot stress any similarity between the Creator and the creature without stressing a bigger difference."[87] How could one say this if there were not an awareness of it? Nobody has *seen* God says christian Scripture,[88] but he who loves "knows God."[89] Our concern is not christian exegesis, but to point out that there is an awareness of the Divine which allows us to "speak" of it when our *logos* is not severed from the *pneuma*. Reason is not our only faculty that puts us into a conscious contact with reality.

We cannot conceptually understand the *theos*, but we are aware of this third dimension of the cosmotheandric experience and may be able to describe it. The same christian texts just quoted add that "God is Love,"[90]

84 In fact, ἀπό may mean *from* [which] (away), but also *from* [which] (by which).

85 Cf. Eph II, 18; etc.

86 Denzinger Schönmetzer, 804: ". . . una quaedam summa res est, incomprehensibilis quidem et ineffabilis. . . ."

87 Denzinger Schönmetzer, 806: "inter creatorem et creaturam non potest similitudo notari, quin inter eos maior sit dissimilitudo notanda."

88 Cf. Jn I, 18; I Jn IV, 14; etc.

89 Cf. I Jn IV, 7.

90 Cf. I Jn IV, 8, 16.

truth,[91] justice,[92] and the like. We could not say this if the word (not the concept) were not a revelation of silence. The traditional "Presence of God" of many schools of spirituality eastern and western is the awareness of an Absence—which would be a plain contradiction in conceptual thinking.

c) Features of the Divine

What has been just said allows us to "speak" of the Divine presenting some features of the Divine without contradiction. By features I do not mean a conceptual trait but words that symbolize some aspects of that Mystery. I would characterize the symbol of the Divine as having three features: *emptiness, freedom, infinitude.* I do not mention attributes like goodness, truth, power, mercy, and especially love, because all these attributes are to be found in Man, as well as in Nature. I am not trying to detect features exclusive to the Divine. The *communicatio idiomatum* ("circumincessional interpenetration"), which christian theology developed as a feature of the Trinity, is to be seen as a feature of the whole of reality. Nonetheless, there are some aspects that more properly belong to the Divine, and I have chosen these three. As opposed to the analytical bent of contemporary thought, which tends to isolate concepts as much as things in order to clarify or to master them, the holistic vision of any entity will also show these same three features that characterize the divine dimension of that thing.

We cannot enter now into the philosophical garden these three words represent lest we get fascinated by and entangled in it. We shall only survey those flowers from afar, as if smelling their fragrance from the Olympian seat of the Deity because we are going to speak about these divine attributes, not about the awe-inspiring problematic of those notions. In fact these three words were concealed in Pandora's box when she, the "greek Eve," descended on Earth. Emptiness, Freedom, and Infinitude are three terribly destabilizing threats to the human mind, but they walk freely in the heavens of the Gods. Without a reference to the third dimension (the Divine), these three words, like Pandora's "gifts," produce havoc in the human world. This is more than a flight of speech; it is a way of saying that when we exclude the Divine from our philosophical considerations we inextricably fall into quagmires.

(1) Nothingness

In practically all human traditions there is an apophatic school. There appears to be a consensus in recognizing that talk about the Divine is *sui generis*, that our affirmations are only remote approximations, and that

91 Cf. Jn XIV, 17; XV, 26; I Jn V, 6; etc.

92 Cf. I Jn II, 29; etc.

negative statements come closer to the divine Mystery than kataphatic approaches. The Divine is far outside the concerns of today's prevalent human experience. This was not so in other epochs when the Deity was an immediately present factor in all human dealings. The experience of the divine has not always been so distant or hidden as it is today in our dominant culture. This is not necessarily a negative statement, since all too often the predominance of the divine dimension of reality has led to theocratic dictatorship, especially when severed from the other dimensions. Ontonomy is not heteronomy.

We have already indicated three approaches to the Divine: the radical negation of the Divine (nihilism), the negation of all our affirmations (dialectical approach), and the awareness of an empty "space" where the Divine dwells (adualistic experience).

Radical nihilism will simply say that it is all nonsense and, when faced with the historical fact of the presence of the Divine in human consciousness, will interpret it as hallucinations, errors, psychological projections, or simply the illusions of undeveloped minds. What this position does not see is that, although God may be an illusion, it can be a very powerful illusion and therefore real in human history. Certainly, we should not identify God with a substance, but radical nihilism will assert that the name of the Deity in all its possible acceptations does not have any meaning different from what falls directly or indirectly under our senses or our reason. Anything else is nonexistent.

I maintain that such a nihilistic position is untenable within the very premises on which it stands. What changes is the notion of that alleged Deity. I see a "providential" role in such an attitude, to speak paradoxically and with a certain non-offensive irony. Nihilism purifies the idea of the Divine from anthropomorphic and even superstitious images, but pure radical nihilism cannot exist, because the roots are always invisible and the awareness of the invisible already fills the invisible with some meaning. We cannot deny, however, that with or without contradiction such a position is defended by some people.

The dialectical approach, as already intimated, will defend that we come to the idea of Deity by negating all the possible affirmations in the field of our experience, and that this is the most appropriate manner to arrive at Nothingness. God would then be that Nothingness which is obtained by negating Being or the symbol of all that is as entity and even as Being. The very act of negating, however, implies both that which is negated and its negation. God would then be Being and Non-being, *sat* and *asat*.[93]

93 Cf. RV X, 129, 1; TU II, 7; etc.

Man surmises that reality is not suffocated by being what it is, that reality overflows from all sides into something that neither was nor is, nor perhaps shall be. It seems as if Non-being were the most loyal companion of Being. God is not to be stifled by the straitjacket of logical necessity or the strictness of the *is*. Dialectical awareness is never satisfied with acknowledging our ignorance. "Negations are truer than affirmations,"[94] wrote a roman cardinal involved in politics, giving voice to an entire tradition before and after him in the East and in the West. It is this tradition that has led to the dialectical approach to the divine Mystery.

Nothingness suggests a dialectical opposition to Being, and in a certain sense is tied to the negation of Being, which may be a dialectical necessity.

Nothingness suggests the absence of "thingness," which in turn hints at no word, no cause. The french *rien* (from latin *res*), *néant* (*nec entem* or *nec gentem*), and the german *Nichts*, the genitive of *nicht* (*ni-wiht* [*Wicht*], "nobeing," "no-thing," "no demon")—all seem to point to a negation of any entity and ultimately of Being. I shall not discuss the merits or demerits of such an approach, but only signal one aspect of such a position: the strenuous effort not to forfeit rationality. It is reason denying itself that makes room for the Divine. We need to remember again the inherent correlation of everything with everything else. Divine Nothingness is totally nonsensical isolated in itself. We can only make sense of it in relationship with all the "rest" (Being), because at the same time we are aware that there "is" a "more," not as an addition, but as an unknown "factor" to which no "is" applies. It is not the consciousness of a "more," a kind of transcendence, but rather an awareness that it is not, that it is nothing of what we think or say. I have already criticized the notion of God as "Wholly Other"; here we have the homeomorphic equivalent to that insight. The Divine "is" Nothingness,... it cannot be inscribed in any field of our experience. It "is" outside, it "is" not—although the negation is still something, as Bergson's acute criticism convincingly proved.

The *advaitic* approach is the third mentioned attitude. We may designate it with *emptiness* (*śūnyatā*). This word seems to be free from having to assert itself by the negation of Being. *Emptiness* suggests leisure, being vacant, which is also related to *vacuity*. If I had to choose a word, I would say *ākāśaḥ*, usually translated as "space" in the sense of the platonic χώρα, as that symbol which provides "space" for all beings "to live, move and have their being"[95]—for Being to be.[96]

94 Nicholas of Cusa, *De Docta ignorantia* I, 26.

95 Cf. Acts XVII, 28.

96 See Panikkar, "There Is No Outer Without Inner Space," in K. Vatsayayan, ed., *Concepts of Space: Ancient and Modern* (Delhi: Abhinav, 1991), 7-38.

There is a chinese saying that seems pertinent: "The Void is not of the nature of a black abyss / or a bottomless pit. / Rather is its nature vast and expansive / as space itself."[97] Here is the proper locus of *śūnyatā,* or emptiness. There is an important distinction to be made between nothingness and emptiness, between nihility and *śūnyatā* in the words of Keiji Nishitani.[98] We shall not, however, enter into this complex problematic and shall simplify it to the utmost. Suffice to say that this third approach is not dialectic. Emptiness is not *negation* of Being. It is rather *absence* of Being, perhaps closer to the spanish and portuguese *nada* (from *non-natus*) in the sense of "prior" to birth, "prior" to existence, even to Being rather than their negation.

Here may lie a fundamental difference between dialectical and *advaitic* thinking. Not to put the burden on the eastern reflection of *śūnyatā*, I may base this reflection on the spanish and portuguese symbol of *nada*, which incidentally may serve to stress the cultural differences between the iberian peninsula and the rest of europe. Our human spirit is aware of Being. In this very awareness we are conscious that we could not be aware of anything if we were not dimly aware of its limits. This applies also to Being. What do we call this limit? One name is Nothingness as Non-Being; another name is *nada* as absence of Being. Nothingness implies the dialectical approach; *nada* entails the *advaitic* approach.

Nothingness is the negation of Being, it "is" Non-Being. If Non-Being makes any sense, it means that our mind has an astounding power over Being since it can even negate it. Dialectics is the triumph over Parmenides: Being is and Non-Being is not. Our mind reigns sovereign. It can negate Being. Being has to obey the dictates of the mind: thinking commands Being. Even God has to abide by the "sacred principle of non-contradiction" (Thomas Aquinas), which is the exigency of the mind, even if *we* make mind a divine attribute. We cannot convert the *sic* into a *non*, but we are aware of the *sic et non* and can encompass them dialectically—a feat of the Mind indeed. On the other hand, *nada* as the absence of Being is not its negation but the awareness of the emptiness surrounding Being, as it were, the awareness of an Absence that only makes sense together with the Presence of whose absence we are aware. There is not the one without the other; they are not separable, and yet we detect their distinction. This is *advaita*. We are aware of the polarity "prior" to the understanding of the poles.

---

97 Quoted by S. C. Malik in "Dimensionsless Space as Eternal Silence" in K. Vatsyayan, ed., *Concepts of Space: Ancient and Modern* (Delhi: Abhinav, 1991).

98 Cf. Nishitani, *Religion and Nothingness,* (1982), 76-118 and *passim*.

It should be unnecessary to repeat that this overwhelming aspect of the Divine belongs to the whole of reality, so that one can discover this Emptiness in any nook and cranny. Here is where symbolic awareness has its place. To recognize anything as a symbol always includes an "empty space," which is the unbridgeable difference between the symbol and the "symbolized," which is only open to us in the symbol as symbol while at the same time we are aware that there is a difference. What we call reality is only the symbol of it-self, which "is" itself only in the symbol.[99]

In sum, one of the features of everything, and which we especially attribute to the Deity, is this aspect of Emptiness which amounts to recognizing that Being is not bound by logical structures. This brings us to our second feature.

(2) Freedom

There is little space for the experience of freedom in a mechanically organized "universe." There is at most a niche for exceptions to the laws of nature, uncertainty relations, probabilistic laws, or the anthropomorphic concept of chance. Freedom is much more than this. Similarly, there is also little space for freedom in a rigidly rational world, since the alternative is irrationality and chaos. God is not free to make 2 + 3 = 6, or to manipulate events so that the existing Cologne Cathedral was never constructed. Obviously such an absolute Lord over the universe has never existed. If *per impossibilem* 2 + 3 = 6, this would mean that the nature of the old 5 has been transmuted into 6. The principle of non-contradiction at the basis of logical thinking is already presupposed in the hypothesis that God could make 5 and non-5 be the same. There would not be non-5 if the principle of non-contradiction were not employed, precisely in order to set up the non-5 as contradictory to the 5. This is not the question. The question is our notion of freedom, which is much more than indeterminism and has nothing to do with irrationality or chaos.

Freedom is a positive, not a negative, value. The prevalent notion of freedom in our culture is commonly interpreted as something that escapes our control, the control of our mind. When we cannot determine, calculate, predict—in a word, control—a process, we speak of degrees of freedom. The only point of reference is our mind. Nonetheless, freedom defies anthropocentrism; it is the locus of the Divine.

Freedom is the freedom of Being. It means the absence of extrinsic constraint, and amounts to self-constitution. To say "Being is free" is a

99 See Panikkar, *Myth, Faith, and Hermeneutics*, 6-8.

tautology. There is nothing "outside" Being that could constrain it. The just-mentioned pure Emptiness is precisely that which "allows" Being to be free. I said selfconstitution, not self-determination, in order to avoid introducing an anthropomorphic idea of a will acting in view of an extrinsic end. As the jewish Scripture declares: "The Lord has made all things for himself."[100]

A current picture of God is of One who determines, once and for all, the laws of Nature, after which Nature is obliged to stay in those orbits—with the believer's proviso, of course, that the Author of the laws may make exceptions to them if this be the divine pleasure. Neither that God nor those laws exist in a cosmotheandric vision. Laws have no ultimate validity, they are only physical inventions, a way for human reason to tame (or as we say, understand) *ta onta*, beings. Being has no law, reality has no laws. Unless of course, we take law to be the Way in which Being manifests itself, grows, expands, lives, is—without any prior or predetermined prescription, which amounts to no law at all.

Being is free. This follows from the notion of freedom as the absence of external coercion. But what coercion? A being is free when it acts, does, and ultimately is according to what it is. Freedom is the expression of the identity of a being with itself. An identity, however, that is not *semper idem*, always the same (over against a static horizon), but *identidem,* over and over ("again") in the brand-new novelty of the *creatio continua*. As was said before, the identity of Being is its Becoming.

A free being, acts, does, thinks, and moves insofar as it *is*. It is as it is. Each being is ontonomically related to the whole in a relationship of interindependence. Either a heteronomic intrusion or an autonomous rebellion (reaction) tarnishes the freedom of a being. If God were only external to us, if the ethical order were only an external norm, Man would not be free; rather, he would be obliged to follow an external injunction.

It would be sheer caricature to picture God as a wise and powerful controller or guardian of the order of Nature, who takes care that the "rights" of every being are respected. This order does not exist, nor does this God. Freedom is menaced by thought; it cannot even be conceptualized, since it would thereby lose (its) freedom. Freedom is the flow of beings when they are in flux, when they interact in authentic spontaneity.

100 Prv XVI, 4; other versions say: "for its own end," "his own end," or "its own purpose"; the latin tradition reads "Universa propter semetipsum operatus est Dominus" and understood it in the sense that God acts not for the sake of each thing but for himself, although it comes to be the same, since the "will of the Creator" is what creates the nature of the creature—speaking within that worldview.

One could object that we are assuming that reality is order, the final seat of truth, and that by letting the real be, Being will really reach its "fullness." The manner of thinking of this objection, however, turns into a vicious circle. If we speak of reality, we have no criterion "outside" it to judge what is good or evil, true or false, the "ought" or even the "is." Therefore, either freedom is tautological with Being (a qualified tautology)—"Being is Being," each being is, insofar as it is being—or else we superimpose upon Being a world of ideas that will supposedly let us know what the right order of things ought to be.

If we assert, however, that freedom is tautological with Being, this implies that we are aware of it, and thus that we make a distinction between Being and consciousness, between Being and Thinking. Consciousness, however, is bound to the Being of which it is conscious; it is not free. Reality is free; it is not bound by anything—not even by an immutable Itself that is bound to "go on" being itself ("always" in the same manner).

If we assume an Ought over Being, we find here the same dominion of Thought over Being that has predominated in western culture since Parmenides. It assumes Thinking above God and Being. We speak then of a Law of Being superior to Being. The Mind is erected as the supreme Arbiter; God as the supreme Idea: Idealism.

It should be clear that the freedom I am speaking of has nothing to do with "libertinism," with whimsical behavior and selfish actions. On the contrary, only one who knows oneself—which amounts to knowing God, as I have said—is the truly free Man. It is no accident that purity of heart is required by practically all religious traditions as a indispensable condition for entering upon the (religious) path of liberation. It is the experience of freedom that reveals to us what we call the divine dimension of the real.

(3) Infinitude

The Divine is the seat of *Infinitude*. Reality is unlimited; its very limits would belong to reality. Our human intellect is constantly confronted with limits and enigmas; both the infinitely great and the infinitely small overwhelm us. Even the most ordinary things present an opaque side, always a plus, an *incognitum*, a possible surprise, something irreducible to our knowledge and, perhaps, to any knowledge.

I might present this infinity in another light. Things, everything up to and including the universe as a whole, seem to be un-finished, non-finite, not achieved, still on the way, in the making, dynamic, open, still capable of change, growth, explosion, or annihilation. Everything in our human experience, whether sensual, intellectual, or mystical, presents itself as moving, im-perfect, in-finite. We may, of course, attribute this imperfection to ourselves. Or we might consider it the reflection of an infinite God. Or we may begin to experience it as belonging to the nature of reality itself, both distributively and comprehensively.

The dimension of infinity lies in the things themselves, but since this dimension is infinite, it is also outside the things themselves. If something has no limits, it defies immanence and transcendence as separate and separable notions. If something has no boundaries, there is no proper inside and outside. Such divisions are only heuristic devices.

I deliberately said that the Divine is the seat of infinity. This seat is seated everywhere, just as in that famous hermetic definition of God cited earlier, as the sphere whose center is everywhere and circumference nowhere.[101] It is not a throne installed somewhere. It is a seat because it sits in the core of everything, and yet it transcends everything. We cannot locate it. This infinity is real, it is not fictitious. The Divine as infinitude is not imaginary, although it is not imaginable.

There is more. If the infinitude is infinite, it is not just seated in the womb of every being but transcends all things as well. There is a seat of infinity "standing" (not only seated) above everything, defying any and all limitation. Infinity stands on high, as it were, as a symbol for the Divine. This infinitude which inheres in every being is not an epistemic feature. Every being is infinite not because our mind cannot attain its limits but because in itself it has no limits. The "self" of the "itself" is infinite. This infinitude is not spatial or temporal—although our language betrays us. The *creatio continua* to which we made reference may offer perhaps the least inadequate background.

A famous upanishadic verse is almost a condensation of what I have been saying: "Brahman is truth [being], knowledge, infinity hidden in the cave [of heart] and in the highest heaven."[102]

The reader may have surmised that this threefold aspect of the *theos* as emptiness, freedom, and infinitude corresponds to the trinitarian paradigm of Father or Source, Son or Logos, and Spirit or Love irreducible to the Logos (without contra-dicting it—how could she?). I refrain from commenting except to say that the trinitarian *perichōrēsis* is not a mechanical or automatic connection but a real inter-in-dependence.

101 Cf. *Liber XXIV philosophorum*, II.

102 TU II, 1: "satyam jñnam anantam brahma . . . nihitani guhāyām parame uyoman."

VII
The Divine Dimension

If the Divine is reduced to only a dimension of reality, is not spiritual life destroyed? Is not all religion eliminated? Is not this alleged remedy for past abuses and superstitions worse than the malady? I am dealing, of course, with our human approach to that mystery which no name can ultimately name. These legitimate concerns would not be met if the character of this Chapter VII were as theoretical as the previous one. Here I shall speak from a more experiential perspective and try to show that this entire study is not as iconoclastic as some fragments may appear. Criticisms of the present status quo are all the more easy because the present state of affairs is, by and large, far from being satisfying to say the least. I am not defending that the "age of religion" is over or that the "positivistic era" is in. What should be clear by now is, on the contrary, that the coming times present us with a single alternative to a human catastrophe of planetary proportions, and that this alternative is not some return to a golden or gilded past, but rather entails a creative transformation of human culture taking into account the human experience of the last six millennia in its positive and negative aspects.

My first remark is intended to dispel a possible misunderstanding; the second qualifies the word "dimension"; and the third explains that a cosmotheandric attitude does not destroy religion but purifies it from many past excrescences and fosters an authentic fulfillment of all that Man is. I have been trying to rescue the Divine from being considered a separate entity, a supreme and absolutized Being floating somewhere above and beyond the rest of reality. This criticism of pure transcendence or absolute otherness in no way undermines the independence of the Divine, or its dignity and reality. The Divine is not to be confused with everything (pantheism). The divine is different from the world, but cannot be isolated from things in the same way as we would isolate a physical or a chemical substance from a complex compound. Neither of the following two metaphors is adequate. The first says that the gold of a mineral magma (a physical compound) may be difficult to extract, just as God may be difficult to find, but once we have discriminated the gold (God) from the "impure" ore (world) we have it. The second says that the hydrogen of an acid (a chemical compound) may be even more difficult to isolate, but once we isolate the hydrogen, the acid disappears. God is everywhere as hydrogen is in every acid and the acids are all different and some not even acidulous—the "good" God is in every creature and yet not every creature is necessarily good. The hydrogen can exist alone; the acid cannot subsist without hydrogen. Popular hinduism has a simpler metaphor that also falls short. The divine, the hindus say, is like the sound [ah] needed for the pronunciation of every consonant: *ka, ga, ca, . . . ma, na,* and so on. It is in every consonant giving a different sound to each and also outside all them. Yet we should not forget that none of these three similes forms an exact analogy. We already said that the indwelling of the Divine is not like a parasite on things; the Divine *is* in the inmost of things, and yet it is also outside things, as the *Gītā* affirms and as christian theology (among many others) confirms. This God "outside" things, however, is not conceptualizable. If it were possible to conceptually isolate God, this would be the beginning of idolatry. God is everywhere, as even a hebrew psalm reminds us, along with innumerable texts of most traditions.[1] We cannot isolate God from anything without destroying that thing. We cannot "reduce" the Divine to any concept, nor to any entity, not even a Supreme Entity. Perhaps an easy way to understand this point is to say that we cannot locate the Divine without destroying it. We cannot deal with the Divine with merely "terrestrial" categories as if among the many entities there were a Supreme One at the top of the pyramid. Defending our position does not destroy spiritual or religious life. On the contrary, our approach saves such spiritual life from falling into idolatry, which so many religions brand as the capital sin.

Our second question expresses concern about degrading the Divine to nothing but a "dimension." It is important, therefore, to qualify that word as well. I am not reducing the Divine to a contingent "accident" by metaphorically calling it a dimension. A dimension is such because it is a dimension of the whole. Without the whole, there is no dimension, but the dimension is real and without it the whole collapses. Perhaps dimension is not the best word for what I am trying to convey, but I have found no better. The word "ingredient," which our chemical and grammatical similes may suggest, may be a still less adequate name. When saying dimension, I am not referring to what God may be in "Himself," assuming that this expression is legitimate, but only to our human approach to that mystery. To affirm,

1 Ps CXXXIX

as some classical philosophies maintain, that we may know God through or from his works, correct as it may be, seems to me unsatisfactory, since such an affirmation implies both a deductive mental operation (from effect to cause, for instance) and a too-extrinsic "idea" of the Divine (*vestigia Dei*). The difficulty in truly understanding what I am going to say lies in our encrusted idea of a purely transcendent and substantial God as a supreme Entity.

Di-mension should in this context be brought together with *im-mensus*, and with its own greek prefix δıά. The root is obviously *mē*, from which derive *manas, mens*, and mind, as well as *metron, metrus*, measure, and even moon (because it served to measure sublunar time). The di-mension is im-mense because it has "gone through" (δıά) all the measurable planes of reality. The dimension measures but is not measured. Only the mind can measure. When I affirm that the Divine is a dimension of reality, I am indicating that we have to transcend the mental, to go *through*—to pierce the mind, as it were, in order to arrive at the divine Mystery. A dimension is something that does not primarily measure (in this case reality) but allows reality to be approached by the mind when this latter "goes through," surpasses itself (*meta-noia*, beyond the mental). It is in this sense that the Divine is a dimension constitutive of the real. It is through its dimensions that we have access to reality. The divine Mystery, I maintain, is a constitutive dimension of reality.

Third, I argue that a cosmotheandric experience not only does *not* destroy spirituality and religion but purifies them. After all, what counts is not spirituality or religion but Man. The cosmotheandric vision does not destroy the *humanum* but, to the contrary, (re)discovers the infinite dignity of Man and of human life. It gives a renewed meaning to those two words (spirituality and religion) and makes possible a religiousness and a spiritual life for all those who have become painfully aware of the shortcomings of practically all theisms and institutionalizations of religion. It brings Man back from exile in a sociological and institutionalized milieu to his real home—which is reality. An alienated God surely alienates Man. Religion is a human, but also a cosmic affair. Christians as well as others could add that an incarnated God incarnates Man into reality and rescues human beings from being second-class citizens in the order of reality. The key to this unity and distinction, as I have already said, is the radical Trinity.

In short, the cosmotheandric experience "re-links" Man with the Divine as well as with the Cosmos and with his Humanity in a thematically stronger way than up to now. I understand religion (*religare*) as that which *re-links* Man with himself (body, soul, and spirit), with society (the meta-political factor), the earth (ecosophy), and with the Divine (worship) in the nondualistic and interindependent way I have explained.

In saying "dimension," I want to emphasize the interconnection of reality as a whole, which is neither a monolithic One (it has dimensions) nor a plural Many (the dimensions are not the thing). Such dimensions are linked in a total trinitarian *perichōrēsis*.

Modern ideologies have almost succeeded in severing these distinct dimensions of reality. I do not call them aspects so as not to fall again into monism (or docetism in christian theology). We need distinctions, and the distinctions are real but to absolutize or substantialize them would amount to succumbing to an insurmountable dualism or to splitting reality into incompatible fragments (to make a whole). Without the power of abstraction, modern science would not be possible; regional ontologies have to be taken in all their consistency (the world of a lawyer, for instance, is not that of a theoretical physicist). The divine Mystery, however, is not the proper subject matter of any regional ontology—or even, perhaps, of any general ontology either. Yet the modern mentality considers the theologian, and even the mystic, as just one more specialist who may have an experience of a separate Divinity, thereby turning the Divine into a special field of expertise.

The cosmotheandric experience is radically different. It is indeed holistic, but with a qualifying character: it is ever unfinished, and in this sense is an open, never closed experience. Whole does not mean complete, but undivided. The cosmotheandric experience puts us in touch with the real in an undivided manner. Precisely because the real is also divine, this contact with reality is never finished, never completely "touched" or wholly embraced. In a sense, it is the experience of (the dimension of) ineffability, infinity, numinosity, freedom . . . inherent in everything.

The positive changes in understanding the role and nature of religions have been enormous during the last fifty years. Here is just one example that I happened to witness. Shortly before his death in 1959, the italian historian of religions Raffaele Pettazzoni scribbled some comments and annotations while reading the books of Mircea Eliade. Some years before, Pettazzoni had also written short articles on the nature of religion, culture, and religious freedom, as well as on the relation between christianity and other religions. He defended religious freedom, which before the european war was still unacceptable in catholic Italy—the argument being that other religions are false and error has no rights. He further interpreted the christian sacraments without isolating them from those of other religions. The bold steps of Pettazzoni appear both sad and encouraging today. Sad, because they exhibit the narrow conscience of so many christians who condemned such ecumenical openness; encouraging, because Pettazzoni's ideas are acceptable today to most christian theologians. The crisis of modernity within roman catholicism could offer us another telling lesson. Something similar may happen, I expect, regarding many ideas of this book. It appears more and more obvious that true religiousness is not bound to theisms, even for a newly emerging christian consciousness as it begins to (re)discover its trinitarian inspiration after over fifteen centuries of forgetfulness out of fear of breaking with its inherited jewish monotheism.

One does not need to agree with the philosophies of Feuerbach, Marx, Nietzsche, Freud, Russell, or Sartre in order to acknowledge how right they were in castigating traditional religions for generating various forms of alienation, pathology, and disbelief. I am neither humanizing nor materializing God, nor divinizing or materializing Man, nor divinizing or anthropomorphizing Matter. I am simply stressing their constitutive link, which does not blur distinctions or create separations.

A further general observation should be made in this connection. The expression "divine dimension" should not be identified with a monotheistic God. The experience of a divine dimension does not automatically make ourselves divine. We may recognize the "finger of God" somewhere (as the expression goes) and yet we may still be far from being transformed by that recognition. Hell, in the traditional sense of the word, reveals a divine dimension, as Dante's powerful stanza beautifully and shockingly sings:

> Fecemi la divina potestate
> *La summa giustizia,*
> *Il primo amore*
>
> Justice moved my great maker; God eternal
> Wrought me: the power, and the unsearchably
> High wisdom, and the primal love supernal.[2]

* * *

In describing some ways to approach the divine dimension of reality I offer a triadic division so as to keep a trinitarian and traditional pattern. No need to insist again that because everything is connected with everything, the different parts of this study are intrinsically related to each other. This chapter underscores the more personal (subjective) approach to "that" which may be called the Deity. The following pattern can be found across the globe and throughout history, although, of course, one culture in one particular period may emphasize one aspect more than another, and different people themselves may resonate with one approach more than another. I

2 Dante, *Inferno,* Canto III.

remark, however, that the three approaches are complementary more than supplementary so that a mature approach to the Divine requires a cultivation of the three. Our symbols are the Father, the Son, and the Spirit, or in other words, Emptiness, Knowledge, and Love; although we could equally say, mysticism, intellectuality, and action, or again *bhakti, jñāna,* and *karma*.

Plainly speaking, our discovery of the Divine is through neither the "flight of the alone to the Alone,"[3] nor the "way of the mind toward God" (*itinerarium mentis in Deum*)[4], nor the rational path of logical demonstration nor that of speculative knowledge (*jñāna*), nor through the door of the sentiments, cosmic feeling, or whatever. To be sure, all these are gates to the Divine, but the human pilgrimage is a real pilgrimage involving our whole body, our entire intellect, and our undivided spirit—mindful of the greatest of the injunctions of the judeochristian tradition to love God with all our strength, mind, and heart.[5]

I shall start with one of the most important dimensions of the Divine, and one of the most neglected approaches to it.

A. Silence

When all things were in quiet silence . . . thy powerful word, . . . leapt down from heaven. [6]

I begin by saying that silence is not just a human virtue or a physical absence of noise; silence is a kind of "property" of Being prior to Being. I have not said an attribute as if it were some character that we attribute to it—although, obviously, our intellect discovers silence in Being. Rather, it is that Being and Silence cannot be severed from each other, although we can make distinctions. Ultimately, silence is the symbol for the absence of everything, especially sound, although this is only a metaphor leading or rather throwing us toward "the other shore" (another metaphor) of Being. No wonder that a civilization of noise (of all types) finds it difficult to discover the divine dimension of reality. God cannot be experienced in words or even by thinking or doing, but just by silence, that is, by being, because Being is silent. An egyptian prayer says:

---

3 Plotinus, *Enneads* VI, 9, 11: φυγὴ μόνου πρὸς μόνον. These last words of Plotinus should be related to his similar statement in V, 1, 6 that prayer is an aspiration of an alone toward the Alone (μόνου πρὸς μόνον).

4 Title of the famous work of Saint Bonaventure.

5 Cf. Dt VI, 5; Mt XXII, 37; etc.

6 Wis XVIII, 14.

> Thou sweet Well for those who suffer thirst in the desert;
> you are closed to those who speak,
> but open to those who are silent.[7]

And in a more metaphysical vein an Upanishad runs:

> Neither by the word nor by the mind
> nor by the sight can he [Brahman] ever be reached.
> How, then, can he be realized
> except by exclaiming, "He is."[8]

This seems to be a recurrent insight of most human traditions: Pythagoras, the orphic rites, Mithra, and obviously Kung-Fu-ze, Lao-Tzu, Plotinus, Proclus, Dionysius the Aeropagite, Augustine, and the mystics and philosophers of all times up to Kierkegaard, Wittgenstein, Heidegger, and many others could be quoted here.

"Be still and know [σχολάσατε καὶ γνῶτε, says the Septuagint] that I am God," according to the hebrew psalm.[9] Only in stillness we can know God.

There is a more profound reason to begin this chapter with Silence besides the sociological remark on our loud civilization: if we are able to perceive the silent dimension of things we shall be able to become aware of the Divine, not only because the Divine is hidden in Silence, but because the Divine is Silence, as far as the *is* can be applied to the Deity. A great part of the old and modern dialectic between Being and Non-being, including the discourses about *śūnyatā, asat,* and *kenōsis*, emptiness, Non-being, and annihilation, could find a more convincing and less dialectical approach if we were to recognize silence as a central metaphysical category. Silence is not the negation of Being; it is not Non-Being. Silence, as we said, is the absence of everything, and ultimately an absence of Being. It is anterior, prior to Being. Silence in this sense of absence of Being is closer to the spanish *nada* (*non-natum,* un-born) than to the english "nothingness." In a word, to

7 Apud ERE, XI, 512, in a slightly modified form.

8 KathU, 12 completed by VI, 13. I abstain from the exegetical question whether the faith of the *guru* is here hinted at. Cf. also MaitU VI, 19, and many other passages on the ineffability and unthinkability of *brahman*. Another Upanishad mentions the "practice of silence" as the way to discover the ātman (CU VIII, 5, 2).

9 Ps. XLVI, 11. "Lasset und erkennt, daß ich Gott bin," translates M. Buber. The Vulgate says (under XLV (XLVI)) 11: "Desistite et agnoscite me Deum"—eliminating the multisecular mystical tradition, which did comment on *vacare Deo* while most translations report the text given above, the Revised English Bible writes: "Let be then; learn that I am God." Cf. also Ps LXV, 1.

become aware of the silence of Being and the silence of the word is close to discovering the divine dimension.[10]

Our concern here is not so much directed to the "nature" of that divine Mystery as to our human ways of opening up to that experience. Let us only recall that the traditional religious exercise of the "presence of God" is not an act of our mind distracting us from giving due attention to the activity at hand, but rather is a discovery of the divine dimension in the act in which we are engaged. God's transcendence is only visible in his immanence.

I have repeatedly mentioned the "third eye" as the seat for this vision. But I have also insisted on the inseparability of the three eyes. The experience of the Divine is not a specialty of the third eye. It is the vision of our entire being when we do not discard any of our "faculties." This is why I begin with the testimony of our bodily senses.

* * *

Here we stumble on a formidable intercultural and even cultural difficulty: we do not have adequate words, nor do the same words have the same meaning in different cultural backgrounds, let alone when we resort to translations. "Mind" is not the same as *Geist*, nor the same as *esprit*, let alone as *budhi* or *manas*, *cit* or *kokoro*. "Body" is not identical with *Leib*, *sarīsa,* or *karada.* The examples could be multiplied endlessly. These may be "homeomorphic equivalents," but the equivalence is not biunivocal. *Koto* in japanese may mean "matter" as well as "word," and even "mind."

Sanskrit *sarīsa* is more than "body," just as "mind" is not the same as the japanese *shin*, nor does "will" have an exact equivalence in many oriental languages. There is a profound insight in the assertion that the translated Koran is not the Qur'an. In our tripartite division, we would like to utilize those three words (body, mind, and will) as widely as possible, and yet we recognize that multiculturalism is an impossibility.

1. *The Body*

The contemporary mentality begins to rediscover the importance of the body in all human and even spiritual affairs. We not only have a body; we are body. The body is not an accident to Man—nor a mere instrument, let alone an obstacle. It should be a sign of concern, and a challenge to conversion for christians that precisely a religion that has the resurrection of the body, of the flesh actually, at the center of its faith, has neglected the importance of

10 See Panikkar, *The Silence of God: The Answer of the Buddha* (Maryknoll, N.Y.: Orbis Books, 1989).

matter beginning with our bodily selves. The âtman is also body, say more than one Upanishad, and we need only to mention yoga to remind us of the importance of the body for the "highest" meditation techniques. Modern civilization has mistaken the "guard of the senses" (*indriyesu guttadvāro*) for the curbing of the body and is swinging now to the opposite reaction. The traditional guarding of the senses in buddhism and christianity, for instance, is not exerting control by the mind to keep the body under subjection, as was perceived by gnosticisms, manichaeisms, and puritanisms of all sorts following a certain greek anthropology. Rather, the christian and buddhist practices were the purification of the in-sight of the senses so that they may be able to perceive the divine dimension in all sensible objects.[11] In spite of all abuses and exaggerations of inhuman "ascetisms," the underlying idea is that we become what we know. To know *brahman* is to become *brahman* is a classical phrase. If we pay undue attention, by excess, to the body, we become just bodily matter. If we pay undue attention, by neglect, to the body, we become dehumanized. "Who wants to play at being an angel becomes a beast," said Pascal.[12]

In sum, the body is of paramount importance. It is in and through the body that we live. For this reason the custody of the senses is as important as the cultivation of the mind and the attention to the spirit. I repeat, we are body. This sentence needs a double negative qualification: we are not only body (we are more than just bodily beings) and we are not only *our* body (we are also body which does not belong to us as private property). The body that we are (like our reason) has boundaries of which we are not always conscious. The body is not always totally visible to our optical makeup. The simile with reason may sound exaggerated to a modern mentality, and it may need qualifications, but overall it stands. My reason is my reason as my body is my body, and yet the boundaries of my reason are not limited to my individuality. There is something like an *intellectus agens* (without entering now into that momentous question). There is also something like a *corpus mysticum*, a *buddhakāya*, a karmic body and the like. There is something undeniable in the principle of individuation located in our bodies (*materia signata quantitates*), but there is something disturbing in reducing our individuality (and worse, our personality) to a body count. Our body consciousness is more than individualistic consciousness. It entails also the awareness of a divine dimension. The body is often silent, but the silence of the body is obtained not by the subjugation of the body but by

---

11 Cf. the *Sâmaññaphalasutta (Digha Nikâya, II)* for buddhism and Mt V, 28; XV, 2, 17-20; etc. for christianity.

12 Pascal, *Pensées*: "Qui veut faire l'ange, fait la bête."

the enhancement of the body, discovering its divine dimension, the ātman, the "temple of the spirit," the risen body, and the like. The *tantra*, that is, the sacramental vision of the world, could be adduced here as representing similar insights, notwithstanding all abuses and caricatures.

I may go so far as to say that without the silence of the body we shall not be able to reach the silence of the mind, and without it the vision of our third eye remains blurred. I am obliged to insert here an only apparent side reflection that in fact belongs to the very kernel of our subject. Modern science began with the fascinating calculus of the acceleration of material bodies, although they were confusingly called "bodies." The acceleration of mass is a natural phenomenon, and although we can also artificially accelerate our bodies up to a certain extent, once we overstep our limits we harm ourselves. Our minds, like our bodies, have their own rhythms, and rhythm is a harmony between stillness and movement. To break the rhythm amounts to inflicting a wound on the silent factor of any being. It is a sin in the classic and etymological sense. To live with intensity does not mean to accelerate life. Machines can speed up our doings, but they cannot accelerate our being. Or, to put it rather pointedly, there is no epistemology without somatology.

There is a proliferating literature in our times about techniques that try to cultivate and recover the eurhythmia of our lives, beginning with our bodies. Obviously, as techniques they may be more or less useful or harmful, but the problem lies deeper. The body is not an object; the body is a subject. Modern medicine learns slowly (too slowly) that it has to overcome its dualistic stance of cartesian origins. I am not saying: "leave the body alone; it knows." I am saying: "let's not kill the body by severing it from the soul and the spirit."

There is no contradiction in what has been said so far concerning silence as absence and the silence of the body. Absence means the lack of all that does not appertain to that being. The body loves to work in silence and even more to move rhythmically. If our stomach makes its presence felt, then it is not functioning properly. Spontaneity is the feature of a sound body. We should let the body be, and only when something goes wrong may we interfere. The silence of the body does not mean neglect. It means precisely the utmost respect to its spontaneity, listening to the body only to untie its bondages. The freedom of the body is its ontonomic relation with the whole of our being. For this, we need to educate the mind.

The buddhist tradition speaks of the *ṣaḍ-āyatana* or six senses probably following the upanishadic expression of the same idea. In some passages there is a rather popular way of describing the ambition of each the six senses to be the most important of all and to work independently. Besides the fact that *prāṇa* (the vital breath, life) wins the contest, the lesson is that all are interconnected and that they are inseparable.[13] Ultimately the six senses (five in some cases) are also connected with all our being so as to form a unity, but we should not now pursue this rather interesting topic.[14] Suffice to say that the awareness of our complex being discloses to us the harmony between all "components" of our beings, not only among themselves, but also with the entire universe.

I must renounce elaboration of the different bodies of Man, of the world as the body of God and of the corporate (from *corpus*, "body") nature of humanity. It suffices to hint at the human experience of the sacredness of the body as temple of the Divine. This would be the place for mentioning the importance of the immobility of the body as an introduction to the silence of the mind. Here we can only emphasize the central point that the silence of the body is based on trust in ourselves, and ultimately on a cosmic confidence in reality.

To sum up: the experience and the cultivation of our bodily silence are an introduction to the experience of the divine dimension of reality. No wonder that our noisy and accelerated civilization makes this experience exceedingly difficult.

2. *The Mind*

Instead of commenting on the silence of thought, fashionable and important as it is, I prefer to introduce the topic with a beautiful sufi story:

> "What makes one wise?" asked the disciple. "Wisdom," replied the Master.
> "What is wisdom?" was retorted.
> "It is simply the ability to recognize," said the Master. "To recognize what?" the disciple asked.
> "Spiritual wisdom," the Master answered, "is the power to recognize the butterfly in a caterpillar, the eagle in an egg, the saint in the sinner."

Only a silent mind is capable of this recognizing power. Already Plotinus

---

13 Cf. BU VI, 1, 1ff.; CU VU, 1ff., etc. The senses are breath, speech, eyes, ears, mind, and generative organs.

14 Cf. KausU III, 1ff. Besides those six, life, intelligence, body, feet, and hands are also mentioned.

spoke of a "silent *logos*" (λόγος σιωπῶν)[15] and of silence as a condition to know ourselves.[16] I wonder whether it is only the silent *logos* that allows us to understand without judging. From a certain disincarnated viewpoint it is easy to idealize the sinner and to pretend to love a nonexistent repentant sinner. But the sinner is sinner, not an already repentant sinner. Ultimately, the metaphysical problem of evil is lurking behind the scene. If one has to love the sinner while hating sin, as it is often said, we turn sin into an abstraction and evil into a banality or, if not, into an irreconcilable enemy that we have to fight up to the bitter end; that is, we fall into the dualism of accepting a Principle of Evil (notwithstanding the eschatological consolation), and then we cannot recognize the saint in the sinner. We would then turn wisdom into "wishful thinking." Or, we could then say that wisdom is to expect the sinner to convert, and we could even pray for the sinner, but that would not be to recognize the saint in the sinner.

The butterfly may potentially be in the caterpillar, and the eagle's egg, if fecundated, may become an eaglet. However, if human freedom means anything, the sinner may not turn into a saint for a saint is surely not a sinner. The recognition of the saint in the sinner is not a passive phenomenological verification—because the saint *is* not the sinner. The sinner may forever remain a sinner. The sinner cannot be at once severed from and united with the absolutely simple Supreme and sinless Being. An active transformation of the sinner, conversion is the watchword here, is required. This is possible because wisdom and ignorance, sinner and sin, the Divine, the Human, and the Material are, after all, distinct but not separated. There is a *perichōrēsis* running through the entire reality. The real "God" is still with the sinner—as the cosmotheandric insight would say, but to think of something as possible is not to recognize the possible as actual.

A common answer to the presence of those latent possibilities of the caterpillar, the egg, and the sinner is to aver that in potency they are butterfly, eagle, and saint. Ever since Aristotle we are prone to distinguish pure potency from the real potency of actually becoming what a being may be capable of becoming. That Man is *capax Dei*, capable of becoming divinized, was a traditional christian *theologoumenon*. For a typical asian mentality the problem is similar. The sinner "is" a saint (the *jīva* "is" *brahman*, the Man in bondage "is"— already—liberated), only that the sinner does not know it. However, if to know is to reach the known, and ultimately to become it, then the passage from ignorance (*avidyā*) to knowledge (*jñāna*) is a real

15 Plotinus, *Enneads* III, 3, 5, 9; III, 8, 6, 11-17.

16 Ibid., V, 3, 3, 17; V, 3, 10, 46.

transit and it can fail, at least for the time being (if we reckon with successive reincarnations). At any rate, the ignorant *can* become knowers. It is not impossible. On the other hand, whether a stone has the same "potency" is a highly disputed issue. *De potentia Dei absoluta* was the debated scholastic question impinging on the nature both of beings and of God, as to whether God had power over the logically impossible. We have already mentioned this question in our previous chapter.

I do not want to pursue further this fascinating problematic, but simply place it in relation to our question. The caterpillar is-not the butterfly. The caterpillar is-not an angel. The caterpillar, however, can become a butterfly, but it cannot become an angel, much less a square circle. The material dimension of reality makes the first case possible. Physical caterpillars in fact become butterflies. Our intellect, however, could think of a caterpillar becoming an angel. It is thinkable. The physical caterpillar inasmuch as it is an entity could by a seconddegree miracle become an angel. It would no longer be a caterpillar; but a butterfly is also no longer a caterpillar. Yet the third case, that of becoming a square circle, is not thinkable by the mind because the square circle is self-contradictory. Here is the locus of the divine dimension about which we should keep silent and say nothing. We cannot say anything because our whole answer moves within the field of intelligibility, and intelligibility is governed by the principle of non-contradiction, and here we trespass it. This is the crux of the entire problem. Saint Thomas says it in a lapidary way: "Nothing falls under God's omnipotence that implies contradiction,"[17] and he gives the reason: "Those things which imply contradiction do not come within the scope of divine omnipotence because they cannot have the reason of possible things."[18]

Thomas had previously written that it could be a vicious circle were we to say that God can do all things that are possible to his power. The difference here is that he assumes the objectivity of the principle of non-contradiction so that being and non-being (at the same time) are incompatible with the notion of an absolutely possible thing so that we should not say that God cannot do it, but that it cannot be because, as Thomas goes on to say in the

17 Thomas Aquinas, *Summ. Theol.* I, q. 25, a. 4: "Sub omnipotentia Dei non cadit aliquid quod contradictionem implicat."

18 The longer text reads: "Quaecumque igitur contradictionem non implicat, sub illis possibilibus continentur, respectu quorum dicitur Deus omnipotens." (Therefore, everything that does not imply a contradiction belongs to those possible things in respect of which God is said to be omnipotent.") *Summ. Theol.* I, q. 25, a. 3: "Ea vero quae contradicitonem implicant, sub divina omnipotentia non continentur: quia non possunt habere possibilium rationem."

same place, the thing has not the nature of a feasible or possible thing (*Sed quia non potest habere rationem factibilis neque possibilis*). I cannot see how this is not also a vicious circle, all the more important because allowing that God can do only those things which the finite power of the creature cannot do reduces the Divine to a Supreme Mind governed by the same principles as our human intellect. We encounter here again the shadow of Parmenides: What cannot be thought cannot be. A contra-diction is something that goes "against" any "diction," and we assume that what cannot be said (with meaning), cannot be thought, which is fair enough; but from here we jump to what cannot be. This is logical monotheism. God is the supreme Intelligence and warrants the truthfulness of our reason when properly used. What we think true must be the case, must be true in its own field. Otherwise thinking loses all meaning. The *cogito ergo sum* of René Descartes offers us a paradigmatic example of the need of our infallible Intellect to act as the final foundation of our reason.

We think that a square circle is not possible because it is not thinkable, because we cannot think of it as a logical or ontological possibility. We affirm that such a case is impossible because it is unthinkable, but we would trespass against the power of our mind if we were to affirm that the unthinkable does not "exist"—understanding existence here just as the charter of being real. We are bound to say it *cannot* be thought and we cannot speak about it, unless our language is to lose all its justification: we cannot think the unthinkable as possible—as possible to think. Possibility is a logical category. Thus, we are forced to affirm that it is impossible for our mind to think it as possible. Nonetheless, we cannot say anything about its reality unless we equate thinking and being—as I have already indicated. We enter into utter silence—into emptiness.

This is not irrationalism. It would be sheer irrationalism if we were to claim that a square circle is possible for a divine Intellect. Possibly it is not—if we are to respect the meaning of words. It is not possible if possibility means non-contradiction. It would be irrationalism to deny the power of reason and undermine the very possibility of our thinking. A square circle is meaningless, unthinkable, and the unthinkable is impossible to any thinking. Our mind stops here and it has to stop here.

Our spirit, however, seems to not want to stop here. If it were to proceed further on that intellectual plane, that would again be irrationalism, and I may not hesitate to say hubris, arrogance, pride. Ἀναγκὴ στῆναι! the greeks said, "We have to stop!" Yet nothing forbids a jump into another dimension—provided we keep in mind, yes in mind, that the springboard from where we jump is an intellectual board. I feel obliged to insist repeatedly that the third eye is third, neither first nor second. We remain at the threshold. To stop proceeding further does not mean to deny the intellect since it is the intellect itself that knows that the door is closed. It means that the intellect has stumbled on an obstacle that it cannot overcome or intellectually assimilate. It appears irrational and we are bound to say it. On the level of the intellect a square circle is undoubtedly irrational. A square circle is not intelligible and therefore not a concept.

I have given a classical geometrical example which, on the one hand, manifests its irrationality but, on the other hand, obliges us to make an unnecessary jump. One could argue that the geometrical example, besides being a contradiction is non-sensical. We call a circle a particular geometrical figure and a square another one. We should respect language if we use it. The proper contradiction would be "a circle and a non-circle." The indic classical example may be more pertinent here: "the son of a barren woman," is not non-sensical, but it is equally a contradiction: "the child of a woman that can have no child." Such a concept is certainly not a concept. It is self-contradictory. Such a son *cannot* be thought of; it is a thinking impossibility; but does it exist? Our thinking has to answer in the negative. That "son" either is not the son of the barren mother or the woman has ceased to be barren if she has given birth to a child.

Here, I said, is the locus of the Divine. On any other field we simply do not need such a transgression of logical thinking. If our language has to have some meaning "the son of a barren woman" is an unintelligible phrase and therefore cannot raise any claim to an intelligible truth. Yet talk about the Divine, if we do not reduce it to talk about another entity, does not need to follow our logical rules.

We may easily agree that the "son of a barren woman" does not exist, because we ourselves have set the meaning of the contradictory words used in the expression. The quoted sufi story, however, seems to say that wisdom is the recognition of the impossible just as the archangel Gabriel seems to have said to the Virgin Mary.[19] In that ultimate realm are there laws? Are there exigencies binding on the same Supreme Intelligence? I am tempted to say that wisdom consists in recognizing freedom as an ultimate structure of the universe and therefore that things and events are not bound to follow fixed and supreme laws. To reach that experience is to "touch" the divine dimension. This is *jñāna* and seems to be a universal testimony of history. It would be unwise and against the humanness of our ancestors to label

19 Lk I, 34-35.

as arrogance, folly, or superstition all those witnesses who "speak" of μὴ ὂν ἀγνωσία, *docta ignorantia*, cloud of unknowing, *mu*, *wu*, *śūnyatā*, *asat*, and similar expressions. We should not be uncritical toward the past, but neither should we be too proud about the present because of some scientific achievements. At any rate, we may transcend reason, but we cannot and should not renounce rationality. Here again the Trinity rescues us from sheer irrationalism. Our rational mind has a divine (ultimate) foundation indeed. This ground is the divine *Logos*, but the *logos* is not All. The *logos* is neither the Father nor the Spirit and yet is inseparable from them. We shall come back to this relationship without offering a chapter of explicit christian theology. This book may be taken as a "confession" of christian faith, but not as an exposition of christian beliefs.

In a word, there "is" an invisible, ineffable, mysterious, dark dimension of the Divine, where the light of the intellect does not enter—it would be proper to say that the intellect "cannot" enter. The "can" belongs already to the field of logical possibility, and we remain simply at the threshold. The door is closed or the chamber is utterly dark, but we are aware of the door and the existence of darkness. We can only see God from behind, says the judeo-christian-muslim tradition. What is this awareness?—if this is the right word. How do we dare to speak about what we do not know? We do not know it, but we know our ignorance of it. What is this *docta ignorantia*?—this ἀγνωσία, "cloud of unknowing," *sad-asad-anirvacanīya*? "Nobody has seen God"[20] is a common statement in most cultures of the world. Or as a psalm cryptically expresses it: "and made darkness his hidden place."[21]

This repeats a common trait of the hindu vision, which says that the Gods love darkness and dwell in obscurity, a reminder of the heraclitean dictum that Nature loves to hide herself.[22] As a christian genius of the fourth century (Evagrius Ponticus) declared, "Blessed are those who have attained infinite ignorance." We have already seen an upanishadic text,[23] and could also call on the witnesses of the entire tradition of negative or apophatic theology, East and West, North and South: "Those who know do not talk, those who talk do not know."[24]

20 Jn I, 18.

21 Ps XVIII, 11 (LXX XVII, 12): καὶ ἔθετο σκότος ἀποκρυφὴν αὐτοῦ, which the Vulgata translates: "et posuit tenebras latibulum suum."

22 Heraclitus, *Fragm.* 123.

23 KenU II, 3.

24 *Tao Te Ching*, 56, a famous passage that should be related to the last chapter of the book: "those who know are not learned, the learned do not know" (81).

What do they mean, all these assertions of mystics, thinkers, poets, and common folk of practically all human traditions since the dawn of humanity? Tellingly enough, even if the most visible, not to say vociferous, part of contemporary civilization seems to have hidden it from the "mass media," those witnesses of the mystical are as alive today as ever.

I sum up all these citations pointing toward the ineffable with a universal and simple symbol: Silence. I take at random one contemporary catalan poet who seems to be inspired by the plotinian phrase "all happens in the silence":[25]

> In the beginning, there was only Silence.
> God was not yet born.
> God was born of Silence
> to create an ever flowing life,
> an endless throbbing.
>
> The universe emerged
> and it was blue.
> . . . .
> Beyond the fear,
> beyond the voices,
> in the heart of the world,
> only Silence lives.[26]

Silence does not speak. If anything, it allows us to listen—if our heart is pure. Silence does not think. It may facilitate thinking, if other conditions are met. Silence is prior to language. It is from silence that language emerges, as Irenaeus affirmed when writing on the Trinity (*De Trinitate*). This sentence has been repeated time and again (because it springs from the same intuition) from Proclus[27] up to Heidegger, who sounds as if he were echoing the oriental classics: "the essence of language has its origin in silence."[28]

---

25 Plotinus, *Enneads* III, 8, 5.

26 Translated by Carles Duarte i Montserat. The original reads: "Al principi només era el silenci. / Déu no havia nascut. / Déu nasqué del silence / per crear-hi una vida incessant, / un batec sense fi. / En sorgí l'univers / i era blau . . . / Més enllà de la por, / més enllà de la veu, / al cor del món, / només viu el silenci."

27 Proclus, *De philosophia chaldaica* IV, 18: τὴν τὸν λόγον ὑποστήσασαν εἶναι σιγήν ("Silence, from which the logos comes, is the foundation of the logos").

28 I may quote the entire sentence: "Das höchste denkerische Sagen besteht darin, im Sagen das eigentlich zu Sagende nicht einfach zu verschweigen, sondern es so zu sagen, daß es im Nichtsagen genannt wird: das Sagen des Denkens ist nicht Erschweigen. Dieses Sagen entspricht auch dem tiefsten Wesen der Sprache, die ihren Ursprung im Schweigen hat," Heidegger, *Nietzsche* (Pfullingen: Neske, 1961). The same idea is repeated in many of his

Silence is a symbol for the divine dimension. It is void of sound, empty of content, absent of Being. It is a symbol, not a concept. It symbolizes the Origin, the Beginning, Emptiness, the Abyss, the *Ungrund*, the Father, *fons et origo totius Trinitatis* as ancient Councils loved to repeat. In addition, silence cannot be experienced. It may be compared to the awareness of absence, which is only the concomitant consciousness of a remembered presence, or of an expected manifestation.[29]

In sum, the experience of the Divine is not the experience of an object, of something separate, or "other." It may be an experience of a positive "absence," of an "other dimension" that gives shape and reality to the empirical and intelligible dimensions, but it is not the experience of an "absolute" other. The experience of the Divine is an experience not of an isolated aspect but of the entire reality in one of its dimensions—an experience that is aware of a glimmering, more or less intense, that shines through the empirical and the noetical. It may be brought together with the experience of *ākāśa*, that "space" which makes everything possible and, as I said earlier, bestows (gift, grace, creation . . .) reality on the other two constituents of the real.

The silence of the mind is obviously not the thought of thoughtlessness, nor is it the repression of thought. *Samadhi, satori*, illumination, awakening, *ekstasis*, thoughtless meditation, and so on, are all words pointing to that experience, but that experience is not reserved to the highest peaks attained by "mystical" people. This experience is the authentic human experience. Man reaches his complete identity when he discovers himself as an icon of the whole reality—an image of the entire humanity, a *microcosmos* and a *microtheos*. This is the experience of being the *puruṣa*. This is self-knowledge, knowledge of the Self—and not self-identity of a rational animal. This is a most traditional idea in both East and West: to know oneself is to know God (and all things); to know the self is to realize the *tat tvam asi* (that thou art).

The "silence of the mind" in this context is a subjective genitive. It does not mean a silent mind, a mind that keeps silence. The silence of the mind, which discovers the divine dimension in all things, is a mind that is itself silence; that is to say, it is absent in the experience of the Divine. The mind is not there; only pure awareness is present. Mind is an ambiguous word; here it stands for rational comprehension and not for the simple intellectual

---

other works. Cf. "Die Sprache selbst hat ihren Ursprung im Schweigen" (*Collected Works*, vol. XXXIX, 218).

29 See Panikkar, "The Silence of the Word: Non-dualistic Polarities," *Cross-Currents* 24 (1974), 154-71; see also Panikkar, *The Trinity and the Religious Experience of Man: Icon, Person, Mystery* (Maryknoll, N.Y.: Orbis Books, 1975).

apprehension of pure awareness. I have been saying time and again that the experience of the Divine is beyond conceptual knowledge.

The silence of the mind in this sense is the absence of the mind which has drawn into itself, as it were, and has made a place for a pure awareness that does not judge and is simply aware of the things or the events in their "naked" fact of being here. God lets the sun rise on the evil and the good alike and the rain to fall on the just and unjust as well, to borrow a christian expression.[30] This is the innocent sight, and it is written that the pure of heart shall see God.[31]

3. *The Will*

We are exploring the ways to approach the divine dimension present in all things as their "inmost self,"[32] or as the Qur'an says, God is closer to us than our jugular vein. Once we become aware of the reality of the Divine, nothing seems more natural than to strive toward it, or at least to discover its traces. Here again we encounter the same paradox: the will to better know and realize this dimension is a necessary condition and at the same time an insurmountable obstacle to approaching that selfsame dimension.

There is a fundamental distinction to be made between *desire* and *aspiration*. Both could be ascribed to a movement of the will, but while *desire* elicits the will from the outside presenting a "desirable" to be reached, *aspiration* moves the will from the inside as a result of an inspiration coming from the indwelling spirit of Man. Yet both are free acts of will—this human "faculty" which is one of the pillars of western civilization. Without the movement of our will to approach the divine dimension we do not direct our steps to the divine light inherent in every being and we let life slip under our feet. The divine dimension is present in every being. God is everywhere by his substance (essence), presence, and power says the scholastic tradition,[33] but if our will does not direct our attention to this presence, the divine passes us by or we do not discover the true nature of that presence.

---

30 Cf. Mt V, 45.

31 Cf. Mt V, 8.

32 SU VI, 11.

33 Thomas Aquinas, *Summ. Theol.* I q. VIII, art. 3. Thomas refers to the text of Gregory the Great, who says, "Deus communi modo est in omnibus rebus praessentia, potentia et substantia: tamen familiare modo dicitur esse in aliquibus per gratiam" (cf. Cant. V, 17) ("In the ordinary way God exists by his presence, power, and substance, but he is said to exist in some things in a more familiar way by grace").

We have to dispose ourselves to look for that hidden divine presence in everything, but as soon as we set our will to such a search, that very will becomes the highest obstacle. We need also here the silence of the will. The reason should be clear. We can only search for something that we more or less surmise. *Nil volitum quin praecognitum*,[34] said the ancients, "nothing is willed if it is not previously known." Although hidden as an ordinary aspect, the divine dimension of things is not a superficial quality, as when we detect something to be heavy, agreeable, or even beautiful or good. The divine dimension is certainly the most intimate dimension of everything, but it is divine, mysterious, ineffable, infinite. Our will therefore is an obstacle because it can only will an object of the will, but the Divine is not an object. It has to be the Divine itself which attracts us to it. The aristotelian God, unmoved and immobile in itself, moves us ὡς ἐρώμενον, as allowing us to love him, "as being loved." "Nobody goes to the Father if the Father does not draw him to himself."[35] A more feminine attitude is needed. We shall know as we are known.[36] The initiative has not come from us. The desire for *nirvāṇa* needs to be overcome in order to reach it. Buddhism, Śaiva Sidhanta, and christianity among many other religious traditions are explicit on this point: Grace is needed. Our will alone is countereffective. It would be a mere projection of ourselves, as the telling story of Huang Po describes: Huang Po, desiring the supreme experience, goes into solitude to listen to the divine voice. His loud prayers are answered, since he hears that voice from the top of the mountain. He climbs it, but on the top is only silence. He descends disappointed and perseveres in his laments and prayers. He hears again the voice and, panting, climbs the mountain for a second time. On the top there is no voice to be heard. He goes down another time, and the same voice is audible. The scene is repeated innumerable times until the last time, when he no longer longs for the divine revelation and keeps quiet. He realizes then that the voice he heard from the mountain was his own echo.

The will helps and does not help. Without the frustrating climbing he may have not discovered his own impotence, but all that we want and can wish is only a projection of ourselves. The crux of the story is whether, after having realized the illusion, there is still a truly divine voice calling not from the mountaintop but from the depth of every being. There is no proof that this voice is real; and there cannot be any proof unless we make the *probans* stronger and more credible than the *probandum*. We said already that silence

34 Common axiom of the Middle Ages quoted, for example, by Saint Thomas, *Summ. Theol. sup*. q. 51, 1; and by al-Farabi.

35 Jn XIV, 6.

36 1 Cor XII, 12.

is silence and has no hidden agenda. It neither proves nor speaks. "He who has ears to hear, hears."[37]

The silence of the will is one of the most important aspects of spiritual life. We cannot pretend anything. If quietism lies on the one extreme, activism and willpower lie on the other. We cannot silence our will at the command of our will. If we discover ourselves desiring something, no amount of good reasons or willing efforts will eliminate the desire. We may curb our wishful actions to get to the desired goal, but the desire is not eliminated by not yielding to it. What purifies or pollutes us does not come from the exterior, but from the heart.[38]

What allows us to "hear" is not our acoustic system or our rational acuteness, but again our heart as the symbol of our entire being. The ideogram of the japanese word for listening, *kiku*, has three graphic elements: ears, eyes, and heart. If our heart is closed, our ears are of no avail.

It is one of the most central aspects, I said, and one of the most difficult to discover in an age of patriarchal dominance, which, after dethroning Reason, has given the royal scepter to the Will. I have already mentioned the experience of grace, that all is a gratuitous gift bestowed upon us beginning with ourselves. This does not trigger a fatalistic mood; this elicits in us an attitude of thankfulness, and consequently of joy, which is another human reality that does not depend on the will. To ascribe thankfulness and joy to "humors" or to "genes" is simply a category mistake, besides coming close to falling into a vicious circle. Already William James asked whether I cry because I am sad or I am sad because I cry. The fact that an injection of adrenaline makes me tense does not prove that I am tense (facing a danger, for instance) because I discharged adrenaline. In short, the experience of grace has nothing to do with the "law" of causality. It has to do with the world of freedom.

Causal thinking has its place in a mechanistic universe. In a human world the motivation of an action is not necessarily its cause—unless we enlarge the concept of cause to any process of correlation. I would submit, parenthetically, that the disrepute of astrology as a science as well as of the so-called law of *karma* is based on a causal interpretation of these understandings. Even the buddhist *pratītyasamutpāda* or dependent origination is not synonymous with the modern law of causality, all degrees of freedom and indeterminacy principles notwithstanding.

37 Mk IV, 9.

38 Mt XV, 18.

The experience of grace, namely, that the most important events and facts of our lives are a gift, does not mean that the law of causality is not valid in its field, nor does it mean that the discovery of something as a gift already points to a giver to whom I owe thankfulness. The human attitude of thankfulness is not necessarily linked with a monotheistic God who is the ultimate Cause of everything. In short, the silence of the will opens us to the discovery of the divine dimension of reality by helping us to realize that not all depends on will and that there is a dimension of freedom in every being.

B. Logos

All our talk about Silence proves that Silence is never alone. It is primordial, but not alone. Silence needs the word in order to be silence. It is the actual absence of the word. The relation is mutual. In truth, silence is always the silence of the word—in the sense of the subjective genitive. Reality has an element of Silence. This Silence belongs to the divine dimension, but it needs the word or rather it is not without the word. Silence has no expression, or rather it begets the expression, the Language, the Word, the Logos.

It should be clear by now that this holistic approach distinguishes but does not separate. Saying *logos*, we do not reduce it to an exclusively immaterial or intellectual phenomenon. *Logos* also entails corporality: sound, voice, gesture, dance, and all our senses. Language, for instance, is an expression of our body as well as a movement of our soul. The *logos* in all its authentic aspects discloses a divine dimension. That famous definition of Man as a rational animal is a distorted version of what Aristotle said and meant: "a living (being) through which the *logos* transits."[39] We are very close to Heraclitus and the later tradition, which saw in the *logos* the main feature of the Divine permeating precisely all that there is by the power of the word[40] by which all things are sustained, according to the Christian Letter to the Hebrews (I, 3) and of which the *homo loquens* is an incarnation. Man is an offspring of the God precisely because he is endowed with *logos*. The aristotelian "definition" is a theological statement: Man is a living being endowed with a divine gift, the *logos*—just the contrary of the way it was later interpreted. The awareness of being begotten by the word is perhaps our highest dignity, since it brings us in touch with the most conspicuous divine dimension. We are born of the word and thus share the nature of the word.

It is from the sharing in the *logos* that we speak. Man can use this divine

39 Aristotle, *Metaphysics* 998b.14.

40 Heraclitus, *Fragm.* 1, 72.

gift of the *logos* to speak with his fellow beings, with the divine or with things. For clarity's sake I call the first speech; the second worship, and the third action— well aware that this is only a heuristic device. The classification of human realities is never like scientific classification of objectifiable entities. A single atom more converts a chemical substance into another with quite different properties; heavy water (H_2O_2) is not water (H_2O). Sulfuric acid (SO_4H_2) is not sulfurous acid (SO_3H_2). This is not the case with living realities in which all is interconnected and interpenetrated. These we cannot compartmentalize so neatly. Reason, intellect, and intuition cannot be separated as if they were three separate entities; they overlap, as it were. *Logos* means language, but also word, reason, intellect, and love as well. We could adduce many other words, which we should distinguish but cannot separate.

1. *Speech*

Many african traditions, as well as those of jewish, hindu, christian, and other religions, link the mystery of language with God, or equate, with necessary qualifications, God with the Word. For many cultures the experience of language amounts to a divine experience. In fact, the experience of oneself as a speaking being, *homo loquens*, amounts to self-knowledge, and self-knowledge is synonymous with knowledge of the Divine, as Socrates, Plotinus, the Upanishads, the *Gītā*, and the christian and muslim traditions assert. To discover oneself speaking is truly sharing in the creating power of the divine.

I may insert here a sociological observation which bears an all-too-often forgotten theological meaning: the pleasure of human conversation, just for the sake of it. Man is a conversant being. Conversation belongs to Man's nature. The use of the word "conversation" in english was adopted from the italian *conversazione,* to stay "at home" for a *soirée* just for speaking. The spanish *tertulia*, as the culture of our humanness by conversation, holds a profound meaning. Moreover, the Vulgate translates the greek *politeuma* as "conversation," which modern english renders as citizenship. The citizen is the one who has the right to speak in the *polis*.

Hardly any human settlement is without its *agora*, a house of the "palaver," a "plaza," a marketplace, a "bazaar," a central street, a roundtable, a commons— the parliament being a modern and highly bureaucratized example of the same. I still remember the bewilderment of some "natives" when they realized that their bazaars and markets are considered by the tourists as supermarkets for buying products and not as places of encounter. Man is a speaking being and in speech realizes an aspect of the divine dimension. *Dābār, logos, vāk, verbum* . . . are divine names. Rhetoric was more than the art of the sophists; it was the proper use of a divine gift, and therefore had the right and duty to be beautiful, that is, eloquent: "the heavenly rhetoric of thine eye" wrote Shakespeare.[41] The art and science of conversation is not a "waste of time" if it is not directed to more or less pragmatic transactions. On the contrary, it is a cultivation of that precious divine gift that Man has. Indeed, the proper use of language is not chatter, gossip, *Gerede*. It is significant that Aristotle uses the word *anthrōpologein* in this pejorative sense, probably because the real *legein* is *theolegein*, a re-enactment of the activity of the Word—as the Gospel of John (XII, 50) says.

I may quote the very beginning of a fundamental work on language that sums up within one particular culture an almost universal conviction: "Without beginning or end Brahman, the primordial Word, imperishable Sound / which manifests itself in the form of [all] beings and from which the entire world comes."[42] The origins of this idea are to be found in the Vedas, that intrinsically relate Brahman with *vāk*, the Word, from which all proceeds and by which everything has come into existence.[43] What interests us here is the personal experience that when I discover myself speaking, truly speaking—that is, uttering sacramental and thus truthful words—I am experiencing a divine power in myself, sensing that the Divine is descending upon me, being, as it were, incarnated in myself.

Śabdabrahman is not just *brahman* as word; it is as well the word as *brahman*. The theory of the evolution of human speech from the hypothetical humanoids to *homo sapiens* within the matrix of a linear conception of time does not explain the origin of the word, "infinite, immense, beyond all this,"[44] which was *agre*,[45] ἐν ἀρξῄ[46] (*in principio*), "the highest point on which dwell all the Gods."[47] This is the word that comes out of Silence and in which we can also share when our words are begotten in and by Silence. I am bound to say that this is not just nominalistic poetry or primitive mentality. It sprouts from a genuine human experience: the experience of being a prophet in the

41 William Shakespeare, *The Passionate Pilgrim*, III. Cf. also Shakespeare, *Love's Labour's Lost*, IV, 3.

42 In Bhartṛhari's own words in Vākyapadīya, I, 1 (ed. 1972): "anādinidhanaṁ brahma śabdatattvaṁ yad aksaram / vivartate 'rthabhāvena prakriyā jagato yataḥ."

43 See, for example, RV X, 125; AitBr. IV, 21, 1; etc.

44 TB II, 8, 8, 4.

45 TMB XX, 14, 2.

46 Jn I, 1.

47 RV I, 164, 39

classical sense of the spokesman of God. The christian confirmation makes Man a priest (mediator), a king (a free Lord over himself), and a prophet (a right interpreter of the word).

It is in the same spirit, and no exaggeration, when the Gospel says that we are going to be judged on every "not-efficient word" (ῥῆμα ἀργὸν ἀ-ἔργον [without energy, action, force]) we utter—on any word that is not a sacramental word.[48]

Our modern world, however, does not believe that "it is by your words you will be justified, and by your words condemned"[49] because the words have been interpreted as terms (signs) and have ceased to be considered as words (symbols).

One of the deleterious effects of nominalism is the loss of this link between the Divine and the Word, including our human words.[50] To really speak is to share in the divine nature, the *Rig-Veda* says.[51] The Word is a divine dimension of the real. To truly speak is to be in touch with this divine dimension. A sad example, sad from both sides, is the recent condemnation to death of an author of a book for an alleged blasphemy against the "Prophet." Blasphemy means little in the modern western world, but is the highest crime in a strict muslim country. Now, in defending the sacredness of the Word, and of human words, I am not defending the Ayatollah Khomeini's sentence. No human act is exclusively an objective action. A fact isolated from its mythical background loses its meaning and power. What one side saw as a real injury the other side saw as freedom of expression. The reaction would certainly have been different if Salman Rushdie had propagated a nazi ideology.

Once we lose the sense of the sacredness of language, it sounds like a ridiculous exaggeration to affirm that any authentic word is a ritual—that is, a sacred action. Monotheistic religions have reserved the "words of God" for revelation, which is consistent with the belief in an exclusively transcendent God: divine words come down to us; our human words cannot ascend to heaven. Human language becomes desacralized. Old catholic Spain was known for such blasphemies as curses and interjections. The habit has become obsolete because the words have become irrelevant; they have lost

48 Mt XII, 36. *Verbum otiosum,* says the Vulgate, any "idle word," also translated as "careless," "thoughtless," "unfounded," etc.

49 Mt XII, 37.

50 See Panikkar, "La parola, creadora de realitat," in R. Panikkar, ed., *Llenguatge i identitat* (Barcelona: Publicacions de L'Abadia de Montserrat, 1994), 11-61.

51 RV I, 164, 37; X, 71; etc.

their power. The basic function of human language, however, is not to be a vehicle of information, but to share humanly in the dynamics of our common destiny. The Divine is a silent partner of any authentic conversation, which in no way diminishes the special power of divine revelation.

When Silence and Word are kept separate, the Silence is terrifying and the Word ceases to be "Word of God," becoming only our words about God; theo-logy loses its sacredness (λόγος τοῦ θεοῦ) and becomes our scrutiny of the Inscrutable. God has gone to heaven and we try in vain to climb to it. Not all who cry "Lord, Lord!" reach heaven.[52] This divine dimension of the ordinary word is not always conspicuous in the speaker or conscious in the listener. The old practices of speaking in "the presence of God" or beginning any speech invoking his Name, uttering a prayer before a meal, lighting a lamp to a *murti* (sacred image) before any speech, or greeting each other with a divine name at the beginning of any encounter, point to this same intuition. Yet all too often, owing to multiple reasons, routine has crept in or such practices have been abandoned.

Abhinavagupta has a hymn in the *Parātrīśikā* that contains a beautiful metaphor to explain how the Supreme Reality is only visible in the things themselves. In other words, the divine dimension is only visible in the other dimensions of reality, in the things themselves, as a fine rain is only perceptible as it drizzles against the dark roof of the house:

> Slender [*pratanu*] rain falling continuously is not visible in the far-spreading sky but it is clearly visible in juxtaposition with the trees of the forest or the eaves of the roof of the house. Even so, the Supreme Bhairava, being too subtle, never appears in the range of experience. Under the circumstances which depend on space, form, time, pattern, and state, that consciousness is generated instantaneously in them in whom the awareness of Bhairava is subdued—the consciousness that is indicative of thy presence, O Lord![53]

Reality has a divine dimension. This dimension is both transcendent and immanent—both in heaven and on earth. Its name is *logos* and its meaning polysemic: word, idea, intellect, reason, . . . or, in a more ontological interpretation, the divine energies, the angelic universe, the imaginal world, the κόσμος νοητός (intelligible cosmos), the first (and second) Sephirot, etc. Language, however, is also the preeminent manifestation of the Divine to and in Man. Not only does Man speak to the Divine, but the Divine speaks

52 Mt VII, 21.

53 Abhinavagupta, *Parātrīśikā*, 8 (p. 22 of the Singh translation).

to Man. In language, the human and the divine worlds communicate, each in its proper way. As I said before, the Divine and the Human share in the Word.

I am not attempting to determine what degree of reality belongs to the different manifestations of the Divine. It is enough for my purpose to signal the existence of this divine dimension, which is the Logos in its variety of meanings. I already hinted at the use and abuse of our human language and gave my opinion that human language is not only a divine gift but also a share in that divine dimension. The life of the intellect implies the cultivation of this most precious gift. The βίος θεωρητικός, or intellectual life about which the ancients spoke, is a participation in the divine Life. The traditional *otium* or the *vacare Deo* was not laziness or selfishness (in spite of the abuses), and needs a new understanding today. One extreme, however, does not justify the other.

The sacredness of human language does not at all mean that our conversations should be all times solemn and humorless. On the contrary, to have neglected the often ironic sense of holy Scripture, for instance, and to have stuck to strictly literal meanings is one of the causes of the decline of the authority of sacred books. The truthfulness of human speech does not mean mathematical accuracy or the seriousness of a court of law.

2. *Worship*

Our *logos* is not limited to speaking to each other with all that that entails. Our *logos* also opens us up to the divine, to something other, superior, more than us. An old english word with no exact equivalent in many european languages is “worship” as the proper attitude in front of the numinous.[54] Worship comprises adoration, awe, and many other human reactions in front of that absent Presence that I called the Mystery. For our purposes we do not need to deal with all of them. I am going to single out only two manifestations of the *logos* in our contact with the divine dimension.

a) Glory

One of the most profound and traditional responses of Man to the wonder of existence takes the form of thankfulness for the gift of Life, and thankfulness expresses itself in glory in its multiple aspects. In a theistic worldview it takes the form of adoration, which includes praising God, glorifying him, thanking him because he exists, since his existence makes our existence possible. It is the *canticum novum* of the christian liturgy,

54 See Panikkar, *Worship and Secular Man* (Maryknoll, N.Y.: Orbis Books, 1973).

taken from the Psalms of the hebrew Bible, an ever-renewed canticle to the glory of Creator and creation. Ramon Llull beautifully begins his *Libre de Contemplació* by saying in the first chapter that Man has to rejoice in the bare fact that God exists, and he follows with a second chapter in which he deepens and enlarges this joy in the consciousness that Man personally exists. The third chapter continues in the same vein, explaining how a further source of joy is the existence of neighbors. The flavor of the original is of such exquisite innocence that it is worth reproducing at least the titles of these three chapters:

> How it behooves Man to be glad since God *is* in Being. [exists]
> How it behooves Man to be glad since (he) *is* in Being. [exists]
> How it behooves Man to be glad for the Being of his neighbors.[55]

This is an expression, or rather an explosion, of sheer joy because there is Being. It is a song to pure existence, an existence that we share with all that there is, a totally unselfish joy. This joy permeates human consciousness and, in and through it, pervades the whole universe. This joy is a dimension of the real before any thought about optimism or pessimism. Brahman is ānanda, bliss, says one version of an Upanishad[56] elaborated later in the vedantic philosophy into a full theology of the Divine as *sat-cit-ānanda*: Being, Consciousness, Joy.

Joy is a fundamental religious category. It belongs to the Ultimate. Paradoxically enough, the clichéd image of East-West is here reversed. Brahman is the source of joy. For the medieval mystic of Mallorca, Existence is gladness and our consciousness of it is what scatters joy. Praise and glory belong to the foremost expression of the *logos*. Language is not just a vehicle for passing on more or less useful information, or a device to convey concepts. Language is the foremost human manifestation, since it manifests what Man feels, thinks, . . . *is*. This pure *is* has one name once we become conscious of it: Glory. We reveal ourselves to our fellow beings by letting them share not only in what we have but in what we are. This is our deepest Being, which shines in and through us once our ego has been overcome. In many cultures of the world the oral greeting is preceded or accompanied by a bodily touch so as to symbolize the revelation of our naked existence. We even take our gloves off before shaking hands. Scholars write books about the ways of greeting of the polynesian peoples, yet often we forget the profound symbolism of our own culture.

---

55 Llull, *Libre de Contemplació*, I, 1 (also 2 and 3): "Libre de Com hom se deu alegrar per ço com Déus és en ésser. Com hom se deu alegrar per ço com és en ésser. Com hom se deu alegrar de l'ésser de son proïsme."

56 Cf. TU. Another version reads *ananta*, "infinite."

A sacred text within the indic context, which sees in sacrifice the fundamental contribution of Man to the destiny of the universe, says: "When mind and speech are united they convey the sacrifice of the Gods."[57] This text communicates an insight similar to the *sacrificium laudis*, the "oblation of praise" of the judeo-christian tradition. It should be clear that *yajña* and *sacrificium* do not mean what this word has come to mean in many circles.[58]

The divine dimension of reality that is manifest in every being triggers this spontaneous reaction of praise and glory. This reaction, within a certain vision of the world, is directed to a person, human or divine—and in a theistic milieu to a Supreme Being. Nonetheless, the spontaneous movement of our spirit, this cry of Man in the face of Beauty, Truth, and Goodness, is not necessarily directed to "another." It is important to recognize that this chant of praise and shout of glory is not exclusively that of theistic believers.

When praise and glory are not explicitly directed to anybody but emerge freely from our being, they are purified of any desire to please, entreat, or even flatter. This does not mean, of course, that most monotheistic worship is of that type. The language of thankfulness and praise is a natural manifestation of the human spirit. This human sentiment of glory, active and passive, is essentially religious because it shows an openness to transcendence from our very immanence, but it is not necessarily directed to a Supreme Being. It may even be experienced while performing the chores of daily life. If we get up in the morning to work, even if our activity is not labor but some creative task, the classical *taedium vitae* or at least fatigue will sooner or later creep in. Is our work really worth the effort? Only if we undergo the naked experience of Life—of that Life which enlivens every being, of that Light which enlightens every creature—only if we are able to some degree to displace the center of gravity from ourselves to an infinite Self, divine Being, or simply the Divine and to feel a communion with it, only then does our existence seem to have a meaning that is superior to the impediments and frustrations that deaden our daily routine. This displacement of the center, however, should not mean alienation; it should not mean working for another, even if exalted as Lord. It certainly should be a going outside oneself, but only in order to converge with the Infinite, to reawaken our sense of belonging to the adventure of reality as a whole. It is this that produces the exhilarating awareness described by Ramon Llull, in which the three manifestations of joy come together.

In our times there seems to be a reaction of alienation if we are told that the aim of our lives is to be like angels in heaven, praising and offering incense

---

57 SB I, 4, 4, 1.

58 See Panikkar, *Le mystére du culte dans l'indouisme et le christianisme* (Paris: Cerf, 1970).

to that Great Monarch in the Skies, and chanting His glories. Perhaps we are too sensitive to the political overand undertones of any spirituality devoted to God the Creator, Viṣṇu the Lord, Christ the King, etc., who, we are told, look on mere humans as little worms, miserable slaves of the Supreme Lord. Once again, we react by throwing out the baby with the bathwater. But it would be falling into another extreme if we were to interpret this human urge to converge with the Infinite as if it were an oceanic movement toward a pantheistic universe. We need a personalistic touch, as it were—and this is a strength of monotheism— but this is not the only possible hypothesis.

Cosmotheandric spirituality allows the glory of existence to flower without the anthropomorphic and monarchic connotations of the Glory to the *parama vyoman* of the Vedas, or similar attitudes in many traditional religions. We are part of a cosmic venture, a human history and a divine destiny; we are partners in that symphony, even free players in it. We transcend ourselves, and yet we do so from our very immanence.

In other words, we jump outside our little selves by discovering the mystery of reality, the wonder of existence, and at the same moment by recognizing that we are part of this very mystery. We do not sing to ourselves, nor do we necessarily praise a Supreme Being as if it should take all the credit for itself. In an ecstatic mood we praise those qualities we discover in reality which we can only call divine, but we do not need to hypostatize them into a Single, Transcendent, Separate, Supreme Being. We recognize this All as the very divine—but also very cosmic and human—reality. It all comes together in one triple experience: ecstatic, enstatic, and reflexive. We are in awe, love, astonishment, joy . . . that Being is, reality exists, and the Divine is not a dream. We can trust. . . .

All of a sudden we are proud to be alive, called into being, given awareness, freedom, and the grace to witness it all and to co-operate with this very life of the real. We give a human twist to the metaphysical question and do not ask *why,* but simply wonder that there is Being rather than Nothingness. At the same time, we are conscious that a task has been entrusted to us, that we are also responsible for this very existence and, consequently, that we may fail to play our role.

It would be easy to quote poets or simply see for ourselves the beauty of the world or the goodness of a human heart. We find one thing in common: not an outer referent but the ecstatic and purifying character of the song of glory. It liberates us from our petty selves; it raises us up to the infinite; only our ego-centeredness prevents us from enjoying the wonder of Existence. The most spontaneous outlet for this attitude is in song. A german distich expresses it beautifully: Wo man singt da lässt dich nieder, Böse Menschen haben keine Lieder. ("Where people sing you may well dwell, / bad people have no songs").

Where our heart rests joyfully, where we find peace and happiness we experience a dimension of the divine—which does not mean, as we remarked in the beginning, that it may not turn into our perdition if disconnected from the whole. There is an intrinsic connection between religion, rightly understood, and joy, *ānanda*, peace, and resurrection or new life. There is a real danger of losing it all if we close ourselves into our small selfish shell. The same phrase "my God" may express a most sublime experience of intimacy with longing for union with the Divine or a most blasphemous attitude of selfishly possessing what does not belong to us. To put it in a crude way: To "liberate" the Divine from the burden of being "God" allows a recovery of precisely this sense of the Mystery, human freedom, and concomitant responsibility. Nevertheless, this human attitude, which I have only sketched and oversimplified, is only half of the picture, and needs to be complemented by further considerations.

b) Prayer

We do not only sing for joy and fill our heart with gratitude. We also cry out in suffering and feel our heart loaded with distress. Our human experience also includes ugliness, violence, evil. All our faith in the Divine cannot free us from indignation, anxiety, and sometimes even despair. This is also a very natural human attitude. It would seem unfair to credit a monotheistic God with all the good aspects of reality and debit us or a malign Spirit with all the negative features. It is, however, also unnecessary to project all the negative aspects of reality onto an omnipotent God who allows such evils while capable of letting them not happen.

Yet the incontrovertible fact is that Man is not self-sufficient. People need each other, but people also require something more—grace. They need the gratuitious help that comes from one another and also from providence, chance, heaven, the Gods, *karma*, or destiny from on high. We cannot foresee everything, we cannot calculate every event and its possibilities. We need prayer, but not as an outlet for our weaknesses, or an expression of our superstitions. We need prayer as a manifestation both of our solidarity with one another and of our communion with that aspect of the universe that we have been calling the Divine Mystery. We need worship, not to beg alms from an all-powerful Lord, but to connect ourselves, by a series of human acts, with this otherwise inexpressible aspect of reality.

When a mother blesses her son, she is not simply giving rational advice on how to choose a wife or succeed in business; she is invoking the powers that be to inspire her son; she is giving expression to a wish that cannot be put into so many words. She is conveying what otherwise cannot be said, and the son thereby experiences not only maternal love but also a link with all his ancestors, a connection with the human race. He feels that freedom implies risk, and that risk demands daring, and daring a certain trust in reality, and that for this he needs luck, God's blessings, good vibrations, mastery of *karma*, the benevolence of the Gods, a fortunate constellation of factors, a positive syntropy, and that all of this is conjured up or expressed by his mother's blessing. Any ritual, after all, is a re-enactment of something that defies immediate causality. Any ritual trusts in Life, God, luck, chance, the stars, other people, circumstances—in a word, grace. I do not lump all these words together as if they mean the same or have the same value. I am giving a voice to the sentiments of the son, who may not be an "orthodox" believer, but who nevertheless has an orthodox humanness. Yet all the words I used bear witness to the sentiment of precariousness that all too often befalls our human condition. Here the very wisdom encoded in the word brings close to us that "prayer," which is trigged by the feelings of our "precariousness," and which spontaneously drives us to cry, claim, shout, speak, ask, . . . in a word, pray.

Now we do not pray to a lifeless dimension of reality. Yet, on the other hand, prayer is something more than simply entreating a mighty Lord to protect my son or heal my ailments—especially when I know the causes at work in the disgrace of my son or the reasons for my malady. This type of prayer may not be the final remedy for such events, but to dispense with a certain naive belief or to be purified of a superstition does not justify going to the other extreme of destroying all those links to reality that I do not understand or cannot foresee and master.

I am not attempting to describe the world of prayer. I am only saying that what goes under this name belongs to the nature of Man. We do not need to have studied Heisenberg's "uncertainty principle" to discover that any observation modifies the observed. Any shaman knows this, and any prayerful person can experience something similar without physics and without magic. The divine dimension links everything with everything. If the physical observation of a microscopic phenomenon can modify it, how much more so may spiritual attention to a human phenomenon modify a human situation! Not all connections in the universe are causal or mechanical. The magic I referred to is nothing but the wrong application of a mechanical causality to much more subtle correlations.

There is a paradox here. Prayer is the manifestation of our impotency. We pray to the powers that be for what we cannot obtain by ourselves. At the same time, prayer is the very extension of our power. A Man of prayer can move the heavens and defeat armies. Although I would have preferred *orison*, which has to do with our mouth uttering a word or making a gesture, like adoration, prayer is the consecrated name for that human activity which leads us to listen to the Beyond (to use only one name) and react freely to it. Prayer is the meeting point between Silence and Word (as was hinted in the beginning of this chapter) and the creative response in language and deed to the embrace of the two. "Thy will be done" is neither the unnecessary tautology of a fatalistic attitude in front of an omnipotent Will, nor the childish attitude to expect to change God's will to fit our little will in competition with the will of our neighbors who pray for sun while we pray for rain. "Thy will be done" in spite of an anthropomorphic language is neither "my will be done by striving to change 'your' Will" nor my blind submission to "your will" but our forging together that "divine will" (to continue that way of speaking) as the Force that directs the destiny of the universe (or of events)—continuing still the same metaphorical language.

The paradox is worth pondering. In prayer I feel both weak and powerful. Weak, therefore I pray; powerful, since in the state of prayer I sense that an "energy" is given to "me" when the *ego* has withdrawn from me. This is why a Man of prayer cannot "use" that power to pursue his will, but only that "thy will be done," which comes to be precisely at that moment.

If glory is the centrifugal dynamism from immanence to transcendence, prayer is a centripetal movement from transcendence toward immanence—in spite of the common meaning of the latin word *precare,* "to beg," "to ask," "to question," "to implore" (from the root *prek* [*perek*]). We would not question if we were not questioned to open ourselves to that ineffable Mystery that defies all names and definitions.

c) Listening

"Who has ears to hear, let them hear."[59] "Thus I have heard"[60] was a traditional japanese response to the "thus has been said"[61] of various buddhist scriptures referring the alleged word of the Buddha. *Śruti*, "what has been heard," is the canonical word for the Vedas. They are not "what has been said," but "what has been heard." To listen, cognate to the sanskrit *śṛṣṭi*

59 Cf. Mt XIII, 9; etc.: "Qui habet aures audiendi, audiet," ὁ ἔχων ὦτα ἀκουέτω.

60 *Nyoze gamon* (apud Forzani [2000] 9).

61 *Ityuktaka*, the name of a collection of short texts attributed to the Buddha himself.

(obedience) means to obey (*ob-audire*), to obey the Voice of the Spirit, of *śabdabrahman*, the word that is *brahman*. A jewish psalm states of Yahweh: "Semel locutus est Deus, duo haec audivi,"[62] and Meister Eckhart interprets this as saying that the Father utters only one single Word and we, pilgrims on the way, understand it as a revelation of the split between Creator and creature. We hear the single Word of God as split between Creator and creature. We could cite this text as expressing an insight similar to Vimalakirti's intriguing sentence: "Buddha expresses the Dharma in a single Sound and the living beings hear it understanding it each in its own way."[63] We could introduce this subsection with scores of other ancient and modern witnesses about the central importance of Listening. The silence does not speak, we said already. Strictly "speaking," we cannot hear silence. We can hear the word; the word speaks, but in order to hear the word speak, we must be silent. The ears are to listen, but if we are not in silence the ears will not hear. *Aures audiendi*, the "ears to hear"—they are for hearing, but they hear only if other sounds do not prevent them from hearing.

We commented on speech, song, and prayer; but they are truly speech, song, and prayer if they are original and not mere repetition, if they are creative, that is, if they come out of nothing, out of silence. What effects their emerging out of nothingness so that each speech, song, and prayer is authentic, genuine, and new each moment is our capacity for pure listening to the Source—wherever and whatever it may be. We listen only if we are attentive; we are attentive if we are interested; and we are interested if we are void of other conflicting interests, if our heart is pure; and our heart is pure if it has been purified by that very Silence which prompted us to listen. Here we have again the vital circle of Life.

It is all a question of listening, of conscious listening, even if we may not understand. It is a matter of listening, not conceptualizing. This listening is hearing the divine dimension.

This divine dimension is not a hidden feature, an esoteric extra sound concealed in the closed chamber of everything. It is, on the contrary, the most salient aspect of each being. Reversing the aristotelian-thomistic idea that the principle of individuation is matter I would maintain that what "individualizes" each being and makes it what it *is* (in its individuality) is not an undifferentiated material structure or intellectual "ingredient," but precisely its divine dimension, which, because infinite, can take any form. In sum, the divine dimension of any entity is its uniqueness, which we discover

62 Ps LXI, 12: "God hath spoken once, these two things I have heard."

63 Apud Forzani (2000) 75.

when we love that thing. In listening lovingly to each being we discover its divine dimension, or in the language of the Gospel, we reach eternal life.

I have repeatedly stated that talk about the divine should not be limited to the use of categories. We need the insight of the third eye. A famous christian text says: "God is spirit and those who worship God must worship in spirit and truth."[64] This might fairly be restated as "Those who want to strike the right method to approach God must do it in spirit and truth." This should be a golden rule of worship. No liturgy is authentic if it is not accompanied by an attentive listening as a kind of background music. Here I am not referring to listening to the word, but rather to that divine dimension which only listening discloses. In a significant passage in vedic scripture, Prajāpati, father of the Gods, decided in favor of the mind (*manas*) against the word (*vāc*) in performing a worship as if saying that rituals, and rules of all types are of no avail without the attention of the mind knowing what we are doing. I am tempted to read into that text a warning from God about modern media of communication. *Vāc* (the word) indeed pleads in her favor that without her no communication is possible. Prajāpati decides against her.[65]

3. *Doing*

The *logos* is undoubtedly a divine dimension, and we experience it when we speak, sing, pray, listen—and understand, as we are still going to see in the following chapter. But the *logos* "is" or rather *does* something more. Innumerable traditions affirm that the word is creative, and some of them explicitly that all has come to be through the logos.[66] To reduce the *logos* to reason or even to intellect or mind is a sad reductionism that has had very negative consequences in many cultures and religions. It has led to unnatural quietism and lopsided idealisms, denying the reality of the material world or degrading the importance of "doing" as if the truly spiritual life could be reduced to "theory" and the highest human activity to mere "understanding" without any true involvement or practical commitment to what we "understand." The *logos* is surely word, but the word is more than just meaning; the word is also sound and action. A word is intrinsically performative; a real word does, and makes; it is *praxis* and *poiēsis*.

We also encounter the divine dimension in doing and making. "Entre los pucheros anda Dios" is a sentence attributed to that contemplative nun of

64 Jn IV, 24.

65 Cf. SB I, 4, 5, 8-12.

66 Jn I, 3; TMB XX, 14, 2; AV IV, 1; etc.

the sixteenth century, Teresa de Jesus: "among the pots (also) walks God"—in the kitchen and in any human activity, however humble. We would have a very inadequate notion of the divine if we were to reduce it to a divine Intellect only. In spite of the anthropomorphic and ultimately wrong idea of a divine Maker, Architect, or, worse, Engineer, there is a profound insight in the vision that any activity contains a divine dimension. This is one of the central aspects of a cosmotheandric spirituality. Among the many aspects one could mention, I am going to select three that emphasize in a special way one feature of a cosmotheandric spirituality.

a) Transformation of the Cosmos

Man is much more than a mere part of the cosmos, as if he were like any other part; Man is much more than a rational animal; he belongs certainly to the cosmos and to the realm of the animals; but his "kingdom is not of this world";[67] his realm (*conversatio, politeuma*, citizenship) is in heaven; he is the center of that consciousness which pervades everything and allows Man to give voice to that awareness, to "express the way" (*dotoku*) as Dogen, the thirteenthcentury Zen master put it.[68] He stands in the middle between the cosmic and the divine—although, as we said, "Man" is already an abstraction of the integral reality, but he is the "platform" from which we see it. We are more than passive inhabitants of the cosmos. We are the watchtower from which the entire reality is perceived; this is our function and responsibility.

The transformation of the cosmos about which christian tradition speaks is the divinization of all created structures, so that at the end God will be all in all.[69] The *ātman-brahman* realization of hinduism, which in a non-historical fashion perhaps tends to leave the material world behind as a stepping stone, not to mention the more recent movements for the *consecratio mundi*, are all forms of a cosmotheandric spirituality. Man here does not have a minor supporting role or a merely passive one, but is a crucial factor in the process, part and parcel of the very destiny of reality, so much so that we can "effect," or provoke the failure of, the entire adventure of Being. The dignity of Man is not just transmitted or received; it is constitutive. Man may not be the absolute king of creation, but certainly is its gardener.[70]

Traditional judaism, early catholicism, along with eastern orthodoxy, mahāyāna buddhism, and some of the hindu religions are not concerned

67 Jn XVIII, 36.

68 A chapter of his main work *Shobogenzo* (apud Forzani [2000], 19ff.).

69 1 Cor XV, 28.

70 Gn II, 15.

with individualistic salvation, but aspire to a universal transformation of the entire "creation"—the ἀποκατάστασις τῶν πάντων (the beginning and end of all things) of christian Scripture.[71] A cosmotheandric spirituality goes a step further. There is no "other" world where one might take refuge or attain individual salvation. One has to discover that "this" world, if the "this" is not reduced to a rationally graspable "this," contains or rather *is* also "that" world—as an Upanishad forcefully puts it: *etad vai tat,*[72] "This [is] truly that," that "other world," *altera terra*, in a tempiternal present.

This task of transforming the cosmos is not achieved by a merely passive attitude nor by sheer activism. It is brought about by being co-operators (*synergoi*) with the Divine.[73] This co-operation is not accidental. The world does not "go" independently from us. We are also active factors in the destiny of the cosmos. Otherwise, discourse about the dignity of Man, his divinization or his divine character is an illusion. One of the mature traits of our so rightly criticized epoch is the acute awareness of what I call *sacred secularity*.[74] This world (*saeculum*) is sacred and our secular moves have transcendent repercussions. Pico della Mirandola, Paracelsus, and many alchemists wrote that Man is an unfinished "product" of the hands of the Creator because the human task is to achieve the unfinished portions by bringing to fulfillment both oneself and the surrounding world.

An *objection* could be raised as to whether it is not utopian, or simply arrogant, to believe that it is incumbent on us is to transform the world? Do we not realize that each of us is only one individual among more than six billion people, standing on a planet in which we are a tiny minority among the living beings, inhabiting a little planet that turns around an insignificant sun in a corner of a minor galaxy lost in the immensity of the universe? This is the objection stemming from the quantitative fallacy which has lost sight of quality and is blind to other dimensions of the real. If numerical quantity is absolute monarch in the realm of Being, my idea is not only preposterous but simply ridiculous. If a space is a newtonian-einsteinian "box" where the universe expands and Man is also located, the idea that "One single thought of Man is worth more than the entire world; therefore we have to direct it only to God as its worthy partner"[75] is simply foolish. The forceful sentence

71 Rv I, 8.

72 KathU II, 1, 3 (IV, 3) and ff.

73 1 Cor III, 9.

74 See Panikkar, *El mundanal silencio* (Barcelona: Martínez Roca, 1999).

75 St. John of the Cross, "*Avisos y sentencias*" ("*Dichos de la luz y amor*"), no. 34: "Un solo pensamiento del hombre vale más que todo el mundo; por tanto sólo a Dios se debe."

of John of the Cross may be an exaggeration in the other direction, but we will have neither hope nor mental health if we believe in the primacy of an atomistic quantitative reality.

This objection highlights in a simple way a fundamental divergence of two anthropologies and ultimately two worldviews. The first says that if Man is an individual, that is, essentially a numerable entity, and if numbers are paramount, then we are justified (up to the "gas chambers") in eliminating any number of individuals *if* they are a real threat to the existence of a greater number of individuals. I say "individuals" because if I kill a person I wound a whole community and eventually the whole world. The other anthropology considers Man to be a microcosm, and eventually even a "microtheos."

The very shift of meaning of the greek word *metron*, which meant "measure" as moderation, to mean quantity *poson* (how big, how much?) is a sign of our times. *Posotēs* would mean quantity, which no greek would mistake for *metron*. In other words, the objection to the transformative role of Man would be valid only if reality is reduced to one single quantitative element, and even then at the price of swallowing all the other features of matter. However, we should not dodge the objection by "spiritualizing" the answer.

The cosmos we are asked to transform is not the "spiritual" world alone. The real cosmos is neither purely spiritual nor merely material; its many dimensions are interrelated and interindependent. Transformation of the world may be a frightening phrase since modern civilization by and large makes the cosmic rule of Man difficult to experience, and thus to believe in. Yet most people feel they should strive for "a better world." Our participation in the dynamism of the cosmos is a sharing in the divine dimension. From the most ancient times the sage was considered a powerful force in the cosmos and the saint was thought to have the power to perform "miracles"—although there is no need to subscribe literally to those ritual beliefs in order to agree with what I am trying to say. A "better world" is neither the dream of an earthly paradise nor the inner self (*antar ātman*[76]) alone; it is a world with less hatred and more love, with less violence and more justice. This world in which we exist and of which we are members is a human world indeed, but it embraces the Whole. With our body we commune with matter, not excluding celestial matter; with our soul we embrace all of humanity, not excluding past and future; with our spirit we cooperate with angels and other spiritual powers, not excluding the Godhead.

76 KathU II, 1, 1 (IV, 1).

I can better explain what I mean by descending from metaphysical spheres into the field of history—allowing for the irony of using "history" as a heuristic device by someone critical of the myth of history. One of the major revolutions in human life is what may be called the passage from prehistory into history, the transition from the late paleolithic to the neolithic period. At this latter period, instead of just subsisting on earth (hunting and food-gathering), Man became an active partner in the world by utilizing the jealously guarded gift of the Gods, fire, or by sharing in the very nature of the divine mediator, Agni. In plain terms, Man engages in metallurgy. From earliest times this power of fashioning and shaping the gifts of Nature was seen as a human task in cooperation with divines forces for the transformation of the universe—even if those skills were sometimes used against other fellow humans, as with weapons, or against the Divine, as seems to have been the case in the episode of the Tower of Babel.[77]

It was understood that although no longer inhabiting an earthly paradise, Man was a heavenly spark whose task is to be the *trikarma-kṛt*, the "doer of the triple work," to bring harmony in the three worlds—precisely by means of the fire-sacrifice as said in the Katha Upanishad.[78]

I am so critical of modern science precisely because I recognize its capital importance in human history and therefore I take it very seriously. This is what prompts me to feel justified making this general statement. In the last six to eight thousand years, the historical period, the prevalent human culture has been a culture of war. Many states have still "ministries of war," although nowadays the euphemism is "defense." War was ultimately an art and understood in the heraclitean sense of ἔρις and the noble meaning of *polemos*. In many african cultures it could be translated as sport and sportive competition. Today it has ceased to be an art and has become a technology of killing and destroying. Bombing from forty thousand feet could be called a technological feat, but not an art.

For human survival we need another mutation in the destiny of reality, compared to which the shift from pre-history to history seems like child's play.[79] I am not naïvely optimistic; I am simply saying that the alternative is the end of human life. This transformation, as I have just affirmed, is for the realization of a better world, but it has no blueprint. There is no pre-programmed model for the destiny of the planet. The transformation

77 Cf. Gn XI.

78 KathU I, 1, 17 (I, 17).

79 See Panikkar, *The Cosmotheandric Experience: Emerging Religious Consciousness* (Maryknoll, N.Y.: Orbis Books, 1993).

of the cosmos is left to the freedom of Being in which Man participates. This freedom moves us to act from within and without constraint, but such an interior urge is an inspiration from the Spirit within. Here lies our responsibility.

If someone complains that I am making of Man a little God, my answer is that I am not in bad company. A great part of humanity believed and still believes that Man is a partner of the Divine, of divine nature, Buddha nature, offspring of the God, an incarnated spirit, an emanation from above or the like. A pure monotheistic belief asks with astonishment, "What is Man that you are mindful of him?"[80] I am no less astonished, but I make the query more credible by not reducing it to a rhetorical question, which is what the christian Scripture tries to do by applying the question to Christ,[81] and by leaving further application open to every Man.[82] To find the divine dimension we first have to find it in ourselves. My topic here, however, is to describe this divine dimension as it is integrated in us.

This last paragraph would explain what I called the irony of my historical argument. If Man is more than an evolved ape, with great respect to apes and to the theory of evolution (this time without irony), then the individual and historical destiny of Man is not all that there is in that reality we call Man. Without theorizing now on the "after life" or the "immortality of the soul," the human person would feel outraged if told that she is just a link in the cosmic chain of Being, be it a mechanical or non-mechanical link, and that she is just an individual who, like a bee, lives and dies for the beehive. Man is much more than this. Our topic is human consciousness that cooperates in the transformation of the cosmos with all that this entails. We share in the divine dimension.

b) The Case of the Human Household

In Japan, India, and many other countries we find household divinities. For example, enshrined in the *atrium* of any roman house were the *lares* and *penates*, the household Gods that presided over all the activities of the extended family so that the "economy," the just order (*nomos*) of the house (*oikos*), might be preserved. In theological language οἰκονομία meant and means the divine "government" of the entire world. Paradoxically enough, modern "economy" has converted the governing of the world into a new household, only that this time it is not divine but monetary—the name of yet another Goddess, Juno Moneta, to continue the paradox with irony.

80 Ps VIII, 4.

81 Cf. Heb II, 6.

82 Cf. I Pet I, 4; I Jn III, 1; etc.

If the sense of cosmic responsibility and governance looms distant in today's common human consciousness of western civilization, the awareness of our "ecological" responsibility has dawned upon contemporary Man in a very promising way—even if the cause may be that we seem to have touched bottom in the sustainability of the earth in supporting our technological "wonder." The moon turns around the earth without waste of energy. Some forty thousand planes move daily around our planet sustained by an artificial *oikonomia* (to say the least). Ecological consciousness is a step in the right direction, but it does not bring us in touch with the divine dimension.

If ecology amounts only to a certain sensitivity regarding the planet, or a sentimental attitude toward the earth, it will not offer any effective resistance to the onslaught of present-day technocracy. It will do no more than delay some of the damage, rationalize some of the exploitation, encourage perhaps a little more recycling, and prolong the agony. If the ecological consciousness does not strike deeper roots in something like cosmotheandric spirituality, it will prove to be only a cosmetic change, and not prevent unscrupulous people from ignoring all ecological warnings whenever short-term advantages are to be had. No spate of international conferences will effect any change in those who subscribe to the "democracy" of money.

Only if the Godhead, the natural World, and Man are seen to belong intrinsically together in a trinitarian reality will our attitude to the earth cease to be domineering, and become one of real partnering, a partnership with something we ourselves *are*—allowing for all the distinctions necessary to prevent confusion.

The solution is not the divinization of Nature or Nature worship, but neither is it to maintain an extrinsic relationship so as to "better" or more "rationally" utilize her "resources." As I said earlier, we not only have a body; we also *are* body. We not only live "on" the earth or draw sustenance from the earth or have an earth, we are the earth; and we are more than the earth just as we are more than our bodies. We have a common, even if not an identical, destiny. The earth is more than our spaceship for traveling somewhere else. The earth is not some gigantic "Titanic," a sophisticated macro-machine carrying us either on a pleasure cruise or to a destination marked "heaven." The earth is our home, our *humus*, our body, our nature. It is not a rented apartment, as our artificial mobility tends to make us believe.

To have gone to the moon is a great shamanic feat, like leaving the body by means of some powerful forces. "We are very proud to have put a human foot on the moon," boasted a learned scientist. "We are more proud that a God has put a divine foot on earth," an illiterate indian christian added. Our life on earth is not just an accident, not for the human race nor for any one of us, not even for the Gods. Nor are we merely "creatures" under the sway of a Supreme Being, we humans having perhaps some slim chance of coming to a better end than inanimate things. This is human hubris before God, under the cloak of humility. Hardly anybody living today in a technocratic civilization can believe in such a God, who seems, indeed, to be on sabbatical leave these days, or merely a spectator, while Man destroys the whole of creation. If this were the case, our lives would be either unbearable or totally different. If human life here on earth is just *una mala noche en una mala posada* (a bad night in a bad inn), as Teresa de Jesús is supposed to have said in a polemical context, we had better make it as short a stay as possible and not bother about tidying up the place, or patching the pocked hull of our spaceship.

A cosmotheandric attitude does not consider material things to be objects and utensils, but rather members. It is more the way a yogin handles and treats the body than the way an engineer operates with raw or fabricated materials. *Technē*, as I have tried to explain, is much like this yogic play with one's own body and extensions of the body such as first degree tools. It is a yogic *āsana* (posture) for our well-being. It follows the rhythm of Being. Life is a play, a dance, but it is not just for fun. Life is also for work and transformation, and tragedies are not excluded. Metamorphosis does not mean the destruction or alienation of matter; it means what I would call a eucharistic sublimation.

Since *technē* is an art, it requires inspiration to practice it, as any artist knows. It utilizes the first-degree machine with its natural sources of energy. Technology is the replacement of the spirit, needed for art, by the *logos*, understood as mere rationality. It utilizes the second-degree machine with its nonnatural sources of energy.[83]

In order to introduce this vision I use the word *ecosophy*—that is, the "wisdom of the earth." The word emphasizes the subjective genitive over the objective. It is the earth's wisdom of which Man is the interpreter, more than our "human" wisdom about the earth. We need to listen to the earth and learn from her. Ask the birds of the sky and the lilies of the field, and they will teach you, says the Bible.[84]

I am not speaking of an extrinsic moral law that prescribes how we should behave with nature, but rather of a recovery of the instincts for self-preservation and for enjoyment. It is the awareness that we not only belong

83 See Panikkar, "L'émancipation de la technologie," *Interculturale,* no. 26 (1984), 23-37.

84 Mt VI, 26.

to the earth, but that we and the earth *are* together. My being does not end at the tips of my fingernails; I am also *in* the rivers I swim, the water I drink, the soil I tread upon, the air I breathe, the mountains I climb, the streets I walk, and, of course, the people I dwell among. This interpenetration also includes the inspiring stars and the annoying insects. Such an attitude could radically change the meaning of our technocratic civilization. Second-degree machines, for all the ingenuity they represent, are not only inhuman and ill-suited to human well-being; they represent an earthly cancer with predictably lethal consequences.

Paraphrasing the judeo-christian tradition, we may say that it is impossible to love the earth as oneself, if one does not love God above all things, but also vice versa: one cannot love God as God should be loved, if one does not love this earth. Ecosophy, like all *sophia*, has to do with our sensitivities as much as our intellection. The love of the house, like the love of the body is not the result of a command of our intellect; it is a spontaneous movement of our being. My sensitivity, for instance, may tell me that splitting the atom to supply extra energy to support our artificial way of life amounts to a cosmic abortion. Yet such an understanding will not be able to give pragmatic minds, for whom the world offers us "resources" and is not a living thing, convincing reasons that demonstrate that the earth has a life of its own that is neither vegetable nor animal life.

Ecosophy is also wisdom and, despite all love for the earth and consciousness that we share a body with matter, will not identify us with a mere material entity. A telling sentence from the Middle Ages, when christian consciousness had to defend itself from being swallowed by a mere cosmic feeling, put it this way: "The stars are for Man, Man is not for the stars."[85]

It should be clear by now that the divine dimension I have tried to sketch is not a dead and merely impersonal thing. It is that aspect of reality which, without being human or material, pervades the human and the cosmic and yet is not reducible to either.

c) Political Involvement

The foregoing considerations would be incomplete if I totally ignored the immediate field of this transformation. Cosmotheandric spirituality sheds light on one of the most tragic dramas of our times, the political situation. The metaphysical and anthropological questions we have raised also enter into this arena.

85 Albert the Great, *Super De div. nom. (De fato)*, a. 1 arg. 13: "Quoniam stellae factae sunt propter hominem, non homo propter stellas."

Kings "by the 'grace of God'" may have been a superstition, but many peoples believed it, including the kings themselves, and this belief gave monarchies a certain consistency and legitimacy. The "sacredness" of a democratic Constitution, for which neither I nor even my representatives voted because we were not there, has pragmatic value only as long as we believe in it. Modern Man, by and large, believes neither in kings nor in constitutions. The sacredness of the nation or the people is what remains, but then there is no higher instance if a conflict arises. The "law of the jungle" continues, and it is only dulcified by more or less thick cosmetics, such as recourse to ideologies of the lesser evil, deterrence, preemptive invasion, and the like. In sum, the world of politics is in crisis because, on the one hand, it denounces the "law" of the most powerful, and, on the other hand, it has not found any substitute once the will of an omnipotent God was discarded. Ultimately, the appeal to the will of God in politics was another more subtle way of affirming the "law" of the most powerful, with the advantage, however, that its transcendence vouched for a certain impartiality.

The relation between religion and politics has been a sour point in human history. Both are concerned with the well-being of Man, although, on the whole this well-being has been differently understood: mostly otherworldly by the former, and this-worldly by the latter. Nonetheless, Man is a unity, and often there are areas such as moral laws where religion and politics overlap. By politics I mean the human concern about the well-being of the *polis*, taken as a symbol of the freedom and power to influence the direction and destiny of human life as a community. By religion I mean the set of beliefs and practices leading to the definitive well-being of Man in general or in a particular community, taking into account an immanent world and/or a transcendent reality, which may or may not influence the political well-being.[86]

The dilemma is well known. If religion is separated from politics, the human personality is split in the center. If religion has nothing to do with politics, both religion and politics are emasculated. If we give preeminence to religion, politics becomes a negligible field from which we may withdraw with impunity and leave the world as an irredeemable "vale of tears." At best, it would be considered a technique for achieving some irrelevant ends. If we give preeminence to politics, religion becomes a private affair without any relevance for people's lives—like a drug or painkiller, at the price of alienation. Either religion or politics loses its importance, its power, and its significance. Since Man cannot truly live a double life, one of the two will simply be inauthentic.

86 See Panikkar, *L'esperit de la politica* (Barcelona: Edicions 62, 1999).

If we mix them together indiscriminately, Man suffocates under an unbreathable heaven on earth (when religion dominates) or dies from the lack of oxygen from heaven (when politics commands). In dealing with the Divine as an indispensable dimension of reality, therefore, we must touch on the political aspect. If we blend religion and politics, the specters of theocratic totalitarianism and fundamentalism of every stripe loom up to menace our very lives. Here again, the "fusion" may favor either religion or politics. *If we favor religion*, the political order loses its ontonomy and becomes enslaved to religious institutions.

The life of Man on Earth is instrumentalized for allegedly higher concerns, and freedom for "this-worldly" activities is lost. Everything is manipulated for the sake of a higher heteronomous order. *If we emphasize politics*, religion is harnessed to political pursuits. Losing its ontonomy, religion is degraded, left to be only a source of psychological energy to motivate people to political ends. Ancient and modern nationalisms give us all too many examples.

I have argued that only a nondualistic relationship allows for a satisfying answer. The difficulty is that within a rigid monotheism, with its Supreme Being seen as author of both the religious and the political orders, an *advaitic* relationship is hardly possible. Either God becomes a puppet while the political structures are paramount, or God stifles human initiatives, if deemed supreme in all terrestrial affairs.

In a cosmotheandric spirituality, the ontonomic order reigns naturally. This entails, however, an *advaitic* notion both of religion and of politics. Only in such a view do we discover the divine dimension of politics without doing violence to the political order. Nothing is exclusively religious, and nothing is exclusively political, because religion is not essentially the worship of a Supreme Being, and politics is not a mere organization of "worldly" affairs. Man does not have two aims in life, just as reality is not dualistic.

When I spoke of a "tragic" situation earlier, it may have sounded like an overstatement, yet such a strong adjective seems appropriate to me. The situation of the world today is serious enough to call for radical measures. To say that people have always complained, or suffered injustice, and that the world has ever been raped by the human species—besides being simply untrue given the contemporary scale of these abuses—neglects as well a threefold difference. First of all, an increasing number of people are becoming more and more conscious that the situation is intolerable, not only for them individually but also collectively. A certain margin of individual freedom exists today in some corners of the world, which gives some groups enough power to threaten the status quo. Should I mention the danger to the cosmos from the ghoulish armaments which a mad technocracy has developed? For centuries the powers that be could silence slaves, blacks, pariahs, and rebels; it will be not so easy from now on. Significantly enough, the slogan of today's most powerful governments is how to stifle what they call "terrorism."

A second difference is that in bygone times religion served as a promised image of a better future in an afterlife, but this has lost whatever soothing power it might once have had. By and large, religion has ceased to be the good or bad opiate that could console people from clearly man-made injuries. Neither the caste system nor the will of God nor karma helps people to endure human injustice any longer.

A third difference is the temporal factor. We are not condemned to the past. Others may have failed, races may have been wiped out, and rebellions may have been crushed, but we have learned from the past. Resignation and fear have been overcome in many parts of the world. Slaves and proletarians may seem to be quiet, but the thousands of ethnic groups demanding justice or vengeance will not be easily crushed. Complicating the situation even more is the global technological system itself, on which the powers that be rely to suppress dissent, and the oppressed hope to harness to their liberation is more robust and pervasive than ever before.

The world cries out for a radical change that cannot be merely theoretical, without a grounding in praxis. Contrariwise, a shift in external structures only, besides lacking the theoretical fulcrum, would also be a sham and a delusion. The sad reality is that most revolutions have been no more than what the name implies, circular movements that merely flip the hierarchy of given political powers upside down. It has probably been said a thousand times: praxis without theory is blind; theory without praxis is lame. We also require *ta mystika*, not by itself, but fully engaged and integrated with the senses and the mind.

If I stop at this point, however, I would still remain in the field of anthropological or metaphysical speculation. If the ultimate ideals of Man, which are what we call religious questions, are not incarnated in the spatio-temporal structures of social and political life, then both remain sterile. Theisms seem to have lost their convincing power, perhaps because the *anthrōpos* feels that the *theos* always wants to dominate heteronomically—something necessary for a transcendent and "Wholly Other" conception of the Godhead. Again we see that a new conception of the Divine is needed.

Unless we reach the political level, however, very little will be achieved. Movements like Amnesty International, the Permanent Peoples' Tribunal, the Global Forum for Human Survival, Movement for "Religion and Peace," Reconciliation, a "Better World," and hundreds of others constantly run aground on the same reef: Who or what will put a halt to the lethal course of technocracy? More concretely, who will control armaments, polluting industries, cancerous consumerism, and the like? Who will put an end to the unbridled tyranny of money? Not even a dictatorship could do it; it would have to rely on the very technocracy it seeks to overcome. What political order do we want? To give a moralizing answer is neither sufficient nor to the point. The specific problem is not whether individuals are "good" or "bad," but whether the System *as such*— the projects of civilization we support, the technocratic mentality we share—is conducive to human fulfillment on all levels.

Without the political aspects of all these issues, without political alternatives, without a political translation of the problematic—irritation, frustration, and violence will only grow. On the other hand, without a drastic change in the general outlook on reality, no power on earth will mobilize the "managers" of power to give it up, or to deviate one iota from the law of inertia. Together these impediments to transformation form a vicious circle in which theoretical change cannot come about without previous practical modifications.

Let me mention examples from very different fields. If human creativity can be fostered only by tinkering with machines and experimenting with microor macro-gadgets, any talk about change will be interpreted as life-denying, negative asceticism and a sheer impossibility. If the meaning of life can only be found either in conquering the next life, as some still interpret traditional religions, or in conquering this one, as most interpret the modern competitive society, then there is little hope of convincing anybody. Competing for heaven or competing with my neighbor—the main difference seems to be that in heaven there is room for all, while in the modern world there is only place for the executive board. What I am criticizing is the underlying assumption that the motivation for action is victory, not love.

What we have to rediscover is that the meaning of Life will never be found in any such conquest, but only in reaching that fullness of Life to which contemplation, in the sense described earlier, is the way. Plenitude, happiness, creativity, freedom, well-being, achievement, etc., should not be given up but, on the contrary, should be enhanced by this new passage from historical to transhistorical Man.

A second example of another order may be helpful. If the "nation-state" ideology is not discussed politically in the light of a new vision of human life, and a theoretical successor is found that is worthier than preceding ideologies, the project will remain a barren intellectual exercise. Discussion of the nationstate problem is not merely about looking for a new technique for redistributing the products of a "world market," or for keeping the peace by an ever more precarious "balance of power," and the like. The discussion must involve the complete vision of Man and the universe. The nation-state is not merely a "political" problem.

Is there any way out of this tragic situation? After all, our present political system is threatening to destroy the world outright. Without attempting any political, economic, or social forecast, I adduce a double simile from the physical world: the catalysis and crystallization of supersaturated solutions. In both cases, changes are brought about by the minimal intervention of an extraneous factor that serves as a catalyst or nucleus around which crystallization occurs. The processes are distinct in that the catalyst remains "free," unchanged in the transformation it precipitates, while the core of crystallization is "captured" in the eventual crystal. But in either case, the situation (or saturation) obviously has to be mature enough, and the "trans-cultural" element pure enough, to elicit the change. One might reasonably suppose that this declining twentieth century has been sufficiently saturated with disenchantment and bitter experience, on one hand, and that the cross-cultural fertilization has also reached a certain point of maturity (and purity), on the other, so as not to render unthinkable the proposition that something a good deal more radical than what is called a new paradigm may well be ready to emerge.

C. Personalism

1. *Iṣṭadevatā Spirituality*

It is not only permissible but perhaps easier, and for many also more humane (and more anthropomorphic), to focus this primordial sense of existence by projecting it onto the Beloved, the God, the Creator, the divine Person, our innocent childhood, . . . *Iṣṭadevatā* spirituality should be mentioned here, and *ṛ* as well. The cosmotheandric insight recognizes the poetic strain in Man and will not allow every expression to be reduced to a metaphysical formula. Śiva, Viṣṇu, Durgā, Jesus Christ, Father, God, Allah, Yahweh, Justice, Truth, Goodness, and Beauty, to name only a few, are not dead symbols—and every living symbol transcends every crude hypostatization. The symbol is only a symbol of the Mystery that manifests itself precisely in the symbol itself. A symbol is not a sign.

It has been believed for centuries that one of the most insurmountable difficulties for dialogue between monotheism and most of the religions of Asia is the essentially "personal character" of the Godhead in monotheism, as against the "impersonal idea" of the Divine allegedly held by those other "higher religions." The misunderstanding here would appear to be threefold: methodological, philosophical, and historical.

Methodologically, the implied comparison is inadequate for two reasons. First, it is not correct to approach, let alone judge, the insights of one culture with the intellectual instruments of another. When today we still speak of a "world order" (whether capitalism, marxism, democracy, neo-liberalism, or even christianity), we are perpetuating the colonialistic ideology which believed that, with the help of a single culture, one could understand and do justice to the belief systems of all others. The nascent interest in intrareligious dialogue and intercultural studies may have a pioneering function here. I already referred to it when criticizing the common western idea concerning "polytheism." This extrapolation of a method unfit to the task is at the root of misunderstandings that have considerable political consequences. Second, the method is inadequate for the reason stated above that the question about the Divine can be neither merely subjective nor purely objective, and requires a sharing in the sphere of the Divine—even to refute it. In order to say that the Divine is merely an illusion, we (or others) must "know" what we are talking about. Religious phenomenology is here an indispensable instrument—and with this we are already in our second remark.

Philosophically, the approach has been flawed because of the undue superimposition of a notion of person, where it can be experienced only as a foreign cultural body and a disturbing element. To make a long story short I simply remark that the very reasons why Thomas Aquinas defends the personality of God (because the Deity has to have, in an eminent way, what we discover here on earth to be the highest perfection: intelligence and free will) are also the reasons why Śankara denies personality to the Divine (namely, in order not to fall into a crude anthropomorphism).

What is person? The late japanese philosopher Keiji Nishitani interprets the passage in Matthew V, 43-48, in which it is stated that God lets the sun shine on evil and good people alike and the rain fall on the just and the unjust without discrimination as saying that God is impersonal: God is indifferent, just as impersonal Nature is indifferent. The Matthean passage reminds me of something reported to have been said by Porphyry: "Beautiful are all things to God, but Men have judged some unjust, and others as just."[87]

87 Heraclitus, *Fragm.* 22: τῷ μὲν θεῷ καλὰ πάντᾳ.

Nishitani, of course, is speaking, somewhat paradoxically, of an "indifference of love . . . that transcends the distinctions men make between good and evil, justice and injustice." I will not make an exegesis of the text or an analysis of the notion of person. The latter is a somewhat artificial name to refer to a much elaborated philosophical meaning. There is no exact name for it in most non-western languages—unless somewhat artificially translated, as in modern japanese (*jinkaku*) and the sanskrit equivalent (*pātra*).

Half a century ago, the common distinction, based on the separation between the natural and the supernatural, was that monotheistic religions worship the "living God" and asian religions only the "Ground of Being." This is simply not valid. A "heaven" into which I would be dragged by force would not be a heaven for me. Similarly, a God that I would not recognize as a God would not be a God for me. We need to realize that the discourse about God is *sui generis*.

Furthermore, the relatively recent distinction between the natural and the supernatural order stemmed from a legitimate christian defense of an appropriate discourse about the Divine once the role of the human intellect is reduced to a one-dimensional reason. Nonetheless, this distinction, valid in its western historical context, is unnecessary and even deleterious in most asian traditions, which do not accept that dichotomy either epistemologically or ontologically. Not even a tree can be transplanted without some of the earth which nurtured its roots.

Historically, we are bound to recognize that the different peoples of the world have had different conceptions of God and even used different names. We may defend our conception of the Divine as the correct one and be convinced that the other notions of the Godhead are erroneous, but to say that the other religions adore false Gods is to commit the sin of intellectual idolatry, identifying our notion with the absolutely true representation of the divine Mystery. The others may be entertaining an erroneous notion of God, perhaps with deleterious effects, but they may just as much be "meaning" and referring to what we may call the "living God." Once again, God is not an object. To consider our allegedly "true" conception of God as the only way to reach the real "God" constitutes one of the tragedies of human history.

Instead, it would be useful to consider the so-called impersonal character of the Godhead as standing for its transcendence, whereas the personal feature stands for our relationship with this divine Mystery. Utter transcendence obviously needs a more humane complement.

Here I would like to introduce a symbol that may be helpful, and which may be approached as a reinterpretation of a traditional hindu notion. This is the idea of the *iṣṭadevatā*, developed mostly in *tantra* and the *shakti* schools. Though *iṣṭadevatā* has little to do with henotheism as conceived by Schelling or Max Müller and is different from the icon conception of orthodox Christianity, all three notions ultimately reflect an urge of the human being and a feature of reality itself.

The notion of *iṣṭadevatā* has often been misunderstood, interpreted individualistically as the *deva* of my *iṣṭa*, choice, desire, pleasure. This is an example of a "katachronic" interpretation—so typical of modernity. Traditionally, it is the guru or master who discovers (not just chooses) the proper *iṣṭadevatā* of the śisy\ *a*, disciple, according to the latter's (the *sādhaka*'s, aspirant's) *guṇa* and *bhāva* (properties and character). The traditional explanation of the *vigraha*, or image of the Divine, consists in making the distinction between idol and icon, or rather, in understanding the *vigraha* as a symbolic re-presentation of *brahman*, or absolute and formless Deity. (The *vigraha* can be *arūpa*, formless, or *sarūpa*, with form, anthropomorphic or otherwise.) The act of re-presenting is essential for the presence of the Deity, and this act is performed by the *sādhaka* or worshiper by having a sensible symbol for the Divine. The very word *vi-graha*, suggesting a firm, concrete grasp (from *gṛh*, to grasp), indicates that the *vigraha* is there precisely in order to allow for a human grasp of the Divine Mystery.

I would like to rescue such an idea from a solely individualistic interpretation and apply it to other traditions as well. The *iṣṭadevatā* spirituality is not sheer relativism, as if the idea of the Deity did not matter and anybody could choose at whim between Jesus Christ and Vinoba Bhave, or Kung-fu-tze and Martin Luther King. Because I find inspiration in the life of Vinoba does not necessarily convert him into my chosen Deity. The *iṣṭadevatā* is not the idol of my sympathies, or the God of my choosing. You do not choose your God. It is the Divine, if at all, who chooses you. The religion one adheres to is not a political party one chooses, a president one votes for, or any individual concoction according to taste. A severe criticism of eclecticism understood in this way is surely appropriate. *Iṣṭadevatā* spirituality, as I am interpreting it, has nothing to do with some liberal, individualistic notion of a democratically elected particular Deity.

A brief example will make my point. Let us assume that Christ is my *iṣṭadevatā*. This does not mean I have chosen Christ because I have examined all the divine candidates in a wide pantheon and Jesus has convinced me more than the others. Neither does it mean that, objectively speaking, I am convinced that Christ is "superior" to all other images of the Divine. Allah is certainly superior, *qua* God, to Jesus of Nazareth—who, after all, was truly Man, much as I may equate him with one of the Trinity. A comparison with Krishna on this existential plane would be equally out of place. Should we decide, for instance, according to the criterion of which one has the greater sense of humor? Does Christ as *iṣṭadevatā* entail rating a theology of Lord Shiva as inferior? Not at all. We are not comparing notions of Deity or weighing sympathies; we are on an existential and personal plane.

Christ as *iṣṭadevatā* means that, owing to a number of factors, Christ has become, for me, the symbol of that third dimension—albeit including also the other two. The reasons may be birth, conversion, culture, history, conviction of superiority (also), personal experience, initiation, or whatever. *How* it has become the *iṣṭadevatā* accounts neither for *why* nor for the bare fact *that* it has become such. We may say it is grace, or *karma*, or providence, or that the *iṣṭadevatā* has manifested herself to me.

This encounter with the *iṣṭadevatā* conditions how I interpret the meaning of life, the moral code, fundamental sentiments, the basic attitudes of my existence. Christ becomes the divine symbol. This may be very conventional or very personal. It may be due to a predominantly intellectual conviction, or to a much more intimate relationship. It may allow me to be called a christian, or it may not, if I do not meet the sociological requirements of a given historical christian community. At any rate, the personal image of the Divine will be shaped by Christ. This certainly does not mean that one may not also recognize all the other great symbols as equally powerful, or that one should be exclusive in an intolerant way. As the re-presentation of the Divine, the *iṣṭadevatā* is what allows a personal relationship with the divine Mystery.

It is not by chance that the *iṣṭadevatā* spirituality has thrived in a *bhakti* atmosphere—that is, where the approach to the divine Mystery has considered love to be the most important way to the Godhead and to personal realization. Within that sphere there is no place for competitiveness. If I have encountered my Beloved, also on the human level, there is no room for jealousy if somebody else has discovered another lover.

The *iṣṭadevatā* spirituality has still another feature. It is difficult to maintain our lives at the highest "mystical" level of reality. As the chinese say, we cannot stand all the time on the tips of our toes. The Divine, as a constitutive dimension of reality, is a wonderful thing, but if we suppress or repress the personal aspect of the Godhead, our hearts may be left cold and our minds blank. We need *la presencia y la figura* (Juan de la Cruz). The *iṣṭadevatā* comes into the picture as the incarnation, the figure, the *nāma,* and the *rūpa* of this dimension. The figure of the Beloved could not survive for the devotees, *bhaktas*, of every religion without a living manifestation of the Divine Mystery. We need Krishna, Bhagavan, Buddha, Tukaram, Jesus, Our Lady, Archangel Michael, guardian angels or whatever. Of course, many of them do not claim to be God, but all are, at different levels, expressions of the Divine Mystery and perform the function not only of focusing our psychology, but of assuaging our metaphysics.

I am not saying that all *iṣṭadevatā* have the same value or perform an identical function, but each covers the ineffability of the Divine Mystery with a beautiful robe. Here is the place to mention the important aspect of aesthetics in the description of the divine dimension. The body, the senses, and beauty are essential aspects in this. In our times, when a dry "theology" seems to have reserved for herself the right to talk about God, the role of aesthetics in uncovering the divine dimension is paramount. Every artist knows or rather feels it—whereby we should stress that true knowledge is also sensible and authentic sentiment is intelligent. Within the field of contemporary christian theology, to mention the name of Hans Urs von Balthasar is a duty.

I am tempted to advance a somewhat daring interpretation of an *iṣṭadevatā* spirituality—which may atone for the all-too-frequent misinterpretations of its so-called polytheism. It could well be that there is a kind of "polytheism" that is only a sort of "iconolatry"—to be distinguished from idolatry. This alleged polytheism would see the living symbol of the Divine in the symbol which in that particular instance "embodies" the divine Mystery, and as such worships it in and at that particular moment of time and space.

One could equally relate the *iṣṭadevatā* as a homeomorphic equivalent to the figure of the *avatāra* (descent, manifestation of the divine)—but we are not indulging now in comparisons. Our point is to stress the multiple manifestations of the divine dimension. If I could hope not to be misunderstood, I would even add that the *iṣṭadevatā* is a sort of incarnation of the Divine. It is in a certain way that real divine symbol with whom we may have a personal relationship.

God has created human beings in his likeness and resemblance. This means not only that we are images of God but also that God sees his image reflected in us. We are theomorphous because God is anthropomorphous. The *iṣṭadevatā* is the link, the mediator. Between the christian idea of the incarnation and this conception of the *iṣṭadevatā* there is surely a homeomorphic equivalence.

2. *Contemplation*

The iconic attitude is fundamental to religion not only because of our body and our nature but also because the divine dimension of reality is intrinsically connected with us. The divine dimension, however, is not exhausted in its symbol, just as I am body (and do not merely have one) and yet I am "more" than my body. There is an invisible factor which makes my body body without being only body and yet inseparable from it. Similarly, there is an invisible aspect of the divine dimension that becomes manifest to the third eye of mystical contemplation.

Contemplation is an essential element in all religions because it corresponds to a fundamental trait of Man. It may be rendered as meditation, orison, quiet, silence, or as presence of God, vocal prayers, prayer of the heart, and the like. I purposely am not using any of the specialized names like *hēsychia*, *mantra*, *dhikr*, *dhyāna*, and *zen*.

The cosmotheandric spirituality recovers the place and the power of this most human activity, too often obscured by external and apparently practical exercises that accompany a superficial idea of religion. I choose the word contemplation to describe what could be rendered by almost any of the other names I have cited. I am not adhering now to any particular school of spirituality. I may, however, start with the wisdom of this word.

Since Cicero, at least, the latin word *contemplatio* was used to translate the greek *theōria* (θεωρία), which had a brilliant career in hellenic thought. The βίος θεωρητικός was the life of the authentic philosopher who "sees'" through to the ideas, the essences, the reality of things. The underlying root of the word is *thea* (θέα) vision, with connotations of paying attention to, observing, caring for, keeping an eye on. Plato and Aristotle were masters of this contemplative life, which was contrasted with actively busying oneself in the immediate chores of ordinary existence. Seneca also expounded upon this in his masterful way.

The literal use of the word allowed one to speak of both αἰσθήσει θεωρητόν (*aisthēsei theōr*ēton), sensory "contemplation," and λόγῳ θεωρητόν (*logō theōr*ēton), intellectual "contemplation." After Plato, Plotinus became the great theoretician of *theōria*. One had to overcome the "vision" of the *nous* (equivalent to *gnōsis*) in order to attain the authentic *theōria*. The confrontation between *theōria* and *gnōsis* had a long and complex relationship in antiquity. A text from hebrew scripture (Wisdom VII, 17) was often quoted in this context: γνῶσις τῶν ὄντων (knowledge of things) and contrasted to θεωρία τῶν ὄντων (vision of the beings) or even θεωρία τῶν γεγονότων (vision of things that have become—that is, of created things).

The christian "twist" was curiously helped along by one of those effective, although grammatically spurious etymologies: θεὸν ὁγρᾶν[88] ("seeing God"). Theory would then mean nothing less than "to see God." In fact, the word *theōria* was often understood as coming from *theos*, God, and not from *thea*, "vision," "to see." The Pseudo-Plutarch still thought that not only *theōrein*, but also *theatron*, "theatre," came from *theos*, so that the first purpose of theater was to honor the Gods, as in the Dionysian festivals celebrated theatrically at Ephesus.[89]

For the christian tradition, *theōreia* meant to look for and eventually to see God, although *en ainigmati* only.[90] Or, in a more concrete way, it meant to see Christ in whom all the riches and treasures of the Godhead are hidden and contained.[91] In this tradition, action and contemplation go together and develop an interesting dialectic. The main principle, based on the Gospels, may still be Origen's often repeated phrase: "Praxis is the ascent to contemplation."[92] Or, in the same place: "There is neither theory without praxis, nor praxis without theory."

This introduces an ambivalence that has persisted to our own times. On the one hand, we have the opposition between *praxis* and *theōria*. On the other, we have *contemplatio*, which, like *theōria,* is opposed to *actio*, but which most christian writers interpret as the highest form of action. Union with God, Creator and Redeemer, cannot be just looking at things, or even at the divine essence, without an active participation in that creation and in the redemption of the world in particular. *Vita contemplativa* in this sense is not opposed to *vita activa*. Ignatius of Loyola's formula—*in actione contemplativus, in contemplatione activus*, "contemplative in action, active in contemplation"—was preceded by the dominican motto: *contemplata aliis tradere*, "To pass on to others the wisdom of contemplation."

Contemplatio comes, of course, from *templum*, the temple as sacred precinct, that is, as a space "cut off" or set apart, where the augurs might observe the sacred birds whose flights follow, re-enact, and thus reveal the course of events in the cosmos at large. *Templum* is related to the greek *temenos*, "sacred enclosure," temple, the root of which, *temnein*, means "to cut." The sacred, for the entire western tradition, is thus segregated, cut off from the profane sphere.

88 Callistus Cataphugiota, *De vita contemplativa* 2 (PG 147:836).

89 Pseudo-Plutarch, *De musica* 27.

90 1 Cor XIII, 12.

91 Col II, 3; etc.

92 Origen, *In Lucam*, fragm. 39 (P.G. 13, 1801): πρᾶξις γὰρ θεωρίας ἀνάβασις.

Taking into account the tradition of *theōreia and contemplatio*, I would like to interpret contemplation as that human activity which transcends the mental and overcomes the *praxis/theōria* split, so that contemplation is a movement both of things and of the spirit, a transformation of objects as well as subjects.

In brief, contemplation is the operation of *ta mystika*, the opening of a truly third eye—the phrase used by Richard of Saint Victor. I mean that activity of Man in which our "three organs" of contact with reality, which correspond to the three dimensions of the real, are equally open and active so as to allow the plenitude of the *humanum*. On one hand, this contemplation implies praxis, that is, activity, good works in traditional parlance, secular involvement, concern for the daily events of one's surroundings, for people and for the land. It also includes, on the other hand, intellectual activity, study, knowledge, the operation of the *nous*, authentic scientific investigation, and what Hegel calls *Anstrengung des Begriffes*. Contemplation, however, further demands not only a marriage of the two but the fruit of that union, a third element that impinges directly on the very course of the universe (as so many connotations of the word still suggest). "By their fruits you shall know them."[93]

Thus, contemplation does not mean just "praying" to God—as if it were necessary to remind divine providence to perform its proper duties. Nor is it only to "meditate" on the nature of things ephemeral (to despise them), or things eternal (to love them), etc. It is rather to unify one's own life by bringing together praxis and theory, action and knowledge, immediate involvement and effective non-attachment (the *asakti* of the *Gītā*).[94] This contemplation is a cosmotheandric act. Man shares in the destiny of the universe by touching, knowing, loving, and doing. This universe is not some gigantic corpse reeling in the void at the speed of light, but a living organism. Our contemplation does not alter the explosions of Sirius in Canis Major. Yet it sounds a unique note whose resonances may reach the very heart of this living mesocosm organically connected with all of reality. This contemplation cannot be the act of a rational animal, it is not a more or less intelligent "program," or even a sensitive praxis for "arranging" the world. It is not the activity of an "artificial intelligence" trying to instill or to find a rational order within a framework in which there is no place for freedom. It is not a merely theoretical grasp of the Whole, or of the world, or of any particular situation. Nor is it merely sentimental or emotional involvement in

93 Mt VII, 16; etc.

94 BG XIII, 9.

the travails of the human world. It is not the specific activity of an exceptional species among living beings that is capable of detecting the evolution of life on the planet. It is a *templum* which gathers and confronts the Whole, *rota in rotae*, a wheel inside a wheel, as the jewish prophet indicated.[95] It is much more than an intelligent influence on the world, as a secularized mentality might say; the ancients would call it a divine act.

As I have hinted, contemplation does not mean to "contemplate" things, but to contemplate the seer, to see the contemplator. Since the Upanishads, we have known that we cannot see the seer, as Augustine wondered: *Videntem videre... Visio Dei viventis et videntis* ("to see the One seeing... the vision of the living and seeing God").[96] But we may become the seer—not by seeing it, but by seeing with the seer, by sharing that vision. The word vision here is of course active and not passive; the vision is in the seeing. The word, obviously, stands for the active becoming not just of the seen, but of the seer, which is seer only when it sees.

My intention is not to describe the nature of contemplation but to underscore its importance and the way in which a cosmotheandric spirituality may enhance and correct imbalances in many a tradition. All too often the mystical aspect has been allowed to atrophy, or been severed from the rest of life.

I have not spoken of the *intuitus animi* of Bernard of Clairvaux,[97] or of the *intuitus veritatis* of Thomas Aquinas,[98] as of so many other christian writers, or of the *fruitio Dei* of the more volitional spiritual directions in the christian tradition. Nor do we dwell on the homeomorphic equivalents of contemplation in other religious traditions. It is nonetheless worth emphasizing this much: contemplation is neither synonymous with mysticism, nor with union with God, nor with a merely intellectual vision. I would like to recover the underlying sense of the word, the deepest participation of Man in the mystery of reality by means of all possible "organs" for entering into contact with the real. I would like to maintain the use of this word in the western world, despite the degeneration of its main thrust. By now, of course, flight from the world, *fuga mundi*, castration of the senses, or of the mind, escapisms of all sorts, and *a posteriori* justifications for every kind of lopsided spirituality have been widely criticized, although such aberrations still persist.

95 Ez X, 10.

96 Augustine, *Sermon 69.*

97 Bernard of Clairvaux, *De consideratione* II, 2 (PL 182:745 b).

98 Thomas Aquinas, *Summ. Theol.* II-II, q. 180, a. 3, ad 1.

In any case, the solidarity (*buddhakāya*, *karman*, *corpus mysticum*, . . .) of reality as a whole is a fact, although the contemporary features of this *solidum* may be different, and our priorities diverse. The *templum* of contemplation may be intriguingly connected with the *tempus* of our temporality, and the *temperantia* of our temperament.

It should remain clear that the contemplation I am describing ought not be equated with an individualistic perfection. It underscores, to the contrary, the transformation of the cosmos, the engagement of Man in the overall dynamism of the universe, and thereby rounds out the very idea of personal perfection.

VIII
The Emerging Mythos

We have been saying that only a holistic insight into the nature of reality will orient us in the jungle of multiple opinions and specialized branches of knowledge. We have also criticized the old models, not because they were wrong but because we now discover them not to take sufficiently into account the objective data of the present, nor the subjective requirements of our contemporary demands. They are simply of the past, and at least need to be reenacted anew. We have, further, suggested the cosmotheandric insight as a possible hypothesis for such an enterprise. Finally, we have concentrated on the role and nature of the Divine in the perennial triad of Cosmos, Man, and God, meanwhile taking care not to sever this dimension from the whole of reality.

We will now try to relate this vision to our world. It is the world in which we live, in which we believe we live, and which offers the context for our ideas about God and Man. The predominant worldview of our times is the scientific cosmology, but this cosmology is a product of modern western culture and is not the only vision of the world. The immensity of the topic allows only for some sketches.

All too often philosophers and thinkers have remained in the lofty realm of ideas and have consciously or unconsciously shunned delving into the "real world" in the parlance not only of common people but also of the scientific community. The well-known and highly criticized gap between theory and praxis exists also between what we call the humanities or *Geisteswissenschaften* and what is labeled as the natural sciences.[1] The incursions of philosophers have reached into sociological fields (marxism is an example), but more rarely into the technological realm. We cannot offer immediate solutions, but we cannot avoid the problem. We should look for

1 This was the problem I studied in my first writings of the 1940s and '50s republished later in *Ontonomía de la ciencia: sobre el sentido de la ciencia y sus relaciones con la* filosofiia (Madrid: Gredos, 1963).

hints of some fundamental areas for change in our worldview, or in what I would like to call our *world-mythos*.

A. A New Kosmology

1. Cosmology and Kosmology

Although the modern scientific cosmology has triumphed over the old cosmologies, the modern vision has not corrected many errors of the old cosmologies, but rather *seems* to have merely displaced or found functional substitutes for certain key elements. Therefore, in order to stress continuity, on the one hand, and novelty, on the other, I have chosen to change the ordinary spelling of the new cosmology (to kosmology) instead of introducing any new name (such as *cosmosophia*, as I am tempted to do). The continuity is obvious. Kosmology continues cosmology. We cannot ignore the important discoveries of the modern scientific cosmology. The novelty consists in overcoming the reductionism of "reducing" the nature of the cosmos to what the modern scientific picture of the universe tells us. Modern science, when aware of its specific method and of its limits, does not pretend to furnish a complete worldview. It is only a description of the quantifiable parameters of the world. Yet because of its spectacular achievements and the poverty of the old views, a great part of our contemporaries, not excluding many in the scientific community, tends to identify the modern scientific cosmology with a fairly complete picture of the real world. In short, the cosmology of Copernicus is incomparably more correct than that of Ptolemy concerning the movement of lifeless bodies, but the latter may indeed be richer in its contents.

By *Kosmology* I understand the science (in its classical meaning of *scientia, gnōsis, jñâna . . .*) about the holistic sense of the *kosmos*, the *logos* on and about the *kosmos*, the "word of the cosmos." Kosmology is a *kosmos-legein*, a "reading" of the kosmos, the disclosure of the world to our human consciousness by means of all the forms of knowledge we may possess. Kosmology is mainly understood here in the sense of the subjective genitive: the *logos*, the word of the kosmos that Man should try to hear and to understand by attuning himself to the music of this world, to the mysteries of the kosmos. We are aware that the kosmos speaks differently to different cultures and that Man hears and interprets this *logos* in many ways. Similarly as the person who knows only one religion has the danger of fanaticism, those who know only the modern cosmology have the danger of absolutizing that cosmos just as those who knew only one of the classical cosmologies did, of course. By and large we have relativized the old kosmologies and branded them as obsolete in a manner similar to how certain theologies have discounted other religions. In both cases, one's own worldview is considered the real one, or at least the decisive point of reference. Interculturality tries to address this great challenge, and this is one area where religious consciousness seems, for once, to be ahead of modern science, although science is still considered by many to be superior to religion and more universal.[2]

Cosmology, on the other hand, is the result of the scientific *ratio* applied to the cosmos, which is open to the rational *logos*. Cosmology is expressed in the current "cosmological" doctrines derived by means of modern scientific methods. Cosmology is mainly understood as an objective genitive: our *logos* about the *cosmos*. Kosmology, on the other hand, deals rather with how Man envisions the universe, with how the kosmos displays itself to Man, and with the experience that Man has of the universe of which we happen to form part and that leads us to discover the real universe in which we live.

Neither traditional kosmologies nor modern cosmologies are totally objectifiable sciences. Both are the prevalent myths that reign in their respective cultures and which confer plausibility on the interpretation of what we call the world. There is an intimate connection between kosmology and cosmology. Both deal with the cosmos, but the latter is a special case of the former. Scientific cosmology has yielded useful and splendid results, but it does not even pretend to embrace the knowledge of the kosmos.

There is a fundamental difference between scientific cognition and human knowledge. Scientific cognition is connected to the study of those phenomena that appear (φαίνεσθαι) to the scientific method. In this way we have analyzed the components of the earth and even of living beings; we have predicted the behavior of celestial and terrestrial bodies, and so on. Scientific discoveries, however, are one particular case of "knowledge," which I call "cognition." When we truly know something, on the other hand, we become that something, we embrace it as part of ourselves, although we need to draw necessary distinctions, since the identification has degrees. Knowledge, properly speaking, is not the result of the activity of our reasoning mind that, after being fed some data, functions like a sophisticated computer. Nor is knowledge an activity of our mind alone; it is an act of our entire being; ultimately it is an act of the whole Being. Knowledge is not a mere epistemological device; it has an ontological nature, and love is an intrinsic part of the act of knowing.

Kosmology aspires to a knowledge of the kosmos in a manner similar

2 See Panikkar, "Politics, Religion, and Interculturality," in K. L. Nandan, ed., *The Earth Has No Corners* (Delhi: Shipra, 2001).

to the way theology aspired to a knowledge of God and thus claimed to have saving power. The novelty of this cosmotheandric kosmology is that it also claims to possess saving power for the wholeness (salvation) of Man, a microcosm. This is why traditional kosmologies considered the kosmos to be the home of Man where he finds doom or well-being. The limits of the *kosmos* are not just geographical or even astronomical. The kosmos is the body of God, say some religions. Christianity likewise claims that the kosmos is the body of Christ, and qualifies this by saying that this body is still in pangs of birth and on the way to an *eschaton* that will be reached by every realized (liberated) person. This cosmotheandric kosmology is the religious novelty of our times that I have called *sacred secularity.*[3]

Kosmology tries to understand and interpret, more or less profoundly, whatever enters into the field of our consciousness. Cosmology only admits what has passed the scientific examination, what has passed through the assessment of our analytical cognition. I offer two examples.

First, *Aether* is a homeomorphic equivalent to the indic *ākāśa*; both stand for the unlimited empty space, as the fifth element of ("material") reality, and both could perhaps be related to the platonic χώρα. Aether, however, could not be apprehended by the parameters of modern science, and, like God, was discounted as a superfluous hypothesis in modern physics. The *actio in distans*, that is, how to explain the transition of energy through an "empty" space, has been empirically and scientifically solved. The cosmological theories about ether (the change in spelling is also significant) are obsolete and have been abandoned. They are not needed to explain any physical phenomenon. The word belongs to the history of science and has practically disappeared from modern dictionaries—except as a literary metaphor. The ether simply does not exist in modern cosmology—unlike *ākāśa* of indian kosmology. A link between matter and spirit has disappeared, and, likewise, an important element for modern japanese philosophy of nothingness, *śūnyatā*, has also been abolished, because it has no place, no function in modern cosmology.

A second example: Since angels are not the subject matter of scientific cognition and modern science shapes our worldview, there is no place for angels in a modern cosmology. Within the modern cosmological myth "we" have no knowledge of them. Of course, this would be the modern discourse: we may take into account the fact that other peoples believe in angels; we may respect and even accept their beliefs, but our epistemological situation is radically different. Taking notice that other people believe in angels, we try to imagine what their belief may mean, but we speak only from hearsay,

3 See Panikkar, *El mundanal silencio* (Barcelona: Martínez Roca, 1999).

since angels are not in our world. In spite of all our epistemological efforts, our ontological situation is different and we cannot believe in angels. Belief is not the belief in the belief of others. We cannot allow angels to disobey the second principle of thermodynamics.

Myths naturally evolve and change, and this is true also for the myth of modern cosmology. When the symbolic structure of a civilization is destroyed, that civilization collapses. The case of the arunta people, whose symbolic totem was destroyed, or of the amerindian civilizations, whose symbolic universe was "superseded" by that of the *conquistadores*, are powerful examples. Both cultures practically died. This should be a call for nonviolence and a warning for any exclusively iconoclastic attitude. As much as I am a critic of modern cosmology I am not for the destruction of it—due not only to ethical scruples (it would be bad) or tactical strategy (technology is more powerful), but also for metaphysical reasons (if technocracy pervades the world there must be some ground for it and crusades will not provide the solution). The new kosmology I am envisioning is neither an updating of the old "worldviews" nor a mere reform of the new (or newest) cosmology, but a transformation of both.

Be that as it may, in stressing the difference between kosmology and cosmology I am trying to dispel a crypto-kantian assumption regarding scientific cognition: There is no world *an sich*; a "world in itself" does not exist. The word "worldview" (*Weltanschauung*) may be misleading. The word tends to make us assume that it is all a question of different views of the same world, a world that is "obviously" described by "our" cosmology. If we are also world and not only in the world, then we cannot eliminate the subjective factor of the cosmos, but neither can we dispense with its objective aspect.

Man is not totally objectifiable. Man is a subject, a subject of understanding, even a subject of self-understanding, and this self-understanding belongs to the essence of Man. Self-understanding is not only my understanding of myself, but is also all the understandings that our fellow beings have of themselves. The *kosmos* is not a mere object of epistemology. *Kosmos* and Man belong together, and human self-understanding cannot be severed from the world in which Man lives. The historical experience of Man is also a kosmological factor. Hence the importance of the predominant scientific cosmology, which we cannot peremptorily dismiss without painting ourselves into a solipsistic corner.

The new kosmology cannot be idealistic; it cannot be a result of the mind alone. Modern Man has had too much experience of the hardness of life, the resistance of matter, and the objectivity of science to put everything on the side of the subject. But it cannot be materialistic either. To begin with, science is too conscious of its own limits and limitations. The numinous appears everywhere, each new answer opens up scores of new questions, and human experience has been too painful to permit everything to be reduced to a mechanistic dialectic— projecting into the future what it cannot answer now.

Nor can it be a theological kosmology. The monotheistic God, despite virtuoso performances by some theologians, has *de facto* not "delivered the goods." A purely transcendent God may be all very well for some philosophers, but can hardly seem convincing for most people. Either God's presence is visible everywhere—I do not say intellectually evident—or God will have little credibility. One need only immerse oneself in a traditional culture—in Asia or Africa, for instance—to sense the ubiquitous presence of the Divine. To convert God into some mysterious proto-energy moving the universe over the eons is a facile but unconvincing solution, the continuation of a discarded monotheism at its lowest ebb. But such a casual dismissal of the divine cannot be a lasting solution; God returns all too often as the leading figure in extreme fundamentalisms, or merely esoteric movements. The problem is not physical but metaphysical. Here metaphysics does not mean what is behind (or underneath) *this* physical world. The *meta* is not epistemological but ontological; it points to a "world," which is not a concept but a symbol in the sense that the symbol is prior to subjectobject epistemological knowledge. As we said earlier, a symbol is symbol only for those who recognize it as a symbol. I could sum it up by saying that the *kosmos* of traditional kosmology is a symbol, whereas the cosmos of cosmology is a concept. It is a methodological error to assume that ancient kosmologies, for instance, did not know anything about those distant galaxies invisible to the naked eye because they did not have a clear concept of them. They knew "them" as part of this world, which had room for the unknown and even the unknowable beyond. Eschatological reflection, for instance, as a metaphysical ingredient of some kosmologies, did not refer to an astronomic big-bang coming to an end, but to the end of creation in its metaphysical meaning. It is naive to consider our ancestors mentally retarded because they did not know today's marvelous physical sciences. They lived in "another" world. I should add that for the new kosmology the world is both symbol and concept. At this juncture we can simply say without further elaboration that the world is neither one nor two. Each world presents an *advaitic* relationship with the people living in it.

2. *The Conflict of Kosmologies*

The kosmological problem is paramount. An increasing number of perceptive thinkers seem to agree that humanity is facing its greatest crisis today. There are so many studies from all corners of the world that it is no longer easy to dismiss it all as the ill-tempered reactions of some prophets of doom, or to ignore the crisis because we, as over-privileged members of society, can still manage fairly well. The world crisis of our times stems from a conflict of kosmologies.

It is too simplistic to reduce the tension of the human world to a dialectical "white and black," to a fight between good and bad people, *deva* and *asura*— even if called right and left, law-abiding and terrorists. The struggle is between different kosmologies, and the victory of the one over the other will never lead to peace—as it never has done. Here we meet again the political importance of interculturality.

I may give an example of a nonviolent effort at transforming the presentday cosmology. The north american cultural historian and theologian Thomas Berry is one of the most articulate voices in this regard. In calling for a "New Story," specifically a new and scientifically credible creation story, he charges christian theology with giving undue emphasis to redemption while neglecting the more basic issue of creation.[4] Indeed, he is not alone in this criticism, to which I subscribe from another perspective.

In his "Twelve Principles for Understanding the Universe," Berry, a catholic priest, does not lay stress on God or on religion. He speaks of the universe as a unity, recognizes its "psychic as well as physical reality," and underlines the "inter-communion of all living and non-living components of the earth community."[5]

It is obvious that any theistic interference would distract him from this overall picture. Berry calls himself a "geologian" rather than a theologian, dispensing with all theisms, religions, and spiritualities. Rightly so, if he has to use those words in the way in which they are mainly used in the english-speaking world. Teilhard de Chardin, whose footsteps this past president of the American Teilhard Association follows, spoke of the Cosmic Christ and the Omega Point out of a predominantly christian inspiration. Berry is not primarly concerned to reconcile religion and modern science. He largely ignores the first while trying to reinterpret the second. Of course a

4 Thomas Berry and Brian Swimme, *The Universe Story: From the Primordial Flaring Forth to the Ecozoic Era* (San Francisco: HarperSanFranciso, 1992).

5 Thomas Berry, *The New Story* (Chambersburg, Pa.: Anima Books, 1978), 107-8.

truly cross-cultural approach might be less linear and serve to relativize both western religious "dogmas" and the achievements of modern science. My point here, however, is simply to stress the need for a new kosmology and to recognize that the theistic traditions are unable to cope with today's human and earthly condition. In a similar vein, scores of other thinkers also attempt to adapt modern religiousness to the world of techno-science.[6]

From the scientific perspective Stephen Hawking also attempts to relate the contemporary religious situation and the modern scientific cosmology, but his underlying theological framework is inadequate.[7] He would like to find a place for God in the universe of astrophysics. Good scientist that he is, he has to confess, in the words of Carl Sagan's introduction to his book, there is "nothing for a creator to do." The "anthropic principle" is another highly sophisticated attempt in a similar direction.[8] One can well understand Heidegger and Berry preferring not to speak about such a God.

We need a new *mythos*, a deeper horizon from which the *mythologoumenon*, the Story for our age, may emerge, but myths are not created or manipulated at will. We may narrate the *mythologoumena* only when the underlying myth makes the story credible and speakable; at present we are hardly ready to hear it, although poets have already borne witness to its emergence. We tolerate them because, we say, they live in another world. Nevertheless, Man cannot live in two worlds without suffering cultural schizophrenia. The new Kosmology is aware of this and looks for a remedy.

Even if the time is not quite ripe for a new myth, we have lost our innocence with the old ones, and we no longer believe in them. Progress, science, technology, history, democracy, and similar other stories in which most of our predecessors believed, and to which many of our contemporaries still cling, are no longer held to be true by a multitude of people or by responsible thinkers from the most diverse walks of life and persuasions. The main difficulty lies in the fact that a constructive and realistic alternative is still far away.

Myths cannot be manipulated, because they have to be believed—and believing is a free act and not the conclusion of a syllogism. Myths are myths only when they are so much taken for granted that we do not acknowledge the need to prove them. We simply believe. Myths are expressed in symbols, and

6 See, for example, the work of the catalan jesuit, M. Corbí.

7 Stephen Hawking, *A Brief History of Time: From the Big Bang to Black Holes* (New York: Bantam, 1988).

8 John D. Barrow and Frank J. Tipler, *The Anthropic Cosmological Principle* (Oxford: Oxford University Press, 1988).

symbols defy any hermeneutics. The myth recedes when we think it through; interpretation only destroys the symbol and replaces it with another. That through which we interpret a symbol then becomes the real symbol because it displays its symbolizing power by needing no further interpretation.

Man cannot live without myths. All peoples and cultures possess such a set of more or less articulated beliefs which they hold in common in order to express what they stand for in this life, and how they see the universe in which they live. Individuals have myths, and such myths die hard. Children reject their parents' stories, yet when they become adults and parents, they begin in their turn to tell similar stories to their children. Man is a mythmaker and myth-enjoyer, a "myth-eater," some languages would say—a "honey-eater" (*madhvāda*), says an Upanishad of the person who has the (direct) experience.[9]

To every demythicization corresponds a new remythicization. This is part of the dialectic between *mythos and logos*.[10] The entire process is a dynamic one. We do not yet know the New Story, but its *dramatis personae*—*kosmos, anthrōpos, theos*—have already been introduced. To suppress any of the three is to fall into reductionism, although the elements of reality are so intertwined that any one of the three personages inheres in the other two. Berry also discovers a trinity, which he calls "the three basic laws of the universe," valid "at all levels of reality": "differentiation, subjectivity, and communion."

My critique of Berry's grand presentation is that what he is narrating is based mainly on the modern scientific story, and I wonder whether modern science can sustain such a life-giving *mythos*. It is instructive to observe how innocently the Teilhards, Berrys, and scores of other modern intellectuals believe in "Science." Hardly anyone dares to point out that "the Emperor is not fully clothed." It is not my intention to criticize Berry's cosmology. It is a powerful effort to raise the consciousness of his fellow north americans that even science can be redeemed. His Story may not convince me—and with me more than half of humanity who do not believe in the scientific *mythos*—but for those for whom modern science offers a paradigm of the universe, his Story is convincing and indeed insightful. His Story, the scientific reinterpretation of a desacralized biblical creation myth, may be the right way to rescue us from the technocratic slavery.

---

9 KathU II, 1, 5 (IV, 5).

10 See Panikkar "Die Unmythologisierung in der Begegnung des Christentums mit dem Hinduismus," *Kerygma und Mythos* 6 (1963), 211-35.

Berry quotes Brian Swimme, speaking at a center dedicated to the "search for a new metaphysics for our living planet": "You scientists have this stupendous story of the universe. . . . But so long as you persist in understanding it solely in a quantitative mode you fail to hear its music. That's what the spiritual traditions can provide. Tell the story, but tell it with a feel for its music."

Beautifully said. My only doubt is whether merely juxtaposing science and spirituality is enough: libretto and music go together. I hope that by listening to the music, science may alter its text. I have omitted a sentence from the quotation. It is this sentence which gives rise to my criticism—unless I should take as a rhetorical *captatio benevolentiae*. The ellipsis reads: "It breaks outside all previous cosmologies." *Evviva la Scienza!*

My concern is not to narrate a New Story, but rather to gather some elements of the possible Story by drawing on human beliefs through the ages, without subscribing to the modern myth that science has at last given us a clear, objective, and calculable picture of the universe for the first time.

* * *

The cosmotheandric *mythos,* which is slowly being formed, retells on another level the majority of myths humanity has held regarding the meaning of the universe. Hence, I am not telling the Story of science, but retelling the Story of humanity. Yet, as every storyteller knows, each authentic narration is alive and unique in each new telling.

Whether it is the vedic struggle between the *devas* and *asuras*; the babylonian, biblical, and islamic stories of heavenly combats; the gnostic legends; or many of the african myths, all those stories tell of the common destiny of the universe. The battles are not just about the evolutionary survival of the fittest, or about the political conquest of additional territory. The struggle of existence is a cosmic, divine, and human conflict that involves all three worlds. According to a widespread definition, which for me is obsolete, mythologies are stories about the Gods. In a way, however, it is not so wrongheaded, since the Gods also implicate Man and the Cosmos. In other words, myths are stories about reality, and because the *mythos* of modern scholarship had forgotten the Gods in its overall picture of the universe, what most strikes modern scholars about ancient myths is the presence of the Gods. So these scholars suppose that myths deal only or mainly with the Gods, whereas such stories also deal with us and the world.

Scores of scholars have been retelling these primordial stories of our ancestors. What they come down to is that we are all engaged in the same destiny; we are all in the same boat, as Cicero literally said. A mythic story encompasses us all. It is a hiero-history, a sacred story that belongs to myth but not to history or science. Such stories we ought to retell time and again and ever new. Without abusing the metaphor, I would say that the stories have the same basic music, but different lyrics. Human destiny is not independent of the destiny of the Gods and the fate of the stars. Individual history is not the whole story; the universe has *a* Destiny—*la dramaturgie théogénique* in the words of Henry Corbin.

Most of the ancient myths have an air of drama but not of tragedy. There is rebellion, fall, disobedience, evil, and death, but there is also the final triumph of the good cause, the hero, the good God. There is redemption, forgiveness, reconciliation, *apokatastasis* ("reconciliation"), *anakephalaiōsis* ("recapitulation"), and the like. To be sure, Gilgamesh is thwarted, Adam falls, and immortality seems to elude all human efforts. This appears to be the human condition: although the end looms far distant and difficult, hope is ultimately not lost. There is resurrection and a new earth, Odysseus returns, and in the *purāṇa* even Yudhishthira's dog is allowed to enter heaven. The traditional universe is hierarchical, and the supreme role is performed by the Deity, although Man also has much to say. The later tragedies are all human tragedies, not divine, that is, not ultimate. One might say that these tragedies represent the irreparable clash between Men and the Gods. In any case, the ultimate fate of the universe was not at stake. If one aeon may collapse, another will succeed; if one race sins, another endures the trial. To each *prālaya*, or cosmic destruction, another world follows. It may be that now, for the first time, humanity envisages an ultimate metaphysical catastrophe, such a total annihilation that not even the "evil God" will win. Everything is wiped out. By whom? By nobody in particular; by a universal Unbecoming. . . .

I have said that the new kosmology has to take the scientific cosmology seriously. This cosmology reckons with an end of the universe. The "years" of our solar system are numbered and "we" have calculated the age when the universe will die. For those who do not believe in any God, that will be the End. The so-called believers will "console" themselves by placing God above time and beyond space, and some philosophers may speak of eternal return. But what of the "living God"? Will such a God have something to do with the destiny of the universe? Could "creation" simply be a form of cruel entertainment performed for a monstrous Creator? Is our resistance to accepting that cold fate of the cosmos only sentimentalism? Yet where does this concern for the end come from? Since a new kosmology cannot ignore this, eschatology must be integrated into kosmology. The emerging myth is not only a story about the origins, or a paradigmatic account of the dealings of the Gods. It also has to be an eschatological narrative, but with a fundamental difference from classical eschatologies. In those tales, something, somebody, even the whole world, reaches the end, the *eschaton*—because there is a meta-eschatological Entity to receive the pilgrim at the end of the journey. Today, however, we are envisaging the possibility not just of the curtain coming down at the end of the drama, but the end of the actors themselves and the collapse of the stage. Could it be a bomb? To foresee the material end of the material universe may be a physico-mathematical problem, although if "end" means "end of time," everything is at stake because time is much more than a scientific parameter. Furthermore, such a finalé entails the end of Man, not the death of an individual or even of millions of them. Something more fundamental is in play—although the "bomb" may have awakened us to such a possibility.

Personalities as different as Albert Einstein, Arnold Toynbee, and Karl Jaspers warned us decades ago about the more than ecological dangers involved in splitting the atom. More recently, Jonathan Schell popularized what had long since been known: the terrifying possibility of an atomic holocaust.[11] That this "utterly new historical situation" demands "changes in our religious symbolism" is slowly being recognized in theological circles.[12] Indeed, in this context religion itself may be coherently redefined as the "way to peace." To be sure, consciousness does not need to be identified with its present bearer: historical Man, but have we any right, or rather any "ground," to ask questions transcending time? Can we trespass the threshold of time?

3. The Metaphysical Problem

Metaphysicians have traditionally asked why there is Being rather than Nothing. For simplification's sake, I am not dealing with the entire problematic here, and I shall not make the capital distinction between entity and being. Our argument here includes all entities inasmuch as they represent Being, and Being has Non-being or Nothingness as its counterpart.

Let us reformulate the problem. Our question is not asking for a *why*, be it a "Cause" or a "Sufficient Reason"—although this is a related inquiry. Rather, our question asks whether Being that *is*, and is Becoming, as we have seen, could not cease to be, to "turn" (I do not say "return") into Nothingness?

---

11 Jonathan Schell, *The Fate of the Earth* (New York: Knopf, 1982).

12 Gordon Kaufman *In Face of Mystery: A Constructive Theology* (Cambridge, Mass.: Harvard University Press, 1993); and *The Theological Imagination: Constructing the Concept of God* (Philadelphia: Westminster Press, 1981).

This question assumes a certain superiority of Thinking over Being. Being is, and it is our Thinking that questions Being. It is a "legitimate" question inasmuch as it is grounded in the Being that we are or in which we share. A legitimate question abides by the "law" of non-contradiction; it is a non-contradictory question. To ask *why* I exist is legitimate, to ask whether I exist is not legitimate—unless the existing I that asks gives a double meaning to existence. To ask whether there *is* non-being ("non-is") is contradictory. We do not know what we ask. To ask whether the notion of non-being may play any role in our conception of being is a legitimate question. Being can question. Nothingness cannot question. We ask about Non-being based on (our) Being; we, thinking beings, by virtue of our own "existing" thinking, ask about the possible meaning of that radical negation which questions not only Being but also Thinking, since even the Thinking would disappear if Nothing should prevail. If the question arises, we cannot dismiss it as if it had not arisen. It arises out of that Being which is our Thinking—although we may respond that we are incapable of giving any satisfactory answer. Not all legitimate questions need to have an answer. If we answer that we do not know whether Being can turn into Nothing, we recognize that the question is a possible question, that we understand the question, although we do not know the answer. If this were the case, we could not deny that a possible answer might be in the affirmative and give priority to Nothing over Being. In this case we would fall into a "black hole" from where there is no exit.

Once we concede this autonomy of Thinking from Being (Thinking questions Being) we cannot stop the more formidable question in the opposite direction: Can Nothing ever come to Being? If the Non-being is the nihility that is-not, from where has it the power to break the shell of Non-being and emerge as Being. *Ex nihilo nihil* fit, said Leibniz quite cogently. The christian *creatio ex nihilo* does not fall under Leibniz's indictment. The proper context of the Christian belief is not nothingness but the negation of the platonic background of a "Demiurge" shaping the kosmos out of a primordial matter (πρώτη ὕλη), the christian God creates *ex nihilo*, that is, without this first matter. The christian creation, however, is *a Deo*, by God, who is not Nothing.[13] Yet a problem still remains. If our thinking and rationality have any meaning and do not collapse in sheer chaos, we have to face the following dilemma: either we admit a universe without beginning or end, an *ewige Wiederkehr* ("eternal return"), a continuous creation, infinite "dependent origination," and the like, or we admit a God, Being, Reality, . . . that stands above the dialectic Being/Non-being—as many of

13 See Panikkar, *Mysterio y revelación: Hinduismo y cristianismo, encuentro de dos culturas* (Madrid: Marova, 1971).

the most acute metaphysicians, East and West, assumed—a "One," "Origin," "x" above Being and Non-being. Either we divinize the world and it exists without beginning and end, moving by its proper infinite impulse, or there is a different but inseparable factor in the world, one of whose names is the "Deity." In between, as it were, our human consciousness witnesses this dynamism. In so many words, this latter world forms the cosmotheandric kosmology.

Of course, we could have cut it all short from the very beginning by negating the proviso that we intercalated, and by saying that the question of Being ceasing to Be has no meaning at all. Being is Being *because* it is being and not nothing. If, however, we give this answer, we are already given a ground for why Being cannot cease to Be: Being has the ground in itself. This is what the scholastics called *Esse a se* ("Being *from* itself"). There is a difference in saying "Being has no Foundation" and "Being is its own Foundation." The first sentence contradicts itself or pushes us on a *recursus ad infinitum*. The second sentence opens the Pandora's box as to what is this Being *a se*. We cannot escape touching a limit, and this limit cannot be ignored in any kosmology.

We arrive at the limit and we ask again: Why may there be Nothing rather than Being? Why will there be Non-being instead of Being persevering? Why should Being be everlasting? Or is the last only a pseudo-question? It may be argued on *two accounts* that this is a spurious problem.

The first argument is that the universe is larger than the planet. There is the physical possibility of "terracide," but not of causing the universe to collapse. The human race may have power over itself and life on this planet, but not over the entire cosmos. The cosmos is not threatened; we cannot kill *all space*.

The second argument is more to the point. I have been describing the inextricable interrelatedness of the entire universe. If we destroy matter, we may well be destroying the soul in ways we cannot even surmise. This universal connectedness, however, is not only between matter and soul but also between past and present, and entails a tempiternal dimension.

This reminds us that we cannot kill *all time*. We may succeed in smashing the future, but cannot annihilate the past. What has been has been, and, in consequence, from the perspective of that past, is and shall be, even if there is no further future. The traditional arguments are well known. The tempiternal reality is linked with time, but also with eternity. If, to put it crudely, time can destroy eternity, eternity can also redeem time. Assuming that time could destroy eternity—since once time ceases to be, the concomitant eternal side also ceases to be—one should equally be able to assume that eternity could "save" time, redeem the lost temporality, inasmuch as the eternal side is concomitant with the temporal and eternity "remains." Putting it differently, an eternal God, once having created something, needs an eternal heaven, or hell. Once there is Being, it cannot cease to be—or it would have done so already. Eternity is not a never-ending time, but is impervious to the bite of any temporality. Being (*esse a se*) is not reversible into Nothingness.

In sum, in this view, although time may be reversible, Being is not. Once something has come to be, this fact is indestructible. This reasoning assumes the traditional idea of a Being above and beyond time who can "play" with temporality. Traditional christian theology says it clearly: *De potentia Dei absoluta*, God could annihilate us. If so, it could be argued, then, that God would have to undergo a change of "mind," since we were created for some "reason." That reason, in God, has to be eternal, immutable, ever valid. Hence, God cannot annihilate its own creation. The argument is not fully sound, however, since God's reason could have been to create the universe just for some time—some *kalpa*.

The problem gets worse if we doubt the existence of such an atemporal and separated Supreme Being. Or, putting it less iconoclastically: Does our trust in God imply that God will prevent the ultimate human folly of self-destruction? History teaches us that this God seems to have been rather insensitive to the fate of slaves, kurds, africans, armenians, jews, kampucheans, and millions of our contemporaries who will never emerge from their subhuman lives because our own economic and political structures make it impossible.

I would like to follow the arguments based not on a belief in the power of God but on the consciousness of human dignity. In this context, we find that the two counterarguments have weaknesses. We may blow up the planet, the first argument said, but not the universe. Fair enough. The weakness of this argument is its assumption that human life is only one more flourishing flower in the earthly garden, and that human consciousness, with its capacity for reflection, questioning, and its moral sense, is just another specimen in the zoo of life. That this may not be the case is brought home by considering precisely this uncanny power of Man to destroy not just animals and plants but also the material basis of that other type of life which we call human. The issue is not whether we will blow up the Andromeda Galaxy, but whether we will destroy that for which Andromeda has any meaning—for example, as the daughter of Cassiopeia. To console ourselves with hypothetical extraterrestrials again betrays a peculiar modern blindness to the uniqueness of Man and to spiritual reality. It is like foreseeing a nuclear holocaust that will obliterate all the enemies, but consoling ourselves because we "westerners" will survive. The earthlings may be "kaput," but the "Galactic Federation" goes on unperturbed in its evolution. I am afraid that those who accept such a hypothesis as plausible have not reached enlightened self-consciousness, or experienced timelessness, or surmised the infinite side of beauty, truth, or goodness.

The problem is not the survival of one or many of the living species of the universe, including the human race, in such a catastrophe. This way of putting the problem may well be an example of how one thinks once the Divine has been totally eliminated and human dignity has been unconsciously degraded. Then one is free to think: all "rational" animals will surely disappear, yet this would be no more than a ripple in the immense oceans of the astronomic universe; and cytobiology may suffer a setback of millions of years, but the universe has billions ahead of it. What this mind-set cannot see is that the question is whether another dimension of reality, one ever so closely interlocked with biological existence, would also be threatened. When life disappears, is that dimension that is not an appearance also annihilated? Could it be that the disappearance of life is only an elimination of the appearances? Or is the core of reality also touched, wounded, and even broken?

It is in dealing with these problems that we become aware of our deep dependence on our respective kosmologies. We have paved the way to meeting the second counterargument by responding to the first. What needs to be criticized here is the dualism of time/eternity. The counterargument says that we may destroy the temporal, but the eternal will remain untouched. In that case we no longer know what we are talking about when we utter the word eternity. In point of fact, almost all traditions admit a link between the two. Even buddhism, which takes the most radical attitude regarding transcendence, will say that extinction, or blowing out all creatureliness (*samskāra* [volitions, impulses], *dharma* [elements of existence, phenomena] ...) opens up *nirvāṇa*, as the word itself suggests. If the destruction of time brings about eternity, this eternity is only another name for sheer Nothingness, total annihilation—which brings us back to our initial problem.

The voices that still speak from within traditional kosmologies would laugh at our concern. They would remind us, as Suhrawardī says, that the angel of humanity can only speak to the lowest of the celestial hierarchies.[14]

14 Henry Corbin, *Creative Imagination in the Sufism of Ibn 'Arabi* (Princeton, N.J.: Princeton University Press, 1981), 49ff.

We cannot even surmise what is above or beyond this universe. Although we have our world, and our great angel, the rest is closed to us. Not only are we not alone in the universe, but this very universe of ours is but one universe, probably among the lowest in the celestial hierarchies. Hence, we are still left with two apparently contradictory groups of ideas. On the one hand, there is the imminent possibility of the end of the world, all the more threatening if we take spiritual reality seriously and are sensitized to its interpenetration with the *saeculum*, with time, space, and matter. On the other hand, this universe of ours appears to be just a tiny little universe for our private use, enjoyment, and perhaps eventual doom. It does not much matter if we destroy it all before its proper hour.

The metaphysical problem leads us back to the anthropic problem. We cannot understand the metaphysical question without understanding the myth of the questioner. There is not necessarily a contradiction here, but rather we find two perspectives, two scales, two kosmologies. The difficulty is that the traditional myths have today receded from the memory of western Man and are considered by many to be implausible, obsolete, and no more than playthings for poets. *Denken* ("thinking") is no longer *dichten* ("making poetry"), much less linked with *danken* ("thanking"). The best we can do with myth these days is science fiction, which would hardly be so entertaining if we took it seriously. The plurality of possible universes bandied about by modern science has virtually nothing to do with the cosmic display of the glory of the Lord.

All possible universes aside, however, there is more involved here than just trying to rehabilitate the old stories so that they would once again be believable. The more is this: If we take the life of the spirit as earnestly as it deserves, we may respect all these mythologies, heed what they mean to tell us, and integrate them on another level without subscribing literally to their stories. We may not reach a cosmological or a divine infinity, but should nonetheless discover that in our own way we are somewhat infinite. The very fact that we are able to know indicates that we can become every knowable thing. The soul, human life, the *psychē* is *panta pōs,* or *quadammodo omnia*, as we said before. Saint Thomas says in relation to this: "It appertains to the nature of the intellect to be one, that is, not to be directed to anything. Its only nature is that it can be everything."[15] The intellect has no nature of its own, since it has the actual possibility of becoming everything. This

15 Thomas Aquinas, *De anima*, III, Lect. 7: "Non contingit naturam intellectus esse neque unam, idest nullam determinatam, sed hanc solam naturam habet quod est possibilis omnium."

is not mere scholastic aristotelianism. It reflects the human experience of transcending individuality and overcoming the presumption of rationality as our specific human difference. In fact, the text says that, as intellectual "souls," we do not have any fixed nature, nor are we a fixed nature. Our only nature is that we can become everything.

A fundamental distinction is in order here. Are we indeterminate, amorphous beings and therefore universal (*ens nullo modo determinatum*)? Or are we concrete and determined beings open to all things (*ens determinatum omni modo*)?—just to quote Jakob Böhme.

These two interpretations can also be rendered by contrasting the well-known principle that *omnis determinatio est negatio*, every determination is a negation, with the other principle that *omnis determinatio est positio*, every determination is a position, as Franz von Baader felicitously formulated it.

What are we? Many a kosmology would reformulate the question: Are we the lowest of the spirits or the highest of the animals? What is our nature? An incarnated spirit, a prisoner of the body, a divine spark gone somewhat astray by ensouling matter? Or an intelligent animal, a rational mammal, a *roseau pensant*, a thinking machine?

Here are two understandings of what it is to be human. In the traditional one, Man is the manifestation of an emanation from on high embodied in an animal body. It reveals a descendant or incarnational (emanationistic) vision. For the modern one, Man is the summit of an animal body showing signs of an intellectual energy. It reveals an ascendant or progressivistic (evolutionistic) vision.

Although both responses present difficulties, their main common difficulty is dualism. If the body is our prison, *sōma/sēma* as the greeks say, our humanness will be reduced to an impossible angelic ideal. We will have to ignore our body to become ourselves. If reason is our specific difference, our humanness will be reduced to the equally impossible ideal of bridging the gulf between the body and the soul, the *res externa* and the *res cogitans*.

My contention is that Man loses its identity if absorbed either by the Divine above or by Matter below. Man is neither a servant of God, nor the king of creation, meaningful as both these expressions may be within their respective contexts. Man may be both, but only provided the *humanum* recovers its proper place in reality and the unique role it has to play there. There is something unique in Man, irreducible to God or to Matter.

B. The Scientific Paradigm

Modern science proceeds in terms of laws, objectivity, experiment, and ultimately puts everything into quantitative parameters. What cannot be measured is not scientific, and what is not scientific has no power and thus need not be given serious consideration. Generally speaking, modern science is applied mathematics, and mathematics has taken over the ancient throne of theology as the "Queen of the Sciences." Mathematics now bestows new titles on the nobility of the sciences. (In spite of a counter-lobby in german scholarship, one of the most ancient banned societies carries the title *Religionswissenschaft*. "Humanities" is still called *Geisteswissenschaft* in most of the academic world.) Hence the effort from all quarters of western civilization to make theology, philosophy, literature, psychology, sociology, and every other discipline also appear to be scientific. Modern science, in its turn and to its credit, is currently making a correlative effort to reestablish the lost dialogue with philosophy, theology, and the other human disciplines.

Contemporary studies in the philosophy of science are serious attempts to correlate a certain philosophical approach to reality with the findings of modern science, but most of them use the *forma mentis* of scientific method, the scientific way of "thinking." This is understandable, because either science is met in its own field, or there is no dialogue—science is monolingual. If we do not speak the scientific language, science will tell us that it does not understand what we are talking about or that we are talking at cross purposes. It is similar to the case of modern democracy: it accepts dialogue on its own terms only. Otherwise we are non-scientific or anti-democratic. Without defending irrationalism or advocating violence, I would venture that these are not the only alternatives.

Most studies on philosophy and science may well be correct in what they conclude, and coherent in what they propound, but the real kosmological issue is not whether two "disciplines" of western culture that have been divorced for centuries can be reconciled, as welcome as this would be. Although of western origin and carrying western archetypes, modern science has penetrated so widely all over the world and so deeply into the minds of many who have identified science with its cosmology so as to require something more than going back to the "good old days," which, incidentally, hardly existed. Furthermore, the "philosophy" in question has also undergone such a change that even with the best of intentions the couple would not be able to recognize the former partner. The problem is not between two disciplines but between cultures. To which we should add that it is no longer between two cultures (the scientific and the philosophical), but between many other cultures, which until now were simply ignored. This is the intercultural challenge of our times.

This is a reason why a mere paradigm shift is inadequate. The required change is much more radical. The issue is whether modern cosmology offers a picture of the real world where man can unfold all his possibilities and reach that fullness of life to which every one of us aspires. Does modern cosmology offer a home for Man? Scientific cosmology cannot offer such a world where we feel at home unless Man is reduced to a rational "thinking" machine and "thinking" to problem solving. This would cripple both reality and human experience. We cannot identify reality with what science tells us of it, nor presume that science offers the only possible understanding of reality. The quantitative method assumes that quantitative parameters are appropriate categories for approaching and knowing reality, and tends to suggest that they are the best (most "effective," most "manageable," most "significant") categories. The problem, however, is more complex. Neither can traditional kosmologies offer such a kosmos where we may find a humane habitat. We have to learn from them, but their *kairos* is over. Those *kosmoi* are no longer our world, not even for those who originally used to live in such kosmologies. Minor alterations are not enough.

Even if modern science were to overcome its quantitative parameters, it cannot give up conceptual thinking and algebraic formulations without ceasing to be what it is—nor should it. Yet reality is not graspable in mathematical language, and even if reality were written in mathematical language, it would only be language, a language about reality, not reality. What I am saying is that we cannot go back. The problem is new, even though we may, and must, learn much from and be inspired by traditional wisdoms.

Meanwhile, modern science has also lately been undergoing important changes. Not only mechanicism, but also objectivism are on their way to being overcome by a more complex pattern in which indeterminacy and the place of the observer are no longer discrepancies incidental to the calculation. Science today is ready to accept anything, provided it passes the mathematical test, and even this test, after Gödel, does not need to be a fixed and rigid frame. The skepticism about mathematics, after all, is not new. The greeks, and probably the babylonians and the indians, already knew that what were called irrational numbers defy the laws of logic, but modern scientific optimism has paid little attention to them. It is profoundly strange that the relation between the hypotenuse and the cathetus in an isosceles triangle can be mathematically "proved" to be even and odd at the same time. At any event, the crisis lies deeper. It lies, on the one hand, with philosophy and, on the other hand, with the very method of the scientific project.

1. Method

The ways in which we reach for something depend both on the instruments that we utilize and on our pre-understanding about the nature of that thing. We would not use a microscope to search for the soul, but we do use it to "investigate" blood. The inertia of the mind plays an important role in explaining continuities, and the much vaunted "paradigm shift" in western culture, as important as it is, shows how much modern science is intrinsically linked with a hellenistic-christian postmedieval model. The new kosmology is something much more radical than a "scientific revolution" within western cosmology. When I said that thinking is not problem-solving, I meant that human thinking does not necessarily and exclusively need mathematical rails. Thinking is not just induction and deduction or guessing at new hypotheses by a creative imagination, which are afterwards confirmed by experiment and/or mathematical coherence. As a human and creative act by which we become aware of Being (of which thinking itself is an activity), thinking does not need a paradigm. Paradigms are useful and even needed for heuristic reasons, once the *heurēka* (εὕρημα, invention, discovery) has already taken place. Modern science offers a powerful paradigm and is shifting it in very promising ways, but it is only one paradigm (among many), a paradigm for a particular art of thinking. Thinking does not follow the paradigm of a well-charted highway; it is rather walking cross country and stopping where we want. Creative thinking builds its own paradigms

I pause for a moment on this issue, which has shaped modern thinking since the birth of modern science and for which Kant found a genial justification. I recall Eddington's metaphor about the first unbeatable scientific law of fishing when all the nets we use have meshes of two square inches: "No fish in the ocean has a diameter of less than two inches"—since in all our experiments we have not found a single exception to the law. But Kant had already explained that, in order to know, we must throw into the sea of things the net of our *a priori* forms. We can only understand the things that get entangled in the net of our categories. With such presuppositions, thinking becomes representational thinking and our consciousness only a net for catching objects. Oriental philosophies and pre-cartesian western thinking, on the other hand, do not operate under such a scheme. One of the contributions of the Kyoto school of contemporary japanese philosophy is to have called into question the limitations of a human consciousness reduced to merely subject-object forms of awareness.

The scientific paradigm has projected the mathematical net in order to take cognizance of a certain structure of the world, which is not the same as "to understand the world." Since this method has been widely imitated by intellectuals in all the so-called humanities, psychological, sociological, and historical laws were quickly discovered. All this has brought about the proliferation of specializations, not only in scientific disciplines but in many other intellectual activities, and even in ways of life. The separation of philosophy, theology, and religion, for instance, is seen by most oriental cultures as a straitjacket that stifles the free flow of human life and imprisons the reality expressed by those words behind the bars of analytical rationality.

I single out one example, knowing full well that many other factors have also played decisive roles in the complex and fascinating birth trauma of modern science. It is perhaps only now that we are no longer the children but the grandchildren of modern science that we are properly situated to understand what our grandparents did. We need neither attack nor defend our parents, or come to blows as past generations did over the problems of "religion versus science" and "faith versus reason." If passion and strong emotions are still not absent in such disputes today, nonetheless, both sides are prepared to enter a much deeper dialogue without feeling threatened.

We have said that the proper way or method to study the nature of a thing depends on our prior idea of that thing. Once embarked in one method, however, the method can become so powerful that it conditions our further investigation making it increasingly difficult to take the "step back" the artist (and the philosopher) need in order to contemplate the object. Analogous to the well-studied "hermeneutical circle" there exists the *methodological circle.* This applies to modern sciences in a special way: in order to investigate the nature of a phenomenon we need a method that depends on the nature of the phenomenon, but subsequently the method will also be applied to disclose to us the nature of that phenomenon. It will be difficult to dispense with the mathematical net when it has helped us so much in fishing in the ocean of the real. Here is an example.

The meaning of life in the time of Galileo, which one may consider the approximate birth date of modern science, gravitated around belief in the noble and human ideals of freedom, fulfillment, and felicity. These ideals were understood, so to speak, to be built into human nature. The means, that is, the method to attain them was *power*, in the best and also the worst sense of the word. Until that era, power had rested mainly in the hands of two classes, privileged since time immemorial. We should not forget that at stake here is the dislodging of an inveterate pattern that had survived for millennia: *brahmins* and *kshatriyas*, priests and nobles, church and state held the power, and with it the keys to the good life to which Man naturally aspires. By the time of Galileo a third class, the burghers of the Edinburghs, Regensburgs, Strasbourgs, Freiburgs, Burgos, Salzburgs, Peterburgs, and other free cities had begun to proliferate. In parallel, a third source of power came to the fore made possible by nominalism and reinforced by the Renaissance: modern science, by which was meant not just knowledge, *scientia, gnōsis, jñāna*, but the capacity to foresee events and to build instruments capable of interfering in the events themselves. Power had always been linked to church and state. Tradition combined with family and hereditary rules would produce plenty of people to serve church and state and so win eternal life. Both had the people, but needed money. Modern science became a new source of money, and thus of power, although money slowly turned into plutocracy (Pluto was a God) and later on into "argentocracy," which did not need any "divine" sanction.

Modern science is based not on pure speculation (polishing the "mirror" [*speculum*] of our intellect) in order to see and enjoy reality, but on the experiment (interference) into reality in order to foresee its behavior and control it. For this we need the instrument (Galileo's telescope). If the cultivation of our inner tools (contemplation) deepens our view, the cultivation of our external tools (action) enlarges our vision. Modern science needs instruments. To deal with them we do not much need thinking but rather calculating, not experience but experiment. Inwardness was taken for granted and/or forgotten. *Otium* ("leisure, contemplation") may give inner peace and happiness, but the *negotium* ("business, activity"), produces money, the new source of power.

The "third estate" acquires power not from church or state, but from the skillful use of instruments provided by newly appearing methods. The monarchic principle shifted from a caste or class to Man, "King of creation." But this "Man" was no longer the member of a body (church, state, caste, or guild), but an individual. Any individual with scientific skills (method), that is, by the use of instruments, can make money and acquire power. The hierarchical principle was no longer seen as necessary for the cohesion of society. Initiation began to be secondary. Scribes and readers were no longer needed since in principle anybody could read and write. Individualism was strengthened, and democracy dawned. The process was long and not always smooth, but gradually a new elite tried to monopolize those new technologies.

This concatenation of factors triggered the explosive and spectacular success of modern science. This form of science does not need to encumber itself with theology or philosophy; it does not require a holistic approach.

One can have science independently of any cosmology and theology, as Galileo argued against Bellarmino. What we (today!) call politics has nothing to do with ethics, as Machiavelli taught. The method is justified by its apparent success—in the double sense of the adjective. The movements of falling bodies are predictable, and even the planets seem to obey laws discovered by Man. These must be— indubitably, it was thought—the laws of nature. God must have been quite a mathematician—an architect and even an engineer. The past tense of that statement marks the inroads made by deism, *ante litteram*, on monotheism. Creation was believed to be something that happened in the past, leaving us with nothing but its laws. Mechanicism was making gigantic strides—not due to materialism or a lack of religious belief—but because it was the most immediate and fruitful field for applied mathematics.

Mathematics became the strongest basis of and support for modern science. Mathematics is neither metaphysical speculation nor experimental science, but it furnishes the proof for the latter. One can easily understand the enthusiasm of the emerging new sciences when they could verify (truly verify) that nature did obey calculus—which was upgraded from counting stones [*calculi*] to being the mirror of the universe and even the language of the divine. Mathematics is the reign of abstraction, and this kingdom, which has no king, has become the absolute monarch in our techno-scientific civilization. Abstraction deals with concepts. As long as concepts are linked ontologically with the things from which they are abstracted they cannot reach their full autonomy. By affirming that names are sheer pragmatic labels, nominalism cut the umbilical cord between things and names and gave free rein to algebraic operations. Now, the most astounding thing, which confers on mathematics the authority it has, is the already mentioned pliability (or obedience) of nature to our logical manipulation of abstract concepts. We do not need to know *what* gravitation, acceleration, electricity, and energy are; we need only to know *how* the phenomena meant by those words function. Calculating a bridge with abstract equations, and even irrational numbers, the bridge stands. Modern cosmology cannot be so easily dismantled. In fact it should not be dismantled, but only eventually dislodged, or, following our overcondensed description, simply freed from its monarchic mantle. The kosmos is not only the scientific cosmos; the mathematical method is not the only way to approach reality.

It is well known that the way becomes the goal not because one is necessarily on the right path but because we tend to see only what is directly in front of us. Modern science was supposed to bring us power as the means for living a full and free human life, but, slowly at first, it became more exclusive and sophisticated than philosophy and theology. All too soon modern science began to seek power not for human fulfillment but for the sake of ever enhancing power itself. The method became the thing; the means became the end. Science soon became equivalent to scientific method. A scientist is a skillful knower of the particular methods specific to a given branch of science.

It is also well known that we only find variations of what we are looking for. We begin looking for matrices for quantification, and increasingly find them in fields we did not at the outset even suspect could be quantified. Psychology and sociology are recent cases of investigation by quantification; chemistry and physics are among the most ancient and well-known. After Galileo, time, space, speed, and mass soon became quantities; now performance, diet and health, even intelligence and opinion, etc., are following suit. The crisis today stems from the suspicion that the proper approach to reality, and the adequate way to reach freedom, fulfillment, and felicity, may not be the scientific method—but we cannot seem to see any other way open to us.

2. *Monotheistic Cosmology*

The phrase may seem far-fetched in the West, but for the rest of the world it sounds almost redundant if we take mono-theism in the earlier described sense of a mono-principle out of which our thinking proceeds and into which it tends. Am I unnecessarily provocative calling the modern scientific cosmology monotheistic? If I called it monarchic, the word might be equally disturbing to those whose only language has been reduced to simplistic slogans. Just as an-archy is not the only response to mon-archy, a-theism is not the only alternative to monotheism. The trinity again provides an answer, if we keep well aware that trinity means neither three principles nor one, and that *advaita* is the key to understanding the trinity. To try to comprehend reality under one single principle leads to monotheism. If we approach reality with the single instrument of our "reason," we cannot do otherwise. Any vision of the world under one single light is bound to be monotheistic. Whether this principle be called *theos*, reason, matter—or on another level, money or market. Only a "three-eyed" vision saves us from rationalistic reductionism. The vision of the third eye is not a *luxus* for "romantics," "mystics," or special people. There is an intrinsic relation between any idea and the context in which that idea is alive, as a cell needs its plasma or a fish water. In a similar vein, the ancient indian logicians discussed whether the meaning of a name lies in the word or in the sentence.

In sum, no doctrine can be understood without a kosmological framework. The ancient kosmologies were efforts at understanding the world, but it was a kosmos populated by gods, spirits, qualities, magic, telluric forces and heavenly energies. Christian philosophy undertook a profound cleansing of the kosmos from most of those "obscure forces" condemned as superstitious. God, angels, and qualities remained for a long time, but most of them went on the decline and were slowly replaced by measurable masses and energies. Gravitation and a few other forces remained unexplained. Newton believed that the planets were moved by angels; well-known is his *hypothesis non fingo*. The universe was polyphonic, and to understand it we had to stand-under the spell of its music and be enthralled and even entranced by it. All our faculties had to be alert. The purity of heart demanded by most traditions was not primarily an ethical injunction; it was an anthropological condition for knowledge.

With the complex changes occurring in european societies around the sixteenth century the mysterious kosmos turned into a no less enigmatic world, but at least a measurable one. Mechanicism made gigantic strides and astonishing discoveries. The "mathematization" of the world began its triumphant course.

The history of science is an ecstatic history. Man is an observer. He knows himself as an observer, but is ultimately not much interested in that. What counts is the observation, the "objective" picture of reality. What fascinates is light years, galaxies, expansion of the universe, black holes, big bangs, quarks, elementary particles, the manifestation of energy and its transformation, genetic codes, chemical reactions, and physical laws, all neatly wrapped up in mathematical language, expressed in extraordinarily appealing and sometimes rather simple formulae, which embrace more and more behaviors on the way to the "Grand Unified Theory" (of Everything) that is always "just around the corner." Man is in ecstasy before all that the human mind has discovered. Man has forgotten himself. If in past centuries there was a pathos to see everything *sub specie aeternitatis*, there is now a similar pathos to see everything *sub specie quantitatis*.

The history of science is the Story of Holy Matter expanding and expanding, getting cooler and cooler, evolving, differentiating, and growing, and at least in one corner of that immensity, appearing in the form of an observer capable of measuring such magnitudes. Of course, between the telescope and the microscope, between astrophysics and atomic physics, there was also the business of applying all those detailed laws to the regulation of the human organism and the management of social organizations. We can apply the same methods to these arenas of life, and also obtain astounding results—pharmaceuticals, surgery, psychohistory and all the rest.

There is more. This reasoning by induction and deduction has conditioned the western ways of thinking so much that symbolic knowledge gets relegated to a corner reserved for artists and is replaced by the conceptual cognition proper to mathematics. One example will allow me to explain the point without the need for lengthy analysis. The example is the so-called argument from design. There is a designer say the theists; there is no designer respond the atheists. In both cases we are within a monotheistic cosmology.

There is order in the universe. Indeed, there is an amazing and stupendous order. One does not need to descend into the awesome abyss of the atoms, or to ascend to the dizzying heights of the galaxies to discover it. One does not need to adduce an "anthropic cosmological principle" or a "cosmic blueprint" to be convinced of it. It suffices to watch a child, to smell a flower, to rest at night, to talk with a friend, to be a potter, a shoemaker, or to engage in agriculture (although perhaps not in agri-business). Nobody can deny that there is a design; one need only look.

Disorders of all types, and even the question of evil, appear as such only because disorder and evil are confronted and judged by the overall pattern of an ordered design. Dis-order implies at least an idea of order. The design is everywhere. We have only to read the signs. Now, the rational mind cannot stop here, and not fully experiencing (enjoying) the design jumps by deduction (according to some) or by induction (in the opinion of others) to the designer, in response to which the atheist will make every effort to criticize the logical cogency of the arguments.

Yet the designer is nowhere to be found. It is even problematic to infer a designer. The principle "any effect requires a cause" is a mere tautology: an effect is that which requires a cause. To recognize something as an effect begs the question. It presupposes already that it comes from a cause. Nor should we forget that the so called proofs for the existence of God are neither mathematical nor ontological. Otherwise the existence of God would depend on the power of our calculus or the strength of our (contingent) being. These "ways" merely show that the belief in God is not against reason.

Even if we have arrived at such a designer, this creates as many problems as it solves. We have to artificially sustain this designer, hide its faults, excuse its nonappearance, explain its absences, and defend this supreme Being whom nobody has ever seen—or at least justify his existence (*theodicea*).

The need for a designer appears when a certain mentality anthropomorphically links design with designer, so that if there is no designer the design seems inexplicable. An inexplicable design is projected onto an even more inexplicable designer. Many christian philosophers still have not learned to look at the lilies of the field.[16] They want so badly to see their Author that they trample the flowers underfoot. The scientists are no better. In search of the "cause" or other "laws" of the lily, they uproot the plant and tear every petal off its flowers in order to find "it." The "look" of the Gospel is a holistic look. In that look, God, the fields, the growth, our trust and even Solomon are included in it. I am defending neither atheism nor an anti-scientific attitude, but the possibility of overcoming both attitudes. I am still looking at the lilies, thinking about them and enjoying them, and—why not?—using them, with care and with love, of course, lest they fade away. I am proposing that it is possible to go beyond this dualistic attitude and overcome the theistic/atheistic paradigm lurking behind most studies on the subject.

After all I have said, it should be sufficiently clear that contesting the existence of a transcendent designer does not mean maintaining the atheistic position and declaring that the design has come about by spontaneous generation, sheer chance, or mere probability. On the contrary, the design is so marvelous that it is its own revelation. It is not, however, the revelation of a designer— which would only pass the problem on to the putative designer. The revelation of the design is the unveiling of the sign that the design signifies: a deeper dimension inherent in the design, impervious to measurement but open to the simple eye. Once again, I invoke the Tao Te Ching and the Gospels, and not pantheism, because to stress divine immanence does not exclude transcendence.

I am referring, of course, to the contemplative look without which our vision of reality, being incomplete, tends to search for an outside cause. A muslim mystic said that, when he went to Mecca for the first time, he saw the Kaaba, but not its Lord; when he went a second time he saw its Lord, but not the Kaaba; on a third pilgrimage he saw neither the Kaaba nor its Lord.[17] This represents a mood close but not equal to part of the sequence of the ten ox-herding pictures of zen when there is "ox lost, man remaining," "no ox, no man," "returning to the source," and finally "in town with helping hands."[18] I could suggest a fourth journey to Mecca when the pilgrim *sees*,

16 Cf. Mt VI, 28; Lk XII, 27.

17 Quoted from Abu Yazid in A. J. Arberry, *Muslim Saints and Mystics* (Chicago: University of Chicago Press, 1966), 121.

18 Ji Bong, *The Ten Ox-Herding Pictures: Allegories for Our Practice.*

all in one, the Kaaba, its Lord, and Nothing—echoing Meister Eckhart. The contemplative look, "looking" the lilies (and not just "looking at" them), sees the entire reality, not through, but "in" the lilies or "as" lilies—and here again grammar betrays us. If our look remains in a quantitative pattern, affirming that the lilies *are* the whole reality is plainly absurd; reality is much "bigger" and "contains" many other things. A lily is not the whole garden, a tree is not the forest, and a beloved person is not all of humanity. No wonder that acceleration and change are modern obsessions and we are soon tired of the same "thing"—even if it is a spouse. I am not defending immobilism. In the story of the Kaaba, which we could apply to people as well, I see all things as "things" and "divine," but also as "nothingness" at the same time so that I am not stuck in them, and, of course, I am on a pilgrimage. *Abgeschiedenheit, resasimiento, asakti*, holy indifference, detachment, and similar notions are not the special witness of highly gifted spiritualists, but belong to anyone with a non-reductionistic notion of Man within the traditional tripartite anthropologies of many cultures.

It is crude anthropomorphism to assume a designer, and it is crude mechanistic attitude to presuppose that there has to be a cause behind it all. Ultimately, such attitudes signal a lack of contemplation. *Per ea quae facta sunt, intellecta conspiciuntur*, says the Vulgate's literal translation of the concise greek in Paul's Romans I, 20 (τοῖς ποιήμασιν νοούμενα καθορᾶται), a quandary to translators and a headache to theologians: ("The invisible things [τὰ ἀόρατα] of God] have been understood through the things made"). This famous passage does not formulate a rational conclusion, but presents us with the intelligibility of the invisible things when our hearts are pure. Those who do not "see" have no excuse, not because their mind is weak, but because their heart has hardened and does not see. It is a question not of discovering God but of seeing the invisible; τὰ γὰρ ἀόρατα αὐτοῦ ἀπὸ κτίσεως κόσμου τοῖς ποιήμασιν νοούμενα καθορᾶται.[19] I do not read this passage as necessarily saying that there is a designer behind. I am not affirming that the design is the designer. This would be pantheism, which is not what I am defending. I am saying that the design is the design, that when I contemplate the design the otherwise invisible complete design appears in all its *divine* splendor. "The pure of heart shall see God"[20]—precisely in everything and everywhere.

One of the most elaborated contemporary studies on these subjects is *The Anthropic Cosmological Principle.*[21] There is a universe, our authors say.

---

19 Rom I, 20. Heb XI, 3 also speaks of rendering visible the invisible: "ex invisibilis visibilia firent" [ἐκ φαινομένων τὸ βλεπόμενον γεγονέναι].

20 Matt V, 8.

21 Barrow and Tipler, *Anthropic Cosmological Principle*, 24.

This universe is the actual one, but we cannot know for sure whether there are not also many other worlds, even an infinite number of them. Ultimately, it would not matter, since modern science would understand it in terms of "all collections of laws and particles which ever did, does, or ever will exist."[22] This may be the cosmological monotheistic universe of modern science, but it is certainly not the universe of the kosmologies that have been the habitat of the world's civilizations for millennia. I am tackling here what is a minor question for the authors, but an eyeopener for us. They write:

> Although the FAP [Final Anthropic Principle] is a statement of physics and hence, *ipso facto** has no ethical or moral content, it nevertheless is closely connected with moral values, for the validity of the FAP is the physical precondition for moral values to arise and to continue to exist in the Universe. . . .[23]

The asterisk (*) declares:

> Physical assumptions and moral assumptions belong to different logical categories. Physical assumptions . . . are declarative sentences. Moral assumptions . . . are imperative sentences, which contain the word "ought" or its equivalent.[24]

Yet in defining the "FAP" the authors say: "Intelligent information-processing *must* come into existence in the Universe, and, once it comes into existence, *it will never die out.*"[25] I have added the emphasis to show that the condition of not containing any *ought* or its equivalent is not fulfilled, even in sentences about physical assumptions. The "must" in this definition makes it an imperative sentence. I am not minimizing the importance of the Anthropic Principle, but am pointing to this welcome contradiction to indicate that the previous compartmentalization of disciplines and specialties is no longer possible. The Anthropic Principle is moral and may even be one of the foundations of morals—and therefore cannot be proven by physics alone. Try as we might, we can no more separate morals from science than we can sever science from theology. Barrow and Tipler correctly insist that "no moral values of any sort exist in a lifeless cosmology." But this unification under the aegis of Reason is precisely the cosmological monotheism I am criticizing: the "Big Bang" (God?) was at the Beginning.

A trinitarian kosmology is no longer monotheistic. The Trinity is not three substances. That would be tritheism. The trinity is pure relation, and

---

22 Ibid., 121.

23 Ibid., 26.

24 Ibid.

25 Ibid., 23 (my emphasis).

we are also incorporated in this relationship, as the christian Incarnation affirms. This trinitarian view may, on the one hand, enter into conflict with the prevalent scientific cosmology, while, on the other hand, it may offer a more positive solution than that of mutual respect at the price of total separation between the scientific and the religious realms.[26]

3. *The Scientific Story*

The picture drawn by science looks somewhat like this—and I ask the reader to forgive my not ill-intended irony, which allows me to make the description more vivid and shorter: There is the universe, which is fundamentally a material amount of mass and/or energy. It develops temporally and spatially, and at a certain moment Man appears, the observer of this very universe, who evolves up to the present pinnacle from which some among the humans can survey the whole situation and venture something like a cosmology. The human being may be a unique exemplar in the universe, or only one specimen of a variety of humanoids scattered among finite or infinite times and spaces. No trace of any of them has ever been found, but science is open-minded and does not consider this an impossibility. Everything not contradictory is possible. Science has no tools to decide, or even to speculate about, whether we are at the end of our evolution or heading toward a Superman of unknown properties (although presumably a step above and beyond mere humanity). There is, above all, a kind of genetic code which works one wonder after another. We are a particle of organic matter in the immensity of the universe, and yet we have developed a power of reflection that makes us wonder. We are pilgrims from a surmised humble origin in a Big Bang on our way to an unknown destination, Omega, Zero, or somewhere in between. Perhaps Deity was simply a word to express that Mystery that science is prompted to investigate, and which leads it to decipher more and more without ever being sure that it has turned over every rock and exhausted every avenue of inquiry. For some scientists, God, if at all, would be (at) the final point of the Evolution, not at the initial stage. So much would they concede. For the moment we do not need "Him."

Within this picture there is plenty of room for humans to go about their business and unfold their creativity in the encounter with "hard" reality. No doubt there is a fascinating history. We know this reality is real because it offers a certain resistance to our essays and experiments. There may remain a small, private sphere of sentimentality, intimacy, perhaps even of love and

26 This would have become the constructive part of a project of the author which was imprudently announced decades ago under the title *Conflict of Kosmologies*.

longing, to which it may be pragmatic or diplomatic to give the name of religion, the Divine or the like. The principle of complementarity so dear to Niels Bohr may take care of this. *Homo religiosus* may represent one facet of *homo sapiens*, whose structure has been worked out, of course, by *homo scientificus*. If you are a "believer," well and good, so long as you are not a fanatic and allow freedom of research for all scientific investigations. Anatomists were long barred from experimenting with human corpses because religious authorities considered them sacred. Genetic engineering of humans is not (yet?) allowed today because nervous political powers fear we may convert humans into sheep, producing hybrids of all types who will be only too "happy" to work for society and will not make trouble. Such scruples repeat the pattern of those days when moralists in catholic countries seriously argued about the length of women's skirts, so to remove "occasions of sin." Today they discuss the lengths to which genetic manipulation may go before such experimentation becomes sinful. We are told, God is no longer interested in women's skirts, but in this interference with human life.

I understand quite well that there is a difference between genes and skirts, but not so long ago moralists were equally convinced there was a moral difference in the styles of hemlines, which could be measured in inches. Has God retreated from the battlefield of feminine fashions to take up arms in the field of genetics, to do battle there at the bacterial level among the petri dishes? Where do we draw the dividing line, if at all? More cunning than Galileo, modern science will not discuss its purposes openly. It will comply externally and proceed with private or "classified" research. Remembering that electricity, too, was once considered demonic, science has learned to wait, believing time is on its side. Genetic engineering is simply the hot issue today.

The naive enthusiasm of the past century is fading away and, having reached a high point in scientific evolution, pure science may perhaps be allowed to ask an embarrassing question. Why on earth should we put external brakes on scientific research out of (ethical) reasons extrinsic to the nature of science? Should religious concerns curtail freedom of research as in the worst old times? Centuries ago christian theology, considered "queen of the sciences," established guidelines for scientific research against which the nascent sciences reacted vigorously. Within that kosmology the logic was impeccable. On what grounds does modern ethics, which does not even claim to be grounded on a metaphysical insight, dare to dictate from the exterior, what scientific research should or should not do? Once we accept the autonomy of the sciences, is it not immoral to dictate from the exterior the norms of research of any discipline? If politicians, for pragmatic reasons, forbid putting some results into practice, much as they put speed limits on the highways (in spite of the fact that cars are capable of exceeding those restrictions), that may be their right, but they should not invoke ethical reasons to bind our consciences, especially since ethics has been severed from religion. Society may sign a moral contract, as many voices claim today, but on what grounds, except coercion, are the non-signatories bound to respect it? The commandments of the Law of Moses were not external commandments of a legislator, but they were chiseled in the very heads of Men as the biblical Prophets time and again proclaimed, and Saint Paul repeats in Romans II, 15. Not to lie or do harm is not the command of a legislator but an inner injunction of my own heart. We should agree with the scientific reaction against any imposition from outside once we accept its premises.

I would also use the same argument the other way round. If a human activity, a scientific activity not excepted, does not find in its own heart, in its own structure, the proper *ontonomic* norm of its activity, then said activity has lost its health and it is immoral to propagate it. A healthy body has its own homeostasis and does not grow beyond its proper limits. When the cells of the body grow beyond their proper limit, for example, it is called cancer. Could it be that the unbridled proliferation of modern research shows oncological symptoms?

Once we disconnect everything from everything, once we forgo the ontonomic order, only a heteronomic force can put order in the world. In plain words, once we have split reality into compartments, only police, hell, force, or violence, be it legitimate or illegitimate, can maintain a certain order. Once community is an empty word and reduced to a sum of individuals, only the power of votes, numbers, arms, or money will keep order in human society.

An intercultural outlook is so important here. I shall put a delicate example. Nobody in the western world, as far as I know, protested against the split of the unsplittable (*atomos*). Only when the atom bomb was produced did the Einsteins, Oppenheimers, and many others open their eyes. Seen from the sensitivity of other cultures, the split of the atom, for whatever good purposes, amounts to a cosmic abortion: we open violently the vagina of matter (*atomos*) because we badly need extra energy for an artificial standard of life.

"What is so unnatural about thermonuclear bombs when they occur all the time in the sun?" a scientist once asked me. To which I quickly and jokingly responded, "What would be so unnatural about me killing you if you are going to die anyway?" The human factor is not just another variable in the big matrix of the universe. My qualms are not merely ethical; my misgivings are anthropological and kosmological.

Here is the crux. If Man is just another specimen in the universe, even if we solemnly intone paeans to Man's formidable gifts, if Man is just a rational animal, one among the millions of living species on the planet, let alone a single individual in a perhaps countless number of galaxies, why should anyone complain if I make such a caricature of the traditional morality? Why should scientists not do whatever they can do without anyone impinging on the freedom of research? Were it not for experimenting on animals, modern medicine would still be in its infancy. Why should we treat Man any differently if we can thereby gain scientific knowledge? I am being sarcastic, but where do we draw the line?

The scientific answer is to look to the law of the greatest numbers, leaving it to historians of religion and sociologists to talk about ethical principles, taboos, and patterns of behavior. The first scientific discoveries created quite a stir, as did the first divorcée in a traditional hindu or christian country, to put examples quite far apart. Slaves were a matter of fact, and slavery a "moral" institution at that, not so long ago, a minor evil. Techno-scientific society has learned to let the hot issues cool down a bit. We bide our time and quietly go on with our chemical weapons, brain research, and molecular genetic biochemistry. Who can stop it? For years "the Russians are doing it," was the slogan for promoting military "research and development" in the United States. The nazis are not the only ones who have utilized prisoners for "medical research." On what grounds are we to call a halt to experimentation? Punishment for "crimes" is still accepted as a moral act.

Arnold Toynbee has brilliant pages about "the industrialization of historical thought" and historical research following the centuries-long exploitation of raw materials.[27] The history of the "industrial revolution" with its advantages and victims is well documented. Once ethics has been deprived of its religious foundations, only sheer power can maintain the "order" of the status quo. The person seems either lost in awe over all this, or supremely unimportant in the whole process. What matters now is not the person, but rather statistics for the sociologists, and the brain or the stomach, the virus or the genes, and the correct prediction or production or prescription for the specialists. In this sense it is surely true that the scientific outlook is not sentimental. We can take this grand plan of applied physical laws right up to the scientific organization of society under a theoretically perfect world

27 Arnold J. Toynbee, *A Study of History*, revised and abridged by the author and Jane Caplan (London: Oxford University Press; Thames & Hudson, 1972), 32ff.

democratic government, which would take care of any imaginable number of individuals, having foreseen everybody's every imaginable need.

The computer—and if need be, an artificial intelligence—will take care, and take over. In the privacy of their mobile homes, and in time off from their increasingly automated productivity, individuals will "enjoy" the undisturbed freedom to push any button and select any channel in order to be informed and entertained. A few pious souls can be tolerated, as long as they do not disturb our technocratic civilization.

Obviously, this picture is not complete. There are many positive features in the overall scenario, but if left to itself, techno-science is going to implant its worldview into the *forma mentis* of the intellectual elite. My main critique is not of science; it is of philosophy, which has abdicated her role, a role that has nothing to do with a return to being an absolute Queen but rather involves inspiring Man to overcome his cultural schizophrenia. The scientific story cannot be disconnected from human history. So-called fundamental research cannot ignore the technological civilization that utilizes it for its own purposes. The old argument "science is good and not responsible for the use of it" is too naïve in itself, even if we ignore the fact that scientific research is impossible today without the sponsorship of some profit-making organization. It is like saying "religion is good and the wars of religion are there because people are bad." Things are much more complex. Our cynicism and greed sometimes rise to unbelievable heights. When discussing a possible ban on antipersonnel mines, which are still creating havoc in many countries, weapons manufacturers and their governmental salesmen have argued that if "they," meaning consumers of such goods like generalismos, dictators and the leaders of military-industrial complexes, do not want the land mines, nobody obliges them to buy. Therefore we should be allowed to go on producing such weapons in a "free" market.

I am not at all advocating "going back" to primitivism or to an idyllic society, which has never existed. I am only saying that the alternative is either a radical change in mind and heart (they go together) or a catastrophe of cosmic proportions. I am not a puritan, and although I believe plants and animals are alive, I am not a vegetarian out of some principled ideal, but rather I partake in a chain of life that likewise passes through the triple world. I also believe, for instance, that matter is alive, albeit with another type of life than that of plants and animals. Hence, how we treat matter and the intentions we hold vis-à-vis the material world matter. The intentions that guide our actions count not only for the acting subject but also for the result of the act. The intention of the hunter is different from the intention of a meat industry, just as the intentions of Madame Curie and Becquerel were not the same as those of the laboratories at Los Alamos and Livermore, where the first atom bombs were designed. Surgery may be needed in an unhealthy organism, including atomic surgery; but if the intention of manipulating matter is money or war, even if called "progress" or defense, this type of action is fundamentally corrupt. Here too the change needs to be radical.

C. Fragments of the New Story

The scientific myth is a powerful one. Inasmuch as people believe in it, it conveys the truth they live by. Logical arguments have no power in front of a myth. A doctrine can be refuted in the arena of logic. A myth, which is a matter of faith, has myriad subterfuges: "I do not know the answer, but the sages of my church, party, community will explain it." Or, as we hear all too often, "we, the scientists, do not understand it *yet*, but in the future we shall," or "we shall have to make some changes in the premises, but the pattern remains," since without that pattern we lose the ground under our feet. Again, "we do not know, and probably shall never know; it is a mystery," nevertheless, we remain within the myth. Millennia ago people discovered that divine omnipotence and goodness are incompatible, that women are not, *qua* person, inferior to men; for centuries people have known that the earth is round and the sun is the center of the solar system; for decades we have known that the wave and particle theories are not necessarily incompatible—and yet the basic myths remained. "Scientific revolutions" may need a change of paradigm, but the displacement of one myth by another follows other rhythms. All too often a violence against a myth only reinforces the myth. A violent attack against a particular nationalism will only reinforce the nationalistic myth among the "victims." It is interesting to recognize that in socialist countries of the old soviet regime, where religious institutions were controlled or persecuted, scientists tended to be more aware of the lopsidedness of a solely scientific ideology and discussed more religious-metaphysical issues than their colleagues of the bourgeoisie in the capitalistic countries. In the interaction between a philosophical and a scientific vision of the world we are dealing with powerful myths and not just two doctrines.

All too often when professional philosophers undertake to criticize science they are likely to display their own ignorance. The reverse is also generally the case. When scientists embark upon philosophical speculation, they betray the same estrangement. The very fact that the languages (and not just the idioms) are different should indicate that the two worlds of discourse reflect two diverse universes. Both sides tend to lead the discussions within the parameters of their own respective fields.

To question a myth is a much more delicate and emotional operation than to debate logical propositions. In the latter case there is a neutral arena, the correct use of logic, which allows for detachment from one's opinions (on the firm grounds of logic) and confidence in the partner who accepts the same procedure (because of fidelity to the same or a similar logic). Not so with myths. Barrow and Tipler's statement that "whereas many philosophers and theologians appear to possess an emotional attachment to their theories and ideas which requires them to believe them, most scientists tend to regard their ideas differently," is most revealing.[28] While this is true when it is a matter of "formulating many logically consistent possibilities,"[29] it is hardly the case when the scientists are challenged with regard to what they believe lies at the very basis of science. My own experience leads me to endorse S. H. Nasr's remark about "scientists who claim to look upon all things from a detached scientific point of view but react with violent passion when the theory of evolution is discussed critically."[30]

I myself have had to soften some statements in the previous section because I did not want to offend the sensibilities of some scientists, whereas some theologians have reacted with more detachment when hearing my critique of monotheism. I repeat that I am neither against science nor against monotheism. I am only saying that the challenge of the new century is the awareness of the radical insufficiency of both.

My point is that we have to go deeper into the problematic and examine whether we are discussing a particular question or asking after the meaning of human life and human activities. We should not discuss texts outside their contexts, and we must also know the pretext of the discussion and the personal factor as well. Philosophy is neither a logical game nor a matter of "formulating many consistent possibilities" regarding a more or less interesting view of reality. Authentic philosophy is not a specialty, it is the intellectual and contemplative activity of Man, a conscious involvement in the very life of reality, and this fact makes Man co-responsible with reality itself. This philosophy may be found in basic research as well as in contemplative thinking; it may be cultivated in solitude or in conversation, and within the sciences and the humanities alike. After all, everyone is, in this respect, a

28 Barrow and Tipler, *Anthropic Cosmological Principle*, 15.

29 Ibid.

30 Seyyed Hossein Nasr, *Ideals and Realities of Islam*, 2nd ed. (London: Allen & Unwin, 1975), 234; see also his *Islam and the Plight of Modern Man* (London/New York: Longman, 1975).

lover of wisdom, a person committed to the search for truth, beauty, and goodness. Our current tendency to relegate professional philosophy to the status of an elite speciality does not truly represent what the "Wisdom of Love" has traditionally meant. This is also the reason why the best scientists are authentic philosophers.

The current philosophic vision, like the modern scientific myth, is inadequate; both leave aside or ignore dimensions of the human being which for the majority of humanity have been central and decisive. This does not mean that the scientific myth is wrong; strictly speaking, no myth is wrong—because a myth is our myth if we believe in it. What I am saying is that the modern scientific myth departs from the common experience of humanity through the ages. To accept it would be to throw overboard the immense riches that humankind has gathered over millennia, thereby enormously impoverishing our human condition as well as our prospects for a human life in the future. Of course, if we assume that all our ancestors were undeveloped people because they had no inkling of quantum mechanics, and primitive because they could not fly and had no electricity, we have already accepted the schism of modernity without much resistance. However, if we still keep a sense of human solidarity with historical Man based not only on sentimental grounds but also on recognizing intellectual ties, it will be a good deal more difficult to believe that all the peoples of the world until now were living in a kind of limbo and that at long last we are on the road to genuine humanity and a verifiable knowledge of reality.

* * *

The traditional criticism of the scientific paradigm consists in saying that it leaves no place for God, to which the scientist responds that there is no need for one. In contrast, my criticism of the scientific paradigm maintains that it leaves no place for Man. The great absentee in the scientific *mythos* is Man. Gods there are aplenty, in the form of black holes, galaxies, and infinities great and small, limits, thresholds, and so forth. Devils are legion; biomolecular sciences provide a virology quite as imposing as any medieval demonology, and modern "medicated" Man proceeds in fear and trembling in a world of invisible germs and viruses of all sorts. Matter and especially energy are all-pervasive, as are time and space. Only Man does not come into the picture. There is an observer there, of course, a so-called intelligent observer, who may even have programmed the computer, and who doubles from time to time as the onlooker agog at what can be observed. Man, however, cannot be located among the data. It would be considered suspicious if the observer were found to be manipulating the information too much for the sake of a particular experiment. On the contrary, Man is in a certain way *the obstacle* to pure information. One reckons with Man mainly as a disturbing factor, a modifying parameter—necessary, to be sure, but somehow obscuring the purity of the measurements.

Man as an object, of course, appertains also in the field of science. Everything Man *has*, including genes, may be conveniently digitized, homogenized, and fed into the latest supercomputer, but this does not tell us what Man is, or *who* Man is, much less who I am. Modern science has been as wary of anthropocentrism as classical theology was of anthropomorphism, so that anthropology now seems to be afraid of its own subject matter unless it is reduced to sociological or scientific parameters. We know that technocracy has overstepped the human scale of cities, businesses, countries, speeds, and displacements of every sort, thus providing certainly all kinds of individual comforts. The cost, however, has been that technocracy has let Man *qua* Man evaporate. The fact that for many american english-speaking people, the very word "Man" suggests exclusively the male is another example of the loss of the *anthrōpos*, that being between Heaven and Earth, that unique character who is neither an animal nor a God, as some traditions still interpret the word. Abhinavagupta says: "Therefore both you and I are genderless."[31]

Only the reified "third person" is he, she, or it. (We should also distinguish between gender and sex.) The person transcends that difference. Man is not only a biped, but the meeting place of all reality, that complex being who as a mesocosm combines all that there is. Man may not be the center, if by center we understand an egotistic and narcissistic individual or collective ego that wants to be the mid-point of the universe. Man, the microcosm, is not a mere miniaturization of the macrocosm, the bigger "paradigm." Man is the icon of God, the infinite Being, affirm many traditions—only that many individuals do not (yet) know that they are *brahman* says vedānta philosophy. What some oriental spiritualities term illumination, enlightenment, realization, *jîvan-mukti*, *satori*, etc., is nothing but this experience of being icon.

In the christian tradition, Mary, who is called mother of God and not just of Christ, gathers and ponders all things in her heart, re-enacting the life of her Son, who brings with him all humanity. As such, this heart of Mary is a symbol of human dignity and destiny. This type of understanding is common in the indic traditions; the ātman is the "microtheos" or "microcosm" of the whole reality.

The expression *mana hṛdaya-vyomni* is used by Bhairava to say that the process of creation (*kaulika vidhi*) inheres in "the heaven of my heart."

31 Abhinavagupta, *Parātrīśikā*, 71.

Abhinavagupta comments: "Heart in this context means the receptacle of all existents."[32]

This echoes a common insight of East and West, for which we give only one more example: "Subtler than the subtle, greater than the great, the ātman lies hidden in the heart of every creature,"[33] and this ātman is *brahman*, the Upanishads repeatedly add. No authentic spirituality exists without an experience of this correlation between ourselves and the Self, the spiritual body, the whole, humanity . . .

I am not reducing science to anthropology, but I am not separating them either. The subject matter of the whole of the "New Story" is neither the cosmos nor Man, but the Kosmos inhabited by God and Man, this latter understood neither as a product of the earth nor as an immigrant from heaven, but as a constitutive member of reality. Man is not only the object of scientific study; Man is also the subject of this study. Moreover, as long as we split knowledge into an epistemic dualism between subject and object, the "New Story" will be fragmented and incomplete. Symbolic knowledge has not yet received the *scientific* input that conceptual knowledge has received from the time of Socrates onwards—using now the word "science" in its pristine sense. Such input remains a grand task for cosmotheandric knowledge.

Something similar could be said regarding the Divine. We may introduce the topic with a quotation from the annals of science: "Most modern, philosophically minded theologians would contend that such a distinction [between God and the physical universe] can be made, but that the physical universe is actually a proper subset of God: the physical universe is *in* God, but God is more than the physical universe. This position was termed *panentheism*."[34]

Whether Krause intended such a crude classification is hardly important. What is characteristic is this formalization of the discourse about God: God as the set of all possible sets, a subset of which would be our physical universe. The scientific language may be a useful metaphor, but language about God cannot be reduced to that. Fortunately enough, nobody has yet found such a God. Of course this form of thinking will never arrive at a living Godhead, unless this Godhead is confused with a mathematical matrix that, however elegant, is lifeless and abstract.

32 Ibid., 78.

33 KathU I, 2, 20 (SU III, 20).

34 Barrow and Tipler, *Anthropic Cosmological Principle*, 121.

My point, however, penetrates deeper. No such way of thinking will ever find a "creature" called Creator and identify it with God. This God does not exist, and I submit that the traditional thinking of most of the peoples of the world did not maintain such a crude idea of the Divine. Symbolic thinking is not rooted in structural or formal abstractions. The living God of common people is not a set containing the world as a subset. The God believed in by traditional theologians is not a being among the beings, or some huge generalized Being embracing all the others. In this context one could understand Pascal's famous "Memorial": "God of Abraham, Isaac and Jacob, not the God of the philosophers." Nevertheless, the scientific paradigm has purified the idea of the Divine from many an excrescence, and probably made it unbelievable today in any theistic form. In brief: God is neither an idol nor a formula, neither a thing nor a concept.

I should not close this thought without a least mentioning the extraordinary contribution of modern literature in rescuing the idea of God from the grips of "microdoxic" doctrines and institutions. It is quite revealing to realize that from Camus to Saramago, to mention only two Nobel prize winners, most literary attacks against christianity insist on defending the person of Jesus.

I cannot narrate the whole story of the New Myth, but perhaps I can describe some fragments already cropping up here and there. I limit myself to a couple of considerations focused on the interrelation of those three dimensions. First, the Divine exists, is real. It is not merely a human dream, projection, or idea. The Divine is not another name for the World or for Man. This does not mean that the Divine has a separate existence, a disconnected reality, nor does it imply that its existence is the same as that of Man and/or the World. Here I am leaning on an almost universal human belief. There is something "more," something "different." The Divine is irreducible to Man or World.

The "more" and the "different" need immediate qualification, not only because every culture has had its own opinions on the nature of this Mystery, but also because both notions have Man as the implicit point of reference. This is the reason why the conception of the Divine is intrinsically connected to the notion Man has of his own humanity. "Image and likeness," many cultures say, using a phrase that can be interpreted to mean either that we are like the Divine, and the center is shifted there, or that the Divine is like us, and we become the center.

At this particular historical juncture, we may have accumulated enough experience and maturity to no longer be blind or insensitive to the havoc wreaked by anthropocentrisms, cosmocentrisms, and theocentrisms of all colors. We cannot eliminate Man from the picture, nor can we reduce the Divine to a mere illusion. We can, however, overcome the dominion of the one over the other in both directions. This does not mean egalitarian partnership. The entire power and reality of the Divine lie in the fact that they are irreducible to anything human or anything cosmic. Otherwise we could promptly eliminate the Divine altogether. The relationship is neither heteronomous (God the boss, we, along with the cosmos, the creatures), nor autonomous (God has divine rights, we our human rights). Theocentrism, cosmocentrism, and anthropocentrism are no longer tenable, because of sad historical experiences as well as to a certain intellectual maturity we have reached. Monotheism/atheism is not the only alternative. The center does not need to be anywhere. A circle has a center, an ellipse two quasi-centers, a parabola none.

We cannot degrade Matter either and convert it into an epiphenomenon of the real. We should neither divinize Matter (or Man) as the only reality nor deny the hierarchical "equality" of the material universe. Here the contribution of modern science is paramount. Thanks to it we have come to know matter in its own right and not as a mere servant of the soul or the spirit. Matter has its own ontonomy, just as God and Man have. This is the interindependence of which we spoke.

"Hierarchical equality" is not "egalitarian partnership," as we wrote concerning the correlation between God and Man. The notion of hierarchy is not a quantifiable notion. A cow as individual cow is not inferior to a human being. It has its own dignity and deserves respect, and yet the hierarchical order of the cows is different from the hierarchical place of Man in the universe, and killing a cow for some reason is not the same as a homicide.

In this entire problematic, the trinitarian symbol is enlightening. The Divine is real, a real but different dimension of the universe, neither independent nor separable. This dimension pervades everything, because no thing is without this dimension. It is not directly detectable, as a body is, or intelligible, as an idea may be. Otherwise we could reduce the Divine to a material or intelligible reality. Yet Man constantly discovers that the "more" and "different" is not an addition or a separation, but, as it were, an ingredient of reality itself. Something similar should be said regarding Man and the Cosmos. Consciousness as well as Matter pervades everything, and nothing is without these dimensions. They are not always directly detectable, and yet we cannot get rid of them, as we tried to explain before.

There is a *perichōrēsis* between the three. The Divine contains, and is everything, but so are Man and the World as well. Each is the Whole, and not just in a particular mode. The three are not merely modalities of the real. The puzzle, if it were one, cannot be solved statically. As three beings, it is a flat contradiction—one is not three. As one being, it comes to no more than modalism. Yet reality is neither one nor three. What we have is a "complex" reality, because we see it from one particular vantage point, precisely from the human one. The one is by "becoming" the others, and also vice versa. The traditional expression in terms of the christian trinity is that the One is by begetting and inspiring the others, and the others are by being begotten and inspired. We may want to look for better metaphors, but the point is to try to understand this fluxus *quo* of reality itself, as the very rhythm of Being. If we look at reality in this dynamic way, we may say that every being is an I, a Thou, and an It, that the speaker is not the spoken to nor the spoken about, but all speech demands the three together. Otherwise there is no speaking, no speaker, and nothing spoken.

Abhinavagupta has a dense page in this regard that I would like to summarize. After repeating the tantric *trika* with its trinitarian principle that "all is inherent in all" (*sarvaṁṁ hi sarvātmakam iti*)—that is, that everything is related to everything, he goes on to say that language permits us the experience of the three personal pronouns applied to any thing, any subject, and to the Divine Itself: "This is a mountain," "Listen, O mountains," and "Of mountains, I am Meru." In the first case we have the third person, the second person in the following example, and the first person when quoting the sentence from the *Gītā* where Krishna says "I am Mount Meru." This is more than a way of speaking. Abhinavagupta adduces the typical example of the identification that comes about in love, when the lover says to the beloved: "O loved one, thou art I." In this understanding, everything is *Śiva*, *śakti*, and *nara* (God, power, and Man). "Each of this triad without giving up its nature, becomes of three forms, viz. singular [*Śiva-bhāva*], dual [*Śakti-bhāva*], and plural [*nara-bhāva*]."[35]

Imagination and fantasy are useful and powerful human faculties, but they may easily mislead us if left on their own. These faculties, combined with logical thinking, have made of the Divine Mystery a separate and Supreme Being, a substance in the crudest sense of the word. This is precisely the *mythos* that is deteriorating and collapsing all around us.

The new *mythos* will certainly contain elements from all the strata of humanity, but it will need a glue, so to speak, a leading thread, a dynamic force that will meld old and new into something we cannot yet properly

35 Abhinavagupta, *Parātrīśikā*, 72-73.

foresee. I believe that the cosmotheandric insight may have sufficient traditional elements, and just enough of a revolutionary character, to serve as that catalyst for hope.

Indeed, the cosmotheandric trinity is not an ideology but a myth. It therefore does not and could not claim to inform only one creed, a single religion, a homogeneous set of beliefs, a unified world culture, or anything of the sort. A myth allows for communication and discussion; it allows for quarrels and helps in overcoming misunderstandings. Although it provides a language, it does not automatically create unanimity or consensus. By its very nature a myth is polysemic, and therefore not incompatible with pluralism.

Summing up: a new *mythos* may be emerging. Signs are everywhere. I have already given many names to fragments of this dawning: cosmotheandric insight, sacred secularity, kosmology, ontonomy, radical trinity, interindependence, radical relativity, and so on. I may also use a consecrated name: *advaita,* which is the equivalent of the radical Trinity. Everything is related to everything but without monistic identity or dualistic separation. I have tried to spell it out throughout these pages.

Epilogue

Since delivering the Gifford Lectures twenty years ago, I have hesitated to publish this book, because of the last chapter, which was supposed to be titled "The Survival of Being." No matter how I reflected on that topic, the results did not satisfy me. On the contrary, what I wrote seemed to be lucubration, a solemn literary work about something we do not and cannot know anything about. I could only move forward to publication and approve the final revisions when I decided to omit chapter 9.

Led by the enthusiasm aroused by the Gifford Lectures in 1989, I imagined I could tackle a subject that proved to transcend the powers of my intellect.

I must admit that all ultimate questions cannot have final answers, but that we can at least be aware of the problem we have presented. I have touched the limits of my understanding and must stop here. The Tree of Knowledge again and again tempts one at the cost of neglecting the more important tree, the Tree of Life.

How can human thinking grasp the destiny of life itself, when we are not its owners?

This is my humble conclusion to much presumptuous research. It has taken me twenty years to admit this, and I apologize.

Raimon Panikkar
Tavertet, Catalunya
4 September 2009

Index

T

U

V

W

Z